C# Cookbook™

Other Microsoft .NET resources from O'Reilly

Related titles	Programming C#	ADO.NET in a Nutshell
	C# in a Nutshell	.NET Windows Forms in a Nutshell
	Programming Visual Basic .NET	.NET Framework Essentials
	Programming ASP.NET	Mastering Visual Studio .NET
	ASP.NET in a Nutshell	

.NET Books Resource Center

dotnet.oreilly.com is a complete catalog of O'Reilly's books on .NET and related technologies, including sample chapters and code examples.

ONDotnet.com provides independent coverage of fundamental, interoperable, and emerging Microsoft .NET programming and web services technologies.

Conferences

O'Reilly & Associates brings diverse innovators together to nurture the ideas that spark revolutionary industries. We specialize in documenting the latest tools and systems, translating the innovator's knowledge into useful skills for those in the trenches. Visit *conferences.oreilly.com* for our upcoming events.

Safari Bookshelf (*safari.oreilly.com*) is the premier online reference library for programmers and IT professionals. Conduct searches across more than 1,000 books. Subscribers can zero in on answers to time-critical questions in a matter of seconds. Read the books on your Bookshelf from cover to cover or simply flip to the page you need. Try it today with a free trial.

C# Cookbook™

Stephen Teilhet and Jay Hilyard

O'REILLY®

Beijing · Cambridge · Farnham · Köln · Paris · Sebastopol · Taipei · Tokyo

C# Cookbook™
by Stephen Teilhet and Jay Hilyard

Published by O'Reilly Media, Inc., 1005 Gravenstein Highway North, Sebastopol, CA 95472.

O'Reilly Media, Inc. books may be purchased for educational, business, or sales promotional use. On-line editions are also available for most titles (*safari.oreilly.com*). For more information, contact our corporate/institutional sales department: (800) 998-9938 or *corporate@oreilly.com*.

Editor:	Brian Jepson
Production Editor:	Marlowe Shaeffer
Cover Designer:	Emma Colby
Interior Designer:	David Futato

Printing History:

January 2004:	First Edition.

 This book uses RepKover™, a durable and flexible lay-flat binding.

ISBN: 0-596-00339-0
[M]   [7/04]

To my mom, dad, and my brother Justin, thanks
for all your help, support, and guidance.

—Stephen

To Brooke, thank you for everything. I love you
and couldn't have done this without you.

—Jay

Table of Contents

Preface xv

1. **Numbers** 1

    1.1   Determining Approximate Equality Between a Fraction
          and Floating-Point Value   2

    1.2   Converting Degrees to Radians   3

    1.3   Converting Radians to Degrees   4

    1.4   Using the Bitwise Complement Operator with Various Data Types   5

    1.5   Test for an Even or Odd Value   6

    1.6   Obtaining the Most- or Least-Significant Bits of a Number   7

    1.7   Converting a Number in Another Base to Base10   9

    1.8   Determining Whether a String Is a Valid Number   10

    1.9   Rounding a Floating-Point Value   12

    1.10   Different Rounding Algorithms   13

    1.11   Converting Celsius to Fahrenheit   14

    1.12   Converting Fahrenheit to Celsius   14

    1.13   Safely Performing a Narrowing Numeric Cast   15

    1.14   Finding the Length of Any Three Sides of a Right Triangle   25

    1.15   Finding the Angles of a Right Triangle   27

2. **Strings and Characters** 28

    2.1   Determining the Kind of Character   28

    2.2   Determining Whether a Character Is Within a Specified Range   32

    2.3   Controlling Case Sensitivity when Comparing Two Characters   33

    2.4   Finding All Occurrences of a Character Within a String   35

    2.5   Finding the Location of All Occurrences of a String Within
          Another String   37

    2.6   The Poor Man's Tokenizer   41

2.7	Controlling Case Sensitivity when Comparing Two Strings	43
2.8	Comparing a String to the Beginning or End of a Second String	44
2.9	Inserting Text into a String	45
2.10	Removing or Replacing Characters Within a String	46
2.11	Encoding Binary Data as Base64	49
2.12	Decoding a Base64-Encoded Binary	50
2.13	Converting a String Returned as a Byte[ ] Back into a String	51
2.14	Passing a String to a Method that Accepts Only a Byte[ ]	53
2.15	Converting Strings to Their Equivalent Value Type	55
2.16	Formatting Data in Strings	58
2.17	Creating a Delimited String	61
2.18	Extracting Items from a Delimited String	62
2.19	Setting the Maximum Number of Characters a String Can Contain	63
2.20	Iterating Over Each Character in a String	64
2.21	Improving String Comparison Performance	66
2.22	Improving StringBuilder Performance	69
2.23	Pruning Characters from the Head and/or Tail of a String	72

3. Classes and Structures **73**

3.1	Creating Union-Type Structures	75
3.2	Allowing a Type to Represent Itself as a String	77
3.3	Converting a String Representation of an Object into an Actual Object	83
3.4	Polymorphism via Concrete or Abstract Base Classes	85
3.5	Making a Type Sortable	90
3.6	Making a Type Searchable	95
3.7	Indirectly Overloading the +=, -=, /=, and *= Operators	99
3.8	Indirectly Overloading the &&, ||, and ?: Operators	102
3.9	Improving the Performance of a Structure's Equals Method	105
3.10	Turning Bits On or Off	108
3.11	Making Error-Free Expressions	111
3.12	Minimizing (Reducing) Your Boolean Logic	114
3.13	Converting Between Simple Types in a Language Agnostic Manner	117
3.14	Determining Whether to Use the Cast Operator, the as Operator, or the is Operator	124
3.15	Casting with the as Operator	125
3.16	Determining a Variable's Type with the is Operator	127
3.17	Polymorphism via Interfaces	130
3.18	Calling the Same Method on Multiple Object Types	133

3.19 Adding a Notification Callback Using an Interface   136
3.20 Using Multiple Entry Points to Version an Application   144
3.21 Preventing the Creation of an Only Partially Initialized Object   146
3.22 Returning Multiple Items from a Method   148
3.23 Parsing Command-Line Parameters   150
3.24 Retrofitting a Class to Interoperate with COM   158
3.25 Initializing a Constant Field at Runtime   163
3.26 Writing Code that Is Compatible with the Widest Range
      of Managed Languages   165
3.27 Implementing Nested foreach Functionality in a Class   167
3.28 Building Cloneable Classes   174
3.29 Assuring an Object's Disposal   177
3.30 Releasing a COM Object Through Managed Code   180
3.31 Creating an Object Cache   181
3.32 The Single Instance Object   191
3.33 Choosing a Serializer   195
3.34 Creating Custom Enumerators   201
3.35 Rolling Back Object Changes   207
3.36 Disposing of Unmanaged Resources   214
3.37 Determining Where Boxing and Unboxing Occur   221

4. **Enumerations** **224**
    4.1 Displaying an Enumeration Value as a String   225
    4.2 Converting Plain Text to an Equivalent Enumeration Value   227
    4.3 Testing for a Valid Enumeration Value   228
    4.4 Testing for a Valid Enumeration of Flags   230
    4.5 Using Enumerated Members in a Bitmask   232
    4.6 Determining Whether One or More Enumeration Flags Are Set   235

5. **Exception Handling** **238**
    5.1 Verifying Critical Parameters   244
    5.2 Indicating Where Exceptions Originate   246
    5.3 Choosing when to Throw a Particular Exception   247
    5.4 Handling Derived Exceptions Individually   249
    5.5 Assuring Exceptions are Not Lost when Using Finally Blocks   251
    5.6 Handling Exceptions Thrown from Methods Invoked
         via Reflection   254
    5.7 Debugging Problems when Loading an Assembly   257
    5.8 HRESULT-Exception Mapping   258
    5.9 Handling User-Defined HRESULTs   262

5.10 Preventing Unhandled Exceptions   263
5.11 Displaying Exception Information   265
5.12 Getting to the Root of a Problem Quickly   268
5.13 Creating a New Exception Type   269
5.14 Obtaining a Stack Trace   279
5.15 Breaking on a First Chance Exception   281
5.16 Preventing the Nefarious TypeInitializationException   284
5.17 Handling Exceptions Thrown from an Asynchronous Delegate   288

6. Diagnostics **290**
6.1 Controlling Tracing Output in Production Code   290
6.2 Providing Fine-Grained Control Over Debugging/Tracing Output   294
6.3 Creating Your Own Custom Switch Class   297
6.4 A Custom Trace Class that Outputs Information in an XML Format   301
6.5 Conditionally Compiling Blocks of Code   310
6.6 Determining Whether a Process Has Stopped Responding   312
6.7 Using One or More Event Logs in Your Application   314
6.8 Changing the Maximum Size of a Custom Event Log   321
6.9 Searching Event Log Entries   322
6.10 Watching the Event Log for a Specific Entry   326
6.11 Finding All Sources Belonging to a Specific Event Log   327
6.12 Implementing a Simple Performance Counter   330
6.13 Implementing Performance Counters that Require a Base Counter   333
6.14 Enable/Disable Complex Tracing Code   336

7. Delegates and Events **340**
7.1 Controlling when and if a Delegate Fires Within a
     Multicast Delegate   340
7.2 Obtaining Return Values from Each Delegate in a
     Multicast Delegate   344
7.3 Handling Exceptions Individually for Each Delegate in a
     Multicast Delegate   346
7.4 Converting a Synchronous Delegate to an Asynchronous Delegate   348
7.5 Adding Events to a Sealed Class   351
7.6 Passing Specialized Parameters to and from an Event   357
7.7 An Advanced Interface Search Mechanism   363
7.8 An Advanced Member Search Mechanism   366
7.9 Observing Additions and Modifications to a Hashtable   372
7.10 Using the Windows Keyboard Hook   380
7.11 Using Windows Hooks to Manipulate the Mouse   386

8. Regular Expressions **388**

    8.1 Enumerating Matches   389

    8.2 Extracting Groups from a MatchCollection   392

    8.3 Verifying the Syntax of a Regular Expression   395

    8.4 Quickly Finding Only the Last Match in a String   396

    8.5 Replacing Characters or Words in a String   397

    8.6 Augmenting the Basic String Replacement Function   400

    8.7 A Better Tokenizer   403

    8.8 Compiling Regular Expressions   405

    8.9 Counting Lines of Text   407

    8.10 Returning the Entire Line in Which a Match Is Found   410

    8.11 Finding a Particular Occurrence of a Match   413

    8.12 Using Common Patterns   415

    8.13 Documenting Your Regular Expressions   418

9. Collections **420**

    9.1 Swapping Two Elements in an Array   422

    9.2 Quickly Reversing an Array   423

    9.3 Reversing a Two-Dimensional Array   425

    9.4 Reversing a Jagged Array   427

    9.5 A More Flexible StackTrace Class   429

    9.6 Determining the Number of Times an Item Appears in an ArrayList   435

    9.7 Retrieving All Instances of a Specific Item in an ArrayList   439

    9.8 Inserting and Removing Items from an Array   443

    9.9 Keeping Your ArrayList Sorted   446

    9.10 Sorting a Hashtable's Keys and/or Values   448

    9.11 Creating a Hashtable with Max and Min Size Boundaries   451

    9.12 Creating a Hashtable with Max and Min Value Boundaries   455

    9.13 Displaying an Array's Data as a Delimited String   458

    9.14 Storing Snapshots of Lists in an Array   460

    9.15 Creating a Strongly Typed Collection   461

    9.16 Persisting a Collection Between Application Sessions   465

10. Data Structures and Algorithms **467**

    10.1 Creating a Hash Code for a Data Type   467

    10.2 Creating a Priority Queue   475

    10.3 Creating a More Versatile Queue   483

    10.4 Determining Where Characters or Strings Do Not Balance   492

    10.5 Creating a One-to-Many Map (MultiMap)   496

10.6 Creating a Binary Tree 503
10.7 Creating an n-ary Tree 514
10.8 Creating a Set Object 524

11. Filesystem I/O **537**
11.1 Creating, Copying, Moving, and Deleting a File 537
11.2 Manipulating File Attributes 540
11.3 Renaming a File 543
11.4 Determining Whether a File Exists 543
11.5 Choosing a Method of Opening a File or Stream
     for Reading and/or Writing 544
11.6 Randomly Accessing Part of a File 552
11.7 Outputting a Platform-Independent EOL Character 556
11.8 Create, Write to, and Read from a File 557
11.9 Determining Whether a Directory Exists 564
11.10 Creating, Moving, and Deleting a Directory 565
11.11 Manipulating Directory Attributes 567
11.12 Renaming a Directory 569
11.13 Searching for Directories or Files Using Wildcards 571
11.14 Obtaining the Directory Tree 576
11.15 Parsing a Path 578
11.16 Parsing Paths in Environment Variables 579
11.17 Verifying a Path 581
11.18 Using a Temporary File in Your Application 583
11.19 Opening a File Stream with just a File Handle 585
11.20 Write to Multiple Output Files at One Time 587
11.21 Launching and Interacting with Console Utilities 589
11.22 Locking Subsections of a File 591
11.23 Watching the Filesystem for Specific Changes to One or More
     Files or Directories 594
11.24 Waiting for an Action to Occur in the Filesystem 599
11.25 Comparing Version Information of Two Executable Modules 601

12. Reflection **605**
12.1 Listing Imported Assemblies 605
12.2 Listing Exported Types 607
12.3 Finding Overridden Methods 609
12.4 Finding Members in an Assembly 613
12.5 Finding Members Within an Interface 614
12.6 Obtaining Types Nested Within a Type 616

12.7 Displaying the Inheritance Hierarchy for a Type   617

12.8 Finding the Subclasses of a Type   619

12.9 Finding All Serializable Types Within an Assembly   621

12.10 Controlling Additions to an ArrayList Through Attributes   623

12.11 Filtering Output when Obtaining Members   626

12.12 Dynamically Invoking Members   631

13. Networking **635**

13.1 Converting an IP Address to a Hostname   635

13.2 Converting a Hostname to an IP Address   636

13.3 Parsing a URI   637

13.4 Forming an Absolute URI   639

13.5 Handling Web Server Errors   640

13.6 Communicating with a Web Server   642

13.7 Going Through a Proxy   644

13.8 Obtaining the HTML from a URL   645

13.9 Writing a TCP Server   646

13.10 Writing a TCP Client   648

13.11 Simulating Form Execution   649

13.12 Downloading Data from a Server   652

13.13 Using Named Pipes to Communicate   653

14. Security **670**

14.1 Controlling Access to Types in a Local Assembly   670

14.2 Encrypting/Decrypting a String   679

14.3 Encrypting and Decrypting a File   683

14.4 Cleaning Up Cryptography Information   688

14.5 Verifying that a String Is Uncorrupted During Transmission   690

14.6 Wrapping a String Hash for Ease of Use   693

14.7 A Better Random Number Generator   699

14.8 Securely Storing Data   700

14.9 Making a Security Assert Safe   706

14.10 Preventing Malicious Modifications to an Assembly   708

14.11 Verifying that an Assembly Has Been Granted Specific Permissions   710

14.12 Minimizing the Attack Surface of an Assembly   711

15. Threading **713**

15.1 Creating Per-Thread Static Fields   713

15.2 Providing Thread Safe Access to Class Members   716

15.3 Preventing Silent Thread Termination   721

15.4 Polling an Asynchronous Delegate   723
15.5 Timing Out an Asynchronous Delegate   726
15.6 Being Notified of the Completion of an Asynchronous Delegate   729
15.7 Waiting for Worker Thread Completion   731
15.8 Synchronizing the Reading and Writing of a Resource Efficiently   732
15.9 Determining Whether a Request for a Pooled Thread
     Will Be Queued   735
15.10 Waiting for All Threads in the Thread Pool to Finish   738
15.11 Configuring a Timer   739
15.12 Storing Thread-Specific Data Privately   742

16. Unsafe Code **746**
16.1 Controlling Changes to Pointers Passed to Methods   747
16.2 Comparing Pointers   751
16.3 Navigating Arrays   753
16.4 Manipulating a Pointer to a Fixed Array   755
16.5 Returning a Pointer to a Particular Element in an Array   756
16.6 Creating and Using an Array of Pointers   758
16.7 Creating and Using an Array of Pointers to Unknown Types   760
16.8 Switching Unknown Pointer Types   762
16.9 Breaking Up Larger Numbers into Their Equivalent Byte Array
     Representation   764
16.10 Converting Pointers to a Byte[], SByte[], or Char[] to a String   766

17. XML **769**
17.1 Reading and Accessing XML Data in Document Order   769
17.2 Reading XML on the Web   772
17.3 Querying the Contents of an XML Document   773
17.4 Validating XML   775
17.5 Creating an XML Document Programmatically   779
17.6 Detecting Changes to an XML Document   781
17.7 Handling Invalid Characters in an XML String   784
17.8 Transforming XML to HTML   786
17.9 Tearing Apart an XML Document   791
17.10 Putting Together an XML Document   796

Index **803**

Preface

C# is a language targeted at developers for the Microsoft .NET platform who have already worked with a C-like language such as C, C++, or Java. Unlike previous versions of C or C++ for the Microsoft Windows platform, C# code runs under a *managed execution environment*. While C and C++ developers using Visual Studio .NET can now write managed code using the Managed Extensions for C++, C# offers a middle path between C++'s overall power but sometimes difficult code and the higher-level task orientation provided by Visual Basic .NET. Microsoft portrays C# as a modern and innovative language for .NET development that will be familiar to current C++ programmers while allowing more runtime control over the executing code.

C# allows you to perform many C/C++-like functions such as direct memory access via pointers and operator overloading that are not supported in Visual Basic .NET. Many of the interesting enhancements for .NET languages are slated to appear first in C#, such as generics. (You can think of generics as templates with a twist.) C# is the system-level programming language for .NET. You can still do great application-level work in C#, but it really shines when you need to build code a little closer to the framework.

If you have seen C#, you may have noticed that it looks a lot like Java; Java programmers will feel very much at home in C# once they learn the Framework SDK. C# can also be a great language for Visual Basic .NET programmers when they need a little more control over what the code is doing and don't want to have to write C++ to gain an advantage. There is a large community on the Web of people doing really neat things with C# and there is tons of sample code on sites such as *http://www.gotdotnet.com*, *http://www.codeproject.com*, and *http://www.4guysfromrolla.com*.

We put this book together based on programming problems we ran into when first learning C# as well as during our continued use of it. We hope that it will help you get past some of the common (and not-so-common) pitfalls and initial questions everyone has when learning a new language. There are recipes dealing with things we found missing from the .NET Framework Class Library (FCL), even though Microsoft has provided tons of functionality to keep folks from reinventing the wheel. Some of these solutions you might immediately use and some may never darken your door, but we hope this book helps you get the most out of C# and the .NET Framework.

The book is laid out with respect to the types of problems you will solve as you progress through your life as a C# programmer. These solutions are called *recipes*; each recipe consists of a single problem, its solution, a discussion of the solution and other relevant related information, and finally where you can look for more information about the classes used from the FCL, other books addressing this topic, related articles, and other recipes. The question–answer format provides complete solutions to problems, making the book easy to read and use. Nearly every recipe contains a complete, documented code sample showing you how to solve the specific problem, as well as a discussion of how the underlying technology works and a list of alternatives, limitations, and other considerations, when appropriate.

Who This Book Is For

You don't have to be an experienced C# or .NET developer to use this book—it is designed for users of all levels. This book provides solutions to problems that developers face every day as well as some that may come along infrequently. The recipes are targeted at the real-world developer who needs to solve problems now, not learn lots of theory first before being able to solve the problem. While reference or tutorial books can teach general concepts, they do not generally provide the help you need in solving real-world problems. We chose to teach by example, the natural way for most people to learn.

The majority of the problems addressed in this book are frequently faced by C# developers, but some of the more advanced problems call for more intricate solutions that combine many techniques. Each recipe is designed to help you quickly understand the problem, learn how to solve it, and find out any potential tradeoffs or ramifications to help you solve your problems quickly, efficiently, and with minimal effort.

To save you even the effort of typing in the solution, we provide the sample code for the book on the O'Reilly web site to facilitate the "editor inheritance" mode of development (copy and paste) as well as to help less experienced developers see good programming practice in action. The sample code provides a running test harness that exercises each of the solutions, but enough of the code is provided in each solution in the book to allow you to implement the solution without the sample code. The sample code is available from the book's catalog page: *http://www.oreilly.com/catalog/csharpckbk*.

What You Need to Use This Book

To run the samples in this book, you need a computer running Windows 2000 or later (if you are using Windows NT 4.0, you can use many, but not all, of the examples in this book; in particular, ASP.NET and .NET web services do not run on NT

4.0). A few of the networking and XML solutions require Microsoft Internet Information Server (IIS) Version 5 or later.

To open and compile the samples in this book, you need Visual Studio .NET 2003. If you are proficient with the downloadable Framework SDK and its command-line compilers, you should not have any trouble following the text of this book and the code samples.

How This Book Is Organized

This book is organized into seventeen chapters, each of which focuses on a particular topic in creating C# solutions. The following paragraphs summarize each chapter to give you an overview of this book's contents:

Chapter 1, *Numbers*
> This chapter focuses on the numeric data types used in C# code. Recipes cover such things as numeric conversions, using bitwise operators on numbers, and testing strings to determine whether they contain a numeric value.

Chapter 2, *Strings and Characters*
> This chapter covers both the String data type as well as the Char data type. Various recipes show how to compare strings in various ways, encode/decode strings, break strings apart, and put them back together again, to name a few.

Chapter 3, *Classes and Structures*
> This large chapter contains recipes dealing with both class and structure data types. This chapter covers a wide range of recipes from design patterns to converting a class to interoperating with COM.

Chapter 4, *Enumerations*
> This chapter covers the enum data type. Recipes display, convert and test enumeration types. In addition, there are recipes on using enumerations that consist of bit flags.

Chapter 5, *Exception Handling*
> The recipes in this chapter focus on the best ways to implement exception handling in your application. Preventing unhandled exceptions, reading and displaying stack traces, and throwing/rethrowing exceptions are included recipes. In addition, specific recipes show how to overcome some tricky situations, such as exceptions from late-bound called methods.

Chapter 6, *Diagnostics*
> This chapter explores recipes that use data types that fall under the System. Diagnostics namespace. Recipes deal with the Trace/Debug classes, event logs, processes, and performance counters.

Chapter 7, *Delegates and Events*
> This chapter's recipes show how both delegates and events can be used in your applications. Recipes allow manipulation of delegates that call more than one

method, synchronous delegates, asynchronous delegates, and Windows keyboard hooks.

Chapter 8, *Regular Expressions*

This chapter covers a very useful set of classes that are used to run regular expressions against strings. Recipes enumerate regular expression matches, break up strings into tokens, find/replace characters, and verify the syntax of a regular expression. A recipe is also included that contains many common regular expression patterns.

Chapter 9, *Collections*

This chapter examines recipes that make use of collections. The collection recipes make use of—as well as extend the functionality of—the array (single, multi, and jagged), the ArrayList, and the Hashtable. The various ways to create your own strongly typed collection are also discussed.

Chapter 10, *Data Structures and Algorithms*

This chapter goes a bit outside of what is provided for you in the .NET Framework Class Library and implements certain data structures and algorithms that are not in the FCL, or possibly are not in existence exactly the way you would like to use them, but ones that you have used to solve problems before. Items such as queues, maps, trees, and hashes are explored.

Chapter 11, *Filesystem I/O*

This chapter deals with filesystem interactions in four distinct ways. The first way is to look at typical file interactions; the second way looks at directory- or folder-based interactions; the third way deals with paths and temporary files; and the fourth way deals with advanced filesystem I/O topics.

Chapter 12, *Reflection*

This chapter shows ways to use the built-in assembly inspection system provided by the .NET Framework to determine what types, interfaces, and methods are implemented within an assembly and how to access them in a late-bound fashion.

Chapter 13, *Networking*

Networking explores the connectivity options provided by the .NET Framework and how to programmatically access network resources. Accessing a web site and its content as well as lower-level TCP/IP tasks are covered. This chapter also includes a recipe for using named pipes via P/Invoke.

Chapter 14, *Security*

There are many ways to write secure code and protect data using the .NET Framework, and in this chapter, we explore areas such as controlling access to types, encryption and decryption, random numbers, securely storing data, and using programmatic and declarative security.

Chapter 15, *Threading*

This chapter addresses the subject of using multiple threads of execution in a .NET program and issues like how to implement threading in your application, protecting resources from and allowing safe concurrent access, storing per-thread data, and the use of asynchronous delegates for processing.

Chapter 16, *Unsafe Code*

This chapter discusses how C# allows you to step outside of the safe environment of managed code and write code that is considered unsafe by the .NET Framework. The possibilities and restrictions of using unsafe code in C# are addressed by illustrating solutions to problems using unsafe code.

Chapter 17, *XML*

If you use .NET, it is likely that you will be dealing with XML to one degree or another; in this chapter, we explore some of the uses for XML, including XPath and XSLT, and topics such as the validation of XML and transformation of XML to HTML.

In some cases, certain recipes are related. In these cases, the See Also section of the recipe as well as some text in the Discussion will note the relation.

What Was Left Out

This book is not a reference or a primer about C#. Some good primers and reference books are *C# in a Nutshell*, *C# Language Pocket Reference*, and *Learning C#*, all titles available from O'Reilly. The MSDN Library is also invaluable. It is included with Visual Studio .NET and available online at *http://msdn.microsoft.com/library/default.asp*.

This book is not about how to use Visual Studio .NET to build, compile, and deploy applications. See *Mastering Visual Studio .NET* (O'Reilly) for excellent coverage of these topics.

Conventions Used in This Book

This book uses the following typographic conventions:

Italic

Used for URLs, names of directories and files, options, and occasionally for emphasis.

`Constant width`

Used for program listings, and for code items such as commands, options, switches, variables, attributes, keys, functions, types, classes, namespaces, methods, modules, properties, parameters, values, objects, events, event handlers, XML tags, HTML tags, macros, the contents of files, and the output from commands.

`Constant width bold`

Used in program listings to highlight an important part of the code.

```
//...
```
Ellipses in C# code indicate text that has been omitted for clarity.
```
<!-- ... -->
```
Ellipses in XML schemas and documents' code indicate text that has been omitted for clarity.

 This icon indicates a tip, suggestion, or general note.

 This icon indicates a warning or caution.

About the Code

Nearly every recipe in this book contains one or more code samples. These samples are not just fragments, but rather a complete solution that takes the form of either a Windows Forms or a Console application. Most of the code samples are written within a class or structure, making it easier to use within your applications. In addition to this, any using directives are included for each recipe so that you will not have to search for which ones to include in your code.

Complete error handling is included only in critical areas, such as input parameters. This allows you to easily see what is correct input and what is not. Many recipes omit error handling. This makes the solution easier to understand by focusing on the key concepts.

Using Code Examples

This book is here to help you get your job done. In general, you may use the code in this book in your programs and documentation. You do not need to contact us for permission unless you're reproducing a significant portion of the code. For example, writing a program that uses several chunks of code from this book does not require permission. Selling or distributing a CD-ROM of examples from O'Reilly books *does* require permission. Answering a question by citing this book and quoting example code does not require permission. Incorporating a significant amount of example code from this book into your product's documentation *does* require permission.

We appreciate, but do not require, attribution. An attribution usually includes the title, author, publisher, and ISBN. For example: "*C# Cookbook* by Stephen Teilhet and Jay Hilyard. Copyright 2004 O'Reilly & Associates, Inc., 0-596-00339-0."

If you feel your use of code examples falls outside fair use or the permission given above, feel free to contact us at *permissions@oreilly.com*.

Platform Notes

The solutions in this book are developed using Visual Studio .NET Version 1.1. The differences between Version 1.1 and Version 1.0 of the .NET Framework are not very significant and the sample code is not affected much. A complete list of differences between Version 1.1 and Version 1.0 of the .NET Framework can be found at *http://www.gotdotnet.com/team/upgrade/apiChanges.aspx*.

Comments and Questions

Please address any comments or questions concerning this book to the publisher:

O'Reilly & Associates
1005 Gravenstein Highway North
Sebastopol, CA 95472
800-998-9938 (in the U.S. or Canada)
707-829-0515 (international or local)
707-829-0104 (fax)

We have a web page for this book, where we list errata, examples, and any additional information. You can access this page at:

http://www.oreilly.com/catalog/csharpckbk

To comment or ask technical questions about this book, send email to:

bookquestions@oreilly.com

For more information about our books, conferences, Resource Centers, and the O'Reilly Network, see our web site at:

http://www.oreilly.com

Acknowledgments

This book is the completion of a journey that started out two years ago with Steve and an idea. Through various trials and tribulations, the book traveled and metamorphosed into the current incarnation you hold. Along the way, Jay was graciously given the opportunity to broaden his writing horizons by having Steve as a writing partner and together, we bring you our take on C#. This book would have been impossible without the following people and we'd like to acknowledge all of their efforts.

Brian Jepson, our editor, who taught us to hear different voices (active vs. passive), helped bring things together for the home stretch, and made late nights seem a bit less bleak when he'd respond to an email immediately we sent at 1:00 a.m. Thank you, Brian, for all of this and for asking the questions to make us think.

Ian Griffiths, our technical editor, gave such feedback as every writer should be blessed with. Ian not only kept us honest, but made many great suggestions, and without his efforts this book would have been a much lesser work.

Nathan Torkington, the cookbook guru at O'Reilly, showed us the light, then proved it wasn't a train. Thank you for starting this series and seeing it through.

From Steve Teilhet

Jay Hilyard worked incredibly hard to make this book great. This book would never have made it to the shelves without you.

Kandis Teilhet, my wife, was there every step of the way to give me the strength to persevere and finish this work. Words cannot express my love for you.

Patrick and Nicholas Teilhet, my two sons, made the rough patches smooth. I couldn't wish for two better sons.

Jim Barton, a longtime friend, provided solid feedback, great ideas, and pointed out errors that I would have otherwise missed.

Thanks to the entire DevPartner Code Review team at the Compuware NuMega Lab: Bill Holmes helped me sort through several of the diagnostics chapter recipes (and yes, the book is done now); Bob Meagher helped me sort out some rather insidious bugs; Jeff Simmons provided some great ideas for recipes. Thanks also to all of the others who contributed: Allan Gaithuma, Eliza Lecours, Paul Pelski, David Headley, Ken Naroff, and Ann-Marie Makenna. Thanks for all your help and support—I think this calls for a celebration.

From Jay Hilyard

Thanks to Steve Teilhet, without whom I never would have had this opportunity and whom I was glad to help. Now get back to work. :)

My wife Brooke is better to me than I deserve and helped me find the stamina and desire to write even in the tough times. No one could have given more support than my "true companion." I love you.

My sons, Owen and Andrew, who for all those times that "Daddy's in the cellar working," still had laughter and smiles for me when I came up and needed them.

Thanks to Steve Munyan, Barry Tannenbaum, Craig Neth, and Kit Von Sück for their insights on life and programming that helped shape my view of .NET.

And thanks to Greg Park, Keith Ludwig, David Fowler and Cleo O'Donnell for believing I would write someday.

And to my family and friends for asking about a book they don't understand and still being interested while helping to keep me on an even keel.

CHAPTER 1

Numbers

Simple types are value types that are a subset of the built-in types in Visual C# .NET, although, in fact, the types are defined as part of the .NET Framework Class Library (.NET FCL). Simple types are made up of several numeric types and a bool type. These numeric types consist of a decimal type (decimal), nine integral types (byte, char, int, long, sbyte, short, uint, ulong, ushort), and two floating-point types (float, double). Table 1-1 lists the simple types and their fully qualified names in the .NET Framework.

Table 1-1. The simple data types

Fully qualified name	Reserved C# keyword	Value range
System.Boolean	bool	true or false
System.Byte	byte	0 to 255
System.SByte	sbyte	−128 to 127
System.Char	char	0 to 65535
System.Decimal	decimal	−79,228,162,514,264,337,593,543,950,335 to 79,228,162,514,264,337,593,543,950,335
System.Double	double	−1.79769313486232e308 to 1.79769313486232e308
System.Single	float	−3.402823e38 to 3.402823e38
System.Int16	short	−32768 to 32767
System.Uint16	ushort	0 to 65535
System.Int32	int	−2,147,483,648 to 2,147,483,647
System.UInt32	uint	0 to 4,294,967,295
System.Int64	long	−9,223,372,036,854,775,808 to 9,223,372,036,854,775,807
System.UInt64	ulong	0 to 18,446,744,073,709,551,615

The C# reserved words for the various data types are simply aliases for the fully qualified type name. Therefore, it does not matter whether you use the type name or the reserved word: the C# compiler will generate identical code.

It should be noted that the following types are not CLS-compliant: sbyte, ushort, uint, and ulong. These types do not conform to the rules governing CLS types and therefore, they might not be supported by other .NET languages. This lack of support might limit or impede the interaction between your C# code and code written in another CLS-compliant language, such as Visual Basic .NET.

1.1 Determining Approximate Equality Between a Fraction and Floating-Point Value

Problem

You need to compare a fraction with a value of type double or float to determine whether they are within a close approximation to each other. Take, for example, the result of comparing the expression 1/6 and the value 0.16666667. These seem to be equivalent, except that 0.16666666 is precise to only 8 places to the right of the decimal point, and 1/6 is precise to the maximum number of digits to the right of the decimal point that the data type will hold.

Solution

Verify that the difference between the two values is within an acceptable tolerance:

```
using System;

public static bool IsApproximatelyEqualTo(double numerator,
                                          double denominator,
                                          double dblValue,
                                          double epsilon)
{
    double difference = (numerator/denominator) - dblValue;

    if (Math.Abs(difference) < epsilon)
    {
        // This is a good approximation
        return (true);
    }
    else
    {
        // This is NOT a good approximation
        return (false);
    }
}
```

Replacing the type double with float allows you to determine whether a fraction and a float value are approximately equal.

Discussion

Fractions can be expressed as a numerator over a denominator; however, storing them as a floating-point value might be necessary. Storing fractions as floating-point values introduces rounding errors that make it difficult to perform comparisons. Expressing the value as a fraction (e.g., 1/6) allows the maximum precision. Expressing the value as a floating-point value (e.g., 0.16667) can limit the precision of the value. In this case, the precision depends on the number of digits that the developer decides to use to the right of the decimal point.

You might need a way to determine whether two values are approximately equal to each other. This comparison is achieved by defining a value (epsilon) that is the smallest positive value, greater than zero, in which the absolute value of the difference between two values (numerator/denominator - dblValue) must be less than. In other words, by taking the absolute value of the difference between the fraction and the floating-point value and comparing it to a predetermined value passed to the epsilon argument, we can determine whether the floating-point value is a good approximation of the fraction.

Consider a comparison between the fraction 1/7 and its floating-point value, 0.14285714285714285. The following call to the IsApproximatelyEqualTo method indicates that there are not enough digits to the right of the decimal point in the floating-point value to be a good approximation of the fraction (there are 6 digits, although 7 are required):

```
bool Approximate = Class1.IsApproximatelyEqualTo(1, 7, .142857, .0000001);
// Approximate == false
```

Adding another digit of precision to the third parameter of this method now indicates that this more precise number is what we require for a good approximation of the fraction 1/7:

```
bool Approximate = Class1.IsApproximatelyEqualTo(1, 7, .1428571, .0000001);
// Approximate == true
```

See Also

See the "Double.Epsilon Field" and "Single.Epsilon Field" topics in the MSDN documentation.

1.2   Converting Degrees to Radians

Problem

When using the trigonometric functions of the Math class, all units are in radians. You have one or more angles measured in degrees and want to convert these to radians in order to use them with the members of the Math class.

Solution

To convert a value in degrees to radians, multiply it by $\pi/180$:

```
using System;

public static double ConvertDegreesToRadians (double degrees)
{
    double radians = (Math.PI / 180) * degrees;
    return (radians);
}
```

Discussion

All of the static trigonometric methods in the Math class use radians as their unit of measure for angles. It is very handy to have conversion routines to convert between radians and degrees, especially when a user is required to enter data in degrees rather than radians.

The equation for converting degrees to radians is shown here:

```
radians = (Math.PI / 180) * degrees
```

The static field Math.PI contains the constant π.

1.3   Converting Radians to Degrees

Problem

When using the trigonometric functions of the Math class, all units are in radians; instead, you require a result in degrees.

Solution

To convert a value in radians to degrees, multiply it by $180/\pi$:

```
using System;

public static double ConvertRadiansToDegrees(double radians)
{
    double degrees = (180 / Math.PI) * radians;
    return (degrees);
}
```

Discussion

All of the static trigonometric methods in the Math class use radians as their unit of measure for angles. It is very handy to have conversion routines to convert between radians and degrees, especially when displaying degrees to a user is more informative than displaying radians.

The equation for converting radians to degrees is shown here:

```
degrees = (180 / Math.PI) * radians
```

The static field `Math.PI` contains the constant π.

1.4   Using the Bitwise Complement Operator with Various Data Types

Problem

The bitwise complement operator (~) is overloaded to work directly with `int`, `uint`, `long`, `ulong`, and enumeration data types consisting of the underlying types `int`, `uint`, `long`, and `ulong`. However, you need to perform a different bitwise complement operation on a data type.

Solution

You must cast the resultant value of the bitwise operation to the type you wish to work. The following code demonstrates this technique with the byte data type:

```
byte y = 1;
byte result = (byte)~y;
```

The value assigned to `result` is 254.

Discussion

The following code shows incorrect use of the bitwise complement operator on the byte data type:

```
byte y = 1;
Console.WriteLine("~y = " + ~y);
```

This code outputs the following surprising value:

```
-2
```

Clearly, the result from performing the bitwise complement of the byte variable is incorrect; it should be 254. In fact, byte is an unsigned data type, so it cannot be equal to a negative number. If we rewrite the code as follows:

```
byte y = 1;
byte result = ~y;
```

we get a compile-time error: "Cannot implicitly convert type 'int' to 'byte.'" This error message gives some insight into why this operation does not work as expected. To fix this problem, we must explicitly cast this value to a byte before we assign it to the `result` variable, as shown here:

```
byte y = 1;
byte result = (byte)~y;
```

This cast is required because the bitwise operators are only overloaded to operate on six specific data types: int, uint, long, ulong, bool, and enumeration data types. When one of the bitwise operators is used on another data type, that data type is converted to the next closest data type of the six supported data types. Therefore, a byte data type is converted to an int before the bitwise complement operator is evaluated:

```
0x01        // byte y = 1;
0xFFFFFFFE  // The value 01h is converted to an int and its
            //    bitwise complement is taken
0xFE        // The resultant int value is cast to its original byte data type
```

Notice that the int data type is a signed data type, unlike the byte data type. This is why we receive -2 for a result instead of the expected value 254. This conversion of the byte data type to its nearest equivalent is called *numeric promotion*. Numeric promotion also comes into play when you use differing data types with binary operators, including the bitwise binary operators.

 Numeric promotion is discussed in detail in the C# Language Specification document in section 7.2.6 (this document is found in the directory \Microsoft Visual Studio .NET 2003\Vc7\1033 below the .NET 2003 installation directory). Understanding how numeric promotion works is essential when using operators on differing data types and when using operators with a data type that it is not overloaded to handle. Knowing this can save you hours of debugging time.

1.5   Test for an Even or Odd Value

Problem

You need a simple method to test a numeric value to determine whether it is even or odd.

Solution

The solution is actually implemented as two methods. To test for an even integer value, use the following method:

```
public static bool IsEven(int intValue)
{
    return ((intValue & 1) == 0);
}
```

To test for an odd integer value, use the following method:

```
public static bool IsOdd(int intValue)
{
    return ((intValue & 1) == 1);
}
```

Discussion

Every odd number always has its least-significant bit set to 1. Therefore, by checking whether this bit is equal to 1, we can tell whether it is an odd number. Conversely, testing the least-significant bit to see whether it is 0 can tell you whether it is an even number.

To test whether a value is even we AND the value in question with 1 and then determine whether the result is equal to zero. If the result is zero, we know that the value is an even number; otherwise, the value is odd. This operation is part of the IsEven method.

On the other hand, we can determine whether a value is odd by ANDing the value with 1, similar to how the even test operates, and then determine whether the result is 1. If the result is set to 1, we know that the value is an odd number; otherwise, the value is even. This operation is part of the IsOdd method.

Note that you do not have to implement both the IsEven and IsOdd methods in your application, although implementing both methods might improve the readability of your code.

The methods presented here accept only 32-bit integer values. To allow this method to accept other numeric data types, you can simply overload it to accept any other data types that you require. For example, if you need to also determine whether a 64-bit integer is even, you could modify the IsEven method as follows:

```
public static bool IsEven(long longValue)
{
    return ((longValue & 1) == 0);
}
```

Only the data type in the parameter list needs to be modified.

1.6 Obtaining the Most- or Least-Significant Bits of a Number

Problem

You have a 32-bit integer value that contains information in both its lower and upper 16 bits. You need a method to get the 16 most-significant bits and/or the 16 least-significant bits of this value.

Solution

To get the most-significant bits (MSB) of an integer value, perform a bitwise and between it and the value shown in the following method:

```
public static int GetMSB(int intValue)
{
    return (intValue & 0xFFFF0000);
}
```

To get the least-significant bits (LSB) of a value, use the following method:

```
public static int GetLSB(int intValue)
{
    return (intValue & 0x0000FFFF);
}
```

This technique can easily be modified to work with other sizes of integers (e.g., 8-bit, 16-bit, or 64-bit); this trick is shown in the Discussion section.

Discussion

In order to determine the values of the MSB of a number, use the following bitwise AND operation:

```
uint intValue = Int32.MaxValue;
uint MSB = intValue & 0xFFFF0000;

// MSB == 0xFFFF0000
```

This method simply ANDs the number to another number with all of the MSB set to 1. This method will zero out all of the LSB, leaving the MSB intact.

In order to determine the values of the LSB of a number, use the following bitwise AND operation:

```
uint intValue = Int32.MaxValue;
uint LSB = intValue & 0x0000FFFF;

// LSB == 0x0000FFFF
```

This method simply ANDs the number to another number with all of the LSB set to 1, which zeroes out all of the MSB, leaving the LSB intact.

The methods presented here accept only 32-bit integer values. To allow this method to accept other numeric data types, you can simply overload this method to accept any other data types that you require. For example, if you need to also acquire the least-significant byte or most-significant byte of a 16-bit integer, you could modify the GetMSB method as follows:

```
public static int GetMSB(short shortValue)
{
    return (shortValue & 0xFF00);
}
```

The GetLSB method is modified as shown here:

```
public static int GetLSB(short shortValue)
{
    return (shortValue & 0x00FF);
}
```

1.7 Converting a Number in Another Base to Base10

Problem

You have a string containing a number in base2 (binary), base8 (octal), base10 (decimal), or base16 (hexadecimal). You need to convert this string to its equivalent integer value and display it in base10.

Solution

Use the overloaded static Convert.ToInt32 method on the Convert class:

```
string base2 = "11";
string base8 = "17";
string base10 = "110";
string base16 = "11FF";

Console.WriteLine("Convert.ToInt32(base2, 2) = " +
                  Convert.ToInt32(base2, 2));

Console.WriteLine("Convert.ToInt32(base8, 8) = " +
                  Convert.ToInt32(base8, 8));

Console.WriteLine("Convert.ToInt32(base10, 10) = " +
                  Convert.ToInt32(base10, 10));

Console.WriteLine("Convert.ToInt32(base16, 16) = " +
                  Convert.ToInt32(base16, 16));
```

This code produces the following output:

```
Convert.ToInt32(base2, 2) = 3
Convert.ToInt32(base8, 8) = 15
Convert.ToInt32(base10, 10) = 110
Convert.ToInt32(base16, 16) = 4607
```

Discussion

The static Convert.ToInt32 method has an overload that takes a string containing a number and an integer defining the base of this number. This method then converts the numeric string into an integer and returns this number displayed as base10.

The other static methods of the Convert class, such as ToByte, ToInt64, and ToInt16, also have this same overload, which accepts a number as a string and a base type for this number. Unfortunately, these methods convert from base2, base8, base10, and base16 only to a value of base10. They do not convert a value to any other base types.

See Also

See the "Convert Class" and "Converting with System.Convert" topics in the MSDN documentation.

1.8 Determining Whether a String Is a Valid Number

Problem

You have a string that possibly contains a numeric value. You need to know whether this string contains a valid number.

Solution

Use the static `Parse` method of any of the numeric types. For example, to determine whether a string contains an integer, use the following method:

```
public static bool IsNumeric(string str)
{
    try
    {
        str = str.Trim( );
        int foo = int.Parse(str);
        return (true);
    }
    catch (FormatException)
    {
        // Not a numeric value
        return (false);
    }
}
```

If you instead needed to test whether a string is a floating-point value, change the second line in the try block to the following:

```
int foo = float.Parse(str);
```

A more compact way of testing a string for a numeric value—and one that does not have the overhead of throwing an exception—is to use the `double.TryParse` method:

```
public static bool IsNumericFromTryParse(string str)
{
    double result = 0;
    return (double.TryParse(str, System.Globalization.NumberStyles.Float,
            System.Globalization.NumberFormatInfo.CurrentInfo, out result));
}
```

The following `IsNumericRegEx` method does not incur the overhead of throwing an exception and it allows more flexibility in determining what type of number to test for. The `IsNumericRegEx` method tests for a number that can be signed/unsigned, contain a decimal point, and be displayed in scientific notation. This method accepts a string, possibly containing only a number, and returns true or false, depending on whether this string conforms to a numeric value:

```
private static Regex r = new Regex(@"^[\+\-]?\d*\.?[Ee]?[\+\-]?\d*$",
                                   RegexOptions.Compiled);

public static bool IsNumericRegEx(string str)
{
    str = str.Trim();
    Match m = r.Match(str);
    return (m.Value);
}
```

Discussion

This recipe shows three ways of determining whether a string contains only a numeric value. The IsNumeric method uses the Parse method, which throws a FormatException if the string cannot be converted to the appropriate type. The second method, IsNumericFromTryParse, uses the built-in double.TryParse method; this method also returns a value of type double if the string contains a valid number. The third method, IsNumericRegEx, uses a regular expression to determine whether the value of a string conforms to the various formats of a numeric value, such as an integer, a floating-point value, or a number written in scientific notation.

The method you choose can have a performance impact on your application. It's not just a question of whether it's called many times, it's also about whether a valid number exists within the string passed in to these methods. In some scenarios IsNumeric will be fastest, even if you call it many times. In others, the IsNumericFromTryParse or IsNumericRegEx will be fastest. It all depends on how often the string will not be a valid number. If you expect the string to contain non-numeric data most of the time (or even half the time), you should consider using the IsNumericFromTryParse or IsNumericRegEx methods. Otherwise, the IsNumeric method will give you the best performance.

The IsNumericRegEx method uses the static IsMatch method on the Regex class to attempt to match a numeric value contained in the string str. This static method returns true if the match succeeds and false if it does not. Notice also that the regular expression starts with the ^ character and ends with the $ character. This forces the regular expression to match everything within the string, not just part of the string. If these characters were not included, the IsMatch method would return true for the following string "111 West Ave".

The IsNumericRegEx method has a drawback: it cannot determine the data type of the number contained within the string. For example, the int.Parse method will accept only strings that contain a valid integer value; likewise, the float.Parse method will accept only strings containing valid float values. The regular expression will return true for any type of numeric value matched. To enhance the regular expression, use the following method to determine whether a value is a non-floating-point number:

```
public static bool IsIntegerRegEx(string str)
{
    str = str.Trim();
    return (Regex.IsMatch(str, @"^[\+\-]?\d+$"));
}
```

We could also use the following method to determine whether the string contains an unsigned number:

```
public static bool IsUnsignedIntegerRegEx(string str)
{
    str = str.Trim();
    return (Regex.IsMatch(str, @"^\+?\d+$"));
}
```

Note also that the Trim method can be excluded if you want to find numbers within strings that contain no beginning or ending whitespace.

1.9   Rounding a Floating-Point Value

Problem

You need to round a number to a whole number or to a specific number of decimal places.

Solution

To round any number to its nearest whole number, use the overloaded static Math. Round method, which takes only a single arguments:

```
int x = (int)Math.Round(2.5555);        // x == 3
```

If you need to round a floating-point value to a specific number of decimal places, use the overloaded static Math.Round method, which takes two arguments:

```
decimal x = Math.Round(2.5555, 2);        // x == 2.56
```

Discussion

The Round method is easy to use; however, you need to be aware of how the rounding operation works. The Round method follows the IEEE Standard 754, section 4 standard. This means that if the number being rounded is halfway between two numbers, the Round operation will always round to the even number. An example will show what this means to you:

```
decimal x = Math.Round(1.5);        // x == 2
decimal y = Math.Round(2.5);        // y == 2
```

Notice that 1.5 is rounded up to the nearest even whole number and 2.5 is rounded down to the nearest even whole number. Keep this in mind when using the Round method.

See Also

See Recipe 1.1; see the "Math Class" topic in the MSDN documentation.

1.10   Different Rounding Algorithms

Problem

The Math.Round method will round the value 1.5 to 2; however, the value 2.5 will also be rounded to 2 using this method. Always round to the greater number in this type of situation (e.g., round 2.5 to 3). Conversely, you might want to always round to the lesser number (e.g., round 1.5 to 1).

Solution

Use the static Math.Floor method to always round up when a value is halfway between two whole numbers:

```
public static double RoundUp(double valueToRound)
{
    return (Math.Floor(valueToRound + 0.5));
}
```

Use the following technique to always round down when a value is halfway between two whole numbers:

```
public static double RoundDown(double valueToRound)
{
    double floorValue = Math.Floor(valueToRound);
    if ((valueToRound - floorValue) > .5)
    {
        return (floorValue + 1);
    }
    else
    {
        return (floorValue);
    }
}
```

Discussion

The static Math.Round method rounds to the nearest even number (see Recipe 1.9 for more information). However, there are some times that you do not want to round a number in this manner. The static Math.Floor method can be used to allow for different manners of rounding.

```
    if (sourceValue <= short.MaxValue && sourceValue >= short.MinValue)
    {
        destinationValue = (short)sourceValue;
    }
    else
    {
        // Inform the application that a loss of information will occur
    }
```

Instead of placing this conditional throughout your code, you can use the following overloaded methods to determine whether an integral type will lose data in a cast:

```
// Overloaded methods to check conversions from unsigned integral types
//     to any other type
public static bool IsSafeToConvert(byte valueToConvert,
                                   string typeToConvertTo)
{
    return (IsSafeToConvert((ulong)valueToConvert, typeToConvertTo));
}

public static bool IsSafeToConvert(ushort valueToConvert,
                                   string typeToConvertTo)
{
    return (IsSafeToConvert((ulong)valueToConvert, typeToConvertTo));
}

public static bool IsSafeToConvert(uint valueToConvert,
                                   string typeToConvertTo)
{
    return (IsSafeToConvert((ulong)valueToConvert, typeToConvertTo));
}

public static bool IsSafeToConvert(ulong valueToConvert,
                                   string typeToConvertTo)
{
    bool isSafe = false;

    switch(typeToConvertTo)
    {
        case "byte":
            if(valueToConvert <= byte.MaxValue && valueToConvert >= 0)
                isSafe = true;
            break;

        case "sbyte":
            if(valueToConvert <= (ulong)sbyte.MaxValue &&
               valueToConvert >= 0)
                isSafe = true;
            break;

        case "short":
            if(valueToConvert <= (ulong)short.MaxValue &&
               valueToConvert >= 0)
                isSafe = true;
            break;
```

```csharp
        case "ushort":
            if(valueToConvert <= ushort.MaxValue && valueToConvert >= 0)
                isSafe = true;
            break;

        case "int":
            if(valueToConvert <= int.MaxValue && valueToConvert >= 0)
                isSafe = true;
            break;

        case "uint":
            if(valueToConvert <= uint.MaxValue && valueToConvert >= 0)
                isSafe = true;
            break;

        case "long":
            if(valueToConvert <= long.MaxValue && valueToConvert >= 0)
                isSafe = true;
            break;

        case "ulong":
            if(valueToConvert <= ulong.MaxValue && valueToConvert >= 0)
                isSafe = true;
            break;

        case "char":
            if(valueToConvert <= char.MaxValue && valueToConvert >= 0)
                isSafe = true;
            break;

        default:
            isSafe = true;
            break;
    }

    return (isSafe);
}

// Overloaded methods to check conversions from signed integral types
//      to any other type
public static bool IsSafeToConvert(sbyte valueToConvert,
                                   string typeToConvertTo)
{
    return (IsSafeToConvert((long)valueToConvert, typeToConvertTo));
}

public static bool IsSafeToConvert(short valueToConvert,
                                   string typeToConvertTo)
{
    return (IsSafeToConvert((long)valueToConvert, typeToConvertTo));
}

public static bool IsSafeToConvert(int valueToConvert,
                                   string typeToConvertTo)
```

```
{
    return (IsSafeToConvert((long)valueToConvert, typeToConvertTo));
}

public static bool IsSafeToConvert(char valueToConvert,
                                   string typeToConvertTo)
{
    return (IsSafeToConvert((long)valueToConvert, typeToConvertTo));
}

public static bool IsSafeToConvert(long valueToConvert,
                                   string typeToConvertTo)
{
    bool isSafe = false;

    switch(typeToConvertTo)
    {
        case "byte":
            if(valueToConvert <= byte.MaxValue &&
               valueToConvert >= byte.MinValue)
                isSafe = true;
            break;

        case "sbyte":
            if(valueToConvert <= sbyte.MaxValue &&
               valueToConvert >= sbyte.MinValue)
                isSafe = true;
            break;

        case "short":
            if(valueToConvert <= short.MaxValue &&
               valueToConvert >= short.MinValue)
                isSafe = true;
            break;

        case "ushort":
            if(valueToConvert <= ushort.MaxValue &&
               valueToConvert >= ushort.MinValue)
                isSafe = true;
            break;

        case "int":
            if(valueToConvert <= int.MaxValue &&
               valueToConvert >= int.MinValue)
                isSafe = true;
            break;

        case "uint":
            if(valueToConvert <= uint.MaxValue &&
               valueToConvert >= uint.MinValue)
                isSafe = true;
            break;
```

```csharp
        case "long":
            if(valueToConvert <= long.MaxValue &&
               valueToConvert >= long.MinValue)
                isSafe = true;
            break;

        case "ulong":
            if(valueToConvert >= 0)
                isSafe = true;
            break;

        case "char":
            if(valueToConvert <= char.MaxValue &&
               valueToConvert >= char.MinValue)
                isSafe = true;
            break;

        default:
            isSafe = true;
            break;
    }

    return (isSafe);
}

// Overloaded methods to check conversions from a float type
//     to any other type
public bool IsSafeToConvert(float valueToConvert, string typeToConvertTo)
{
    bool isSafe = false;

    switch(typeToConvertTo)
    {
        case "byte":
            if(valueToConvert <= byte.MaxValue &&
               valueToConvert >= byte.MinValue)
                isSafe = true;
            break;

        case "sbyte":
            if(valueToConvert <= sbyte.MaxValue &&
               valueToConvert >= sbyte.MinValue)
                isSafe = true;
            break;

        case "short":
            if(valueToConvert <= short.MaxValue &&
               valueToConvert >= short.MinValue)
                isSafe = true;
            break;

        case "ushort":
            if(valueToConvert <= ushort.MaxValue &&
               valueToConvert >= ushort.MinValue)
```

```
                isSafe = true;
            break;

        case "int":
            if(valueToConvert <= int.MaxValue &&
               valueToConvert >= int.MinValue)
                isSafe = true;
            break;

        case "uint":
            if(valueToConvert <= uint.MaxValue &&
               valueToConvert >= uint.MinValue)
                isSafe = true;
            break;

        case "long":
            if(valueToConvert <= long.MaxValue &&
               valueToConvert >= long.MinValue)
                isSafe = true;
            break;

        case "ulong":
            if(valueToConvert <= ulong.MaxValue &&
               valueToConvert >= ulong.MinValue)
                isSafe = true;
            break;

        case "char":
            if(valueToConvert <= char.MaxValue &&
               valueToConvert >= char.MinValue)
                isSafe = true;
        break;

        case "double":
            if(valueToConvert <= double.MaxValue &&
               valueToConvert >= double.MinValue)
                isSafe = true;
            break;

        case "decimal":
            if(valueToConvert <= (float)decimal.MaxValue &&
               valueToConvert >= (float)decimal.MinValue)
                isSafe = true;
            break;

        default:
            isSafe = true;
            break;
    }

    return (isSafe);
}

// Overloaded methods to check conversions from a double type
//    to any other type
```

```csharp
public bool IsSafeToConvert(double valueToConvert, string typeToConvertTo)
{
    bool isSafe = false;

    switch(typeToConvertTo)
    {
        case "byte":
            if(valueToConvert <= byte.MaxValue &&
                valueToConvert >= byte.MinValue)
                isSafe = true;
            break;

        case "sbyte":
            if(valueToConvert <= sbyte.MaxValue &&
                valueToConvert >= sbyte.MinValue)
                isSafe = true;
            break;

        case "short":
            if(valueToConvert <= short.MaxValue &&
                valueToConvert >= short.MinValue)
                isSafe = true;
            break;

        case "ushort":
            if(valueToConvert <= ushort.MaxValue &&
                valueToConvert >= ushort.MinValue)
                isSafe = true;
            break;

        case "int":
            if(valueToConvert <= int.MaxValue &&
                valueToConvert >= int.MinValue)
                isSafe = true;
            break;

        case "uint":
            if(valueToConvert <= uint.MaxValue &&
                valueToConvert >= uint.MinValue)
                isSafe = true;
            break;

        case "long":
            if(valueToConvert <= long.MaxValue &&
                valueToConvert >= long.MinValue)
                isSafe = true;
            break;

        case "ulong":
            if(valueToConvert <= ulong.MaxValue &&
                valueToConvert >= ulong.MinValue)
                isSafe = true;
            break;
```

```
            case "char":
                if(valueToConvert <= char.MaxValue &&
                   valueToConvert >= char.MinValue)
                    isSafe = true;
                break;

            case "float":
                if(valueToConvert <= float.MaxValue &&
                   valueToConvert >= float.MinValue)
                    isSafe = true;
                break;

            case "decimal":
                if(valueToConvert <= (double)decimal.MaxValue &&
                   valueToConvert >= (double)decimal.MinValue)
                    isSafe = true;
                break;

            default:
                isSafe = true;
                break;
    }

    return (isSafe);
}

// Overloaded methods to check conversions from a decimal type
//     to any other type
public bool IsSafeToConvert(decimal valueToConvert,
                            string typeToConvertTo)
{
    bool isSafe = false;

    switch(typeToConvertTo)
    {
        case "byte":
            if(valueToConvert <= byte.MaxValue &&
               valueToConvert >= byte.MinValue)
                isSafe = true;
            break;

        case "sbyte":
            if(valueToConvert <= sbyte.MaxValue &&
               valueToConvert >= sbyte.MinValue)
                isSafe = true;
            break;

        case "short":
            if(valueToConvert <= short.MaxValue &&
               valueToConvert >= short.MinValue)
                isSafe = true;
            break;
```

```
        case "ushort":
            if(valueToConvert <= ushort.MaxValue &&
                valueToConvert >= ushort.MinValue)
                isSafe = true;
            break;

        case "int":
            if(valueToConvert <= int.MaxValue &&
                valueToConvert >= int.MinValue)
                isSafe = true;
            break;

        case "uint":
            if(valueToConvert <= uint.MaxValue &&
                valueToConvert >= uint.MinValue) .
                isSafe = true;
            break;

        case "long":
            if(valueToConvert <= long.MaxValue &&
                valueToConvert >= long.MinValue)
                isSafe = true;
            break;

        case "ulong":
            if(valueToConvert <= ulong.MaxValue &&
                valueToConvert >= ulong.MinValue)
                isSafe = true;
            break;

        case "char":
            if(valueToConvert <= char.MaxValue &&
                valueToConvert >= char.MinValue)
                isSafe = true;
            break;

        default:
            isSafe = true;
            break;
    }

    return (isSafe);
}
```

Discussion

A *narrowing conversion* occurs when a larger type is cast down to a smaller type. For instance, consider casting a value of type Int32 to a value of type Int16. If the Int32 value is smaller or equal to the Int16.MaxValue field and the Int32 value is higher or equal to the Int16.MinValue field, the cast will occur without error or loss of information. Loss of information occurs when the Int32 value is larger than the Int16. MaxValue field or the Int32 value is lower than the Int16.MinValue field. In either of these cases, the most-significant bits of the Int32 value would be truncated and discarded, changing the value after the cast.

If a loss of information occurs in an unchecked context, it will occur silently without the application noticing. This problem can cause some very insidious bugs that are hard to track down. To prevent this, check the value to be converted to determine whether it is within the lower and upper bounds of the type that it will be cast to. If the value is outside these bounds, then code can be written to handle this situation. This code could force the cast not to occur and/or possibly to inform the application of the casting problem. This solution can aid in the prevention of hard-to-find arithmetic bugs from appearing in your applications.

You should understand that both techniques shown in the Solution section are valid. However, the technique you use will depend on whether you expect to hit the overflow case on a regular basis or only occasionally. If you expect to hit the overflow case quite often, you might want to choose the second technique of manually testing the numeric value. Otherwise, it might be easier to use the checked keyword, as in the first technique.

In C#, code can run in either a *checked* or *unchecked* context; by default, the code runs in an unchecked context. In a checked context, any arithmetic and conversions involving integral types are examined to determine whether an overflow condition exists. If so, an OverflowException is thrown. In an unchecked context, no OverflowException will be thrown when an overflow condition exists.

A checked context can be set up by using the /checked{+} compiler switch, by setting the Check for Arithmetic Overflow/Underflow project property to true, or by using the checked keyword. An unchecked context can be set up using the /checked- compiler switch, by setting the Check for Arithmetic Overflow/Underflow project property to false, or by using the unchecked keyword.

Notice that floating-point and decimal types are not included in the code that handles the conversions to integral types in this recipe. The reason is that a conversion from any integral type to a float, double, or decimal will not lose any information; therefore, it is redundant to check these conversions.

In addition, you should be aware of the following when performing a conversion:

- Casting from a float, double, or decimal type to an integral type results in the truncation of the fractional portion of this number.
- Casting from a float or double to a decimal results in the float or double being rounded to 28 decimal places.
- Casting from a double to a float results in the double being rounded to the nearest float value.
- Casting from a decimal to a float or double results in the decimal being rounded to the resulting type (float or double).

- Casting from int, uint, or long to a float could result in the loss of precision, but never magnitude.
- Casting from long to a double could result in the loss of precision, but never magnitude.

See Also

See the "checked" keyword and "Checked and Unchecked" topics in the MSDN documentation.

1.14 Finding the Length of Any Three Sides of a Right Triangle

Problem

You need to calculate the length of one side of a triangle when either the lengths of two sides are known or one angle and the length of a side are known.

Solution

Use the Math.Sin, Math.Cos, and Math.Tan methods of the Math class to find the length of one side. The equations for these methods are as follows:

```
double theta = 40;
double hypotenuse = 5;
double oppositeSide;
double adjacentSide;

oppositeSide = Math.Sin(theta) * hypotenuse;
oppositeSide = Math.Tan(theta) * adjacentSide;
adjacentSide = Math.Cos(theta) * hypotenuse;
adjacentSide = oppositeSide / Math.Tan(theta);
hypotenuse   = oppositeSide / Math.Sin(theta);
hypotenuse   = adjacentSide / Math.Cos(theta);
```

where theta(Θ) is the known angle, and the oppositeSide variable is equal to the length of the side *opposite* to the angle theta, and the adjacentSide variable is equal to the length of the side *adjacent* to the angle theta. The hypotenuse variable is equal to the length of the *hypotenuse* of the triangle. See Figure 1-1.

In addition to these three static methods, the length of the hypotenuse of a right triangle can be calculated using the Pythagorean theorem. This theorem states that the hypotenuse of a right triangle is equal to the square root of the sum of the squares of the other two sides. This equation can be realized through the use of the Math.Pow and Math.Sqrt static methods of the Math class, as follows:

```
double hypotenuse = Math.Sqrt(Math.Pow(xSide, 2) + Math.Pow(ySide, 2))
```

where xSide and ySide are the lengths of the two sides that are *not* the hypotenuse of the triangle.

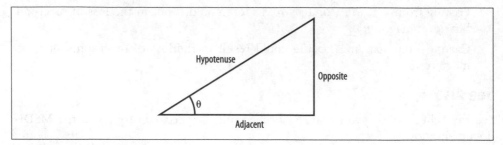

Figure 1-1. A right triangle

Discussion

Finding the length of a side of a right triangle is easy when an angle and the length of one of the sides are known. Using the trigonometric functions sine, cosine, and tangent, we can derive the lengths of either of the two unknown sides. The equations for sine, cosine, and tangent are defined here:

```
sin(Theta) = oppositeSide / hypotenuseSide
cos(Theta) = adjacentSide / hypotenuseSide
tan(Theta) = oppositeSide / adjacentSide
```

where theta is the value of the known angle. Rearranging these equations allows us to derive the following equations:

```
oppositeSide = sin(theta) * hypotenuse;
oppositeSide = tan(theta) * adjacentSide;
adjacentSide = cos(theta) * hypotenuse;
adjacentSide = oppositeSide / tan(theta);
hypotenuse   = oppositeSide / sin(theta);
hypotenuse   = adjacentSide / cos(theta);
```

These equations give us two methods to find the length of each side of the triangle.

In the case where none of the angles are known, but the lengths of two of the sides are known, use the Pythagorean theorem to determine the length of the hypotenuse. This theorem is defined as follows:

```
Math.Sqrt(Math.Pow(hypotenuse)) = Math.Sqrt(Math.Pow(xSide, 2) + Math.Pow(ySide, 2))
```

Simplifying this equation into a syntax usable by C#, we obtain the following code:

```
double hypotenuse = Math.Sqrt(Math.Pow(xSide, 2) + Math.Pow(ySide, 2));
```

where hypotenuse is equal to the length of the hypotenuse, and xSide and ySide are the lengths of the other two sides.

See Also

See the "Math Class" topic in the MSDN documentation.

1.15 Finding the Angles of a Right Triangle

Problem

You need to calculate an angle of a triangle when the lengths of two sides are known.

Solution

Use the Math.Atan, Math.Acos, or Math.Asin static methods of the Math class. The following code calculates the angle theta and returns the value in *radian* measure:

```
double theta = Math.Atan(OppositeSide / AdjacentSide);
theta = Math.Acos(AdjacentSide / Hypotenuse);
theta = Math.Asin(OppositeSide / Hypotenuse);
```

To get the angle in degrees, use the following code:

```
double theta = Math.Atan(oppositeSide / adjacentSide) * (180 / Math.PI);
theta = Math.Acos(adjacentSide / hypotenuse) * (180 / Math.PI);
theta = Math.Asin(oppositeSide / hypotenuse) * (180 / Math.PI);
```

where theta is the known angle value, the oppositeSide is equal to the length of the side *opposite* to the angle, and adjacentSide is equal to the length of the side *adjacent* to the angle. The hypotenuse is the length of the *hypotenuse* of the triangle. See Figure 1-1 in Recipe 1.14 for a graphical representation of these sides of a right triangle.

Discussion

In some cases, we need to determine an angle of a right triangle when only the lengths of two sides are known. The three trigonometric functions arcsine, arccosine, and arctangent allow us to find any angle of a right triangle, given this information. The static methods Math.Atan, Math.Acos, and Math.Asin on the Math class provide the functionality to implement these trigonometric operations.

See Also

See Recipe 1.14; see the "Math Class" topic in the MSDN documentation.

CHAPTER 2

Strings and Characters

String usage abounds in just about all types of applications. The System.String type does not derive from System.ValueType and is therefore considered a reference type. The string alias is built into C# and can be used instead of the full name.

The FCL does not stop with just the string class; there is also a System.Text. StringBuilder class for performing string manipulations and the System.Text. RegularExpressions namespace for searching strings. This chapter will cover the string class and the System.Text.StringBuilder class.

The System.Text.StringBuilder class provides an easy, performance friendly, method of manipulating string objects. This class duplicates much of the functionality of a string class. However, this duplicated functionality provides a more efficient manipulation of strings than is obtainable by using the string class.

2.1   Determining the Kind of Character

Problem

You have a variable of type char and wish to determine the kind of character it contains—a letter, digit, number, punctuation character, control character, separator character, symbol, whitespace, or surrogate character. Similarly, you have a string variable and want to determine the kind of character in one or more positions within this string.

Solution

Use the built-in static methods on the System.Char structure shown here:

```
Char.IsControl
Char.IsDigit
Char.IsLetter
Char.IsNumber
```

```
Char.IsPunctuation
Char.IsSeparator
Char.IsSurrogate
Char.IsSymbol
Char.IsWhitespace
```

Discussion

The following examples demonstrate how to use the methods shown in the Solution section in a function to return the kind of a character. First, create an enumeration to define the various types of characters:

```
public enum CharKind
{
    Control,
    Digit,
    Letter,
    Number,
    Punctuation,
    Separator,
    Surrogate,
    Symbol,
    Whitespace,
    Unknown
}
```

Next, create a method that contains the logic to determine the type of a character and to return a CharKind enumeration value indicating that type:

```
public static CharKind GetCharKind(char theChar)
{
    if (Char.IsControl(theChar))
    {
        return CharKind.Control;
    }
    else if (Char.IsDigit(theChar))
    {
        return CharKind.Digit;
    }
    else if (Char.IsLetter(theChar))
    {
        return CharKind.Letter;
    }
    else if (Char.IsNumber(theChar))
    {
        return CharKind.Number;
    }
    else if (Char.IsPunctuation(theChar))
    {
        return CharKind.Punctuation;
    }
    else if (Char.IsSeparator(theChar))
```

See Also

See the "Char Structure" topic in the MSDN documentation.

2.2   Determining Whether a Character Is Within a Specified Range

Problem

You need to determine whether a character in a char data type is within a range, such as between 1 and 5 or between A and M.

Solution

Use the built-in comparison support for the char data type. The following code shows how to use the built-in comparison support:

```
public static bool IsInRange(char testChar, char startOfRange, char endOfRange)
{
    if (testChar >= startOfRange && testChar <= endOfRange)
    {
        // testChar is within the range
        return (true);
    }
    else
    {
        // testChar is NOT within the range
        return (false);
    }
}
```

There is only one problem with that code. If the startOfRange and endOfRange characters have different cases, the result may not be what you expect. By adding the following code, which makes all characters uppercase, to the beginning of the method in Recipe 2.7, we can solve this problem:

```
testChar = char.ToUpper(testChar);
startOfRange = char.ToUpper(startOfRange);
endOfRange = char.ToUpper(endOfRange);
```

Discussion

The IsInRange method accepts three parameters. The first is the testChar character that you need to check on, to test if it falls between the last two parameters on this method. The last two parameters are the starting and ending characters, respectively, of a range of characters. The testChar parameter must be between startOfRange and endOfRange or equal to one of theses parameters for this method to return true; otherwise, false is returned.

The `IsInRange` method can be called in the following manner:

```
bool inRange = IsInRange('c', 'a', 'g');
bool inRange = IsInRange('c', 'a', 'b');
bool inRange = IsInRange((char)32, 'a', 'g');
```

The first call to this method returns `true`, since `c` is between `a` and `g`. The second method returns `false`, since `c` is not between `a` and `b`. The third method indicates how an integer value representative of a character would be passed to this method.

Note that this method tests whether the `testChar` value is inclusive between the range of characters `startOfRange` and `endOfRange`. If you wish to determine only whether `testChar` is between this range exclusive of the `startOfRange` and `endOfRange` character values, you should modify the `if` statement, as follows:

```
if (testChar > startOfRange && testChar < endOfRange)
```

2.3   Controlling Case Sensitivity when Comparing Two Characters

Problem

You need to compare two characters for equality, but you need the flexibility of performing a case-sensitive or case-insensitive comparison.

Solution

Use the `Equals` instance method on the char structure to compare the two characters:

```
public static bool IsCharEqual(char firstChar, char secondChar)
{
    return (IsCharEqual(firstChar, secondChar, false));
}

public static bool IsCharEqual(char firstChar, char secondChar,
                               bool caseSensitiveCompare)
{
    if (caseSensitiveCompare)
    {
        return (firstChar.Equals(secondChar));
    }
    else
    {
        return (char.ToUpper(firstChar).Equals(char.ToUpper(secondChar)));
    }
}
```

The first overloaded `IsCharEqual` method takes only two parameters: the characters to be compared. This method then calls the second `IsCharEqual` method with three parameters. The third parameter on this method call defaults to `false` so that when this method is called, you do not have to pass in a value for the `caseSensitiveCompare` parameter—it will automatically default to `false`.

Discussion

Using the `ToUpper` method in conjunction with the `Equals` method on the `string` class allows us to choose whether to take into account the case of the strings when comparing them. To perform a case-sensitive comparison of two `char` variables, simply use the `Equals` method, which, by default, performs a case-sensitive comparison. Performing a case-insensitive comparison requires that both characters be converted to their uppercase values (they could just as easily be converted to their lowercase equivalents, but for this recipe we convert them to uppercase) before the `Equals` method is invoked. Setting both characters to their uppercase equivalents removes any case-sensitivity between the character values, and they can be compared using the case-sensitive `Equals` comparison method as though it were a case-insensitive comparison.

You can further extend the overloaded `IsCharEqual` methods to handle the culture of the characters passed in to it:

```
public static bool IsCharEqual(char firstChar, CultureInfo firstCharCulture,
                               char secondChar, CultureInfo secondCharCulture)
{
    return (IsCharEqual(firstChar, firstCharCulture,
            secondChar, secondCharCulture, false));
}

public static bool IsCharEqual(char firstChar, CultureInfo firstCharCulture,
                               char secondChar, CultureInfo secondCharCulture,
                               bool caseSensitiveCompare)
{
    if (caseSensitiveCompare)
    {
        return (firstChar.Equals(secondChar));
    }
    else
    {
        return (char.ToUpper(firstChar, firstCharCulture).Equals
                    (char.ToUpper(secondChar, secondCharCulture)));
    }
}
```

The addition of the `CultureInfo` parameters to these methods allows us to pass in the culture information for the strings that we are calling `ToUpper` on. This information allows the `ToUpper` method to correctly uppercase the character based in the culture-specific details of the character (i.e., the language, region, etc., of the character).

Note that you must include the following using directives to compile this code:

```
using System;
using System.Globalization;
```

2.4 Finding All Occurrences of a Character Within a String

Problem

You need a way of searching a string for multiple occurrences of a specific character.

Solution

Use IndexOf in a loop to determine how many occurrences of a character exist, as well as identify their location within the string:

```
using System;
using System.Collections;

public static int[] FindAllOccurrences(char matchChar, string source)
{
    return (FindAllOccurrences(matchChar, source, -1, false));
}

public static int[] FindAllOccurrences(char matchChar, string source,
                                       int maxMatches)
{
    return (FindAllOccurrences(matchChar, source, maxMatches, false));
}

public static int[] FindAllOccurrences(char matchChar, string source,
                                       bool caseSensitivity)
{
    return (FindAllOccurrences(matchChar, source, -1, caseSensitivity));
}

public static int[] FindAllOccurrences(char matchChar, string source,
                                       int maxMatches, bool caseSensitivity)
{
    ArrayList occurrences = new ArrayList();
    int foundPos = -1;    // -1 represents not found
    int numberFound = 0;
    int startPos = 0;
    char tempMatchChar = matchChar;
    string tempSource = source;

    if (!caseSensitivity)
    {
        tempMatchChar = char.ToUpper(matchChar);
        tempSource = source.ToUpper();
    }

    do
    {
        foundPos = tempSource.IndexOf(matchChar, startPos);
        if (foundPos > -1)
```

```
        {
            startPos = foundPos + 1;
            numberFound++;

            if (maxMatches > -1 && numberFound > maxMatches)
            {
                break;
            }
            else
            {
                occurrences.Add(foundPos);
            }
        }
    }while (foundPos > -1);

    return ((int[])occurrences.ToArray(typeof(int)));
}
```

Discussion

The FindAllOccurrences method is overloaded to allow the last two parameters (maxMatches and caseSensitivity) to be set to a default value if the developer chooses not to pass in one or both of these parameters. The maxMatches parameter defaults to -1, indicating that all matches are to be found. The caseSensitivity parameter defaults to false to allow for a case-insensitive search.

The FindAllOccurrences method starts out by determining whether case sensitivity is turned on. If false was passed in to the caseSensitivity parameter, both matchChar and source are set to all uppercase. This prevents a case-sensitive search.

The main loop in this method is a simple do loop that terminates when foundPos returns -1, meaning that no more matchChar characters can be found in the source string. We use a do loop so that the IndexOf operation would be executed at least one time before the check in the while clause is performed to determine whether there are any more character matches to be found in the source string.

Once a match is found by the IndexOf method, the numberFound variable is incremented by one to indicate that another match was found, and startPos is moved past the previously found match to indicate where the next IndexOf operation should start. The startPos is increased to the starting position of the last match found plus one. The +1 is needed so that we do not keep matching the same character that was previously matched. An infinite loop would occur in the code if at least one match was found in the source string.

Finally, a check is made to determine whether we are done searching for matchChar characters. If the maxMatches parameter is set to -1, the code keeps searching until it arrives at the end of the source string. Any other number indicates the maximum number of matchChar characters to search for. The maxMatches parameter limits the number of matches that can be made in the source string. If this check indicates that we are able to keep this match, it is stored in the occurrences ArrayList.

2.5   Finding the Location of All Occurrences of a String Within Another String

Problem

You need to search a string for every occurrence of a specific string. In addition, the case-sensitivity, or insensitivity, of the search needs to be controlled.

Solution

Using IndexOf or IndexOfAny in a loop, we can determine how many occurrences of a character or string exist as well their locations within the string. To find each occurrence of a case-sensitive string in another string, use the following code:

```
using System;
using System.Collections;

public static int[] FindAll(string matchStr, string searchedStr, int startPos)
{
    int foundPos = -1;    // -1 represents not found
    int count = 0;
    ArrayList foundItems = new ArrayList();

    do
    {
        foundPos = searchedStr.IndexOf(matchStr, startPos);
        if (foundPos > -1)
        {
            startPos = foundPos + 1;
            count++;
            foundItems.Add(foundPos);

            Console.WriteLine("Found item at position: " + foundPos.ToString());
        }
    }while (foundPos > -1 && startPos < searchedStr.Length);

    return ((int[])foundItems.ToArray(typeof(int)));
}
```

If the FindAll method is called with the following parameters:

```
int[] allOccurrences = FindAll("Red", "BlueTealRedredGreenRedYellow", 0);
```

the string "Red" is found at locations 8 and 19 in the string searchedStr. This code uses the IndexOf method inside a loop to iterate through each found matchStr string in the searchStr string.

To find a case-sensitive character in a string, use the following code:

```
public static int[] FindAll(char MatchChar, string searchedStr, int startPos)
{
    int foundPos = -1;    // -1 represents not found
    int count = 0;
    ArrayList foundItems = new ArrayList();
```

```
      do
      {
          foundPos = searchedStr.IndexOf(MatchChar, startPos);
          if (foundPos > -1)
          {
              startPos = foundPos + 1;
              count++;
              foundItems.Add(foundPos);

              Console.WriteLine("Found item at position: " + foundPos.ToString());
          }
      }while (foundPos > -1 && startPos < searchedStr.Length);

      return ((int[])foundItems.ToArray(typeof(int)));
}
```

If the FindAll method is called with the following parameters:

```
int[] allOccurrences = FindAll('r', "BlueTealRedredGreenRedYellow", 0);
```

the character 'r' is found at locations 11 and 15 in the string searchedStr. This code uses the IndexOf method inside a do loop to iterate through each found matchChar character in the searchStr string. Overloading the FindAll method to accept either a char or string type avoids the performance hit of boxing the char type to a string type.

To find each case-insensitive occurrence of a string in another string, use the following code:

```
public static int[] FindAny(string matchStr, string searchedStr, int startPos)
{
    int foundPos = -1;    // -1 represents not found
    int count = 0;
    ArrayList foundItems = new ArrayList();

    // Factor out case-sensitivity
    searchedStr = searchedStr.ToUpper();
    matchStr = matchStr.ToUpper();

    do
    {
        foundPos = searchedStr.IndexOf(matchStr, startPos);
        if (foundPos > -1)
        {
            startPos = foundPos + 1;
            count++;
            foundItems.Add(foundPos);

            Console.WriteLine("Found item at position: " + foundPos.ToString());
        }
    }while (foundPos > -1 && startPos < searchedStr.Length);

    return ((int[])foundItems.ToArray(typeof(int)));
}
```

If the `FindAny` method is called with the following parameters:

```
int[] allOccurrences = FindAll("Red", "BlueTealRedredGreenRedYellow", 0);
```

the string "Red" is found at locations 8, 11, and 19 in the string `searchedStr`. This code uses the `IndexOf` method inside a loop to iterate through each found `matchStr` string in the `searchStr` string. The search is rendered case-insensitive by using the `ToUpper` method on both the `searchedStr` and the `matchStr` strings.

To find a character in a string, use the following code:

```
public static int[] FindAny(char[] MatchCharArray, string searchedStr, int startPos)
{
    int foundPos = -1;    // -1 represents not found
    int count = 0;
    ArrayList foundItems = new ArrayList();

    do
    {
        foundPos = searchedStr.IndexOfAny(MatchCharArray, startPos);
        if (foundPos > -1)
        {
            startPos = foundPos + 1;
            count++;
            foundItems.Add(foundPos);

            Console.WriteLine("Found item at position: " + foundPos.ToString());
        }
    }while (foundPos > -1 && startPos < searchedStr.Length);

    return ((int[])foundItems.ToArray(typeof(int)));
}
```

If the `FindAll` method is called with the following parameters:

```
int[] allOccurrences = FindAll(new char[] MatchCharArray = {'R', 'r'},
                           "BlueTealRedredGreenRedYellow", 0);
```

the characters 'r' or 'R' are found at locations 8, 11, 15, and 19 in the string `searchedStr`. This code uses the `IndexOfAny` method inside a loop to iterate through each found `matchStr` string in the `searchStr` string. The search is rendered case-insensitive by using an array of `char` containing all characters, both upper- and lowercase, to be searched for.

Discussion

In the example code, the `foundPos` variable contains the location of the found character/string within the `searchedStr` string. The `startPos` variable contains the next position in which to start the search. The `IndexOf` or `IndexOfAny` method is used to perform the actual searching. The `count` variable simply counts the number of times the character/string was found in the `searchedStr` string.

The example used a do loop so that the IndexOf or IndexOfAny operation would be executed at least one time before the check in the while clause is performed to determine whether there are any more character/string matches to be found in the searchedStr string. This loop terminates when foundPos returns -1 (meaning that no more character/strings can be found in the searchedStr string) or when an out-of-bounds condition exists. When foundPos equals -1, there are no more instances of the match value in the searchedStr string; therefore, we can exit the loop. If, however, the startPos overshoots the last character element of the searchedStr string, an out-of-bounds condition exists and an exception is thrown. To prevent this, always check to make sure that any positioning variables that are modified inside of the loop, such as the startPos variable, are within their intended bounds.

Once a match is found by the IndexOf or IndexOfAny method, the if statement body is executed to increment the count variable by one and to move the startPos up past the previously found match. The count variable is incremented by one to indicate that another match was found. The startPos is increased to the starting position of the last match found plus 1. Adding 1 is necessary so that we do not keep matching the same character/string that was previously matched, which would cause an infinite loop to occur in the code if at least one match was found in the searchedStr string. To see this behavior, remove the +1 from the code.

There is one potential problem with this code. Consider the case where:

```
searchedStr = "aa";
matchStr = "aaaa";
```

The code contained in this recipe would match "aa" three times.

```
(aa)aa
a(aa)a
aa(aa)
```

This situation may be fine for some applications, but not if you need it to return only the following matches:

```
(aa)aa
aa(aa)
```

To do this, change the following line in the while loop:

```
startPos = foundPos + 1;
```

to this:

```
startPos = foundPos + matchStr.Length;
```

This code moves the startPos pointer beyond the first matched string, disallowing any internal matches.

To convert this code to use a while loop rather than a do loop, the foundPos variable must be initialized to 0 and the while loop expression should be as follows:

```
while (foundPos >= 0 && startPos < searchStr.Length)
{
    foundPos = searchedStr.IndexOf(matchChar, startPos);
    If (foundPos > -1)
    {
        startPos = foundPos + 1;
        count++;
    }
}
```

See Also

See the "String.IndexOf Method" and "String.IndexOfAny Method" topics in the MSDN documentation.

2.6   The Poor Man's Tokenizer

Problem

You need a quick method of breaking up a string into a series of discrete tokens or words.

Solution

Use the Split instance method of the string class. For example:

```
string equation = "1 + 2 - 4 * 5";
string[] equationTokens = equation.Split(new char[1]{' '});

foreach (string Tok in equationTokens)
    Console.WriteLine(Tok);
```

This code produces the following output:

```
1
+
2
-
4
*
5
```

The Split method may also be used to separate people's first, middle, and last names. For example:

```
string fullName1 = "John Doe";
string fullName2 = "Doe,John";
string fullName3 = "John Q. Doe";

string[] nameTokens1 = fullName1.Split(new char[3]{' ', ',', '.'});
string[] nameTokens2 = fullName2.Split(new char[3]{' ', ',', '.'});
string[] nameTokens3 = fullName3.Split(new char[3]{' ', ',', '.'});
```

```
foreach (string tok in nameTokens1)
{
    Console.WriteLine(tok);
}
Console.WriteLine("");

foreach (string tok in nameTokens2)
{
    Console.WriteLine(tok);
}
Console.WriteLine("");

foreach (string tok in nameTokens3)
{
    Console.WriteLine(tok);
}
```

This code produces the following output:

```
John
Doe

Doe
John

John
Q

Doe
```

Notice that a blank is inserted between the '.' and the space delimiters of the fullName3 name; this is correct behavior. If you did not want to process this space in your code, you can choose to ignore it.

Discussion

If you have a consistent string whose parts, or *tokens*, are separated by well-defined characters, the Split function can tokenize the string. Tokenizing a string consists of breaking the string down into well-defined, discrete parts, each of which is considered a token. In the two previous examples, the tokens were either parts of a mathematical equation (numbers and operators) or parts of a name (first, middle, and last).

There are several drawbacks to this approach. First, if the string of tokens is not separated by any well-defined character(s), it will be impossible to use the Split method to break up the string. For example, if the equation string looked like this:

```
string equation = "1+2-4*5";
```

we would clearly have to use a more robust method of tokenizing this string (see Recipe 8.7 for a more robust tokenizer).

A second drawback is that a string of tokenized words must be entered consistently in order to gain meaning from the tokens. For example, if we ask users to type in their names, they may enter any of the following:

```
John Doe
Doe John
John Q Doe
```

If one user enters in his name the first way and another user enters it the second way, our code will have a difficult time determining whether the first token in the string array represents the first or last name. The same problem will exist for all of the other tokens in the array. However, if all users enter their names in a consistent style, such as *First Name*, space, *Last Name*, we will have a much easier time tokenizing the name and understanding what each token represents.

See Also

See Recipe 8.7; see the "String.Split Method" topic in the MSDN documentation.

2.7   Controlling Case Sensitivity when Comparing Two Strings

Problem

You need to compare the contents of two strings for equality. In addition, the case sensitivity of the comparison needs to be controlled.

Solution

Use the `Compare` static method on the `string` class to compare the two strings. Whether the comparison is case-insensitive is determined by the third parameter of one of its overloads. For example:

```
string lowerCase = "abc";
string upperCase = "AbC";

int caseSensitiveResult = string.Compare(lowerCase, upperCase, false);
int caseInsensitiveResult = string.Compare(lowerCase, upperCase, true);
```

The `caseSensitiveResult` value is -1 (indicating that `lowerCase` is "less than" `upperCase`) and the `caseInsensitiveResult` is zero (indicating that `lowerCase` "equals" `upperCase`).

Discussion

Using the static `string.Compare` method allows us the freedom to choose whether to take into account the case of the strings when comparing them. This method returns an integer indicating the lexical relationship between the two strings. A zero means that the two strings are equal, a negative number means that the first string is less than the second string, and a positive number indicates that the first string is greater than the second string.

By setting the last parameter of this method (the *IgnoreCase* parameter) to true or false, we can determine whether the Compare method takes into account the case of both strings when comparing. Setting this parameter to true forces a case-insensitive comparison and setting this parameter to false forces a case-sensitive comparison. In the case of the overloaded version of the method with no *IgnoreCase* parameter, comparisons are always case-sensitive.

See Also

See the "String.Compare Method" topic in the MSDN documentation.

2.8 Comparing a String to the Beginning or End of a Second String

Problem

You need to determine whether a string is at the head or tail of a second string. In addition, the case sensitivity of the search needs to be controlled.

Solution

Use the EndsWith or StartsWith instance methods on a string object. Comparisons with EndsWith and StartsWith are always case-sensitive. The following code compares the value in the string variable head to the beginning of the string Test:

```
string head = "str";
string test = "strVarName";
bool isFound = test.StartsWith(head);
```

The following example compares the value in the string variable Tail to the end of the string test:

```
string tail = "Name";
string test = "strVarName";
bool isFound = test.EndsWith(tail);
```

In both examples, the isFound Boolean variable is set to true, since each string is found in test.

To do a case-insensitive comparison, employ the static string.Compare method. The following two examples modify the previous two examples by performing a case-insensitive comparison. The first is equivalent to a case-insensitive StartsWith string search:

```
string head = "str";
string test = "strVarName";
int isFound = string.Compare(head, 0, test, 0, head.Length, true);
```

The second is equivalent to a case-insensitive EndsWith string search:

```
string tail = "Name";
string test = "strVarName";
int isFound = string.Compare(tail, 0, test, (test.Length - tail.Length),
                             tail.Length, true);
```

Discussion

Use the `BeginsWith` or `EndsWith` instance methods to do a case-sensitive search for a particular string at the beginning or end of a string. The equivalent case-insensitive comparison requires the use of the static `Compare` method in the `string` class. If the return value of the `Compare` method is zero, a match was found. Any other number means that a match was not found.

See Also

See the "String.StartsWith Method," "String.EndsWith Method," and "String.Compare Method" topics in the MSDN documentation.

2.9   Inserting Text into a String

Problem

You have some text (either a `char` or a `string` value) that needs to be inserted at a specific location inside of a second string.

Solution

Using the `Insert` instance method of the `string` class, a `string` or `char` can easily be inserted into a string. For example, in the code fragment:

```
string sourceString = "The Inserted Text is here -><-";

sourceString  = sourceString.Insert(28, "Insert-This");
Console.WriteLine(sourceString);
```

the string `sourceString` is inserted between the > and < characters in a second string. The result is:

```
The Inserted Text is here ->Insert-This<-
```

Inserting the character in `sourceString` into a second literal string between the > and < characters is shown here:

```
string sourceString = "The Inserted Text is here -><-";
char insertChar = '1';

sourceString  = sourceString.Insert(28, Convert.ToString(insertChar));
Console.WriteLine(sourceString);
```

There is no overloaded method for `Insert` that takes a `char` value, so using a string of length one is the next best solution.

Discussion

There are two ways of inserting strings into other strings, unless, of course, you are using the regular expression classes. The first involves using the Insert instance method on the string class. This method is also slower than the others since strings are immutable, and, therefore, a new string object must be created to hold the modified value. In this recipe, the reference to the old string object is then changed to point to the new string object. Note that the Insert method leaves the original string untouched and creates a new string object with the inserted characters.

To add flexibility and speed to your string insertions, use the Insert instance method on the StringBuilder class. This method is overloaded to accept all of the built-in types. In addition, the StringBuilder object optimizes string insertion by not making copies of the original string; instead, the original string is modified.

If we use the StringBuilder class instead of the string class to insert a string, our code appears as:

```
StringBuilder sourceString =
  new StringBuilder("The Inserted Text is here ->< -");
sourceString.Insert (28, "Insert-This");
Console.WriteLine(sourceString);
```

The character insertion example would be changed to the following code:

```
char charToInsert = '1';
StringBuilder sourceString =
  new StringBuilder("The Inserted Text is here ->< -");
sourceString.Insert (28, charToInsert);
Console.WriteLine(sourceString);
```

Note that when using the StringBuilder class, you must also use the System.Text namespace.

See Also

See the "String.Insert Method" topic in the MSDN documentation.

2.10   Removing or Replacing Characters Within a String

Problem

You have some text within a string that needs to be either removed or replaced with a different character or string. Since the replacing operation is somewhat simple, you do not require the overhead of using a regular expression to aid in the replacing operation.

Solution

To remove a substring from a string, use the `Remove` instance method on the `string` class. For example:

```
string name = "Doe, John";
name = name.Remove(3, 1);
Console.WriteLine(name);
```

This code creates a new string and then sets the `name` variable to refer to it. The string contained in `name` now looks like this:

```
Doe John
```

If performance is critical, and particularly if the string removal operation occurs in a loop so that the operation is performed multiple times, you can instead use the `Remove` method of the `StringBuilder` object. The following code modifies the `str` variable so that its value becomes 12345678:

```
StringBuilder str = new StringBuilder("1234abc5678", 12);
str.Remove(4, 3);
Console.WriteLine(str);
```

To replace a delimiting character within a string, use the following code:

```
string commaDelimitedString = "100,200,300,400,500";
commaDelimitedString = commaDelimitedString.Replace(',', ':');
Console.WriteLine(commaDelimitedString);
```

This code creates a new string and then makes the `commaDelimitedString` variable refer to it. The string in `commaDelimitedString` now looks like this:

```
100:200:300:400:500
```

To replace a place-holding string within a string, use the following code:

```
string theName = "Mary";
string theObject = "car";
string ID = "This <ObjectPlaceholder> is the property of <NamePlaceholder>.";
ID = ID.Replace("<ObjectPlaceholder>", theObject);
ID = ID.Replace("<NamePlaceholder>", theName);
Console.WriteLine(ID);
```

This code creates a new string and then makes the `ID` variable refer to it. The string in `ID` now looks like this:

```
This car is the property of Mary.
```

As when removing a portion of a string, you may, for performance reasons, choose to use the `Replace` method of the `StringBuilder` class instead. For example:

```
string newName = "John Doe";

str = new StringBuilder("name = <NAME>");
str.Replace("<NAME>", newName);
Console.WriteLine(str.ToString( ));
```

```
str.Replace('=', ':');
Console.WriteLine(str.ToString());

str = new StringBuilder("name1 = <FIRSTNAME>, name2 = <FIRSTNAME>");
str.Replace("<FIRSTNAME>", newName, 7, 12);
Console.WriteLine(str.ToString());
str.Replace('=', ':', 0, 7);
Console.WriteLine(str.ToString());
```

This code produces the following results:

```
name = John Doe
name : John Doe
name1 = John Doe, name2 = <FIRSTNAME>
name1 : John Doe, name2 = <FIRSTNAME>
```

Note that when using the `StringBuilder` class, you must use the `System.Text` namespace.

Discussion

The `string` class provides two methods that allow easy removal and modification of characters in a string: the `Remove` instance method and the `Replace` instance method. The `Remove` method deletes a specified number of characters starting at a given location within a string. This method returns a new `string` object containing the modified string.

The `Replace` instance method that the `string` class provides is very useful for removing characters from a string and replacing them with a new character or string. At any point where the `Replace` method finds an instance of the string passed in as the first parameter, it will replace it with the string passed in as the second parameter. The `Replace` method is case-sensitive and returns a new `string` object containing the modified string. If the string being searched for cannot be found in the original string, the method returns a copy of the original `string` object.

The `Replace` and `Remove` methods on a `string` object always create a new `string` object that contains the modified text. If this action hurts performance, consider using the `Replace` and `Remove` methods on the `StringBuilder` class.

The `Remove` method of the `StringBuilder` class is not overloaded and is straightfoward to use. Simply give it a starting position and the number of characters to remove. This method returns a reference to the same instance of the `StringBuilder` object whose `Replace` method modified the string value.

The `Replace` method of the `StringBuilder` class allows for fast character or string replacement to be performed on the original `StringBuilder` object. These methods return a reference to the same instance of the `StringBuilder` object whose `Replace` method was called.

Note that this method is case-sensitive.

See Also

See the "String.Replace Method," "String.Remove Method," "StringBuilder.Replace Method," and "StringBuilder.Remove Method" topics in the MSDN documentation.

2.11 Encoding Binary Data as Base64

Problem

You have a byte[], which could represent some binary information such as a bitmap. You need to encode this data into a string so that it can be sent over a binary-unfriendly transport such as email.

Solution

Using the static method Convert.ToBase64CharArray on the Convert class, a byte[] may be encoded to a char[] equivalent, and the char[] can then be converted to a string:

```
using System;

public static string Base64EncodeBytes(byte[] inputBytes)
{
    // Each 3-byte sequence in inputBytes must be converted to a 4-byte
    // sequence
    long arrLength = (long)(4.0d * inputBytes.Length / 3.0d);
    if ((arrLength % 4) != 0)
    {
        // increment the array length to the next multiple of 4
        //    if it is not already divisible by 4
        arrLength += 4 - (arrLength % 4);
    }

    char[] encodedCharArray = new char[arrLength];
    Convert.ToBase64CharArray(inputBytes, 0, inputBytes.Length, encodedCharArray, 0);

    return (new string(encodedCharArray));
}
```

Discussion

The Convert class makes encoding between a byte[] and a char[] and/or a string a simple matter. The ToBase64CharArray method fills the specified character array with converted bytes, and also returns an integer specifying the number of elements in the resulting byte[], which, in this recipe, is discarded. As you can see, the parameters for this method are quite flexible. It provides the ability to start and stop the conversion at any point in the input byte array and to add elements starting at any position in the resulting char[].

To encode a bitmap file into a string that can be sent to some destination via email, you could use the following code:

```
FileStream fstrm = new FileStream(@"C:\WINNT\winnt.bmp", FileMode.Open, FileAccess.
Read);
BinaryReader reader = new BinaryReader(fstrm);
byte[] image = new byte[reader.BaseStream.Length];
for (int i = 0; i < reader.BaseStream.Length; i++)
{
    image[i] = reader.ReadByte( );
}
reader.Close( );
fstrm.Close( );
string bmpAsString = Base64EncodeBytes(image);
```

The bmpAsString string can then be sent as the body of an email message.

To decode an encoded string to a byte[], see Recipe 2.12.

See Also

See Recipe 2.12; see the "Convert.ToBase64CharArray Method" topic in the MSDN documentation.

2.12 Decoding a Base64-Encoded Binary

Problem

You have a string that contains information such as a bitmap encoded as base64. You need to decode this data (which may have been embedded in an email message) from a string into a byte[] so that you can access the original binary.

Solution

Using the static method Convert.FromBase64CharArray on the Convert class, an encoded char[] and/or string may be decoded to its equivalent byte[]:

```
using System;

public static byte[] Base64DecodeString(string inputStr)
{
    byte[] decodedByteArray =
        Convert.FromBase64CharArray(inputStr.ToCharArray( ),
                                    0, inputStr.Length);
    return (decodedByteArray);
}
```

Discussion

The static FromBase64CharArray method on the Convert class makes decoding an encoded base64 string a simple matter. This method returns a byte[] that contains the decoded elements of the string.

If you receive a file via email, such as an image file (.bmp), that has previously been converted to a string, to convert it back into its original bitmap file, you could do something like the following:

```
byte[] imageBytes = Base64DecodeString(bmpAsString);
fstrm = new FileStream(@"C:\winnt_copy.bmp", FileMode.CreateNew, FileAccess.Write);
BinaryWriter writer = new BinaryWriter(fstrm);
writer.Write(imageBytes);
writer.Close();
fstrm.Close();
```

In this code, the bmpAsString variable was obtained from the code in the Discussion section of Recipe 2.11. The imageBytes byte[] is the bmpAsString string converted back to a byte[], which can then be written back to disk.

To encode a byte[] to a string, see Recipe 2.13.

See Also

See Recipe 2.11; see the "Convert.FromBase64CharArray Method" topic in the MSDN documentation.

2.13   Converting a String Returned as a Byte[ ] Back into a String

Problem

Many methods in the FCL return a byte[] consisting of characters instead of a string. Some of these methods include:

```
System.Net.Sockets.Socket.Receive
System.Net.Sockets.Socket.ReceiveFrom
System.Net.Sockets.Socket.BeginReceive
System.Net.Sockets.Socket.BeginReceiveFrom
System.Net.Sockets.NetworkStream.Read
System.Net.Sockets.NetworkStream.BeginRead
System.IO.BinaryReader.Read
System.IO.BinaryReader.ReadBytes
System.IO.FileStream.Read
System.IO.FileStream.BeginRead
System.IO.MemoryStream // Constructor
System.IO.MemoryStream.Read
System.IO.MemoryStream.BeginRead
System.Security.Cryptography.CryptoStream.Read
System.Security.Cryptography.CryptoStream.BeginRead
System.Diagnostics.EventLogEntry.Data
```

In many cases, this byte[] might contain ASCII or Unicode encoded characters. You need a way to recombine this byte[] to obtain the original string.

Solution

To convert a byte array of ASCII values to a complete string, use the following method:

```
using System;
using System.Text;

public static string FromASCIIByteArray(byte[] characters)
{
    ASCIIEncoding encoding = new ASCIIEncoding( );
    string constructedString = encoding.GetString(characters);

    return (constructedString);
}
```

To convert a byte array of Unicode values (UTF-16 encoded) to a complete string, use the following method:

```
public static string FromUnicodeByteArray(byte[] characters)
{
    UnicodeEncoding encoding = new UnicodeEncoding( );
    string constructedString = encoding.GetString(characters);

    return (constructedString);
}
```

Discussion

The GetString method of the ASCIIEncoding class converts 7-bit ASCII characters contained in a byte array to a string. Any value larger than 127 is converted to the ? character. The ASCIIEncoding class can be found in the System.Text namespace. The GetString method is overloaded to accept additional arguments as well. The overloaded versions of the method convert all or part of a string to ASCII and then store the result in a specified range inside a byte array.

The GetString method returns a string containing the converted byte array of ASCII characters.

The GetString method of the UnicodeEncoding class converts Unicode characters into 16-bit Unicode values. The UnicodeEncoding class can be found in the System.Text namespace. The GetString method returns a string containing the converted byte array of Unicode characters.

See Also

See the "ASCIIEncoding Class" and "UnicodeEncoding Class" topics in the MSDN documentation.

2.14 Passing a String to a Method that Accepts Only a Byte[ ]

Problem

Many methods in the FCL accept a byte[] consisting of characters instead of a string. Some of these methods include:

```
System.Net.Sockets.Socket.Send
System.Net.Sockets.Socket.SendTo
System.Net.Sockets.Socket.BeginSend
System.Net.Sockets.Socket.BeginSendTo
System.Net.Sockets.NetworkStream.Write
System.Net.Sockets.NetworkStream.BeginWrite
System.IO.BinaryWriter.Write
System.IO.FileStream.Write
System.IO.FileStream.BeginWrite
System.IO.MemoryStream.Write
System.IO.MemoryStream.BeginWrite
System.Security.Cryptography.CryptoStream.Write
System.Security.Cryptography.CryptoStream.BeginWrite
System.Diagnostics.EventLog.WriteEntry
```

In many cases, you might have a string that you need to pass into one of these methods or some other method that only accepts a byte[]. You need a way to break up this string into a byte[].

Solution

To convert a string to a byte array of ASCII values, use the GetBytes method on an instance of the ASCIIEncoding class:

```
using System;
using System.Text;

public static byte[] ToASCIIByteArray(string characters)
{
    ASCIIEncoding encoding = new ASCIIEncoding( );
    int numberOfChars = encoding.GetByteCount(characters);
    byte[] retArray = new byte[numberOfChars];

    retArray = encoding.GetBytes(characters);

    return (retArray);
}
```

To convert a string to a byte array of Unicode values, use the UnicodeEncoding class:

```
public static byte[] ToUnicodeByteArray(string characters)
{
    UnicodeEncoding encoding = new UnicodeEncoding( );
    int numberOfChars = encoding.GetByteCount(characters);
```

```
        byte[] retArray = new byte[numberOfChars];

        retArray = encoding.GetBytes(characters);

        return (retArray);
    }
```

Discussion

The GetBytes method of the ASCIIEncoding class converts ASCII characters—contained in either a char array or a string—into a byte array of 7-bit ASCII values. Any value larger than 127 is converted to the ? character. The ASCIIEncoding class can be found in the System.Text namespace. The GetBytes method is overloaded to accept additional arguments as well. The overloaded versions of the method convert all or part of a string to ASCII and then store the result in a specified range inside a byte array, which is returned to the caller.

The GetBytes method of the UnicodeEncoding class converts Unicode characters into 16-bit Unicode values. The UnicodeEncoding class can be found in the System.Text namespace. The GetBytes method returns a byte array, each element of which contains the Unicode value of a single character of the string.

A single Unicode character in the source string or in the source char array corresponds to two elements of the byte array. For example, the following byte array contains the ASCII value of the letter 'S':

```
        byte[] sourceArray = {83};
```

However, for a byte array to contain a Unicode representation (UTF-16 encoded) of the letter 'S', it must contain two elements. For example:

```
        byte[] sourceArray = {83, 0};
```

The Intel architecture uses a little-endian encoding, which means that the first element is the least-significant byte and the second element is the most-significant byte. Other architectures may use big-endian encoding, which is the opposite of little-endian encoding. The UnicodeEncoding class supports both big-endian and little-endian encodings. Using the UnicodeEncoding instance constructor, you can construct an instance that uses either big-endian or little-endian ordering. In addition, you have the option to indicate whether a byte order mark preamble should be generated so that readers of the file will know which endianness is in use.

See Also

See the "ASCIIEncoding Class" and "UnicodeEncoding Class" topics in the MSDN documentation.

2.15 Converting Strings to Their Equivalent Value Type

Problem

You have a string that represents the equivalent value of a number ("12"), char ("a"), bool ("true"), or a color enumeration ("Red"). You need to convert this string to its equivalent value type. Therefore, the number "12" would be converted to a numeric value such as int, short, float, etc. The string "a" would be converted to a char value 'a', the string "true" would be converted to a bool value, and the color "Red" could be converted to an enumeration value (if an enumeration were defined that contained the element Red).

Solution

Use the Parse static method of the type that the string is to be converted to. To convert a string containing a number to its numeric type, use the following code:

```
// This code requires the use of the System and System.Globalization namespaces

string longString = "7654321";
int actualInt = Int32.Parse(longString);    // longString = 7654321

string dblString = "-7654.321";
double actualDbl = Double.Parse(dblString, NumberStyles.AllowDecimalPoint |
        NumberStyles.AllowLeadingSign);    // longString = "-7654.321
```

To convert a string containing a Boolean value to a Boolean type, use the following code:

```
// This code requires the use of the System namespace

string boolString = "true";
bool actualBool = Boolean.Parse(boolString);    // actualBool = true
```

To convert a string containing a char value to a char type, use the following code:

```
// This code requires the use of the System namespace

string charString = "t";
char actualChar = char.Parse(charString);    // actualChar = 't'
```

To convert a string containing an enumeration value to an enumeration type, use the following code:

```
// This code requires the use of the System namespace

enum Colors
{
    red, green, blue
}
```

```
string colorString = "blue";
// Note that the Parse method below is a method defined by System.Enum, not by Colors
Colors actualEnum = (Colors)Colors.Parse(typeof(Colors), colorString);
    // actualEnum = blue
```

Discussion

The static `Parse` method on certain types derived from the `ValueType` data types allows easy conversion from a string value to the value of that specific value type. The `Parse` method is supported by the following types:

Boolean	Int64
Byte	SByte
Decimal	Single
Double	UInt16
Int16	UInt32
Int32	UInt64

In addition to the `Parse` methods that take a single `string` parameter and convert it to the target data type, each numeric type has a second overloaded version of the `Parse` method that includes a second parameter of type `System.Globalization.NumberStyles`. This allows the `Parse` method to correctly handle specific properties of numbers, such as leading or trailing signs, decimal points, currency symbols, thousands separators, etc. `NumberStyles` is marked as a flag-style enumeration, so you can bitwise `OR` more than one enumerated value together to allow a group of styles to be used on the string.

The `NumberStyles` enumeration is defined as follows:

AllowCurrencySymbol
> If the string contains a number with a currency symbol, it is parsed as currency; otherwise, it is parsed as a number.

AllowDecimalPoint
> Allows a decimal point in the number.

AllowExponent
> Allows the number to be in exponential notation format.

AllowHexSpecifier
> Allows characters that specify a hexadecimal number.

AllowLeadingSign
> Allows a leading sign symbol.

AllowLeadingWhite
> Ignores any leading whitespace.

AllowParentheses
> Allows parentheses.

AllowThousands
> Allows group separators.

AllowTrailingSign
>   Allows a trailing sign symbol.

AllowTrailingWhite
>   Ignores any trailing whitespace.

Any
>   Applies any of the previous styles. This style simply ORs together all of the preceding styles.

Currency
>   Same as the All style, except that the AllowExponent style is omitted.

Float
>   Equivalent to AllowLeadingWhite | AllowTrailingWhite | AllowLeadingSign | AllowDecimalPoint | AllowExponent

HexNumber
>   Equivalent to AllowLeadingWhite | AllowTrailingWhite | AllowHexSpecifier

Integer
>   Equivalent to AllowLeadingWhite | AllowTrailingWhite | AllowLeadingSign

None
>   Applies none of the styles.

Number
>   Equivalent to AllowLeadingWhite | AllowTrailingWhite | AllowLeadingSign | AllowTrailingSign | AllowDecimalPoint | AllowThousands

If the NumberStyle parameter is not supplied when it is required (as when, for example, a numeric string includes a thousands separator), or if the NumberStyle enumeration is used on a string that does not contain a number in the supplied NumberStyle format, a FormatException exception will be thrown. If the size of the number in the string is too large or too small for the data type, an OverFlowException exception will be thrown. Passing in a null for the SourceString parameter will throw an ArgumentNullException exception.

The Parse method of the two non-numeric data types, bool and char, also deserve some additional explanation. When calling Boolean.Parse, if a string value contains anything except a value equal to the static properties Boolean.FalseString, Boolean.TrueString, or the string literals "false" or "true" (which are case-insensitive), a FormatException exception is thrown. Passing in a null for the SourceString parameter throws an ArgumentNullException exception.

When invoking char.Parse, if a string value containing more than one character is passed as its single argument, a FormatException exception is thrown. Passing in a null for the string parameter throws an ArgumentNullException exception.

The static Enum.Parse method returns an Object of the same type as specified in the first parameter of this method (EnumType). This value is viewed as an Object type and must be cast to its correct enumeration type.

This method throws an ArgumentException exception if the *Value* parameter cannot be matched to a string in the enumeration. An ArgumentNullException exception is thrown if a null is passed in to the *Value* parameter.

2.16 Formatting Data in Strings

Problem

You need to format one or more embedded pieces of information inside of a string, such as a number, character, or substring.

Solution

The static string.Format method allows you to format strings in a variety of ways. For example:

```
int ID = 12345;
double weight = 12.3558;
char row = 'Z';
string section = "1A2C";

string output = string.Format(@"The item ID = {0:G} having weight = {1:G}
            is found in row {2:G} and section {3:G}", ID, weight, row, section);
Console.WriteLine(output);
output = string.Format(@"The item ID = {0:N} having weight = {1:E}
            is found in row {2:E} and section {3:E}", ID, weight, row, section);
Console.WriteLine(output);
output = string.Format(@"The item ID = {0:N} having weight = {1:N}
            is found in row {2:E} and section {3:D}", ID, weight, row, section);
Console.WriteLine(output);
output = string.Format(@"The item ID = {0:(#####)} having weight = {1:0000.00 lbs}
                is found in row {2} and section {3}", ID, weight, row, section);
Console.WriteLine(output);
```

The output is as follows:

```
The item ID = 12345 having weight = 12.3558 is found in row Z and section 1A2C
The item ID = 12,345.00 having weight = 1.235580E+001 is found in row Z and section
1A2C
The item ID = 12,345.00 having weight = 12.36 is found in row Z and section 1A2C
The item ID = (12345) having weight = 0012.36 lbs is found in row Z and section 1A2C
```

To simplify things, the string.Format method could be discarded and all the work could have been done in the System.Console.WriteLine method, which calls string.Format internally, as shown here:

```
Console.WriteLine(@"The item ID = {0,5:G} having weight = {1,10:G} " +
        "is found in row {2,-5:G} and section {3,-10:G}",
        ID, weight, row, section);
```

The output of this WriteLine method is:

```
The item ID = 12345 having weight =    12.3558 is found in row Z     and section 1A2C
```

Discussion

The `string.Format` method allows a wide range of formatting options for string data. The first parameter of this method can be passed a string that may look similar to the following:

```
"The item ID = {0,5:G}"
```

The text The item ID = will be displayed as is, with no changes. The interesting part of this string is the section enclosed in braces. This section has the following form:

```
{index, alignment:formatString}
```

The section can contain the following three parts:

index

A number identifying the zero-based position of the section's data in the *args* parameter array. The data is to be formatted accordingly and substituted for this section. This number is required.

alignment

The number of spaces to insert before or after this data. A negative number indicates left justification (spaces are added to the right of the data), and a positive number indicates right justification (spaces are added to the left of the data). This number is optional.

formatString

A string indicating the type of formatting to perform on this data. This section is where most of the formatting information usually resides. Tables 2-2 and 2-3 contain valid formatting codes that can be used here. This part is optional.

Table 2-2. The standard formatting strings

Formatting character(s)	Meaning
C or c	Use the currency format. A precision specifier can optionally follow, indicating the number of decimal places to use.
D or d	Use the decimal format for integral types. A precision specifier can optionally follow, which represents the minimum number of digits in the formatted number.
E or e	Use scientific notation. A precision specifier can optionally follow, indicating the number of digits to use after the decimal point.
F or f	Use fixed-point format. A precision specifier can optionally follow, which represents the number of digits to display to the right of the decimal point.
G or g	Use the general format. The number is displayed in its shortest form. A precision specifier can optionally follow, which represents the number of significant digits to display.
N or n	Use the number format. A minus sign is added to the beginning of a negative number, and thousands separators are placed accordingly in the number. A precision specifier can optionally follow, which represents the number of digits to display to the right of the decimal point.
P or p	Use the percent format. The number is converted to a percent representation of itself. A precision specifier can optionally follow, indicating the number of decimal places to use.

Table 2-2. The standard formatting strings (continued)

Formatting character(s)	Meaning
R or r	Use the round-trip format. This format allows the number to be formatted to a representation that can be parsed back to its original form by using the Parse method. Any precision specifier is ignored.
X or x	Use the hexadecimal format. The number is converted to its hexadecimal representation. The uppercase X produces a hexadecimal number with all capital letters A through F. The lowercase x produces a hexadecimal number with all lowercase letters a through f. A precision specifier can optionally follow, which represents the minimum number of digits in the formatted number.

Table 2-3. Custom formatting strings

Formatting character(s)	Meaning
0	Use the zero placeholder format. If a digit in the original number exists in this position, display that digit. If there is no digit in the original string, display a zero.
#	Use the digit placeholder format. If a digit in the original number exists in this position, display that digit. If there is no digit in the original string, display nothing.
.	Use the decimal point format. The decimal point is matched up with the decimal point in the number that is to be formatted. Formatting to the right of the decimal point operates on the digits to the right of the decimal point in the original number. Formatting to the left of the decimal point operates in the same way.
,	Use the thousands separator format. A thousands separator will be placed after every three digits starting at the decimal point and moving to the left.
%	Use the percentage placeholder format. The original number is multiplied by 100 before being displayed.
E or e	Use the scientific notation format. A precision specifier can optionally follow, indicating the number of digits to use after the decimal point.
\	Use the escape character format. The \ character and the next character after it are grouped into an escape sequence.
Any text within single or double quotes such as "aa" or 'aa'	Use no formatting; display as is and in the same position in which the text resides in the format string.
;	Used as a section separator between positive, negative, and zero formatting strings.
Any other character	Use no formatting; display as is and in the same position in which it resides in the format string.

In addition to the string.Format and the Console.WriteLine methods, the overloaded ToString instance method of a value type may also use the previous formatting characters in Table 2-3. Using ToString, the code would look like this:

```
float valueAsFloat = 122.35;
string valueAsString = valueAsFloat.ToString("[000000.####]");
```

The valueAsString variable would contain the formatted number contained in valueAsFloat. The formatted number would look like this:

```
[000122.35]
```

The overloaded `ToString` method accepts a single parameter of type `IFormatProvider`. The `IFormatProvider` provided for the `valueAsFloat.ToString` method is a string containing the formatting for the value type plus any extra text that needs to be supplied.

See Also

See the "String.Format Method," "Standard Numeric Format Strings," and "Custom Numeric Format Strings" topics in the MSDN documentation.

2.17   Creating a Delimited String

Problem

You have an array of strings to format as delimited text and possibly to store in a text file.

Solution

Using the static `Join` method of the `string` class, the array of strings can be easily joined in as little as one line of code. For example:

```
string[] infoArray = new string[5] {"11", "12", "Checking", "111", "Savings"};
string delimitedInfo = string.Join(",", infoArray);
```

This code sets the value of `delimitedInfo` to the following:

```
11,12,Checking,111,Savings
```

Discussion

The `Join` method concatenates all the strings contained in a string array. Additionally, a specified delimiting character(s) is inserted between each string in the array. This method returns a single string object with the fully joined and delimited text.

Unlike the `Split` method of the `string` class, the `Join` method accepts only one delimiting character at a time. In order to use multiple delimiting characters within a string of values, subsequent `Join` operations must be performed on the information until all of the data has been joined together into a single string. For example:

```
string[] infoArray = new string[4] {"11", "12", "Checking", "Savings"};
string delimitedInfoBegin = string.Join(",", infoArray, 0, 2);
string delimitedInfoEnd = string.Join(",", infoArray, 2, 2);
string[] delimitedInfoTotal = new string[2] {delimitedInfoBegin,
        delimitedInfoEnd};
string delimitedInfoFinal = string.Join(":", delimitedInfoTotal);
Console.WriteLine(delimitedInfoFinal);
```

produces the following delimited file:

```
11,12:Checking,Savings
```

See Also

See the "String.Join Method" topic in the MSDN documentation.

2.18   Extracting Items from a Delimited String

Problem

You have a string, possibly from a text file, which is delimited by one or more characters. You need to retrieve each piece of delimited information as easily as possible.

Solution

Using the Split instance method on the string class, we can place the delimited information into an array in as little as a single line of code. For example:

```
string delimitedInfo = "100,200,400,3,67";
string[] discreteInfo = delimitedInfo.Split(new char[1] {','});

foreach (string Data in discreteInfo)
    Console.WriteLine(Data);
```

The string array discreteInfo holds the following values:

```
100
200
400
3
67
```

Discussion

The Split method, like most methods in the string class, is simple to use. This method returns a string array with each element containing one discrete piece of the delimited text split on the delimiting character(s).

In the Solution, the string delimitedInfo was comma-delimited. However, it could have been delimited by any type of character or even by more than one character. When there is more than one type of delimiter, use code like the following:

```
string[] discreteInfo = delimitedInfo.Split(new char[3] {',', ':', ' '});
```

This line splits the delimitedInfo string whenever one of the three delimiting characters (comma, colon, or space character) is found.

The Split method is case-sensitive. To split a string on the letter "a" in a case-insensitive manner, use code like the following:

```
string[] discreteInfo = delimitedInfo.Split(new char[1] {'a', 'A'});
```

Now, anytime the letter "a" is encountered, no matter what its case, the Split method views that character as a delimiter.

See Also

See the "String.Join Method" topic in the MSDN documentation.

2.19 Setting the Maximum Number of Characters a String Can Contain

Problem

You want to ensure that the data entered by a user and assigned to a string does not exceed a certain number of characters.

Solution

Use the overloaded constructor of the `StringBuilder` class, which accepts a maximum capacity. The following code creates a `StringBuilder` object that has a maximum size of 10 characters:

```
System.Text.StringBuilder sbMax = new System.Text.StringBuilder(10, 10);
sbMax.Append("123456789");
sbMax.Append("0");
```

This code creates a `StringBuilder` object, `sbMax`, which has a maximum length of 10 characters. Nine characters are appended to this string and then a tenth character is appended without a problem. However, if the next line of code is executed:

```
sbMax.Append("#");
```

The length of `sbMax` goes beyond 10 characters and an `ArgumentOutOfRangeException` is thrown.

Discussion

The `string` object is immutable and, as such, does not have a built-in method to prevent its length from going beyond a certain point. Fortunately, the `StringBuilder` object contains an overloaded constructor that allows the maximum size of its string to be set. The `StringBuilder` constructor that we are concerned with is defined as follows:

```
public StringBuilder(int initialCapacity, int maxCapacity)
```

For most applications, the *initialCapacity* and *maxCapacity* can be identical. This way gives you the best performance, overall. If these two parameters are not identical, it is critical that these two parameters can coexist. Take, for example, the following code:

```
System.Text.StringBuilder sbMax = new System.Text.StringBuilder(3, 12);
sbMax.Append("1234567890");
sbMax.Append("0");
sbMax.Append("#");
```

which will throw an ArgumentOutOfRangeException as the final # character is appended. This configuration incorrectly allows a maximum of only 11 characters instead of the 12 indicated.

The following line of code:

```
System.Text.StringBuilder sbMax = new System.Text.StringBuilder(30, 12);
```

also throws an ArgumentOutOfRangeException. This time, the *initialCapacity* parameter is larger than *maxCapacity*, causing the exception. While you may not be explicitly writing these values for your application, if you are calculating them using some type of expression, you may run into these problems.

To handle an attempt to append characters to the StringBuilder string, forcing it beyond the maximum size, wrap any code to append text to the StringBuilder object in a try-catch block:

```
try
{
    sbMax.Append("New String");
}
catch(ArgumentOutOfRangeException rangeE)
{
    // Handle overrun here
}
```

In addition to the Append method, you should also wrap any AppendFormat, Insert, and Replace methods of the StringBuilder object in a try-catch block. Any of these methods can allow characters to be added to the StringBuilder string, potentially causing its length to exceed its maximum specified length.

See Also

See the "StringBuilder.Append Method" topic in the MSDN documentation.

2.20   Iterating Over Each Character in a String

Problem

You need to iterate over each character in a string efficiently in order to examine or process each character.

Solution

C# provides two methods for iterating strings. The first is by using a foreach loop, as follows:

```
string testStr = "abc123";
foreach (char c in testStr)
{
    Console.WriteLine(c.ToString());
}
```

This method is quick and easy. Unfortunately, it is somewhat less flexible than the second method, which uses the for loop instead of a foreach loop to iterate over the string. For example:

```
string testStr = "abc123";
for (int counter = 0; counter < testStr.Length; counter++)
{
    Console.WriteLine(testStr[counter].ToString( ));
}
```

Discussion

The foreach loop is simpler and thus less error-prone, but it lacks flexibility. In contrast, the for loop is slightly more complex, but it makes up for that in flexibility.

The for loop method uses the indexer of the string variable testStr to get the character located at the position indicated by the counter loop index. Care must be taken not to run over the bounds of the string array when using this type of looping mechanism.

A for loop is flexible enough to change how looping over characters in a string is performed. For example, the loop could be quickly modified to start and end at a specific point in the string by simply changing the *initializer* and *conditional* expressions of the for loop. Characters can be skipped by changing the *iterator* expression to increment the counter variable by more than one. The string can also be iterated in reverse order by changing the for loop expressions, as shown:

```
for (int counter = testStr.Length - 1; counter >= 0; counter--)
{
    Console.WriteLine(testStr[counter].ToString( ));
}
```

This example allows a string to be created containing the characters of the original string in reverse order:

```
string revTestStr = "";
for (int counter = testStr.Length - 1; counter >= 0; counter--)
{
    revTestStr += testStr[counter];
}
Console.WriteLine(revTestStr);
```

It should be noted that each of these methods was compiled using the /optimize compiler option. However, adding or removing this option has very little impact on the resulting IL code.

The compiler optimizes the use of a foreach loop iterating through a *vector array*—one that starts at zero and has only one dimension. Converting a foreach loop to another type of loop, such as a for loop, may not produce any noticeable increases in performance.

2.21 Improving String Comparison Performance

Problem

Your application consists of many strings that are compared frequently. You have been tasked with improving performance and making more efficient use of resources.

Solution

Use the intern pool to improve resource usage and, in turn, improve performance. The Intern and IsInterned instance methods of the string class allow you to use the intern pool. Use the following static methods to make use of the string intern pool:

```
using System;
using System.Text;

public class InternedStrCls
{
    public static void CreateInternedStr(char[] characters)
    {
        string NonInternedStr = new string(characters);
        String.Intern(NonInternedStr);
    }

    public static void CreateInternedStr(StringBuilder strBldr)
    {
        String.Intern(strBldr.ToString());
    }

    public static void CreateInternedStr(string str)
    {
        String.Intern(str);
    }

    public static void CreateInternedStr(string[] strArray)
    {
        foreach(string s in strArray)
        {
            String.Intern(s);
        }
    }
}
```

Discussion

The CLR automatically stores all string literals declared in an application in an area of memory called the *intern pool*. The intern pool contains a unique instance of each string literal found in your code, which allows for more efficient use of resources by not storing multiple copies of strings that contain the same string literal. Another benefit is speed. When two strings are compared using either the == operator or the Equals instance method of the string class, a test is done to determine whether each string variable reference is the same; if they are not, then each string's length is checked; if both string's lengths are equal, each character is compared individually. However, if we could guarantee that the references, instead of the string contents, could be compared, much faster string comparisons can be made. String interning does just that: it guarantees that the references to equivalent string values are the same, eliminating the possibility of attempting the length and character-by-character checks. This yields better performance in situations where the references to two equal strings are different and the length and character-by-character comparisons have to be made.

Note that the only strings automatically placed in this intern pool by the compiler are string literals—strings surrounded by double quotes—found in code by the compiler. The following lines of code will place the string "foo" into the intern pool:

```
string s = "foo";
StringBuilder sb = new StringBuilder("foo");
StringBuilder sb = new StringBuilder().Append("foo");
```

The following lines of code will not place the string "foo" into the intern pool:

```
char[] ca = new char[3] {'f','o','o'};
StringBuilder sb = new StringBuilder().Append("f").Append("oo");

string s1 = "f";
string s2 = "oo";
string s3 = s1 + s2;
```

You can programmatically store a new string created by your application in the intern pool using the static string.Intern method. This method returns a string referencing the string literal contained in the intern pool, or, if the string is not found, the string is entered into the intern pool and a reference to this newly pooled string is returned.

There is also another method used in string interning called IsInterned. This method operates similarly to the Intern method, except that it returns null if the string is not in the intern pool, rather than adding it to the pool. This method returns a string referencing the string literal contained in the intern pool, or, if the string is not found, it returns null.

An example of using this method is shown here:

```
string s1 = "f";
string s2 = "oo";
string s3 = s1 + s2;
if (String.IsInterned(s3) == null)
{
    Console.WriteLine("NULL");
}
```

However, if we add the highlighted line of code, the IsInterned test returns a non-null string object:

```
string s1 = "f";
string s2 = "oo";
```

```
    string s3 = s1 + s2;
    InternedStrCls.CreateInternedStr(s3);
    if (String.IsInterned(s3) == null)
    {
        Console.WriteLine("NULL");
    }
```

The Intern method is useful when you need a reference to a string, even if it does not exist in the intern pool.

The IsInterned method can optimize the comparison of a single string to any string literal or manually interned string. Consider that you need to determine whether a string variable contains any string literal that has been defined in the application. Call the string.IsInterned method with the string variable as the parameter. If null is returned, there is no match in the intern pool, and thus there is no match between the string variable's value and any string literals:

```
    string s1 = "f";
    string s2 = "oo";
    string s3 = s1 + s2;

    if (String.IsInterned(s3) != null)
    {
        // If the string "foo" has been defined in the app and placed
        //   into the intern pool, this block of code executes.
    }
    else
    {
        // If the string "foo" has NOT been defined in the app NOR been placed
        //   into the intern pool, this block of code executes.
    }
```

Exercise caution when using the string interning methods. Calling the Intern method for every possible string that could be created by your application would actually cause the application's performance to slow considerably, since this method must search the intern pool for the string; if it does not exist in the pool, it is added. The reference to the newly created string in the intern pool is then returned.

Another potential problem with the IsInterned method in particular stems from the fact that every string literal in the application is stored in this intern pool at the start of the application. If you are using IsInterned to determine whether a string exists, you are comparing that string against all string literals that exist in the application, as well as any you might have explicitly interned, not just the ones in the scope in which IsInterned is used.

See Also

See the "String.Intern Method" and "String.IsInterned Method" topics in the MSDN documentation.

2.22 Improving StringBuilder Performance

Problem

In an attempt to improve string-handling performance, you have converted your code to use the StringBuilder class. However, this change has not improved performance as much as you had hoped.

Solution

The chief advantage of a StringBuilder object over a string object is that it preallocates a default initial amount of memory in an internal buffer in which a string value can expand and contract. When that memory is used, however, .NET must allocate new memory for this internal buffer. You can reduce the frequency with which this occurs by explicitly defining the size of the new memory using either of two techniques. The first approach is to set this value when the StringBuilder class constructor is called. For example, the code:

```
StringBuilder sb = new StringBuilder(200);
```

specifies that a StringBuilder object can hold 200 characters before new memory must be allocated.

The second approach is to change the value after the StringBuilder object has been created, using one of the following properties or methods of the StringBuilder object:

```
sb.Capacity = 200;
sb.EnsureCapacity(200);
```

Discussion

As noted in previous recipes in this chapter, the string class is immutable; once a string is assigned to a variable of type string, that variable cannot be changed in any way. So changing the contents of a string variable entails the creation of a new string containing the modified string. The reference variable of type string must then be changed to reference this newly created string object. The old string object will eventually be marked for collection by the garbage collector, and, subsequently, its memory will be freed. Because of this intensive behind-the-scene action, code that performs intensive string manipulations using the string class suffers greatly from having to create new string objects for each string modification, and greater pressure is on the garbage collector to remove unused objects from memory more frequently.

The StringBuilder class solves this problem by preallocating an internal buffer to hold a string. The contents of this string buffer are manipulated directly. Any operations performed on a StringBuilder object do not carry with it the performance penalty of creating a whole new string or StringBuilder object and, consequently, filling up the managed heap with many unused objects.

There is one caveat with using the StringBuilder class, which, if not heeded, can impede performance. The StringBuilder class uses a default initial capacity to contain the characters of a string, unless you change this default initial capacity through one of the StringBuilder constructors. Once this space is exceeded, by appending characters, for instance, a new string buffer is allocated double the size of the original buffer. For example, a StringBuilder object with an initial size of 20 characters would be increased to 40 characters, then to 80 characters, and so on. The string contained in the original internal string buffer is then copied to this newly allocated internal string buffer along with any appended or inserted characters.

The default capacity for a StringBuilder object is 16 characters; in many cases, this is much too small. To increase this size upon object creation, the StringBuilder class has an overloaded constructor that accepts an integer value to use as the starting size of the preallocated string. Determining an initial size value that is not too large (thereby allocating too much unused space) or too small (thereby incurring a performance penalty for creating and discarding a large number of StringBuilder objects) may seem like more of an art than a science. However, determining the optimal size may prove invaluable when your application is tested for performance.

 In cases where good values for the initial size of a StringBuilder object cannot be obtained mathematically, try running the applications under a constant load while varying the initial StringBuilder size. When a good initial size is found, try varying the load while keeping this size value constant. You may discover that this value needs to be tweaked to get better performance. Keeping good records of each run, and committing them to a graph, will be invaluable in determining the appropriate number to choose. As an added note, using PerfMon (Administrative Tools → Performance Monitor) to detect and graph the number of garbage collections that occur might also provide useful information in determining whether your StringBuilder initial size is causing too many reallocations of your StringBuilder objects.

The most efficient method of setting the capacity of the StringBuilder object is to set it in the call to its constructor. The overloaded constructors of a StringBuilder object that accept a capacity value are defined as follows:

```
public StringBuilder(int capacity)
public StringBuilder(string str, int capacity)
public StringBuilder(int capacity, int maxCapacity)
public StringBuilder(string str, int startPos, int length, int capacity)
```

In addition to the constructor parameters, one property of the StringBuilder object allows its capacity to be increased (or decreased.) The Capacity property gets or sets an integer value that determines the new capacity of this instance of a StringBuilder object. Note that the Capacity property cannot be less than the Length property.

A second way to change the capacity is through the EnsureCapacity method, which is defined as follows:

```
public int EnsureCapacity(string capacity)
```

This method returns the new capacity for this object. If the capacity of the existing object already exceeds that of the value in the *capacity* parameter, the initial capacity is retained, and this value is also returned by this method.

There is one problem with using these last two members. If any of these members increases the size of the StringBuilder object by even a single character, the internal buffer used to store the string has to be reallocated. However, minimizing the capacity of the object does not force a reallocation of a new, larger internal string buffer. These methods are useful if they are used in exceptional cases when the StringBuilder capacity may need an extra boost, so that fewer reallocations are performed in the long run.

The StringBuilder object also contains a Length property, which, if increased, appends spaces to the end of the existing StringBuilder object's string. If the Length is decreased, characters are truncated from the StringBuilder object's string. Increasing the Length property can increase the Capacity property, but only as a side effect. If the Length property is increased beyond the size of the Capacity property, the Capacity property value is set to the new value of the Length property. This property acts similarly to the Capacity property:

```
sb.Length = 200;
```

 The string and StringBuilder objects are considered *nonblittable*, which means that they must be marshaled across any managed/unmanaged boundaries in your code. The reason is that strings have multiple ways of being represented in unmanaged code, and there is no one-to-one correlation between these representations in unmanaged and managed code. In contrast, types such as byte, sbyte, short, ushort, int, uint, long, ulong, IntPtr, and UIntPtr are *blittable* types and do not require conversion between managed and unmanaged code. One-dimensional arrays of these blittable types, as well as structures or classes containing only blittable types, are also considered blittable and do not need extra conversion when passed between managed and unmanaged code.

The string and StringBuilder objects take more time to marshal, due to conversion between managed and unmanaged types. Performance will be improved when calling unmanaged code through P/Invoke methods if only blittable types are used. Consider using a byte array instead of a string or StringBuilder object, if at all possible.

See Also

See the "StringBuilder Class" topic in the MSDN documentation.

2.23 Pruning Characters from the Head and/or Tail of a String

Problem

You have a string with a specific set of characters, such as spaces, tabs, escaped single/double quotes, any type of punctuation character(s), or some other character(s), at the beginning and/or end of a string. You want a simple way to remove these characters.

Solution

Use the Trim, TrimEnd, or TrimStart instance methods of the String class:

```
string foo = "--TEST--";
Console.WriteLine(foo.Trim(new char[1] {'-'}));              // Displays "TEST"

foo = ",-TEST-,-";
Console.WriteLine(foo.Trim(new char[2] {'-',','}));          // Displays "TEST"

foo = "--TEST--";
Console.WriteLine(foo.TrimStart(new char[1] {'-'}));         // Displays "TEST--"

foo = ",-TEST-,-";
Console.WriteLine(foo.TrimStart(new char[2] {'-',','}));     // Displays "TEST-,-"

foo = "--TEST--";
Console.WriteLine(foo.TrimEnd(new char[1] {'-'}));           // Displays "--TEST"

foo = ",-TEST-,-";
Console.WriteLine(foo.TrimEnd(new char[2] {'-',','}));       // Displays "-,-TEST"
```

Discussion

The Trim method is most often used to eliminate whitespace at the beginning and end of a string. In fact, if you call Trim without any parameters on a string variable, this is exactly what would happen. The Trim method is overloaded to allow you to remove other types of characters from the beginning and end of a string. You can pass in a char[] containing all the characters that you want removed from the beginning and end of a string. Note that if the characters contained in this char[] are located somewhere in the middle of the string, they are not removed.

The TrimStart and TrimEnd methods remove characters at the beginning and end of a string, respectively. These two methods are not overloaded, similar to the Trim method. Rather, these two methods accept only a char[]. If you pass a null into either one of these methods, only whitespace is removed from the beginning or the end of a string.

See Also

See the "String.Trim Method," "String.TrimStart Method," and "String.TrimEnd Method" topics in the MSDN documentation.

CHAPTER 3

Classes and Structures

Structures, like any other value type, implicitly inherit from System.ValueType. At first glance, a structure is similar to a class, but they are actually very different. Knowing when to use a structure over a class will help tremendously when designing an application. Using a structure incorrectly can result in inefficient and hard-to-modify code. Both structures and simple types inherit from ValueType.

Structures have two performance advantages over reference types. First, if a structure is allocated on the stack (i.e., it is not contained within a reference type), access to the structure and its data is somewhat faster than access to a reference type on the heap. Reference type objects must follow their reference, or *pointer*, onto the heap in order to get at their data. However, this performance advantage pales in comparison to the second performance advantage of structures: namely, that cleaning up the memory allocated to a structure on the stack requires a simple change of the address to which the stack pointer points, which is done at the return of a method call. This call is extremely fast compared to allowing the garbage collector to automatically clean up reference types for you in the managed heap.

Structure performance falls short in comparison to that of classes when they are passed by value to other methods. Because they reside on the stack, a structure and its data have to be copied to a new local variable (the method's parameter that is used to receive the structure) when it is passed by value to a method. This copying takes more time than passing a single reference to a class's object by value to a method—unless the structure is the same size as or smaller than the machine's pointer size; thus, a structure with a size of 32 bits is just as cheap to pass as a reference (which happens to be the size of a pointer) on a 32-bit machine. Keep this in mind when choosing between a class and a structure. While creating, accessing, and destroying a class's object may take longer, it also might not balance the performance hit when a structure is passed by value a large number of times to one or more methods. Keeping the size of the structure small minimizes the performance hit of passing it around by value.

Structures can also cause degradation in performance when they are passed to methods that require a reference type, such as any of the collection types in the FCL. Passing a structure (or any simple type, for that matter) into a method requiring a reference type causes the structure to be boxed. *Boxing* is wrapping a value type in an object. When the method returns, the value type will be *unboxed*, which means that the value type will be extracted from its object wrapper. Both of these operations are time-consuming and may degrade performance.

As concerns the object-oriented capabilities of classes and structures, classes have far more flexibility. A structure cannot contain a user-defined default constructor, since the C# compiler automatically provides a default constructor that initializes all the fields in the structure to their default values. This is also why no field initializers can be added to a structure. If you need to override the default field values, a structure might not be the way to go. However, a parameterized constructor can be created that initializes the structure's fields to any value that is necessary.

Structures, like classes, can inherit from interfaces; but unlike classes, structures cannot inherit from a class or a structure. This limitation precludes creating structure hierarchies, as you can with classes. Polymorphism as implemented through an abstract base class is also prohibited when using a structure, since a structure cannot inherit from another class.

Use a class if:

- Its identity is important. Structures get copied implicitly when being passed by value into a method. You could pass a structure by reference, but then another object might not be able to hold a reference to the structure.

- It will have a large memory footprint.

- Its fields need initializers.

- You need to inherit from a base class.

- You need polymorphic behavior. That is, you need to implement an abstract base class from which you will create several similar classes that inherit from this abstract base class. (Note that polymorphism can be implemented via interfaces as well, but it is usually not a good idea to place an interface on a value type, since a boxing operation will occur if the structure is converted to the interface type.) For more on polymorphism through interfaces, see Recipe 3.17.

Use a structure if:

- It will act like a primitive type (int, long, byte, etc.).

- It must have a small memory footprint.

- You are calling a P/Invoke method that requires a structure to be passed in by value. *Platform Invoke*, or P/Invoke for short, allows managed code to call out to an unmanaged method exposed from within a DLL. Many times an unmanaged DLL method requires a structure to be passed in to it; using a structure is an efficient method of doing this and is the only way if the structure is being passed by value.

- You need to avoid the overhead of garbage collection.
- Its fields need to be initialized only to their default values. This value would be zero for numeric types, false for Boolean types, and null for reference types.
- You do not need to inherit from a base class (other than ValueType, from which all structs inherit).
- You do not need polymorphic behavior.

3.1   Creating Union-Type Structures

Problem

You need to create a data type that operates similar to a union type in C++. A union type is useful mainly in interop scenarios where the unmanaged code accepts and/or returns a union type; we suggest that you do not use it in other situations.

Solution

Use a structure and mark it with the StructLayout attribute (specifiying the LayoutKind.Explicit layout kind in the constructor). In addition, mark each field in the structure with the FieldOffset attribute. The following structure defines a union in which a single signed numeric value can be stored:

```
using System.Runtime.InteropServices;

[StructLayoutAttribute(LayoutKind.Explicit)]
struct SignedNumber
{
    [FieldOffsetAttribute(0)]
    public sbyte Num1;

    [FieldOffsetAttribute(0)]
    public short Num2;

    [FieldOffsetAttribute(0)]
    public int Num3;

    [FieldOffsetAttribute(0)]
    public long Num4;

    [FieldOffsetAttribute(0)]
    public float Num5;

    [FieldOffsetAttribute(0)]
    public double Num6;

    [FieldOffsetAttribute(0)]
    public decimal Num7;
}
```

The next structure is similar to the `SignedNumber` structure, except that it also can contain a `String` type in addition to the signed numeric value:

```
[StructLayoutAttribute(LayoutKind.Explicit)]
struct SignedNumberWithText
{
    [FieldOffsetAttribute(0)]
    public sbyte Num1;

    [FieldOffsetAttribute(0)]
    public short Num2;

    [FieldOffsetAttribute(0)]
    public int Num3;

    [FieldOffsetAttribute(0)]
    public long Num4;

    [FieldOffsetAttribute(0)]
    public float Num5;

    [FieldOffsetAttribute(0)]
    public double Num6;

    [FieldOffsetAttribute(0)]
    public decimal Num7;

    [FieldOffsetAttribute(16)]
    public string Text1;
}
```

Discussion

Unions are structures usually found in C++ code; however, there is a way to duplicate that type of structure using a C# structure data type. A *union* is a structure that accepts more than one type at a specific location in memory for that structure. For example, the `SignedNumber` structure is a union-type structure built using a C# structure. This structure accepts any type of signed numeric type (sbyte, int, long, etc.), but it accepts this numeric type at only one location, or offset, within the structure.

 Since `StructLayoutAttribute` can be applied to both structures and classes, a class can also be used when creating a union data type.

Notice the `FieldOffsetAttribute` has the value zero passed to its constructor. This denotes that this field will be at the zeroth offset (this is a byte offset) within this structure. This attribute is used in tandem with the `StructLayoutAttribute` to manually enforce where the fields in this structure will start (that is, at which offset from the beginning of this structure in memory each field will start at). The

`FieldOffsetAttribute` can be used only with a `StructLayoutAttribute` set to `LayoutKind.Explicit`. In addition, it cannot be used on static members within this structure.

Unions can become problematic, since several types are essentially laid on top of one another. The biggest problem is extracting the correct data type from a union structure. Consider what happens if you choose to store the `long` numeric value `long.MaxValue` in the `SignedNumber` structure. Later, you might accidentally attempt to extract a byte data type value from this same structure. In doing so, you will get back only the first byte of the long value.

Another problem is starting fields at the correct offset. The `SignedNumberWithText` union overlays numerous signed numeric data types at the zeroth offset. The last field in this structure is laid out at the sixteenth byte offset from the beginning of this structure in memory. If you accidentally overlay the string field `Text2` on top of any of the other signed numeric data types, you will get an exception at runtime. The basic rule is that you are allowed to overlay a value type on another value type, but you cannot overlay a reference type over a value type. If the `Text2` field were marked with the following attribute:

```
[FieldOffsetAttribute(14)]
```

this exception is thrown at runtime (note that the compiler does not catch this problem):

```
An unhandled exception of type 'System.TypeLoadException' occurred in
Chapter_Code.exe.

Additional information: Could not load type Chapter_Code.SignedNumberWithText from
assembly 14 because it contains an object field at offset 14 that is incorrectly
aligned or overlapped by a non-object field.
```

It is imperative to get the offsets correct when using complex unions in C#.

See Also

See the "StructLayoutAttribute Class" topic in the MSDN documentation.

3.2 Allowing a Type to Represent Itself as a String

Problem

Your class or structure needs to control how its information is displayed when its `ToString` method is called. For example, when creating a new data type, such as a `Line` class, you might want to allow objects of this type to be able to display themselves in a textual format. In the case of a `Line` object, it would display itself as `"(x1, y1)(x2, y2)"`.

Solution

Override and/or implement the IFormattable.ToString method to display numeric information, such as for a Line structure:

```csharp
using System;
using System.Text;
using System.Text.RegularExpressions;

public struct Line : IFormattable
{
    public Line(int startX, int startY, int endX, int endY)
    {
        x1 = startX;
        x2 = endX;
        y1 = startY;
        y2 = endY;
    }

    public int x1;
    public int y1;
    public int x2;
    public int y2;

    public double GetDirectionInRadians()
    {
        int xSide = x2 - x1;
        int ySide = y2 - y1;

        if (xSide == 0)      // Prevent divide-by-zero
            return (0);
        else
            return (Math.Atan (ySide / xSide));
    }

    public double GetMagnitude()
    {
        int xSide = x2 - x1;
        int ySide = y2 - y1;
        return (Math.Sqrt( Math.Sqrt((xSide * xSide) + (ySide * ySide))-));
    }

    // This overrides the Object.ToString method
    //   This override is not required for this recipe
    //   and is included for completeness
    public override string ToString()
    {
        return (String.Format("({0},{1}) ({2},{3})", x1, y1, x2, y2));
    }

    public string ToString(string format)
    {
        return (this.ToString(format, null));
    }
```

```
    public string ToString(IFormatProvider formatProvider)
    {
        return (this.ToString(null, formatProvider));
    }

    public string ToString(string format, IFormatProvider formatProvider)
    {
        StringBuilder compositeStr = new StringBuilder("");

        if ((format != null) && (format.ToUpper().Equals("V")))
        {
            double direction = this.GetDirectionInRadians();
            double magnitude = this.GetMagnitude();

            string retStringD = direction.ToString("G5", formatProvider);
            string retStringM = magnitude.ToString("G5", formatProvider);

            compositeStr.Append("magnitude = ").Append(retStringM).Append
                            ("\tDirection = ").Append(retStringD);
        }
        else
        {
            string retStringX1 = this.x1.ToString(format, formatProvider);
            string retStringY1 = this.y1.ToString(format, formatProvider);
            string retStringX2 = this.x2.ToString(format, formatProvider);
            string retStringY2 = this.y2.ToString(format, formatProvider);

            compositeStr.Append("(").Append(retStringX1).Append(",").Append
                            (retStringY1).Append(")(").Append(retStringX2).Append
                            (",").Append(retStringY2).Append(")");
        }
        return (compositeStr.ToString());
    }
}
```

Discussion

The ToString method provides a convenient way to display the current contents, or state, of a structure (this recipe works equally well for reference types). The solution section of this recipe shows the various implementations of ToString for both numeric and textual data. The Line class contains two points in space that form the endpoints of a line. This line data is then fed into the ToString methods for that class to produce formatted output.

The following code exercises the ToString methods of the Line class:

```
using System.Globalization;

public void TestLineToString()
{
    Line V1 = new Line(0, 0, 40, 123);
    Line V2 = new Line(0, -2, 1, 11);
    Line V3 = new Line(0, 1, 0, 1);
```

```
        Console.WriteLine("\r\nTest Default ToString method");
        Console.WriteLine("V1 = " + V1);
        Console.WriteLine("V2 = " + V2);
        Console.WriteLine("V1.ToString() = {0:V}", V1.ToString());
        Console.WriteLine("V2.ToString() = {0:V}", V2.ToString());

        Console.WriteLine("\r\nTest overloaded ToString(format) method");
        Console.WriteLine("V1.ToString(\"D\") = {0:D}", V1);
        Console.WriteLine("V1.ToString(\"D5\") = {0:D5}", V1);
        Console.WriteLine("V2.ToString(\"F\") = {0:F}", V2);
        Console.WriteLine("V1.ToString(\"N\") = {0:N}", V1);
        Console.WriteLine("V2.ToString(\"n\") = {0:n}", V2);
        Console.WriteLine("V1.ToString(\"E\") = {0:E}", V1);
        Console.WriteLine("V2.ToString(\"X\") = {0:X}", V2);

        Console.WriteLine("\r\nTest overloaded ToString(formatProvider) method");
        NumberFormatInfo NullFormatter = null;
        NumberFormatInfo Formatter = new NumberFormatInfo();
        Formatter.NegativeSign = "!";
        Formatter.PositiveSign = "+";
        Console.WriteLine("V2.ToString(Formatter) = " + V2.ToString(Formatter));
        Console.WriteLine("V2.ToString(Formatter) = " + V2.ToString(Formatter));
        Console.WriteLine("V2.ToString(null) = " + V2.ToString(NullFormatter));
        Console.WriteLine("V2.ToString(null) = " + V2.ToString(NullFormatter));
        Console.WriteLine("V2.ToString(new CultureInfo(\"fr-BE\")) = "
                + V2.ToString(new CultureInfo("fr-BE")));  //French - Belgium
        Console.WriteLine("V2.ToString(new CultureInfo(\"fr-BE\")) = "
                + V2.ToString(new CultureInfo("fr-BE")));  //French - Belgium


        Console.WriteLine
                ("\r\nTest overloaded ToString(format, formatProvider) method");
        Console.WriteLine("V2.ToString(\"D\", Formatter) = " + V2.ToString("D",
                        Formatter));
        Console.WriteLine("V2.ToString(\"F\", Formatter) = " + V2.ToString("F",
                        Formatter));
        Console.WriteLine("V2.ToString(\"D\", null) = " + V2.ToString("D", null));
        Console.WriteLine("V2.ToString(\"F\", null) = " + V2.ToString("F", null));
        Console.WriteLine("V2.ToString(\"D\", new CultureInfo(\"fr-BE\")) = "
                + V2.ToString("D", new CultureInfo("fr-BE")));  //French - Belgium
        Console.WriteLine("V2.ToString(\"F\", new CultureInfo(\"fr-BE\")) = "
                + V2.ToString("F", new CultureInfo("fr-BE")));  //French - Belgium

        Console.WriteLine("\r\nTest overloaded ToString(\"V\", formatProvider) method");
        Console.WriteLine("V2.ToString(\"V\", Formatter) = " + V2.ToString("V",
                        Formatter));
        Console.WriteLine("V2.ToString(\"V\", null) = " + V2.ToString("V", null));
    }
```

This code displays the following results:

```
Test Default ToString method
V1 = (0,0) (40,123)
V2 = (0,-2) (1,11)
V1.ToString() = (0,0) (40,123)
V2.ToString() = (0,-2) (1,11)
```

```
Test overloaded ToString(format) method
V1.ToString("D") = (0,0)(40,123)
V1.ToString("D5") = (00000,00000)(00040,00123)
V2.ToString("F") = (0.00,-2.00)(1.00,11.00)
V1.ToString("N") = (0.00,0.00)(40.00,123.00)
V2.ToString("n") = (0.00,-2.00)(1.00,11.00)
V1.ToString("E") = (0.000000E+000,0.000000E+000)(4.000000E+001,1.230000E+002)
V2.ToString("X") = (0,FFFFFFFE)(1,B)

Test overloaded ToString(formatProvider) method
V2.ToString(Formatter) = (0,!2)(1,11)
V2.ToString(Formatter) = (0,!2)(1,11)
V2.ToString(null) = (0,-2)(1,11)
V2.ToString(null) = (0,-2)(1,11)
V2.ToString(new CultureInfo("fr-BE")) = (0,-2)(1,11)
V2.ToString(new CultureInfo("fr-BE")) = (0,-2)(1,11)

Test overloaded ToString(format, formatProvider)        method
V2.ToString("D", Formatter) = (0,!2)(1,11)
V2.ToString("F", Formatter) = (0.00,!2.00)(1.00,11.00)
V2.ToString("D", null) = (0,-2)(1,11)
V2.ToString("F", null) = (0.00,-2.00)(1.00,11.00)
V2.ToString("D", new CultureInfo("fr-BE")) = (0,-2)(1,11)
V2.ToString("F", new CultureInfo("fr-BE")) = (0,00,-2,00)(1,00,11,00)

Test overloaded ToString("V", formatProvider) method
V2.ToString("V", Formatter) = magnitude = 3.6109        direction = 1.494
V2.ToString("V", null) = magnitude = 3.6109      direction = 1.494
```

This method prints out the two x and y coordinates that make up the start and end points of a line for the Line class. An example output of the Line.ToString() method is:

```
(0,0) (40,123)
```

This output could also be displayed as a vector that starts at the origin of the Cartesian plane and points straight up along the positive y-axis. Another choice for this would be to print out the magnitude and direction of this line. This result is demonstrated in the overloaded ToString method that accepts both a format string and an IFormatProvider.

The next overloaded ToString method takes a single argument, *format*, which is a String containing the formatting information of the type. This method calls the last overloaded ToString method and passes the format information as the first parameter and a null as the second parameter. The following ToString method operates similarly to the previous ToString method, except that it accepts an IFormatProvider data type as its only parameter. The format parameter of the last ToString method is set to null when called by this method.

The final ToString method is where all the real work takes place. This method accepts two parameters, a String (format) containing formatting information and an IFormatProvider (formatProvider) containing even more specific formatting information. The format string makes use of predefined formats such as "D", "d", "F", "f",

"G", "g", "X", and "x", to name a few. (See Recipe 2.16 for more information on the formatting character codes.) These formats specify whether the information will be displayed as decimal ("D" or "d"), general ("G" or "g"), hexadecimal ("X" or "x"), or one of the other types. As a note, calling ToString with no parameters always sets the format type to general. In addition, this method also takes a special format character "V" or "v". This character formatting code is not one of the predefined formatting codes; instead, it is one that we added to provide special handling of a Line object's output in vector format. This code allows the Line type to be displayed as a magnitude and a direction:

```
magnitude = 13.038      direction = 1.494
```

The second parameter accepts any data type that implements the IFormatProvider interface. There are three types in the FCL that implement this interface: CultureInfo, DateTimeFormatInfo, or NumberFormatInfo. The CultureInfo class contains formatting information specific to the various supported cultures that exist around the world. The DateTimeFormatInfo class contains formatting information specific to date and time values; similarly, the NumberFormatInfo class contains formatting information specific to numbers.

This ToString method sets up a variable, compositeStr, which will contain the final formatted value of the Line type. Next, the format parameter is checked for null. Remember, the previous ToString method that accepts the IFormatProvider parameter will call this form of the ToString method and pass in a format value of null. So we must be able to handle a null value gracefully at this point. If the format parameter passed in to the Line type is not null and is equal to the character "V", we are able to provide a string to display this line as a magnitude and a direction. The direction and magnitude values are obtained for this object and are displayed in a General format with five significant digits of precision. If, on the other hand, any other type of formatting character code was passed in—including null—each of the individual coordinates are formatted using the ToString method of the Int32 structure. These coordinates are concatenated into a string and returned to the caller to be displayed.

The method:

```
public string ToString(string format, IFormatProvider formatProvider)
```

must be implemented, since the structure implements the IFormattable interface. The IFormattable interface provides a consistent interface for this ToString method:

```
public interface IFormattable
{
    string ToString(string format, IFormatProvider formatProvider);
}
```

For the Line structure, the IFormattable.ToString method passes its parameters to the Int32 structure's ToString method with the same method signature, which provides a more uniform formatting capability for Line values.

Using the IFormattable interface forces you to implement the IFormattable.ToString method to more effectively display your type's value(s). However, you do not have to implement it, as you can see for yourself by removing this interface from the Line structure's declaration. In fact, for performance's sake, it is best to not implement this interface on structures, due to the cost of boxing the structure. Implementing this interface on a class does not incur a performance penalty.

See Also

See Recipe 2.16; see the "IFormatProvider Interface" topic in the MSDN documentation.

3.3 Converting a String Representation of an Object into an Actual Object

Problem

You need a way of accepting a string containing a textual representation of an object and converting it to an object usable by your application. For example, if you were provided with the string representation of a line (x1, y1)(x2, y2), you would want to convert it into a Line structure.

Solution

Implement a Parse method on your Line structure:

```
using System;
using System.Text;
using System.Text.RegularExpressions;

public struct Line
{
    public Line(int startX, int startY, int endX, int endY)
    {
        x1 = startX;
        x2 = endX;
        y1 = startY;
        y2 = endY;
    }

    public int x1;
    public int y1;
    public int x2;
    public int y2;

    public static Line Parse(string stringLine)
    {
```

```
    if (stringLine == null)
    {
        throw (new ArgumentNullException("stringLine",
                "A null cannot be passed into the Parse method."));
    }

    // Take this string (x1,y1)(x2,y2) and convert it to a Line object
    int X1 = 0;
    int Y1 = 0;
    int X2 = 0;
    int Y2 = 0;

    MatchCollection MC = Regex.Matches(stringLine,
            @"\s*\(\s*(?<x1>\d+)\s*\,\s*(?<y1>\d+)\s*\)\s*
                \(\s*(?<x2>\d+)\s*\,\s*(?<y2>\d+)\s*\)" );

    if (MC.Count == 1)
    {
        Match M = MC[0];
        X1 = int.Parse(M.Groups["x1"].Value);
        Y1 = int.Parse(M.Groups["y1"].Value);
        X2 = int.Parse(M.Groups["x2"].Value);
        Y2 = int.Parse(M.Groups["y2"].Value);
    }
    else
    {
        throw (new ArgumentException(
            "The value " + stringLine + " is not a well formed Line value."));
    }

    return (new Line(X1, Y1, X2, Y2));
    }
}
```

Discussion

The `Parse` method is used to reconstruct one data type—in this case, a `String`—into the data type containing that `Parse` method. For example, if the string "123" were passed into the `int.Parse` method, the numeric data type 123 would be extracted and then returned. Many other types in the FCL use a `Parse` method to reconstruct an object of its own type from another data type, such as a string. Note that you are not limited as far as the type and number of parameters that can be passed into this method. As an example, see how the `DateTime.Parse` and `DateTime.ParseExact` methods are defined and overloaded.

The parsing of a string containing the start and end coordinates of a line is a little more difficult. To make things easier, we use a regular expression to extract the beginning and ending X and Y coordinates.

The regular expression parses out the individual coordinate values provided by the `stringLine` string parameter. Each found coordinate is passed on to the static `int.Parse` method on the int structure. This final step obtains the final parsed integer values from the matches produced by the regular expression. If the regular expression does not extract the required coordinates, we can assume that the stringLine parameter does not contain a well-formed string that can be converted to a Line object.

The following code:

```
Console.WriteLine("Line.Parse(\"(12,2)(0,45)\") = " + Line.Parse("(12,2)(0,45)"));
Console.WriteLine("Line.Parse(\"(0,0)(0,0)\") = " + Line.Parse("(0,0)(0,0)"));
```

produces this output:

```
Line.Parse("(12,2)(0,45)") = (12,2) (0,45)
Line.Parse("(0,0)(0,0)") = (0,0) (0,0)
```

 When implementing a Parse method on your own types, you need to consider the situation where invalid data is passed to this method. When this happens, an ArgumentException should be thrown. When a null is passed in, you should instead throw an ArgumentNullException.

See Also

See the "Parse Method" topic; see the Parse Sample under the ".NET Samples—How To: Base Data Types" topic in the MSDN documentation.

3.4 Polymorphism via Concrete or Abstract Base Classes

Problem

You need to build several classes that share many common traits. These classes may share common properties, methods, events, delegates, and even indexers; however, the implementation of these may be different for each class. These classes should not only share common code but also be polymorphic in nature. That is to say, code that uses an object of the base class should be able to use an object of any of these classes in the same manner.

Solution

Use an abstract base class to create polymorphic code. To demonstrate the creation and use of an abstract base class, here is an example of three classes, each defining a media type: magnetic, optical, and punch card. An abstract base class, Media, is created to define what each derived class will contain:

```
public abstract class Media
{
    public abstract void Init( );
    public abstract void WriteTo(string data);
```

```
    public abstract string ReadFrom( );
    public abstract void Close( );

    private IntPtr mediaHandle = IntPtr.Zero;

    public IntPtr Handle
    {
        get {return(mediaHandle);}
    }
}
```

Next, the three specialized media type classes, which inherit from Media, are defined to override each of the abstract members:

```
public class Magnetic : Media
{
    public override void Init( )
    {
        Console.WriteLine("Magnetic Init");
    }

    public override void WriteTo(string data)
    {
        Console.WriteLine("Magnetic Write");
    }

    public override string ReadFrom( )
    {
        Console.WriteLine("Magnetic Read");

        string data = "";
        return (data);
    }

    public override void Close( )
    {
        Console.WriteLine("Magnetic Close");
    }
}

public class Optical : Media
{
    public override void Init( )
    {
        Console.WriteLine("Optical Init");
    }

    public override void WriteTo(string data)
    {
        Console.WriteLine("Optical Write");
    }

    public override string ReadFrom( )
    {
```

```
        Console.WriteLine("Optical Read");

        string data = "";
        return (data);
    }

    public override void Close()
    {
        Console.WriteLine("Optical Close");
    }
}

public class PunchCard : Media
{
    public override void Init()
    {
        Console.WriteLine("PunchCard Init");
    }

    public override void WriteTo(string data)
    {
        Console.WriteLine("PunchCard WriteTo");
    }

    public override string ReadFrom()
    {
        Console.WriteLine("PunchCard ReadFrom");

        string data = "";
        return (data);
    }

    public override void Close()
    {
        Console.WriteLine("PunchCard Close");
    }
}
```

The following methods, TestMediaABC and UseMedia, show how any of the three media types can be used polymorphically from within the UseMedia method:

```
public void TestMediaABC()
{
    Media x = new Magnetic();
    UseMedia(x);

    Console.WriteLine();

    x = new Optical();
    UseMedia(x);
}

private void UseMedia(Media media)
{
```

```
    media.Init();
    media.WriteTo("text");
    media.ReadFrom();
    Console.WriteLine(media.Handle);
    media.Close();

    Console.WriteLine(media.ToString());
}
```

The output of these methods is shown here:

```
Magnetic Init
Magnetic Write
Magnetic Read
0
Magnetic Close
Magnetic

Optical Init
Optical Write
Optical Read
0
Optical Close
Optical
```

Discussion

Polymorphism through an abstract base class is a powerful tool. With this tool, you are able to create a method (UseMedia in this solution) that accepts a parameter whose specific type is known only at runtime. Since the use of this parameter is similar for all objects that can be passed in to this method, we do not have to worry about the specific class that is passed in; we need to know only how the abstract base class is defined. It is through this abstract base class definition that we know how to use the specific type.

There are several things to keep in mind when using an abstract base class:

- Neither this class nor its abstract members can be declared as sealed; this would defeat polymorphism.
- The abstract class cannot be instantiated using the new operator, but a variable can be declared as an abstract base class type.
- All abstract members must be overridden in a derived class unless the derived class is also abstract.
- It is implied that an abstract method is also defined as virtual.
- Only methods, properties, indexers, and events may be declared as abstract.
- Abstract methods, properties, and indexers may not be declared as static or virtual.
- If an abstract base class implements an interface, it must provide either an implementation for the interface members or an abstract definition of the interface members. A combination of the two may be applied as well.

- An abstract base class can contain abstract and nonabstract members. It is not required to contain any abstract members, but this omission may confuse those who read this code.

- An abstract class may implement any number of interfaces and may also inherit from a single class. As a note, abstract members may override `virtual` members in the nonabstract base class.

- A derived class can override `abstract` properties and must include at least one accessor method (i.e., get or set.) A property in a base class that overrides an abstract property implementing only a get or a set accessor must override that specific get or set accessor. If the `abstract` property implements both a get and a `set` accessor, the overriding base class property may override one or both accessors.

- A structure cannot implement polymorphism through an abstract base class/ structure. Instead, a structure should consider implementing polymorphism through interfaces (see Recipe 3.17).

It is possible to use interfaces to implement polymorphism; this is discussed at length in Recipe 3.17. There are several advantages to using an abstract base class over an interface:

- Abstract base classes allow more flexibility in versioning. An abstract base class can add a nonabstract member without breaking existing derived classes; an interface cannot. However, adding a new *abstract* member will break the existing derived classes.

- An abstract base class can contain abstract members as well as nonabstract members. An interface may contain only definitions of members with no implementation.

You should also consider using an abstract base class over an interface when a lot of disparate members need to be overridden in the derived classes. For example, if you are implementing a set of members that control searching or sorting of items, you should initially consider interfaces, since this is a focused set of members that may be implemented over a wide range of unrelated classes. If you were implementing a set of members that determines the base functionality for a complete type, such as the `Media` type, you would want to use an abstract base class. See Recipe 3.17 for the advantages of using interface polymorphism over abstract base classes.

Notice that the abstract `Media` class in this recipe could be written as a concrete class (i.e., remove the `abstract` keyword and add implementations to all abstract methods). This would allow you to create objects from the `Media` class. If you do not wish for objects to be created from your base class (`Media`), you should make it abstract.

See Also

See Recipe 3.17; see section 10.1.1.1, "Abstract Classes", in the C# Language Specification.

3.5   Making a Type Sortable

Problem

You have a data type that will be stored as elements in an array or an ArrayList. You would like to use the Array.Sort and ArrayList.Sort methods to allow for a custom sorting of your data types in the array. In addition, you may need to use this structure in a SortedList collection.

Solution

Implement the IComparable interface. The following class, Square, implements this interface in a way so that the Array, ArrayList, and SortedList objects can sort and search an array or collection of these Square objects:

```
public class Square : IComparable
{
    public Square( ){}
    public Square(int height, int width)
    {
        this.height = height;
        this.width = width;
    }

    private int height;
    private int width;

    public int Height
    {
        get{ return (height); }
        set{ height = value; }
    }

    public int Width
    {
        get{ return (width); }
        set{ width = value; }
    }

    public int CompareTo(object obj)
    {
        if (this.GetType( ) != obj.GetType( ))
        {
            throw (new ArgumentException(
                "Both objects being compared must be of type Square."));
        }
        else
        {
            Square square2 = (Square)obj;

            long area1 = this.Height * this.Width;
            long area2 = square2.Height * square2.Width;
```

```
            if (area1 == area2)
            {
                return (0);
            }
            else if (area1 > area2)
            {
                return (1);
            }
            else if (area1 < area2)
            {
                return (-1);
            }
            else
            {
                return (-1);
            }
        }
    }

    public override string ToString()
    {
        return ("Height:" + height + "  Width:" + width);
    }
}
```

Discussion

By implementing the IComparable interface on your class (or structure), you can take advantage of the sorting routines of the Array, ArrayList, and SortedList classes. The algorithms for sorting are built into these classes; all you have to do is tell them how to sort through your classes via the code you implement in the IComparable. CompareTo method.

When an array of Square objects is passed to the Array.Sort static method, the array is sorted using the IComparable interface of the Square objects. The same goes for the ArrayList.Sort method. The Add method of the SortedList class uses this interface to sort the objects as they are being added to the SortedList.

The algorithm that the Array.Sort and ArrayList.Sort methods use to sort an array's elements is the QuickSort algorithm.

IComparer is designed to solve the problem of allowing objects to be sorted based on different criteria in different contexts. This interface also allows us to sort types that we did not write. If we wanted to also be able to sort the Square objects by height, we could create a new class called CompareHeight, which would also implement the IComparer interface:

```
public class CompareHeight : IComparer
{
```

```csharp
    public int Compare(object obj1, object obj2)
    {
        if (!(obj1 is Square) || !(obj2 is Square))
        {
            throw (new ArgumentException("Both parameters must be of type Square."));
        }
        else
        {
            Square square1 = (Square)obj1;
            Square square2 = (Square)obj2;

            if (square1.Height == square2.Height)
            {
                return (0);
            }
            else if (square1.Height > square2.Height)
            {
                return (1);
            }
            else if (square1.Height < square2.Height)
            {
                return (-1);
            }
            else
            {
                return (-1);
            }
        }
    }
}
```

This class is then passed in to the IComparer parameter of the Sort routine. Now we can specify different ways to sort our Square objects.

 For best performance, keep the CompareTo method short and efficient, since it will be called multiple times by the Sort methods. For example, in sorting an array with 4 items, the Compare method was called 10 times.

The following method shows how to use the Square and CompareHeight structures with the Array, ArrayList, and SortedList classes:

```csharp
    public static void TestSort()
    {
        Square[] arrayOfSquares = new Square[4] {new Square(1,3),
                                                 new Square(4,3),
                                                 new Square(2,1),
                                                 new Square(6,1)};

        ArrayList arrayListOfSquares = new ArrayList();
        arrayListOfSquares.Add(new Square(1,3));
        arrayListOfSquares.Add(new Square(4,3));
```

```
arrayListOfSquares.Add(new Square(2,1));
arrayListOfSquares.Add(new Square(6,1));

IComparer HeightCompare = new CompareHeight();

// Test an ARRAY
Console.WriteLine("ARRAY");
Console.WriteLine("Original array");
foreach (Square s in arrayOfSquares)
{
    Console.WriteLine(s.ToString());
}

Console.WriteLine();
Console.WriteLine("Sorted array using IComparer=HeightCompare");
Array.Sort(arrayOfSquares, HeightCompare);
foreach (Square s in arrayOfSquares)
{
    Console.WriteLine(s.ToString());
}

Console.WriteLine();
Console.WriteLine("Sorted array using IComparable");
Array.Sort(arrayOfSquares);
foreach (Square s in arrayOfSquares)
{
    Console.WriteLine(s.ToString());
}

// Test an ARRAYLIST
Console.WriteLine();
Console.WriteLine();
Console.WriteLine("ARRAYLIST");
foreach (Square s in arrayListOfSquares)
{
    Console.WriteLine(s.ToString());
}

Console.WriteLine();
Console.WriteLine("Sorted ArrayList using IComparer=HeightCompare");
arrayListOfSquares.Sort(HeightCompare);
foreach (Square s in arrayListOfSquares)
{
    Console.WriteLine(s.ToString());
}

Console.WriteLine();
Console.WriteLine("Sorted ArrayList using IComparable");
arrayListOfSquares.Sort();
foreach (Square s in arrayListOfSquares)
{
    Console.WriteLine(s.ToString());
}
```

```
// Test a SORTEDLIST
SortedList SortedListOfSquares = new SortedList();
SortedListOfSquares.Add(0, new Square(1,3));
SortedListOfSquares.Add(2, new Square(4,3));
SortedListOfSquares.Add(1, new Square(2,1));
SortedListOfSquares.Add(3, new Square(6,1));

Console.WriteLine();
Console.WriteLine();
Console.WriteLine("SORTEDLIST");
foreach (DictionaryEntry s in SortedListOfSquares)
{
    Console.WriteLine(s.Key + " : " + ((Square)s.Value).ToString());
}
}
```

This code displays the following output:

```
ARRAY
Original array
Height:1  Width:3
Height:4  Width:3
Height:2  Width:1
Height:6  Width:1

Sorted array using IComparer=HeightCompare
Height:1  Width:3
Height:2  Width:1
Height:4  Width:3
Height:6  Width:1

Sorted array using IComparable
Height:2  Width:1
Height:1  Width:3
Height:6  Width:1
Height:4  Width:3

ARRAYLIST
Height:1  Width:3
Height:4  Width:3
Height:2  Width:1
Height:6  Width:1

Sorted ArrayList using IComparer=HeightCompare
Height:1  Width:3
Height:2  Width:1
Height:4  Width:3
Height:6  Width:1

Sorted ArrayList using IComparable
Height:2  Width:1
Height:1  Width:3
Height:6  Width:1
Height:4  Width:3
```

```
SORTEDLIST
0 : Height:1  Width:3
1 : Height:2  Width:1
2 : Height:4  Width:3
3 : Height:6  Width:1
```

See Also

See Recipe 3.6; see the "IComparable Interface" topic in the MSDN documentation.

3.6   Making a Type Searchable

Problem

You have a data type that will be stored as elements in an array or an ArrayList. You would like to use the Array.BinarySearch and ArrayList.BinarySearch methods to allow for custom searching of your data types in the array.

Solution

Use the IComparable and IComparer interfaces. The Square class, from Recipe 3.5, implements these in a way so that the Array, ArrayList, and SortedList objects can sort and search an array or collection of Square objects.

Discussion

By implementing the IComparable interface on your class (or structure), you can take advantage of the search routines of the Array, ArrayList, and SortedList classes. The algorithms for searching are built into these classes; all you have to do is tell them how to search through your classes via the code you implement in the IComparable. CompareTo method.

To implement the CompareTo method, see Recipe 3.5.

The Array and ArrayList classes provide a BinarySearch method to perform a search on the elements in that array. The elements are compared against an object passed to the BinarySearch method in the object parameter. The SortedList class does not have a BinarySearch method; instead, it has Contains, ContainsKey, and ContainsValue methods to perform a linear search when searching for values. This linear search uses the Equals method of the elements in the SortedList collection to do its work (to overload the Equals method, see Recipe 3.9), the Compare and CompareTo methods do not have any effect on the operation of the linear search performed in the SortedList class, but they do have an effect on binary searches.

To perform an accurate search using the BinarySearch methods of the Array and ArrayList classes, you must first sort the Array or ArrayList using its Sort method. In addition, if you pass an IComparer interface to the BinarySearch method, you must also pass the same interface to the Sort method. Otherwise, the BinarySearch method might not be able to find the object you are looking for.

The following method shows how to use the Square and CompareHeight structures with the Array, ArrayList, and SortedList classes:

```
public static void TestSort( )
{
    Square[] arrayOfSquares = new Square[4] {new Square(1,3),
                                             new Square(4,3),
                                             new Square(2,1),
                                             new Square(6,1)};

    ArrayList arrayListOfSquares = new ArrayList( );
    arrayListOfSquares.Add(new Square(1,3));
    arrayListOfSquares.Add(new Square(4,3));
    arrayListOfSquares.Add(new Square(2,1));
    arrayListOfSquares.Add(new Square(6,1));

    IComparer HeightCompare = new CompareHeight( );

    // Test an ARRAY
    Console.WriteLine("ARRAY");
    Console.WriteLine("Original array");
    foreach (Square s in arrayOfSquares)
    {
        Console.WriteLine(s.ToString( ));
    }

    Console.WriteLine( );
    Console.WriteLine("Sorted array using IComparer=HeightCompare");
    Array.Sort(arrayOfSquares, HeightCompare);
    foreach (Square s in arrayOfSquares)
    {
        Console.WriteLine(s.ToString( ));
    }

    Console.WriteLine( );
    Console.WriteLine("Search using IComparer=HeightCompare");
    int found = Array.BinarySearch(arrayOfSquares, new Square(1,3), HeightCompare);
    Console.WriteLine("found (1,3): " + found);

    Console.WriteLine( );
    Console.WriteLine("Sorted array using IComparable");
    Array.Sort(arrayOfSquares);
    foreach (Square s in arrayOfSquares)
    {
        Console.WriteLine(s.ToString( ));
```

```
    }
    Console.WriteLine("Search using IComparable");
    found = Array.BinarySearch(arrayOfSquares,
                            new Square(6,1), null);  // Use IComparable
    Console.WriteLine("found (6,1): " + found);

    // Test an ARRAYLIST
    Console.WriteLine();
    Console.WriteLine();
    Console.WriteLine("ARRAYLIST");
    foreach (Square s in arrayListOfSquares)
    {
        Console.WriteLine(s.ToString());
    }

    Console.WriteLine();
    Console.WriteLine("Sorted ArrayList using IComparer=HeightCompare");
    arrayListOfSquares.Sort(HeightCompare);
    foreach (Square s in arrayListOfSquares)
    {
        Console.WriteLine(s.ToString());
    }

    Console.WriteLine();
    Console.WriteLine("Search using IComparer=HeightCompare");
    found = arrayListOfSquares.BinarySearch(new Square(1,3), HeightCompare);
    Console.WriteLine("found (1,3): " + found);

    Console.WriteLine();
    Console.WriteLine("Sorted ArrayList using IComparable");
    arrayListOfSquares.Sort();
    foreach (Square s in arrayListOfSquares)
    {
        Console.WriteLine(s.ToString());
    }

    Console.WriteLine();
    Console.WriteLine("Search using IComparable");
    found = arrayListOfSquares.BinarySearch(new Square(6,1), null);
    Console.WriteLine("found (6,1): " + found);

    // Test a SORTEDLIST
    SortedList SortedListOfSquares = new SortedList();
    SortedListOfSquares.Add(0, new Square(1,3));
    SortedListOfSquares.Add(2, new Square(4,3));
    SortedListOfSquares.Add(1, new Square(2,1));
    SortedListOfSquares.Add(3, new Square(6,1));

    Console.WriteLine();
    Console.WriteLine();
    Console.WriteLine("SORTEDLIST");
    foreach (DictionaryEntry s in SortedListOfSquares)
    {
```

```
            Console.WriteLine(s.Key + " : " + ((Square)s.Value).ToString());
        }

        Console.WriteLine();
        bool foundBool = SortedListOfSquares.Contains(2);
        Console.WriteLine("SortedListOfSquares.Contains(2): " + foundBool);

        foundBool = SortedListOfSquares.ContainsKey(2);
        Console.WriteLine("SortedListOfSquares.ContainsKey(2): " + foundBool);

        // Does not use IComparer or IComparable
        // -- uses a linear search along with the Equals method, which has not been
        //      overloaded; if the Square object were to be used as the key
        //      rather than the value, a binary search would be performed when searching
        //      for this Square object.
        Square value = new Square(6,1);
        foundBool = SortedListOfSquares.ContainsValue(value);
        Console.WriteLine
            ("SortedListOfSquares.ContainsValue(new Square(6,1)): " + foundBool);
    }
```

This code displays the following:

```
ARRAY
Original array
Height:1   Width:3
Height:4   Width:3
Height:2   Width:1
Height:6   Width:1

Sorted array using IComparer=HeightCompare
Height:1   Width:3
Height:2   Width:1
Height:4   Width:3
Height:6   Width:1

Search using IComparer=HeightCompare
found (1,3): 0

Sorted array using IComparable
Height:2   Width:1
Height:1   Width:3
Height:6   Width:1
Height:4   Width:3
Search using IComparable
found (6,1): 2

ARRAYLIST
Height:1   Width:3
Height:4   Width:3
Height:2   Width:1
Height:6   Width:1

Sorted ArrayList using IComparer=HeightCompare
Height:1   Width:3
```

```
Height:2  Width:1
Height:4  Width:3
Height:6  Width:1

Search using IComparer=HeightCompare
found (1,3): 0

Sorted ArrayList using IComparable
Height:2  Width:1
Height:1  Width:3
Height:6  Width:1
Height:4  Width:3

Search using IComparable
found (6,1): 2

SORTEDLIST
0 : Height:1  Width:3
1 : Height:2  Width:1
2 : Height:4  Width:3
3 : Height:6  Width:1

SortedListOfSquares.Contains(2): True
SortedListOfSquares.ContainsKey(2): True
SortedListOfSquares.ContainsValue(new Square(6,1)): False
```

See Also

See Recipes 3.5 and 3.9; see the "IComparable Interface" and "IComparer Interface" topics in the MSDN documentation.

3.7   Indirectly Overloading the +=, -=, /=, and *= Operators

Problem

You need to control the handling of the +=, -=, /=, and *= operators within your data type; unfortunately, these operators cannot be directly overloaded.

Solution

Overload these operators indirectly by overloading the +, -, /, and * operators:

```
public class Foo
{
    // Other class members...

    // Overloaded binary operators
    public static Foo operator +(Foo f1, Foo f2)
    {
        Foo result = new Foo();
```

```
        // Add f1 and f2 here...
        // Place result of the addition into the result variable

        return (result);
    }

    public static Foo operator +(int constant, Foo f1)
    {
        Foo result = new Foo( );

        // Add the constant integer and f1 here...
        // Place result of the addition into the result variable

        return (result);
    }

    public static Foo operator +(Foo f1, int constant)
    {
        Foo result = new Foo( );

        // Add the constant integer and f1 here...
        // Place result of the addition into the result variable

        return (result);
    }

    public static Foo operator -(Foo f1, Foo f2)
    {
        Foo result = new Foo( );

        // Subtract f1 and f2 here...
        // Place result of the subtraction into the result variable

        return (result);
    }

    public static Foo operator -(int constant, Foo f1)
    {
        Foo result = new Foo( );

        // Subtract the constant integer and f1 here...
        // Place result of the subtraction into the result variable

        return (result);
    }

    public static Foo operator -(Foo f1, int constant)
    {
        Foo result = new Foo( );

        // Subtract the constant integer and f1 here...
        // Place result of the subtraction into the result variable
```

```
        return (result);
    }

    public static Foo operator *(Foo f1, Foo f2)
    {
        Foo result = new Foo( );

        // Multiply f1 and f2 here...
        // Place result of the multiplication into the result variable

        return (result);
    }

    public static Foo operator *(int multiplier, Foo f1)
    {
        Foo result = new Foo( );

        // Multiply multiplier and f1 here...
        // Place result of the multiplication into the result variable

        return (result);
    }

    public static Foo operator *(Foo f1, int multiplier)
    {
        return (multiplier * f1);
    }

    public static Foo operator /(Foo f1, Foo f2)
    {
        Foo result = new Foo( );

        // Divide f1 and f2 here...
        // Place result of the division into the result variable

        return (result);
    }

    public static Foo operator /(int numerator, Foo f1)
    {
        Foo result = new Foo( );

        // Divide numerator and f1 here...
        // Place result of the division into the result variable

        return (result);
    }

    public static Foo operator /(Foo f1, int denominator)
    {
        return (1 / (denominator / f1));
    }
}
```

Discussion

While it is illegal to try and overload the +=, -=, /=, and *= operators directly, you can overload them indirectly by overloading the +, -, /, and * operators. The +=, -=, /=, and *= operators then use the overloaded +, -, /, and * operators for their calculations.

The four operators +, -, /, and * are overloaded by the methods in the Solution section of this recipe. You might notice that each operator is overloaded three times. This is intentional, since a user of your object may attempt to add, subtract, multiply, or divide it by an integer value. The unknown here is which position the integer constant will be in; will it be in the first parameter or the second? The following code snippet shows how this might look for multiplication:

```
Foo x = new Foo();
Foo y *= 100;    // Uses: operator *(Foo f1, int multiplier)
y = 100 * x;     // Uses: operator *(int multiplier, Foo f1)
y *= x;          // Uses: operator *(Foo f1, Foo f2)
```

The same holds true for the other overloaded operator.

If these operators were being implemented in a class, you would first check whether any were set to null. The following code for the overloaded addition operator has been modified to do this:

```
public static Foo operator +(Foo f1, Foo f2)
{
    if (f1 == null || f2 == null)
    {
        throw (new ArgumentException("Neither object may be null."));
    }

    Foo result = new Foo();

    // Add f1 and f2 here...
    // Place result of the addition into the result variable

    return (result);
}
```

See Also

See the "Operator Overloading Usage Guideline," "Overloadable Operators," and "Operator Overloading Tutorial" topics in the MSDN documentation.

3.8 Indirectly Overloading the &&, ||, and ?: Operators

Problem

You need to control the handling of the &&, ||, and ?: operators within your data type; unfortunately, these operators cannot be directly overloaded.

Solution

Overload these operators indirectly by overloading the &, |, true, and false operators:

```
public class ObjState
{
    public ObjState(int state)
    {
        this.state = state;
    }

    public int state = 0;

    public static ObjState operator &(ObjState obj1, ObjState obj2)
    {
        if (obj1.state >= 0 && obj2.state >= 0)
            return (new ObjState(1));
        else
            return (new ObjState(-1));
    }

    public static ObjState operator |(ObjState obj1, ObjState obj2)
    {
        if (obj1.state < 0 && obj2.state < 0)
            return (new ObjState(-1));
        else
            return (new ObjState(1));
    }

    public static bool operator true(ObjState obj)
    {
        if (obj.state >= 0)
            return (true);
        else
            return (false);
    }

    public static bool operator false(ObjState obj)
    {
        if (obj.state >= 0)
            return (true);
        else
            return (false);
    }

    public override string ToString()
    {
        return (state.ToString());
    }
}
```

This technique gives you complete control over the operations of the &&, ||, and ?: operators.

Alternatively, you can simply add an implicit conversion to `bool`:

```
public class ObjState
{
    public ObjState(int state)
    {
        this.state = state;
    }

    public int state = 0;

    public static implicit operator bool(ObjState obj)
    {
        if (obj.state == 0)
        {
            throw new InvalidOperationException();
        }

        return (obj.state > 0);
    }
}
```

This technique implements strict Boolean logic; the first technique (overriding the &&, ||, and ?: operators) gives you more freedom to stray from implementing strict Boolean logic.

Discussion

While you cannot overload the &&, ||, and ?: operators directly, you can overload them indirectly by overloading the &, |, true, and false operators. The &&, ||, and ?: operators then use the overloaded &, |, true, and false operators for their calculations.

The && operator indirectly uses the false and & operators to perform a short-circuiting And operation. Initially, the false operator is invoked to determine whether the first object is equal to false. If so, the operation stops and whatever is on the lefthand side of the && operator is returned. If the false operator returns a true, the & operator is invoked next to perform the ANDing operation on the two objects. This initial test using the false operator enables the operator to short-circuit the operation.

The || operator works the same as the && operator, except that the initial test is done using the true operator rather than the false operator.

The ?: operator only requires the overloading of the true operator to be indirectly overloaded. Note that overloading the true operator requires the overloading of the false operator for symmetry. The ?: operator takes a conditional expression as input and evaluates either its true or false expression. This operator can be defined as follows:

```
conditional-expression ? true-expression : false-expression
```

The ?: operator invokes the true operator to determine which expression of this operator should be evaluated. Note that if an implicit conversion to bool exists, it will be used in preference to the true operator.

When implementing these operators, you would first check to determine whether any parameters in the overloaded operator methods were set to null. The code for the overloaded & operator has been modified to do this:

```
public static ObjState operator &(ObjState obj1, ObjState obj2)
{
    if (obj1 == null || obj2 == null)
    {
        throw (new ArgumentNullException("Neither object may be null."));
    }

    if (obj1.state >= 0 && obj2.state >= 0)
        return (new ObjState(1));
    else
        return (new ObjState(-1));
}
```

See Also

See the "Operator Overloading Usage Guidelines," "Overloadable Operators," and "Operator Overloading Tutorial" topics in the MSDN documentation.

3.9   Improving the Performance of a Structure's Equals Method

Problem

You need to provide a better performing Equals method than the default Equals method on a structure. The default implementation of Equals on a ValueType uses reflection to compare the fields of two ValueTypes, resulting in poor performance. Note that this recipe does not hold true for classes; although the same techniques apply if you want to overload the Equals method in a class.

Solution

Override the Equals method. When this method is overridden, you must also override the GetHashCode method:

```
public struct Line
{
    public Line(int startX, int startY, int endX, int endY)
    {
        x1 = startX;
        x2 = endX;
        y1 = startY;
        y2 = endY;
    }

    private int x1;
    private int y1;
```

```
    private int x2;
    private int y2;

    public override bool Equals(object obj)
    {
        bool isEqual = false;

        if (obj == null || (this.GetType() != obj.GetType()))
        {
            isEqual = false;
        }
        else
        {
            Line theLine = (Line)obj;
            isEqual = (this.x1 == theLine.x1) &&
                      (this.y1 == theLine.y1) &&
                      (this.x2 == theLine.x2) &&
                      (this.y2 == theLine.y2);
        }
        return (isEqual);

    }

    public override int GetHashCode()
    {
        return (x1+109*(x2+113*(y1+127*y2)));
    }
}
```

In addition, a strongly typed Equals method can be added to further streamline this operation:

```
public bool Equals(Line lineObj)
{
    bool isEqual = (this.x1 == lineObj.x1) &&
                   (this.y1 == lineObj.y1) &&
                   (this.x2 == lineObj.x2) &&
                   (this.y2 == lineObj.y2);

    return (IsEqual);
}
```

In this recipe, we chose a Line structure arbitrarily. However, your focus should be on the details of overriding an Equals method. In addition, we chose to define the equivalence of two Line objects as having the exact same starting and ending coordinates.

Discussion

All structures come with a predefined Equals method that internally uses reflection. Take a look at the IL code for the Equals method of the System.ValueType class in the *mscorlib.dll* using Ildasm. You will notice that the implementation of this Equals method first checks to see whether the object passed in to this method is null. If it is not, the next check is to determine whether the object implementing the Equals method is the same type as the one passed in to it. If so, a check is made using the internally implemented method `ValueType.CanCompareBits`. If this method determines that the bits of the two objects can be compared successfully, a call is made to `ValueType.FastEqualsCheck`. If this faster check for equivalence cannot be made, reflection—which performs slower—is used to obtain all the instance fields of both objects and compare them individually within a loop. This may not be the best way to go for your custom `ValueType`—from both a performance and a logic point of view.

Performance-wise, the `Equals` methods provided in this recipe are faster. From a logic point of view, you can create your own equivalence algorithm, and not depend on what the default implementation considers equivalence. For example, your `ValueType` could contain many different instance fields, but the equivalence of two of these `ValueTypes` may depend only on a subset of these instance fields. By overriding the `Equals` method, we can solve both of these problems at one time.

By creating a strongly typed `Equals` method, we can take performance one step farther. The overridden `Equals` method must confirm that the object type passed in to it is not only non-null, but that it is also of the same type. If both of these tests pass, an unboxing operation must be performed when the object that is passed is cast to its corresponding `ValueType`. Note also that a boxing operation must occur when the `Equals` method is called.

 There are several rules that you should follow when determining when to override the `Equals` method. The `Equals` method should be overridden when implementing the `IComparable` interface on your structure/class. If the object passed as a parameter to this method is either `null` or not of the same type as this object, return a `false`. Finally, exceptions should not be explicitly thrown in this method, as it might confuse other developers that are trying to debug code using your object. These rules are valid for reference types as well.

Whenever the `Equals` method is overloaded, you should overload the `GetHashCode` method. If you fail to do so, the code will compile, but a warning will be issued stating that the `GetHashCode` method should be overridden.

Overriding the `GetHashCode` method is desirable for several reasons. Most importantly, overriding this method allows your `ValueType` to be used as a key in a `System.Collection.HashTable` object. The second reason is performance. If you take a look at the IL for the `ValueType.GetHashCode` method in the *mscorlib.dll* using Ildasm, you will see that it also uses reflection to obtain the first non-null instance field of the `ValueType`. Once it obtains this field, that field's `GetHashCode` method is called to return a hash code value. If no valid fields exist in the `ValueType`, the internal method `ValueType.GetMethodTablePtrAsInt` is called to get a hash code. The final reason for overloading this method is to control more precisely the algorithm for obtaining a hash code.

As a final note, when overloading the Equals method, you should strongly consider overloading the == and != operators. This overloading will provide consistency within your type. For example, some clients of your type may use the Equals method and some may attempt to use the == or != operators. Providing overrides to all three of these members allows consistent use of your type. The code to overload these two operators for the Line type is as follows:

```
public static bool operator ==(Line l1, Line l2)
{
    return (l1.Equals(l2));
}

public static bool operator !=(Line l1, Line l2)
{
    return (!l1.Equals(l2));
}
```

See Also

See the "ValueType.Equals Method" topic in the MSDN documentation.

3.10 Turning Bits On or Off

Problem

You have a numeric value or an enumeration that contains bit flags. You need a method to turn on (set the bit to 1) or turn off (set the bit to 0) one or more of these bit flags. In addition, you also want a method to flip one or more bit flag values; that is, change the bit(s) to their opposite value.

Solution

The following method turns one or more bits on:

```
public static int TurnBitOn(int value, int bitToTurnOn)
{
    return (value | bitToTurnOn);
}
```

The following method turns one or more bits off:

```
public static int TurnBitOff(int value, int bitToTurnOff)
{
    return (value & ~bitToTurnOff);
}
```

The following method flips a bit to its opposite value:

```
public static int FlipBit(int value, int bitToFlip)
{
    return (value ^ bitToFlip);
}
```

Discussion

When a large number of flags are required, and particularly when combinations of flags can be set, it becomes cumbersome and unwieldy to use Boolean variables. In this case, using the binary representation of a number, we can assign each bit to indicate a specific Boolean value. Each Boolean value is called a *bit flag*. For example, we have a number defined as a byte data type. This number is comprised of eight binary bit values, which can be either a 1 or a 0. Supposing we assign a color to each bit, our number would be defined as follows:

```
byte colorValue = 0;  // colorValue initialized to no color

//   colorValue    Bit position
//     red       0 (least-significant bit)
//     green     1
//     blue      2
//     black     3
//     grey      4
//     silver    5
//     olive     6
//     teal      7 (most-significant bit)
```

By setting each bit to 0 or 1, we can define a color value for the colorValue variable. Unfortunately, the colorValue variable does not take into account all colors. We can remedy this by allowing multiple bits to be set to 1. This trick allows us to combine red (bit 0) and green (bit 1) to get the color yellow; red (bit 0) and blue (bit 2) to get violet; or red, green, and blue to get white.

 Note that we have used the byte data type in defining our colorValue bitmask. This is because it is more convenient to use unsigned data types for bit flag variables. The other unsigned integers supported by C# are ushort, uint, and ulong. This makes it easier to create the bitmask values to use with the bit flag variable. Simply put, you do not have to worry about negative values of the data type when using unsigned data types.

Now that we have our bit flags set up in the colorValue variable, we need a way to set the individual bits to a 0 or 1, as well as a way to determine whether one or more bits (colors) are turned on. To do this, we use a *bitmask*. A bitmask is a constant number, usually of the same type as the target type containing the bit flags. This bitmask value will be ANDed, ORed, or XORed with the number containing the bit flags to determine the state of each bit flag or to set each bit flag to a 0 or 1:

```
[Flags]
public enum ColorBitMask
{
    NoColorBitMask = 0,    //binary value == 00000000
    RedBitMask = 1,        //binary value == 00000001
    GreenBitMask = 2,      //binary value == 00000010
    BlueBitMask = 4,       //binary value == 00000100
```

```
    BlackBitMask = 8,      //binary value == 00001000
    GreyBitMask = 16,      //binary value == 00010000
    SilverBitMask = 32,    //binary value == 00100000
    OliveBitMask = 64,     //binary value == 01000000
    TealBitMask = 128,     //binary value == 10000000
    YellowBitMask = 3,     //binary value == 00000011
    VioletBitMask = 5,     //binary value == 00000101
    WhiteBitMask = 7,      //binary value == 00000111
}
```

One common use for the & operator is to set one or more bits in a bit flag value to 0. If we AND a binary value with 1, we always obtain the original binary value. If, on the other hand, we AND a binary value with 0, we always obtain 0. Knowing this, we can use the bitmask values to remove various colors from the colorValue variable:

```
ColorBitMask color = YellowBitMask;
ColorBitMask newColor = color & ~ColorBitMask.RedBitMask);
```

This operation removes the RedBitMask from the color value. This value is then assigned to the newColor variable. The newColor variable now contains the value 2 (00000010 in binary), which is equal to the GreenBitMask value. Essentially, we removed the color red from the color yellow and ended up with the color green, which is a constituent color of yellow.

The | operator can also be used to set one or more bits to 1. If we OR a binary value with 0, we always obtain the original binary value. If, on the other hand, we OR a binary value with 1, we always obtain 1. Using this knowledge, we can use the bitmask values to add various colors to the color variable. For example:

```
ColorBitMask color = ColorBitMask.RedBitMask;
ColorBitMask newColor = color | ColorBitMask.GreenBitMask;
```

This operation ORs the GreenBitMask to the color value, which is currently set to the value RedBitMask. This value is then assigned to the newColor variable. The newColor variable now contains the value 3 (00000011 in binary); this value is equal to the YellowBitMask value. Essentially, we added the color green to the color red and obtained the color yellow.

The ^ operator is often used to flip or invert one or more bits in a bit flag value. It returns a 1 only when either bit is set to 1. If both bits are set to 1s or 0s, this operator returns a 0. This operation provides a convenient method of flipping a bit:

```
ColorBitMask color = ColorBitMask.RedBitMask;
ColorBitMask newColor = color ^ ColorBitMask.RedBitMask;
```

The code shown here flips the least-significant bit (defined by the RedBitMask operation) to its opposite value. So if the color were red, it would become 0, or no defined color, as shown here:

```
    00000001 == Color (red)
^   00000001 == RedBitMask
    00000000
```

If we XOR this result a second time with the bitmask `RedBitMask`, we get our original color (red) back again, as shown here:

```
  00000000 == Color (red)
^ 00000001 == RedBitMask
  00000001 == red
```

If this operation is performed on the color yellow, we can obtain the color other than red that makes up this color. This operation is shown here along with the code:

```
ColorBitMask color = ColorBitMask.YellowBitMask;
ColorBitMask newColor = color ^ ColorBitMask.RedBitMask;

  00000011 == Color (yellow)
^ 00000001 == RedBitMask
  00000010 == green
```

Use the AND (&) operator to set one or more bits to 0.

Use the OR (|) operator to set one or more bits to 1.

Use the XOR (^) operator when flipping one or more bits to their opposite values.

See Also

See Recipe 1.4; see the "C# Operators" topic in the MSDN documentation.

3.11 Making Error-Free Expressions

Problem

A complex expression in your code is returning incorrect results. For example, if you wanted to find the average area given two circles, you might write the following expression:

```
double radius1 = 2;
double radius2 = 4;
double aveArea = .5 * Math.PI * Math.Pow(radius1, 2) + Math.PI *
                Math.Pow(radius2, 2);
```

However, the result is always incorrect.

Complex mathematical and Boolean equations in your code can easily become the source of bugs. You need to write bug-free equations, while at the same time making them easier to read.

Solution

The solution is quite simple: use parentheses to explicitly define the order of operations that will take place in your equation. To fix the expression presented in the Problem section, rewrite it as follows:

```
double radius1 = 2;
double radius2 = 4;
double aveArea = .5 * (Math.PI * Math.Pow(radius1, 2) + Math.PI *
                Math.Pow(radius2, 2));
```

Notice the addition of the parentheses; these parentheses cause the area of the two circles to be calculated and added together first. Then the total area is multiplied by .5. This is the behavior we are looking for. An additional benefit is that the expression can become easier to read as the parentheses provide clear distinction of what part of the expression is to be evaluated first. This technique works equally well with Boolean equations.

Discussion

Parentheses are key to writing maintainable and bug-free equations. Not only is your intention clearly spelled out, but you also override any operator precedence rules that you might not have taken into account. In fact, the only way to override operator precedence is to use parentheses (you can use temporary variables to hold partial results, which aids in readability, but can increase the size of the IL code). Consider the following equation:

```
int x = 1 * 2 - -50 / 4 + 220 << 1;
Console.WriteLine("x = " + x);
```

The value 468 is displayed for this equation.

This is the same equation written with parentheses:

```
int y = ((1 * 2) - ((-50) / 4) + 220) << 1;
Console.WriteLine("y = " + y);
```

The same value (468) is also displayed for this equation. Notice how it is much easier to read and understand how this equation works when parentheses are used. It is possible to get carried away with the use of parentheses in an equation:

```
int z = ((((1 * 2) - ((-50) / 4)) + 220) << (1));
Console.WriteLine("z = " + z);
```

This equation also evaluates to 468, but due to the overuse of parentheses, you can get lost determining where one set of parentheses begins and where it ends. You should try to balance your placement of parentheses in strategic locations to prevent oversaturating your equation with parentheses.

Another place where you can get into trouble with operator precedence is when using the ternary operator (?:). The ternary operator is defined as follows:

boolean-expression ? *true-case-expression* : *false-case-expression*

Each type of expression used by this operator is defined as follows:

boolean-expression
> This expression must evaluate to a Boolean value or to a value whose type has an implicit conversion to bool or one that has a true operator. Depending on the

outcome of this expression, either the *true-case-expression* or the *false-case-expression* will be executed.

true-case-expression

This expression is evaluated when the *boolean-expression* evaluates to true.

false-case-expression

This expression is evaluated when the *boolean-expression* evaluates to false.

Either the *true-case-expression* or the *false-case-expression* will be evaluated; never both.

The ternary operator is able to compact several lines of an if-else statement into a single expression that can fit easily on a single line. This ternary statement is also usable inline with a statement or another expression. The following code example shows the use of the ternary operator inline with an expression:

```
byte x = 8 + ((foo == 1) ? 4 : 2);
```

By examining the order of operator precedence, we see that the == operator is evaluated first and then the ternary operator. Depending on the result of the Boolean expression foo == 1, the ternary operator will produce either the value 4 or 2. This value is then added to 8 and assigned to the variable x.

This operator is considered to have *right-associative* properties, similar to the assignment operators. Because of this, you can get into trouble using ternary expressions as expressions within other ternary expressions. Consider the following code:

```
// foo currently equals 1
// Assume that all methods will always return a Boolean true, except for Method3,
//      which always returns a Boolean false
Console.WriteLine(Method1() ? Method2() : Method3() ? Method4() : Method5());
```

Which methods will be called? If you started evaluating this expression from the left, your expression would essentially look like the following:

```
Console.WriteLine((Method1() ? Method2() : Method3()) ? Method4() : Method5());
```

Notice the extra highlighted parentheses added to clarify how the expression will be evaluated in this manner. The answer that the methods Method1, Method2, and Method4 will be called is wrong. The ternary operators are evaluated from right to left, not left to right, as are most other common operators. The correct answer is that only Method1 and Method2 would be called. Extra highlighted parentheses have been added to this expression, in order to clarify how it is evaluated:

```
Console.WriteLine(Method1() ? Method2() : (Method3() ? Method4() : Method5()));
```

This technique will cause Method1 and Method2 to be called in that order. If any of these methods produced side effects, the application might produce unexpected results.

 If you must use nested ternary expressions, make liberal use of parentheses around each ternary expression to clearly specify your intentions.

3.12 Minimizing (Reducing) Your Boolean Logic

Problem

Many times a Boolean equation quickly becomes large, complex, and even unmanageable. You need a way to manage this complexity while at the same time verifying that your logic works as designed.

Solution

To fix this situation, try applying the theorems shown in Table 3-1 to minimize these types of equations.

Table 3-1. Boolean theorems

Theorem ID	Theorem definition
T0	!(!x) == x
T1	x | x == x
T2	x | !x == true
T3 (DeMorgan's Theorem)	!x | !y == !(x & y)
T4	x & x == x
T5	x & !x == false
T6 (DeMorgan's Theorem)	!x & !y == !(x | y)
T7 (Commutative Law)	x | y == y | x
T8 (Associative Law)	(x | y) | z == x | (y | z)
T9 (Distributive Law)	x & y | x & z == x & (y | z)
T10	x | x & y = x
T11	x & y | x & !y = x
T12	(x & y) | (!x & z) | (y & z) == (x & y) | (!x & z)
T13 (Commutative Law)	x & y == y & x
T14 (Associative Law)	(x & y) & z == x & (y & z)
T15 (Distributive Law)	(x | y) & (x | z) == x | (y & z)
T16	x & (x | y) = x
T17	(x | y) & (x | !y) = x
T18	(x | y) & (!x | z) & (y | z) == (x | y) & (!x | z)
T19	x | x | x | ... | x == x
T20	!(x | x | x | ... | x) == !x & !x & !x & ... & !x
T21	x & x & x & ... & x == x
T22	!(x & x & x & ... & x) == !x | !x | !x | ... | !x
T23	(x | y) & (w | z) == (x & w) | (x * z) | (y & w) | (y * z)
T24	(x & y) | (w & z) == (x | w) & (x | z) & (y | w) & (y | z)

In Table 3-1, assume that w, x, y, and z are all variables of type bool. The Theorem ID column in this table allows easy identification of which theorems are being used in the Boolean equations that are being minimized in the Discussion section.

Discussion

Simplifying your Boolean logic will benefit your code by making it less cluttered and making its logic clearer and more readily understood. This simplification will lessen the number of potential locations in your logic where bugs can hide and at the same time improve maintainability.

Let's walk through several examples to show how the process of minimizing your logic works. These examples use the three Boolean variables X, Y, and Z. The names have been kept simple so that we can concentrate on minimizing the logic and not have to worry about what the code is trying to do.

The first example uses only the X and Y Boolean variables:

```
if (!X & !Y) {...}
```

From this if statement, we extract the following Boolean logic:

```
!X & !Y
```

Using theorem T6, we can eliminate one operator from this equation:

```
!(X | Y)
```

Now this equation only requires two Boolean operators to be evaluated instead of three. By the way, you might notice that this equation is a logical NOR operation.

The second example uses the X and Y Boolean variables in a seemingly complex equation:

```
if ((!X & Y) | (X & !Y) | (X & Y)){...}
```

From this if statement, we extract the Boolean logic:

```
(!X & Y) | (X & !Y) | (X & Y)
```

Using theorem T11, we can simplify the last two parenthesized expressions into the following:

```
(!X & Y) | X
```

This equation is much simpler than the initial equation. In fact, we reduced the number of operators from 7 to 3, which is greater than a 2:1 ratio.

Some equations might not seem like they can be simplified very much, but looks can be deceiving. Let's try to simplify the following equation:

```
(!X & Y) | (X & !Y)
```

Using theorem T24, we can derive the following expression:

```
(!X + X) & (!X | !Y) & (Y | X) & (Y | !Y)
```

Using theorem T2, we can remove the first and last parenthesized expressions:

```
(!X | !Y) & (Y | X)
```

Finally, using theorem T3, we can minimize the equation once again to the following form:

```
!(X & Y) & (Y | X)
```

We were only able to remove a single operator from this equation. This optimization might or might not improve the performance and readability of your code, since it is such a minor change that requires some effort.

You may think that this expression is in its most reduced form. However, if you examine this expression more closely, you may notice that it is the equation for the XOR operator. Knowing this, we can simplify the equation to the following:

```
X ^ Y
```

This technique really shines when you are faced with a large and complex Boolean expression, such as the one shown here:

```
(!X & !Y & !Z) | (!X & Y & Z) | (X & !Y & !Z) | (X & !Y & Z) |
(X & Y & Z)
```

Using theorem T9, we get the following equation:

```
(!X & ((!Y & !Z) | (Y & Z))) | (X & ((!Y & !Z) | (!Y & Z) |
(Y & Z)))
```

Notice that the equation (!Y & !Z) | (Y & Z) is the equivalent of the NOT XOR operation on Y and Z. So we can simplify this equation much further:

```
(!X & !(Y ^ Z)) | (X & ((!Y & !Z) | (!Y & Z) | (Y & Z)))
```

Using theorem T9, once again, we get the following equation:

```
(!X & !(Y ^ Z)) | (X & (!Y & (!Z | Z) | (Y & Z)))
```

Using theorem T2, we get the final equation:

```
(!X & !(Y ^ Z)) | (X & (!Y | (Y & Z)))
```

This equation is much simpler than the original and requires much less processing to evaluate, as well.

 While it is unnecessary in most cases to commit all of these theorems to memory, you should try to understand them all. In addition, memorizing some of the simpler theorems can come in quite handy in many circumstances.

The theorems outlined in this recipe should be complete enough to allow you to play around with minimizing your Boolean equations.

See Also

See the "C# Operators" topic in the MSDN documentation.

3.13 Converting Between Simple Types in a Language Agnostic Manner

Problem

You need to convert between any two of the following types: bool, char, sbyte, byte, short, ushort, int, uint, long, ulong, float, double, decimal, DateTime, and string. Different languages sometimes handle specific conversions differently; you need a way to perform these conversions in a consistent manner across all .NET languages. One situation where this recipe is needed is when VB.NET and C# components communicate within the same application.

Solution

Different languages sometimes handle casting of larger numeric types to smaller numeric types differently—these types of casts are called narrowing conversions. For example consider the following Visual Basic .NET (VB.NET) code which casts a Single to an Integer:

```
' Visual Basic .NET Code:
Dim initialValue As Single
Dim finalValue As Integer

initialValue = 13.499
finalValue = CInt(initialValue)
Console.WriteLine(finalValue.ToString())

initialValue = 13.5
finalValue = CInt(initialValue)
Console.WriteLine(finalValue.ToString())

initialValue = 13.501
finalValue = CInt(initialValue)
Console.WriteLine(finalValue.ToString())
```

This code outputs the following:

```
13
14
14
```

Notice that using the CInt cast in VB.NET uses the fractional portion of the number to round the resulting number.

Now let's convert this code to C# using the explicit casting operator:

```
// C# Code:
float initialValue = 0;
int finalValue = 0;
```

```
initialValue = (float)13.499;
finalValue = (int)initialValue;
Console.WriteLine(finalValue.ToString());

initialValue = (float)13.5;
finalValue = (int)initialValue;
Console.WriteLine(finalValue.ToString());

initialValue = (float)13.501;
finalValue = (int)initialValue;
Console.WriteLine(finalValue.ToString());
```

This code outputs the following:

```
13
13
13
```

Notice that the resulting value was not rounded. Instead, the C# casting operator simply truncates the fractional portion of the number.

Consistently casting numeric types in any language can be done through the static methods on the Convert class. The previous C# code can be converted to use the ToInt32 method:

```
// C# Code:
finalValue = Convert.ToInt32((float)13.449);
Console.WriteLine(finalValue.ToString());

finalValue = Convert.ToInt32((float)13.5);
Console.WriteLine(finalValue.ToString());

finalValue = Convert.ToInt32((float)13.501);
Console.WriteLine(finalValue.ToString());
```

This code outputs the following:

```
13
14
14
```

Discussion

All conversions performed using methods on the Convert class are considered to be in a checked context in C#. VB.NET does not have the concept of a checked or unchecked context, so all conversions are considered to be in a checked context—an unchecked context cannot be created in VB.NET. An OverflowException will be thrown in a checked context when a narrowing conversion results in a loss of information. This exception is never thrown in an unchecked context when a narrowing conversion results in a loss of information.

The various conversion methods are listed in Table 3-2.

Table 3-2. Conversion methods on the Convert class

Method	Use
ToBoolean	Convert a type to a `bool`
ToChar	Convert a type to a `char`
ToString	Convert a type to a `string`
ToDateTime	Convert a type to a `DateTime`
ToInt16	Convert a type to a `short`
ToInt32	Convert a type to an `int`
ToInt64	Convert a type to a `long`
ToUInt16	Convert a type to a `ushort`
ToUInt32	Convert a type to a `uint`
ToUInt64	Convert a type to a `ulong`
ToByte	Convert a type to a `byte`
ToSByte	Convert a type to an `sbyte`
ToSingle	Convert a type to a `float`
ToDecimal	Convert a type to a `decimal`
ToDouble	Convert a type to a `double`

Converting between any of the data types listed in Table 3-2 is a simple matter. All of the listed methods are static and exist on the Convert class. Converting one type to another is performed by first choosing the correct method on the Convert class. This method will be named after the type you are converting to (e.g., if you are converting to a char type, the method name would be ToChar). Next, you need to pass the type that will be casted as the parameter to the Convert method. Finally, set a variable of the resultant cast type equal to the return value of the Convert method. The following code converts the value in variable Source—defined as a short that contains a number between 0 and 9—to a char type. This char value is then returned by the Convert method and assigned to the variable destination. The variable destination must be defined as a char:

```
destination = Convert.ToChar(source);
```

There are cases in which conversions will do nothing. Converting from one type to that same type will do nothing except return a result that is equivalent to the source variable's value. Take, for example, using the Convert.ToInt32 method to convert a source variable of type Int32 to a destination variable of type Int32. This method takes the value obtained from the source variable and places it in the destination variable.

Some conversions cause exceptions to occur because there is no clear way of converting between the two types; these attempted conversions are listed in Table 3-3. Because some conversions might or might not throw an exception—such as converting from an sbyte to a byte—it is good programming practice to enclose the static conversion method within a try/catch block. The following code wraps a conversion between numeric types in a try/catch block:

```
try
{
    finalValue = Convert.ToInt32(SomeFloat);
}
catch(OverflowException oe)
{
    // Handle narrowing conversions that result in a loss
    //    of information here.
}
catch(InvalidCastException ice)
{
    // Handle casts that cannot be performed here.
}
```

The following code wraps a conversion from a string type to an Int32 in a try/catch block:

```
try
{
    finalValue = Convert.ToInt32(SomeString);
}
catch(OverflowException oe)
{
    // Handle narrowing conversions that result in a loss
    //    of information here.
}
catch(ArgumentException ae)
{
    // Handle nulls passed into the Convert method here.
}
catch(FormatException fe)
{
    // Handle attempts to convert a string that does not contain
    //    a value that can be converted to the destination type here.
}
catch(Exception e)
{
    // Handle all other exceptions here.
}
```

Table 3-3. Cases where a Source to Destination type conversion throws an exception

Destination	Source	Exception type
bool	char DateTime	InvalidCastException
byte	DateTime	InvalidCastException
char	bool DateTime decimal double float	InvalidCastException

Destination	Source	Exception type
DateTime	bool byte sbyte char decimal double short int long ushort uint ulong object float	InvalidCastException
decimal	char DateTime	InvalidCastException
double	char DateTime	InvalidCastException
short	DateTime	InvalidCastException
int	DateTime	InvalidCastException
long	DateTime	InvalidCastException
sbyte	DateTime	InvalidCastException
float	char DateTime	InvalidCastException
ushort	DateTime	InvalidCastException
uint	DateTime	InvalidCastException
ulong	DateTime	InvalidCastException
byte	sbyte	OverFlowException (if Source is out of the range of Destination)
sbyte	byte ushort uint ulong	OverFlowException (if Source is out of the range of Destination)
short	byte sbyte ushort	OverFlowException (if Source is out of the range of Destination)
ushort	byte sbyte short	OverFlowException (if Source is out of the range of Destination)
int	byte sbyte short ushort uint	OverFlowException (if Source is out of the range of Destination)

Table 3-3. Cases where a Source to Destination type conversion throws an exception (continued)

Destination	Source	Exception type
uint	byte sbyte short ushort int	OverFlowException (if Source is out of the range of Destination)
long	byte sbyte short ushort int uint ulong	OverFlowException (if Source is out of the range of Destination)
ulong	byte sbyte short ushort int uint long	OverFlowException (if Source is out of the range of Destination)
decimal	byte sbyte short ushort int uint long ulong	OverFlowException (if Source is out of the range of Destination)
float	byte sbyte short ushort int uint long ulong	OverFlowException (if Source is out of the range of Destination)
double	byte sbyte short ushort int uint long ulong	OverFlowException (if Source is out of the range of Destination)
Any type	string	ArgumentException (if source string is null) or FormatException (if source string represents an invalid value for the Destination type)

Notice that the string type can be converted to any type, and that any type may be converted to a string type—assuming that the source string is not null and conforms to the destination type's range.

The most insidious problems can occur when a larger type is converted to a smaller type in an unchecked context; the potential exists for information to be lost. Code runs in an unchecked context if the conversion is contained in an unchecked block or if the /checked compiler option is set to false (by default, this compiler option is set to false in both debug and release builds). An example of code contained in an unchecked block is as follows:

```
short destination = 0;
int source = Int32.MaxValue;
unchecked(destination = (short)source);
```

or:

```
unchecked
{
    short destination = 0;
    int source = Int32.MaxValue;
    destination = (short)source;
}
```

A checked context is when the conversion is contained in a checked block or if the /checked compiler option is set to true. An example of code contained in a checked block is as follows:

```
short destination = 0;
int source = Int32.MaxValue;
checked(destination =(short)source);
```

or:

```
checked
{
    short destination = 0;
    int source = Int32.MaxValue;
    destination = (short)source;
}
```

This code throws an OverflowException exception if any loss of information would occur. This allows the application to be notified of the overflow condition and to handle it properly.

The Convert method is always considered to operate in a checked context, even when no other type of checked context wraps the code performing the conversion.

See Also

See the "checked" keyword, "unchecked" keyword, "Checked and Unchecked," and "Convert Class" topics in the MSDN documentation.

3.14 Determining Whether to Use the Cast Operator, the as Operator, or the is Operator

Problem

You need to determine which operator is best in your situation the cast—(*type*)– operator, the as operator, or the is operator.

Solution

Use the information provided in the Discussion section to determine which operator is best to use.

Discussion

The cast operator should be used when:

- It is acceptable for the InvalidCastException to be thrown. To prevent this exception from being thrown, consider using either the as or is operators.
- You are casting a reference type to a reference type.
- You are casting a value type to a value type.
- You are performing a boxing or unboxing conversion.
- You are invoking a user-defined conversion. The is and as operators cannot handle this type of cast.

The as operator should be used when:

- It is *not* acceptable for the InvalidCastException to be thrown. The as operator will instead return a null if the cast cannot be performed.
- You are casting a reference type to a reference type.
- You are *not* casting a value type to a value type. The cast operator must be used in this case.
- You are performing a boxing conversion.
- You are *not* performing an unboxing conversion. The cast operator must be used in this case.
- You are *not* invoking a user defined conversion. The cast operator must be used in this case.

The is operator should be used when:

- You need a fast method of determining whether a cast can be performed before the actual cast is attempted.
- You do not need to actually cast a variable from one data type to another; you just need to determine if the variable can be cast to a specific type.

- It is not acceptable for the `InvalidCastException` to be thrown.
- You are casting a reference type to a reference type.
- You are *not* casting a value type to a value type. The cast operator must be used in this case.
- You are *not* invoking a user defined conversion. Unlike the as operator, a compile-time error is not displayed when using the is operator with a user-defined conversion. This is operator will instead always return a `false` value, regardless of whether the cast can successfully be performed.

See Also

See Recipes 3.15 and 3.16; see the "() Operator," "as Operator," and "is Operator" topics in the MSDN documentation.

3.15 Casting with the as Operator

Problem

Ordinarily, when you attempt a casting operation, the .NET Common Language Runtime generates an `InvalidCastException` if the cast fails. Often, though, you cannot guarantee in advance that a cast will succeed, but you also do not want the overhead of handling an `InvalidCastException`.

Solution

Use the as operator. The as operator attempts the casting operation, but if the cast fails, the expression returns a `null` instead of throwing an exception. If the cast succeeds, the expression returns the converted value. The following code shows how the as operator is used:

```
public static void ConvertObj(Base baseObj)
{
    Specific specificObj = baseObj as Specific;
    if (specificObj == null)
    {
        // Cast failed
    }
    else
    {
        // Cast was successful
    }
}
```

where the `Specific` type derives from the `Base` type:

```
public class Base {}
public class Specific : Base {}
```

In this code fragment, the as operator is used to attempt to cast the `specificObj` to the type `Base`. The next lines contain an if-else statement that tests the variable `baseObj` to determine whether it is equal to null. If it is equal to null, you should prevent any use of this variable, since it might cause a NullReferenceException to be thrown.

Discussion

The as operator has the following syntax:

```
expression as type
```

The expression and type are defined as follows:

expression
    A reference type.

type
    The type to which to cast the object defined by *expression*.

This operation returns *expression* cast to the type defined by *type* if the cast succeeds. If the cast fails, a null is returned, and an InvalidCastException is not thrown. Because of this, you should always check the result for null.

This operator does not work with user-defined conversions (both explicit and implicit). A user-defined conversion method extends one type to allow it to be converted to another type. This is done by adding a method, such as the following, to a class or structure:

```
public struct MyPoint
{
    public static explicit operator MyPoint(System.Drawing.Point pt)
    {
        // Convert a Point structure to a MyPoint structure type
        return (new MyPoint());
    }
}
```

This method allows a System.Drawing.Point structure to be cast to an object of type MyPoint. Due to the use of the explicit keyword, the cast must be explicitly defined:

```
System.Drawing.Point systemPt = new System.Drawing.Point(0, 0);
MyPoint pt = (MyPoint)systemPt;
```

If you attempt to use the as operator in a user-defined conversion, the following compiler error is shown:

```
Cannot convert type 'Chapter_Code.Vector32' to 'string' via a built-in conversion
```

This type of conversion does not work with unboxing conversions, either. An unboxing conversion converts a previously boxed value type to its original value type, such as with the following code:

```
int x = 5;
object obj = x;          // Box x
int originalX = obj as int;   // Attempt to unbox obj into an integer
```

If you attempt to use the as operator in an unboxing conversion, the following compiler error is shown:

```
The as operator must be used with a reference type ('int' is a value type)
```

because as indicates that the cast cannot be performed by returning null, but there is no such thing as a null value for an int.

See Also

See Recipes 3.14 and 3.16; see the "() Operator," "as Operator," and "is Operator" topics in the MSDN documentation.

3.16 Determining a Variable's Type with the is Operator

Problem

A method exists that creates an object from one of several types of classes. This object is then returned as a generic object type. Based on the type of object that was initially created in the method, you want to branch to different logic.

Solution

Use the is operator. This operator returns a Boolean true or false indicating whether the cast is legal, but the cast never actually occurs.

Suppose we have four different point classes:

```
public class Point2D {...}
public class Point3D {...}
public class ExPoint2D : Point2D {...}
public class ExPoint3D : Point3D {...}
```

Next, we have a method that accepts an integer value and, based on this value, one of the four specific point types are returned:

```
public object CreatePoint(int pointType)
{
    switch (pointType)
    {
        case 0:
            return (new Point2D( ));
        case 1:
            return (new Point3D( ));
        case 2:
            return (new ExPoint2D( ));
        case 3:
            return (new ExPoint3D( ));
        default:
            return (null);
    }
}
```

Finally, we have a method that calls the CreatePoint method. This method handles the point object type returned from the CreatePoint method based on the actual point object returned:

```
public void CreateAndHandlePoint( )
{
    // Create a new point object and return it
    object retObj = CreatePoint(3);

    // Handle the point object based on its actual type
    if (retObj is ExPoint2D)
    {
        Console.WriteLine("Use the ExPoint2D type");
    }
    else if (retObj is ExPoint3D)
    {
        Console.WriteLine("Use the ExPoint3D type");
    }
    else if (retObj is Point2D)
    {
        Console.WriteLine("Use the Point2D type");
    }
    else if (retObj is Point3D)
    {
        Console.WriteLine("Use the Point3D type");
    }
    else
    {
        Console.WriteLine("Invalid point type");
    }
}
```

Notice that the tests for the ExPoint2D and ExPoint3D objects are performed before the tests for Point2D and Point3D. This order will allow us to differentiate between base classes and their derived classes (ExPoint2D derives from Point2D and ExPoint3D derives from Point3D). If we had reversed these tests, the test for Point2D would evaluate to true for both the Point2D class and its derivatives (ExPoint2D).

Discussion

The is operator is a fast and easy method of predetermining whether a cast will work. If the cast fails, you have saved yourself the overhead of trying the cast and handling a thrown exception. If the is operator determines that this cast can successfully be performed, all you need to do is perform the cast.

The is operator is defined as follows:

expression **is** *type*

The expression and type are defined as follows:

expression
    A reference type.

Type

    The type to which to cast the reference type defined by *expression*.

This expression returns a Boolean value: true if the cast is able to succeed or false if the cast would fail. For example:

```
if (SpecificObj is Base)
{
    // It is of type Base
}
else
{
    // Cannot cast SpecificObj to a Base type object
}
```

> Never use the is operator with a user-defined conversion (either explicit or implicit). The is operator always returns false when used with these types of conversions, regardless of whether the cast can be performed.

This operator does not work with user-defined conversions (both explicit and implicit). Unlike the as operator, a compile-time error will not be displayed; instead, the is operator will always return false. This operator should never be used with user-defined conversions, since the result will always be in question. Also, unlike the as operator, the is operator will work with unboxing conversions.

The following code determines whether an unboxing operation can be performed:

```
// An int is passed in to this method and boxed
public void SomeMethod(object o)
{
    if (o is int)
    {
        // o can be unboxed
        // It is now possible to cast o to an int
        x = (int)o;
    }
    else
    {
        // Cannot unbox o
    }
}
```

This code first declares an integer variable x and boxes it into an object variable o. The is operator is then used to determine whether o can be unboxed back into the integer variable x. This is the one case where it is absolutely necessary to use is if you want to avoid an exception. You can't use as here because there is no such thing as a null int, so it cannot tell you if the unboxing fails.

See Also

See Recipes 3.14 and 3.15; see the "() Operator," "as Operator," and "is Operator" topics in the MSDN documentation.

3.17 Polymorphism via Interfaces

Problem

You need to implement polymorphic functionality on a set of existing classes. These classes already inherit from a base class (other than Object), thus preventing the addition of polymorphic functionality through an abstract or concrete base class.

In a second situation, you need to add polymorphic functionality to a structure. Abstract or concrete classes cannot be used to add polymorphic functionality to a structure.

Solution

Implement polymorphism using an interface instead of an abstract or concrete base class. The code shown here defines two different classes that inherit from ArrayList:

```
public class InventoryItems : ArrayList
{
    // ...
}

public class Personnel : ArrayList
{
    // ...
}
```

We want to add the ability to print from either of these two objects polymorphically. To do this, an interface called IPrint is added to define a Print method to be implemented in a class:

```
public interface IPrint
{
    void Print();
}
```

Implementing the IPrint interface on the InventoryItems and Personnel classes gives us the following code:

```
public class InventoryItems : ArrayList, IPrint
{
    public void Print()
    {
        foreach (object obj in this)
        {
            Console.WriteLine("Inventory Item: " + obj);
```

```
        }
      }
    }

    public class Personnel : ArrayList, IPrint
    {
        public void Print()
        {
            foreach (object obj in this)
            {
                Console.WriteLine("Person: " + obj);
            }
        }
    }
```

The following two methods TestIPrintInterface and CommonPrintMethod show how any object that implements the IPrint interface can be passed to the CommonPrintMethod polymorphically and printed:

```
    public void TestIPrintInterface()
    {
        // Create an InventoryItems object and populate it
        IPrint obj = new InventoryItems();
        ((InventoryItems)obj).Add("Item1");
        ((InventoryItems)obj).Add("Item2");

        // Print this object
        CommonPrintMethod(obj);

        Console.WriteLine();

        // Create a Personnel object and populate it
        obj = new Personnel();
        ((Personnel)obj).Add("Person1");
        ((Personnel)obj).Add("Person2");

        // Print this object
        CommonPrintMethod(obj);
    }
    private void CommonPrintMethod(IPrint obj)
    {
        Console.WriteLine(obj.ToString());
        obj.Print();
    }
```

The output of these methods is shown here:

```
    InventoryItems
    Inventory Item: Item1
    Inventory Item: Item2

    Personnel
    Person: Person1
    Person: Person2
```

Discussion

The use of interfaces is found throughout the Framework Class Library (FCL). One example is the IComparer interface: this interface requires a class to implement the Compare method, which compares two objects to determine if one is greater than, less than, or equal to another object. This method is used by the Array.Sort and Array. BinarySearch static methods to allow sorting and searching to be performed on the elements contained in an array. For example, if an array contained objects that implemented a custom IComparer interface, the static Sort and BinarySearch methods would use this interface to customize its sorting/searching of elements in that array.

Another example is found in the IEnumerable and IEnumerator interfaces. These interfaces let you iterate over items in a container using the foreach loop. It does not matter what the contained items are or what the containing object is. The foreach loop can simply use these interfaces regardless of the type of objects that implement them.

In many cases, you will choose to implement polymorphism through abstract base classes; however, there are some cases where interfaces are superior. Interfaces should be considered before abstract base classes in the following cases:

- When several unrelated classes need to implement a common subset of their functionality polymorphically. The Solution to this recipe demonstrates this concept.

- If one or more of the classes already inherits from a base class, an interface may be added to implement polymorphism. If you look at the Solution for this recipe, you'll see that our InventoryItem class could have inherited from an existing Item class. This would make it impossible to use an abstract base class. An interface can be added in this case to implement polymorphism.

- If, in future versions of your data type, you will want to add new polymorphic functionality without breaking the existing interface of your data type. Interface polymorphism provides better versioning than abstract or concrete base classes. To add new polymorphic functionality, implement a new interface containing this functionality on your existing data type.

- When you need to implement polymorphism on value types.

Implementing polymorphism through interfaces works not only on reference types, but also with value types. Value types cannot derive from any other type except ValueType; this makes them unable to implement an abstract base class. We must instead use interfaces to implement polymorphism. This can be shown by changing the following class declarations:

```
public class InventoryItems : ArrayList
public class Personnel : ArrayList
```

to this:

```
public struct InventoryItems : ArrayList, IPrint
public struct Personnel : ArrayList, IPrint
```

These structures now can act polymorphically on the IPrint interface. When implementing an interface on a structure, be aware that a boxing operation will be performed whenever the value is cast to the interface type (in this case, the IPrint interface). The boxed object is a copy of the original structure. This means that if you modify the boxed object, using a reference to the interface, you will be modifying a copy of the original structure.

See Also

See the "interface" keyword in the MSDN documentation.

3.18 Calling the Same Method on Multiple Object Types

Problem

You need to perform a particular action on a set of dissimilar objects contained within an array or collection, preferably without having to know each individual object's type.

Solution

Use interfaces in a polymorphic manner. The following interface contains a single method, Sort, which allows sorting to be performed on the object that implements this interface:

```
public interface IMySort
{
    void Sort();
}
```

The next three classes implement the IMySort interface. These classes all share the same Sort method, but each class implements it in a different way:

```
public class CharContainer : IMySort
{
    public void Sort()
    {
        // Do character type sorting here

        Console.WriteLine("Characters sorted");
    }
}

public class NumberContainer : IMySort
{
    public void Sort()
    {
        // Do numeric type sorting here
```

```
            Console.WriteLine("Numbers sorted");
        }
    }

    public class ObjectContainer : IMySort
    {
        public void Sort()
        {
            // Do object type sorting here

            Console.WriteLine("Objects sorted");
        }
    }
```

The SortAllObjects method accepts an array of objects:

```
    public void SortAllObjects(IMySort[] sortableObjects)
    {
        foreach (IMySort m in sortableObjects)
        {
            m.Sort();
        }
    }
```

If this method is called as follows:

```
    Obj.SortAllObjects(new IMySort[3] {new CharContainer(),
                                       new NumberContainer(),
                                       new ObjectContainer()});
```

the following is displayed:

```
    Characters sorted
    Numbers sorted
    Objects sorted
```

Discussion

The foreach loop is useful not only for iterating over individual elements in a collection or an array, but also in iterating over a specific interface implemented by each element in a collection or array. Using this technique, interface members may be used in a similar manner on each element, even if the elements are unrelated object types. Consider the following array of objects:

```
    Object[] objs = new Object[6] {new CharContainer(),
                                   new NumberContainer(),
                                   new CharContainer(),
                                   new ObjectContainer(),
                                   new NumberContainer(),
                                   new ObjectContainer()});
```

This array contains several objects of differing types. The one thread of similarity that runs through each type is the implementation of the IMySort interface, defined as follows:

```
public interface IMySort
{
    void Sort();
}
```

Passing the Objects array in to the following method allows each Sort method to be
called from each object in the Objects array:

```
public void SortAllObjects(object[] sortableObjects)
{
    foreach (IMySort m in sortableObjects)
    {
        m.Sort();
    }
}
```

The foreach loop in this method is able to treat each object in the sortableObjects
array in the same way because each object in the sortableObjects array is cast to its
IMySort interface and used as such.

If the foreach loop encounters a sortableObjects array that contains one or more
objects that do not implement the IMySort interface, an InvalidCastException will be
thrown. To prevent an exception from being thrown while at the same time allowing
the foreach loop to iterate over all elements in the sortableObjects array, you can
use the following modified code:

```
public void SortAllObjects(object[] sortableObjects)
{
    foreach (object o in sortableObjects)
    {
        IMySort sortObject = o as IMySort;
        if (sortObject!= null)
        {
            sortObject.Sort();
        }
    }
}
```

This modified method will now test each element of the sortableObjects array to
first determine whether it can be cast to an IMySort interface. If it can be cast to this
interface type, the variable sortObject will not be null and the if statement will
allow the Sort method on that object to be called.

See Also

See the "interface" keyword, "Base Class Usage Guidelines," and "When to Use
Interfaces" topics in the MSDN documentation.

3.19 Adding a Notification Callback Using an Interface

Problem

You need a flexible, well-performing callback mechanism that does not make use of a delegate because you need more than one callback method. So the relationship between the caller and the callee is more complex than can easily be represented through the one method signature that you get with a delegate.

Solution

Use an interface to provide callback methods. The INotificationCallbacks interface contains two methods that will be used by a client as callback methods. The first method, FinishedProcessingSubGroup, is called when an amount specified in the amount parameter is reached. The second method, FinishedProcessingGroup, is called when all processing is complete:

```
public interface INotificationCallbacks
{
    void FinishedProcessingSubGroup(int amount);
    void FinishedProcessingGroup();
}
```

The NotifyClient class implements the INotificationCallbacks interface. This class contains the implementation details of each of the callback methods:

```
public class NotifyClient : INotificationCallbacks
{
    public void FinishedProcessingSubGroup(int amount)
    {
        Console.WriteLine("Finished processing " + amount + " items");
    }

    public void FinishedProcessingGroup()
    {
        Console.WriteLine("Processing complete");
    }
}
```

The Task class is the main class that implements its callbacks through the NotifyClient object. The Task class contains a field called notificationObj, which stores a reference to the NotifyClient object that is passed to it either through construction or through the AttachToCallback method. The UnAttachCallback method removes the NotifyClient reference from this object. The ProcessSomething method implements the callback methods:

```
public class Task
{
    public Task(NotifyClient notifyClient)
```

```
    {
        notificationObj = notifyClient;
    }

    NotifyClient notificationObj = null;

    public void AttachToCallback(NotifyClient notifyClient)
    {
        notificationObj = notifyClient;
    }

    public void UnAttachCallback()
    {
        notificationObj = null;
    }

    public void ProcessSomething()
    {
        // This method could be any type of processing

        for (int counter = 0; counter < 100; counter++)
        {
            if ((counter % 10) == 0)
            {
                if (notificationObj != null)
                {
                    notificationObj.FinishedProcessingSubGroup(counter);
                }
            }
        }

        if (notificationObj != null)
        {
            notificationObj.FinishedProcessingGroup();
        }
    }
}
```

The CallBackThroughIFace method uses callback features of the Task class as follows:

```
public void CallBackThroughIFace()
{
    NotifyClient notificationObj = new NotifyClient();
    Task t = new Task(notificationObj);
    t.ProcessSomething();

    Console.WriteLine();

    t.UnAttachCallback();
    t.ProcessSomething();

    Console.WriteLine();

    t.AttachToCallback(notificationObj);
    t.ProcessSomething();
```

```
        Console.WriteLine( );

        t.UnAttachCallback( );
        t.ProcessSomething( );
    }
```

This method displays the following:

```
Finished processing 0 items
Finished processing 10 items
Finished processing 20 items
Finished processing 30 items
Finished processing 40 items
Finished processing 50 items
Finished processing 60 items
Finished processing 70 items
Finished processing 80 items
Finished processing 90 items
Processing complete

Finished processing 0 items
Finished processing 10 items
Finished processing 20 items
Finished processing 30 items
Finished processing 40 items
Finished processing 50 items
Finished processing 60 items
Finished processing 70 items
Finished processing 80 items
Finished processing 90 items
Processing complete
```

Discussion

Using an interface mechanism for callbacks is a simple but effective alternative to using delegates. The interface mechanism is only slightly faster than using a delegate since you are simply making a call through an interface.

This interface mechanism requires a notification client (NotifyClient) to be created that implements a callback interface (INotificationCallbacks). This notification client is then passed to an object that is required to call back to this client. This object is then able to store a reference to the notification client and use it appropriately whenever its callback methods are used.

When using the callback methods on the notificationObj, you should test to determine whether the notificationObj is null; if so, you should not use it or else a NullReferenceException will be thrown:

```
if (notificationObj != null)
{
    notificationObj.FinishedProcessingGroup( );
}
```

Interface callbacks cannot always be used in place of delegates. The following list indicates where to use each type of callback:

- Use a delegate if you require ease of coding over performance.
- Use the interface callback mechanism if you need potentially complex callbacks. An example of this could be adding a single callback interface method that will call back to an overloaded method. The number and types of parameters determine the method chosen.

The current Task class is designed to allow only a single notification client to be used; in many cases, this would be a severe limitation. The Task class could be modified to handle multiple callbacks, similar to a multicast delegate. The MultiTask class is a modification of the Task class to do just this:

```
public class MultiTask
{
    public MultiTask(NotifyClient notifyClient)
    {
        notificationObjs.Add(notifyClient);
    }

    ArrayList notificationObjs = new ArrayList();

    public void AttachToCallback(NotifyClient notifyClient)
    {
        notificationObjs.Add(notifyClient);
    }

    public void UnAttachCallback(NotifyClient notifyClient)
    {
        notificationObjs.Remove(notifyClient);
    }

    public void UnAttachAllCallbacks()
    {
        notificationObjs.Clear();
    }

    public void ProcessSomething()
    {
        // This method could be any type of processing

        for (int counter = 0; counter < 100; counter++)
        {
            if ((counter % 10) == 0)
            {
                foreach (NotifyClient callback in notificationObjs)
                {
                    callback.FinishedProcessingSubGroup(counter);
                }
            }
        }
    }
```

```
        foreach (NotifyClient callback in notificationObjs)
        {
            callback.FinishedProcessingGroup();
        }
    }
}
```

The `MultiCallBackThroughIFace` method uses callback features of the `MultiTask` class as follows:

```
public void MultiCallBackThroughIFace()
{
    NotifyClient notificationObj = new NotifyClient();
    MultiTask t = new MultiTask(notificationObj);
    t.ProcessSomething();

    Console.WriteLine();

    t.AttachToCallback(notificationObj);
    t.ProcessSomething();

    Console.WriteLine();

    t.UnAttachCallback(notificationObj);
    t.ProcessSomething();

    Console.WriteLine();

    t.UnAttachAllCallbacks();
    t.ProcessSomething();
}
```

This method displays the following:

```
Finished processing 0 items
Finished processing 10 items
Finished processing 20 items
Finished processing 30 items
Finished processing 40 items
Finished processing 50 items
Finished processing 60 items
Finished processing 70 items
Finished processing 80 items
Finished processing 90 items
Processing complete

Finished processing 0 items
Finished processing 0 items
Finished processing 10 items
Finished processing 10 items
Finished processing 20 items
Finished processing 20 items
Finished processing 30 items
Finished processing 30 items
Finished processing 40 items
```

```
Finished processing 40 items
Finished processing 50 items
Finished processing 50 items
Finished processing 60 items
Finished processing 60 items
Finished processing 70 items
Finished processing 70 items
Finished processing 80 items
Finished processing 80 items
Finished processing 90 items
Finished processing 90 items
Processing complete
Processing complete

Finished processing 0 items
Finished processing 10 items
Finished processing 20 items
Finished processing 30 items
Finished processing 40 items
Finished processing 50 items
Finished processing 60 items
Finished processing 70 items
Finished processing 80 items
Finished processing 90 items
Processing complete
```

Another shortcoming exists with both the Task and MultiTask classes. What if you need several types of client notification classes? For example, we already have the NotifyClient class, what if we added a second class NotifyClientType2 that also implements the INotificationCallbacks interface? This new class is shown here:

```
public class NotifyClientType2 : INotificationCallbacks
{
    public void FinishedProcessingSubGroup(int amount)
    {
        Console.WriteLine("[Type2] Finished processing " + amount + " items");
    }

    public void FinishedProcessingGroup()
    {
        Console.WriteLine("[Type2] Processing complete");
    }
}
```

The current code base cannot handle this new client notification type. To fix this problem, we can replace all occurrences of the type NotifyClient with the interface type INotificationCallbacks. This will allow us to use any type of notification client with our Task and MultiTask objects. The modifications to these classes are highlighted in the following code:

```
public class Task
{
    public Task(INotificationCallbacks notifyClient)
    {
```

```
            notificationObj = notifyClient;
    }

    INotificationCallbacks notificationObj = null;

    public void AttachToCallback(INotificationCallbacks notifyClient)
    {
        notificationObj = notifyClient;
    }

    ...
}

public class MultiTask
{
    public MultiTask(INotificationCallbacks notifyClient)
    {
        notificationObjs.Add(notifyClient);
    }

    ArrayList notificationObjs = new ArrayList();

    public void AttachToCallback(INotificationCallbacks notifyClient)
    {
        notificationObjs.Add(notifyClient);
    }

    public void UnAttachCallback(INotificationCallbacks notifyClient)
    {
        notificationObjs.Remove(notifyClient);
    }

    ...

    public void ProcessSomething()
    {
        // This method could be any type of processing

        for (int counter = 0; counter < 100; counter++)
        {
            if ((counter % 10) == 0)
            {
                foreach (INotificationCallbacks callback in notificationObjs)
                {
                    callback.FinishedProcessingSubGroup(counter);
                }
            }
        }

        foreach (INotificationCallbacks callback in notificationObjs)
        {
            callback.FinishedProcessingGroup();
        }
    }
}
```

Now we can use either of the client notification classes interchangeably. This is shown in the following modified methods MultiCallBackThroughIFace and CallBackThroughIFace:

```
public void CallBackThroughIFace( )
{
    INotificationCallbacks notificationObj = new NotifyClient( );
    Task t = new Task(notificationObj);
    t.ProcessSomething( );

    Console.WriteLine( );

    t.UnAttachCallback( );
    t.ProcessSomething( );

    Console.WriteLine( );

    INotificationCallbacks notificationObj2 = new NotifyClientType2( );
    t.AttachToCallback(notificationObj2);
    t.ProcessSomething( );

    Console.WriteLine( );

    t.UnAttachCallback( );
    t.ProcessSomething( );
}

public void MultiCallBackThroughIFace( )
{
    INotificationCallbacks notificationObj = new NotifyClient( );
    MultiTask t = new MultiTask(notificationObj);
    t.ProcessSomething( );

    Console.WriteLine( );

    INotificationCallbacks notificationObj2 = new NotifyClientType2( );
    t.AttachToCallback(notificationObj2);
    t.ProcessSomething( );

    Console.WriteLine( );

    t.UnAttachCallback(notificationObj);
    t.ProcessSomething( );

    Console.WriteLine( );

    t.UnAttachAllCallbacks( );
    t.ProcessSomething( );
}
```

The highlighted code has been modified from the original code.

See Also

See the "interface" keyword, "Base Class Usage Guidelines," and "When to Use Interfaces" topics in the MSDN documentation.

3.20   Using Multiple Entry Points to Version an Application

Problem

Some companies reuse the same duplicated, but slightly modified, application, with each version built especially for a particular client or group of clients. Bug fixes, testing, adding, and modifying code in each of these code bases can get very confusing as the number of duplicated applications grows. You need a way of managing this increasing complexity.

Solution

Instead of copying the entire application to a different area, modifying the duplicated code, and creating a special build script for it, you could compile the same application (with all modifications included, of course) and use a different entry point based on the client. To do this, add a new class with a new Main entry point method, one for each client or group of clients:

```
public class ClientABC
{
    public static void Main()
    {
        //Startup/Initialization code for client ABC
    }
}

public class ClientXYZ
{
    public static void Main()
    {
        //Startup/Initialization code for client XYZ
    }
}
```

The build scripts can be modified to build the same application using a different entry point that matches up to one or more clients:

```
csc /out:AppABC.exe *.cs /main:ClientABC
csc /out:AppXYZ.exe *.cs /main:ClientXYZ
```

Discussion

It is very difficult to work with several slightly different copies of the same application. If a bug is found and fixed in one application, it must be fixed in all of the copies as well. This can be a time-consuming and arduous task. To make things easier on your coding team, consider using multiple entry points into your application, one for each client or set of clients. Using this technique, you can fix code in one place as opposed to fixing the same bug over multiple applications.

The /main compiler switch controls the class in which the compiler looks for a public static Main method that it can use as an entry point. If the compiler finds a /main switch, the Main method at the location specified in this switch is used as the entry point and all other Main methods in the application are considered as regular methods and nonentry points.

You should note that only one Main entry point method is allowed per class. If two or more are found in a single class, a compiler error will result. You can have entry points in both a nested class and its parent class, as shown here:

```
public class ClientABC
{
    public static void Main()
    {
        //Startup/Initialization code for client ABC
    }

    public class ClientXYZ
    {
        public static void Main()
        {
            //Startup/Initialization code for client XYZ
        }
    }
}
```

The /main compiler option would have to be modified in this case to the following:

```
csc /out:AppABC.exe *.cs /main:ClientABC
csc /out:AppXYZ.exe *.cs /main:ClientABC.Clientxyz
```

Also note that if classes ClientABC and ClientXYZ were nested in a namespace—the MyCompany namespace, for instance—the namespace would also have to be added to this compiler switch, as follows:

```
csc /out:AppABC.exe *.cs /main:MyCompany.ClientABC
csc /out:AppXYZ.exe *.cs /main:MyCompany.ClientABC.Clientxyz
```

The /main switch can be modified through the Visual Studio .NET Property Pages dialog box. If you open this dialog box, drill down to the Common Properties → General → Startup Object property. The fully qualified class name containing the Main method entry point can be entered in this property.

See Also

See the "/main" compiler option and the "Main" topic in the MSDN documentation.

3.21   Preventing the Creation of an Only Partially Initialized Object

Problem

You need to force a client to use an overloaded constructor, which accepts parameters to fully initialize the object, rather than a default constructor, which may not fully initialize the object. Often a default constructor cannot fully initialize an object since it may not have the necessary information to do it. Using a default constructor, the client is required to perform a multistep process; for instance, create the object and then initialize its fields either through various properties and/or methods.

Solution

By removing the default constructor and strictly using parameterized constructors, the client is forced to provide the necessary initialization parameters during object creation. The following Log class will not initialize its LogStream field to a StreamWriter object on construction:

```
public class Log
{
    private StreamWriter logStream = null;

    public StreamWriter LogStream
    {
        get {return (logStream);}
        set {logStream = value;}
    }

    // use the LogStream field...
    public void Write(string text)
    {
        logStream.Write(text);
    }
}
```

The C# compiler will automatically create a default constructor that calls the default constructor of its base class, if you omit the constructor for a class. The following modified class will prevent the default constructor from being created:

```
public class Log
{
    public Log(StreamWriter logStream)
    {
        this.logStream = logStream;
    }

    private StreamWriter logStream = null;

    public StreamWriter LogStream
```

```
    {
        get {return (logStream);}
        set {logStream = value;}
    }

    // use the LogStream field...
    public void Write(string text)
    {
        logStream.Write(text);
    }
}
```

When a client creates an object from this class, the client is forced to initialize the LogStream field.

Discussion

There is a small problem with not supplying a default constructor. If a class inherits from Log and does not supply a constructor of its own, the C# compiler will produce the rather cryptic error "No overload for method 'Log' takes '0' arguments." The following class produces this error:

```
public class EnhancedLog : Log
{
    public EnhancedLog (string s)
    {
        // Initialize...
    }
}
```

What this means is that Log does not contain a default constructor. The C# compiler automatically adds a call to the base class's default constructor, if you do not specify otherwise. Therefore, the EnhancedLog constructor contains an unseen call (this call can be seen using Ildasm) to the default constructor of the Log class.

This problem can be solved in one of several ways. First, we could simply add a protected default constructor to the Log class. This would prevent the creation of a Log object using the default constructor, but would allow classes inheriting from Log to do so without problems. A second method is to use the base keyword to direct the constructor to call a particular constructor in the base class. The following EnhancedLog class uses the base keyword to call the parameterized constructor of the base Log class, passing in a StreamWriter object:

```
public class EnhancedLog : Log
{
    public EnhancedLog (string s) : base(new StreamWriter(@"C:\test.log"))
    {
        // Initialize...
    }
}
```

A third way to solve this problem is to make the Log class noninheritable by adding the sealed keyword to the class declaration. While this prevents the problem of calling the default constructor, it also prevents others from inheriting from and extending the Log class. For many cases, this third solution is not the best one.

3.22 Returning Multiple Items from a Method

Problem

In many cases, a single return value for a method is not enough. You need a way to return more than one item from a method.

Solution

Use the out keyword on parameters that will act as return parameters. The following method accepts an inputShape parameter and calculates height, width, and depth from that value:

```
public void ReturnDimensions(int inputShape,
                             out int height,
                             out int width,
                             out int depth)
{
    height = 0;
    width = 0;
    depth = 0;

    // Calculate height, width, depth from the inputShape value
}
```

This method would be called in the following manner:

```
// Declare output parameters
int height;
int width;
int depth;

// Call method and return the height, width, and depth
Obj.ReturnDimensions(1, out height, out width, out depth);
```

Another method is to return a class or structure containing all the return values. The previous method has been modified to return a structure instead of using out arguments:

```
public Dimensions ReturnDimensions(int inputShape)
{
    // The default ctor automatically defaults this structure's members to 0
    Dimensions objDim = new Dimensions();

    // Calculate objDim.Height, objDim.Width, objDim.Depth from the inputShape value

    return (objDim);
}
```

where `Dimensions` is defined as follows:

```
public struct Dimensions
{
    int Height;
    int Width;
    int Depth;
}
```

This method would now be called in this manner:

```
// Call method and return the Height, Width, and Depth
Dimensions objDim = obj.ReturnDimensions(1);
```

Discussion

Marking a parameter in a method signature with the out keyword indicates that this parameter will be initialized and returned by this method. This trick is useful when a method is required to return more than one value. A method can, at most, have only one return value, but through the use of the out keyword, we can mark several parameters as a kind of return value.

To set up an out parameter, the parameter in the method signature is marked with the out keyword, shown here:

```
public void ReturnDimensions(int inputShape,
                             out int height,
                             out int width,
                             out int depth)
{
    ...
}
```

To call this method, we must also mark the calling method's arguments with the out keyword, shown here:

```
obj.ReturnDimensions(1, out height, out width, out depth);
```

The out arguments in this method call do not have to be initialized; they can simply be declared and passed in to the ReturnDimensions method. Regardless of whether they are initialized before the method call, they must be initialized before they are used within the ReturnDimensions method. Even if they are not used through every path in the ReturnDimensions method, they still must be initialized. That is why this method starts out with the following three lines of code:

```
height = 0;
width = 0;
depth = 0;
```

You may be wondering why you couldn't use a ref parameter instead of the out parameter, as they both allow a method to change the value of an argument marked as such. The answer is that an out parameter makes the code somewhat self-documenting. You know that when an out parameter is encountered, this parameter is acting as a return value. In addition, an out parameter does not require the extra work to be initialized before it is passed in to the method, which a ref parameter does.

The out parameter was originally designed for marshaling scenarios. An out parameter does not have to be marshaled when the method is called; rather, it is marshaled once when the method returns the data to the caller. Any other type of call (by-value or by-reference) requires that the value be marshaled in both directions. Using the out keyword in marshaling scenarios improves performance.

3.23   Parsing Command-Line Parameters

Problem

You require your applications to accept one or more command-line parameters in a standard format. You need to access and parse the entire command line passed to your application.

Solution

Use the following class to help with parsing command-line parameters:

```
using System;
using System.Diagnostics;

public class ParseCmdLine
{
    // All args are delimited by tab or space
    // All double-quotes are removed except when escaped '\"'
    // All single-quotes are left untouched

    public ParseCmdLine( ) {}

    public virtual string ParseSwitch(string arg)
    {
        arg = arg.TrimStart(new char[2] {'/', '-'});

        return (arg);
    }

    public virtual void ParseSwitchColonArg(string arg, out string outSwitch,
                                            out string outArgument)
    {
        outSwitch = "";
        outArgument = "";

        try
        {
            // This is a switch or switch/argument pair
            arg = arg.TrimStart(new char[2] {'/', '-'});
```

```
            if (arg.IndexOf(':') >= 0)
            {
                outSwitch = arg.Substring(0, arg.IndexOf(':'));
                outArgument = arg.Substring(arg.IndexOf(':') + 1);

                if (outArgument.Trim( ).Length <= 0)
                {
                    throw (new ArgumentException(
                        "Command-Line parameter error: switch " +
                        arg +
                        " must be followed by one or more arguments.", arg));
                }
            }
            else
            {
                throw (new ArgumentException(
                        "Command-Line parameter error: argument " +
                        arg +
                        " must be in the form of a 'switch:argument}' pair.",
                        arg));
            }
        }
        catch (ArgumentException ae)
        {
            // Re-throw the exception to be handled in the calling method
            throw;
        }
        catch (Exception e)
        {
            // Wrap an ArgumentException around the exception thrown
            throw (new ArgumentException("General command-Line parameter error",
                                    arg, e));
        }
    }

    public virtual void ParseSwitchColonArgs(string arg, out string outSwitch,
                                        out string[] outArguments)
    {
        outSwitch = "";
        outArguments = null;

        try
        {
            // This is a switch or switch/argument pair
            arg = arg.TrimStart(new char[2] {'/', '-'});

            if (arg.IndexOf(':') >= 0)
            {
                outSwitch = arg.Substring(0, arg.IndexOf(':'));
                string Arguments = arg.Substring(arg.IndexOf(':') + 1);

                if (Arguments.Trim( ).Length <= 0)
                {
                    throw (new ArgumentException(
```

```
                    "Command-Line parameter error: switch " +
                    arg +
                    " must be followed by one or more arguments.", arg));
            }

            outArguments = Arguments.Split(new char[1] {';'});
        }
        else
        {
            throw (new ArgumentException(
                "Command-Line parameter error: argument " +
                arg +
                " must be in the form of a 'switch:argument{;argument}' pair.",
                arg));
        }
    }
    catch (Exception e)
    {
        // Wrap an ArgumentException around the exception thrown
        throw ;
    }
}

public virtual void DisplayErrorMsg()
{
    DisplayErrorMsg("");
}

public virtual void DisplayErrorMsg(string msg)
{
    Console.WriteLine
        ("An error occurred while processing the command-line arguments:");
    Console.WriteLine(msg);
    Console.WriteLine();

    FileVersionInfo version =
                Process.GetCurrentProcess().MainModule.FileVersionInfo;
    if (Process.GetCurrentProcess().ProcessName.Trim().Length > 0)
    {
        Console.WriteLine(Process.GetCurrentProcess().ProcessName);
    }
    else
    {
        Console.WriteLine("Product Name: " + version.ProductName);
    }

    Console.WriteLine("Version " + version.FileVersion);
    Console.WriteLine("Copyright " + version.LegalCopyright);
    Console.WriteLine("TradeMarks " + version.LegalTrademarks);

    DisplayHelp();
}

public virtual void DisplayHelp()
```

```
        {
            Console.WriteLine("See help for command-line usage.");
        }
    }
```

Discussion

Before command-line parameters can be parsed, a common format must first be decided upon. The format for this recipe follows the command-line format for the Visual C# .NET language compiler. The format used is defined as follows:

- All command-line arguments are separated by one or more spaces and/or tabs.

- Each argument may start with either a - or / character, but not both. If it does not, that argument is considered a literal, such as a filename.

- Each argument that starts with either the - or / character may be divided up into a switch followed by a colon followed by one or more arguments separated with the ; character. The command-line parameter -sw:arg1;arg2;arg3 is divided up into a switch (sw) and three arguments (arg1, arg2, and arg3). Note that there should not be any spaces in the full argument; otherwise, the runtime command-line parser will split up the argument into two or more arguments.

- Strings delineated with double quotes, such as "c:\test\file.log" will have their double quotes stripped off. This is a function of the runtime interpreting the arguments passed in to your application.

- Single quotes are not stripped off.

- To preserve double quotes, precede the double quote character with the \ escape sequence character.

- The \ character is handled only as an escape sequence character when followed by a double quote—in which case, only the double-quote is displayed.

- The ^ character is handled by the *runtime* command-line parser as a special character.

Fortunately, the runtime command-line parser (for Visual Studio .NET, this would be *devenv.exe*) handles most of this before your application receives the individual parsed arguments.

The runtime command-line parser passes a string[] containing each parsed argument to the entry point of your application. The entry point can take one of the following forms:

```
public static void Main()
public static int Main()
public static void Main(string[] args)
public static int Main(string[] args)
```

The first two accept no arguments, but the last two accept the array of parsed command-line arguments. Note that the static Environment.CommandLine property will also return a string containing the entire command line and the static Environment. GetCommandLineArgs method will return an array of strings containing the parsed command-line arguments. The individual arguments in this array can then be passed to the various methods of the ParseCmdLine class. The following code shows how this can be accomplished:

```
[STAThread]
public static void Main(string[] args)
{
    // The application should be initialized here assuming no command-line
    //     parameters were found.

    ParseCmdLine parse = new ParseCmdLine();

    try
    {
        // Create an array of all possible command-line parameters
        // and how to parse them
        object[,] mySwitches = new object[2, 4] {
                {"file", "output", "trialmode", "debugoutput"},
                {ArgType.Simple, ArgType.Compound, ArgType.SimpleSwitch,
                ArgType.Complex}};

        // Loop through all command-line parameters
        for (int counter = 0; counter < args.Length; counter++)
        {
            args[counter] = args[counter].TrimStart(new char[2] {'/', '-'});

            // Search for the correct ArgType and parse argument according to
            //     this ArgType
            for (int index = 0; index <= mySwitches.GetUpperBound(1); index++)
            {
                string theSwitch;
                string theArgument;
                string[] theArguments;

                if (args[counter].StartsWith((string)mySwitches[0, index]))
                {
                    // Parse each argument into switch:arg1;arg2...
                    switch ((ArgType)mySwitches[1, index])
                    {
                        case ArgType.Simple:
                            theSwitch = args[counter];
                            break;

                        case ArgType.SimpleSwitch:
                            theSwitch = parse.ParseSwitch(args[counter]);
                            break;

                        case ArgType.Compound:
                            parse.ParseSwitchColonArg(args[counter],out theSwitch,
                                                        out theArgument);
                            break;
```

```csharp
                    case ArgType.Complex:
                        parse.ParseSwitchColonArgs(args[counter],out theSwitch,
                                                    out theArguments);
                        break;

                    default:
                        throw (new ArgumentException(
                            "Cmd-Line parameter error: ArgType enumeration " +
                            mySwitches[1, index].ToString() +
                            " not recognized."));
                }

                // Implement functionality to handle each parsed
                //    command-line parameter
                switch ((string)mySwitches[0, index])
                {
                    case "file":
                        // Handle this switch here...
                        break;

                    case "output":
                        // Handle this switch here...
                        break;

                    case "trialmode":
                        // Handle this switch and its argument here...
                        break;

                    case "debugoutput":
                        // Handle this switch and its arguments here...
                        break;

                    default:
                        throw (new ArgumentException(
                            "Cmd-Line parameter error: Switch " +
                            mySwitches[0, index].ToString() +
                            " not recognized."));
                }
            }
        }
    }
}
catch (ArgumentException ae)
{
    parse.DisplayErrorMsg(ae.ToString());
    return;
}
catch (Exception e)
{
    // Handle other exceptions here
    // ...
}
}
```

The `ArgType` enumeration is defined as follows:

```
enum ArgType
{
    Simple = 0,        // A simple file name with no preceding '/' or '-' chars
    SimpleSwitch = 1,  // A switch preceded by '/' or '-' chars
    Compound = 2,      // A 'switch:argument' pair preceded by '/' or '-' chars
    Complex = 3        // A 'switch:argument{;argument}' pair with multiple args
                       //    preceded by '/' or '-' chars
}
```

Passing in the following command-line arguments to this application:

```
MyApp c:\input\infile.txt -output:d:\outfile.txt -trialmode
     /debugoutput:c:\test1.log;\\myserver\history\test2.log
```

results in the following parsed switches and arguments:

```
Literal:     c:\input\infile.txt

Switch:      output
Argument:    d:\outfile.txt

Switch:      trialmode

Switch:      debugoutput
Arguments:   c:\test1.log
             \\myserver\history\test2.log
```

If we input incorrectly formed command-line parameters, such as forgetting to add arguments to the -output switch, we get the following output:

```
An error has occured while processing the command-line arguments:
System.ArgumentException: Command-Line parameter error: argument output must be
in the form of a 'switch:argument{;argument}' pair.
Parameter name: output
   at Chapter_Code.ParseCmdLine.ParseSwitchColonArg(String arg,
       String& outSwitch, String& outArgument)
       in c:\book cs cookbook\code\chapter3.cs:line 238
   at Chapter_Code.Class1.Main(String[] args)
       in c:\book cs cookbook\code\main.cs:line 55

CHAPTER_CODE.EXE
Version 1.0.1009.12739
Copyright
TradeMarks
See help for command-line usage.
```

This may be too much output to show to the user; for example, you might not want the entire exception to be displayed. In addition, the last line in the message indicates that you should see the help files for information on the correct command-line usage. It would be more useful to display the correct command-line arguments and some brief information on their usage. To do this, we can extend the `ParseCmdLine` class and make our own specialized class to use in our application. The following class shows how this is accomplished:

```csharp
public class SpecializedParseCmdLine : ParseCmdLine
{
    public SpecializedParseCmdLine() {}

    public override string ParseSwitch(string arg)
    {
        if (arg.IndexOf(':') < 0)
        {
            throw (new ArgumentException("Command-Line parameter error: switch " +
                    arg + " must not be followed by one or more arguments.", arg));
        }

        return (base.ParseSwitch(arg));
    }

    public virtual void DisplayErrorMsg()
    {
        DisplayErrorMsg("");
    }

    public virtual void DisplayErrorMsg(string msg)
    {
        Console.WriteLine(
            "An error has occurred while processing the command-line arguments:");
        Console.WriteLine();

        FileVersionInfo version =
                Process.GetCurrentProcess().MainModule.FileVersionInfo;
        if (Process.GetCurrentProcess().ProcessName.Trim().Length > 0)
        {
            Console.WriteLine(Process.GetCurrentProcess().ProcessName);
        }
        else
        {
            Console.WriteLine("Product Name: " + version.ProductName);
        }

        Console.WriteLine("Version " + version.FileVersion);
        Console.WriteLine("Copyright " + version.LegalCopyright);
        Console.WriteLine("TradeMarks " + version.LegalTrademarks);

        DisplayHelp();
    }
    public override void DisplayHelp()
    {
        // Display correct input args
        base.DisplayHelp();

        Console.WriteLine("Chapter_Code [file | /output:projectfile | /trialmode |
                        /debugoutput:file{;file}]");
        Console.WriteLine();
        Console.WriteLine("Available command-line switches:");
        Console.WriteLine("\tfile        : The file to use as input.");
        Console.WriteLine("\toutput      : The file to use as output.");
```

```
Console.WriteLine("\ttrialmode   : Turns on the trial mode, if present.");
Console.WriteLine("\tdebugoutput : One or more files in which to dump
                     debug information into.");
    }
}
```

This class overrides four methods of the ParseCmdLine class. The DisplayHelp method is overridden to display the relevant information needed to correctly use the command-line parameters in our application. The overloaded DisplayErrorMsg methods are overridden to prevent the lengthy exception message from being displayed. Finally, the ParseSwitch method is overridden to add some more preventative code that will disallow any arguments from being added to a switch that should not have any arguments. By overriding other methods in the ParseCmdLine class, you can modify this class to handle many other situations specific to your application.

See Also

See the "Main" and "Command-Line Arguments" topics in the MSDN documentation.

3.24 Retrofitting a Class to Interoperate with COM

Problem

An existing C# class needs to be usable by a COM object or will need to be usable sometime in the future. You need to make your class work seamlessly with COM.

Solution

Microsoft has made COM interop quite easy. In fact, you really have to do only two minor steps to make your code visible to COM:

1. Set the Register for COM interop field in the project properties to True. This produces a type library that can be used by a COM client.

2. Use the *Regasm.exe* command-line tool to register the class. For example, to register the type library for the *ClassLibrary1.dll,* you would do the following:

   ```
   regasm ClassLibrary1.dll /tlb:ClassLibrary1.tlb
   ```

By default, this tool will make many decisions for you. For example, new GUIDs are created for your classes and interfaces unless you specify a particular GUID to use. This can be a bad thing; it is usually a good idea to explicity specify which GUIDs your classes and interfaces are to use. To take control of how your C# code is viewed and used from a COM client, you need to use a few attributes. Table 3-4 contains a list of attributes and their descriptions that can be used to control these things.

Table 3-4. Attributes to control how a COM client views and is able to use your C# code

Attribute name	Description
GuidAttribute	Places a GUID on an assembly, class, struct, interface, enum, or delegate. Prevents the Tlbimp (the type library converter tool, which converts a COM type library into the equivalent metadata) from creating a new GUID for this target.
ClassInterfaceAttribute	Defines the class interface type that will be applied to an assembly or class. Valid interface types are: *AutoDispatch* The interface will support only late binding. This is the default. *AutoDual* The interface will support both early and late binding. *None* An interface will not be explicitly provided. Therefore, only late-bound access is allowed through an IDispatch interface.
InterfaceTypeAttribute	Defines how an interface is exposed to COM clients. This attribute may only be used on interfaces. Valid interface types are: *InterfaceIsDual* The interface will be exposed as a dual interface. *InterfaceIsIDispatch* The interface will be exposed as a dispinterface. *InterfaceIsIUnknown* The interface will be exposed as deriving from IUnknown. If this attribute is not used, the interface defaults to being exposed as a dual interface.
ProgIdAttribute	Force the ProgId of a class to a defined string. An automatically generated ProgId consists of the namespace and type name. If your ProgId may exceed 39 characters (i.e., your namespace is equal to or greater than 39 characters), you should use this attribute to manually set a ProgId that is 39 characters or less. By default the ProgId is generated from the full namespace and type name (e.g., Namespace1.Namespace2.TypeName).

ComVisibleAttribute	Allows fine grained control over which C# code is visible to a COM client. To limit the exposed types, set the ComVisibleAttribute to false at the assembly level:
	
	 `[assembly: ComVisibleAttribute(false)]`
	
	 and then set each type and/or member's visibility individually using the following syntax:
	
	 `[ComVisibleAttribute(true)]`
	 `public class Foo {...}`

These attributes are used in conjunction with the previous two steps mentioned to create and register the assembly's classes. Several other COM interop attributes exist in the FCL, but the ones mentioned here provide the most basic control over how your assembly is viewed and used by COM clients.

Discussion

To show how these attributes are applied, we use the Foo class, defined within the Chapter_Code namespace:

```
using System;

namespace Chapter_Code
{
    public class Foo
    {
        public Foo( ) {}

        private int state = 100;

        public string PrintMe( )
        {
            return("TEST SUCCESS");
        }

        public int ShowState( )
        {
            return (state);
        }

        public void SetState(int newState)
        {
            state = newState;
        }
    }
}
```

To allow the Foo type to be exposed to a COM client, we would first add an interface, IFoo, describing the members of Foo, that are to be exposed. Adding an interface in this manner is optional, especially if you are exposing classes to scripting clients. If the AutoDual interface type is used with the ClassInterfaceAttribute, early-bound clients will not need this interface either. Even though it is optional, it is still a good idea to use an interface in this manner.

Next, an unchanging GUID is added to the assembly, the IFoo interface, and the Foo class using the GuidAttribute. A ProgId is also added to the Foo class. Finally, the class interface type is defined as an AutoDispatch interface, using the ClassInterfaceAttribute. The new code is shown here with the changes highlighted:

```
using System;
using System.Runtime.InteropServices;

[assembly: GuidAttribute("D4E77B72-43C8-45f1-B0C0-D47685EC18C2")]

namespace Chapter_Code
{
    [GuidAttribute("1C6CD700-A37B-4295-9CC9-D7392FDD425D")]
    public interface IFoo
```

```
    {
        string PrintMe( );
        int ShowState( );
        void SetState(int newState);
    }

    [GuidAttribute("C09E2DD6-03EE-4fef-BB84-05D3422DD3D9")]
    [ClassInterfaceAttribute(ClassInterfaceType.AutoDispatch)]
    [ProgIdAttribute("Chapter_Code.Foo")]
    public class Foo : IFoo
    {
        public Foo( ) {}

        private int state = 100;

        public string PrintMe( )
        {
            return("TEST SUCCESS");
        }

        public int ShowState( )
        {
            return (state);
        }

        public void SetState(int newState)
        {
            state = newState;
        }
    }
}
```

The code to use the exposed C# code from VBScript using COM interop is shown here:

```
<script runat=server>
    Sub TestCOMInterop( )
        'ClassLibrary1 was created using Regasm in the Solution section
        'of this recipe
        Dim x As New ClassLibrary1.Foo

        MsgBox ("Current State: " & x.ShowState( ))
        x.SetState (-1)
        MsgBox ("Current State: " & x.ShowState( ))
        MsgBox ("Print String: " & x.PrintMe( ))
    End Sub
</script>
```

The first Dim statement creates a new instance of the Foo type that is usable from the VBScript code. The rest of the VBScript code exercises the exposed members of the Foo type.

There are some things to keep in mind when exposing C# types to COM clients:

- Only public members or explicit interface member implementations are exposed to COM clients. Explicit interface member implementations are not public, but if the interface itself is public, it may be seen by a COM client.

- Constant fields are not exposed to COM clients.

- You must provide a default constructor in your exposed C# type.

- Parameterized constructors are not exposed to COM clients.

- Static members are not exposed to COM clients.

- Interop flattens the inheritance hierarchy so that your exposed type and its base class members are all available to the COM client. For example, the methods ToString( ) and GetHashCode( ), defined in the base Object class, are also available to VBScript code:

  ```
  Sub TestCOMInterop( )
      Dim x As New ClassLibrary1.Foo

      MsgBox (x.ToString( ))
      MsgBox (x.GetHashCode( ))
  End Sub
  ```

- It is a good idea to explicitly state the GUIDs for any types exposed to COM clients, including any exposed interfaces, through the use of the GuidAttribute. This prevents Tlbexp/Regasm from creating new GUIDs every time your interface changes. A new GUID is created by the Regasm tool every time you choose the Build → Rebuild Solution or Build → Rebuild *ProjectName* menu item. These actions cause the date/time of the module (*dll* or *exe*) to change, as well as the version number for your assembly, which, in turn, can cause a different GUID to be calculated. A new GUID will be calculated for a rebuilt assembly even if no code changes within that assembly. Explicitly adding a GUID to your exposed types will cause your registry to greatly expand during the development stage as more new GUIDs are added to it.

- It is also a good idea to limit the visibility of your types/members through judicial use of the ComVisibleAttribute. This can prevent unauthorized use of specific types/members that could possibly corrupt data or be used to create a security hole by malicious code.

- Exposed types should implement an interface (for example, IFoo) that allows you to specify exactly what members of that type are exposed to COM. If such an explicit interface is not implemented, the compiler will default to exposing what it can of the type.

See Also

See the "Assembly Registration Tool (Regasm.exe)," "Type Library Exporter (Tlbexp.exe)," "Type Library Importer (Tlbimp.exe)," and "Assembly to Type Library Conversion Summary" topics in the MSDN documentation.

3.25 Initializing a Constant Field at Runtime

Problem

A field marked as const can be initialized only at compile time. You need to initialize a field at runtime to a valid value, not at compile time. This field must then act as if it were a constant field for the rest of the application's life.

Solution

When declaring a constant value in your code, there are two choices. You can use a readonly field or a const field. Each has its own strengths and weaknesses. However, if you need to initialize a constant field at runtime, you should use a readonly field:

```
public class Foo
{
    public readonly int bar;

    public Foo( ) {}

    public Foo(int constInitValue)
    {
        bar = constInitValue;
    }

    // Rest of class...
}
```

This is not possible using a const field. A const field can be initialized only at compile time:

```
public class Foo
{
    public const int bar;        // This line causes a compile-time error

    public Foo( ) {}

    public Foo(int constInitValue)
    {
        bar = constInitValue;    // This line also causes a compile-time error
    }

    // Rest of class...
}
```

Discussion

A readonly field allows initialization to take place only in the constructor at runtime, whereas a const field must be initialized at compile time. Therefore, implementing a readonly field is the only way to allow a field that must be constant to be initialized at runtime.

There are only two ways to initialize a readonly field. The first is by adding an initializer to the field itself:

```
public readonly int bar = 100;
```

The second way is to initialize the readonly field through a constructor. This is demonstrated through the code in the Solution to this recipe.

If you look at the following class:

```
public class Foo
{
    public readonly int x;
    public const int y = 1;

    public Foo() {}

    public Foo(int roInitValue)
    {
        x = roInitValue;
    }

    // Rest of class...
}
```

You'll see it is compiled into the following IL:

```
.class public auto ansi beforefieldinit Foo
    extends [mscorlib]System.Object
{
.field public static literal int32 y = int32(0x00000001)  //<<-- const field
.field public initonly int32 x                            //<<-- readonly field
.method public hidebysig specialname rtspecialname
        instance void   .ctor(int32 input) cil managed
{
    // Code size       14 (0xe)
    .maxstack  8
//001659: }
//001660: }

//001666: public class Foo
//001667: {
//001668: public readonly int x;
//001669: public const int y = 1;
//001670:
//001671: public Foo(int roInitValue)
    IL_0000:  ldarg.0
    IL_0001:  call        instance void [mscorlib]System.Object::.ctor()
//001672: {
//001673: x = input;
    IL_0006:  ldarg.0
    IL_0007:  ldarg.1
    IL_0008:  stfld       int32 Foo::x
//001674 }
    IL_000d:  ret
```

```
} // end of method Foo::.ctor

} // end of class Foo
```

Notice that a const field is compiled into a static field, and a readonly field is compiled into an instance field. Therefore, you need only a class name to access a const field.

 A common argument against using const fields is that they do not version as well as readonly fields. If you rebuild a component that defines a const field, and the value of that const changes in a later version, any other components that were built against the old version won't pick up the new value.

The following code shows how to use a readonly field:

```
Foo obj1 = new Foo(100);
Console.WriteLine(obj1.bar);
```

Those two lines compile into the following IL:

```
IL_0013:  ldc.i4      0xc8
IL_0018:  newobj      instance void Foo::.ctor(int32)
IL_001d:  stloc.1
IL_001e:  ldloc.1
IL_001f:  ldfld       int32 Foo::bar
```

Since the const field is already compiled into the application as a static member field, only one simple IL instruction is needed to use this const field at any point in the application:

```
IL_0029:  ldc.i4.1
```

Notice that the compiler compiled away the const field and uses the value it was initialized to, which is 1. This is faster than using a readonly field. However, const fields are inflexible as far as versioning is concerned.

See Also

See the "const" and "readonly" keywords in the MSDN documentation.

3.26 Writing Code that Is Compatible with the Widest Range of Managed Languages

Problem

You need to make sure your C# code will interoperate with all other managed languages that are CLS-compliant consumers, such as VB.NET.

Solution

Mark the assembly with the `CLSCompliantAttribute`:

```
[assembly: CLSCompliantAttribute(true)]
```

Discussion

By default, your C# assemblies created with VS.NET are not marked with the `CLSCompliantAttribute`. This does not mean that the assembly will not work in the managed environment. It means that this assembly may use elements that are not recognized by other Common Language Specification (CLS)-compliant languages. For example, unsigned numeric types are not recognized by all managed languages, but they can be used in the C# language. The problem occurs when C# returns an unsigned data type, such as `uint`, either through a return value or a parameter to a calling component in another language that does not recognize unsigned data types—VB.NET is one example.

> CLS compliance is enforced only on types/members marked public or protected. This makes sense because components written in other languages will only be able to use the public or protected types/members of components written in C#.

Marking your assembly as CLS-compliant means that any CLS-compliant language will be able to seamlessly interoperate with your code; that is, it enables CLS-compliance checking. It should also be noted that if you have types and/or members within those types that are not CLS-compliant, a compiler error will be generated. This makes it much easier on developers to catch problems before they manifest themselves, especially in an environment where multiple managed languages are being used on a single project. Marking your entire assembly to be CLS-compliant is done with the following line of code:

```
[assembly: CLSCompliantAttribute(true)]
```

Sometimes you just can't be 100% CLS-compliant, but you don't want to have to throw away the benefit of compiler checking for the 99.9% of your methods that are CLS-compliant just so you can expose one method that is not. To mark these types or members as not being CLS-compliant, use the following attribute:

```
[CLSCompliantAttribute(false)]
```

By passing a value of `false` to this constructor's `isCompliant` parameter, any type/member marked as such will not cause any compiler errors due to non-CLS-compliant code.

> Many types/members in the FCL are not CLS-compliant. This is not a problem when using C# to interact with the FCL. However, this is a problem for other languages. To solve this dilemma, the authors of the FCL usually included a CLS-compliant type/member where possible to mirror the non-CLS-compliant type/member.

The following is a list of some of the things that can be done to make code non-CLS-compliant when using the C# language:

- Two identifiers with the same name that differ only by case
- Using unsigned data types (byte, ushort, uint, ulong)
- Use of the UIntPtr type
- Boxed value types
- The use of operator overloading
- An array of non-CLS-compliant types, such as unsigned data types
- An enumeration type having a non-CLS-compliant underlying data type

See Also

See the "CLSCompliantAttribute Class" topic in the MSDN documentation.

3.27 Implementing Nested foreach Functionality in a Class

Problem

You need a class that contains an array of objects; each of these objects in turn contains an array of objects. You want to use a nested foreach loop to iterate through all objects in both the outer and inner arrays in the following manner:

```
foreach (SubSet aSubSet in Set)
{
    foreach (Item i in aSubSet)
    {
        // Operate on Item objects contained in the innermost object collection
        //   SomeSubSet, which in turn is contained in another outer collection
        //    called Set
    }
}
```

Solution

Implement IEnumerable on the top-level class as usual, but also implement IEnumerable on each of the objects returned by the top-level enumeration. The following class set contains an ArrayList of SubGroup objects, and each SubGroup object contains an ArrayList of Item objects:

```
using System;
using System.Collections;

//----------------------------------------
//
//  The top-level class
```

```
//
//----------------------------------------
public class Set : IEnumerable
{
    //CONSTRUCTORS
    public Set( ) {}

    //FIELDS
    private ArrayList setArray = new ArrayList( );

    //PROPERTIES
    public int Count
    {
        get{return(setArray.Count);}
    }

    //METHODS
    public IEnumerator GetEnumerator( )
    {
        return(new SetEnumerator(this));
    }

    public int AddGroup(string name)
    {
        return(setArray.Add(new SubGroup(name)));
    }

    public SubGroup GetGroup(int setIndex)
    {
        return((SubGroup)setArray[setIndex]);
    }

    //NESTED ITEMS
    public class SetEnumerator : IEnumerator
    {
        //CONSTRUCTORS
        public SetEnumerator(Set theSet)
        {
            setObj = theSet;
        }

        //FIELDS
        private Set setObj;
        private int index = -1;

        //METHODS
        public bool MoveNext( )
        {
            index++;
            if (index >= setObj.Count)
            {
                return(false);
            }
            else
```

```
            {
                return(true);
            }
        }

        public void Reset( )
        {
            index = -1;
        }

        public object Current
        {
            get{return(setObj.setArray[index]);}
        }
    }
}

//----------------------------------------
//
//   The inner class
//
//----------------------------------------
public class SubGroup : IEnumerable
{
    //CONSTRUCTORS
    public SubGroup( ) {}

    public SubGroup(string name)
    {
        subGroupName = name;
    }

    //FIELDS
    private string subGroupName = "";
    private ArrayList itemArray = new ArrayList( );

    //PROPERTIES
    public string SubGroupName
    {
        get{return(subGroupName);}
    }

    public int Count
    {
        get{return(itemArray.Count);}
    }

    //METHODS
    public int AddItem(string name, int location)
    {
        return(itemArray.Add(new Item(name, location)));
    }

    public Item GetSubGroup(int index)
```

```
    {
        return((Item)itemArray[index]);
    }

    public IEnumerator GetEnumerator()
    {
        return(new SubGroupEnumerator(this));
    }

    //NESTED ITEMS
    public class SubGroupEnumerator : IEnumerator
    {

        //CONSTRUCTORS
        public SubGroupEnumerator(SubGroup SubGroupEnum)
        {
            subGroup = SubGroupEnum;
        }

        //FIELDS
        private SubGroup subGroup;
        private int index = -1;

        //METHODS
        public bool MoveNext()
        {
            index++;
            if (index >= subGroup.Count)
            {
                return(false);
            }
            else
            {
                return(true);
            }
        }

        public void Reset()
        {
            index = -1;
        }

        public object Current
        {
            get{return(subGroup.itemArray[index]);}
        }
    }
}


//-------------------------------------------
//
//   The lowest-level class
//
//-------------------------------------------
```

```
public class Item
{
    //CONSTRUCTOR
    public Item(string name, int location)
    {
        itemName = name;
        itemLocation = location;
    }

    private string itemName = "";
    private int itemLocation = 0;

    public string ItemName
    {
        get {return(itemName);}
        set {itemName = value;}
    }

    public int ItemLocation
    {
        get {return(itemLocation);}
        set {itemLocation = value;}
    }
}
```

Discussion

Building functionality into a class to allow it to be iterated over using the foreach loop is not extremely difficult; however, building functionality into embedded classes to allow a nested foreach idiom to be used requires keeping careful track of the classes you are building.

The ability of a class to be used by the foreach loop requires the use of two interfaces: IEnumerable and IEnumerator. The IEnumerable interface contains the GetEnumerator method, which accepts no parameters and returns an enumerator object. It is this enumerator object that implements the IEnumerator interface. This interface contains the methods MoveNext and Reset along with the property Current. The MoveNext method accepts no parameters and returns a bool indicating whether the MoveNext method has reached the last element in the collection. The Reset method also accepts no parameters and returns a void. This method simply moves to the position in the collection that is immediately before the first element. Once in this state, the MoveNext method must be called in order to access the first element. The Current property is read-only and returns an object, which is the current element in the collection.

The code for this recipe is divided among five classes. The top-level class is the Set class, which contains an ArrayList of SubGroup objects. The SubGroup object also contains an ArrayList, but this ArrayList contains Item objects. The Set and SubGroup classes each contain a nested class, which is the enumerator class (i.e., it implements

IEnumerator). The Set and SubGroup classes both implement the IEnumerable interface. The class structure looks like this:

```
Set (Implements IEnumerable)
SetEnumerator (Implements IEnumerator and is nested within the Set class)
    SubGroup (Implements IEnumerable)
    SubGroupEnumerator (Implements IEnumerator and is nested within the SubGroup
        class)
        Item
```

By examining the Set class, we can see how classes usable by a foreach loop are constructed. This class contains:

- A simple ArrayList, which will be iterated over by the class enumerator.
- A property, Count, which returns the number of elements in the ArrayList.
- A method, GetEnumerator, which is defined by the IEnumerable interface. This method returns a SetEnumerator object. As you shall see later, this object allows the foreach loop to do its work.
- A method, AddGroup, which adds a SubGroup object to the ArrayList.
- A method, GetGroup, which returns a SubGroup object in the ArrayList.

The SetEnumerator class, which is nested within the Set class, contains:

- A constructor that accepts a Set object. This Set object will be iterated over by the foreach loop.
- Two fields to hold the current index (index) and the Set object (setObj).
- A method, MoveNext, which is defined by the IEnumerator interface. This method moves the current index (index) to the next position in the Set object's ArrayList. If the index is moved past the last element in the ArrayList, a false is returned. Otherwise, the index is incremented by one, and a true is returned.
- A method Reset, which is defined by the IEnumerator interface. This method moves the current index (index) to a position immediately before the first element in the ArrayList of the Set object (i.e., -1).
- A method Current, which is defined by the IEnumerator interface. This method returns the SubGroup object in the Set object's ArrayList, which is pointed to by the index field.

To create the SubGroup and SubGroupEnumerator class, we follow the same pattern, except that the SubGroup class contains an ArrayList of Item objects and the SubGroupEnumerator operates on a SubGroup object.

The final class is the Item class. This class is the lowest level of this structure and contains data that has been grouped within the SubGroup objects, all of which is contained in the Set object. There is nothing out of the ordinary with this class; it simply contains data and the means with which to set and retrieve this data.

Using these classes is quite simple. The following method shows how to create a Set object that contains multiple SubGroup objects, which, in turn, contain multiple Item objects:

```
public void CreateNestedObjects()
{
    Set topLevelSet = new Set();

    // Create two groups under the TopLevelSet object
    topLevelSet.AddGroup("sg1");
    topLevelSet.AddGroup("sg2");

    // For each SubGroup object in the TopLevelSet object, add two Item objects
    foreach (SubGroup SG in TopLevelSet)
    {
        SG.AddItem("item1", 100);
        SG.AddItem("item2", 200);
    }
}
```

The CreateNestedObjects method first creates a topLevelSet object and creates two SubGroups within it called sg1 and sg2. Each of these SubGroup objects in turn is filled with two Item objects called item1 and item2.

The next method shows how to read all of the Item objects contained within the Set object that was created in the CreateNestedObjects method:

```
public void ReadNestedObjects(Set TopLevelSet)
{
    Console.WriteLine("TopLevelSet.Count: " + TopLevelSet.Count);

    // Outer foreach to iterate over all SubGroup objects
    //in the Set object
    foreach (SubGroup SG in TopLevelSet)
    {
        Console.WriteLine("\tSG.SubGroupName:  " + SG.SubGroupName);
        Console.WriteLine("\tSG.Count: " + SG.Count);

        // Inner foreach to iterate over all Item objects
        //in the current SubGroup object
        foreach (Item i in SG)
        {
            Console.WriteLine("\t\ti.ItemName:     " + i.ItemName);
            Console.WriteLine("\t\ti.ItemLocation: " + i.ItemLocation);
        }
    }
}
```

This method displays the following:

```
TopLevelSet.Count: 2
        SG.SubGroupName:  sg1
        SG.Count: 2
                I.ItemName:     item1
```

```
                I.ItemLocation: 100
                I.ItemName:      item2
                I.ItemLocation: 200
        SG.SubGroupName:  sg2
        SG.Count: 2
                I.ItemName:      item1
                I.ItemLocation: 100
                I.ItemName:      item2
                I.ItemLocation: 200
```

The outer foreach loop is used to iterate over all SubGroup objects that are stored in
the top-level Set object. The inner foreach loop is used to iterate over all Item objects
that are stored in the current SubGroup object.

See Also

See the "IEnumerable Interface" and "IEnumerator Interface" topics in the MSDN
documentation.

3.28 Building Cloneable Classes

Problem

You need a method of performing a shallow cloning operation, a deep cloning operation, or both on a data type that may also reference other types.

Solution

Shallow copying means that the copied object's fields will reference the same objects
as the original object. To allow shallow copying, add the following Clone method to
your class:

```
using System;
using System.Collections;

public class ShallowClone : ICloneable
{
    public int data = 1;
    public ArrayList listData = new ArrayList();
    public object objData = new object();

    public object Clone()
    {
        return (this.MemberwiseClone());
    }
}
```

Deep copying or *cloning* means that the copied object's fields will reference new copies of the original object's fields. This method of copying is more time-consuming
than the shallow copy. To allow deep copying, add the following Clone method to
your class:

```
using System;
using System.Collections;
using System.Runtime.Serialization.Formatters.Binary;
using System.IO;

[Serializable]
public class DeepClone : ICloneable
{
    public int data = 1;
    public ArrayList listData = new ArrayList();
    public object objData = new object();

    public object Clone()
    {
        BinaryFormatter BF = new BinaryFormatter();
        MemoryStream memStream = new MemoryStream();

        BF.Serialize(memStream, this);
        memStream.Flush();
        memStream.Position = 0;

        return (BF.Deserialize(memStream));
    }
}
```

Add an overloaded Clone method to your class to allow for deep or shallow copying. This method allows you to decide at runtime how your object will be copied. The code might appear as follows:

```
using System;
using System.Collections;
using System.Runtime.Serialization.Formatters.Binary;
using System.IO;

[Serializable]
public class MultiClone : ICloneable
{
    public int data = 1;
    public ArrayList listData = new ArrayList();
    public object objData = new object();

    public object Clone(bool doDeepCopy)
    {
        if (doDeepCopy)
        {
            BinaryFormatter BF = new BinaryFormatter();
            MemoryStream memStream = new MemoryStream();

            BF.Serialize(memStream, this);
            memStream.Flush();
            memStream.Position = 0;

            return (BF.Deserialize(memStream));
        }
        else
```

```
        {
            return (this.memberwiseClone());
        }
    }

    public object Clone()
    {
        return (Clone(false));
    }
}
```

Discussion

Cloning is the ability to make an exact copy (a clone) of an instance of a type. Cloning may take one of two forms: a shallow copy or a deep copy. Shallow copying is relatively easy. It involves copying the object that the Clone method was called on. The reference type fields in the original object are copied over, as are the value type fields. This means that if the original object contains a field of type StreamWriter, for instance, the cloned object will point to this same instance of the original object's StreamWriter; a new object is not created.

 There is no need to deal with static fields when performing a cloning operation. There is only one memory location reserved for each static field per class. Besides, the cloned object will have access to the same static fields as the original.

Support for shallow copying is implemented by the MemberwiseClone method of the Object class, which serves as the base class for all .NET classes. So the following code allows a shallow copy to be created and returned by the Clone method:

```
public object Clone()
{
return (this.MemberwiseClone());
}
```

Making a deep copy is the second way of cloning an object. A deep copy will make a copy of the original object just as the shallow copy does. However, a deep copy will also make separate copies of each reference type field in the original object. Therefore, if the original object contains a StreamWriter type field, the cloned object will also contain a StreamWriter type field, but the cloned object's StreamWriter field will point to a new StreamWriter object, not the original object's StreamWriter object.

Support for deep copying is not automatically provided by the Clone method or the .NET Framework. Instead, the following code illustrates an easy way of implementing a deep copy:

```
BinaryFormatter BF = new BinaryFormatter();
MemoryStream memStream = new MemoryStream();

BF.Serialize(memStream, this);
```

```
memStream.Flush( );
memStream.Position = 0;

return (BF.Deserialize(memStream));
```

Basically, the original object is serialized out to a memory stream using binary serialization, then it is deserialized into a new object, which is returned to the caller. Note that it is important to flush memory and reposition the memory stream pointer back to the start of the stream before calling the Deserialize method; otherwise, an exception indicating that the serialized object contains no data will be thrown.

Performing a deep copy using object serialization allows the underlying object to be changed without having to modify the code that performs the deep copy. If you performed the deep copy by hand, you'd have to make a new instance of all the instance fields of the original object and copy them over to the cloned object. This is a tedious chore in and of itself. If a change is made to the fields of the object being cloned, the deep copy code must also change to reflect this modification. Using serialization, we rely on the serializer to dynamically find and serialize all fields contained in the object. If the object is modified, the serializer will still make a deep copy without any code modifications. Two reasons you would possibly want to do a deep copy by hand are:

1. It can be faster in terms of application performance.
2. The serialization technique presented in this recipe works properly only when everything in your object is serializable. Of course, manual cloning doesn't always help there either—some objects are just inherently nonclonable. Suppose you have a network management application where an object represents a particular printer on your network. What's it supposed to do when you clone it? Fax a purchase order for a new printer?

One problem inherent with deep copying is performing a deep copy on a nested data structure with circular references. This recipe manages to make it possible to deal with circular references, although it's a tricky problem. So, in fact, you don't need to avoid circular references if you are using this recipe.

See Also

See the "ICloneable Interface" and "Object.MemberwiseClone Method" topics in the MSDN documentation.

3.29   Assuring an Object's Disposal

Problem

You require a way to always have the Dispose method of an object called when that object's work is done or it goes out of scope.

Solution

Use the using statement:

```
using System;
using System.IO;

// ...

using(FileStream FS = new FileStream("Test.txt", FileMode.Create))
{
    FS.WriteByte((byte)1);
    FS.WriteByte((byte)2);
    FS.WriteByte((byte)3);

    using(StreamWriter SW = new StreamWriter(FS))
    {
        SW.WriteLine("some text.");
    }
}
```

Discussion

The using statement is very easy to use and saves you the hassle of writing extra code. If the solution had not used the using statement, it would look like this:

```
FileStream FS = new FileStream("Test.txt", FileMode.Create);
try
{
    FS.WriteByte((byte)1);
    FS.WriteByte((byte)2);
    FS.WriteByte((byte)3);

    StreamWriter SW = new StreamWriter(FS);
    try
    {
        SW.WriteLine("some text.");
    }
    finally
    {
        if (SW != null)
        {
            ((IDisposable)SW).Dispose();
        }
    }
}
finally
{
    if (FS != null)
    {
        ((IDisposable)FS).Dispose();
    }
}
```

There are several points about the using statement.

- There is a using directive, such as
  ```
  using System.IO;
  ```
  which should be differentiated from the using statement. This is potentially confusing to developers first getting into this language.
- The variable(s) defined in the using statement clause must all be of the same type, and they must have an initializer. However, you are allowed multiple using statements in front of a single code block, so this isn't a significant restriction.
- Any variables defined in the using clause are considered read-only in the body of the using statement. This prevents a developer from inadvertently switching the variable to refer to a different object and causing problems when an attempt is made to dispose of the object that the variable initially referenced.
- The variable should not be declared outside of the using block and then initialized inside of the using clause.

This last point is described by the following code:

```
FileStream FS;
using(FS = new FileStream("Test.txt", FileMode.Create))
{
    FS.WriteByte((byte)1);
    FS.WriteByte((byte)2);
    FS.WriteByte((byte)3);

    using(StreamWriter SW = new StreamWriter(FS))
    {
        SW.WriteLine("some text.");
    }
}
```

For this example code, we will not have a problem. But consider that the variable FS is usable outside of the using block. Essentially, we could revisit this code and modify it as follows:

```
FileStream FS;
using(FS = new FileStream("Test.txt", FileMode.Create))
{
    FS.WriteByte((byte)1);
    FS.WriteByte((byte)2);
    FS.WriteByte((byte)3);

    using(StreamWriter SW = new StreamWriter(FS))
    {
        SW.WriteLine("some text.");
    }
}
FS.WriteByte((byte)4);
```

This code compiles but throws an `ObjectDisposedException` on the last line of this code snippet because the `Dispose` method has already been called on the `FS` object. The object has not yet been collected at this point and still remains in memory in the disposed state.

See Also

See Recipes 3.30 and 3.36; see the "IDispose Interface," "Using foreach with Collections," and "Implementing Finalize and Dispose to Clean Up Unmanaged Resources" topics in the MSDN documentation.

3.30 Releasing a COM Object Through Managed Code

Problem

You need to release a COM object from managed code without forcing a garbage collection to occur.

Solution

Use the static `ReleaseComObject` method of the `Marshal` class:

```
int newRefCount = System.Runtime.InteropServices.Marshal.ReleaseComObject(COMObj);
```

where *COMObj* is a reference to the runtime callable wrapper (RCW) of a COM object.

Discussion

If the COM object is holding on to resources that need to be released in a timely manner, we will want to decrement the reference count on the COM object as quickly as possible, once we've finished using the COM object and have set it to `null`. The GC needs to run in order to collect the unreferenced RCW around our COM object, thereby decrementing the reference count on the COM object. Unfortunately, there is no guarantee that the GC will run in order to collect the RCW anytime in the near future.

To solve this problem, we could call `GC.Collect` ourselves to try to free the RCW, but this might be overkill. Instead, use the `ReleaseComObject` method to manually force the RCW to decrement its reference count on the COM object without having to force a collection to occur.

The static `ReleaseComObject` method returns an `int` indicating the current reference count contained in the RCW object after this method has finished decrementing its reference count. Remember that this method decrements the reference count contained in the RCW, not the COM object's reference count. When the RCW reference count goes to zero, it releases its COM object. At this point, the GC can collect the RCW.

Care must be used when calling the ReleaseComObject method. Misuse of this method can cause a COM object to be released by the RCW too early. Since the ReleaseComObject method decrements the reference count in the RCW, you should call it no more than one time for every object that contains a pointer to the RCW. Calling it multiple times might cause the RCW to release the COM object earlier than expected. Any attempt to use a reference to an RCW that has had its reference count decremented to zero results in a NullReferenceException exception. The RCW might not have been collected yet, but its reference to the COM object has been terminated.

See Also

See Recipes 3.29 and 3.36; see the "Marshal.ReleaseComObject Method" topic in the MSDN documentation.

3.31 Creating an Object Cache

Problem

Your application creates many objects that are expensive to create and/or have a large memory footprint—for instance, objects that are populated with data from a database or a web service upon their creation. These objects are used throughout a large portion of the application's lifetime. You need a way to not only enhance the performance of these objects—and as a result, your application—but also to use memory more efficiently.

Solution

Create an object cache to keep these objects in memory as long as possible, without tying up valuable heap space and possibly resources. Since cached objects may be reused at a later time, you also forego the process of having to create similar objects many times.

You can reuse the ASP.NET cache that is located in the System.Web.Caching namespace or you can build your own lightweight caching mechanism. The See Also section at the end of this recipe provides several Microsoft resources that show you how to use the ASP.NET cache to cache your own objects. However, the ASP.NET cache is very complex and may have a nontrivial overhead associated with it, so using a lightweight caching mechanism like the one shown here is a viable alternative.

The following class, ObjCache, represents a type that allows the caching of SomeComplexObj objects:

```
using System;
using System.Collections;

public class ObjCache
{
```

```csharp
// Constructors
public ObjCache( )
{
    Cache = new Hashtable( );
}

public ObjCache(int initialCapacity)
{
    Cache = new Hashtable(initialCapacity);
}

// Fields
private Hashtable cache = null;

// Methods
public SomeComplexObj GetObj(object key)
{
    if (!cache.ContainsKey(key) || !IsObjAlive(key))
    {
        AddObj(key, new SomeComplexObj( ));
    }

    return ((SomeComplexObj)((WeakReference)cache[key]).Target);
}

public object GetObj(object key, object obj)
{
    if (!cache.ContainsKey(key) || !IsObjAlive(key))
    {
        return (null);
    }
    else
    {
        return (((WeakReference)cache[key]).Target);
    }
}

public void AddObj(object key, SomeComplexObj item)
{
    WeakReference WR = new WeakReference(item, false);

    if (cache.ContainsKey(key))
    {
        cache[key] = WR;
    }
    else
    {
        cache.Add(key, WR);
    }
}

public void AddObj(object key, object item)
{
    WeakReference WR = new WeakReference(item, false);
```

```csharp
        if (cache.ContainsKey(key))
        {
            cache[key] = WR;
        }
        else
        {
            cache.Add(key, WR);
        }
    }

    public bool IsObjAlive(object key)
    {
        if (cache.ContainsKey(key))
        {
            return (((WeakReference)cache[key]).IsAlive);
        }
        else
        {
            return (false);
        }
    }

    public int AliveObjsInCache()
    {
        int count = 0;

        foreach (DictionaryEntry item in cache)
        {
            if (((WeakReference)item.Value).IsAlive)
            {
                count++;
            }
        }

        return (count);
    }

    public int ExistsInGeneration(object key)
    {
        int retVal = -1;

        if (cache.ContainsKey(key) && IsObjAlive(key))
        {
            retVal = GC.GetGeneration((WeakReference)cache[key]);
        }

        return (retVal);
    }

    public bool DoesKeyExist(object key)
    {
        return (cache.ContainsKey(key));
    }
```

```
public bool DoesObjExist(object complexObj)
{
    return (cache.ContainsValue(complexObj));
}

public int TotalCacheSlots()
{
    return (cache.Count);
}
```

> The SomeComplexObj class can be replaced with any type of class you choose. For this recipe, we will use this class, but for your code, you can change it to whatever class or structure type you need.

The SomeComplexObj is defined here (realistically, this would be a much more complex object to create and use; however, for the sake of brevity, this class is written as simply as possible):

```
public class SomeComplexObj
{
    public SomeComplexObj(){}

    private int idcode = -1;

    public int IDCode
    {
        set{idcode = value;}
        get{return (idcode);}
    }
}
```

ObjCache, the caching object used in this recipe, makes use of a Hashtable object to hold all cached objects. This Hashtable allows for fast lookup when retrieving objects and generally for fast insertion and removal times. The Hashtable object used by this class is defined as a private field and is initialized through its overloaded constructors.

Developers using this class will mainly be adding and retrieving objects from this object. The GetObj method implements the retrieval mechanism for this class. This method returns a cached object if its key exists in the Hashtable and the WeakReference object is considered to be alive. An object that the WeakReference type refers to has not been garbage collected. The WeakReference type can remain alive long after the object to which it referred is gone. An indication of whether this WeakReference object is alive is obtained through the read-only IsAlive property of the WeakReference object. This property returns a bool indicating whether this object is alive (true) or not (false). When an object is not alive, or when its key does not exist in the Hashtable, this method creates a new object with the same key as the one passed in to the GetObj method and adds it to the Hashtable.

The AddObj method implements the mechanism to add objects to the cache. This method creates a WeakReference object that will hold a weak reference to our object. Each object in the cache is contained within a WeakReference object. This is the core of the caching mechanism used in this recipe. A WeakReference that references an object (its target) allows that object to later be referenced through itself. When the target of the WeakReference object is also referenced by a strong (i.e., normal) reference, the GC cannot collect the target object. But if no references are made to this WeakReference object, the GC can collect this object to make room in the managed heap for new objects.

After creating the WeakReference object, the Hashtable is searched for the same key that we want to add. If an object with that key exists, it is overwritten with the new object; otherwise, the Add method of the Hashtable class is called.

The ObjCache class has been written to cache either a specific object type or multiple object types. To do this, a method called GetAnyTypeObj has been added that returns an object. Additionally, the AddObj method is overloaded to accept an object as its second parameter type. The following code uses the strongly typed GetObj method to return a SomeComplexObj object:

```
SomeComplexObj SCO2 = OC.GetObj("ID2");
```

The following code uses the generic GetAnyTypeObj method to return some other type of object:

```
Obj SCO2 = (Obj)OC.GetAnyTypeObj("ID2");
if (SCO2 == null)
{
    OC.AddObj("ID2", new Obj());
    SCO2 = (Obj)OC.GetAnyTypeObj("ID2");
}
```

where Obj is an object of any type. Notice that it is now the responsibility of the caller to verify that the GetObj method does not return null.

Quite a bit of extra work is required in the calling code to support a cache of heterogeneous objects. More responsibility is placed on the user of this cache object, which can quickly lead to usability and maintenance problems if not written correctly.

The code to exercise the ObjCache class is shown here:

```
// Create the cache here
ObjCache OC = new ObjCache();

public void TestObjCache()
{
    OC.AddObj("ID1", new SomeComplexObj());
    OC.AddObj("ID2", new SomeComplexObj());
    OC.AddObj("ID3", new SomeComplexObj());
    OC.AddObj("ID4", new SomeComplexObj());
    OC.AddObj("ID5", new SomeComplexObj());
```

```
Console.WriteLine("\r\n--> Add 5 weak references");
Console.WriteLine("OC.TotalCacheSlots = " + OC.TotalCacheSlots());
Console.WriteLine("OC.AliveObjsInCache = " + OC.AliveObjsInCache());
Console.WriteLine("OC.ExistsInGeneration('ID1') = " +
    OC.ExistsInGeneration("ID1"));

/////////////// BEGIN COLLECT ///////////////
GC.Collect();
GC.WaitForPendingFinalizers();
///////////////  END COLLECT  ///////////////

Console.WriteLine("\r\n--> Collect all weak references");
Console.WriteLine("OC.TotalCacheSlots = " + OC.TotalCacheSlots());
Console.WriteLine("OC.AliveObjsInCache = " + OC.AliveObjsInCache());

OC.AddObj("ID1", new SomeComplexObj());
OC.AddObj("ID2", new SomeComplexObj());
OC.AddObj("ID3", new SomeComplexObj());
OC.AddObj("ID4", new SomeComplexObj());
OC.AddObj("ID5", new SomeComplexObj());

Console.WriteLine("\r\n--> Add 5 weak references");
Console.WriteLine("OC.TotalCacheSlots = " + OC.TotalCacheSlots());
Console.WriteLine("OC.AliveObjsInCache = " + OC.AliveObjsInCache());

CreateObjLongMethod();
Create135();
CollectAll();
}

private void CreateObjLongMethod()
{
    Console.WriteLine("\r\n--> Obtain ID1");
    if (OC.IsObjAlive("ID1"))
    {
        SomeComplexObj SCOTemp = OC.GetObj("ID1");
        SCOTemp.IDCode = 100;
        Console.WriteLine("SCOTemp.IDCode = " + SCOTemp.IDCode);
    }
    else
    {
        Console.WriteLine("Object ID1 does not exist...Creating new ID1...");
        OC.AddObj("ID1", new SomeComplexObj());

        SomeComplexObj SCOTemp = OC.GetObj("ID1");
        SCOTemp.IDCode = 101;
        Console.WriteLine("SCOTemp.IDCode = " + SCOTemp.IDCode);
    }
}

private void Create135()
{
    Console.WriteLine("OC.ExistsInGeneration('ID1') = " +
        OC.ExistsInGeneration("ID1"));
```

```csharp
        Console.WriteLine("\r\n--> Obtain ID1, ID3, ID5");
        SomeComplexObj SCO1 = OC.GetObj("ID1");
        SomeComplexObj SCO3 = OC.GetObj("ID3");
        SomeComplexObj SCO5 = OC.GetObj("ID5");
        SCO1.IDCode = 1000;
        SCO3.IDCode = 3000;
        SCO5.IDCode = 5000;
        Console.WriteLine("OC.ExistsInGeneration('ID1') = " +
          OC.ExistsInGeneration("ID1"));

        ////////////// BEGIN COLLECT //////////////
        GC.Collect();
        GC.WaitForPendingFinalizers();
        //////////////  END COLLECT  //////////////

        Console.WriteLine("\r\n--> Collect all weak references");
        Console.WriteLine("OC.TotalCacheSlots = " + OC.TotalCacheSlots());
        Console.WriteLine("OC.AliveObjsInCache = " + OC.AliveObjsInCache());
        Console.WriteLine("OC.ExistsInGeneration('ID1') = "
          + OC.ExistsInGeneration("ID1"));

        Console.WriteLine("SCO1.IDCode = " + SCO1.IDCode);
        Console.WriteLine("SCO3.IDCode = " + SCO3.IDCode);
        Console.WriteLine("SCO5.IDCode = " + SCO5.IDCode);

        Console.WriteLine("\r\n--> Get ID2, which has been collected.  ID2 Exists ==" +
          OC.IsObjAlive("ID2"));
        SomeComplexObj SCO2 = OC.GetObj("ID2");
        Console.WriteLine("ID2 has now been re-created.  ID2 Exists == " +
          OC.IsObjAlive("ID2"));
        Console.WriteLine("OC.AliveObjsInCache = " + OC.AliveObjsInCache());
        SCO2.IDCode = 2000;
        Console.WriteLine("SCO2.IDCode = " + SCO2.IDCode);

        ////////////// BEGIN COLLECT //////////////
        GC.Collect();
        GC.WaitForPendingFinalizers();
        //////////////  END COLLECT  //////////////

        Console.WriteLine("\r\n--> Collect all weak references");
        Console.WriteLine("OC.TotalCacheSlots = " + OC.TotalCacheSlots());
        Console.WriteLine("OC.AliveObjsInCache = " + OC.AliveObjsInCache());
        Console.WriteLine("OC.ExistsInGeneration('ID1') = " +
          OC.ExistsInGeneration("ID1"));
        Console.WriteLine("OC.ExistsInGeneration('ID2') = " +
          OC.ExistsInGeneration("ID2"));
        Console.WriteLine("OC.ExistsInGeneration('ID3') = " +
          OC.ExistsInGeneration("ID3"));
    }

    private void CollectAll()
    {
        ////////////// BEGIN COLLECT //////////////
        GC.Collect();
```

```
            GC.WaitForPendingFinalizers( );
            //////////////  END COLLECT  //////////////

            Console.WriteLine("\r\n--> Collect all weak references");
            Console.WriteLine("OC.TotalCacheSlots = " + OC.TotalCacheSlots( ));
            Console.WriteLine("OC.AliveObjsInCache = " + OC.AliveObjsInCache( ));
            Console.WriteLine("OC.ExistsInGeneration('ID1') = " +
                OC.ExistsInGeneration("ID1"));
            Console.WriteLine("OC.ExistsInGeneration('ID2') = " +
                OC.ExistsInGeneration("ID2"));
            Console.WriteLine("OC.ExistsInGeneration('ID3') = " +
                OC.ExistsInGeneration("ID3"));
            Console.WriteLine("OC.ExistsInGeneration('ID5') = " +
                OC.ExistsInGeneration("ID5"));
        }
```

The output of this test code is shown here:

```
--> Add 5 weak references
OC.TotalCacheSlots = 5
OC.AliveObjsInCache = 5
OC.ExistsInGeneration('ID1') = 0

--> Collect all weak references
OC.TotalCacheSlots = 5
OC.AliveObjsInCache = 0

--> Add 5 weak references
OC.TotalCacheSlots = 5
OC.AliveObjsInCache = 5

--> Obtain ID1
SCOTemp.IDCode = 100
OC.ExistsInGeneration('ID1') = 0

--> Obtain ID1, ID3, ID5
OC.ExistsInGeneration('ID1') = 0

--> Collect all weak references
OC.TotalCacheSlots = 5
OC.AliveObjsInCache = 3
OC.ExistsInGeneration('ID1') = 1
SCO1.IDCode = 1000
SCO3.IDCode = 3000
SCO5.IDCode = 5000

--> Get ID2, which has been collected.  ID2 Exists == False
ID2 has now been re-created.  ID2 Exists == True
OC.AliveObjsInCache = 4
SCO2.IDCode = 2000

--> Collect all weak references
OC.TotalCacheSlots = 5
OC.AliveObjsInCache = 4
OC.ExistsInGeneration('ID1') = 2
```

```
OC.ExistsInGeneration('ID2') = 1
OC.ExistsInGeneration('ID3') = 2

--> Collect all weak references
OC.TotalCacheSlots = 5
OC.AliveObjsInCache = 0
OC.ExistsInGeneration('ID1') = -1
OC.ExistsInGeneration('ID2') = -1
OC.ExistsInGeneration('ID3') = -1
OC.ExistsInGeneration('ID5') = -1
```

Discussion

Caching involves storing frequently used objects in memory that are expensive to create and recreate for fast access. This technique is in contrast to recreating these objects through some time-consuming mechanism (e.g., from data in a database or from a file on disk) every time they are needed. By storing frequently used objects such as these—so that we do not have to create them nearly as much—we can further improve the performance of the application.

When deciding which types of items can be cached, you should look for objects that take a long time to create and/or initialize. For example, if an object's creation involves one or more calls to a database, to a file on disk, or to a network resource, it can be considered as a candidate for caching. In addition to selecting objects with long creation times, these objects should also be frequently used by the application. Selection depends on a combination of the frequency of use and the average time for which it is used in any given usage. Objects that remain in use for a long time when they are retrieved from the cache may work better in this cache than those that are frequently used but for only a very short period of time.

If you know that the number of cached objects will be equal to or less than 10, you can substitute a ListDictionary for the Hashtable. The ListDictionary is optimized for 10 items or fewer. If you are unsure of whether to pick a ListDictionary or a Hashtable, consider using a HybridDictionary object instead. A HybridDictionary object uses a ListDictionary when the number of items it contains is 10 or fewer. When the number of contained items exceeds 10, a Hashtable object is used. The switch from a ListDictionary to a Hashtable involves copying the elements from the ListDictionary to the Hashtable. This can cause a performance problem if this type of collection will usually contain more than 10 items. In addition, if the initial size of a ListDictionary is set above 10, a Hashtable is used by the HybridDictionary exclusively, again reducing the effectiveness of the HybridDictionary.

If you do not want to overwrite cached items having the same key as the object you are attempting to insert into the cache, the AddObj method must be modified. The code for the AddObj method could be modified to this:

```
public void AddObj(object key, SomeComplexObj item)
{
    WeakReference WR = new WeakReference(item, false);
```

```
        if (!cache.ContainsKey(key))
        {
            cache.Add(key, WR);
        }
        else
        {
            throw (new Exception("Attempt to insert duplicate keys."));
        }
    }
```

We could also add a mechanism to calculate the cache-hit-ratio for this cache. The cache-hit-ratio is the ratio of hits—every time an existing object is requested from the Hashtable—to the total number of calls made to attempt a retrieval of an object. This can give us a good indication of how well our ObjCache is working. The code to add to this class to implement a cache-hit-ratio is shown highlighted here:

```
    private float numberOfGets = 0;
    private float numberOfHits = 0;

    public float HitMissRatioPcnt()
    {
        if (numberOfGets == 0)
        {
            return (0);
        }
        else
        {
            return ((numberOfHits / numberOfGets) * 100);
        }
    }

    public SomeComplexObj GetObj(object key)
    {
        ++numberOfGets;

        if (!cache.ContainsKey(key) || !IsObjAlive(key))
        {
            AddObj(key, new SomeComplexObj());
        }
        else
        {
            ++numberOfHits;
        }

        return ((SomeComplexObj)((WeakReference)cache[key]).Target);
    }
```

The numberOfGets field tracks the number of calls made to the GetObj retrieval method. The numberOfHits field tracks the number of times that an object to be retrieved exists in the cache. The HitMissRatioPcnt method returns the numberOfHits divided by the numberOfGets as a percentage. The higher the percent, the better our cache is operating (100% is equal to a hit every time the GetObj method is called). A lower percentage indicates that this cache object is not working efficiently (0% is equal to a miss every time the GetObj method is called). A very low percentage indicates that the cache object may not be the correct solution to your problem or that you are not caching the correct object(s).

The WeakReference objects created for the ObjCache class do not track objects after they are finalized. This would add much more complexity than is needed by this class. Moreover, we would have the responsibility of dealing with resurrected objects that are in an undefined state. This is a dangerous path to follow.

Remember, a caching scheme adds complexity to your application. The most a caching scheme can do for your application is to enhance performance and possibly place less stress on memory resources. You should consider this when deciding whether to implement a caching scheme such as the one in this recipe.

See Also

To use the built-in ASP.NET cache object independently of a web application, see the following topics in MSDN:

- "Caching Application Data"
- "Adding Items to the Cache"
- "Retrieving Values of Cached Items"
- "Deleting Items from the Cache"
- "Notifying an Application when an Item Is Deleted from the Cache"
- "System.Web.Caching Namespace"

In addition, see the Datacache2 Sample under ".NET Samples—ASP.NET Caching" in MSDN; see the sample links to the Page Data Caching example in the ASP.NET QuickStart Tutorials.

Also see the "WeakReference Class" topic in the MSDN documentation.

3.32   The Single Instance Object

Problem

You have a data type that will be used by several clients. This data type will create and hold a reference to another object that takes a long time to create; this could be a database connection or an object that is made up of many internal objects, which also must be created along with their containing object. Rather than allow this data type to be instantiated many times by many different clients, you would rather have a single object that is instantiated only one time and used by everyone.

Solution

The following two code examples illustrate the two *singleton design patterns*. The first design always returns the same instance of the OnlyOne class through its GetInstance method:

```
public sealed class OnlyOne
{
    private OnlyOne() {}

    private static OnlyOne theOneObject = null;

    public static OnlyOne GetInstance()
    {
        lock (typeof(OnlyOne))
        {
            if (theOneObject == null)
            {
                OnlyOne.theOneObject = new OnlyOne();
            }

            return (OnlyOne.theOneObject);
        }
    }

    public void Method1() {}
    public void Method2() {}
}
```

The second design uses only static members to implement the singleton design pattern:

```
public sealed class OnlyStaticOne
{
    private OnlyStaticOne() {}

    // Use a static constructor to initialize the singleton
    static OnlyStaticOne() {}

    public static void Method1() {}
    public static void Method2() {}
}
```

Discussion

The *singleton design pattern* allows one and only one instance of a class to exist in memory at any one time. Singleton classes are useful when you need a single way of accessing a resource such as a database connection or a file on a network. Many times, manager objects are created as singletons. For example, an object pool manager most likely would be a singleton; this allows a single access point to the pool for the entire application. Several examples of the singleton class can be found in the FCL, such as the System.Diagnostics.Trace, System.Diagnostics.Debug, and System.IO.Path classes, to name a few.

The OnlyOne class implements the singleton pattern by using a static field of the same type as its containing class—the OnlyOne type, in this case—and a common access point called GetInstance. The GetInstance method is called by the client code to obtain the one and only instance of the OnlyOne class. If there are no instantiated OnlyOne classes, a new one is created and returned. Once the OnlyOne object is created for the first time by the GetInstance method, a reference to it is placed in the theOneObject static field. This field contains a reference to the only OnlyOne object running in the application. Note that because static fields do not cross application domain boundaries, a single instance of the OnlyOne object is created for each application domain in a process. On successive calls to GetInstance, the OnlyOne object referenced by theOneObject field is returned. All access to the OnlyOne object is performed on the object returned by the GetInstance method.

The default constructor for this class has its accessibility made private to prevent code from accidentally creating an instance of this class. Setting the default constructor to private and disallowing any nonprivate constructors in this class is critical to a good singleton pattern. If code were to accidentally create a second or third class of this type, your application code would then have more than one access point to a resource, or you might have more than one manager type object managing a set of objects. When setting the default constructor to private, or if there is no default constructor in your class, you should mark the class with the sealed keyword. This keyword prevents any class from inheriting from this class. If a class were to inherit from this class, and if this new class did not provide an explicit constructor, a default constructor would be provided by the compiler. This default constructor is written to automatically call the base class's default constructor. If the base class's default constructor is private, it is inaccessible to its subclasses. The compiler will catch this type of error, but it makes the code more readable and maintainable if the sealed keyword is used to mark a singleton class.

The OnlyStaticOne class implements the singleton pattern in a much different way. This class makes exclusive use of static members to allow only one access point to this class's members (the use of the word "instance" would be misleading here— static members do not operate on an actual instance of an object, but rather on the type itself). Similar to the previous singleton pattern example, this class is also marked as sealed, and it has a private default constructor.

There are advantages and disadvantages to using each of these implementations of the singleton design pattern. The advantages of using the OnlyOne style are:

- Converting the class into a nonsingleton class can be done easily. To do this, eliminate the sealed keyword on the class, make the constructor public, and remove the GetInstance method and the theOneObject field.
- Modifying this pattern to allow a fixed number of instances of this type of object to be instantiated is fairly easy to do. The code to do this is shown here:

```
public sealed class OnlyThree
{
```

```
        private OnlyThree()
        {
            count++;
        }

        private static OnlyThree[] anObject = new OnlyThree[3];
        private static int count = 0;
        private static int lastObjReturned = 0;
        private const int maxInstances = 3;

        public static OnlyThree GetInstance()
        {
            if (count < maxInstances)
            {
                OnlyThree.anObject[count] = new OnlyThree();
                lastObjReturned = count;
            }
            else
            {
                if (lastObjReturned == 1)
                {
                    lastObjReturned = maxInstances;
                }
                else
                {
                    lastObjReturned--;
                }
            }

            return (OnlyThree.anObject[lastObjReturned -1]);
        }

        public void Method1() {}
        public void Method2() {}
    }
```

- Subclassing and overriding/hiding members of this class are possible. Note that you must remove the sealed keyword first.

The disadvantages to this style are:

- The code is a bit more complex than simply using all static members.

- You must always obtain an object reference to the one instance of this class through the GetInstance method.

- If coded incorrectly, this type of singleton could allow more than one of these objects to be created. For instance, this could happen if the default constructor's accessibility was not set to private and you forgot to write the constructor in this class.

The advantages to using the OnlyStaticOne style of the singleton class are:

- It is easy to read and therefore easy to maintain.

- It is easy to write.

- It is easy to use since there is no `GetInstance` method to call.
- Making the default constructor (or any other constructor) nonprivate would have little impact on the use of this class, since instantiating a class with no instance members other than an instance constructor is of little use.

The disadvantages to this style are:

- This style may be more difficult to convert to a regular nonsingleton class if future requirements demand it.
- A single instance of the `OnlyOne` object is created for each application domain in a process. If your process will be hosting more than one application domain, you should consider using the first style of singleton class.
- Subclassing this class requires more work than the previous singleton style.

See Also

See the "sealed" keyword and "lock Statement" topic in the MSDN documentation.

3.33 Choosing a Serializer

Problem

The FCL contains several classes to allow objects to be serialized into different formats. Choosing the correct format for your task and remembering how to use that format can become a chore, especially when there is a mixture of different formats and all of them are on disk. You need some way of simplifying the serialization interfaces to make serialization easy without worrying about the underlying differences in the serialization classes. This will also allow other developers on your team to become proficient with the use of the various serializers more quickly.

Solution

Use the *façade design pattern* to create the following `Serializer` class:

```
using System;
using System.Collections;
using System.IO;
using System.Runtime.Serialization.Formatters.Binary;
using System.Xml.Serialization;
using System.Runtime.Serialization.Formatters.Soap;

// Note that you must also add a reference to the following assembly:
//   System.Runtime.Serialization.Formatters.Soap.dll

[Serializable]
public class Serializer
{
    public Serializer() {}
```

```csharp
    protected Hashtable serializationMap = new Hashtable();
    protected Hashtable serializationTypeOfMap = new Hashtable();

    // Serialize an object
    public void SerializeObj(object obj, string destination)
    {
        SerializeObj(obj, destination, SerializationAction.Default);
    }

    public void SerializeObj(
      object obj, string destination, SerializationAction action)
    {
        if (action == SerializationAction.RetainAssemblyInfo    ||
            action == SerializationAction.RetainPrivateMembers  ||
            action == SerializationAction.SmallestFootprint     ||
            action == SerializationAction.Default)
        {
            BinarySerializeObj(obj, destination);
            serializationMap.Add(destination.ToUpper(), DeserializationType.Binary);
        }
        else if (action == SerializationAction.MakePortable ||
                 action == SerializationAction.AsSOAPMsg)
        {
            SoapSerializeObj(obj, destination);
            serializationMap.Add(destination.ToUpper(), DeserializationType.SOAP);
        }
        else  if (action == SerializationAction.AsXML ||
                  action == SerializationAction.SendToXMLWebService)
        {
            XmlSerializeObj(obj, destination);
            serializationMap.Add(destination.ToUpper(), DeserializationType.XML);
            serializationTypeOfMap.Add(destination.ToUpper(),
              obj.GetType().FullName);
        }
    }

    private void BinarySerializeObj(object obj, string destination)
    {
        BinaryFormatter binFormatter = new BinaryFormatter();
        Stream fileStream = new FileStream(destination, FileMode.Create,
          FileAccess.Write, FileShare.None);
        binFormatter.Serialize(fileStream, obj);
        fileStream.Close();
    }

    private void SoapSerializeObj(object obj, string destination)
    {
        SoapFormatter SOAPFormatter = new SoapFormatter();
        Stream fileStream = new FileStream(destination, FileMode.Create,
          FileAccess.Write, FileShare.None);
        SOAPFormatter.Serialize(fileStream, obj);
        fileStream.Close();
    }
}
```

```csharp
private void XmlSerializeObj(object obj, string destination)
{
    XmlSerializer XMLFormatter = new XmlSerializer(obj.GetType( ));
    Stream fileStream = new FileStream(destination, FileMode.Create,
        FileAccess.Write, FileShare.None);
    XMLFormatter.Serialize(fileStream, obj);
    fileStream.Close( );
}

// DeSerialize an object
public object DeSerializeObj(string source)
{
    return (DeSerializeObj(source,
        (DeserializationType)serializationMap[source.ToUpper( )]));
}

public object DeSerializeObj(string source, DeserializationType type)
{
    object retObj = null;

    if (type == DeserializationType.Binary)
    {
        retObj = BinaryDeSerializeObj(source);
        serializationMap.Remove(source.ToUpper( ));
    }
    else if (type == DeserializationType.SOAP)
    {
        retObj = SoapDeSerializeObj(source);
        serializationMap.Remove(source.ToUpper( ));
    }
    else if (type == DeserializationType.XML)
    {
        retObj = XmlDeSerializeObj(source);
        serializationMap.Remove(source.ToUpper( ));
        serializationTypeOfMap.Remove(source.ToUpper( ));
    }

    return (retObj);
}

private object BinaryDeSerializeObj(string source)
{
    BinaryFormatter binFormatter = new BinaryFormatter( );
    Stream fileStream = new FileStream(source, FileMode.Open, FileAccess.Read,
                                    FileShare.None);
    object DeserializedObj = binFormatter.Deserialize(fileStream);
    fileStream.Close( );

    return (DeserializedObj);
}

private object SoapDeSerializeObj(string source)
{
    SoapFormatter SOAPFormatter = new SoapFormatter( );
```

```
        Stream fileStream = new FileStream(source, FileMode.Open, FileAccess.Read,
                                           FileShare.None);
        object DeserializedObj = SOAPFormatter.Deserialize(fileStream);
        fileStream.Close();

        return (DeserializedObj);
    }

    private object XmlDeSerializeObj(string source)
    {
        XmlSerializer XMLFormatter = new
            XmlSerializer(Type.GetType((string)serializationTypeOfMap
                                 [source.ToUpper()]));
        Stream fileStream = new FileStream(source, FileMode.Open,
            FileAccess.Read, FileShare.None);
        object DeserializedObj = XMLFormatter.Deserialize(fileStream);
        fileStream.Close();

        return (DeserializedObj);
    }
}

public enum SerializationAction
{
    Default = 0,
    RetainAssemblyInfo,
    RetainPrivateMembers,
    MakePortable,
    SmallestFootprint,
    SendToXMLWebService,
    AsSOAPMsg,
    AsXML
}

public enum DeserializationType
{
    Binary = 0,
    SOAP,
    XML
}
```

Discussion

The *façade design pattern* uses a façade class to provide a simple interface to a group of underlying objects that do similar work. Any client that wants to use one of the underlying objects can go through the façade object. In effect, the façade pattern abstracts away the complexities and disparities between the underlying classes. This allows a uniform, and much easier to use, interface to be presented to the clients that wish to use any of these underlying objects.

The façade object can decide which underlying object will be used to perform the action requested, but it is not required to do so. The user could even pass in one or more arguments allowing the façade object to determine which underlying object to use. The nice thing about this pattern is that if the client decides that they need more flexibility than is provided by the façade object, they can choose to use the underlying objects and contend with their individual complexities. Also, if other serialization classes are created, they can easily be added to the façade object without breaking the existing code.

The class that acts as the façade in this recipe is the `Serializer` class. This class abstracts away the various interfaces to the various serializers that ship with the FCL, namely:

```
System.Runtime.Serialization.Formatters.Binary.BinaryFormatter
System.Xml.Serialization.XmlSerializer
System.Runtime.Serialization.Formatters.Soap.SoapFormatter
```

In addition, this class provides an enumeration called `SerializationAction`, which can be passed to the `SerializeObj` method for the `Serializer` to choose the best type of serialization object to use to serialize the input data. The various values of the `SerializationAction` enumeration and their meanings are:

Default
> Uses the default serialization object, which is `BinaryFormatter`.

RetainAssemblyInfo
> Uses the `BinaryFormatter`. This value is used when the assembly information needs to be retained by the serialization process.

RetainPrivateMembers
> Uses the `BinaryFormatter`. This value is used when private members need to be added to the serialization stream.

SmallestFootprint
> Uses the `BinaryFormatter`. This value is used when the client wants the serialization data in the most compact form possible. As an added benefit, this serialization method is also the fastest.

MakePortable
> Uses the `SoapFormatter`. This value is used when the serialization data needs to be in the most portable form (i.e., SOAP).

AsSOAPMsg
> Uses the `SoapFormatter`. This value tells the façade object to explicitly use the `SoapFormatter`.

SendToXMLWebService
> Uses the `XmlSerializer`. This value is used when the serialized object will be sent to an ASP.NET XML web service.

AsXML
> Uses the `XmlSerializer`. This value tells the façade object to explicitly use the `XmlSerializer`.

The interface to the Serializer object contains two sets of overloaded methods: SerializeObj and DeSerializeObj. Both SerializeObj methods accept an object to be serialized in the *obj* parameter and a location to store the serialized object in the *destination* parameter. The second SerializeObj method also has a parameter that accepts a SerializationAction enumeration, which was previously discussed. The first SerializeObj method does not have this parameter and so defaults to using the SerializationAction.Default enumeration value.

 You need to have permissions to open a FileStream directly from your code in order to use this recipe. This recipe cannot be used in a partial-trust environment where you are obliged to get your FileStreams either from IsolatedStorage or from a FileDialog.

Both DeSerializeObj methods accept a source string indicating where the serialized object is located. The second overloaded DeSerializeObj method also accepts a DeserializationType enumeration. This enumeration contains three values—Binary, SOAP, and XML—and is used to explicitly inform the underlying Deserialize methods of which serialization objects to use. If the first DeSerializeObj method is called, the values cached in the SerializeObj methods are used to deserialize the object without the client having to remember various small details about the serialization process used to initially serialize the object. If the SerializeObj methods are not used to serialize the object, one of the various DeserializationType enumeration values can be explicitly passed as an argument to inform the DeSerializeObj method which underlying deserialization method to call.

The serializationMap and serializationTypeOfMap Hashtables are used to cache various pieces of information during the serialization process. The SerializeObj methods use the serializationMap Hashtable to map the destination of the serialized object to the type of serialization process used. This allows the DeSerializeObj methods to use the source parameter to locate the pertinent information in the serializationMap Hashtable. The serializationTypeOfMap is used only when the XmlSerializer object is used for serialization. Upon deserialization, the XmlSerializer uses the serializationTypeOfMap to locate the full type name that is to be deserialized.

The following code serializes an integer array to the file TestBinSerXML.txt and then deserializes it into the retArray variable:

```
Serializer s = new Serializer();
s.SerializeObj(new int[10] {1,2,3,4,5,6,7,8,9,10}, @"C:\TestBinSerXML.txt",
            SerializationAction.AsXML);
int[] retArray = (int[])s.DeSerializeObj(@"c:\TestBinSerXML.txt");
```

See Also

See the "Serializing Objects," "Introducing XML Serialization," and "Serialization Guidelines" topics in the MSDN documentation.

3.34 Creating Custom Enumerators

Problem

You need to add foreach support to a class, but the normal way of adding an IEnumerator class is not flexible enough. Instead of simply iterating from the first element to the last, you also need to iterate from the last to the first, and you need to be able to step over, or skip, a predefined number of elements on each iteration. All of these types of iterators should be available to your class.

Solution

The following interfaces allow polymorphic use of the foreach method:

```
using System.Collections;

public interface IRevEnumerator
{
    IEnumerator GetEnumerator( );
}

public interface IStepEnumerator
{
    IEnumerator GetEnumerator( );
}
```

The following class acts as a container for a private ArrayList called InternalList and is used in the foreach loop to iterate through the private InternalList:

```
public class Container : IEnumerable, IRevEnumerator, IStepEnumerator
{
    public Container( )
    {
        // Add dummy data to this class
        internalList.Add(-1);
        internalList.Add(1);
        internalList.Add(2);
        internalList.Add(3);
        internalList.Add(4);
        internalList.Add(5);
        internalList.Add(6);
        internalList.Add(7);
        internalList.Add(8);
        internalList.Add(9);
        internalList.Add(10);
        internalList.Add(200);
        internalList.Add(500);
    }

    private ArrayList internalList = new ArrayList( );
    private int step = 1;
```

```csharp
IEnumerator IEnumerable.GetEnumerator()
{
    return (new ContainerIterator(this));
}

IEnumerator IRevEnumerator.GetEnumerator()
{
    return (new RevContainerIterator(this));
}

IEnumerator IStepEnumerator.GetEnumerator()
{
    return (new StepContainerIterator(this, step));
}

public int ForeachStep
{
    get {return (step);}
    set {step = value;}
}

public ArrayList List
{
    get {return (internalList);}
    set {internalList = value;}
}

// Nested classes
// This class iterates from the first element to the last element
// in the internalList
public class ContainerIterator : IEnumerator
{
    public ContainerIterator(Container c)
    {
        this.c = c;
        Reset();
    }

    private int index = -1;
    private Container c = null;

    public void Reset()
    {
        index = -1;
    }

    public object Current
    {
        get {return (c.internalList[index]);}
    }

    public bool MoveNext()
    {
        ++index;
```

```csharp
            if (index < c.internalList.Count)
            {
                return (true);
            }
            else
            {
                return (false);
            }
        }
    }

    // This class iterates from the last element to the first element
    // in the internalList
    public class RevContainerIterator : IEnumerator
    {
        public RevContainerIterator(Container c)
        {
            this.c = c;
            Reset();
        }

        private int index = -1;
        private Container C = null;

        public void Reset()
        {
            index = c.internalList.Count;
        }

        public object Current
        {
            get {return (c.internalList[index]);}
        }

        public bool MoveNext()
        {
            --index;

            if (index >= 0)
            {
                return (true);
            }
            else
            {
                return (false);
            }
        }
    }

    // This class iterates from the first element to the last element
    // int the internalList and skips a predefined number of elements
    // in the internalList on each iteration
    public class StepContainerIterator : IEnumerator
    {
```

```
                public StepContainerIterator(Container c, int step)
                {
                    this.c = c;
                    this.step = step;
                    Reset();
                }

                private int index = -1;
                private int step = 1;
                private Container c = null;

                public void Reset()
                {
                    index = -1;
                }

                public object Current
                {
                    get {return (c.internalList[index]);}
                }

                public bool MoveNext()
                {
                    if (index == -1)
                    {
                        ++index;
                    }
                    else
                    {
                        index += step;
                    }

                    if (index < c.internalList.Count)
                    {
                        return (true);
                    }
                    else
                    {
                        return (false);
                    }
                }
            }
        }
```

Discussion

The *iterator design pattern* provides an easy method of moving from item to item contained within an object. This object could be an array, a collection, or some other similar type of container. This technique is similar to using a for loop to iterate over each item contained in an array. The difference is that, with the iterator design pattern, you do not need advance knowledge about how the elements are stored in the container or where the elements are located in the container. In contrast, when using

---

a `for` loop, you need to know what elements are stored in the container. And you need some type of direct or indirect access, via a method or indexer, to the contained list of elements. This is not so with the `foreach` loop.

The FCL provides two special interfaces, `IEnumerable` and `IEnumerator`, that allow us to easily implement this design pattern. The `IEnumerable` interface defines a single method:

```
IEnumerator GetEnumerator()
```

This method accepts no parameters and returns an `IEnumerator` interface object. The `IEnumerator` type that is returned is another interface that has the following property and two methods:

```
object Current {get;}
bool MoveNext()
void Reset()
```

The `Current` method returns the current element being accessed. The `MoveNext` method moves to the next element. If this method successfully moves to the next element, it returns true. If there are no more elements in the list, it returns `false` as an indication to stop the iteration. The `Reset` method resets the current element pointer to the position immediately before the first element in the list.

Implementing these two interfaces allows us to use a familiar looping mechanism: the `foreach` loop. With the `foreach` loop, you do not have to worry about moving the current element pointer to the beginning of the list or even about incrementing this pointer as you move through the list. In addition, you do not have to watch for the end of the list, preventing you from going beyond the bounds of the list. The best part about the `foreach` loop and the iterator pattern is that you do not have to know how to access the list of elements within its container—indeed, you do not even have to have access to the list of elements; the `IEnumerator` and `IEnumerable` interfaces implemented on the container do this for you.

The `Container` class contains a private `ArrayList` of items called `internalList`. The `GetEnumerator` method on this class is implemented to return a class called `ContainerIterator`, which is nested within the `Container` class. This `ContainerIterator` class implements the `IEnumerator` interface and contains all of the intelligence to control how the `foreach` loop operates and what data it operates on.

The `ContainerIterator` class uses a private variable, `index`, as the pointer to the current element in the `Container.internalList` `ArrayList`. Remember that this `ArrayList` is private and cannot be seen by the client code. A second private variable, `c`, holds a pointer to the outer class `Container`. A nested class is used because it can see all private members of the outer class; therefore, it is not a problem to access the `internalList` from the nested `ContainerIterator` class.

The `ContainerIterator` class is designed to move from the first element in the `ArrayList` to the last. The `foreach` loop may not change this. However, we may add code to the `ContainerIterator` class to move across the elements in the `ArrayList` in different manners. For example, if we always wanted to iterate the `ArrayList` in ascending order, we could modify the `ContainerIterator` class constructor by calling the `ArrayList.Sort` method, as follows:

```
public ContainerIterator(Container c)
{
    this.c = c;
    Reset();
    c.internalList.Sort();
}
```

The `ContainerIterator` may also be modified to start at the last element in the `ArrayList` and work its way to the first element. The `RevContainerIterator` class demonstrates this. A third class called `StepContainerIterator` demonstrates a way to step over a specified number of elements in the `ArrayList`. This is similar to the following VB.NET and C# code:

```
' VB.NET Code
For i = 0 to 100 Step 2
...
Next
```

```
// C# Code
for (int i = 0; i <= 100; i += 2) {...}
```

In both of these loops, every other element in the list is skipped. The `StepContainerIterator` allows this by accepting an integer value in its constructor that determines how many items will be skipped. This is the *step* parameter in this constructor.

There is also a way to choose which `IEnumerator` interface to use with a `foreach` loop. Since the `GetEnumerator` method returns only an `IEnumerator` interface instead of a concrete object, we can nest all three of these `IEnumerator` type classes within our `Container` class and tell the `foreach` loop which iterator it will use.

To enable this, our `Container` class needs to implement three distinct interfaces, `IEnumerator`, `IRevEnumerator`, and `IStepEnumerator`. The `IEnumerator` interface is defined by the FCL. Notice that all three interfaces define the same `GetEnumerator` method. The `Container` class implements the methods on these three interfaces as explicit interface methods. This allows us to choose which `GetInterface` method to use by casting the `Container` class to one of these three interface types.

To use the `ContainerIterator`, we do not have to do anything to the `foreach` loop; this is the default `IEnumerator` type that is returned by `GetEnumerator`. The code for this is as follows:

```
Container cntnr = new Container();
foreach (int i in cntnr)
{
    Console.WriteLine(i);
}
```

If we do not know that cntnr contains an ArrayList of integers, we could write the following to iterate over each element:

```
foreach (object i in cntnr)
{
    Console.WriteLine(i.ToString( ));
}
```

To use RevContainerIterator, we cast the cntnr object to the interface that has the GetEnumerator method to return a RevContainerIterator. This code is written as follows:

```
Container cntnr = new Container( );
foreach (int i in ((IRevEnumerator)cntnr))
{
    Console.WriteLine(i);
}
```

Again, to use the StepContainerIterator, we cast the cntnr object to the correct interface, IStepEnumerator. This code is written as follows:

```
Container cntnr = new Container( );
cntnr.ForeachStep = 2;
foreach (int i in ((IStepEnumerator)cntnr))
{
    Console.WriteLine(i);
}
```

Notice the extra step with this interface: the ForeachStep property in the Container object needs to be set to an integer value. This value then is passed to the StepContainerIterator constructor to be used in skipping over that number of elements in the list.

See Also

See the "IEnumerator Interface," "Using foreach with Collections," and "Collection Classes Tutorial" topics in the MSDN documentation.

3.35   Rolling Back Object Changes

Problem

You have an object that allows its state to be changed. However, you do not want these changes to become permanent if other changes to the system cannot be made at the same time. In other words, you want to be able to roll back the changes if any of a group of related changes fails.

Solution

Use the *memento design pattern* to allow your object to save its original state in order
to roll back changes. The SomeDataOriginator class defined for this recipe contains
data that must be changed only if other system changes occur. Its source code is:

```
using System;
using System.Collections;

public class SomeDataOriginator
{
    public SomeDataOriginator() {}

    public SomeDataOriginator(int state, string id, string clsName)
    {
        this.state = state;
        this.id = id;
        this.clsName = clsName;
    }

    private int state = 1;
    private string id = "ID1001";
    private string clsName = "SomeDataOriginator";

    public string ClassName
    {
        get {return (clsName);}
        set {clsName = value;}
    }

    public string ID
    {
        get {return (id);}
        set {id = value;}
    }

    public void ChangeState(int newState)
    {
        state = newState;
    }

    public void Display()
    {
        Console.WriteLine("State: " + state);
        Console.WriteLine("Id: " + id);
        Console.WriteLine("clsName: " + clsName);
    }

    // Nested Memento class used to save outer class's
       state internal class Memento
    {
```

```
        internal Memento(SomeDataOriginator data)
        {
            this.state = data.State;
            this.id = data.id;
            this.clsName = data.clsName;
            originator = data;
        }

        private SomeDataOriginator originator = null;
        private int state = 1;
        private string id = "ID1001";
        private string clsName = "SomeDataOriginator";

        internal void Rollback()
        {
            originator.clsName = this.clsName;
            originator.id = this.id;
            originator.state = this.state;
        }
    }
}
```

The MementoCareTaker is the caretaker object, which saves a single state that the originator object can roll back to. Its source code is:

```
public class MementoCareTaker
{
    private SomeDataOriginator.Memento savedState = null;

    internal SomeDataOriginator.Memento Memento
    {
        get {return (savedState);}
        set {savedState = value;}
    }
}
```

MultiMementoCareTaker is another caretaker object that can save multiple states to which the originator object can roll back. Its source code is:

```
public class MultiMementoCareTaker
{
    private ArrayList savedState = new ArrayList();

    internal SomeDataOriginator.Memento this[int index]
    {
        get {return ((SomeDataOriginator.Memento)savedState[index]);}
        set {savedState[index] = (SomeDataOriginator.Memento)value;}
    }

    internal void Add(SomeDataOriginator.Memento memento)
    {
        SavedState.Add(memento);
    }
```

```
        internal int Count
        {
            get {return (savedState.Count);}
        }
    }
}
```

Discussion

The *memento design pattern* allows object state to be saved so that it can be restored in response to a specific situation. The memento pattern is very useful for implementing undo/redo or commit/rollback actions. This pattern usually has an *originator object*—a new or existing object that needs to have an undo/redo or commit/rollback style behavior associated with it. This originator object's state—the values of its fields—will be mirrored in a *memento object*, which is an object that can store the state of an originator object. Another object that usually exists in this type of pattern is the *caretaker object*. The caretaker is responsible for saving one or more memento objects, which can then be used later to restore the state of an originator object. This recipe makes use of two caretaker objects. The first, MementoCareTaker, saves a single object state that can later be used to roll an object back. The second, MultiMementoCareTaker, uses an ArrayList object to save multiple object states, thereby allowing many levels of rollbacks to occur. You can also think of MultiMementoCareTaker as storing multiple levels of undo/redo state.

The originator class, SomeDataOriginator, has the state, id, and clsName fields to store information. The originator class has a nested Memento class that needs to access the fields of the originator directly.

One thing we have to add to the class, that will not affect how it behaves or how it is used, is a nested Memento class. This nested class is used to store the state of its outer class. We use a nested class so that it can access the private fields of the outer class. This allows the Memento object to get copies of all the needed fields of the originator object without having to add special logic to the originator to allow it to give this field information to the Memento object.

The Memento class contains only private fields that mirror the fields in the outer object that you want to store. Note that you do not have to store all fields of an outer type, just the ones that you want to roll back or undo. The Memento object also contains a constructor that accepts a SomeDataOriginator object. The constructor saves the pointer to this object as well as its current state. There is also a single method called Rollback. The Rollback method is central to restoring the state of the current SomeDataOriginator object. This method uses the originator pointer to this object to set the SomeDataOriginator object's fields back to the values contained in this instance of the Memento object.

The caretaker objects store any Memento objects created by the application. The application can then specify which Memento objects to use to roll back an object's state. Remember that each Memento object knows which originator object to roll back.

Therefore, you need to tell the caretaker object only to use a Memento object to roll back an object, and the Memento object takes care of the rest.

There is a potential problem with the caretaker objects that is easily remedied. The problem is that the caretaker objects are not supposed to know anything about the Memento objects. The caretaker objects in this recipe see only one method, the Rollback method, that is specific to the Memento objects. So, for this recipe, this is not really a problem. However, if you decide to add more logic to the Memento class, you need a way to shield it from the caretaker. You do not want another developer to add code to the caretaker objects that may allow it to change the internal state of any Memento objects they contain.

To the caretaker objects, each Memento object should simply be an object that contains the Rollback method. To make the Memento objects appear this way to the caretaker objects, we can place an interface on the Memento class. This interface is defined as follows:

```
public interface IMemento
{
    void Rollback();
}
```

The Memento class is then modified as follows (changes are highlighted):

```
internal class Memento : IMemento
{
    public void Rollback()
    {
        originator.clsName = this.clsName;
        originator.id = this.id;
        originator.state = this.state;
    }

    // The rest of this class does not change
}
```

The caretaker classes are modified as follows (changes are highlighted):

```
internal class MementoCareTaker
{
    private IMemento savedState = null;

    internal IMemento Memento
    {
        get {return (savedState);}
        set {savedState = value;}
    }
}

internal class MultiMementoCareTaker
{
    private ArrayList savedState = new ArrayList();
```

```
    internal IMemento this[int index]
    {
        get {return ((SomeDataOriginator.Memento)savedState[index]);}
        set {savedState[index] = (SomeDataOriginator.Memento)value;}
    }

    internal void Add(IMemento memento)
    {
        savedState.Add(memento);
    }

    internal int Count
    {
        get {return (savedState.Count);}
    }
}
```

Implementing the IMemento interface serves two purposes. First, it prevents the care-taker classes from knowing anything about the internals of the Memento objects they contain. Second, it allows the caretaker objects to handle any type of Memento object, so long as it implements the IMemento interface.

The following code shows how the SomeDataOriginator, Memento, and caretaker objects are used. It uses the MementoCareTaker object to store a single state of the SomeDataOriginator object and then rolls the changes back after the SomeDataOriginator object is modified:

```
// Create an originator and default its internal state
SomeDataOriginator data = new SomeDataOriginator();
Console.WriteLine("ORIGINAL");
data.Display();

// Create a caretaker object
MementoCareTaker objState = new MementoCareTaker();

// Add a memento of the original originator object to the caretaker
objState.Memento = new SomeDataOriginator.Memento(data);

// Change the originator's internal state
data.ChangeState(67);
data.ID = "foo";
data.ClassName = "bar";
Console.WriteLine("NEW");
data.Display();

// Rollback the changes of the originator to its original state
objState.Memento.Rollback();
Console.WriteLine("ROLLEDBACK");
data.Display();
```

The use of the MultiMementoCareTaker object is very similar to the MementoCareTaker object, as the following code shows:

```
SomeDataOriginator data = new SomeDataOriginator( );
Console.WriteLine("ORIGINAL");
data.Display( );

MultiMementoCareTaker multiObjState = new MultiMementoCareTaker( );
multiObjState.Add(new SomeDataOriginator.Memento(data));

data.ChangeState(67);
data.ID = "foo";
data.ClassName = "bar";
Console.WriteLine("NEW");
data.Display( );
multiObjState.Add(new SomeDataOriginator.Memento(data));

data.ChangeState(671);
data.ID = "foo1";
data.ClassName = "bar1";
Console.WriteLine("NEW1");
data.Display( );
multiObjState.Add(new SomeDataOriginator.Memento(data));

data.ChangeState(672);
data.ID = "foo2";
data.ClassName = "bar2";
Console.WriteLine("NEW2");
data.Display( );
multiObjState.Add(new SomeDataOriginator.Memento(data));

data.ChangeState(673);
data.ID = "foo3";
data.ClassName = "bar3";
Console.WriteLine("NEW3");
data.Display( );

for (int Index = (multiObjState.Count - 1); Index >= 0; Index--)
{
    Console.WriteLine("\r\nROLLBACK(" + Index + ")");
    multiObjState[Index].Rollback( );
    data.Display( );
}
```

This code creates a SomeDataOriginator object and changes its state several times. At every state change, a new Memento object is created to save the SomeDataOriginator object's state at that point in time. At the end of this code, a for loop iterates over each Memento object stored in the MultiMementoCareTaker object, from the most recent to the earliest. On each iteration of this loop, the Memento object is used to restore the state of the SomeDataOriginator object.

3.36 Disposing of Unmanaged Resources

Problem

Your class references unmanaged resources such as some type of handle, or it manipulates a block of memory or a file via P/Invoke methods or your class uses a COM object that requires some cleanup method to be called before it is released. You need to make sure that the resources are released properly and in a timely manner. In a garbage-collected environment, such as that used by the Common Language Runtime (CLR), you cannot assume either will happen.

Solution

Implement the *dispose design pattern*, which is specific to .NET. The class that contains a reference to the unmanaged resources is shown here as Foo. This object contains references to a COM object called SomeCOMObj, a FileStream object called FStream, and an ArrayList that may or may not contain references to unmanaged resources. The source code is:

```
using System;
using System.Collections;
using System.IO;

[DllImport("Kernel32.dll", SetLastError = true)]
private static extern IntPtr CreateSemaphore(IntPtr lpSemaphoreAttributes,
        int lInitialCount, int lMaximumCount, string lpName);

[DllImport("Kernel32.dll", SetLastError = true)]
private static extern bool ReleaseSemaphore(IntPtr hSemaphore, int lReleaseCount,
        out IntPtr lpPreviousCount);

public class Foo : IDisposable
{
    public Foo() {}

    // Replace SomeCOMObj with your COM object type
    private SomeCOMObj comObj = new SomeCOMObj();
    private FileStream fileStream = new FileStream(@"c:\test.txt",
      FileMode.OpenOrCreate);
    private ArrayList aList = new ArrayList();
    private bool hasBeenDisposed = false;
    private IntPtr hSemaphore = IntPtr.Zero;   // Unmanaged handle

    // Protect these members from being used on a disposed object
    public void WriteToFile(string text)
    {
        if(hasBeenDisposed)
        {
            throw (new ObjectDisposedException(this.ToString(),
                                    "Object has been disposed"));
        }
```

```csharp
        UnicodeEncoding enc = new UnicodeEncoding();
        fileStream.Write(enc.GetBytes(text), 0, text.Length);
    }

    public void UseCOMObj()
    {
        if(hasBeenDisposed)
        {
            throw (new ObjectDisposedException(this.ToString(),
                                    "Object has been disposed"));
        }

        Console.WriteLine("GUID: " + comObj.GetType().GUID);
    }

    public void AddToList(object obj)
    {
        if(hasBeenDisposed)
        {
            throw (new ObjectDisposedException(this.ToString(),
                                    "Object has been disposed"));
        }

        aList.Add(obj);
    }

    public void CreateSemaphore()
    {
        // Create unmanaged handle here
        hSemaphore = CreateSemaphore(IntPtr.Zero, 5, 5, null);
    }

    // The Dispose methods
    public void Dispose()
    {
        Dispose(true);
    }

    protected virtual void Dispose(bool disposeManagedObjs)
    {
        if (!hasBeenDisposed)
        {
            if (disposeManagedObjs)
            {
                // Dispose all items in an array or ArrayList
                foreach (object obj in aList)
                {
                    IDisposable disposableObj = obj as IDisposable;
                    if (disposableObj != null)
                    {
                        disposableObj.Dispose();
                    }
                }
```

```
            // Dispose managed objects implementing IDisposable
            fileStream.Close();

            // Reduce reference count on RCW
            while (Marshal.ReleaseComObject(comObj) > 0);

            GC.SuppressFinalize(this);
        }
        // Release unmanaged handle here
        IntPtr prevCnt = new IntPtr();
        ReleaseSemaphore(hSemaphore, 1, out prevCnt);

        hasBeenDisposed = true;
    }
}

// The destructor
~Foo()
{
    Dispose(false);
}

// Optional Close method
public void Close()
{
    Dispose();
}
}
```

The following class inherits from Foo:

```
// Class inherits from an IDisposable class
public class Bar : Foo
{
    //...

    private bool hasBeenDisposed = false;

    protected override void Dispose(bool disposeManagedObjs)
    {
        if (!hasBeenDisposed)
        {
            try
            {
                if(disposeManagedObjs)
                {
                    // Call Dispose/Close/Clear on any managed objects here...
                }

                // Release any unmanaged objects here...
            }
            finally
            {
                // Call base class' Dispose method
                base.Dispose(disposeManagedObjs);
```

```
                hasBeenDisposed = true;
            }
        }
    }
}
```

Whether this class directly contains any references to unmanaged resources, it should be disposed of as shown in the code.

Discussion

The *dispose design pattern* allows any unmanaged resources held by an object to be cleaned up from within the managed environment. This pattern is flexible enough to allow unmanaged resources held by the disposable object to be cleaned up explicitly (by calling the Dispose method) or implicitly (by waiting for the garbage collector to call the destructor). Finalizers are a safety net to clean up objects when you forget to do it.

This design pattern should be used on any base class that has derived types that hold unmanaged resources. This indicates to the inheritor that this design pattern should be implemented in their derived class as well.

All the code that needs to be written for a disposable object is written within the class itself. First, all disposable types must implement the IDisposable interface. This interface contains a single method, Dispose, which accepts no parameters and returns void. The Dispose method is overloaded to accept a Boolean flag indicating whether any managed objects referenced by this object should also be disposed. If this parameter is true, managed objects referenced by this object will have their Dispose method called, and unmanaged resources are released; otherwise, only unmanaged resources are released.

The IDisposable.Dispose method will forward its call to the overloaded Dispose method that accepts a Boolean flag. This flag will be set to true to allow all managed objects to attempt to dispose of themselves as well as to release unmanaged resources held by this object.

The IDisposable interface is very important to implement. This interface allows the using statement to take advantage of the dispose pattern. A using statement that operates on the Foo object is written as follows:

```
using (Foo f = new Foo())
{
    f.WriteToFile("text");
}
```

Always implement the IDisposable interface on types that contain resources that need to be disposed or otherwise explicitly closed or released. This allows the use of the using keyword and aids in self-documenting the type.

A foreach loop will also make use of the IDisposable interface, but in a slightly different manner. After each iteration of this loop, the Dispose method is called via the enumerator type of the object being enumerated. The enumerator type is usually a nested class that implements IEnumerator, and, in this case, would also implement IDisposable. The foreach loop guarantees that it will call the Dispose method on the enumerator object to allow each individually enumerated object to be disposed of properly.

The overloaded Dispose method that accepts a Boolean flag contains a static method call to GC.SuppressFinalize to force the garbage collector to remove this object from the *fqueue*, or finalization queue. The fqueue allows the garbage collector to run C# destructors at a point after the object has been freed. However, this ability comes at a price: it takes many garbage collection cycles to completely collect an object with a destructor. If the object is placed on the fqueue in generation 0, the object will have to wait until generation 1 is collected, which could be some time, since it usually takes 10 generation 0 collections before generation 1 is collected. The GC.SuppressFinalize method prevents the need for the object to stay in memory for all of these garbage collection cycles. Calling this static method from within the Dispose method is critical to writing better performing classes.

Always call the GC.SuppressFinalize method in the base class Dispose method. Doing so will allow your object to be taken off of the finalization queue in the garbage collector allowing for earlier collection. This will help prevent memory retention and will help your application's performance.

A destructor is also added to this class. The destructor contains code to call the overloaded Dispose method, passing in false as its only argument. Note that all cleanup code should exist within the overloaded Dispose method that accepts a Boolean flag. All other methods should call this method to perform any necessary cleanup. The destructor will pass a false value into the Dispose method to prevent any managed objects from being disposed. Remember, the destructors run in their own thread. Attempting to dispose of objects that may have already been collected or are about to be collected could have serious consequences for your code, such as resurrecting an object into an undefined state. It is best to prevent any references to other objects while the destructor is running.

It is possible to add a Close or even a Clear method to your class to be called as well as the Dispose method. Several classes in the FCL use a Close or Clear method to clean up unmanaged resources:

```
FileStream.Close( )
StreamWriter.Close( )
TcpClient.Close( )
MessageQueue.Close( )
SymmetricAlgorithm.Clear( )
```

```
AsymmetricAlgorithm.Clear()
CryptoAPITransform.Clear()
CryptoStream.Clear()
```

Each of these classes also contains a Dispose method. The Clear method usually calls the Dispose method directly. There is a problem with this design. The Clear method is used extensively throughout the FCL for classes such as ArrayList, Hashtable, and other collection type classes. However, the Clear method of the collection classes performs a much different task; instead of calling the IDisposable.Dispose method, it clears the collection of all its items. This Clear method has nothing to do with releasing unmanaged resources or calling the Dispose method.

Another problem is the confusion with the Close, Clear, and Dispose methods of the CryptoStream class. The Close method simply flushes the pending data and attempts to close the underlying stream object. The Clear method forwards its call on to the Dispose method. The Dispose method cleans up this object, but does not close the underlying stream object. If you look at the base Stream class, it has an implementation of IDisposable, and it will close the stream when you dispose it. But CryptoStream replaces this implementation with its own that fails to close the stream, and which doesn't call back into the Stream base class's Dispose implementation. So it's entirely inconsistent. From this, we can conclude that to completely clean up a CryptoStream object, we must first call Close and then either call Clear or Dispose. When in doubt, always default to calling the Dispose method on an object.

 Consider not implementing a Close method unless it will be obvious to the user or inheritor of this class what it is for, or if you are deriving from a type such as Stream, which does not give you a choice, since the Stream class contains no implementation for this method. Never implement a Clear method that will be used to dispose your object. Instead, use the commonly recognized Dispose method. Otherwise, your code will not operate in a consistent manner with the disposable classes within the FCL.

This implementation does not follow the dispose design pattern. To follow this pattern, the Close method should simply forward its call on to the IDisposable.Dispose method. In addition, the Clear method is never mentioned in the dispose design pattern, so avoid using a Clear method for anything other than to remove elements from a collection type. As a note, this inappropriate usage of the Clear method is unique to the cryptography classes. All other classes in the FCL seem to use it correctly.

The overloaded Dispose method that accepts a Boolean flag will contain all of the logic to release unmanaged resources from this object as well as possibly calling Dispose on types referenced by this object. In addition to these two actions, this method can also reduce the reference count on any COM objects that are referenced by this object. The static Marshal.ReleaseComObject method will decrement the reference count by one on the COM object reference passed in to this method:

```
Marshal.ReleaseComObject(comObj);
```

To force the reference count to go to zero, allowing the COM object to be released and its Runtime Callable Wrapper (RCW) to be garbage collected, you could write the following code:

```
while (Marshal.ReleaseComObject(comObj) > 0);
```

Take great care when forcing the reference count to zero in this manner. If another object is using this COM object, the COM object will be released out from under this other object. This can easily destabilize a system. For more information on using this method, see Recipe 3.30.

Any callable method/property/indexer (basically, any nonprivate method except for the Dispose and Close methods and the constructor(s) and the destructor) should throw the ObjectDisposedException exception if it is called after the object has been disposed—that is, after its Dispose method has been called. A private field called hasBeenDisposed is used as a Boolean flag to indicate whether this object has been disposed; a true confirms that it has been disposed. This flag is checked to determine whether this object has been disposed at the beginning of every method/property/indexer. If it has been disposed, the ObjectDisposedException is thrown. This prevents the use of an object after it has been disposed and potentially placed in an unknown state.

Disposable objects should always check to see if they have been disposed in all of their public methods, properties, and indexers. If a client attempts to use your object after it has been disposed, an ObjectDisposedException should be thrown. Note that a Dispose method can be called multiple times after this object has been disposed without having any side effects (including the throwing of ObjectDisposedExceptions) on the object.

Any classes inheriting from Foo need not implement the IDisposable interface; it is implied from the base class. The inheriting class should implement the hasBeenDisposed Boolean flag field and use this flag in any methods/properties/indexers to confirm that this object has been disposed. Finally, a Dispose method is implemented that accepts a Boolean flag and overrides the same virtual method in the base class. This Dispose method does not have to call the GC.SuppressFinalize(this) static method; this is done in the base class's Dispose method.

The IDisposable.Dispose method should not be implemented in this class. When the Dispose method is called on an object of type Bar, the Foo.Dispose method will be called. The Foo.Dispose method will then call the overridden Bar.Dispose(bool) method, which, in turn, calls its base class Dispose(bool) method, Foo.Dispose(bool). The base class's destructor is also inherited by the Bar class.

All Dispose methods should call their base class's Dispose method.

If the client code fails to call the `Dispose` or `Close` method, the destructor will run and the `Dispose(bool)` method will still be called, albeit at a later time. The destructor is the object's last line of defense for releasing unmanaged resources.

See Also

See Recipes 3.29 and 3.30; see the "Dispose Interface," "Using foreach with Collections," and "Implementing Finalize and Dispose to Clean Up Unmanaged Resources" topics in the MSDN documentation.

3.37   Determining Where Boxing and Unboxing Occur

Problem

You have a project consisting of some very complex code that is a performance bottleneck for the entire application. You have been assigned to increase performance, but you do not know where to start looking.

Solution

A great way to start looking for performance problems is to use a profiling tool to see whether boxing is actually causing you any kind of problem in the first place. A profiler will show you exactly what allocations are occurring and in what volume. There are several profilers on the market; some are free and others are not.

If you have already established through profiling that boxing is definitely causing a problem but you are still having trouble working out where it's occurring, then you can use the Ildasm disassembler tool that is packaged with VS.NET. With Ildasm you can convert an entire project to its equivalent IL code and then dump the IL to a text file. To do this, Ildasm has several command-line switches, one of which is the `/output` switch. This switch is used as follows:

```
ildasm Proj1.dll /output:Proj1.il
```

This command will disassemble the file *Proj1.dll* and then write the disassembled IL to the file *Proj1.il*.

A second useful command-line switch is `/source`. This switch shows the original code (C#, VB.NET, etc.) in which this DLL was written, as well as the IL that was compiled from each of these source lines. Note that the DLL must be built with debugging enabled. This switch is used as follows:

```
ildasm Proj1.dll /output:Proj1.il /source
```

We prefer the second method of invoking Ildasm, since the original source is included, preventing you from getting lost in all of the IL code.

After running Ildasm from the command line, open the resulting IL code file into VS.NET or your favorite editor. Inside the editor, do a text search for the words box and unbox. This will find all occurrences of boxing and unboxing operations.

Using this information, you have pinpointed the problem areas. Now, you can turn your attention to them to see if there is any way to prevent or minimize the boxing/unboxing operations.

Discussion

When a boxing or unboxing operation occurs in code, whether it was implicit or explicit, the IL generated includes the box or unbox command. For example, the following C# code:

```
int valType = 1;
object boxedValType = valType;
valType = (int)boxedValType;
```

compiles to the following IL code:

```
//000883:          int valType = 1;
  IL_0000:  ldc.i4.1
  IL_0001:  stloc.0
//000884:          object boxedValType = valType;
  IL_0002:  ldloc.0
  IL_0003:  box         [mscorlib]System.Int32
  IL_0008:  stloc.1
//000898:          int valType = (int) boxedValType;
  IL_0061:  ldloc.1
  IL_0062:  unbox       [mscorlib]System.Int32
  IL_0067:  ldind.i4
```

Notice the box and unbox commands in the previous IL code. IL makes it very apparent when a boxing or unboxing operation occurs. We can use this to our advantage to find and hopefully prevent a boxing operation from occurring.

The following can help prevent or eliminate boxing:

1. Use classes instead of structures. This usually involves simply changing the struct keyword to class in the structure definition. This very simple and quick change can dramatically improve performance.

2. Do not implement explicit interface members on structures. As the discussion shows, this causes the structure to be boxed before the call to an interface member is made through the interface. This reflects the fact that explicit implementation of a method on an interface is only accessible from the interface type. This means that the structure must be cast to that interface type before the explicitly declared methods of that interface type can be used. An interface is a reference type and therefore causes the structure to be boxed when an explicit interface method is accessed on that structure.

Note that changes to a value type that exists in both boxed and unboxed form occur independently of one another.

See Also

See the "Boxing Conversion" and "Unboxing Conversion" topics in the MSDN documentation.

Below is a list of some available profiling tools:

- Allocation Profiler (free), which can be obtained in the *User Samples* section of the web site *http://www.gotdotnet.com/community/usersamples/*.
- DevPartner Profiler Community Edition (free), which can be obtained at *http://www.compuware.com/products/devpartner/profiler/*.
- DevPartner Studio Professional Edition (purchase), which can be purchased at *http://www.compuware.com/products/devpartner/studio/*. This package contains the code profiler tool as well as many other tools that work with .NET and other .NET code. This package also contains a memory analysis tool that can aid in debugging performance problems.

CHAPTER 4

Enumerations

Enumerations implicitly inherit from System.Enum, which, in turn, inherits from System.ValueType. Enumerations have a single use: to describe items of a specific group. For example, the colors red, blue, and yellow could be defined by the enumeration ValidShapeColor; likewise square, circle, and triangle could be defined by the enumeration ValidShape. These enumerations would look like the following:

```
enum ValidShapeColor
{
    Red, Blue, Yellow
}

enum ValidShape
{
    square = 2, circle = 4, triangle = 6
}
```

Each item in the enumeration receives a numeric value regardless of whether you assign one. Since the compiler automatically adds the numbers starting with zero and increments by one for each item in the enumeration, the ValidShapeColor enumeration previously defined would be exactly the same if it were defined in the following manner:

```
enum ValidShapeColor
{
    Red = 0, Blue = 1, Yellow = 2
}
```

Enumerations are good code-documenting tools. For example, it is more intuitive to write the following:

```
ValidShapeColor currentColor = ValidShapeColor.Red;
```

than it is to write:

```
int currentColor = 0;
```

Either mechanism can work, but the first method is easy to read and understand, especially for a new developer taking over someone else's code.

4.1 Displaying an Enumeration Value as a String

Problem

You need to display the textual or numeric value of an enumeration member.

Solution

Use the `ToString` method that each enumeration member inherits from `System.Enum`.

Using the following `ValidShape` enumeration type as an example, we can obtain the textual and numeric values so that we may display them:

```
enum ValidShape
{
    Square = 0, Circle, Cylinder, Octagon
}
```

Using the `ToString` method of the `ValidShape` enumeration type, we can derive the value of a specific `ValidShape` enumeration value directly:

```
Console.WriteLine(ValidShape.Circle.ToString());
Console.WriteLine(ValidShape.Circle.ToString("G"));
Console.WriteLine(ValidShape.Circle.ToString("D"));
Console.WriteLine(ValidShape.Circle.ToString("F"));
Console.WriteLine(ValidShape.Circle.ToString("X"));
```

This generates the following output:

```
Circle
Circle
1
Circle
00000001
```

If we are working with a variable of type `ValidShape`, the enumeration values can be derived in the same manner:

```
ValidShape shapeStyle = ValidShape.Cylinder;

Console.WriteLine(shapeStyle.ToString());
Console.WriteLine(shapeStyle.ToString("G"));
Console.WriteLine(shapeStyle.ToString("D"));
Console.WriteLine(shapeStyle.ToString("F"));
Console.WriteLine(shapeStyle.ToString("X"));
```

The following is displayed:

```
Cylinder
Cylinder
2
Cylinder
00000002
```

Discussion

Deriving the textual or numeric representation of an enumeration value is a simple matter, using the ToString instance method on the Enum type. This method can accept a character indicating the type of formatting to place on the enumeration value. The character can be one of the following: G, g, F, f, D, d, X, or x. See Table 4-1 for a description of these formatting types.

Table 4-1. Formatting types

Formatting type	Description
G or g	(General) Displays the string representation of the enumeration value.
F or f	(Flag) Displays the string representation of the enumeration value. The enumeration is treated as if it were a bit field.
D or d	(Decimal) Displays decimal equivalent of the enumeration.
X or x	(Hexadecimal) Displays hexadecimal equivalent of the enumeration.

When printing out the values of an enumeration with the Flags attribute, the information displayed takes into account that more than one of the enumeration values may have been ORed together. The output will be all of the enumerations printed out as strings separated by commas or as the ORed numeric value, depending on the formatting chosen. For example, consider if the Flags attribute were added to the ValidShape enumeration as follows:

```
[Flags]
enum ValidShape
{
    Square = 0, Circle = 1, Cylinder = 2, Octagon = 4
}
```

and if we changed the code for this recipe as follows:

```
ValidShape shapeStyle = ValidShape.Circle | ValidShape.Cylinder;

Console.WriteLine(shapeStyle.ToString());
Console.WriteLine(shapeStyle.ToString("G"));
Console.WriteLine(shapeStyle.ToString("D"));
Console.WriteLine(shapeStyle.ToString("F"));
Console.WriteLine(shapeStyle.ToString("X"));
```

we would see the following output:

```
Circle, Cylinder
Circle, Cylinder
3
Circle, Cylinder
00000003
```

This technique provides a flexible way of extracting the flags that we are currently using on an enumeration type.

See Also

See the "Enum.ToString" method and "Enumeration Format Strings" topic in the MSDN documentation.

4.2   Converting Plain Text to an Equivalent Enumeration Value

Problem

You have the textual value of an enumeration element, possibly from a database or text file. This textual value needs to be converted to a usable enumeration type.

Solution

The static `Parse` method on the `Enum` class allows the textual value of an enumeration element to be converted to a usable enumeration value. For example:

```
try
{
    Language proj1Language = (Language)Enum.Parse(typeof(Language), "VBNET");
    Language proj2Language = (Language)Enum.Parse(typeof(Language), "UnDefined");
}
catch (ArgumentException e)
{
    // Handle an invalid text value here (such as the "UnDefined" string)
}
```

where the following `Language` enumeration is defined as:

```
enum Language
{
    Other = 0, CSharp = 1, VBNET = 2, VB6 = 3
}
```

Discussion

The static `Enum.Parse` method converts text to a specific enumeration value. This technique is useful when a user is presented a list of values, where each value is defined in an enumeration. When the user selects an item from this list, the text chosen can be easily converted from its string representation to its equivalent enumeration representation using `Enum.Parse`. This method returns an object of the same type as *enumType*. This value must then be cast to the same type as *enumType* in order to use it.

In addition to accepting a single enumeration value as a string, the *enumValue* parameter can also accept the enumeration value as a corresponding numeric value. For example, the following line:

```
Language proj1Language = (Language)Enum.Parse(typeof(Language), "VBNET");
```

could be rewritten as follows to perform the exact same action:

```
Language proj1Language = (Language)Enum.Parse(typeof(Language), "2");
```

This is assuming that the `Language.VBNET` enumeration is equal to 2.

Another interesting feature of the parse method is that it can accept a comma-delimited list of enumeration names or values and then logically OR them together. The following example creates an enumeration with the languages VBNET and CSharp ORed together:

```
Language proj1Language = (Language)Enum.Parse(typeof(Language), "CSharp, VBNET");
```

or:

```
Language proj1Language = (Language)Enum.Parse(typeof(Language), "1, 2");
```

Each individual element of the comma-delimited list is trimmed of any whitespace, so it does not matter if you add any whitespace between each item in this list.

See Also

See the "Enum.Parse" method in the MSDN documentation.

4.3   Testing for a Valid Enumeration Value

Problem

When a numeric value is passed to a method that accepts an enumeration type, it is possible that the numeric value does not exist in the parameter that accepts the enumeration value. You want to perform a test before using this numeric value to determine whether it is indeed listed in this enumeration type.

Solution

Use the static `Enum.IsDefined` method on the `Enum` class.

Using the following `Language` enumeration:

```
enum Language
{
    Other = 0, CSharp = 1, VBNET = 2, VB6 = 3
}
```

If we have a method that accepts the `Language` enumeration such as the following method:

```
public void HandleEnum(Language language)
{
    // Use language here...
}
```

Discussion

The static `Enum.IsDefined` method determines whether an enumeration value actually exists within an enumeration of a particular type. `Enum.IsDefined` is a check used to determine whether the values exist in the enumeration before they are used in your code. This method returns a `bool` value, where a `true` indicates that the enumeration value is defined in this enumeration and `false` indicates that it is not.

The `Enum.IsDefined` method should be used to determine whether a valid enumeration value has been passed to any method that accepts an enumeration value as a parameter. In particular, this `Enum.IsDefined` should always be used whenever the method is visible to external objects. Any external object can invoke methods with public visibility; therefore, any enumerated value passed in to this method should be screened before it is actually used. Methods with `internal`, `protected`, and `internal protected` visibility have a much smaller scope than public methods but could still suffer from the same problems as the `public` methods. Methods with `private` visibility may not need this extra level of protection. Use your own judgment on whether to use `Enum.IsDefined` to evaluate enumeration values passed in to private methods. Note that calling this method adds a little overhead to your method. This slight performance hit can be magnified if this method is called many times throughout your application.

The `HandleEnum` method can be called in several different ways. Two of these ways are shown here:

```
HandleEnum(Language.CSharp)
HandleEnum((Language)1)
```

Any of these method calls are valid. In addition, the following method calls are also valid:

```
HandleEnum((Language)100)

someVar = 100;
```

These method calls will also compile without errors, but odd behavior will result if the code in `HandleEnum` tries to use the value passed in to it (in this case, the value 100). In many cases an exception will not even be thrown and the CLR will attempt to handle the value 100 as part of the `Language` enumeration.

To prevent this from happening, use the static `Enum.IsDefined` method to determine if these are valid `Language` enumeration values. The following code shows the modified body of the `HandleEnum` method:

```
public void HandleEnum(Language language)
{
    if (Enum.IsDefined(typeof(Language), language))
    {
        // Use language here...
    }
    else
```

```
    {
        // Deal with the invalid language value here...
    }
}
```

See Also

To test for a valid enumeration within an enumeration marked with the [Flags] attribute, see Recipe 4.4; see the "Enum.IsDefined" method in the MSDN documentation.

4.4 Testing for a Valid Enumeration of Flags

Problem

You need to determine whether a given value is a valid enumeration value or a valid combination of enumeration values (i.e., bit flags ORed together in an enumeration marked with the Flags attribute).

Solution

There is a problem with using Enum.IsDefined with an enumeration marked with the Flags attribute. Consider the situation if the Language enumeration were written as follows:

```
[Flags]
enum Language
{
    CSharp = 1, VBNET = 2, VB6 = 4
}
```

Valid values for Language include the set of numbers {1, 2, 3, 4, 5, 6, 7}; however, the values 3, 5, 6, and 7 are not explicitly represented in this enumeration. The value 3 is equal to the CSharp and VBNET enumeration members ORed together and the value 7 is equal to all of the enumeration members ORed together. This means that for the values 3, 5, 6, and 7, the Enum.IsDefined method will return false, indicating that these are not valid values, when, in fact, they are. We need a way to determine whether a correct set of flags has been passed into a method.

To fix this problem, we can add a new member to the Language enumeration to define all values for which the Language enumeration is valid. In our case, the Language enumeration would be rewritten as:

```
[Flags]
enum Language
{
    CSharp = 1, VBNET = 2, VB6 = 4,
    All = (CSharp | VBNET | VB6)
}
```

The new `All` enumeration member is equal to all other `Language` members ORed together. Now, when we want to validate a `Language` flag, all we have to do is the following:

```
public bool HandleFlagsEnum(Language language)
{
    if ((language & Language.All) == language)
    {
        return (true);
    }
    else
    {
        return (false);
    }
}
```

Discussion

If you want to use the `HandleFlagsEnum` method with existing code, all that is required is to add an `All` member to the existing enumeration. The `All` member should be equal to all the members of the enumeration ORed together.

The `HandleFlagsEnum` method then uses this `All` member to determine whether an enumeration value is valid. This is accomplished by ANDing the `language` value with the `Language.All` value in the `HandleFlagsEnum` method.

This method can also be overloaded to handle the underlying type of the enumeration as well (in this case, the underlying type of the `Language` enumeration is an integer). The following code determines whether an integer variable contains a valid `Language` enumeration value:

```
public static bool HandleFlagsEnum(int language)
{
    if ((language & (int)Language.All) == language)
    {
        return (true);
    }
    else
    {
        return (false);
    }
}
```

The overloaded `HandleFlagsEnum` methods return `true` if the `language` parameter is valid, and `false` otherwise.

See Also

To test for a valid enumeration within an enumeration not marked with the `[Flags]` attribute, see Recipe 4.3.

4.5   Using Enumerated Members in a Bitmask

Problem

An enumeration of values is needed to act as bit flags that can be ORed together to
create a combination of values (flags) in the enumeration.

Solution

Mark the enumeration with the Flags attribute:

```
[Flags]
enum Language
{
    CSharp = 0x0001, VBNET = 0x0002, VB6 = 0x0004, Cpp = 0x0008
}
```

Combining elements of this enumeration is a simple matter of using the bitwise OR
operator (|). For example:

```
Language lang = Language.CSharp | Language.VBNET;
```

Discussion

Adding the Flags attribute to an enumeration marks this enumeration as individual
bit flags that can potentially be ORed together. Using an enumeration of flags is no
different than using a regular enumeration type. It should be noted that failing to
mark an enumeration with the Flags would not generate an exception or a compile-
time error even if the enumeration were used as bit flags.

The addition of the Flags attribute provides you with three benefits. First, if the
Flags attribute is placed on an enumeration, the ToString and ToString("G") methods return a string consisting of the name of the constant(s) separated by commas.
Otherwise, these two methods return the numeric representation of the enumeration
value. Note that the ToString("F") method returns a string consisting of the name of
the constant(s) separated by commas, regardless of whether this enumeration is
marked with the Flags attribute. For an indication of why this works in this manner,
see the "F" formatting type in Table 4-1 in Recipe 4.1.

The second benefit is that when you are using reflection to traverse code and
encounter an enumeration, you are able to determine the developer's intention for
this enumeration. If the developer explicitly defined this enumeration as containing
bit flags (with the Flags attribute), you can use it as such.

The third benefit is similar to the second benefit. If a developer marks an enumeration with the Flags attribute, you know that the developer intended this enumeration to contain only bit flags. This is similar to documenting one's code. Knowing
that this enumeration can be used as a bitmask, you can more easily determine what
is going on within this developer's code.

The flags enumeration can be viewed as a single value or as one or more values combined into a single enumeration value. If you need to accept multiple languages at a single time, you could write the following code:

```
Language lang = Language.CSharp | Language.VBNET;
```

The variable lang is now equal to the bit values of the two enumeration values ORed together. These values ORed together will equal three, as shown here:

```
Language.CSharp    0001
Language.VBNET     0010
ORed bit values    0011
```

The enumeration values were converted to binary and ORed together to get the binary value 0011 or 3 in base10. The compiler views this value both as two individual enumeration values (Language.CSharp and Language.VBNET) ORed together or as a single value (3).

To determine whether a single flag has been turned on in an enumeration variable, we need to use the bitwise AND (&) operator, as follows:

```
Language lang = Language.CSharp | Language.VBNET;

if((lang & Language.CSharp) == Language.CSharp)
    Console.WriteLine("The enum contains the C# enumeration value");
else
    Console.WriteLine("The enum does NOT contain the C# value");
```

This code will display the text "The enum contains the C# enumeration value." The ANDing of these two values will produce either zero, if the variable lang does not contain the value Language.CSharp; or the value Language.CSharp, if lang contains this enumeration value. Basically, ANDing these two values looks like this in binary:

```
Language.CSharp | Language.VBNET    0011
Language.CSharp                     0001
ANDed bit values                    0001
```

This case is dealt with in more detail in Recipe 4.6.

In some cases, the enumeration can grow quite large. We could add many other languages to this enumeration, as shown here:

```
[Flags]
enum Language
{
    CSharp = 0x0001, VBNET = 0x0002, VB6 = 0x0004, Cpp = 0x0008,
    FortranNET = 0x0010, JSharp = 0x0020, MSIL = 0x0080
}
```

In the cases where a Language enumeration value is needed to represent all languages, we would have to OR together each value of this enumeration:

```
Language lang = CSharp | VBNET | VB6 | Cpp | FortranNET | Jsharp | MSIL
```

Instead of doing this, we can simply add a new value to this enumeration that includes all languages as follows:

```
[Flags]
enum Language
{
    CSharp = 0x0001, VBNET = 0x0002, VB6 = 0x0004, Cpp = 0x0008,
    FortranNET = 0x0010, JSharp = 0x0020, MSIL = 0x0080,
    All = 0xFFFF
}
```

or:

```
[Flags]
enum Language
{
    CSharp = 0x0001, VBNET = 0x0002, VB6 = 0x0004, Cpp = 0x0008,
    FortranNET = 0x0010, JSharp = 0x0020, MSIL = 0x0080,
    All = (CSharp | VBNET | VB6 | Cpp | FortranNET | JSharp | MSIL)
}
```

Now there is a single enumeration value, All, that encompasses every value of this enumeration. Notice that there are two methods of creating the All enumeration value. The second method is much easier to read; however, if individual language elements of the enumeration are added or deleted, you will have to modify the All value accordingly.

Similarly, we could also add values to capture specific subsets of enumeration values as follows:

```
[Flags]
enum Language
{
    CSharp = 0x0001, VBNET = 0x0002, VB6 = 0x0004, Cpp = 0x0008,
    FortranNET = 0x0010, JSharp = 0x0020,
    MSIL = 0x0080,
    All = 0x00FF, VBOnly = 0x0006, NonVB = 0x00F9
}
```

or:

```
[Flags]
enum Language
{
    CSharp = 0x0001, VBNET = 0x0002, VB6 = 0x0004, Cpp = 0x0008,
    FortranNET = 0x0010, JSharp = 0x0020,
    MSIL = 0x0080,
    All = (CSharp | VBNET | VB6 | Cpp | FortranNET | Jsharp | MSIL)
    VBOnly = (VBNET | VB6),
    NonVB = (CSharp | Cpp | FortranNET | Jsharp | MSIL)
}
```

Now we have two extra members in the enumerations: one that encompasses VB only languages (Languages.VBNET and Languages.VB6) and one that encompasses non-VB languages.

4.6 Determining Whether One or More Enumeration Flags Are Set

Problem

You need to determine whether a variable of an enumeration type, consisting of bit flags, contains one or more specific flags. For example, given the following enumeration Language:

```
[Flags]
enum Language
{
    CSharp = 0x0001, VBNET = 0x0002, VB6 = 0x0004, Cpp = 0x0008
}
```

Determine, using Boolean logic, whether the variable lang in the following line of code contains a language such as Language.CSharp and/or Language.Cpp:

```
Language lang = Language.CSharp | Language.VBNET;
```

Solution

To determine whether a variable contains a single bit flag that is set, use the following conditional:

```
if((lang & Language.CSharp) == Language.CSharp)
{
    // lang contains at least Language.CSharp
}
```

To determine whether a variable exclusively contains a single bit flag that is set, use the following conditional:

```
if(lang == Language.CSharp)
{
    // lang contains only the Language.CSharp
}
```

To determine whether a variable contains a set of bit flags that are all set, use the following conditional:

```
if((lang & (Language.CSharp | Language.VBNET)) ==
    (Language.CSharp | Language.VBNET))
{
    // lang contains at least Language.CSharp and Language.VBNET
}
```

To determine whether a variable exclusively contains a set of bit flags that are all set, use the following conditional:

```
if((lang | (Language.CSharp | Language.VBNET)) ==
    (Language.CSharp | Language.VBNET))
{
    // lang contains only the Language.CSharp and Language.VBNET
}
```

Discussion

When enumerations are used as bit flags (these enumerations should be marked with the Flags attribute) they usually will require some kind of conditional testing to be performed. This kind of conditional testing requires the use of the bitwise AND (&) and OR (|) operators.

Testing for a variable having a specific bit flag set is done with the following conditional statement:

```
if((lang & Language.CSharp) == Language.CSharp)
```

where lang is of the Language enumeration type.

The & operator is used with a bitmask to determine whether a bit is set to 1. The result of ANDing two bits is 1 only when both bits are 1; otherwise, the result is 0. We can use this operation to determine if a specific bit flag is set to a 1 in the number containing the individual bit flags. If we AND the variable lang with the specific bit flag we are testing for (in this case Language.CSharp), we can extract that single specific bit flag. The expression (lang & Language.CSharp) is solved in the following manner if lang is equal to Language.CSharp:

```
Language.CSharp      0001
lang                 0001
ANDed bit values     0001
```

If lang is equal to another value such as Language.VBNET, the expression is solved in the following manner:

```
Language.CSharp      0001
lang                 0010
ANDed bit values     0000
```

Notice that ANDing the bits together returns the value Language.CSharp in the first expression and 0x0000 in the second expression. Comparing this result to the value we are looking for (Language.CSharp) tells us whether that specific bit was turned on.

This method is great for checking specific bits, but what if you wanted to know if only a specific bit was turned on (and all other bits turned off) or off (and all other bits turned on)? To test whether only the Language.CSharp bit is turned on in the variable lang, we can use the following conditional statement:

```
if(lang == Language.CSharp)
```

Consider the situation if the variable lang contained only the value Language.CSharp. The expression using the OR operator would look like this:

```
Language.CSharp      0001
lang                 0001
ORed bit values      0001
```

Now, add a language value or two to the variable lang and perform the same operation on lang:

```
Language.CSharp      0001
lang                 1101
ORed bit values      1101
```

The first expression results in the same value as we are testing against. The second expression results in a much larger value than Language.CSharp. This result indicates that the variable lang in the first expression only contains the value Language.CSharp and the second expression contains other languages including Language.CSharp.

Using this same formula, we can test multiple bits to determine whether they are both on and all other bits are off. This is done in the following conditional statement:

```
if((lang & (Language.CSharp | Language.VBNET)) ==
    (Language.CSharp | Language.VBNET))
```

Notice that to test for more than one language, we simply OR the language values together. By switching the first & operator for an | operator, we can determine whether at least these bits are turned on. This is done in the following conditional statement:

```
if((lang | (Language.CSharp | Language.VBNET)) ==
    (Language.CSharp | Language.VBNET))
```

When testing for multiple enumeration values, it may be beneficial to add a value to your enumeration, which ORs together all the values you want to test for. If we wanted to test for all languages except Language.CSharp, our conditional statement(s) would grow quite large and unwieldy. To fix this, we could add a value to the Language enumeration that ORs together all languages except Language.CSharp. The new enumeration would look like this:

```
[Flags]
enum Language
{
    CSharp = 0x0001, VBNET = 0x0002, VB6 = 0x0004, Cpp = 0x0008,
    AllLanguagesExceptCSharp = VBNET | VB6 | Cpp
}
```

and our conditional statement might look similar to the following:

```
if((lang | Language.AllLanguagesExceptCSharp) ==
    Language. AllLanguagesExceptCSharp)
```

This statement is quite a bit smaller and is easier to manage and read.

 Use the AND operator when testing whether one or more bits are set to 1. Use the OR operator when testing whether one or more bits are set to 0.

CHAPTER 5

Exception Handling

This chapter contains recipes covering the exception handling mechanism, including the try, catch, and finally blocks. Along with these recipes are others covering the mechanisms used to throw exceptions manually from within your code. The final types of recipes include those dealing with the Exception classes, their uses, and subclassing them to create new types of exceptions.

Often the design and implementation of exception handling is performed later in the development cycle. But with the power and complexities of C# exception handling, you need to plan and even implement your exception handling scheme much earlier in the development cycle. Doing so will increase the reliability and robustness of your code while minimizing the impact of adding exception handling after most or all of the application is coded.

Exception handling in C# is very flexible. It allows you to choose a fine- or coarse-grained approach to error handling and any level between. This means that you can add exception handling around any individual line of code (the fine-grained approach), around a method that calls many other methods (the coarse-grained approach), or use a mix of the two. When using a fine-grained approach, you can intercept specific exceptions that might be thrown from just a few lines of code. The following method sets an object's property to a numeric value using fine-grained exception handling:

```
protected void SetValue(object value)
{
    try
    {
        myObj.Property1 = value;
    }
    catch (Exception e)
    {
        // Handle potential exceptions arising from this call here.
    }
}
```

Consequentially, this approach can add a lot of extra baggage to your code if used throughout your application. This fine-grained approach to exception handling should be used when you have a single line or just a few lines of code that have a high probability of throwing an exception and you need to handle that exception in a specific manner. For example, using the previous SetValue method, we may have to inform the user that an exception occurred and provide a chance to try the action again. If a method exists on myObj that needs to be called whenever an exception is thrown by one of its methods, we should make sure that this method is called at the appropriate time.

Coarse-grained exception handling is quite the opposite; it uses fewer try-catch or try-catch-finally blocks. One example would be to place a try-catch block around all of the code in every public method in an application or component. Doing this allows exceptions to be handled at the highest level in your code. If an exception is thrown at any location in your code, it will be bubbled up the call stack until a catch block is found that can handle it. If try-catch blocks are placed on all public methods (including the Main method), then all exceptions will be bubbled up to these methods and handled. This allows for much less exception handling code to be written, but your ability to handle specific exceptions that may occur in particular areas of your code is diminished. You must determine how best to add exception handling code to your application. This means applying the right balance of fine- and coarse-grained exception handling in your application.

C# allows catch blocks to be written without any parameters. An example of this is shown here:

```
public void CallCOMMethod( )
{
    try
    {
        // Call a method on a COM object.
        myCOMObj.Method1( );
    }
    catch
    {
        // Handle potential exceptions arising from this call here.
    }
}
```

This catch block has no parameters. This is a holdover from C++, where exception objects did not have to be derived from the Exception class. Writing a catch clause in this manner in C++ allows any type of object thrown as an exception to be caught. However, in C#, only objects derived from the Exception base class may be thrown as an exception. Using the catch block with no parameters allows all exceptions to be caught, but you lose the ability to view the exception and its information. A catch block written in this manner:

```
catch
{
```

```
    // NOT Able to write the following line of code.
    //Console.WriteLine(e.ToString);
}
```

is equivalent to this:

```
catch (Exception e)
{
    // Able to write the following line of code.
    Console.WriteLine(e.ToString);
}
```

except that the Exception object can now be accessed.

 Avoid writing a catch block without any parameters. Doing so will prevent you from accessing the actual Exception object that was thrown.

When catching exceptions in a catch block, you should determine up front when exceptions need to be rethrown, when exceptions need to be wrapped in an outer exception and thrown, and when exceptions should be handled immediately and not be rethrown.

Wrapping an exception in an outer exception is a good practice when the original exception thrown would not make sense to the caller. When wrapping an exception in an outer exception, you need to determine what exception is most appropriate to wrap the caught exception. As a rule of thumb, the wrapping exception should always aid in tracking down the original problem.

Another useful practice to use when catching exceptions is to use specific catch blocks to handle specific exceptions in your code. When using specific catch blocks, consider adding a catch block that handles all other exceptions (Exception) if you need to handle any other unexpected exception or make sure that all other exceptions are handled at some point in your code. Also, remember that base class exceptions—when used in a catch block—catch that type as well as all of its subclasses. The following code uses specific catch blocks to handle different exceptions in the appropriate manner:

```
public void CallCOMMethod()
{
    try
    {
        // Call a method on a COM object.
        myCOMObj.Method1();
    }
    catch (System.Runtime.InteropServices.ExternalException exte)
    {
        // Handle potential COM exceptions arising from this call here.
    }
    catch (InvalidOperationException ae)
    {
```

```
        // Handle any potential method calls to the COM object which are
        // not valid in its current state.
    }
}
```

In this code, any `ExternalException` or its derivatives are handled differently than any thrown `InvalidOperationException` or its derivatives. If any other types of exceptions are thrown from the `myCOMObj.Method1`, they are not handled here and are bubbled up until a valid `catch` block is found. If none are found, the exception is considered unhandled and the application will terminate.

At times, cleanup code must be executed regardless of whether an exception is thrown. Any object must be placed in a stable known state when an exception is thrown. In these situations where code must be executed, use a `finally` block. The following code has been modified (see boldface lines) to use a `finally` block:

```
public void CallCOMMethod( )
{
    try
    {
        // Call a method on a COM object.
        myCOMObj.Method1( );
    }
    catch (System.Runtime.InteropServices.ExternalException exte)
    {
        // Handle potential COM exceptions arising from this call here.
    }
    finally
    {
        // Clean up and free any resources here.
        //   For example, there could be a method on myCOMObj to allow us to clean
        //   up after using the Method1 method.
    }
}
```

The `finally` block will always execute, no matter what happens in the `try` and `catch` blocks. The `finally` block even executes if a `return`, `break`, or `continue` statement is executed in the `try` or `catch` blocks, or if a `goto` is used to jump out of the exception handler. This setup allows for a reliable method of cleaning up after the `try` (and possibly `catch`) block code executes.

When determining how to structure your exception handling in your application or component, consider doing the following:

- Use a single `try-catch` or `try-catch-finally` exception handler at locations higher up in your code. These exception handlers could be considered coarse-grained.
- Code farther down the call stack should contain `try-finally` exception handlers. These exception handlers can be considered fine-grained.

The fine-grained `try-finally` exception handlers allow for better control over cleaning up after an exception occurs. The exception is then bubbled up to the coarser-grained try-catch or try-catch-finally exception handler. This technique allows for a more centralized scheme of exception handling, and minimizes the code that you have to write to handle exceptions.

To improve performance, you should programmatically handle the case when an exception could be thrown versus catching the exception after it is thrown. For example, if a method has a good chance of returning a null value, you could test the returned value for null before that value is used, as opposed to using a try-catch block and allowing the NullReferenceException to be thrown. Remember that throwing an exception has a negative impact on performance and exception-handling code has no noticeable impact on performance, as long as an exception is not thrown. To illustrate this, we take a method that uses exception handling code to handle the NullReferenceException:

```
public void SomeMethod( )
{
    try
    {
        Stream s = GetAnyAvailableStream( );
        Console.WriteLine("This stream has a length of " + s.Length);
    }
    catch (Exception e)
    {
        // Handle a null stream here.
    }
}
```

and convert this method to use an if-else conditional to handle the NullReferenceException as:

```
public void SomeMethod( )
{
    Stream s = GetAnyAvailableStream( );

    if (s != null)
    {
        Console.WriteLine("This stream has a length of " + s.Length);
    }
    else
    {
        // Handle a null stream here.
    }
}
```

Additionally, you should also make sure that this stream was closed, by using the finally block in the following manner:

```
public void SomeMethod( )
{
    Stream s = null;
    try
    {
        s = GetAnyAvailableStream( );
```

```
        if (s != null)
        {
            Console.WriteLine("This stream has a length of " + s.Length);
        }
        else
        {
            // Handle a null stream here.
        }
    }
    finally
    {
        s.Close();
    }
}
```

The `finally` block contains the method call that will close the stream, ensuring that there is no data loss.

Consider throwing exceptions instead of returning HRESULTs or some other type of error code. With well-placed exception handling code, you should not have to rely on methods that return error codes such as an HRESULT or a Boolean true/false to correctly handle errors, which makes for much cleaner code. Another benefit is that you do not have to look up any HRESULT values or any other type of error code to understand the code. However, the biggest advantage is that when an exceptional situation arises, you cannot just ignore it as you can with error codes.

This technique is especially useful when writing a managed C# component that is called by one or more COM objects. Throwing an exception is much cleaner and easier to read than returning an HRESULT. The managed wrapper that the runtime creates for your managed object will make a clean and consistent conversion between the exception type and its corresponding HRESULT value.

Throw specific exceptions, not general ones. For example, throw an ArgumentNullException instead of ArgumentException, which is the base class of ArgumentNullException. Throwing an ArgumentException just tells you that there was a problem with a parameter value to a method. Throwing an ArgumentNullException tells you more specifically what the problem with the parameter really is. Another potential problem is that a more general thrown exception may not be caught if you are looking for a more specific type derived from the thrown exception.

There are several types of exceptions built-in to the FCL that you will find very useful to throw in your own code. Many of these exceptions are listed here with a definition of where and when they should be thrown:

- Throw an InvalidOperationException in a property, indexer, or method when one is called while the object is in an inappropriate state. This state could be caused by calling an indexer on an object that has not yet been initialized or calling methods out of sequence.

- Throw ArgumentException if invalid parameters are passed into a method, property, or indexer. The ArgumentNullException, ArgumentOutOfRangeException, and

InvalidEnumArgumentException are three subclasses of the ArgumentException class. It is more appropriate to throw one of these subclassed exceptions since they are more indicative of the root cause of the problem. The ArgumentNullException indicates that a parameter was passed in as null and that this parameter cannot be null under any circumstance. The ArgumentOutOfRangeException indicates that an argument was passed in that was outside of a valid acceptable range. This exception is used mainly with numeric values. The InvalidEnumArgumentException indicates that an enumeration value was passed in that does not exist in that enumeration type.

- Throw a FormatException when an invalid formatting parameter is passed in as a parameter to a method. This technique is mainly used when overriding/overloading methods such as ToString that can accept formatting strings.

- Throw ObjectDisposedException when a property, indexer, or method is called on an object that has already been disposed. This exception should be thrown inside of the called property, indexer, or method.

Many exceptions that derive from the SystemException class, such as NullReferenceException, ExecutionEngineException, StackOverflowException, OutOfMemoryException, and IndexOutOfRangeException are thrown only by the CLR and should not be explicitly thrown with the throw keyword in your code.

5.1 Verifying Critical Parameters

Problem

You have a method, property, or indexer that requires the correct value or set of values to be passed in to it (e.g., cannot be null, must be within a numeric range or a set of numeric ranges, the enumeration value must be a valid value in the enumeration). If an incorrect value is passed in to the method, it must inform the application and handle the invalid value gracefully.

Solution

The parameters passed in to a public method should always be tested for correctness before they are used; however, it may be more appropriate to use Debug.Assert or even to use no tests when checking parameters to nonpublic methods. If one or more fail the test, an ArgumentException, or one of its derivatives, should be thrown to ensure that the application is notified that critical data has possibly been corrupted. (Note that an IndexOutOfRangeException could instead be thrown from within an indexer.)

When a numeric parameter that is out of a specified range is passed, the ArgumentOutOfRangeException should be thrown. The following code checks whether the numberOfItems parameter is greater than an upper bound of 100:

```
if (numberOfItems > 100)
{
```

```
        throw (new ArgumentOutOfRangeException("numberOfItems", numberOfItems,
                "The number of items has exceeded the defined limits."));
    }
```

Many parameters passed to methods may produce strange results when they are null. To prevent this from happening, test the parameters to see whether they are null. If any parameter is null, throw the ArgumentNullException. The following code checks the charToSeek char variable to see whether it is null:

```
    if (charToSeek.Equals(null))
    {
        throw (new ArgumentNullException("charToSeek",
                "The character to seek may not be null."));
    }
```

If a method accepts an enumeration value, a caller may pass a numeric value in lieu of an enumeration value of the parameter's type. This is dangerous since the caller can easily pass in a number that does not exist in the enumeration. To prevent this problem, test the enumeration type parameter using the static IsDefined method on the Enum class. If the parameter contains a bad value, throw the InvalidEnumArgumentException. The following code shows how to test the zooAnimals parameter, of type Animals, for a bad value:

```
    if (!Enum.IsDefined(typeof(Animals), zooAnimals))
    {
        throw (new System.ComponentModel.InvalidEnumArgumentException("zooAnimals",
                (int)zooAnimals, typeof(Animals)));
    }
```

There is a problem with using IsDefined with two or more enumeration values ORed together. See Recipe 4.4.

Discussion

Testing parameters in this way does not have to be done on every method. Instead, you should test the parameters that are passed in to all public methods of public classes and throw an exception only if they are in error. For nonpublic methods, you can add Debug.Assert statements to test these parameters.

Being in control of the code within your assembly makes it much easier for you to know which valid parameters, their ranges, etc., you need to pass to methods within your own assembly. Someone who is unfamiliar with your assembly has a much higher chance of passing in bad arguments to the parameters in your assembly's public interface. Therefore, you should guard against bad parameters from being passed to methods that will be used by developers other than yourself.

Note that the only exception allowing for an inner exception is ArgumentException. The more general exceptions, such as ArgumentException, were designed this way, so that the more specific exceptions, such as ArgumentNullException, can be wrapped with the more general exceptions, such as ArgumentException. This specificity gives a much clearer picture of how and where the exception occurred.

See Also

See the "ArgumentException Class" topic in the MSDN documentation.

5.2 Indicating Where Exceptions Originate

Problem

You want to be able to clearly distinguish which of your objects threw an exception, to aid in tracking down problems.

Solution

You should rethrow the exception in the `catch` clause in which the original exception was handled. The `throw` keyword is used, followed by a semicolon, to rethrow an exception:

```
try
{
    Console.WriteLine("In inner try");
    int z2 = 9999999;
    checked{z2 *= 999999999;}
}
catch(DivideByZeroException dbze)
{
    Console.WriteLine(@"A divide by zero exception occurred. " +
                        "Error message == " + dbze.Message);
    throw;
}
```

Discussion

Rethrowing a caught exception is useful to inform clients of your code that an error has occurred. Consider the case in which a client application contained the `CatchReThrownException` method and the `ReThrowException` method was contained in a separate server application that existed somewhere on the network. When the client application called the `ReThrowException` method and an error occurred, the server application could handle the exception and continue about its business. However, if this exception forced the server application to abort, it should rethrow the exception so that the client application knows what happened and can deal with the same exception in a graceful manner.

 Remember that throwing exceptions is expensive. Try not to needlessly throw and rethrow exceptions since this might bog down your application.

5.3 Choosing when to Throw a Particular Exception

Problem

There are many exceptions to choose from in the FCL. You need an easily accessible list of these exceptions that indicates when and where to use them. By throwing exceptions in a consistent manner (e.g., throwing an IndexOutOfRangeException when an array index is greater than the length of the array), you and others on your team will be able to debug problems more easily.

Solution

Use the list of exceptions and their definitions in Table 5-1 to determine which exception to employ when throwing or catching exceptions.

Discussion

Table 5-1. The built-in exception types

Exception name	Derives from	Description
System.ApplicationException	Exception	Use this class as the base class to user-defined exceptions; a more derived exception should be thrown.
System.ArgumentNullException	ArgumentException	Thrown when a parameter value for a method is null and null is not allowed.
System.ArgumentOutOfRangeException	ArgumentException	Thrown when a parameter value for a method is out of the range of expected values.
System.ArrayTypeMismatchException	SystemException	Thrown when an incompatible data type is assigned to an element in an array.
System.Runtime.InteropServices.COMException	ExternalException	Thrown when an unknown HRESULT is returned from a COM object.
System.Configuration.ConfigurationException	SystemException	Thrown when an invalid configuration setting is encountered.
System.Reflection.CustomAttributeFormatException	FormatException	Thrown when a custom attribute format is incorrect.
System.IO.DirectoryNotFoundException	IOException	Thrown when a file or directory cannot be found.
System.Exception	Object	Base class of all exceptions; you should always throw a more derived exception.
System.FormatException	SystemException	Thrown when an invalid format parameter is passed to a method.

Table 5-1. The built-in exception types (continued)

Exception name	Derives from	Description
System.IndexOutOfRangeException	SystemException	Thrown when you attempt to access an array element with an index value outside the valid range for that array.
System.Configuration.Install.InstallException	SystemException	Thrown during software installation when an error is encountered during uninstall, committing of data, or rolling back of data.
System.ComponentModel.InvalidEnumArgumentException	ArgumentException	Thrown when an invalid enumeration value is passed to a method.
System.InvalidOperationException	SystemException	Thrown when a method is called while the object it resides in is in a state that makes it illegal to call this method.
System.IO.IOException	SystemException	Thrown when a general I/O exception occurs; you should throw a more derived exception.
System.MemberAccessException	SystemException	Thrown when a general error occurs while using a class member; you should throw a more derived exception.
System.MethodAccessException	MemberAccessException	Thrown when a general error occurs while using a method member.
System.NotFiniteNumberException	ArithmeticException	Thrown when a double or single data type is expected to have a finite number and instead it contains NaN, +infinity, or - infinity.
System.NotImplementedException	SystemException	Thrown when a member is accessed that is not yet implemented.
System.NotSupportedException	SystemException	Thrown when a member is accessed that is not yet supported.
System.NullReferenceException	SystemException	Thrown when a reference set to null is used.
System.ObjectDisposedException	InvalidOperation-Exception	Thrown when a disposed object is accessed.
System.ServiceProcess.TimeoutException	SystemException	Thrown when a service times out.
System.ComponentModel.WarningException	SystemException	Thrown when a warning message needs to be displayed. This exception does not imply a serious failure of the application or system.
System.Net.WebException	InvalidOperation-Exception	Thrown when a pluggable protocol causes an error.
System.Xml.XmlException	SystemException	Thrown due to a general error in the XML.

See Also

See the "Exception Class" topic in the MSDN documentation; also see the classes that derive from the Exception class.

5.4 Handling Derived Exceptions Individually

Problem

You have an exception hierarchy that consists of a base exception class and multiple derived exception classes. At some point in your code, you want to handle only one or two of these derived exceptions in a specific manner. All other derived exceptions should be handled in a more generic manner. You need a clean way to target specific exceptions in an exception class hierarchy to be handled differently from the rest.

Solution

The exception handlers for C# allow for multiple catch clauses to be implemented. Each of these catch clauses can take a single parameter—a type derived from the Exception class. An exception handler that uses multiple catch clauses is shown here:

```
try
{
    int d = 0;
    int z = 1/d;
}
catch(DivideByZeroException dbze)
{
    Console.WriteLine("A divide by zero exception occurred. Error message == "
        + dbze.Message);
}
catch(OverflowException ofe)
{
    Console.WriteLine("An Overflow occurred. Error message == " + ofe.Message);
}
catch(Exception e)
{
    Console.WriteLine("Another type of error occurred. Error message == "
        + e.Message);
}
```

This code produces the following output:

```
A divide by zero exception occurred. Error message == Attempted to divide by zero.
```

Discussion

Notice the exception types that each catch clause handles in this try-catch block. These specific exception types will be handled on an individual basis within their own catch block. Suppose the try block looked as follows:

```
try
{
    int z2 = 9999999;
    checked{z2 *= 999999999;}
}
```

We would get the following message:

```
An Overflow occurred. Error message == Arithmetic operation resulted in an overflow.
```

Now, since the OverflowException is being thrown, it is handled in a totally different catch block.

You may be thinking that you could do the same thing in a single catch block using an if-else statement. An example of this is shown here:

```
catch(Exception e)
{
    if (e is OverflowException)
        Console.WriteLine("An Overflow occurred. Error message == " + e.Message);
    else if (e is DivideByZeroException)
        Console.WriteLine("A divide by zero exception occurred. Error message == " +
                        e.Message);
    else
        Console.WriteLine("Another type of error occurred. Error message == " +
                        e.Message);
}
```

The if-else statements are used to check the type of this exception and then execute the appropriate code. This structure has two flaws. The first is that the compiler does not check whether the exceptions are listed in the correct order in the if-else statements. If an exception class is placed in the if-else conditional structure after a class in which it inherits from, the derived class will never be checked. Consider the following modified catch clause:

```
try
{
    int d = 0;
    int z = 1/d;
}
catch(Exception e)
{
    if (e is ArithmeticException)
        Console.WriteLine("The base class exception was chosen.");
    else if (e is OverflowException)
        Console.WriteLine("An Overflow occurred. Error message == " + e.Message);
    else if (e is DivideByZeroException)
        Console.WriteLine("A divide by zero exception occurred. Error message == " +
                        e.Message);
    else
        Console.WriteLine("Another type of error occurred. Error message == " +
                        e.Message);
}
```

This code produces the following output:

The base class exception was chosen.

Even though the `DivideByZeroException` was thrown, the `ArithmeticException` is always found first, as the `DivideByZeroException` and `OverflowException` both have the `ArithmeticException` class as their base class.

The second flaw is one of appearance. Using multiple `catch` clauses is much easier to read due to its natural and consistent structure. This is the way the language should be used, and, therefore, this is what many developers are going to look for. Other developers reading your code may find it more natural to read the multiple `catch` classes rather than the single `catch` clause with a decision structure inside of it. Not everyone may agree with us on this part, but we do consider structure and consistency an integral part of writing good code.

There is one case where we would consider using the single `catch` clause with the decision structure: when large amounts of code would have to be duplicated in each `catch` clause and there is no way to put the duplicated code in a `finally` clause after the `try-catch` block.

See Also

See the "Error Raising and Handling Guidelines" topic in the MSDN documentation.

5.5   Assuring Exceptions are Not Lost when Using Finally Blocks

Problem

You have multiple nested try/catch, try/finally, and try/catch/finally blocks. If a catch block attempts to rethrow an exception, it is possible that the rethrown exception could get discarded and a new and unexpected exception could be caught by an outer exception handler. You want to prevent this situation from occurring.

Solution

Add an inner try/catch block in the `finally` block of the outer exception handler:

```
private void PreventLossOfException()
{
    try
    {
        //...
    }
    catch(Exception e)
    {
        Console.WriteLine("Error message == " + e.Message);
        throw;
    }
    finally
```

```
    {
        try
        {
            //...
        }
        catch(Exception e)
        {
            Console.WriteLine(@"An unexpected error occurred in the finally block.
                        Error message == " + e.Message);
        }
    }
}
```

This block will prevent the original exception from being lost.

Discussion

Consider what would happen if an error were thrown from the inner `finally` block
contained in the ReThrowException method. If the code looked like this:

```
public void PreventLossOfException()
{
    try
    {
        Console.WriteLine("In outer try");
        ReThrowException();
    }
    catch(Exception e)
    {
        Console.WriteLine("In outer catch.   ReThrown error == " + e.Message);
    }
    finally
    {
        Console.WriteLine("In outer finally");
    }
}

private void ReThrowException()
{
    try
    {
        Console.WriteLine("In inner try");
        int z2 = 9999999;
        checked{z2 *= 999999999;}
    }
    catch(OverflowException ofe)
    {
        Console.WriteLine("An Overflow occurred.   Error message == " +
                    ofe.Message);
        throw;
    }
    catch(Exception e)
    {
        Console.WriteLine("Another type of error occurred.   Error message == " +
                    e.Message);
```

```
        throw;
    }
    finally
    {
        Console.WriteLine("In inner finally");
        throw(new Exception("Oops"));
    }
}
```

the following output would be displayed:

```
In outer try
In inner try
An Overflow occurred.    Error message == Arithmetic operation resulted in an
overflow.
In inner finally
In outer catch.    ReThrown error == Oops
In outer finally
```

If we modify the inner finally block to handle its own errors (changes are highlighted), similar to the following code:

```
public void PreventLossOfException()
{
    try
    {
        Console.WriteLine("In outer try");
        ReThrowException();
    }
    catch(Exception e)
    {
        Console.WriteLine("In outer catch.    ReThrown error == " + e.Message);
    }
    finally
    {
        Console.WriteLine("In outer finally");
    }
}

private void ReThrowException()
{
    try
    {
        Console.WriteLine("In inner try");
        int z2 = 9999999;
        checked{z2 *= 999999999;}
    }
    catch(OverflowException ofe)
    {
        Console.WriteLine("An Overflow occurred.    Error message == " +
                            ofe.Message);
        throw;
    }
    catch(Exception e)
    {
```

```
            Console.WriteLine("Another type of error occurred.    " +
                            "Error message == " + e.Message);
            throw;
        }
        finally
        {
            try
            {
                Console.WriteLine("In inner finally");
                throw(new Exception("Oops"));
            }
            catch(Exception e)
            {
                Console.WriteLine(@"An error occurred in the finally block. " +
                                "Error message == " + e.Message);
            }
        }
    }
}
```

we would get the following output:

```
In outer try
In inner try
An Overflow occurred.    Error message == Arithmetic operation resulted in an
overflow.
In inner finally
An error occurred in the finally block.    Error message == Oops
In outer catch.    ReThrown error == Arithmetic operation resulted in an overflow.
In outer finally
```

By handling exceptions within the inner finally block, we assure that the correct re-thrown exception bubbles up to the next outer exception handler.

 When writing a finally block, consider placing a separate try-catch around the code.

See Also

See the "Error Raising and Handling Guidelines" topic and the "throw," "try," "catch," and "finally" keywords in the MSDN documentation.

5.6   Handling Exceptions Thrown from Methods Invoked via Reflection

Problem

Using reflection, you invoke a method that generates an exception. You want to obtain the real exception object and its information in order to diagnose and fix the problem.

Solution

The real exception and its information can be obtained through the InnerException property of the TargetInvocationException exception that is thrown by MethodInfo. Invoke.

Discussion

The following example shows how an exception that occurs within a method invoked via reflection is handled. The Reflect class contains a ReflectionException method that invokes the static TestInvoke method using the reflection classes as shown here:

```
using System;
using System.Reflection;

public class Reflect
{
    public void ReflectionException()
    {
        Type reflectedClass = typeof(Reflect);
        try
        {
            MethodInfo methodToInvoke = reflectedClass.GetMethod("TestInvoke");

            if (methodToInvoke != null)
            {
                object oInvoke = methodToInvoke.Invoke(null, null);
            }
        }
        catch(Exception e)
        {
            Console.WriteLine("MESSAGE: " + e.Message);
            Console.WriteLine("SOURCE: " + e.Source);
            Console.WriteLine("TARGET: " + e.TargetSite);
            Console.WriteLine("STACK: " + e.StackTrace + "\r\n");

            if(e.InnerException != null)
            {
                Console.WriteLine();
                Console.WriteLine("\t**** INNEREXCEPTION START ****");
                Console.WriteLine("\tTYPE THAT THREW EXCEPTION: " +
                            reflectedClass.ToString());
                Console.WriteLine("\tINNEREXCEPTION MESSAGE: " +
                            e.InnerException.Message);
                Console.WriteLine("\tINNEREXCEPTION SOURCE: " +
                            e.InnerException.Source);
                Console.WriteLine("\tINNEREXCEPTION STACK: " +
                            e.InnerException.StackTrace);
                Console.WriteLine("\tINNEREXCEPTION TARGETSITE: " +
                            e.InnerException.TargetSite);
                Console.WriteLine("\t****  INNEREXCEPTION END  ****");
            }
        }
```

```
        Console.WriteLine( );

        // Shows fusion log when assembly cannot be located
        Console.WriteLine(e.ToString( ));
    }
}

    // Method to invoke via reflection
    public static void TestInvoke( )
    {
        throw (new Exception("Thrown from invoked method."));
    }
}
```

This code displays the following text:

```
MESSAGE: Exception has been thrown by the target of an invocation.
SOURCE: mscorlib
TARGET: System.Object InternalInvoke(System.Object, System.Reflection.BindingFlags,
    System.Reflection.Binder, System.Object[], System.Globalization.CultureInfo,
    Boolean, System.Reflection.Assembly, Boolean)
STACK: at System.Reflection.RuntimeMethodInfo.InternalInvoke(Object obj,
    BindingFlags invokeAttr, Binder binder, Object[] parameters, CultureInfo culture,
    Boolean isBinderDefault, Assembly caller, Boolean verifyAccess)
    at System.Reflection.RuntimeMethodInfo.InternalInvoke(Object obj,
    BindingFlags invokeAttr, Binder binder, Object[] parameters, CultureInfo culture,
    Boolean verifyAccess)
    at System.Reflection.RuntimeMethodInfo.Invoke(Object obj, BindingFlags invokeAttr,
    Binder binder, Object[] parameters, CultureInfo culture)
    at System.Reflection.MethodBase.Invoke(Object obj, Object[] parameters)
    at Reflect.ReflectionException( ) in
    c:\book cs cookbook\code\test.cs:line 22

        **** INNEREXCEPTION START ****
        TYPE THAT THREW EXCEPTION: ClassLibrary1.Reflect
        INNEREXCEPTION MESSAGE: Thrown from invoked method.
        INNEREXCEPTION SOURCE: ClassLibrary1
        INNEREXCEPTION STACK: at ClassLibrary1.Reflect.TestInvoke( ) in
            C:\BOOK CS CookBook\Code\Test.cs:line 49
          at ClassLibrary1.Reflect.TestInvoke( ) in
            C:\BOOK CS CookBook\Code\Test.cs:line 49
        INNEREXCEPTION TARGETSITE: Void TestInvoke( )
        ****  INNEREXCEPTION END  ****
```

When the methodToInvoke.Invoke method is called, the TestInvoke method is called and subsequently throws an exception. The outer exception thrown is the TargetInvocationException exception; this is the generic exception thrown when a method invoked through reflection throws an exception. The CLR automatically wraps the original exception thrown by the invoked method inside of the TargetInvocationException object's InnerException property. In this case, the exception thrown by the invoked method is the generic Exception exception. This exception is shown after the section that begins with the text **** INNEREXCEPTION START ****.

In addition to this text, the code also calls e.ToString to print out the exception text. The text output from ToString is:

```
System.Reflection.TargetInvocationException: Exception has been thrown by the target
of an invocation. ---> System.Exception: Thrown from invoked method.
    at ClassLibrary1.Reflect.TestInvoke() in
        C:\BOOK CS CookBook\Code\Test.cs:line 49
    at ClassLibrary1.Reflect.TestInvoke() in
        C:\BOOK CS CookBook\Code\Test.cs:line 49
    --- End of inner exception stack trace ---
    at System.Reflection.RuntimeMethodInfo.InternalInvoke(Object obj, BindingFlags
        invokeAttr, Binder binder, Object[] parameters, CultureInfo culture, Boolean
        isBinderDefault, Assembly caller, Boolean verifyAccess)
    at System.Reflection.RuntimeMethodInfo.InternalInvoke(Object obj, BindingFlags
        invokeAttr, Binder binder, Object[] parameters, CultureInfo culture, Boolean
        verifyAccess)
    at System.Reflection.RuntimeMethodInfo.Invoke(Object obj, BindingFlags invokeAttr,
        Binder binder, Object[] parameters, CultureInfo culture)
    at System.Reflection.MethodBase.Invoke(Object obj, Object[] parameters)
    atReflect.ReflectionException() in c:\book cs cookbook
        \code\test.cs:line 22
```

Using the ToString method is a quick and simple way of displaying the most relevant outer exception information along with the most relevant information for each inner exception.

See Also

See the "Type Class" and "MethodInfo Class" topics in the MSDN documentation.

5.7   Debugging Problems when Loading an Assembly

Problem

You want to use a reflection-based technique, such as the static Assembly.LoadFrom method, to load an assembly. If this method fails, you want to collect as much useful information you can as to why this assembly failed to load.

Solution

Either call the ToString method on the exception object thrown or use the FusionLog property on BadImageFormatException, FileLoadException, or FileNotFoundException. When an exception occurs while using a file, the exception contains extra information that is taken from the fusion log. To see this in action, run the following code:

```
public static void LoadMissingDLL()
{
    // Load the DLL
    try
```

```
    {
        Assembly reflectedAssembly = Assembly.LoadFrom("BadFileName.dll");
    }
    catch (FileNotFoundException fnf)
    {
        // This displays the fusion log information only
        Console.WriteLine(fnf.FusionLog);
    }
    catch (Exception e)    // Note that you would use one catch block or the other,
    {                      //    not both
        // This displays the exception information along
        // with any fusion log information
        Console.WriteLine(e.ToString());
    }
}
```

Discussion

Use this technique to debug problems when loading an assembly from a file. When using the ToString method of the Exception object, notice the bottom part of the error message that starts with "Fusion log follows." This is the section that can provide some clue as to why the reflection APIs could not find your assembly. If you want just the fusion information, you can use the FusionLog property of one of the aforementioned exception objects.

See Also

See the "BadImageFormatException Class," "FileLoadException Class," and "FileNotFoundException Class" topics in the MSDN documentation.

5.8   HRESULT-Exception Mapping

Problem

You need a reference table that maps each COM HRESULT to its managed exception counterpart. This mapping will allow you to throw the correct managed exception in C#, which will map to the expected COM HRESULT in unmanaged code.

Solution

Every managed exception maps to an HRESULT. Table 5-2 lists the managed exception classes and their equivalent HRESULT values. Use this table to determine what type of managed exception to use when throwing an exception back to unmanaged code, as well as what type of exception object to use when handling returned COM/COM+ HRESULT values.

Table 5-2. Mappping .NET exceptions to HRESULTS

.NET exception class name	HRESULT name (hex value of HRESULT)
AccessException	COR_E_MEMBERACCESS (0x8013151A)
AmbiguousMatchException	COR_E_AMBIGUOUSMATCH (0X80138000211D)
AppDomainUnloadedException	MSEE_E_APPDOMAINUNLOADED (0x80131015)
ApplicationException	COR_E_APPLICATION (0x80131600)
ArgumentException	COR_E_ARGUMENT (0x80070057)
ArgumentNullException	E_POINTER (0x80004003)
ArgumentOutOfRangeException	COR_E_ARGUMENTOUTOFRANGE (0x80131502)
ArithmeticException	COR_E_ARITHMETIC (0x80070216)
ArrayTypeMismatchException	COR_E_ARRAYTYPEMISMATCH (0x80131503)
BadImageFormatException	COR_E_BADIMAGEFORMAT (0x8007000B)
CannotUnloadAppDomainException	COR_E_CANNOTUNLOADAPPDOMAIN (0x80131015)
COMException	Any Other HRESULT Defaults To This .NET Exception
ContextMarshalException	COR_E_CONTEXTMARSHAL (0x80131504)
CryptographicException	NTE_FAIL
CryptographicUnexpectedOperationException	CORSEC_E_CRYPTO_UNEX_OPER (0x80131431)
CustomAttributeFormatException	COR_E_FORMAT (0x80131537)
DirectoryNotFoundException	COR_E_DIRECTORYNOTFOUND (0x80070003) STG_E_PATHNOTFOUND (0x80030003)
DivideByZeroException	COR_E_DIVIDEBYZERO (0x80020012)
DllNotFoundException	COR_E_DLLNOTFOUND (0x80131524)
DuplicateWaitObjectException	COR_E_DUPLICATEWAITOBJECT (0x80131529)
EndOfStreamException	COR_E_ENDOFSTREAM (0x801338)
EntryPointNotFoundException	COR_E_TYPELOAD (0x80131522)
Exception	COR_E_EXCEPTION (0x80131500)
ExecutionEngineException	COR_E_EXECUTIONENGINE (0x80131506)
ExternalException	E_FAIL (0x80004005)
FieldAccessException	COR_E_FIELDACCESS (0x80131507)
FileNotFoundException	COR_E_FILELOAD (0x80131621 or 0x80131018)
FileNotFoundException	COR_E_FILENOTFOUND (0x80070002)
FormatException	COR_E_FORMAT (0x80131537)
IndexOutOfRangeException	COR_E_INDEXOUTOFRANGE (0x80131508)
InvalidCastException	COR_E_INVALIDCAST (0x80004002)
InvalidComObjectException	COR_E_INVALIDCOMOBJECT (0x80131527)
InvalidFilterCriteriaException	COR_E_INVALIDFILTERCRITERIA (0x80131601)
InvalidOleVariantTypeException	COR_E_INVALIDOLEVARIANTTYPE (0x80131531)
InvalidOperationException	COR_E_INVALIDOPERATION (0x80131509)

Table 5-2. Mappping .NET exceptions to HRESULTS (continued)

.NET exception class name	HRESULT name (hex value of HRESULT)
InvalidProgramException	COR_E_INVALIDPROGRAM (0x8013153A)
IOException	COR_E_IO (0x80131620)
IsolatedStorageException	ISS_E_ISOSTORE (0x80131450)
MarshalDirectiveException	COR_E_MARSHALDIRECTIVE (0x80131535)
MethodAccessException	COR_E_METHODACCESS (0x80131510)
MissingFieldException	COR_E_MISSINGFIELD (0x80131511)
MissingManifestResourceException	COR_E_MISSINGMANIFESTRESOURCE (0x80131532)
MissingMemberException	COR_E_MISSINGMEMBER (0x80131512)
MissingMethodException	COR_E_MISSINGMETHOD (0x80131513)
MulticastNotSupportedException	COR_E_MULTICASTNOTSUPPORTED (0x80131514)
NotFiniteNumberException	COR_E_NOTFINITENUMBER (0x80131528)
NotImplementedException	E_NOTIMPL
NotSupportedException	COR_E_NOTSUPPORTED (0x80131515)
NullReferenceException	COR_E_NULLREFERENCE (0x80004003)
OutOfMemoryException	COR_E_OUTOFMEMORY (0x8007000E)
OverflowException	COR_E_OVERFLOW (0x80131516)
PathTooLongException	COR_E_PATHTOOLONG (0x8013206)
PlatformNotSupportedException	COR_E_PLATFORMNOTSUPPORTED (0x80131539)
PolicyException	CORSEC_E_POLICY_EXCEPTION
RankException	COR_E_RANK (0x80131517)
ReflectionTypeLoadException	COR_E_REFLECTIONTYPELOAD (0x80131602)
RemotingException	COR_E_REMOTING (0x8013150B)
RemotingTimeoutException	COR_E_REMOTING (0x8013150B)
SafeArrayTypeMismatchException	COR_E_SAFEARRAYTYPEMISMATCH (0x80131533)
SafeArrayRankMismatchException	COR_E_SAFEARRAYRANKMISMATCH (0x80131538)
SecurityException	COR_E_SECURITY (0x8013150A)
SEHException	E_FAIL (0x80004005)
SerializationException	COR_E_SERIALIZATION (0x8013150C)
ServerException	COR_E_SERVER (0x8013150E)
StackOverflowException	COR_E_STACKOVERFLOW (0x800703E9)
SUDSGeneratorException	COR_E_EXCEPTION (0x80131500)
SUDSParserException	COR_E_EXCEPTION (0x80131500)
SynchronizationLockException	COR_E_SYNCHRONIZATIONLOCK (0x80131518)
SystemException	COR_E_SYSTEM (0x80131501)
TargetException	COR_E_TARGET
TargetInvocationException	COR_E_TARGETINVOCATION (0x80131604)

Table 5-2. Mappping .NET exceptions to HRESULTS (continued)

.NET exception class name	HRESULT name (hex value of HRESULT)
TargetParameterCountException	COR_E_TARGETPARAMCOUNT (0x80138002)
ThreadAbortException	COR_E_THREADABORTED (0x80131530)
ThreadInterruptedException	COR_E_THREADINTERRUPTED (0x80131519)
ThreadStateException	COR_E_THREADSTATE (0x80131520)
ThreadStopException	COR_E_THREADSTOP
TypeInitializationException	COR_E_TYPEINITIALIZATION (0x80131534)
TypeLoadException	COR_E_TYPELOAD (0x80131522)
TypeUnloadedException	COR_E_TYPEUNLOADED (0x80131013)
UnauthorizedAccessException	COR_E_UNAUTHORIZEDACCESS (0x80070005)
VerificationException	COR_E_VERIFICATION
WeakReferenceException	COR_E_WEAKREFERENCE

Discussion

Handling exceptions generated by COM/COM+ components involves the following two steps:

1. Handle any specific exceptions that the .NET Common Language Runtime maps the COM/COM+ HRESULTs in which you're interested. The table in the Discussion section lists the standard HRESULT values returned by COM/COM+ objects and the .NET exceptions classes to which they are mapped.

2. Handle any user-defined exceptions that are unique to a specific COM/COM+ component by trapping the COMException exception. The COMException class reflects COM/COM+ HRESULTs that have no mapping to managed exceptions.

The following code fragment illustrates this handling of COM/COM+ exceptions:

```
try
{
    CallCOMMethod( );
}
catch (UnauthorizedAccessException uae)
{
    // Handle COM/COM+ access exceptions here
}
catch (System.Runtime.InteropServices.COMException ce)
{
    // Handle user-defined COM/COM+ exceptions here
}
catch (Exception e)
{
    // Handle all other exceptions here
}
```

See Recipe 5.9 for more information on handling user-defined HRESULTs.

See Also

See Recipe 5.9; see the "Error Raising and Handling Guidelines," "HRESULTs and Exceptions," and "Handling COM Interop Exceptions" topics in the MSDN documentation.

5.9 Handling User-Defined HRESULTs

Problem

A COM object can return a user-defined HRESULT or an HRESULT that has no mapping to a managed exception type. You wish to handle these returned HRESULTs in a more specific manner.

Solution

The following code fragment illustrates the handling of user-defined COM/COM+ exceptions:

```
try
{
    CallCOMMethod( );
}
catch (System.Runtime.InteropServices.COMException ce)
{
    switch ((uint)ce.ErrorCode)
    {
        case 0x80132000:
            // Handle this specific user-defined COM/COM+ exceptions here
            break;
        case 0x80132001:
            // Handle this specific user-defined COM/COM+ exceptions here
            break;
        default:
            // Handle any other specific user-defined COM/COM+
            // exceptions here
            break;
    }
}
catch (Exception e)
{
    // Handle all other exceptions here
}
```

Discussion

Handle any user-defined exceptions that are unique to a specific COM/COM+ component by trapping the COMException exception. This class reflects COM/COM+ HRESULTs that have no mapping to managed exceptions.

The COMException has a property, ErrorCode, in addition to those properties in the base Exception class. This property contains the HRESULT value that the COM/COM+ object returned. Another difference between COMException and Exception is that the InnerException property of a COMException object will always be null.

See Also

See the "Error Raising and Handling Guidelines" and "Handling COM Interop Exceptions" topics in the MSDN documentation.

5.10   Preventing Unhandled Exceptions

Problem

You need to make absolutely sure that every exception thrown by your application is handled and that no exception is bubbled up past the outermost exception handler. Hackers often use these types of exceptions to aid in their analysis of the vulnerabilities of an application.

Solution

Place try-catch or try-catch-finally blocks in strategic places in your application. In addition, use the exception event handler as a final line of defense against unhandled exceptions.

Discussion

If an exception occurs and is not handled, it will cause your application to shut down prematurely. This can leave data in an unstable state, which may only be able to be rectified by manual intervention—meaning that you could be spending a long night cleaning up the data by hand. To minimize the damage, you can place exception handlers in strategic locations throughout your code.

The most obvious location to place exception handling code is inside of the Main method. The Main method is the entry point to executables (files with an *.exe* extension). Therefore, if any exceptions occur inside your executable, the CLR starts looking for an exception handler, starting at the location where the exception occurred. If none are found, the CLR walks the stack until one is found; each method on the stack is examined in turn to determine whether an exception handler exists. If no exception handlers are found in the final method in the stack, the exception is considered unhandled and the application is terminated. In an executable, this final method is the Main method.

In addition, or in place of using try-catch or try-catch-finally blocks at the entry point of your application, you can use the exception event handler to capture unhandled exceptions. Note that Windows Forms applications provide their own unhandled exception trap around exception handlers and never raise the AppDomain level event. There are two steps to setting up an exception event handler. The first is to create the actual event handler. This is done as follows:

```
static void LastChanceHandler(object sender, UnhandledExceptionEventArgs args)
{
    try
    {
        Exception e = (Exception) args.ExceptionObject;

        Console.WriteLine("Unhandled exception == " + e.ToString());
        if (args.IsTerminating)
        {
            Console.WriteLine("The application is terminating");
        }
        else
        {
            Console.WriteLine("The application is not terminating");
        }
    }
    catch(Exception e)
    {
        Console.WriteLine("Unhandled exception in unhandled exception handler == " +
                        e.ToString());
    }
    finally
    {
        // Add other exception logging or cleanup code here.
    }
}
```

Next, you should add code to your application to wire up this event handler. The code to wire up the event handler should be executed as close to the start of the application as possible. For example, by placing this code in the Main method:

```
public static void Main()
{
    AppDomain.CurrentDomain.UnhandledException +=
            new UnhandledExceptionEventHandler(LastChanceHandler);

    //...
}
```

you are assured of being able to clean up after any unhandled exception.

The exception event handler takes two parameters. The first is the sender object, which is the AppDomain object that threw the exception. The second argument is an UnhandledExceptionEventArgs object. This object contains all the relevant information on the unhandled exception. Using this object, we can obtain the actual exception object that was thrown as well as a Boolean flag that indicates whether the application will terminate.

Exception event handlers are a great help when used in multithreaded code. If an unhandled exception is thrown in a thread other than the main thread, that thread aborts. However, only the worker thread, and not the application as a whole, will terminate. But you are not clearly notified when the CLR aborts this thread, which can cause some interesting debugging problems. However, when an exception event handler is used, you can be notified of any unhandled exceptions that occur in any worker thread and that cause it to abort.

The exception event handler captures unhandled exceptions only for the primary application domain. Any application domains created from the primary application domain do not fire this event for unhandled exceptions.

See Also

See the "Error Raising and Handling Guidelines" and "UnhandledException-EventHandler Class" topics in the MSDN documentation.

5.11 Displaying Exception Information

Problem

There are several different methods of displaying exception information. You need to choose the best one to use.

Solution

The .NET platform supports several methods for displaying exception information, depending on the specific type of information that you want to show. The easiest method is to use the ToString method of the thrown exception object, usually in the catch block of an exception handler:

```
catch(Exception e)
{
    Console.WriteLine(e.ToString( ));
}
```

Another method is to manually display the individual properties of the thrown exception and iterate through each inner exception, if any exist. For example, the following custom method is called from a catch block that takes a single exception object as a parameter and proceeds to display its information, including information on all inner exceptions:

```
public void DisplayException(Exception e)
{
    Console.WriteLine("Outer Exception.");
    Console.WriteLine("ExceptionType: " + e.GetType( ).Name);
    Console.WriteLine("HelpLine: " + e.HelpLink);
    Console.WriteLine("Message: " + e.Message);
    Console.WriteLine("Source: " + e.Source);
    Console.WriteLine("StackTrace: " + e.StackTrace);
    Console.WriteLine("TargetSite: " + e.TargetSite);
```

```
        string indent = "\t";
        Exception ie = e;

        while(ie.InnerException != null)
        {
            ie = ie.InnerException;

            Console.WriteLine("Inner Exception.");
            Console.WriteLine(indent + "ExceptionType: " +
                              ie.GetType().Name);
            Console.WriteLine(indent + "HelpLink: " + ie.HelpLink);
            Console.WriteLine(indent + "Message: " + ie.Message);
            Console.WriteLine(indent + "Source: " + ie.Source);
            Console.WriteLine(indent + "StackTrace: " + ie.StackTrace);
            Console.WriteLine(indent + "TargetSite: " + ie.TargetSite);

            indent += "\t";
        }
    }
}
```

Discussion

A typical exception object of type `Exception` displays the following information if its `ToString` method is called:

```
System.Exception: Exception of type System.Exception was thrown.
   at Chapter_Code.Chapter7.TestSpecializedException() in c:\book cs cookbook\code\
      test.cs:line 286
```

There are three pieces of information shown here:

- The exception type (`Exception` in this case) followed by a colon.
- The string contained in the exception's `Message` property.
- The string contained in the exception's `StackTrace` property.

The great thing about the `ToString` method is that information about any exception contained in the `InnerException` property is automatically displayed as well. The following text shows the output of an exception that wraps an inner exception:

```
System.Exception: Exception of type System.Exception was thrown.
---> System.Exception: The Inner Exception
   at Chapter_Code.Chapter7.TestSpecializedException()
     in c:\book cs cookbook\code\
     test.cs:line 306
   --- End of inner exception stack trace ---
   at Chapter_Code.Chapter7.TestSpecializedException()
     in c:\book cs cookbook\code\
     test.cs:line 310
```

The same three pieces of information are displayed for each exception. The output is broken down into the following format:

```
Outer exception type: Outer exception Message property
---> Inner Exception type: Inner exception Message property
Inner Exception StackTrace property
```

```
    --- End of inner exception stack trace ---
  Outer exception StackTrace property
```

If the inner exception contains an exception object in its InnerException property, that exception is displayed as well. In fact, information for all inner exceptions is displayed in this format.

Calling the ToString method is a quick, useful way of getting the most pertinent information out of the exception and displaying it in a formatted string. However, not all of the exception's information is displayed. There might be a need to display the HelpLine or Source properties of the exception. In fact, if this is a user-defined exception, there could be custom fields that need to be displayed or captured in an error log. Also, you might not like the default formatting that the ToString method offers. In these cases, consider writing your own method to display the exception's information.

To illustrate the custom method presented in the Solution section (the DisplayException method), consider the following code, which throws an exception that wraps two inner exceptions:

```
Exception innerInner = new Exception("The innerInner Exception.");
ArgumentException inner = new ArgumentException("The inner Exception.", innerInner);
NullReferenceException se = new NullReferenceException("A Test Message.", inner);
se.HelpLink = "MyComponent.hlp";
se.Source = "MyComponent";

try
{
    throw (se);
}
catch(Exception e)
{
    DisplayException(e);
}
```

If this code were executed, DisplayException would display the following:

```
Outer Exception.
ExceptionType: NullReferenceException
HelpLine: MyComponent.hlp
Message: A Test Message.
Source: MyComponent
StackTrace:    at Chapter_Code.SEH.DisplayException() in c:\book cs cookbook\code\
               test.cs:line 219
TargetSite: Void DisplayException()
inner Exception.
        ExceptionType: ArgumentException
        HelpLink:
        Message: The inner Exception.
        Source:
        StackTrace:
        TargetSite:
inner Exception.
```

```
ExceptionType: Exception
HelpLink:
Message: The innerInner Exception.
Source:
StackTrace:
TargetSite:
```

The outermost exception is displayed first, followed by all of its properties. Next, each inner exception is displayed in a similar manner.

The while loop of the DisplayException method is used to iterate through each inner exception until the innermost exception is reached. The indent variable is used to create the staggered display of inner exception information. Initially, this variable contains a single tab character ('\t'). A single tab character is added to this variable at the end of each iteration of the loop, allowing for the creation of the staggered display.

See Also

See the "Error Raising and Handling Guidelines" and "Exception Class" topics in the MSDN documentation.

5.12   Getting to the Root of a Problem Quickly

Problem

A thrown and caught exception can contain one or more inner exceptions. The innermost exception is usually indicates the origin of the problem. You want to be able to view the original thrown exception and skip all of the outer exceptions, and to view the initial problem.

Solution

The GetBaseException instance method of the Exception class displays information on only the innermost (original) exception; all other exception information is not displayed. This method accepts no parameters and returns the innermost exception. For example:

```
Console.WriteLine(e.GetBaseException().ToString());
```

Discussion

Calling the GetBaseException().ToString() method on an exception object that contains an inner exception produces the same error information as if the ToString method was called directly on the inner exception. However, if the exception object does not contain an inner expression, the information of the provided exception object is displayed. For the following code:

```
Exception innerInner = new Exception("The innerInner Exception.");
ArgumentException inner = new ArgumentException("The inner Exception.", innerInner);
NullReferenceException se = new NullReferenceException("A Test Message.", inner);

try
{
    throw (se);
}
catch(Exception e)
{
    Console.WriteLine(e.GetBaseException( ).ToString( ));
}
```

something similar to this would be displayed:

```
System.Exception: The innerInner Exception.
    at Chapter_Code.EH.MyMethod( ) in c:\book cs cookbook\code\test.cs:line 286
```

Notice that no exception other than the innerInner exception is displayed. This useful technique gets to the root of the problem while filtering out all of the other outer exceptions that you are not interested in.

See Also

See the "Error Raising and Handling Guidelines" and "Exception Class" topics in the MSDN documentation.

5.13   Creating a New Exception Type

Problem

None of the built-in exceptions in the .NET Framework provide the implementation details that you require for an exception that you need to throw. You need to create your own exception class that operates seamlessly with your application, as well as other applications. Whenever an application receives this new exception, it can inform the user that a specific error occurred in a specific component. This report will greatly reduce the time required to debug the problem.

Solution

Create your own exception class. To illustrate, we'll create a custom exception class, RemoteComponentException, that will inform a client application that an error has occurred in a remote server assembly. The complete source code for the RemoteComponentException class is:

```
using System;
using System.IO;
using System.Runtime.Serialization;
using System.Runtime.Serialization.Formatters.Binary;
```

```csharp
[SerializableAttribute]
public class RemoteComponentException :
  ApplicationException, ISerializable
{
    // New exception field
    private string serverName = "";

    // Normal exception ctor's
    public RemoteComponentException( ) : base( )
    {
    }

    public RemoteComponentException(string message) : base(message)
    {
    }

    public RemoteComponentException(string message,
      Exception innerException)
        : base(message, innerException)
    {
    }

    // Exception ctor's that accept the new ServerName parameter
    public RemoteComponentException(string message,
      string serverName) : base(message)
    {
        this.serverName = serverName;
    }

    public RemoteComponentException(string message,
      Exception innerException, string serverName)
            : base(message, innerException)
    {
        this.serverName = serverName;
    }

    // Serialization ctor
    public RemoteComponentException(SerializationInfo exceptionInfo,
            StreamingContext exceptionContext)
            : base(exceptionInfo, exceptionContext)
    {
        this.serverName = exceptionInfo.GetString("ServerName");
    }

    // Read-only property
    public string ServerName
    {
        get{return (serverName.Trim( ));}
    }

    public override string Message
    {
        get
        {
```

```
            if (this.ServerName.Length == 0)
                return (base.Message + Environment.NewLine +
                        "An unnamed server has encountered an error.");
            else
                return (base.Message + Environment.NewLine +
                        "The server " + this.ServerName +
                        " has encountered an error.");
        }
    }

    // Overridden methods
    // ToString method
    public override string ToString()
    {
        string errorString = "An error has occured in a server " +
            "component of this client.";
        errorString += Environment.NewLine + "Server Name: " +
            this.ServerName;
        if (this.InnerException == null)
        {
            errorString += Environment.NewLine +
                "Server component failed to provide an " +
                "underlying exception!";
        }
        else
        {
            string indent = "\t";
            Exception ie = this;
            while(ie.InnerException != null)
            {
                ie = ie.InnerException;
                errorString += Environment.NewLine + indent +
                    "inner exception type thrown by server component: " +
                    ie.GetType().Name.ToString();
                errorString += Environment.NewLine + indent + "Message: "
                    + ie.Message;
                errorString += Environment.NewLine + indent +
                    "StackTrace: " + ie.StackTrace;

                indent += "\t";
            }
        }
        errorString += Environment.NewLine + "StackTrace of client " +
                    "component: " + this.StackTrace;

        return (errorString);
    }

    // Call base.ToString method
    public string ToBaseString()
    {
        return (base.ToString());
    }
```

```csharp
        // GetHashCode
        public override int GetHashCode()
        {
            return (ServerName.GetHashCode());
        }

        // Equals
        public override bool Equals(object obj)
        {
            bool isEqual = false;

            if (obj == null || (this.GetType() != obj.GetType()))
            {
                isEqual = false;
            }
            else
            {
                RemoteComponentException se = (RemoteComponentException)obj;
                if ((this.ServerName.Length == 0)
                  && (se.ServerName.Length == 0))
                    isEqual = false;
                else
                    isEqual = (this.ServerName == se.ServerName);
            }

            return (isEqual);
        }

        // == operator
        public static bool operator ==(RemoteComponentException v1,
           RemoteComponentException v2)
        {
            return (v1.Equals(v2));
        }

        // != operator
        public static bool operator !=(RemoteComponentException v1,
           RemoteComponentException v2)
        {
            return (!(v1 == v2));
        }

        // Used during serialization to capture information about extra fields
        public override void GetObjectData(SerializationInfo exceptionInfo,
                                           StreamingContext exceptionContext)
        {
            base.GetObjectData(exceptionInfo, exceptionContext);
            exceptionInfo.AddValue("ServerName", this.ServerName);
        }
    }
```

Discussion

The code to test the RemoteComponentException class is:

```csharp
public void TestSpecializedException()
{
    // Generic inner exception used to test the
    // RemoteComponentException's inner exception
    Exception inner = new Exception("The inner Exception");

    // Test each ctor
    Console.WriteLine(Environment.NewLine + Environment.NewLine +
      "TEST EACH CTOR");
    RemoteComponentException se1 = new RemoteComponentException ();
    RemoteComponentException se2 =
      new RemoteComponentException ("A Test Message for se2");
    RemoteComponentException se3 =
      new RemoteComponentException ("A Test Message for se3", inner);
    RemoteComponentException se4 =
      new RemoteComponentException ("A Test Message for se4",
                                    "MyServer");
    RemoteComponentException se5 =
      new RemoteComponentException ("A Test Message for se5", inner,
                                    "MyServer");

    // Test new ServerName property
    Console.WriteLine(Environment.NewLine +
      "TEST NEW SERVERNAME PROPERTY");
    Console.WriteLine("se1.ServerName == " + se1.ServerName);
    Console.WriteLine("se2.ServerName == " + se2.ServerName);
    Console.WriteLine("se3.ServerName == " + se3.ServerName);
    Console.WriteLine("se4.ServerName == " + se4.ServerName);
    Console.WriteLine("se5.ServerName == " + se5.ServerName);

    // Test overridden Message property
    Console.WriteLine(Environment.NewLine +
      "TEST -OVERRIDDEN- MESSAGE PROPERTY");
    Console.WriteLine("se1.Message == " + se1.Message);
    Console.WriteLine("se2.Message == " + se2.Message);
    Console.WriteLine("se3.Message == " + se3.Message);
    Console.WriteLine("se4.Message == " + se4.Message);
    Console.WriteLine("se5.Message == " + se5.Message);

    // Test -overridden- ToString method
    Console.WriteLine(Environment.NewLine +
      "TEST -OVERRIDDEN- TOSTRING METHOD");
    Console.WriteLine("se1.ToString() == " + se1.ToString());
    Console.WriteLine("se2.ToString() == " + se2.ToString());
    Console.WriteLine("se3.ToString() == " + se3.ToString());
    Console.WriteLine("se4.ToString() == " + se4.ToString());
    Console.WriteLine("se5.ToString() == " + se5.ToString());

    // Test ToBaseString method
    Console.WriteLine(Environment.NewLine +
      "TEST TOBASESTRING METHOD");
    Console.WriteLine("se1.ToBaseString() == " + se1.ToBaseString());
    Console.WriteLine("se2.ToBaseString() == " + se2.ToBaseString());
    Console.WriteLine("se3.ToBaseString() == " + se3.ToBaseString());
    Console.WriteLine("se4.ToBaseString() == " + se4.ToBaseString());
```

```csharp
Console.WriteLine("se5.ToBaseString() == " + se5.ToBaseString());

// Test -overridden- Equals method
Console.WriteLine(Environment.NewLine +
  "TEST -OVERRIDDEN- EQUALS METHOD");
Console.WriteLine("se1.Equals(se1) == " + se1.Equals(se1));
Console.WriteLine("se2.Equals(se1) == " + se2.Equals(se1));
Console.WriteLine("se3.Equals(se1) == " + se3.Equals(se1));
Console.WriteLine("se4.Equals(se1) == " + se4.Equals(se1));
Console.WriteLine("se5.Equals(se1) == " + se5.Equals(se1));
Console.WriteLine("se5.Equals(se4) == " + se5.Equals(se4));

// Test -overridden- == operator
Console.WriteLine(Environment.NewLine +
  "TEST -OVERRIDDEN- == OPERATOR");
Console.WriteLine("se1 == se1 == " + (se1 == se1));
Console.WriteLine("se2 == se1 == " + (se2 == se1));
Console.WriteLine("se3 == se1 == " + (se3 == se1));
Console.WriteLine("se4 == se1 == " + (se4 == se1));
Console.WriteLine("se5 == se1 == " + (se5 == se1));
Console.WriteLine("se5 == se4 == " + (se5 == se4));

// Test -overridden- != operator
Console.WriteLine(Environment.NewLine +
  "TEST -OVERRIDDEN- != OPERATOR");
Console.WriteLine("se1 != se1 == " + (se1 != se1));
Console.WriteLine("se2 != se1 == " + (se2 != se1));
Console.WriteLine("se3 != se1 == " + (se3 != se1));
Console.WriteLine("se4 != se1 == " + (se4 != se1));
Console.WriteLine("se5 != se1 == " + (se5 != se1));
Console.WriteLine("se5 != se4 == " + (se5 != se4));

// Test -overridden- GetBaseException method
Console.WriteLine(Environment.NewLine +
  "TEST -OVERRIDDEN- GETBASEEXCEPTION METHOD");
Console.WriteLine("se1.GetBaseException() == " + se1.GetBaseException());
Console.WriteLine("se2.GetBaseException() == " + se2.GetBaseException());
Console.WriteLine("se3.GetBaseException() == " + se3.GetBaseException());
Console.WriteLine("se4.GetBaseException() == " + se4.GetBaseException());
Console.WriteLine("se5.GetBaseException() == " + se5.GetBaseException());

// Test -overridden- GetHashCode method
Console.WriteLine(Environment.NewLine +
  "TEST -OVERRIDDEN- GETHASHCODE METHOD");
Console.WriteLine("se1.GetHashCode() == " + se1.GetHashCode());
Console.WriteLine("se2.GetHashCode() == " + se2.GetHashCode());
Console.WriteLine("se3.GetHashCode() == " + se3.GetHashCode());
Console.WriteLine("se4.GetHashCode() == " + se4.GetHashCode());
Console.WriteLine("se5.GetHashCode() == " + se5.GetHashCode());

// Test serialization
Console.WriteLine(Environment.NewLine +
  "TEST SERIALIZATION/DESERIALIZATION");
BinaryFormatter binaryWrite = new BinaryFormatter();
```

```
    Stream ObjectFile = File.Create("se1.object");
    binaryWrite.Serialize(ObjectFile, se1);
    ObjectFile.Close();
    ObjectFile = File.Create("se2.object");
    binaryWrite.Serialize(ObjectFile, se2);
    ObjectFile.Close();
    ObjectFile = File.Create("se3.object");
    binaryWrite.Serialize(ObjectFile, se3);
    ObjectFile.Close();
    ObjectFile = File.Create("se4.object");
    binaryWrite.Serialize(ObjectFile, se4);
    ObjectFile.Close();
    ObjectFile = File.Create("se5.object");
    binaryWrite.Serialize(ObjectFile, se5);
    ObjectFile.Close();

    BinaryFormatter binaryRead = new BinaryFormatter();
    ObjectFile = File.OpenRead("se1.object");
    object Data = binaryRead.Deserialize(ObjectFile);
    Console.WriteLine("----------" + Environment.NewLine + Data);
    ObjectFile.Close();
    ObjectFile = File.OpenRead("se2.object");
    Data = binaryRead.Deserialize(ObjectFile);
    Console.WriteLine("----------" + Environment.NewLine + Data);
    ObjectFile.Close();
    ObjectFile = File.OpenRead("se3.object");
    Data = binaryRead.Deserialize(ObjectFile);
    Console.WriteLine("----------" + Environment.NewLine + Data);
    ObjectFile.Close();
    ObjectFile = File.OpenRead("se4.object");
    Data = binaryRead.Deserialize(ObjectFile);
    Console.WriteLine("----------" + Environment.NewLine + Data);
    ObjectFile.Close();
    ObjectFile = File.OpenRead("se5.object");
    Data = binaryRead.Deserialize(ObjectFile);
    Console.WriteLine("----------" + Environment.NewLine +
       Data + Environment.NewLine  + "----------");
    ObjectFile.Close();

    Console.WriteLine(Environment.NewLine + "END TEST" + Environment.NewLine);
}
```

The exception hierarchy starts with the Exception class; from this, two classes are derived: ApplicationException and SystemException. The SystemException class and any classes derived from it are reserved for the developers of the FCL. Most of the common exceptions, such as the NullReferenceException or the OverflowException exceptions, are derived from SystemException. The FCL developers created the ApplicationException class for other developers using the .NET languages to derive their own exceptions from. This partitioning allows for a clear distinction between user-defined exceptions and the built-in system exceptions. Nothing actively prevents you from deriving a class from the SystemException class, but it is better to be consistent and use the convention of always deriving from the ApplicationException class for user-defined exceptions.

You should follow the naming convention for exceptions when determining the name of your exception. The convention is very simple. Whatever you decide on for the exception's name, add the word Exception to the end of the name (e.g., use UnknownException as the exception name instead of just Unknown). In addition, the name should be camel-cased* and contain no underscore characters.

Every user-defined exception should include *at least* three constructors, described next. This is not a requirement, but it makes your exception classes operate similar to every other exception class in the FCL and minimizes the learning curve for other developers using your new exception. These three constructors are:

The default constructor
  This constructor takes no arguments and simply calls the base class's default constructor.

A constructor with a parameter that accepts a message string
  This message string overwrites the default contents of the Message field of this exception. Like the default constructor, this constructor also calls the base class's constructor, which also accepts a message string as its only parameter.

A constructor that accepts a message string and an inner exception as parameters
  The object contained in the *innerException* parameter is added to the InnerException field of this exception object. Like the other two constructors, this constructor calls the base class' constructor of the same signature.

If this exception will be caught in unmanaged code, such as a COM object, you can also override the HRESULT value for this exception. An exception caught in unmanaged code becomes an HRESULT value. If the exception does not override the HRESULT value, it defaults to the HRESULT value of the base class exception, which, in the case of a user-defined exception object that inherits from ApplicationException, is HRESULT COR_E_APPLICATION, which has a value of 0x80131600. To override the default HRESULT value, simply change the value of this field in the constructor. The following code demonstrates this technique:

```
public class RemoteComponentException : ApplicationException
{
    public RemoteComponentException() : base()
    {
        HResult = 0x80040321;
    }

    public RemoteComponentException(string message) : base(message)
    {
        HResult = 0x80040321;
    }

    public RemoteComponentException(string message, Exception innerException)
        : base(message, innerException)
```

* ThisIsCamelCasing.

```
    {
        HResult = 0x80040321;
    }
}
```

Now the HResult that the COM object will see is the value 0x80040321. See Table 5-2 in Recipe 5.8 for more information on the mapping of HRESULT values to their equivalent managed exception classes.

 It is usually a good idea to override the Message field in order to incorporate any new fields into the exception's message text. Always remember to include the base class's message text along with any additional text you add to this property.

Fields and their accessors should be created to hold data specific to the exception. Since this exception will be thrown as a result of an error that occurs in a remote server assembly, we will add a private field to contain the name of the server or service. In addition, we will add a public read-only property to access this field. Since we added this new field, we should add two constructors that accept an extra parameter used to set the value of the serverName field.

If necessary, override any base class members whose behavior is inherited by the custom exception class. For example, since we have added a new field, we need to determine whether it will need to be added to the default contents of the Message field for this exception. If it does, we must override the Message property.

Notice that the Message field in the base class is displayed on the first line and our additional text is displayed on the next line. This organization takes into account that a user might modify the message that will appear in the Message field by using one of the overloaded constructors that takes a message string as a parameter.

In certain cases (such as remoting), your exception object should be serializable and deserializable. This involves performing the following two additional steps:

1. Add the Serializable attribute to the class definition. This attribute specifies that this class can be serialized or deserialized. A SerializationException is thrown if this attribute does not exist on this class and an attempt is made to serialize this class.

2. The class should implement the ISerializable interface if you want control over how serialization and deserialization are performed, and it should provide an implementation for its single member, GetObjectData. Here we implement it because the base class implements it, which means that we have no choice but to reimplement it if we want the fields we added (e.g., serverName) to get serialized.

In addition, a new overridden constructor is needed that accepts information to deserialize this object.

Even though it is not required, you should make all user-defined exception classes serializable and deserializable.

At this point, the RemoteComponentException class contains everything you need for a complete user-defined exception class. You could stop at this point, but let's continue a bit farther and override some default functionality that deals with the hash code, equality, and inequality:

Overriding the Equals method

It is possible that we might need to override the default implementation of the Equals method and the == and != operators. The default implementation tests each object for reference equality. We may need to test for value equality; in this case, we need to override this method and both operators. The ServerName property value will be used in determining equality between two RemoteComponentException classes. The Equals method returns true only if the ServerName properties of both RemoteComponentException objects return the same value. Otherwise, the two objects are not considered equal. The exception occurs when the ServerName properties of both objects are blank. In this case, both RemoteComponentException objects are considered to be in an unknown state and therefore equality cannot be definitely determined.

Overriding the GetHashCode method

Since we have overridden the Equals method, we should override the GetHashCode method, which overrides the hash code generation algorithm.

Overriding the == and != operators

When overriding the Equals method, both the == and != operators should be overloaded as well. Notice that both operators ultimately use the Equals method to determine equality. Therefore, they are simple to write.

As a final note, it is wise to place all user-defined exceptions in a separate assembly, which allows for easier reuse of these exceptions in other applications, and, more importantly, allows other application domains and remotely executing code to both throw and handle these exceptions correctly no matter where they are thrown. The assembly that holds these exceptions should be signed with a strong name and added to the Global Assembly Cache (GAC) so that any code that uses or handles these exceptions can find the assembly that defines them. See Recipe 14.10 for more information on how to do this.

See Also

See Recipe 14.10; see the "Using User-Defined Exceptions" and "ApplicationException Class" topics in the MSDN documentation.

5.14 Obtaining a Stack Trace

Problem

You need a view of what the stack looks like at any particular point in your application. However, you do not have an exception object from which to obtain this stack trace.

Solution

Use the following line of code to obtain a stack trace at any point in your application:

```
string currentStackTrace = System.Environment.StackTrace;
```

The variable currentStackTrace now contains the stack trace at the location where this line of code was executed.

Discussion

A good use of the Solution is tracking down stack overflow problems. You can obtain the current stack trace at various points in your application and then calculate the stack depth. This depth calculation can then be logged to determine when and why the stack is overflowing or potential trouble spots where the stack may grow very large.

It is very easy to obtain a stack trace using the System.Environment.StackTrace property. Unfortunately, this stack trace also lists three methods defined in the System. Environment class that are called when you use the Environment.StackTrace property. The returned stack trace, using this method, will look something like the following:

```
at System.Environment.GetStackTrace(Exception e)
at System.Environment.GetStackTrace(Exception e)
at System.Environment.get_StackTrace()
at Chapter_Code.Class1.ObtainingStackTrace() in c:\book cs cookbook\test.cs:line 260
at Chapter_Code.Class1.Main(String[] args) in c:\book cs cookbook\main.cs:line 78
```

The first three items in the stack trace are method calls that we are not interested in. To fix this, we can write the following method to find and remove these items from the stack trace:

```
public static string GetStackTraceInfo(string currentStackTrace)
{
    string firstStackTraceCall = "System.Environment.get_StackTrace()";
    int posOfStackTraceCall = currentStackTrace.IndexOf(firstStackTraceCall);
    return (currentStackTrace.Substring(posOfStackTraceCall +
            firstStackTraceCall.Length));
}
```

This method is called using the following line of code:

```
string stackTraceInfo = GetStackTraceInfo(System.Environment.StackTrace);
```

The second line in the GetStackTraceInfo method creates and initializes a string variable to the first called StackTrace method—which is actually a call to the get portion of the StackTrace property. This variable is used in the third line to obtain its starting position in the complete stack trace string. The final line of code grabs the end of the complete stack trace string, starting at the ending of the first called StackTrace method. The FinalStackTrace variable now contains the following string:

```
at Chapter_Code.Class1.ObtainingStackTrace() in c:\book cs cookbook\test.cs:line 260
at Chapter_Code.Class1.Main(String[] args) in c:\book cs cookbook\main.cs:line 78
```

This is the current stack trace at the point in the code where the Environment.StackTrace method was called.

Now that we have a stack trace of our code, we can calculate the stack depth at the point where we call Environment.StackTrace. The following code uses a regular expression to determine the depth of a stack trace:

```
using System;
using System.Text.RegularExpressions;

public static int GetStackTraceDepth(string currentStackTrace)
{
    string firstStackTraceCall = "System.Environment.get_StackTrace()";
    int posOfStackTraceCall = currentStackTrace.IndexOf(firstStackTraceCall);
    string finalStackTrace = currentStackTrace.Substring(posOfStackTraceCall +
            firstStackTraceCall.Length);

    MatchCollection methodCallMatches = Regex.Matches(finalStackTrace,
            @"\sat\s.*(\sin\s.*\:line\s\d*)?");
    return (methodCallMatches.Count);
}
```

This regular expression captures every method call in the stack trace string. Note that, if the correct symbols are located for our assembly, the stack trace might look like this:

```
at Chapter_Code.Class1.ObtainingStackTrace() in c:\book cs cookbook\test.cs:line 260
at Chapter_Code.Class1.Main(String[] args) in c:\book cs cookbook\main.cs:line 78
```

However, if the correct symbols cannot be found, the stack trace string will look similar to the following:

```
at Chapter_Code.Class1.ObtainingStackTrace()
at Chapter_Code.Class1.Main(String[] args)
```

The file and line numbers are not displayed in this case, and the regular expression must take this into account.

To get a count of the stack depth, use the Count property of the MatchCollection object to give the total number of method calls in the stack. In addition, we can obtain each individual method call as an independent string by iterating through the MatchCollection object. The code to do this is:

```
Console.WriteLine("-------------");
foreach(Match m in MethodCallMatches)
{
    Console.WriteLine(m.Value + System.Environment.NewLine + "-------------");
}
```

This code will display the following:

```
-------------
at Chapter_Code.Class1.ObtainingStackTrace( ) in
  c:\book cs cookbook\test.cs:line 260
-------------
at Chapter_Code.Class1.Main(String[] args) in
  c:\book cs cookbook\main.cs:line 78
-------------
```

Each method and its information are contained within a `Match` object within the `MatchCollection` object.

The `Environment.StackTrace` method can be useful as a debugging tool. You can see at various points in your application which methods have been called and their calling order. This can come in very handy when creating and debugging an application that uses recursion. In addition, you can also keep track of the stack depth by using the `Environment.StackTrace` property.

See Also

See the "Environment.StackTrace Property" topic in the MSDN documentation.

5.15   Breaking on a First Chance Exception

Problem

You need to fix a problem with your code that is throwing an exception. Unfortunately, an exception handler is handling the exception, and you are having a tough time pinpointing where and when the exception is being thrown.

Forcing the application to break on an exception before the application has a chance to handle it is very useful in situations where you need to step through the code at the point where the exception is first being thrown. If this exception was thrown and not handled by your application, the debugger would intervene and break on the line of code that caused the unhandled exception. In this case, you can see the context in which the exception was thrown. However, if an exception handler is active when the exception is thrown, the exception handler will handle it and continue on, preventing you from being able to see the context at the point where the exception was thrown. This is the default behavior for all exceptions.

Solution

Select Debug → Exceptions within Visual Studio .NET to display the Exceptions dialog box (see Figure 5-1). Select the exception from the tree that you want to modify

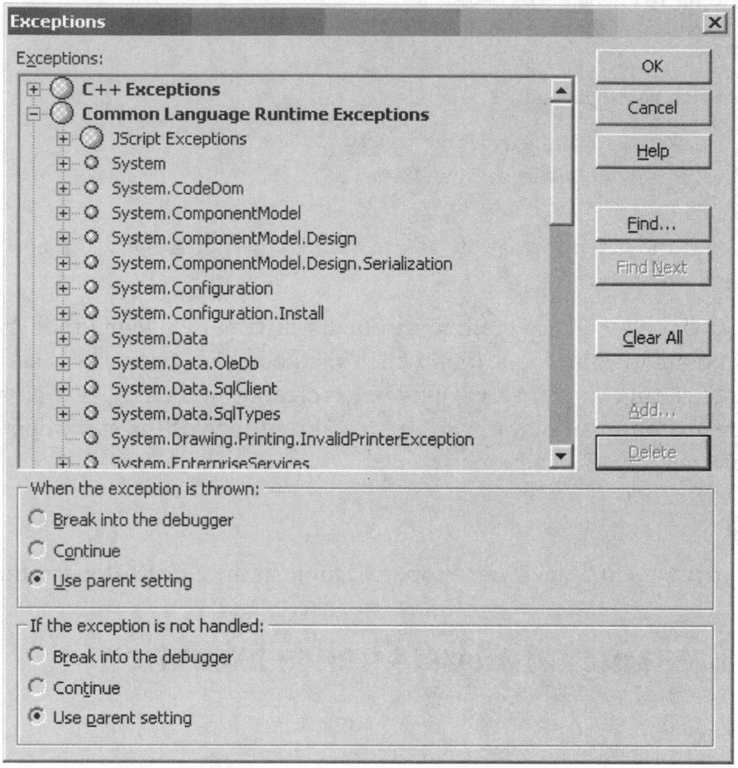

Figure 5-1. The Exceptions dialog box

and then click on the "Break into the debugger" radio button in the "When the exception is thrown" frame. Click the OK button and then run your application. Any time the application throws the type of error you selected in the Exceptions dialog box, the debugger will break on that line of code before your application has a chance to handle it.

Discussion

Using the Exceptions dialog box, you can target specific exceptions or sets of exceptions for which you wish to alter the default behavior. This dialog has three main sections. The first is the TreeView control, which contains the list of categorized exceptions. Using this TreeView, you can choose one or more exceptions or groups of exceptions whose behavior you wish to modify.

The next section on this dialog is the frame with the caption "When the exception is thrown." This frame contains three radio buttons that control the behavior when the exception is first thrown. At this stage, the exception is considered a *first chance exception*. The "Break into the debugger" radio button forces the debugger to intervene when a first chance exception of the type chosen in the TreeView control is thrown. The "Continue" radio button allows the application to attempt to handle the first chance exception. The "Use parent setting" radio button uses the configuration of the parent of this exception when handling it as a first class exception.

The third section on this dialog is the frame with the caption "If the exception is not handled." This frame contains the same three radio buttons as the previous frame. These radio buttons control the behavior when an unhandled exception is thrown by the application. At this stage, the exception is considered a *second chance exception*. The radio buttons operate in the same manner as with the previous frame.

This dialog contains two helpful buttons, Find and Find Next, to allow you to search for an exception rather than dig into the TreeView control and search for it on your own. In addition to these buttons, there are three buttons, Clear All, Add, and Delete, which are used to add and remove user-defined exceptions. For example, we can create our own exception, as we did in Recipe 5.13, and add this exception to the TreeView list. You must add any managed exception such as this to the TreeView node entitled Common Language Runtime Exceptions. This setting tells the debugger that this is a managed exception and should be handled as such.

To add a user-defined exception to the TreeView, click the Add button and the dialog box shown in Figure 5-2 appears.

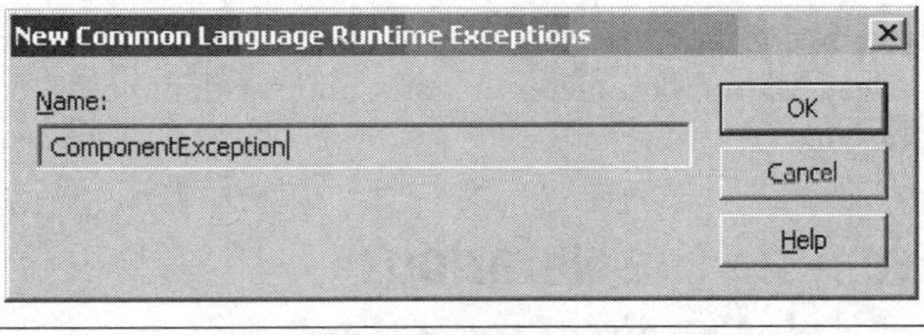

Figure 5-2. Adding a user-defined exception to the TreeView

Type the name of the exception—exactly as its class name is spelled—into the Name field of this dialog box. Do not append any other information to this name, such as the namespace it resides in or a class name that it is nested within. Doing so will cause the debugger to fail to see this exception when it is thrown. Clicking the OK button places this exception into the TreeView under the Common Language Runtime Exceptions node. You can then modify the way this exception will be handled using the radio buttons at the bottom of the Exceptions dialog box. The Exceptions dialog box will look something like the one in Figure 5-3 after you add and modify this user-defined exception.

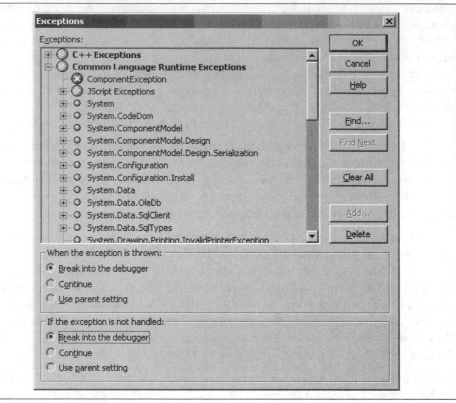

Figure 5-3. The Exceptions dialog box after adding a user-defined exception to the TreeView

The Delete button deletes any selected user-defined exception that you added to the TreeView. The Clear All button deletes any and all user-defined exceptions that have been added to the TreeView.

5.16 Preventing the Nefarious TypeInitializationException

Problem

Problems can occur when initializing a class or a structure's static fields. Some of these problems are serious enough to raise a TypeInitializationException exception. Unfortunately, this exception can be hard to track down and can potentially shut down your application. You want to prevent this from occurring.

Solution

If you are initializing static fields to a value, null, or not initializing them at all, as is the case with the following class:

```
public class TestInit
{
    public static object one;
    public static string two = one.ToString( );
}
```

you should consider rewriting the class to include a static constructor that performs the initialization of the static fields. This will aid in the debugging of your static fields:

```
public class TestInit
{
    static TestInit( )
    {
        try
        {
            one = null;
            two = one.ToString( );
        }
        catch (Exception e)
        {
            Console.WriteLine("CAUGHT EXCEPTION IN .CCTOR: " + e.ToString( ));
        }
    }

    public static object one;
    public static string two;
}
```

Discussion

To see this exception in action, run the following method:

```
public static void Main( )
{
    // Causes TypeInitializationException
    TestInit c = new TestInit( );

    // Replacing this method's code with the following line
    //     will produce similar results
    //TestInit.one.ToString( );
}
```

This code creates an instance of the TestInit class. We are assured that any static fields of the class will be initialized before this class is created, and any static constructors on the TestInit class will be called as well. The TestInit class is written as follows:

```
public class TestInit
{
    public static object one = null;
    public static string two = one.ToString( );
}
```

As you can see, a NullReferenceException should be thrown on the second static field, since it is trying to call ToString on an object set to null. If run from the development environment, you will see two message boxes pop up in sequence. The first is the message box depicted in Figure 5-4. The second message box shown is depicted in Figure 5-5. The application proceeds to shut down at this point.

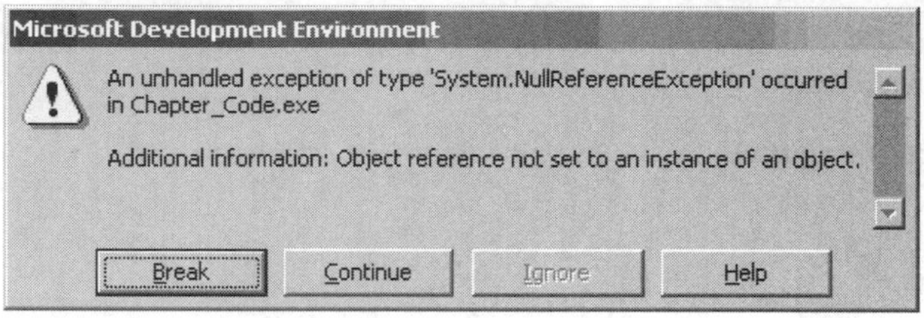

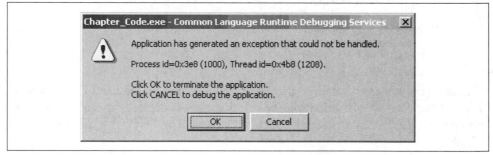

Figure 5-4. An unhandled NullReferenceException

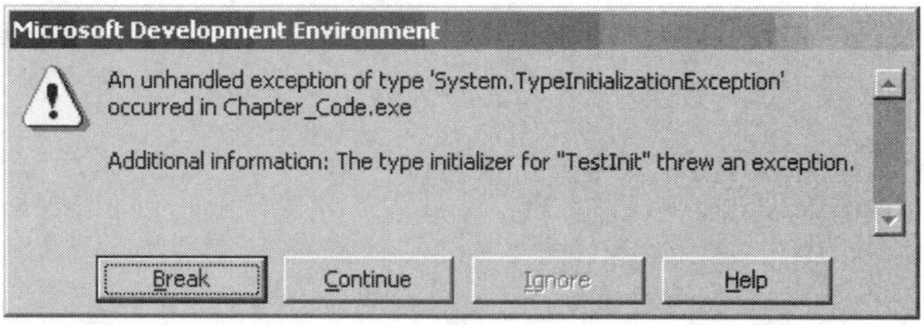

Figure 5-5. An unhandled TypeInitializationException

However, if this executable is run from outside the development environment, the message box shown in Figure 5-6 is displayed and the application shuts down.

Figure 5-6. An unhandled runtime exception

Now, let's add a try-catch block around the `Main` method, as shown here:

```
public static void Main()
{
    try
    {
        // Causes TypeInitializationException
        TestInit c = new TestInit();
    }
    catch(Exception e)
    {
        Console.WriteLine("CAUGHT EXCEPTION IN CREATING METHOD: " + e.ToString());
    }
}
```

When this code is run inside the development environment, the message box in Figure 5-4 appears again, but the `TypeInitializationException` is caught by the new exception handler that we added to the `Main` method. The text displayed by the exception handler is shown here:

```
CAUGHT EXCEPTION IN CREATING METHOD: System.TypeInitializationException:
    The type initializer for "TestInit" threw an exception. --->
    System.NullReferenceException: Object reference not set to an instance
                            of an object.
   at Chapter_Code.TestInit..cctor() in c:\book cs cookbook\code\test.cs:line 200
   --- End of inner exception stack trace ---
   at Chapter_Code.TestInit..ctor()
   at Chapter_Code.Class1.TypeinitExceptionPrevention() in c:\book cs cookbook\
      code\test.cs:line 175
```

The `TypeInitializationException` wraps the `NullReferenceException` that was the original exception thrown. The runtime provides the `TypeInitializationException` wrapper automatically.

A third method of trapping this exception is to use the exception event handler. This exception event handler is described in detail in Recipe 5.10. When only this exception handler is employed with no supporting `try-catch` or `try-catch-finally` blocks, the following events occur when running the executable in the development environment:

1. The message boxes shown in Figures 5-4 and 5-5 are displayed in that order.

2. The event exception handler intercepts the exception before the application is terminated. When the executable is run standalone, the message box in Figure 5-6 is displayed first. Then, the event exception handler intercepts the exception, and, finally, the application is terminated.

The second method seems to work best; use `try-catch` blocks at a minimum around code that will potentially cause static fields to initialize.

There is a way to eliminate the `TypeInitializationException` from the picture. We can simply initialize our class or structure's static fields within the appropriate static constructor(s), shown in the Solution section of this recipe. When this code is executed, the catch block captures the real exception and there is no fear of the application shutting down. The text displayed by the catch block is as follows:

```
CAUGHT EXCEPTION IN .CCTOR: System.NullReferenceException: Object reference not set
to an instance of an object.
    at Chapter_Code.TestInit..cctor() in c:\book cs cookbook\code\test.cs:line 191
```

This is much cleaner and more elegant than the other solutions. In addition, tracking down the source of the bug is much easier. As a note, this exception now operates in the same manner regardless of whether the application is being run in the development environment.

See Also

See the "Error Raising and Handling Guidelines" and "TypeInitializationException Class" topics in the MSDN documentation.

5.17 Handling Exceptions Thrown from an Asynchronous Delegate

Problem

When using a delegate asynchronously, you want to be notified in the calling thread if the delegate has thrown any exceptions.

Solution

Wrap the EndInvoke method of the delegate in a try/catch block:

```
using System;
using System.Threading;

public class AsyncAction
{
    public void PollAsyncDelegate()
    {
        // Create the async delegate to call Method1 and call its BeginInvoke method
        AsyncInvoke MI = new AsyncInvoke(TestAsyncInvoke.Method1);
        IAsyncResult AR = MI.BeginInvoke(null, null);

        // Poll until the async delegate is finished
        while (!AR.IsCompleted)
        {
            System.Threading.Thread.Sleep(100);
            Console.Write('.');
        }
        Console.WriteLine("Finished Polling");

        // Call the EndInvoke method of the async delegate
```

```
        try
        {
            int RetVal = MI.EndInvoke(AR);
            Console.WriteLine("RetVal: " + RetVal);
        }
        catch (Exception e)
        {
            Console.WriteLine(e.ToString());
        }
    }
}
```

The following code defines the AsyncInvoke delegate and the asynchronously invoked static method TestAsyncInvoke.Method1:

```
public delegate int AsyncInvoke();

public class TestAsyncInvoke
{
    public static int Method1()
    {
        throw (new Exception("Method1"));    // Simulate an exception being thrown
    }
}
```

Discussion

If the code in the PollAsyncDelegate method did not contain a call to the delegate's EndInvoke method, the exception thrown in Method1 would simply be discarded and never caught. This behavior is by design; for all unhandled exceptions that occur within the thread, the thread immediately returns to the thread pool and the exception is lost.

If a method that was called asynchronously through a delegate throws an exception, the only way to trap that exception object is to include a call to the delegate's EndInvoke method and wrap this call in an exception handler. The EndInvoke method must be called to retrieve the results of the asynchronous delegate; in fact, the EndInvoke method must be called even if there are no results. These results can be obtained through a return value or any ref or out parameters of the delegate.

See Also

For more on calling delegates asynchronously, see Recipe 7.4.

CHAPTER 6

Diagnostics

The .NET Framework Class Library (FCL) contains many classes to obtain diagnostic information about your application, as well as the environment it is running in. In fact, there are so many classes that a namespace, System.Diagnostics, was created to contain all of them. This chapter contains recipes for instrumenting your application with debug/trace information, obtaining process information, using the built-in Event Log, and taking advantage of performance counters.

Debugging (using the Debug class) is turned on by default in the debug build only, and tracing (using the Trace class) is turned on by default in both debug and release builds. These defaults allow you to ship your application instrumented with tracing code using the Trace class. You ship your code with tracing turned off so that the tracing code is not called (otherwise, the tracing would slow your application). If a problem that you cannot recreate on your development computer occurs on the production machine, you can enable tracing and allow the tracing information to be dumped to a file. This file can be inspected to help pinpoint the real problem. This trick is discussed at length in Recipes 6.1 and 6.2.

Since both the Debug and Trace classes contain the same members with the same names, they can be interchanged in your code by renaming Debug to Trace and vice versa. Most of the recipes in this chapter use the Trace class; you can modify those recipes so that they use the Debug class by replacing each Trace with Debug in the code.

6.1 Controlling Tracing Output in Production Code

Problem

Mysterious bugs often appear at the client's site, even after the application is thoroughly tested. Most of the time these bugs are difficult, if not impossible, to reproduce on your development machine. Knowing this, you want an application with built-in instrumentation that's off by default but can easily be turned on when you need it.

Solution

Use the `Trace` class for any tracing code that you might need to turn on after your application has been deployed. To turn on tracing at a client's site, provide the client with an application configuration file such as this one:

```xml
<?xml version="1.0" encoding="utf-8" ?>
<configuration>
    <system.diagnostics>
        <switches>
            <add name="DatabaseSwitch" value="4"/>
            <!-- 4 == TraceLevel.Verbose -->
        </switches>

        <trace autoflush = "true" indentsize = "2">
            <listeners>
                <add name = "MyListener"
                     type = "System.Diagnostics.TextWriterTraceListener"
                     initializeData = " MyFileName.log"/>
            </listeners>
        </trace>
    </system.diagnostics>
</configuration>
```

Discussion

Allowing tracing code to be enabled and used at a client site can be incredibly useful when debugging problems in release code. This technique is even more useful when the problem cannot easily be reproduced in-house. For this reason, it is—in some cases—a wise practice to use the `Trace` class instead of the `Debug` class when adding tracing code to your application.

To control the trace output at a client site, you can use an XML config file. This XML file must have the same base name as the executable that is to use these switches, followed by an extension of *.exe.config*. For example, if the executable name were *Accounting.exe*, the configuration file would be named *Accounting.exe.config*. This file should be placed in the same directory as the executable *Accounting.exe*.

The application configuration file always consists of the following two outer elements for diagnostic information:

```xml
<configuration>
    <system.diagnostics>
        ...
    </system.diagnostics>
</configuration>
```

However, the `configuration` element may contain other child elements besides the `system.diagnostics` element.

Within these elements, the `switches` and `trace` elements may be added. These two elements contain information specific to switches and listeners. If your code contains a `TraceSwitch` (as shown in the next example) or `BooleanSwitch` object—or any other type derived from the Switch class—you can control this object's trace level setting through the <switches> element in the configuration file:

```
private static TraceSwitch ts = new TraceSwitch("DatabaseSwitch",
        "Only allow database transactions to be logged");
```

The <listeners> element shown in the Solution adds a new TraceListener derived object to the listeners collection. Any Trace or Debug statements will use this new listener.

The switches element of the Solution can contain the three elements defined here:

> Clears any previously added switch.

<add name="*Switch_Name*" value="*Number*"/>
> Adds new switch initialization information to be used at runtime. The name attribute defines the name of the switch that is used in your code. The value attribute is set to a number that either turns the switch on or off, in the case of a BooleanSwitch class, or defines the switch level (e.g., the amount of output you wish to receive), in the case of a TraceSwitch class. To turn on a BooleanSwitch, use a nonzero value (negative numbers work here, too); to turn it off, use zero.

<remove name="*Switch_Name*"/>
> Removes switch initialization information at runtime. The name attribute defines the name of the switch that is used in your code.

Immediately after the switches tags in the solution are the trace tags, although the ordering of these tags is up to you. The trace tags can contain the following two optional attributes:

autoflush = true|false
> Indicates whether the listener automatically flushes its buffer after every write (true) or not (false).

indentsize = "4"
> Specifies the number of indent characters to use when indenting the output.

Within the trace tags are the listeners tags, which, in turn, can contain any of the following defined tags:

> Clears any previously added listeners. This tag also removes the DefaultTraceListener from the listeners collection.

<add name="*MyListener*" type="System.Diagnostics.
TextWriterTraceListener,System" initializeData="*MyFileName.log*"/>
> Adds a new listener to any Trace and Debug classes used in your application. The name attribute defines the name of the listener that is used in your code. The type attribute is set to the listener's class name. The optional initializeData attribute allows a string to be passed in to the constructor of this listener. If you are using

a custom listener, you will need to include a constructor that accepts a string as the only argument to prevent an exception from being thrown.

`<remove name = "MyListener"/>`

Removes a listener at runtime. The `name` attribute defines the name of the listener to be removed. This could be useful if another configuration file, such as the *machine.config* file, has already added a listener or if any listeners were created through your application's code. If more than one listener is added, the output will be written out twice—once for each listener.

Regardless of whether your code defines `TRACE` and/or `DEBUG`, the code will attempt to access this file for switch initialization information if a class derived from `Switch` is instantiated. If you wish to prevent this behavior, place any code that instantiates a switch class inside of a method decorated with the `ConditionalAttribute` attribute:

```
public class Traceable
{
    BooleanSwitch DBSwitch = null;
    BooleanSwitch UISwitch = null;
    BooleanSwitch exceptionSwitch = null;

    [System.Diagnostics.ConditionalAttribute("TRACE")]
    public void EnableTracing()
    {
        DBSwitch = new BooleanSwitch("DatabaseSwitch",
                    "Switch for database tracing");
        UISwitch = new BooleanSwitch("UISwitch",
                    "Switch for user interface tracing");
        exceptionSwitch = new BooleanSwitch("ExceptionSwitch",
                        "Switch for tracing thrown exceptions");
    }
}
```

The `ConditionalAttribute` attribute prevents the switches from attempting to access the application configuration file when `TRACE` is undefined by preventing your application from calling the `EnableTracing` method.

In addition to the application configuration file (*MyApp.exe.config*), there is also a *machine.config* file located in the directory %*<runtime install path>*%*CONFIG*. The configuration tags, and all of its containing elements may be placed in this file as well. However, doing so will enable these switches and listeners on a machine-wide level. This can cause applications that define their own listeners to behave strangely, especially if the listeners are duplicated. Additionally, the application will look for configuration information in the application configuration file first and the *machine. config* file second.

The application configuration file and the machine configuration file are both case-sensitive. Be sure that your tag names and their attributes are in the correct case. However, the string assigned to the `name` attribute does not seem to be case-sensitive, while other strings assigned to attributes are case-sensitive.

See Also

See the "Trace and Debug Settings Schema" topic in the MSDN documentation.

6.2 Providing Fine-Grained Control Over Debugging/Tracing Output

Problem

Your application consists of multiple components. You need, at specific times, to turn on debug/trace output for a select few components, while leaving all other debug/trace output turned off. In addition, you need control over the type and amount of information that is produced by the Trace/Debug statements.

Solution

Use the BooleanSwitch class with an application configuration file (*.config). The following method creates three switches for our application: one that controls tracing for database calls, one that controls tracing for UI components, and one that controls tracing for any exceptions that are thrown by the application:

```
public class Traceable
{
    BooleanSwitch DBSwitch = null;
    BooleanSwitch UISwitch = null;
    BooleanSwitch exceptionSwitch = null;

    public void EnableTracing()
    {
        DBSwitch = new BooleanSwitch("DatabaseSwitch",
                    "Switch for database tracing");
        Console.WriteLine("DBSwitch Enabled = " + DBSwitch.Enabled);

        UISwitch = new BooleanSwitch("UISwitch",
                    "Switch for user interface tracing");
        Console.WriteLine("UISwitch Enabled = " + UISwitch.Enabled);

        exceptionSwitch = new BooleanSwitch("ExceptionSwitch",
                        "Switch for tracing thrown exceptions");
        Console.WriteLine("ExceptionSwitch Enabled = " + exceptionSwitch.Enabled);
    }
}
```

After creating each switch, the Enabled property is displayed, indicating whether the switch is on or off.

Creating these switches without an application configuration file results in every switch getting set to false. To control what state each switch is set to, use an application configuration file, shown here:

```xml
<?xml version="1.0" encoding="utf-8" ?>
<configuration>
    <system.diagnostics>
        <switches>
            <clear/>
            <add name="DatabaseSwitch" value="1" />
            <add name="UISwitch" value="0" />
            <add name="ExceptionSwitch" value="0" />
        </switches>
    </system.diagnostics>
</configuration>
```

The TraceSwitch class can also be used with an application configuration file (*AppName.exe.config*). The following method creates a new TraceSwitch object with a level assigned by the application configuration file:

```csharp
public class Traceable
{
    TraceSwitch DBFilterSwitch = null;
    TraceSwitch UIFilterSwitch = null;
    TraceSwitch exceptionFilterSwitch = null;

    public void SetTracingFilter()
    {
        DBFilterSwitch = new TraceSwitch("DatabaseFilter",
                        "Filter database output");
        Console.WriteLine("DBFilterSwitch Level = " + DBFilterSwitch.Level);

        UIFilterSwitch = new TraceSwitch("UIFilter",
                        "Filter user interface output");
        Console.WriteLine("UIFilterSwitch Level = " + UIFilterSwitch.Level);

        exceptionFilterSwitch = new TraceSwitch("ExceptionFilter",
                            "Filter exception output");
        Console.WriteLine("exceptionFilterSwitch Level = "
                        + exceptionFilterSwitch.Level);
    }
}
```

After creating each filter switch, the Level property is displayed to indicate the switch's level.

Creating these switches at this point results in every switch's level being set to zero. To turn them on, use an application configuration file, shown here:

```xml
<?xml version="1.0" encoding="utf-8" ?>

<configuration>
    <system.diagnostics>
        <switches>
            <clear/>
            <add name="DatabaseFilter" value="4" />
            <add name="UIFilter" value="0" />
```

```
            <add name="ExceptionFilter" value="1" />
        </switches>
    </system.diagnostics>
</configuration>
```

This XML file contains a nested tag called switches. This tag defines switch names and sets a value indicating the level of the switch. The TraceSwitch class accepts five predefined trace levels shown in Table 6-1. The level of the TraceSwitch can be set through code, but that would defeat the flexibility of using a configuration file.

Table 6-1. The TraceSwitch class's tracing levels

Level name	Value	Default
Off	0	Yes
Error	1	No
Warning	2	No
Info	3	No
Verbose	4	No

For more information on the application configuration file, see Recipe 6.1.

Discussion

Turning tracing on or off involves the BooleanSwitch class. When the BooleanSwitch is created, it attempts to locate a switch with the same name as the *displayName* parameter in either the *machine.config* or application configuration files. If it cannot locate this name in either file, BooleanSwitch is set to false.

The application configuration file is an XML file named with the assembly's name followed by *.exe.config*. An application will automatically use a config file with the same name as the executable; however, the config file must be in the same directory as the application. Notice the switches tag nested inside the <system.diagnostics> element. This tag allows switches to be added and their values set. For Boolean switches, a zero turns the switch off, and any other positive or negative number turns it on. The Enabled property of the BooleanSwitch can be set through code, but that would defeat the flexibility of using a configuration file.

This XML file must have the same name as the executable using these switches, followed by *.config*. For example, if the executable name were *Accounting.exe,* the configuration file would be named *Accounting.exe.config*. This file should be placed in the same directory as the executable *Accounting.exe*. For more information on this file, see Recipe 6.1.

The application configuration file can also set trace and debug output levels in this same switches tag. These levels identify the scope of the output, for example, if the output will contain only warnings, only errors, only informational messages, or some combination thereof. Of course, this is only an example, you may define your own levels as well. For more information on controlling these output levels, see Recipe 6.3.

The `TraceSwitch` class operates similarly to the `BooleanSwitch` class, except that the `TraceSwitch` class encapsulates the available levels that control the type and amount of debug/trace output. The `BooleanSwitch` class is simply an on/off switch used to enable or disable debugging/tracing.

When the `TraceSwitch` is created, it attempts to locate a switch with the same name as the *displayName* parameter in either the *machine.config* or application configuration files. If it cannot locate this name in either file, the `TraceSwitch.Level` property is set to zero.

The application configuration file can also enable or disable trace and debug output in this same switches tag. For more information on this topic, see Recipe 6.1.

See Also

See Recipes 6.1 and 6.3; see the "BooleanSwitch Class" and "Trace and Debug Settings Schema" topics in the MSDN documentation.

6.3   Creating Your Own Custom Switch Class

Problem

The `BooleanSwitch` and `TraceSwitch` classes defined in the FCL may not always have the required flexibility or fine-grained control that you need. You want to create you own switch class that provides the level of control and flexibility that you need. For example, creating a class that allows you to set more precise trace levels than those supported by the `TraceSwitch` class. The `TraceSwitch` class provides the following tracing levels:

```
TraceError
TraceWarning
TraceInfo
TraceVerbose
```

However, you need a finer-grained set of levels, such as the following:

```
Disable     MinorError
Note        MediumError
Warning     CriticalError
```

Solution

You can create your own switch class that inherits from `System.Diagnostics.Switch` and provides the level of control that you need. For example, creating a class that allows you to set more precise trace levels than those supported by the `TraceSwitch` class involves the following steps:

1. Define a set of enumerated values that represent the levels to be supported by your switch class:

```
public enum AppSpecificSwitchLevel
{
    Disable = 0,
    Note = 1,
    Warning = 2,
    MinorError = 3,
    MediumError = 4,
    CriticalError = 5
}
```

2. Define a class, such as AppSpecificSwitch, that inherits from System.Diagnostics.Switch:

```
public class AppSpecificSwitch : Switch
{
    protected AppSpecificSwitchLevel level = 0;

    public AppSpecificSwitch(string displayName, string description)
        : base(displayName, description)
    {
        this.Level = (AppSpecificSwitchLevel)base.SwitchSetting;
    }

    // Read/write Level property
    public AppSpecificSwitchLevel Level
    {
        get
        {
            return level;
        }
        set
        {
            if (value < AppSpecificSwitchLevel.Disable)
            {
                level = AppSpecificSwitchLevel.Disable;
            }
            else if (value > AppSpecificSwitchLevel.CriticalError)
            {
                level = AppSpecificSwitchLevel.CriticalError;
            }
            else
            {
                level = value;
            }
        }
    }

    // Read-only properties for the AppSpecificSwitchLevel enum
    public bool Disable
    {
        get
        {
```

```csharp
            if (level <= AppSpecificSwitchLevel.Disable)
            {
                return (true);
            }
            else
            {
                return (false);
            }
        }
    }

    public bool Note
    {
        get
        {
            if (level <= AppSpecificSwitchLevel.Note)
            {
                return (true);
            }
            else
            {
                return (false);
            }
        }
    }

    public bool Warning
    {
        get
        {
            if (level <= AppSpecificSwitchLevel.Warning)
            {
                return (true);
            }
            else
            {
                return (false);
            }
        }
    }

    public bool MinorError
    {
        get
        {
            if (level <= AppSpecificSwitchLevel.MinorError)
            {
                return (true);
            }
            else
            {
                return (false);
            }
        }
```

```
        }

        public bool MediumError
        {
            get
            {
                if (level <= AppSpecificSwitchLevel.MediumError)
                {
                    return (true);
                }
                else
                {
                    return (false);
                }
            }
        }

        public bool CriticalError
        {
            get
            {
                if (level <= AppSpecificSwitchLevel.CriticalError)
                {
                    return (true);
                }
                else
                {
                    return (false);
                }
            }
        }
    }
```

3. In code, you can instantiate this custom class by invoking its constructor:

```
AppSpecificSwitch appSwitch = new AppSpecificSwitch("MyApplication",
                                "My Application Specific Switch");
```

4. Set the switch in the application configuration file. For example, the following configuration file sets the level of our custom switch to `AppSpecificSwitchLevel.CriticalLevel`:

```
<?xml version="1.0" encoding="utf-8" ?>
<configuration>
    <system.diagnostics>
        <switches>
            <add name="MyApplication" value="5" />
        </switches>
    </system.diagnostics>
</configuration>
```

More information on configuration files can be found in Recipes 6.1 and 6.2.

Discussion

The BooleanSwitch and TraceSwitch classes defined in the FCL might not always have the flexibility that you need. In these cases, you can create a class that inherits from the Switch class—the abstract base class of all switch type classes.

The critical part of creating a custom switch class is the constructor. The constructor must call its base class constructor using the :base( ) syntax. If this syntax is omitted, a compiler error will appear indicating that there is no default constructor to call on the base class Switch. You might notice that the Switch class contains a single public constructor that accepts two string parameters. This is designed so that you must use this constructor when building an object of this type or any type derived from it. Calling the base class's constructor also allows the application configuration file to be searched, if one exists, for any initialization value for this switch object.

We can circumvent the configuration file search by writing the constructor as follows:

```
public AppSpecificSwitch(string displayName, string description)
    : base("", description)
{
    this.Level = (AppSpecificSwitchLevel)base.SwitchSetting;
}
```

The other item of interest in this constructor is the one line of code in its body. This line of code grabs the level information acquired from the application configuration file and sets this inherited class's Level property to this value. This line is required because the base class is the one that receives the initialization information from a configuration file, not the inherited class.

This class contains several other properties. The first is the Level property, which gets and sets the current level of this object. The levels are defined in the AppSpecificSwitchLevel enumeration. This class also contains a read-only property for each element in the AppSpecificSwitchLevel enumeration. These can be used to query this object to determine whether its various levels are set.

See Also

See Recipes 6.1 and 6.2; see the "Switch Class" and "Trace and Debug Settings Schema" topics in the MSDN documentation.

6.4 A Custom Trace Class that Outputs Information in an XML Format

Problem

You need to output trace information in an XML format. Unfortunately, the Trace and Debug classes are sealed and therefore cannot be inherited from in order to create more specialized classes. This limitation poses somewhat of a problem if you need to create a Trace or Debug class that outputs XML instead of plain text. You could start from scratch and build new Trace and Debug classes from the ground up, but you would have to handle configuration files, listener collections, and switch information, among other things. This way can become quite time-consuming; you need a better way.

Solution

You could use the Log4Net package found at the SourceForge web site (*http://log4net.sourceforge.net*); it is a complete logging system that can easily be added to your application. However, if you use the XML logging, you should realize that the XML output is not well-formed. This is done by design so that the XML fragments output from Log4Net can be included as external entities in a different XML file to create a well-formed XML file.

Another solution is to create a new trace listener class, such as XMLTraceListener, that inherits from the framework-provided TraceListener class. The XMLTraceListener class is defined as follows (note that the XMLTraceListener does create a well-formed XML document):

```
using System;
using System.Collections;
using System.Diagnostics;
using System.IO;
using System.Xml;

public class XMLTraceListener : TraceListener, IDisposable
{
    // CTORS
    public XMLTraceListener() : this(null, "XMLTraceListener") {}

    // Required to be used by a *.config file
    public XMLTraceListener(string name) : this(null, name) {}

    public XMLTraceListener(Stream stream) :
      this(stream, "XMLTraceListener") {}

    public XMLTraceListener(Stream stream, string name)
    {
        indentLevel = 0;

        if (stream == null)
        {
            string DirName = Environment.CurrentDirectory;

            if (DirName.EndsWith(Path.DirectorySeparatorChar.ToString()) ||
                DirName.EndsWith(Path.AltDirectorySeparatorChar.ToString()))
            {
                DirName += Process.GetCurrentProcess().ProcessName + ".xml";
            }
            else
```

```
        {
            DirName += @"\" + Process.GetCurrentProcess( ).ProcessName +
              ".xml";
        }

        try
        {
            writer = new XmlTextWriter(File.OpenWrite(DirName), null);
        }
        catch (Exception e)
        {
            Debugger.Log(0, "Initialization Error",
              "Could not create StreamWriter");
            Debugger.Log(0, null, e.ToString( ));

            // Re-throw exception
            throw;
        }
    }
    else
    {
        // Create XML writer
        writer = new XmlTextWriter(stream, null);
    }

    // Open the XML document, and write the root element
    writer.WriteStartDocument( );
    writer.WriteStartElement(XmlConvert.EncodeLocalName(
      "XMLDebugOutput"));
}

// FIELDS
private Stack tagHierarchy = new Stack( );
private int indentLevel = 0;
private XmlTextWriter writer = null;

// METHODS
public override void Write(string message)
{
    if (this.NeedIndent)
    {
        this.NeedIndent = true;
    }

    WriteData(message);
}

public override void Write(object obj)
{
    if (obj != null)
    {
        this.Write(obj.ToString( ));
    }
    else
```

```csharp
        {
            this.Write("");
        }
    }

    public override void Write(object obj, string message)
    {
        if (obj != null)
        {
            this.Write(obj.ToString( ), message);
        }
        else
        {
            this.Write("", message);
        }
    }

    public override void Write(string message, string category)
    {
        this.Write(message + ": " + category);
    }

    public override void WriteLine(string message)
    {
        this.Write(message + Environment.NewLine);
    }

    public override void WriteLine(object obj)
    {
        if (obj == null)
        {
            this.Write(obj.ToString( ) + Environment.NewLine);
        }
        else
        {
            // If the obj param is specified to be TraceTag.End
            //    we can close the last opened XML tag
            if (obj is TraceTag)
            {
                if (((TraceTag)obj) == TraceTag.End)
                {
                    WriteEndTag( );
                }
                else
                {
                    throw (new ArgumentException(
                            "This must be specified only " +
                            "as a TraceTag.End tag.",
                            obj.ToString( )));
                }
            }
            else
            {
                this.Write(Environment.NewLine);
            }
    }
```

```csharp
        }
    }

    public override void WriteLine(object obj, string message)
    {
        if (obj == null)
        {
            this.Write(obj.ToString(), message + Environment.NewLine);
        }
        else
        {
            // If the obj param is specified to be TraceTag.Start
            //    we can open the starting XML tag & record it
            if (obj is TraceTag)
            {
                if (((TraceTag)obj) == TraceTag.Start)
                {
                    WriteStartTag(message);
                }
                else
                {
                    throw (new ArgumentException(
                        "This must be specified only " +
                        "as a TraceTag.Start tag.",
                        obj.ToString()));
                }
            }
            else
            {
                this.Write("", message + Environment.NewLine);
            }
        }
    }

    public override void WriteLine(string message, string category)
    {
        this.Write(message, category + Environment.NewLine);
    }

    private new string WriteIndent()
    {
        this.NeedIndent = false;

        string IndentChars = "";
        for (int Counter = 0; Counter < (this.indentLevel); Counter++)
        {
            IndentChars += "\t";
        }

        return (IndentChars);
    }

    private void WriteData(string message)
    {
```

```csharp
        // Write to the debugger output
        if (Debugger.IsAttached && Debugger.IsLogging())
        {
            Debugger.Log(0, null, WriteIndent() + message);
        }

        // Write to the stream output
        writer.WriteString(message);
    }

    public override void Fail(string message)
    {
        Fail(message, null);
    }

    public override void Fail(string message, string detailedMessage)
    {
        WriteStartTag("FAIL");

        // Write to the debugger output
        if (Debugger.IsAttached && Debugger.IsLogging())
        {
            Debugger.Log(0, null, WriteIndent() +
                "!!! Failure Message !!! ");
            Debugger.Log(0, null, message);
            if (detailedMessage != null)
            {
                Debugger.Log(0, null, ": " + detailedMessage);
            }
            Debugger.Log(0, null, Environment.NewLine);
        }

        // Write to the stream output
        writer.WriteString("!!! Failure Message !!!");
        if (message != null)
        {
            writer.WriteString(message);
        }
        if (detailedMessage != null)
        {
            writer.WriteString(": " + detailedMessage);
        }
        WriteEndTag();
    }

    private void WriteStartTag(string tag)
    {
        // Test the tag param for correct xml tag syntax
        if (!System.Security.SecurityElement.IsValidTag(tag) )
        {
            throw (new ArgumentException("Invalid tag.", "tag"));
        }
        else if (tag.Length <= 0)
        {
```

```csharp
            throw (new ArgumentException(
                    "Invalid tag, tag must be greater than zero " +
                    "characters in length.",
                    "tag"));
        }
        else if (char.IsNumber(tag[0]))
        {
            throw (new ArgumentException(
                    "Invalid tag, tag must not start with a " +
                    "numeric character.",
                    "tag"));
        }

        // Output the tag to both the debugger & XmlTextWriter
        Debugger.Log(0, null, WriteIndent() + "<" + tag + ">" +
            Environment.NewLine);
        writer.WriteStartElement(XmlConvert.EncodeLocalName(tag));

        // Increase the indent level
        this.indentLevel++;

        // Push this tag onto the stack
        //    This stack element will be used again in
        // the WriteEndTag method
        tagHierarchy.Push(tag);
    }

    private void WriteEndTag()
    {
        writer.WriteEndElement();

        this.indentLevel--;

        // Write out the ending tag for the next item to be popped
        // off the stack
        if (tagHierarchy.Count > 0)
        {
            Debugger.Log(0, null, WriteIndent() + @"</" +
                    tagHierarchy.Pop().ToString() +
                    ">" + Environment.NewLine);
        }
        else
        {
            throw (new InvalidOperationException(
                    "Cannot close a tag that has not been created."));
        }
    }

    public override void Close()
    {
        this.Dispose();
    }

    public override void Flush()
    {
```

```
            writer.Flush( );
            base.Flush( );
        }

        public new void Dispose( )
        {
            // Close all XmlTextWriter unclosed XML tags
            writer.WriteEndDocument( );

            // Close all Debugger.Log unclosed XML tags
            int tagCount = tagHierarchy.Count;
            for (int counter = 0; counter < tagCount; counter++)
            {
                this.indentLevel--;
                Debugger.Log(0, null, WriteIndent( ) + @"</" +
                            tagHierarchy.Pop( ).ToString( ) +
                            ">" + Environment.NewLine);
            }

            writer.Close( );
            base.Close( );

            GC.SuppressFinalize(this);
        }
    }
```

Here is the enumeration used to indicate to the XMLTraceListener object whether to
write out a starting or an ending tag:

```
    public enum TraceTag
    {
        Start,
        End
    }
```

Discussion

The Trace and Debug classes are sealed and therefore cannot be inherited from to create more specialized classes. This limitation poses somewhat of a problem if we need
to create a specialized Trace or Debug class that outputs XML instead of plain text. As
an alternative plan, we can inherit from the System.Diagnostics.TraceListener class
to create a specialized listener that outputs XML. Our new XMLTraceListener class
can then be added to the collection of listeners contained in either the Trace or Debug
classes. Once the listener is added, we can use the Trace or Debug classes as normal.

The following example shows how the XMLTraceListener class could be used to output trace information as an XML document:

```
    public void TestXMLTraceListener( )
    {
        // The trace information will be displayed in the Output window of the IDE

        // Add our trace listener to the collection of listeners
```

```
            Trace.Listeners.Clear();
            Trace.Listeners.Add(new XMLTraceListener());

            // Test output
            Trace.WriteLine(TraceTag.Start, "one");          // <one>
              Trace.WriteLine("The first element");
              Trace.Fail("FIRST FAIL");
              Trace.Fail("SECOND FAIL", "Details");
              Trace.WriteLine(TraceTag.Start, "two");        // <two>
                Trace.WriteLine("The second element");
                Trace.WriteLine(TraceTag.Start, "three");    // <three>
                  Trace.WriteLine("The third element");
                Trace.WriteLine(TraceTag.End);               // </three>
                Trace.WriteLine(TraceTag.Start, "four");     // <four>
                  Trace.WriteLine("The fourth element");
                Trace.WriteLine(TraceTag.End);               // </four>
                Trace.Assert(false, "FIRST ASSERTION", "Details");
                Trace.Assert(false, "SECOND ASSERTION");
                Trace.Assert(false);
              Trace.WriteLine(TraceTag.End);                 // </two>
            Trace.WriteLine(TraceTag.End);                   // </one>

            // Cleanup
            Trace.Flush();
            Trace.Close();
        }
```

Note that for the Trace class to output any information, the TRACE directive must be defined, either in the project properties dialog box under Configuration Properties → Build → Conditional Compilation Constants or by using a #define directive at the beginning of the file:

```
#define TRACE
```

The main difference between using the XMLTraceListener and any other trace listener is the use of the TraceTag enumeration. This enumeration has two values, Start and End. Start signifies that the current text to be output will be output as a starting tag, and End signifies that the next tag output will close the most recently opened tag. Note that the closing tag text is automatically displayed; you do not have to keep track of this information.

The XMLTraceListener class contains two private methods of interest, WriteStartTag and WriteEndTag. The WriteStartTag method writes the starting tag for an XML block, after verifying that the tag is a valid XML tag. Note that these verification steps are not performed by the XmlTextWriter.WriteStartElement method. The WriteEndTag method writes the ending tag for the last XML tag that you opened. Notice that the WriteEndTag method does not accept any parameters. This method knows which closing tag to write to the Debugger.Log method by using the tagHierarchy Stack object. The last beginning tag written is placed on the top of this stack. All the WriteEndTag method has to do is pop off the last tag from this stack and write out its closing tag. The XmlTextWriter.WriteEndElement method automatically keeps track of the starting and ending tags so no special handling is required.

The `WriteStartTag` is indirectly called by using the `WriteLine` method, which accepts both an `object` and a `string` argument. Passing in the value `TraceTag.Start` for the `object` argument and a tag name for the `string` argument, you can create a beginning tag as shown here:

```
Trace.WriteLine(TraceTag.Start, "one");        // Displays:    <one>
```

To close this tag, call the overloaded `WriteLine` method, which accepts only an `object` argument. The value passed to this argument must be `TraceTag.End` in order to display an ending tag:

```
Trace.WriteLine(TraceTag.End);                 // Displays:    </one>
```

If the default constructor or the constructor that accepts only a `string` argument is called, a default XML file is created and passed to the first parameter of the `XmlTextWriter` constructor. The name of the file will be the process name for the application with the *.xml* extension. The file will be created in the current directory of the executing assembly.

See Also

See the "TraceListener Class" and "XmlTextWriter" topics in the MSDN documentation.

6.5   Conditionally Compiling Blocks of Code

Problem

Specific blocks of code will be used only in a nonrelease build of your application. These blocks of code should not be compiled into the release version of the application. You need a way to conditionally compile specific blocks of code based on the type of build.

Solution

There are two methods of allowing or preventing code from being compiled. The first is to use the C# preprocessor directives. The available preprocessor directives are:

```
#define
#undef
#if
#elif
#else
#endif
```

The `#define` and `#undef` preprocessor directives define and undefine symbols. These symbols are then used by the `#if` and `#elif` preprocessor directives to determine whether the blocks of code they wrap are to be compiled.

The second method of allowing or preventing code from being compiled is to use the ConditionalAttribute attribute to allow a method to be compiled based on a defined symbol. This attribute is used to specify a method as conditionally compiled as follows:

```
#define TRACE

    ...

[ConditionalAttribute("TRACE")]
public void TraceHelp(string message)
{
    ...
}
```

The TraceHelp method is compiled only when the TRACE preprocessing identifier is defined.

Discussion

The ConditionalAttribute attribute can be used only on methods to prevent them from being compiled and called at runtime when the preprocessor identifier passed to the ConditionalAttribute attribute's constructor is undefined. Properties, indexers, and other members cannot have this attribute.

Another limitation of this attribute is that it can be placed only on a method that returns void. This makes sense, since code that invokes this method doesn't expect a return value, and will run successfully whether the method is invoked. For example, in the code:

```
int retValue = Car.GetModelNumber( );
```

if the GetModelNumber method is not compiled, then this code will not be able to function correctly.

Along these same lines, a method marked as override cannot be marked with the ConditionalAttribute attribute. However, the virtual method that a method overrides may be marked with the ConditionalAttribute attribute. If the virtual method is marked with this attribute, all methods overriding it are compiled and called based on whether the virtual method is compiled. In other words, the overriding methods are implicitly marked with the same ConditionalAttribute attribute as the virtual method.

#define and #undef apply only to preprocessor identifiers within a file scope, whereas the /define: compiler option defines preprocessor identifiers for all files in a project. #define and #undef also take precedence over the /define: compiler option. For instance, if the project's /define: compiler option defined TRACE, and one of the files that project contains has the code:

```
#undef TRACE
```

then TRACE will be defined for all files except the one containing the #undef TRACE directive.

To set the project's /define: compiler option in Visual Studio .NET, right-click on the project name in the Solution Explorer tool window, then click the Properties menu item. This step will display the Property Pages dialog box for this project. Next, click the Configuration Properties node in the tree on the left side of this dialog box. In the control to the right of this tree, find the line entitled Conditional Compilation Constants. On this line, you may add or remove any preprocessor identifiers that you want.

The #if and #elif directives determine what code within a member is to be compiled. For example:

```
public void MyMethod( )
{
    #if (TRACE)
        Method1( );
    #elif (DEBUG)
        Method2( );
    #else
        Method3( );
    #endif
}
```

MyMethod will call Method1 when TRACE is defined, Method2 is called if TRACE is undefined and DEBUG is defined, and Method3 is called if both TRACE and DEBUG are undefined.

See Also

See the "C# Preprocessor Directives" and "ConditionalAttribute Class" topics in the MSDN documentation.

6.6   Determining Whether a Process Has Stopped Responding

Problem

You need to watch one or more processes to determine whether they have stopped responding to the system. This functionality is similar to the column in the Task Manager that displays the text Responding or Not Responding, depending on the state of the application.

Solution

Use the following method to determine whether a process has stopped responding:

```
public bool IsProcessResponding(Process process)
{
    if (process.MainWindowHandle == IntPtr.Zero)
    {
        Console.WriteLine("This process does not have a MainWindowHandle");
```

```
            return (true);
        }
        else
        {
            // This process has a MainWindowHandle
            if (!process.Responding)
            {
                Console.WriteLine("Process " + process.ProcessName +
                    " is not responding.");
                return (false);
            }
            else
            {
                Console.WriteLine("Process " + process.ProcessName +
                    " is responding.");
                return (true);
            }
        }
    }
}
```

Discussion

The `IsProcessResponding` method accepts a single parameter, *process*, identifying a process. The `Responding` property is then called on the `Process` object represented by the *process* parameter. This property returns a `true` to indicate that a process is currently responding, or a `false` to indicate that the process has stopped responding.

The `Responding` property always returns `true` if the process in question does not have a `MainWindowHandle`. Processes such as Idle, spoolsv, Rundll32, and svchost do not have a main window handle and therefore the `Responding` property always returns `true` for them. To weed out these processes, you can use the `MainWindowHandle` property of the `Process` class, which returns the handle of the main window for a process. If this property returns zero, the process has no main window.

To determine whether all processes on a machine are responding, you can call the `IsProcessResponding` method as follows:

```
foreach (Process proc in Process.GetProcesses())
{
    if (!MyObject.IsProcessResponding(proc))
    {
        Console.WriteLine("Process " + proc.ProcessName + " is not responding.");
    }
}
```

This code snippet iterates over all processes currently running on your system. The static `GetProcesses` method of the `Process` class takes no parameters and returns an array of `Process` objects that contains process information for all processes running on your system. Each `Process` object is then passed in to our `IsProcessResponding` method to determine whether it is responding. Other static methods on the `Process` class that retrieve `Process` objects are `GetProcessById`, `GetCurrentProcess`, and `GetProcessesByName`.

See Also

See the "Process Class" topic in the MSDN documentation.

6.7   Using One or More Event Logs in Your Application

Problem

You need to add the ability for your application to read and write one or more event logs of specific events that occur in your application, such as startup, shutdown, critical errors, and even security breaches. Along with reading and writing to a log, you need the ability to create, clear, close, and remove logs from the event log.

Your application might need to keep track of several logs at one time. For example, your application might use a custom log to track specific events as they occur in your application, such as startup and shutdown. To supplement the custom log, your application could make use of the Security log already built into the event log system to read/write security events that occur in your application.

Support for multiple logs comes in handy when one log needs to be created and maintained on the local computer, and another duplicate log needs to be created and maintained on a remote machine. (This remote machine might contain logs of all running instances of your application on each user's machine. An administrator could use these logs to quickly find any problems that occur or discover if security is breached in your application. In fact, an application could be run in the background on the remote administrative machine that watches for specific log entries to be written to this log from any user's machine. Recipe 6.10 uses an event mechanism to watch for entries written to an event log and could easily be used to enhance this recipe.)

Solution

Use the event log built into the Microsoft Windows operating system to record specific events that occur infrequently. The following class contains all the methods needed to create and use an event log in your application:

```
using System;
using System.Diagnostics;

public class AppEvents
{
    // Constructors
    public AppEvents(string logName) :
        this(logName, Process.GetCurrentProcess().ProcessName, ".") {}

    public AppEvents(string logName, string source) : this(logName, source, ".") {}

    public AppEvents(string logName, string source, string machineName)
```

```csharp
{
    this.logName = logName;
    this.source = source;
    this.machineName = machineName;

    if (!EventLog.SourceExists(source, machineName))
    {
        EventLog.CreateEventSource(source, logName, machineName);
    }

    log = new EventLog(logName, machineName, source);
    log.EnableRaisingEvents = true;
}

// Fields
private EventLog log = null;
private string source = "";
private string logName = "";
private string machineName = ".";

// Properties
public string Name
{
    get{return (logName);}
}

public string SourceName
{
    get{return (source);}
}

public string Machine
{
    get{return (machineName);}
}

// Methods
public void WriteToLog(string message, EventLogEntryType type,
                       CategoryType category, EventIDType eventID)
{
    if (log == null)
    {
        throw (new ArgumentNullException("log",
            "This Event Log has not been opened or has been closed."));
    }

    log.WriteEntry(message, type, (int)eventID, (short)category);
}

public void WriteToLog(string message, EventLogEntryType type,
                       CategoryType category, EventIDType eventID,
                         byte[] rawData)
{
    if (log == null)
```

```
        {
            throw (new ArgumentNullException("log",
                "This Event Log has not been opened or has been closed."));
        }

        log.WriteEntry(message, type, (int)eventID, (short)category,
            rawData);
    }

    public EventLogEntryCollection GetEntries()
    {
        if (log == null)
        {
            throw (new ArgumentNullException("log",
                "This Event Log has not been opened or has been closed."));
        }

        return (log.Entries);
    }

    public void ClearLog()
    {
        if (log == null)
        {
            throw (new ArgumentNullException("log",
                "This Event Log has not been opened or has been closed."));
        }

        log.Clear();
    }

    public void CloseLog()
    {
        if (log == null)
        {
            throw (new ArgumentNullException("log",
                "This Event Log has not been opened or has been closed."));
        }

        log.Close();
        log = null;
    }

    public void DeleteLog()
    {
        if (EventLog.SourceExists(source, machineName))
        {
            EventLog.DeleteEventSource(source, machineName);
        }

        if (logName != "Application" &&
            logName != "Security" &&
            logName != "System")
        {
```

```
                if (EventLog.Exists(logName, machineName))
                {
                    EventLog.Delete(logName, machineName);
                }
            }

            if (log != null)
            {
                log.Close();
                log = null;
            }
        }
    }
```

The `EventIDType` and `CategoryType` enumerations used in this class are defined as follows:

```
    public enum EventIDType
    {
        NA = 0,
        Read = 1,
        Write = 2,
        ExceptionThrown = 3,
        BufferOverflowCondition = 4,
        SecurityFailure = 5,
        SecurityPotentiallyCompromised = 6
    }

    public enum CategoryType : short
    {
        None = 0,
        WriteToDB = 1,
        ReadFromDB = 2,
        WriteToFile = 3,
        ReadFromFile = 4,
        AppStartUp = 5,
        AppShutDown = 6,
        UserInput = 7
    }
```

Discussion

The `AppEvents` class created for this recipe provides applications with an easy-to-use interface for creating, using, and deleting single or multiple event logs in your application. Support for multiple logs comes in handy when one log needs to be created and maintained on the local computer and another duplicate log needs to be created and maintained on a remote machine. (This remote machine might contain logs of all running instances of your application on each user's machine. An administrator could use these logs to quickly discover whether any problems occur or security is breached in your application. In fact, an application could be run in the background on the remote administrative machine that watches for specific log entries to be written to this log from any user's machine. Recipe 6.10 uses an event mechanism to watch for entries written to an event log and could easily be used to enhance this recipe.)

The methods of the AppEvents class are described as follows:

WriteToLog

This method is overloaded to allow an entry to be written to the event log with or without a byte array containing raw data.

GetEntries

Returns all the event log entries for this event log in an EventLogEntryCollection.

ClearLog

Removes all the event log entries from this event log.

CloseLog

Closes this event log, preventing further interaction with it.

DeleteLog

Deletes this event log and the associated event log source.

An AppEvents object can be added to an array or collection containing other AppEvent objects; each AppEvents object corresponds to a particular event log. The following code creates two AppEvents classes and adds them to a ListDictionary collection:

```
public void CreateMultipleLogs( )
{
    AppEvents appEventLog = new AppEvents("AppLog", "AppLocal");
    AppEvents globalEventLog = new AppEvents("System", "AppGlobal");

    ListDictionary logList = new ListDictionary( );
    logList.Add(appEventLog.Name, appEventLog);
    logList.Add(globalEventLog.Name, globalEventLog);
}
```

To write to either of these two logs, obtain the AppEvents object by name from the ListDictionary object, cast the resultant object type to an AppEvents type, and call the WriteToLog method:

```
((AppEvents)logList[appEventLog.Name]).WriteToLog("App startup",
                EventLogEntryType.Information, CategoryType.AppStartUp,
                EventIDType.ExceptionThrown);

((AppEvents)logList[globalEventLog.Name]).WriteToLog("App startup security check",
                EventLogEntryType.Information, CategoryType.AppStartUp,
                EventIDType.BufferOverflowCondition);
```

Containing all AppEvents objects in a ListDictionary object allows you to easily iterate over all AppEvents objects that your application has instantiated. Using a foreach loop, you can write a single message to both a local and a remote event log:

```
foreach (DictionaryEntry log in logList)
{
    ((AppEvents)log.Value).WriteToLog("App startup", EventLogEntryType.FailureAudit,
            CategoryType.AppStartUp, EventIDType.SecurityFailure);
}
```

To delete each log in the logList object, you can use the following foreach loop:

```
foreach (DictionaryEntry log in logList)
{
    ((AppEvents)log.Value).DeleteLog();
}
logList.Clear();
```

There are several key points that you should be aware of. The first concerns a small problem with constructing multiple AppEvents classes. If you create two AppEvents objects and pass in the same source string to the AppEvents constructor, an exception will be thrown. Consider the following code, which instantiates two AppEvents objects with the same source string:

```
AppEvents appEventLog = new AppEvents("AppLog", "AppLocal");
AppEvents globalEventLog = new AppEvents("Application", "AppLocal");
```

The objects are instantiated without errors, but when the WriteToLog method is called on the globalEventLog object, the following exception is thrown:

```
An unhandled exception of type 'System.ArgumentException' occurred in system.dll.

Additional information: The source 'AppLocal' is not registered in log 'Application'.
(It is registered in log 'AppLog'.) " The Source and Log properties must be matched,
or you may set Log to the empty string, and it will automatically be matched to the
Source property.
```

This exception occurs because the WriteToLog method internally calls the WriteEntry method of the EventLog object. The WriteEntry method internally checks to see whether the specified source is registered to the log you are attempting to write to. In our case, the AppLocal source was registered to the first log it was assigned to—the AppLog log. The second attempt to register this same source to another log, Application, failed silently. You do not know that this attempt failed until you try to use the WriteEntry method of the EventLog object.

One way to prevent this exception from occurring is to modify the AppEvents class constructor to create a new EventLog object with an empty string for the log name parameter. This modified constructor call is highlighted in the following code:

```
public AppEvents(string logName, string source, string machineName)
{
    this.logName = logName;
    this.source = source;
    this.machineName = machineName;

    if (!EventLog.SourceExists(source, machineName))
    {
        EventLog.CreateEventSource(source, logName, machineName);
    }

    log = new EventLog("", machineName, source);
    log.EnableRaisingEvents = true;
}
```

Now, instead of an exception being thrown, the system searches for the log that the source is registered to and uses that log in place of the one specified in the `logName` parameter. If *source* is not registered to any log, the source will be registered with the Application log, and that log will be used by this `EventLog` object as well.

Another key point about the `AppEvents` class is the following code, placed at the beginning of each method (except for the `DeleteLog` method):

```
if (log == null)
{
    throw (new ArgumentNullException("log",
        "This Event Log has not been opened or has been closed."));
}
```

This code checks to see whether the private member variable `log` is a `null` reference. If so, an `ArgumentException` is thrown, informing the user of this class that a problem occurred with the creation of the `EventLog` object. The `DeleteLog` method does not check the `log` variable for `null` since it deletes the event log source and the event log itself. The `EventLog` object is not involved in this process except at the end of this method, where the `log` is closed and set to `null`, if it is not already `null`. Regardless of the state of the `log` variable, the source and event log should be deleted in this method.

The `DeleteLog` method makes a critical choice when determining whether to delete a log. The following code prevents the Application, Security, and System event logs from being deleted from your system:

```
if (logName != "Application" &&
    logName != "Security" &&
    logName != "System")
{
    if (EventLog.Exists(logName, machineName))
    {
        EventLog.Delete(logName, machineName);
    }
}
```

If any of these logs are deleted, so are the sources registered with the particular log. Once the log is deleted, it is permanent; believe us, it is not fun to try and recreate the log and its sources without a backup.

As a last note, the `EventIDType` and `CategoryType` enumerations are designed mainly to log security type breaches as well as potential attacks on the security of your application. Using these event IDs and categories, the administrator can more easily track down potential security threats and do post-mortem analysis after security is breached. These enumerations can easily be modified or replaced with your own to allow you to track different events that occur as a result of your application running.

You should minimize the number of entries written to the event log from your application. The reason for this is that writing to the event log causes a performance hit. Writing too much information to the event log can noticeably slow your application. Pick and choose the entries you write to the event log wisely.

See Also

See Recipe 6.10; see the "EventLog Class" topic in the MSDN documentation.

6.8 Changing the Maximum Size of a Custom Event Log

Problem

Custom event logs are created with a default maximum size of 512K. For some applications, this default may be too small or even too large. You need a way of programmatically modifying this size. If you are a system administrator, you might need to write a utility to modify this value.

Solution

There is no direct way of modifying the maximum size of an event log. However, the following method makes use of the registry to circumvent this limitation:

```
using System;
using Microsoft.Win32;

public void SetCustomLogMaxSize(string logName, int maxSize)
{
    RegistryKey key = Registry.LocalMachine.OpenSubKey
        (@"SYSTEM\CurrentControlSet\Services\Eventlog\" + logName, true);
    if (key == null)
    {
        Console.WriteLine(
            "Registry key for this Event Log does not exist.");
    }
    else
    {
        key.SetValue("MaxSize", maxSize);
        Registry.LocalMachine.Close();
    }
}
```

Discussion

The FCL classes devoted to making use of the event log contain most of the functionality that a developer will ever need. Yet there are some small items that are not directly accessible using the event log API in the FCL. One of these is the manipulation of the maximum size of an event log. Event logs are initialized to a maximum size of 512K, after which the event log entries are overwritten by default.

There are cases where an application may produce many or very few entries in an event log. In these cases, it would be nice to manipulate the maximum size of an event log so that memory is used most efficiently and that critical entries are not lost or overwritten because the event log fills up too fast.

It is possible to set the maximum size of an event log manually through the Event Viewer application. Unfortunately, you might not always have access to the machine to manually do this. In addition, this is a tedious and time-consuming process. You can programmatically set the maximum size by changing the value of a registry entry. If an event log were named MyLog, the properties of this log would reside in the following registry location:

```
HKEY_LOCAL_MACHINE\SYSTEM\CurrentControlSet\Services\Eventlog\MyLog
```

This location contains several value entries containing properties of this event log. The value entry we are interested in is MaxSize. Using the static methods of the Registry class, we can add or modify this value to one of our choosing with code like the following:

```
Microsoft.Win32.RegistryKey lm = Registry.LocalMachine;
Microsoft.Win32.RegistryKey logKey = lm.OpenSubKey(
            @"SYSTEM\CurrentControlSet\Services\Eventlog\RegistryLog", true);
logKey.SetValue("MaxSize", (int) 1024);
logKey.Close;
```

To access this registry value, we first call the RegistryKey.OpenSubKey method. This method returns a RegistryKey object, which, in this case, represents the key containing the MaxSize value entry in which we are interested. The SetValue method of the RegistryKey object is called next to change the value of the MaxSize entry. If this value entry does not exist, it is created with the desired value. This information is then flushed to the registry and the RegistryKey class is closed. Both of these actions are performed though the Close method on the RegistryKey class.

See Also

See the "Registry.LocalMachine Field" and "RegistryKey.Open Method" topics in the MSDN documentation.

6.9   Searching Event Log Entries

Problem

Your application might have produced many entries in the event log. To perform an analysis of how the application operated, how many errors were encountered, and so on, you need to be able to perform a search through all of the entries in an event log. Unfortunately, there are no good built-in search mechanisms for event logs.

Solution

You will eventually have to sift through all the entries your application writes to an event log in order to find the entries that allow you to perhaps fix a bug or improve your application's security system. Unfortunately, there are no good search mechanisms for event logs. This recipe contains an EventLogSearch class, which contains many static methods allowing you to search for entries in an event log based on a criterion. In addition, this search mechanism allows complex searches involving multiple criteria to be performed on an event log at one time. The code for the EventSearchLog class is:

```
using System;
using System.Collections;
using System.Diagnostics;

public sealed class EventLogSearch
{
    private EventLogSearch( ) {}     // Prevent this class from being instantiated.

    public static EventLogEntry[] FindTimeGeneratedAtOrBefore(
        IEnumerable logEntries, DateTime timeGeneratedQuery)
    {
        ArrayList entries = new ArrayList( );

        foreach (EventLogEntry logEntry in logEntries)
        {
            if (logEntry.TimeGenerated <= timeGeneratedQuery)
            {
                entries.Add(logEntry);
            }
        }

        EventLogEntry[] entriesArray = new EventLogEntry[entries.Count];
        entries.CopyTo(entriesArray);
        return (entriesArray);
    }

    public static EventLogEntry[] FindTimeGeneratedAtOrAfter(
        IEnumerable logEntries, DateTime timeGeneratedQuery)
    {
        ArrayList entries = new ArrayList( );

        foreach (EventLogEntry logEntry in logEntries)
        {
            if (logEntry.TimeGenerated >= timeGeneratedQuery)
            {
                entries.Add(logEntry);
            }
        }

        EventLogEntry[] entriesArray = new EventLogEntry[entries.Count];
        entries.CopyTo(entriesArray);
```

```
        return (entriesArray);
    }
}
```

Discussion

Other searchable criteria can be added to this class by following the same coding pattern for each search method. For instance, the following example shows how to add a search method to find all entries that contain a particular username:

```
public static EventLogEntry[] FindUserName(IEnumerable logEntries,
    string userNameQuery)
{
    ArrayList entries = new ArrayList();

    foreach (EventLogEntry logEntry in logEntries)
    {
        if (logEntry.UserName == userNameQuery)
        {
            entries.Add(logEntry);
        }
    }

    EventLogEntry[] entriesArray = new EventLogEntry[entries.Count];
    entries.CopyTo(entriesArray);
    return (entriesArray);
}
```

The methods shown in Table 6-2 list other search methods that could be included in this class and describe which property of the event log entries they search on. (All of these methods are implemented on the code for this book, which can be found at *http://www.oreilly.com/catalog/csharpckbk.*)

Table 6-2. Other possible search methods

Search method name	Entry property searched
FindMachineName	MachineName == MachineNameQuery
FindCategory (overloaded to accept a string type category name)	Category == CategoryNameQuery
FindCategory (overloaded to accept a short type category number)	Category == CategoryNumberQuery
FindSource	Source == SourceQuery
FindEntryType	EntryType == EntryTypeQuery
FindMessage	Message == Message.Query
FindEventID	EventID == EventIDQuery

The FindCategory method can be overloaded to search on either the category name or category number.

The following method makes use of the EventLogSearch methods to find and display entries that are marked as Error log entries:

```
public void FindAnEntryInEventLog()
{
    EventLog Log = new EventLog("System");

    EventLogEntry[] entries = EventLogSearch.FindEntryType(Log.entries,
                                                EventLogEntryType.Error);

    foreach (EventLogEntry Entry in entries)
    {
        Console.WriteLine("Message:      " + Entry.Message);
        Console.WriteLine("EventID:      " + Entry.EventID);
        Console.WriteLine("Category:     " + Entry.Category);
        Console.WriteLine("EntryType:    " + Entry.EntryType.ToString());
        Console.WriteLine("Source:       " + Entry.Source);
    }
}
```

The following method finds and displays entries generated at or after 8/24/2002, are marked as Error type logs, and contain an event ID of 7000:

```
public void FindAnEntryInEventLog()
{
    EventLog log = new EventLog("System");

    EventLogEntry[] entries = EventLogSearch.FindTimeGeneratedAtOrAfter(log.entries,
                        DateTime.Parse("8/24/2002"));
    entries = EventLogSearch.FindEntryType(entries, EventLogEntryType.Error);
    entries = EventLogSearch.FindEventID(entries, 7000);

    foreach (EventLogEntry entry in entries)
    {
        Console.WriteLine("Message:      " + entry.Message);
        Console.WriteLine("EventID:      " + entry.EventID);
        Console.WriteLine("Category:     " + entry.Category);
        Console.WriteLine("EntryType:    " + entry.EntryType.ToString());
        Console.WriteLine("Source:       " + entry.Source);
    }
}
```

Note that this search mechanism can search within only one event log at a time.

To illustrate how searching works, let's assume that you are using the FindEventID method to search on the EventID. Initially, you would call the FindEventID search method, passing in a collection that implements the IEnumerable interface, such as the EventLogEntryCollection collection (that contains all entries in that event log) or an array of EventLogEntry objects. The EventLogEntryCollection collection is returned by the Entries property of the EventLog class. The FindEventID method will return an array of EventLogEntry objects that match the search criteria (the value passed in to the second argument of the FindEventID method).

The real power of this searching method design is that the initial search on the `EventLogEntryCollection` returns an array of `EventLogEntry` objects. This `EventLogEntry` array may then be passed back into another search method to be searched again, effectively narrowing down the search query. For example, the `EventLogEntry` array returned from the `FindEventID` method may be passed into another search method such as the `FindEntryType` method to narrow down the search to all entries that are possibly informational entry types.

See Also

See the "EventLog Class" and "EventLogEntry Class" topics in the MSDN documentation.

6.10   Watching the Event Log for a Specific Entry

Problem

You may have multiple applications that write to a single event log. For each of these applications, you want a monitoring application to watch for one or more specific log entries to be written to the event log. For example, you might want to watch for a log entry that indicates that an application encountered a critical error or shut down unexpectedly. These log entries should be reported in real time.

Solution

Monitoring an event log for a specific entry requires the following steps:

1. Create the following method to set up the event handler to handle event log writes:

```
public void WatchForAppEvent(EventLog log)
{
    log.EnableRaisingEvents = true;
    log.EntryWritten += new EntryWrittenEventHandler(OnEntryWritten);
}
```

2. Create the event handler to examine the log entries and determine whether further action is to be performed. For example:

```
public static void OnEntryWritten(object source,
                                  EntryWrittenEventArgs entryArg)
{
    if (entryArg.Entry.EntryType == EventLogEntryType.Error)
    {
        Console.WriteLine(entryArg.Entry.Message);
        Console.WriteLine(entryArg.Entry.Category);
        Console.WriteLine(entryArg.Entry.EntryType.ToString());
        // Do further actions here as necessary...
    }
}
```

Discussion

This recipe revolves around the EntryWrittenEventHandler delegate, which calls back a method whenever any new entry is written to the event log. The EntryWrittenEventHandler delegate accepts two arguments: a *source* of type object and an *entryArg* of type EntryWrittenEventArgs. The *entryArg* parameter is the most interesting of the two. It contains a property called Entry that returns an EventLogEntry object. This EventLogEntry object contains all the information you need concerning the entry that was written to the event log.

This event log that we are watching is passed as the WatchForAppEvent method's *log* parameter. This method performs two actions. First, it sets log's EnableRaisingEvents property to true. If this property were set to false, no events would be raised for this event log when an entry is written to it. The second action this method performs is to add the OnEntryWritten callback method to the list of event handlers for this event log.

To prevent this delegate from calling the OnEntryWritten callback method, you can set the EnableRaisingEvents property to false, effectively turning off the delegate.

Note that the Entry object returned by the entryArg parameter of the OnEntryWritten callback method is read-only and therefore the entry cannot be modified before it is written to the event log.

See Also

See the "Handling the EntryWritten Event" and "EventLog.EntryWritten Event" topics in the MSDN documentation.

6.11 Finding All Sources Belonging to a Specific Event Log

Problem

You need to determine which sources are attached to a particular event log before the log is examined and/or deleted. A source is a component or application that has registered itself to a particular event log as a source of events.

Solution

Use the following method to extract all of the source names registered to a log (pass the log's name in as the *logName* argument):

```
public ArrayList FindSourceNamesFromLog(string logName)
{
    ArrayList sourceNamesList = new ArrayList();
```

```
string[] eventLogNames = Registry.LocalMachine.OpenSubKey
    (@"SYSTEM\CurrentControlSet\Services\Eventlog").GetSubKeyNames( );
foreach (string log in eventLogNames)
{
    Console.WriteLine("log: " + log);
    if (logName == log)
    {
        string[] sourceNames = Registry.LocalMachine.OpenSubKey
                (@"SYSTEM\CurrentControlSet\Services\Eventlog\" +
                log).GetSubKeyNames( );

        sourceNamesList.Capacity = Registry.LocalMachine.OpenSubKey
                (@"SYSTEM\CurrentControlSet\Services\Eventlog\" +
                log).SubKeyCount;

        for (int i = 0; i < sourceNames.Length; i++)
        {
            sourceNamesList.Add(sourceNames[i]);
            Console.WriteLine("SourceName: " + sourceNames[i]);
        }
    }
}

return (sourceNamesList);
}
```

To obtain a listing of *all* logs and their registered sources, use the following method:

```
public static Hashtable FindSourceNamesFromAllLogs( )
{
    Hashtable logsAndSources = new Hashtable( );

    string[] eventLogNames = Registry.LocalMachine.OpenSubKey
        (@"SYSTEM\CurrentControlSet\Services\Eventlog").GetSubKeyNames( );

    foreach (string log in eventLogNames)
    {
        ArrayList sourceNamesList = new ArrayList( );

        string[] sourceNames = Registry.LocalMachine.OpenSubKey
                (@"SYSTEM\CurrentControlSet\Services\Eventlog\" +
                log).GetSubKeyNames( );

        sourceNamesList.Capacity = Registry.LocalMachine.OpenSubKey
                (@"SYSTEM\CurrentControlSet\Services\Eventlog\" +
                log).SubKeyCount;

        for (int i = 0; i < sourceNames.Length; i++)
        {
            sourceNamesList.Add(sourceNames[i]);
        }

        logsAndSources.Add(log, sourceNamesList);
```

```
        }

        return (logsAndSources);
    }
```

This method returns a Hashtable with the log name as the key and an ArrayList of source names as the Hashtable's value. The information in the Hashtable of ArrayLists can be accessed using the following code:

```
foreach (DictionaryEntry DE in logsAndSources)
{
    Console.WriteLine("Log: " + DE.Key);              // Display the log
    foreach (string source in ((ArrayList)DE.Value))
    {
        // Display all sources for this log
        Console.WriteLine("\tSource: " + source);
    }
}
```

Discussion

This recipe is similar to Recipe 6.8 in that we need to find information concerning an event log that can be obtained only through the registry. If we need to find the sources associated with a log called MyLog, we would look up all of the subkeys contained in the following location:

```
HKEY_LOCAL_MACHINE\SYSTEM\CurrentControlSet\Services\Eventlog\MyLog\
```

If MyLog were associated with two sources called AppSource and MonitorSource, the following keys would exist under the MyLog key:

```
\AppSource
\MonitorSource
```

The full registry path for both keys would be:

```
HKEY_LOCAL_MACHINE\SYSTEM\CurrentControlSet\Services\Eventlog\MyLog\AppSource
HKEY_LOCAL_MACHINE\SYSTEM\CurrentControlSet\Services\Eventlog\MyLog\MonitorSource
```

This recipe makes use of the Registry and RegistryKey classes to look up the subkeys under the event log's key in the registry. See Recipe 6.8 for more information dealing with opening registry keys using the Registry and RegistryKey classes.

The read-only SubKeyCount property and GetSubKeyNames method of the RegistryKey class are used to obtain the number of subkeys that reside under a particular key and a string array containing their names.

The FindSourceNamesFromLog method uses the GetSubKeyNames method to obtain a list of event logs from the EventLog registry key. It then searches these log names until the log name passed to this method through the *logName* parameter is found. Once the correct log is found, its subkeys—representing all of the sources tied to that log—are saved to the sourceNamesList array. This array is then passed back to the caller.

See Also

See Recipe 6.8; see the "Registry.LocalMachine Field" and "RegistryKey.Open Method" topics in the MSDN documentation.

6.12 Implementing a Simple Performance Counter

Problem

You need to use a performance counter to track application-specific information. The simpler performance counters find, for example, the change in a counter value between successive samplings or just count the number of times an action occurs. Other, more complex counters exist but are not dealt with in this recipe. For example, a custom counter could be built to keep track of the number of database transactions, the number of failed network connections to a server, or even the number of users connecting to your web service per minute.

Solution

Create a simple performance counter that finds, for example, the change in a counter value between successive samplings or to simply count the number of times an action occurs. Use the following method to create a simple custom counter:

```
public PerformanceCounter CreateSimpleCounter(string counterName, string counterHelp,
    PerformanceCounterType counterType, string categoryName, string categoryHelp)
{
    CounterCreationDataCollection counterCollection =
            new CounterCreationDataCollection( );

    // Create the custom counter object and add it to the collection of counters
    CounterCreationData counter = new CounterCreationData(counterName, counterHelp,
            counterType);
    counterCollection.Add(counter);

    // Create category
    if (PerformanceCounterCategory.Exists(categoryName))
    {
        PerformanceCounterCategory.Delete(categoryName);
    }

    PerformanceCounterCategory appCategory =
        PerformanceCounterCategory.Create(categoryName,
                                    categoryHelp, counterCollection);

    // Create the counter and initialize it
    PerformanceCounter appCounter =
        new PerformanceCounter(categoryName, counterName, false);
```

```
        appCounter.RawValue = 0;

        return (appCounter);
    }
```

Discussion

The first action this method takes is to create a `counterCollection` object and `CounterCreationData` object. The `CounterCreationData` object is created using the *counterName*, *counterHelp*, and *countertype* parameters passed to the `CreateSimpleCounter` method. The `CounterCreationData` object is then added to the `counterCollection`.

 The ASPNET user account, by default, prevents performance counters from being read. You can either increase the permissions allowed by this account or use impersonation to enable this functionality. However, this then becomes a deployment requirement of your web application. Decreasing security for the ASPNET account may very well be frowned upon by IT folks deploying your application.

If *categoryName*—a string containing the name of the category that is passed as a parameter to the method—is not registered on the system, a new category is created from a `PerformanceCounterCategory` object. If one is registered, it is deleted and created anew from a `PerformanceCounterCategory` object. Finally, the actual performance counter is created from a `PerformanceCounter` object. This object is initialized to zero and returned by the method.

The `CreateSimpleCounter` method returns a `PerformanceCounter` object that will be used by an application. The application can perform several actions on a `PerformanceCounter` object. An application can increment or decrement it using one of these three methods:

```
long value = appCounter.Increment( );
long value = appCounter.Decrement( );
long value = appCounter.IncrementBy(i);

// Additionally, a negative number may be passed to the
// IncrementBy method to mimic a DecrementBy method
// (which is not included in this class). For example:
long value = appCounter.IncrementBy(-i);
```

The first two methods accept no parameters, while the third accepts a `long` containing the number by which to increment the counter. All three methods return a `long` type indicating the new value of the counter.

In addition to incrementing or decrementing this counter, you can also take samples of the counter at various points in the application. A *sample* is a snapshot of the counter and all of its values at a particular instance in time. A sample may be taken using the following line of code:

```
CounterSample counterSampleValue = appCounter.NextSample( );
```

The NextSample method accepts no parameters and returns a CounterSample structure.

At another point in the application, a counter can be sampled again, and both samples can be passed in to the static Calculate method on the CounterSample class. These actions may be performed on a single line of code as follows:

```
float calculatedSample = CounterSample.Calculate(counterSampleValue,
                                    appCounter.NextSample( ));
```

The calculated sample calculatedSample may be stored for future analysis.

The simpler performance counters already available in the .NET Framework are:

CounterDelta32/CounterDelta64
> Determines the difference (or change) in value between two samplings of this counter. The CounterDelta64 counter can hold larger values than CounterDelta32.

CounterTimer
> Calculates the percentage of the CounterTimer value change over the CounterTimer time change.

CounterTimerInverse
> Calculates the inverse of the CounterTimer counter.

CountPerTimeInterval32/CountPerTimeInterval64
> Calculates the number of items waiting (possibly within a queue) over the time elapsed.

ElapsedTime
> Calculates the difference in time between when this counter recorded the start of an event and the current time, measured in seconds.

NumberOfItems32/NumberOfItems64
> This counter returns its raw value. The NumberOfItems64 counter can hold larger values than NumberOfItems32. This counter does not need to be passed to the static Calculate method of the CounterSample class; there are no values that must be calculated. Instead, use the RawValue property of the PerformanceCounter object (i.e., in this recipe, the appCounter.RawValue property would be used).

NumberOfItemsHEX32/NumberOfItemsHEX64
> This counter returns its raw value in hexadecimal format. The NumberOfItemsHEX64 counter can hold larger values than NumberOfItemsHEX32. This counter does not need to be passed to the static Calculate method of the CounterSample class; there are no values that must be calculated. Instead, use the RawValue property of the PerformanceCounter object (i.e., in this recipe, the appCounter.RawValue property would be used).

RateOfCountsPerSecond32/RateOfCountsPerSecond64
> Calculates the RateOfCountsPerSecond* value change over the RateOfCountsPerSecond* time change, measured in seconds. The RateOfCountsPerSecond64 counter can hold larger values than the RateOfCountsPerSecond32 counter.

`Timer100Ns`
> Calculates the percentage of the `Timer100Ns` value change over the `Timer100Ns` time change, measured in 100ns time units.

`Timer100nsInverse`
> Calculates the inverse of the `Timer100Ns` counter.

See Also

See Recipe 6.13; see the "PerformanceCounter Class," "PerformanceCounterType Enumeration," "PerformanceCounterCategory Class," "ASP.NET Impersonation," and "Monitoring Performance Thresholds" topics in the MSDN documentation.

6.13 Implementing Performance Counters that Require a Base Counter

Problem

You need to use some of the more advanced performance counters to accurately track information about your application. This performance counter exists as two counters used together. The first counter is the *main counter*, which is divided by the second counter, called the *base counter*. Essentially, the first counter is the numerator and the second counter is the denominator; the custom counter reports the result of this division operation. The main counter is used in tandem with its base counter type to calculate, for example, the average amount of time it takes for an action (e.g., connecting to a server) to complete or the average number of actions that occur during a single process (e.g., database timeouts).

Solution

Create a complex performance counter, which is used in tandem with the base counter type to calculate, for example, the average amount of time it takes for an action to complete or the average number of actions that occur during a single process. Use the following method to create a complex custom counter:

```
public void CreateComplexCounter(string counterName, string counterHelp,
    PerformanceCounterType counterType, string baseCounterName,
    string baseCounterHelp,  PerformanceCounterType baseCounterType,
    string categoryName, string categoryHelp,
    out PerformanceCounter appCounter,
    out PerformanceCounter appBaseCounter)
{
    CounterCreationDataCollection counterCollection =
      new CounterCreationDataCollection( );

    // Create the custom counter object and its base counter object
    //     and add them to the collection of counters (they must be
    //     added successively)
```

```
        CounterCreationData counter = new CounterCreationData(counterName,
          counterHelp, counterType);
        counterCollection.Add(counter);
        CounterCreationData BaseCounter =
          new CounterCreationData(baseCounterName,
                baseCounterHelp, baseCounterType);
        counterCollection.Add(BaseCounter);

        // Create category
        if (PerformanceCounterCategory.Exists(categoryName))
        {
            PerformanceCounterCategory.Delete(categoryName);
        }

        PerformanceCounterCategory appCategory =
            PerformanceCounterCategory.Create(categoryName, categoryHelp,
              counterCollection);

        // Create the counter and initialize it
        PerformanceCounter newAppCounter =
            new PerformanceCounter(categoryName, counterName, false);
        PerformanceCounter newAppBaseCounter =
            new PerformanceCounter(categoryName, baseCounterName, false);

        newAppCounter.RawValue = 0;
        newAppBaseCounter.RawValue = 0;

        appCounter = newAppCounter;
        appBaseCounter = newAppBaseCounter;
    }
```

Discussion

The `CreateComplexCounter` method returns two `PerformanceCounter` objects as out parameters; one is the counter, and the other is the base counter. These two counters are used in tandem; the base counter controls some aspect of the denominator in the calculation relating these two counters. Since the value of the `appCounter` parameter, returned from this method, depends on the value in the `appBaseCounter` parameter, we are considering these types of counters as complex counters.

 The ASPNET user account, by default, prevents performance counters from being read. You can either increase the permissions allowed by this account or use impersonation to enable this functionality. However, this then becomes a deployment requirement of your web application. Decreasing security for the ASPNET account may very well be frowned upon by IT folks deploying your application.

This method operates similarly to the `CreateSimpleCounter` method described in Recipe 6.12. The one major difference is that two `CounterCreationData` objects are created and added to the `CounterCreationDataCollection` object. This first `CounterCreationData` object is the main counter used in the calculation for this counter. The second is the base counter, used in the denominator of the calculation for this counter. These counters must be added, in order, to the CounterCreationDataCollection object. In addition, the counter defined by the *counterName* parameter must be added before the counter defined by the *baseCounterName* parameter.

The application can perform several actions on these PerformanceCounter objects. An application can increment or decrement a PerformanceCounter object using one of these three methods:

```
long value = newAppCounter.Increment( );
long value = newAppCounter.Decrement( );
long value = newAppCounter.IncrementBy(i);

long value = newAppBaseCounter.Increment( );
long value = newAppBaseCounter.Decrement( );
long value = newAppBaseCounter.IncrementBy(i);

// Additionally, a negative number may be passed in to the IncrementBy method
//    to mimic a DecrementBy method (which is not included in this class)
long value = newAppCounter.IncrementBy(-i);
long value = newAppBaseCounter.IncrementBy(-i);
```

The first two methods accept no parameters, while the third accepts a long containing the number by which to increment the counter. All three methods return a long type indicating the new value of the counter.

In addition to incrementing or decrementing these counters, you can also take samples of these counters at various points in the application. A sample is a snapshot of the counter and all of its values at a particular instance in time. A sample may be taken using the following lines of code:

```
CounterSample counterSampleValue = newAppCounter.NextSample( );
CounterSample counterSampleValue = newAppBaseCounter.NextSample( );
```

The NextSample method accepts no parameters and returns a CounterSample object.

At another point in the application, a counter may be sampled again, and the samples can be passed in to the static *Calculate* method on the CounterSample class. These actions may be performed on a single line of code as follows:

```
float calculatedSample = CounterSample.Calculate(counterSampleValue,
                                        newAppCounter.NextSample( ));
```

Note that you need to pass only the newAppCounter samples; the newAppBaseCounter samples are handled for you. The calculated sample calculatedSample may be stored for future analysis. See Recipe 6.12 for a definition of the Calculate method.

The complex performance counters defined in the .NET Framework are defined here:

AverageCount64

> Calculates the AverageTimer64 value change over the AverageBase value change. This counter uses AverageBase as its base counter type.

`AverageTimer32`

Calculates the `AverageTimer32` value change over the number of ticks per second, all over the `AverageBase` value change. This counter uses `AverageBase` as its base counter type.

`CounterMultiTimer`

Calculates the percentage of `CounterMultiTimer` value change over the `CounterMultiTimer` time change divided by `CounterMultiBase`. This counter uses `CounterMultiBase` as its base counter type.

`CounterMultiTimerInverse`

Calculates the inverse of the `CounterMultiTimer` counter. This counter uses `CounterMultiBase` as its base counter type.

`CounterMultiTimer100Ns`

Calculates the percentage of `CounterMultiTime100Ns` value change over the `CounterMultiTime100Ns` time change divided by `CounterMultiBase`. The value of this counter is measured in 100ns time units. This counter uses `CounterMultiBase` as its base counter type.

`CounterMultiTimer100NsInverse`

Calculates the inverse of the `CounterMultiTimer100Ns` counter. This counter uses `CounterMultiBase` as its base counter type.

`RawFraction`

Calculates a percentage of the `RawFraction` counter value over the `RawBase` counter value. This counter uses `RawBase` as its base counter type.

`SampleCounter`

Calculates the `SampleCounter` value change over their corresponding `SampleBase` value change per second. This counter uses `SampleBase` as its base counter type.

`SampleFraction`

Calculates the percentage of `SampleCounter` value change over the `SampleBase` value change. This counter uses `SampleBase` as its base counter type.

See Also

See Recipe 6.12; see the "PerformanceCounter Class," "PerformanceCounterType Enumeration," "PermformanceCounterCategory Class," "ASP.NET Impersonation," and "Monitoring Performance Thresholds" topics in the MSDN documentation.

6.14 Enable/Disable Complex Tracing Code

Problem

You have an object that contains complex tracing/debugging code. In fact, there is so much tracing/debugging code that to turn it all on would create an extremely large amount of output. You want to be able to generate objects at runtime that contain all of the tracing/debugging code, only a specific portion of this tracing/debugging code, or that contain no tracing/debugging code. The amount of tracing code generated could depend on the state of the application or the environment where it is running. The tracing code needs to be generated during object creation.

Solution

Use the TraceFactory class, which implements the *Simple Factory design pattern* to allow creation of an object that either generates tracing information or does not:

```
#define TRACE
#define TRACE_INSTANTIATION
#define TRACE_BEHAVIOR

using System.Diagnostics;

public class TraceFactory
{
    public TraceFactory() {}

    public Foo CreateObj()
    {
        Foo obj = null;

        #if (TRACE)
            #if (TRACE_INSTANTIATION)
                obj = new BarTraceInst();
            #elif (TRACE_BEHAVIOR)
                obj = new BarTraceBehavior();
            #else
                obj = new Bar();
            #endif
        #else
            obj = new Bar();
        #endif

        return (obj);
    }
}
```

The class hierarchy for the Bar, BarTraceInst, and BarTraceBehavior classes is shown next. The BarTraceInst class would contain only the constructor tracing code, the BarTraceBehavior class contains only tracing code within specific methods, and the Bar class contains no tracing code:

```
public abstract class Foo
{
    public virtual void SomeBehavior()
    {
        //...
    }
}
```

```
public class Bar : Foo
{
    public Bar() {}

    public override void SomeBehavior()
    {
        base.SomeBehavior();
    }
}

public class BarTraceInst : Foo
{
    public BarTraceInst()
    {
        Trace.WriteLine("BarTraceInst object instantiated");
    }

    public override void SomeBehavior()
    {
        base.SomeBehavior();
    }
}

public class BarTraceBehavior : Foo
{
    public BarTraceBehavior() {}

    public override void SomeBehavior()
    {
        Trace.WriteLine("SomeBehavior called");
        base.SomeBehavior();
    }
}
```

Discussion

The *factory design pattern* is designed to abstract away the creation of objects within a system. This pattern allows code to create objects of a particular type by using an intermediate object called a *factory*. In its simplest form, a factory pattern consists of some client code that uses a factory object to create and return a specific type of object. The factory pattern allows changes to be made in the way objects are created, independent of the client code. This design prevents code changes to the way an object is constructed from permeating throughout the client code.

Consider that you could have a class that contained numerous lines of tracing code. If you ran this code to obtain the trace output, you would be inundated with reams of information. This setup is hard to manage and even harder to read to pinpoint problems in your code. One solution to this problem is to use a factory to create an object based on the type of tracing code you wish to output.

To do this, create an abstract base class called Foo that contains all of the base behavior. The Foo class is subclassed to create the Bar, BarTraceInst, and BarTraceBehavior classes. The Bar class contains no tracing code, the BarTraceInst class only contains tracing code in its constructor (and potentially in its destructor), and the BarTraceBehavior class only contains tracing code in specific methods. (The class hierarchy provided in the Solution section is much simpler than classes that you would create; this allows you to focus more on the design pattern and less on the class hierarchy from which the factory creates classes.)

A TraceFactory class is created that will act as our factory to create objects inheriting from the abstract Foo class. The TraceFactory class contains a single public method called CreateObj. This method attempts to instantiate an object that inherits from Foo based on the preprocessor symbols defined in your application. If the following line of code exists:

```
#define TRACE_BEHAVIOR
```

the BarTraceBehavior class is created. If this line exists:

```
#define TRACE_INSTANTIATION
```

the BarTraceInst class is created. If neither of these exists, the Bar class is created. Once the correct class is created, it is returned to the caller. The caller never needs to know which exact object is instantiated, only that it is of type Foo. This allows us to add even more classes to handle varying types and amounts of tracing code.

To instantiate a TraceFactory class, use the following code:

```
TraceFactory factory = new TraceFactory( );
```

Using this factory object, we can create a new object of type Foo:

```
Foo obj = factory.CreateObj( );
Console.WriteLine(obj.ToString( ));
obj.SomeBehavior( );
```

Now we can use the Foo object without regard to the trace output that it will produce. To create and use a different Foo object, all we have to do is define a different preprocessor symbol that controls which subclass of Foo is created.

See Also

See the "C# Preprocessor Directives" and "ConditionalAttribute Class" topics in the MSDN documentation.

CHAPTER 7

Delegates and Events

Delegates contain all that is needed to allow a method, with a specific signature and return type, to be invoked by your code. A delegate can be used similarly to an object; for example, it can be passed to methods and stored in a data structure. A delegate is used when, at design time, you do not know which method you need to call and the information to determine this is available only at runtime.

Another scenario is when the code calling a method is being developed independently of the code that will supply the method to be called. The classic example is a Windows Forms control. If you design a control, you are unlikely to know what method should be called when the application raises an event, so you must use a delegate. However, when others use your control, they will typically decide at design time which method to call. (For example, it's common to connect a `Button`'s click handler to a delegate at design time.)

This chapter's recipes make use of delegates and events. These recipes cover handling each method invoked in a multicast delegate individually, synchronous delegate invocation versus asynchronous delegate invocation, and enhancing an existing class with events, among other topics. If you are not familiar with delegates and events, you should read the MSDN documentation on these topics. There are also good tutorials and example code showing you how to set up and use delegates and events.

7.1 Controlling when and if a Delegate Fires Within a Multicast Delegate

Problem

You have added multiple delegates to create a multicast delegate. When this multicast delegate is fired, each delegate within it is fired in turn. You need to exert more control over such things as the order in which each delegate is fired, firing only a subset of delegates, or firing each delegate based on the success or failure of previous delegates.

Solution

Use the `GetInvocationList` method to obtain an array of `Delegate` objects. Next, iterate over this array using a for loop. You can then invoke each `Delegate` object in the array individually and optionally retrieve its return value.

The following method creates a multicast delegate called `All` and then uses `GetInvocationList` to allow each delegate to be fired individually, in reverse order:

```
public void InvokeInReverse()
{
    MultiInvoke MI1 = new MultiInvoke(TestInvoke.Method1);
    MultiInvoke MI2 = new MultiInvoke(TestInvoke.Method2);
    MultiInvoke MI3 = new MultiInvoke(TestInvoke.Method3);

    MultiInvoke All = MI1 + MI2 + MI3;

    Console.WriteLine("Fire delegates in reverse");
    Delegate[] Delegates = All.GetInvocationList();
    for (int counter = Delegates.Length - 1; counter >= 0; counter--)
    {
        ((MultiInvoke)Delegates[counter])();
    }
}
```

The following method fires every other delegate, starting with the first delegate in the list:

```
public void InvokeEveryOther()
{
    MultiInvoke MI1 = new MultiInvoke(TestInvoke.Method1);
    MultiInvoke MI2 = new MultiInvoke(TestInvoke.Method2);
    MultiInvoke MI3 = new MultiInvoke(TestInvoke.Method3);

    MultiInvoke All = MI1 + MI2 + MI3;

    Delegate[] Delegates = All.GetInvocationList();

    Console.WriteLine("Fire every other delegate");
    for (int counter = 0; counter < Delegates.Length; counter += 2)
    {
        ((MultiInvoke)Delegates[counter])();
    }
}
```

In .NET, all delegates are implicitly multicast—that is, any delegate can invoke multiple methods each time it is itself invoked. In this recipe, we use the term "multicast" to describe a delegate that has been set up to invoke multiple methods. The following delegate defines the `MultiInvoke` delegate:

```
public delegate int MultiInvoke();
```

The following class contains each of the methods that will be called by the
MultiInvoke multicast delegate:

```
public class TestInvoke
{
    public static int Method1()
    {
        Console.WriteLine("Invoked Method1");
        return (1);
    }

    public static int Method2()
    {
        Console.WriteLine("Invoked Method2");
        return (2);
    }

    public static int Method3()
    {
        Console.WriteLine("Invoked Method3");
        return (3);
    }
}
```

It is also possible to decide whether to continue firing delegates in the list based on
the return value of the currently firing delegate. The following method fires each delegate, stopping only when a delegate returns a false value:

```
public void InvokeWithTest()
{
    MultiInvokeTF MI1 = new MultiInvokeTF(TestInvokeTF.Method1);
    MultiInvokeTF MI2 = new MultiInvokeTF(TestInvokeTF.Method2);
    MultiInvokeTF MI3 = new MultiInvokeTF(TestInvokeTF.Method3);

    MultiInvokeTF All = MI1 + MI2 + MI3;

    bool retVal = true;

    Console.WriteLine(
        "Invoke individually (Call based on previous return value):");
    foreach (MultiInvokeTF individualMI in All.GetInvocationList())
    {
        if (retVal)
        {
            retVal = individualMI();
        }
        else
        {
            // This break is not required; it is an optimization to
            // prevent the loop from continuing to execute.
            break;
        }
    }
}
```

The following delegate defines the MultiInvokeTF delegate:

```
public delegate bool MultiInvokeTF();
```

The following class contains each of the methods that will be called by the MultiInvokeTF multicast delegate:

```
public class TestInvokeTF
{
    public static bool Method1()
    {
        Console.WriteLine("Invoked Method1");
        return (true);
    }

    public static bool Method2()
    {
        Console.WriteLine("Invoked Method2");
        return (false);
    }

    public static bool Method3()
    {
        Console.WriteLine("Invoked Method3");
        return (true);
    }
}
```

Discussion

A delegate, when called, will invoke all delegates stored within its *invocation list*. These delegates are invoked sequentially from the first to the last one added. Once the multicast delegate is called, you cannot change when—or if—any delegate in the list is called.

Fortunately, with the use of the GetInvocationList method of the MulticastDelegate class, you can obtain each delegate in the invocation list of a multicast delegate. This method accepts no parameters and returns an array of Delegate objects that corresponds to the invocation list of the delegate on which this method was called. The returned Delegate array contains the delegates of the invocation list in the order in which they would normally be called; that is, the zeroth element in the Delegate array contains the Delegate object that is normally called first.

This application of the GetInvocationList method gives us the ability to control exactly when and how the delegates in a multicast delegate are invoked and allows us to prevent the continued invocation of delegates when one delegate fails. This ability is important if each delegate is manipulating data and one of the delegates fails in its duties but does not throw an exception. If one delegate fails in its duties and the remaining delegates rely on all previous delegates to succeed, you must quit invoking delegates at the point of failure. Note that an exception will force the invocation of delegates to cease, but throwing an exception is an expensive process. This recipe handles a delegate failure more efficiently, and also provides more flexibility in dealing with these errors. For example, you can write logic to specify which delegates are to be invoked, based on the performance of previously invoked delegates.

See Also

See Recipes 7.2 and 7.3; see the "Delegate Class" and "Delegate.GetInvocationList Method" topics in the MSDN documentation.

7.2 Obtaining Return Values from Each Delegate in a Multicast Delegate

Problem

You have added multiple delegates to a single multicast delegate. Each of these individual delegates returns a value that is required by your application. Ordinarily, the values returned by individual delegates in a multicast delegate are lost; all except the value from the last delegate to fire, whose return value is returned to the calling application. You need to be able to access the return value of each delegate that is fired in the multicast delegate.

Solution

Use the GetInvocationList method as in Recipe 7.1. This method returns each individual delegate from a multicast delegate. In doing so, we can invoke each delegate individually and get its return value. The following method creates a multicast delegate called All and then uses GetInvocationList to fire each delegate individually. After firing each delegate, the return value is captured:

```
public void TestIndividualInvokesRetVal()
{
    MultiInvoke MI1 = new MultiInvoke(TestInvoke.Method1);
    MultiInvoke MI2 = new MultiInvoke(TestInvoke.Method2);
    MultiInvoke MI3 = new MultiInvoke(TestInvoke.Method3);

    MultiInvoke All = MI1 + MI2 + MI3;

    int retVal = -1;

    Console.WriteLine("Invoke individually (Obtain each return value):");
    foreach (MultiInvoke individualMI in All.GetInvocationList())
    {
        retVal = individualMI();
        Console.WriteLine("\tOutput: " + retVal);
    }
}
```

The following delegate defines the MultiInvoke delegate:

```
public delegate int MultiInvoke();
```

The following class contains each of the methods that will be called by the
MultiInvoke multicast delegate:

```
public class TestInvoke
{
    public static int Method1()
    {
        Console.WriteLine("Invoked Method1");
        return (1);
    }

    public static int Method2()
    {
        Console.WriteLine("Invoked Method2");
        return (2);
    }

    public static int Method3()
    {
        Console.WriteLine("Invoked Method3");
        return (3);
    }
}
```

Discussion

One quirk with multicast delegates is that if any or all delegates within its invocation
list return a value, only the value of the last invoked delegate is returned; all others
are lost. This loss can become annoying, or worse, if your code requires these return
values. Consider a case in which the All delegate was invoked normally, as in the following code:

```
retVal = All();
Console.WriteLine(retVal);
```

The value 3 would be displayed since Method3 was the last method invoked by the All
delegate. None of the other return values would be captured.

By using the GetInvocationList method of the MulticastDelegate class, we can get
around this limitation. This method returns an array of Delegate objects that can
each be invoked separately. Note that this method does not invoke each delegate; it
simply returns an array of them to the caller. By invoking each delegate separately,
we can retrieve each return value from each fired delegate. (More information on the
GetInvocationList method is presented in Recipe 7.1.)

Note that any out or ref parameters will also be lost when a multicast delegate is
invoked. This recipe allows you to obtain the out and/or ref parameters of each
invoked delegate within the multicast delegate.

However, you still need to be aware that any unhandled exceptions emanating from
one of these invoked delegates will be bubbled up to the method
TestIndividualInvokesRetVal, presented in this recipe. To better handle this situation, see Recipe 7.3.

See Also

See Recipes 7.1 and 7.3; see the "Delegate Class" and "Delegate.GetInvocationList Method" topics in the MSDN documentation.

7.3 Handling Exceptions Individually for Each Delegate in a Multicast Delegate

Problem

You have added multiple delegates to a single multicast delegate. Each of these individual delegates must fire, regardless of whether an unhandled exception is thrown within one of the delegates. But once a delegate in a multicast delegate throws an unhandled exception, no more delegates are fired. You need a way to trap unhandled exceptions within each individual delegate while still allowing the rest of the delegates to fire.

Solution

Use the GetInvocationList method as shown in Recipe 7.1. This method returns each individual delegate from a multicast delegate, and by doing so, allows us to invoke each delegate within an exception handler. The following method creates a multicast delegate called All and then uses GetInvocationList to retrieve each delegate individually. Each delegate is then fired within an exception handler:

```
using System;
using System.Security;

public class DelegateUtilities
{
    public void TestIndividualInvokesExceptions()
    {
        MultiInvoke MI1 = new MultiInvoke(TestInvoke.Method1);
        MultiInvoke MI2 = new MultiInvoke(TestInvoke.Method2);
        MultiInvoke MI3 = new MultiInvoke(TestInvoke.Method3);

        MultiInvoke All = MI1 + MI2 + MI3;

        int retVal = -1;

        Console.WriteLine("Invoke individually (handle exceptions):");
        foreach (MultiInvoke individualMI in All.GetInvocationList())
        {
            try
            {
                retVal = individualMI();
                Console.WriteLine("\tOutput: " + retVal);
            }
```

```
            catch (SecurityException se)
            {
                // Stop everything, malicious code may be attempting
                // to access privileged data
                break;
            }
            catch (Exception e)
            {
                // Display (or log) the exception and continue
                Console.WriteLine(e.ToString());
            }
        }
    }
}
```

The following delegate defines the `MultiInvoke` delegate:

```
public delegate int MultiInvoke();
```

The following class contains each of the methods that will be called by the `MultiInvoke` multicast delegate:

```
public class TestInvoke
{
    public static int Method1()
    {
        Console.WriteLine("Invoked Method1");
        return (1);
    }

    public static int Method2()
    {
        Console.WriteLine("Invoked Method2");
        return (2);
    }

    public static int Method3()
    {
        // Simulate an exception being thrown
        throw (new Exception("Method3"));
        Console.WriteLine("Invoked Method3");
        return (3);
    }
}
```

Discussion

If an exception occurs in a delegate that is invoked from within a multicast delegate and that exception is unhandled, any remaining delegates are not invoked. This is the expected behavior of a multicast delegate. However, in some circumstances, you'd like to be able to handle exceptions thrown from individual delegates and then determine at that point whether to continue invoking the remaining delegates.

In the `TestIndividualInvokesExceptions` method of this recipe, if an exception `SecurityException` is caught, execution of the delegates is immediately stopped to prevent a security breach. However, if another type of `Exception` object is thrown, we just display or log it and continue invoking delegates. This strategy allows for as fine-grained handling of exceptions as you need. Note that if you rethrow an exception, the exception will be bubbled up to the next enclosing exception handler. If the next outer exception handler is outside of the loop used to iterate through each delegate object returned by the `GetInvocationList` method, any remaining delegates will not be invoked.

By adding a `finally` block to this `try/catch` block, you can be assured that code within this `finally` block is executed after every delegate returns. This technique is useful if you want to interleave code between calls to delegates, such as code to clean up objects that are not needed or code to verify that each delegate left the data it touched in a stable state.

See Also

See Recipes 7.1 and 7.2; see the "Delegate Class" and "Delegate.GetInvocationList Method" topics in the MSDN documentation.

7.4 Converting a Synchronous Delegate to an Asynchronous Delegate

Problem

You have determined that one or more delegates invoked synchronously within your application are taking a long time to execute. This delay is making the user interface less responsive to the user. These delegates should be converted to asynchronous delegates.

Solution

A typical synchronous delegate is created in the following manner:

```
using System;

// The delegate declaration
public delegate void SyncInvoke( );

// The class and method that is invoked through the SyncInvoke delegate
public class TestSyncInvoke
{
    public static void Method1( )
    {
        Console.WriteLine("Invoked Method1");
    }
}
```

The code to use this delegate is:

```
public class DelegateUtilities
{
    public void TestSimpleSyncDelegate()
    {
        SyncInvoke SI = new SyncInvoke(TestSyncInvoke.Method1);
        SI();
    }
}
```

This delegate can be called asynchronously on a thread obtained from the thread pool by modifying the code as follows:

```
public class DelegateUtilities
{
    public void TestSimpleAsyncDelegate()
    {
        AsyncCallback CB = new AsyncCallback(DelegateCallback);

        SyncInvoke ASI = new SyncInvoke(TestSyncInvoke.Method1);
        IAsyncResult AR = ASI.BeginInvoke(CB, null);
    }

    // The callback that gets called when Method1 is finished processing
    private static void DelegateCallback(IAsyncResult iresult)
    {
        AsyncResult result = (AsyncResult)iresult;
        AsyncInvoke ASI = (AsyncInvoke)result.AsyncDelegate;

        int retVal = ASI.EndInvoke(result);
        Console.WriteLine("retVal (Callback): " + retVal);
    }
}
```

Of course you might want to also change the TestSyncInvoke class name to TestAsyncInvoke and the SyncInvoke delegate name to AsyncInvoke just to be consistent with your naming.

The previous example shows how to call a delegate that accepts no parameters and returns void. The next example shows a synchronous delegate that accepts parameters and returns an integer:

```
using System;

// The delegate declaration
public delegate int SyncInvoke(string message);

// The class and method that is invoked through the SyncInvoke delegate
public class TestSyncInvoke
{
    public static int Method1(string message)
    {
        Console.WriteLine("Invoked Method1 with message: " + message);
```

```
            return (1);
        }
    }
```

The code to use this delegate is:

```
public class DelegateUtilities
{
    public void TestComplexSyncDelegate()
    {
        SyncInvoke SI = new SyncInvoke(TestSyncInvoke.Method1);
        int retVal = SI("Synchronous call");
        Console.WriteLine("Sync: " + retVal);
    }
}
```

This synchronous delegate can be converted to an asynchronous delegate in the following manner:

```
using System;
using System.Runtime.Remoting.Messaging;

public class DelegateUtilities
{
    public void TestCallbackAsyncDelegate()
    {
        AsyncCallback CB = new AsyncCallback(DelegateCallback);

        SyncInvoke SI = new SyncInvoke(TestSyncInvoke.Method1);
        IAsyncResult AR = SI.BeginInvoke("Asynchronous call message", CB, null);

        Console.WriteLine("WORKING...");
    }

    // The callback that gets called when Method1 is finished processing
    private static void DelegateCallback(IAsyncResult iresult)
    {
        AsyncResult result = (AsyncResult)iresult;
        AsyncInvoke ASI = (AsyncInvoke)result.AsyncDelegate;

        int retVal = ASI.EndInvoke(result);
        Console.WriteLine("retVal (Callback): " + retVal);
    }
}
```

Discussion

Converting a delegate from being invoked synchronously to asynchronously is not an overly complicated procedure. You need to add calls to both `BeginInvoke` and `EndInvoke` on the delegate that is being called synchronously. A callback method, `DelegateCallback`, is added, which gets called when the delegate is finished. This callback method then calls the `EndInvoke` method on the delegate invoked using `BeginInvoke`.

The notification callback method specified in the *callback* parameter accepts a single parameter of type IAsyncResult. This parameter can be cast to an AsyncResult type and used to set up the call to the EndInvoke method. If you want to handle any exceptions thrown by the asynchronous delegate in the notification callback, wrap the EndInvoke method in a try/catch exception handler.

See Also

See the "Delegate Class" and "Asynchronous Delegates" topics in the MSDN documentation.

7.5 Adding Events to a Sealed Class

Problem

Through the use of inheritance, adding events to a nonsealed class is fairly easy. For example, inheritance is used to add events to a Hashtable object. However, adding events to a sealed class, such as System.IO.DirectoryInfo, requires a technique other than inheritance.

Solution

To add events to a sealed class, such as the DirectoryInfo class, wrap it using another class, such as the DirectoryInfoNotify class defined in the next example.

 You can use the FileSystemWatcher class (see Recipes 11.23 and 11.24) to monitor the filesystem changes asynchronously due to activity outside of your program or you could use the DirectoryInfoNotify class defined here to monitor your program's activity when using the filesystem.

```
using System;
using System.IO;

public class DirectoryInfoNotify
{
    public DirectoryInfoNotify(string path)
    {
        internalDirInfo = new DirectoryInfo(path);
    }

    private DirectoryInfo internalDirInfo = null;
    public event EventHandler AfterCreate;
    public event EventHandler AfterCreateSubDir;
    public event EventHandler AfterDelete;
    public event EventHandler AfterMoveTo;

    protected virtual void OnAfterCreate()
    {
```

```csharp
        if (AfterCreate != null)
        {
            AfterCreate(this, new EventArgs());
        }
    }

    protected virtual void OnAfterCreateSubDir()
    {
        if (AfterCreateSubDir != null)
        {
            AfterCreateSubDir(this, new EventArgs());
        }
    }

    protected virtual void OnAfterDelete()
    {
        if (AfterDelete != null)
        {
            AfterDelete(this, new EventArgs());
        }
    }

    protected virtual void OnAfterMoveTo()
    {
        if (AfterMoveTo != null)
        {
            AfterMoveTo(this, new EventArgs());
        }
    }

    // Event firing members
    public void Create()
    {
        internalDirInfo.Create();
        OnAfterCreate();
    }

    public DirectoryInfoNotify CreateSubdirectory(string path)
    {
        DirectoryInfo subDirInfo = internalDirInfo.CreateSubdirectory(path);
        OnAfterCreateSubDir();

        return (new DirectoryInfoNotify(subDirInfo.FullName));
    }

    public void Delete(bool recursive)
    {
        internalDirInfo.Delete(recursive);
        OnAfterDelete();
    }

    public void Delete()
    {
        internalDirInfo.Delete();
        OnAfterDelete();
```

```
    }

    public void MoveTo(string destDirName)
    {
        internalDirInfo.MoveTo(destDirName);
        OnAfterMoveTo();
    }

    // Non-Event firing members
    public string FullName
    {
        get {return (internalDirInfo.FullName);}
    }
    public string Name
    {
        get {return (internalDirInfo.Name);}
    }
    public DirectoryInfoNotify Parent
    {
        get {return (new DirectoryInfoNotify(internalDirInfo.Parent.FullName));}
    }
    public DirectoryInfoNotify Root
    {
        get {return (new DirectoryInfoNotify(internalDirInfo.Root.FullName));}
    }

    public override string ToString()
    {
        return (internalDirInfo.ToString());
    }
}
```

The DirectoryInfoObserver class, shown in the following code, allows you to register any DirectoryInfoNotify objects with it. This registration process allows the DirectoryInfoObserver class to listen for any events to be raised in the registered DirectoryInfoNotify object(s). The only events that are raised by the DirectoryInfoNotify object are after a modification has been made to the directory structure using a DirectoryInfoNotify object that has been registered with a DirectoryInfoObserver object:

```
public class DirectoryInfoObserver
{
    public DirectoryInfoObserver() {}

    public void Register(DirectoryInfoNotify dirInfo)
    {
        dirInfo.AfterCreate += new EventHandler(AfterCreateListener);
        dirInfo.AfterCreateSubDir +=
                new EventHandler(AfterCreateSubDirListener);
        dirInfo.AfterMoveTo += new EventHandler(AfterMoveToListener);
        dirInfo.AfterDelete += new EventHandler(AfterDeleteListener);
    }
```

```
    public void UnRegister(DirectoryInfoNotify dirInfo)
    {
        dirInfo.AfterCreate -= new EventHandler(AfterCreateListener);
        dirInfo.AfterCreateSubDir -=
                new EventHandler(AfterCreateSubDirListener);
        dirInfo.AfterMoveTo -= new EventHandler(AfterMoveToListener);
        dirInfo.AfterDelete -= new EventHandler(AfterDeleteListener);
    }

    public void AfterCreateListener(object sender, EventArgs e)
    {
        Console.WriteLine("Notified after creation of directory--sender: " +
                    ((DirectoryInfoNotify)sender).FullName);
    }

    public void AfterCreateSubDirListener(object sender, EventArgs e)
    {
        Console.WriteLine("Notified after creation of SUB-directory--sender: " +
                    ((DirectoryInfoNotify)sender).FullName);
    }

    public void AfterMoveToListener(object sender, EventArgs e)
    {
        Console.WriteLine("Notified of directory move--sender: " +
                    ((DirectoryInfoNotify)sender).FullName);
    }

    public void AfterDeleteListener(object sender, EventArgs e)
    {
        Console.WriteLine("Notified of directory deletion--sender: " +
                    ((DirectoryInfoNotify)sender).FullName);
    }
}
```

Discussion

There are situations in which this technique might be useful even when a class is not
sealed. For example, if you want to raise notifications when methods that have not
been declared as virtual are called, you'll need this technique. So even if
DirectoryInfo were not sealed, you would still need this technique because you can't
override its Delete, Create, and other methods. And hiding them with the new keyword is unreliable because someone might use your object through a reference of
type DirectoryInfo instead of type DirectoryInfoNotify, in which case they'll end up
using the original methods and not your new methods. So the delegation approach
presented here is the only reliable technique when methods in the base class are non-
virtual, regardless of whether the base class is sealed.

The following code creates two DirectoryInfoObserver objects along with two
DirectoryInfoNotify objects, and then it proceeds to create a directory C:\testdir and
a subdirectory under C:\testdir called new:

```
public void TestDirectoryInfoObserver( )
{
    // Create two observer objects
    DirectoryInfoObserver observer1 = new DirectoryInfoObserver( );
    DirectoryInfoObserver observer2 = new DirectoryInfoObserver( );

    // Create a notification object for the directory c:\testdir
    DirectoryInfoNotify dirInfo = new DirectoryInfoNotify(@"c:\testdir");

    // Register the notification object under both observers
    observer1.Register(dirInfo);
    observer2.Register(dirInfo);

    // Create the directory c:\testdir
    dirInfo.Create( );

    // Change the first observer to watch the new subdirectory
    DirectoryInfoNotify subDirInfo = dirInfo.CreateSubdirectory("new");
    observer1.Register(subDirInfo);

    // Delete the subdirectory first and then the parent directory
    subDirInfo.Delete(true);
    dirInfo.Delete(false);

    // Unregister notification objects with their observers
    observer2.UnRegister(dirInfo);
    observer1.UnRegister(dirInfo);
}
```

This code outputs the following:

```
Notified after creation of directory--sender: c:\testdir
Notified after creation of directory--sender: c:\testdir
Notified after creation of SUB-directory--sender: c:\testdir
Notified after creation of SUB-directory--sender: c:\testdir
Notified of directory deletion--sender: c:\testdir\new
Notified of directory deletion--sender: c:\testdir
Notified of directory deletion--sender: c:\testdir
```

Rather than using inheritance to override members of a sealed class (i.e., the DirectoryInfo class), the sealed class is wrapped by a notification class (i.e., the DirectoryInfoNotify class).

The main drawback to wrapping a sealed class is that each method available in the underlying DirectoryInfo class might have to be implemented in the outer DirectoryInfoNotify class, which can be tedious if the underlying class has many visible members. The good news is that if you know you will not be using a subset of the wrapped class's members, you do not have to wrap each of those members. Simply do not make them visible from your outer class, which is what we have done in the DirectoryInfoNotify class. Only the methods we intend to use are implemented on the DirectoryInfoNotify class. If more methods on the DirectoryInfo class will later be used from the DirectoryInfoNotify class, they can be added with minimal effort.

For a `DirectoryInfoNotify` object to wrap a `DirectoryInfo` object, the `DirectoryInfoNotify` object must have an internal reference to the wrapped `DirectoryInfo` object. This reference is in the form of the `internalDirInfo` field. Essentially, this field allows all wrapped methods to forward their calls to the underlying `DirectoryInfo` object. For example, the `Delete` method of a `DirectoryInfoNotify` object forwards its call to the underlying `DirectoryInfo` object as follows:

```
public void Delete()
{
    // Forward the call
    internalDirInfo.Delete();

    // Raise an event
    OnAfterDelete();
}
```

You should make sure that the method signatures are the same on the outer class as they are on the wrapped class. This convention will make it much more intuitive and transparent for another developer to use.

There is one method, `CreateSubdirectory`, that requires further explanation:

```
public DirectoryInfoNotify CreateSubdirectory(string path)
{
    DirectoryInfo subDirInfo = internalDirInfo.CreateSubdirectory(path);
    OnAfterCreateSubDir();

    return (new DirectoryInfoNotify(subDirInfo.FullName));
}
```

This method is unique since it returns a `DirectoryInfo` object in the wrapped class. However, if we also returned a `DirectoryInfo` object from this outer method, we might confuse the developer attempting to use the `DirectoryInfoNotify` class. If a developer is using the `DirectoryInfoNotify` class, he or she will expect that class to also return objects of the same type from the appropriate members rather than returning the type of the wrapped class.

To fix this problem and make the `DirectoryInfoNotify` class more consistent, a `DirectoryInfoNotify` object is returned from the `CreateSubdirectory` method. The code that receives this `DirectoryInfoNotify` object might then register it with any available `DirectoryInfoObserver` object(s). This technique is shown here:

```
// Create a DirectoryInfoObserver object and a DirectoryInfoNotify object
DirectoryInfoObserver observer = new DirectoryInfoObserver();
DirectoryInfoNotify dirInfo = new DirectoryInfoNotify(@"c:\testdir");

// Register the DirectoryInfoNotify object with the DirectoryInfoObserver object
observer.Register(dirInfo);

// Create the c:\testdir directory and then create a sub directory within that
//    directory this will return a new DirectoryInfoNotify object, which is
//    registered with the same DirectoryInfoObserver object as the dirInfo object
```

```
dirInfo.Create( );
DirectoryInfoNotify subDirInfo = dirInfo.CreateSubdirectory("new");
observer.Register(subDirInfo);

// Delete this subdirectory
subDirInfo.Delete(true);

// Clean up
observer.UnRegister(dirInfo);
```

The observer object will be notified of the following events in this order:

1. When the `dirInfo.Create` method is called

2. When the `dirInfo.CreateSubdirectory` method is called

3. When the `subDirInfo.Delete` method is called

If the second `observer.Register` method were not called, the third event (`subDirInfo.Delete`) would not be caught by the observer object.

The `DirectoryInfoObserver` class contains methods that listen for events on any `DirectoryInfoNotify` objects that are registered with it. The *Xxx*`Listener` methods are called whenever their respective event is raised on a registered `DirectoryInfoNotify` object. Within these *Xxx*`Listener` methods, you can place any code that you wish to execute whenever a particular event is raised.

These *Xxx*`Listener` methods accept a *sender* object parameter, which is a reference to the `DirectoryInfoNotify` object that raised the event. This *sender* object can be cast to a `DirectoryInfoNotify` object and its members may be called if needed. This parameter allows you to gather information and take action based on the object that raised the event.

The second parameter to the *Xxx*`Listener` methods is of type `EventArgs`, which is a rather useless class for our purposes. Recipe 7.6 shows a way to use a class derived from the `EventArgs` class to pass information from the object that raised the event to the *Xxx*`Listener` method on the observer object and then back to the object that raised the event.

See Also

See Recipe 7.6; see the "Event" keyword and "Handling and Raising Events" topic in the MSDN documentation.

7.6   Passing Specialized Parameters to and from an Event

Problem

You have implemented Recipe 7.5, but you want to allow an event listener to be able to cancel an action that raised a particular event. For example, if a class attempts to create a new directory, you want to be able to verify that the directory is being created in the correct location. If the directory is not being created in the correct location (perhaps an insecure location), you want to be able to prevent the directory's creation.

Solution

Use a class derived from `EventArgs` as the second parameter to the event handler. In this example, we use `CancelEventArgs`, a class defined in the .NET Framework Class Library. The Solution for Recipe 7.5 has been modified to include an event that is raised before the `Create` method of the `DirectoryInfoNotify` object actually creates a new path. An object of type `CancelEventArgs` is passed to this new event to allow any listeners of this event to cancel the `Create` method action. The modified class is shown here with the modifications highlighted:

```
using System;
using System.ComponentModel;
using System.IO;

public class DirectoryInfoNotify
{
    public DirectoryInfoNotify(string path)
    {
        internalDirInfo = new DirectoryInfo(path);
    }

    private DirectoryInfo internalDirInfo = null;
    public event CancelEventHandler BeforeCreate;
    public event EventHandler AfterCreate;
    public event EventHandler AfterCreateSubDir;
    public event EventHandler AfterDelete;
    public event EventHandler AfterMoveTo;

    protected virtual void OnBeforeCreate(CancelEventArgs e)
    {
        if (BeforeCreate != null)
        {
            BeforeCreate(this, e);
        }
    }

    protected virtual void OnAfterCreate()
    {
        if (AfterCreate != null)
        {
            AfterCreate(this, new EventArgs());
        }
    }

    protected virtual void OnAfterCreateSubDir()
    {
        if (AfterCreateSubDir != null)
        {
```

```
            AfterCreateSubDir(this, new EventArgs());
        }
    }

    protected virtual void OnAfterDelete()
    {
        if (AfterDelete != null)
        {
            AfterDelete(this, new EventArgs());
        }
    }

    protected virtual void OnAfterMoveTo()
    {
        if (AfterMoveTo != null)
        {
            AfterMoveTo(this, new EventArgs());
        }
    }

    // Event firing members
    public void Create()
    {
        CancelEventArgs args = new CancelEventArgs(false);
        OnBeforeCreate(args);

        if (!args.Cancel)
        {
            internalDirInfo.Create();
            OnAfterCreate();
        }
    }

    public DirectoryInfoNotify CreateSubdirectory(string path)
    {
        DirectoryInfo subDirInfo = internalDirInfo.CreateSubdirectory(path);
        OnAfterCreateSubDir();

        return (new DirectoryInfoNotify(subDirInfo.FullName));
    }

    public void Delete(bool recursive)
    {
        internalDirInfo.Delete(recursive);
        OnAfterDelete();
    }

    public void Delete()
    {
        internalDirInfo.Delete();
        OnAfterDelete();
    }

    public void MoveTo(string destDirName)
    {
```

```
        internalDirInfo.MoveTo(destDirName);
        OnAfterMoveTo();
    }

    // Non-Event firing members
    public virtual string FullName
    {
        get {return (internalDirInfo.FullName);}
    }
    public string Name
    {
        get {return (internalDirInfo.Name);}
    }
    public DirectoryInfoNotify Parent
    {
        get {return (new DirectoryInfoNotify(internalDirInfo.Parent.FullName));}
    }
    public DirectoryInfoNotify Root
    {
        get {return (new DirectoryInfoNotify(internalDirInfo.Root.FullName));}
    }

    public override string ToString()
    {
        return (internalDirInfo.ToString());
    }
}
```

The DirectoryInfoObserver class contains each of the event listeners and is shown here with the modifications highlighted:

```
public class DirectoryInfoObserver
{
    public DirectoryInfoObserver() {}

    public void Register(DirectoryInfoNotify dirInfo)
    {
        dirInfo.BeforeCreate += new CancelEventHandler(BeforeCreateListener);
        dirInfo.AfterCreate += new EventHandler(AfterCreateListener);
        dirInfo.AfterCreateSubDir +=
                new EventHandler(AfterCreateSubDirListener);
        dirInfo.AfterMoveTo += new EventHandler(AfterMoveToListener);
        dirInfo.AfterDelete += new EventHandler(AfterDeleteListener);
    }

    public void UnRegister(DirectoryInfoNotify dirInfo)
    {
        dirInfo.BeforeCreate -= new CancelEventHandler(BeforeCreateListener);
        dirInfo.AfterCreate -= new EventHandler(AfterCreateListener);
        dirInfo.AfterCreateSubDir -=
                new EventHandler(AfterCreateSubDirListener);
        dirInfo.AfterMoveTo -= new EventHandler(AfterMoveToListener);
        dirInfo.AfterDelete -= new EventHandler(AfterDeleteListener);
    }
```

```
    public void BeforeCreateListener(object sender, CancelEventArgs e)
    {
        if (!e.Cancel)
        {
            if (!((DirectoryInfoNotify)sender).Root.FullName.Equals(@"d:\"))
            {
                e.Cancel = true;
            }
            else
            {
                Console.WriteLine(
                        "Notified BEFORE creation of directory--sender: " +
                        ((DirectoryInfoNotify)sender).FullName);
            }
        }
    }

    public void AfterCreateListener(object sender, EventArgs e)
    {
        Console.WriteLine("Notified after creation of directory--sender: " +
                    ((DirectoryInfoNotify)sender).FullName);
    }

    public void AfterCreateSubDirListener(object sender, EventArgs e)
    {
        Console.WriteLine("Notified after creation of SUB-directory--sender: " +
                    ((DirectoryInfoNotify)sender).FullName);
    }

    public void AfterMoveToListener(object sender, EventArgs e)
    {
        Console.WriteLine("Notified of directory move--sender: " +
                    ((DirectoryInfoNotify)sender).FullName);
    }

    public void AfterDeleteListener(object sender, EventArgs e)
    {
        Console.WriteLine("Notified of directory deletion--sender: " +
                    ((DirectoryInfoNotify)sender).FullName);
    }
}
```

Discussion

The code for the modified DirectoryInfoNotify class contains a new event called
BeforeCreate, which is raised from the OnBeforeCreate method. The OnBeforeCreate
method is initially called by the Create method immediately before calling the Create
method of the wrapped DirectoryInfo object. This setup will allow the event listener
for the BeforeCreate event to decide whether the directory creation operation should
be cancelled.

The DirectoryInfoObserver class contains a new method, BeforeCreateListener,
which listens for the BeforeCreate event. In addition, the Register and UnRegister

methods of this class contain logic to add this event to the list of events that will be listened for on any registered DirectoryInfoNotify objects.

The OnBeforeCreate method of the DirectoryinfoNotify class is passed a parameter of a type called CancelEventArgs, which exists in the .NET FCL. This type derives from EventArgs and contains one useful property, called Cancel. This property will be used by the AfterCreateListener method of the DirectoryInfoObserver class to determine whether the Create method should be cancelled before it has a chance to create a new directory.

The CancelEventArgs object will be created in a DirectoryInfoNotify object, and when the BeforeCreate event is raised, the CancelEventArgs object will be passed to the BeforeCreateListener method on the DirectoryInfoObserver object. This method will then determine whether the creation of the directory should proceed or be cancelled. The determination is made by comparing the root drive of the directory to see if it is anything but the *D:* drive; if so, the operation is cancelled. This prevents any registered DirectoryInfoNotify objects from creating a directory on any drive other than the *D:* drive.

If multiple DirectoryInfoObserver objects are listening to the BeforeCreate event and one of those observer objects decides to cancel the operation, the entire operation is cancelled. In other words, the final handler to be called gets the power of veto.

The same CancelEventArgs object is referenced by each observer as well as each object that raised the event. This allows us to read the value of the Cancel property on the returned CancelEventArgs object in the Create method of the DirectoryInfoNotify object. If this property returns true, the operation cannot proceed; otherwise, the operation is permitted.

You are not confined to merely passing EventArgs objects or any of its subclasses found in the FCL; you can subclass the EventArgs class to create a specialized EventArgs type. This would be beneficial if the object passed in to the *sender* parameter of the event does not include all of the information that the *Xxx*Listener methods will need. For example, you could create the following specialized EventArgs class:

```
public class UserEventArgs : EventArgs
{
    public UserEventArgs(string userName)
    {
        this.userName = userName;
    }

    private string userName = "";

    public string UserName
    {
        get {return (userName);}
    }
}
```

This class passes the name of the logged-on user to the *Xxx*Listener methods to allow them to determine whether the operation should continue based on that user's privileges. This is just one example of creating a specialized EventArgs class. You can create others to pass in whatever information your listeners need.

See Also

See Recipe 7.5; see the "Event" keyword, "EventHandler Delegate," and "Handling and Raising Events" topics in the MSDN documentation.

7.7   An Advanced Interface Search Mechanism

Problem

You are searching for an interface using the Type class. However, complex interface searches are not available through the GetInterface and GetInterfaces methods of a Type object. The GetInterface method searches for an interface only by name (using a case-sensitive or -insensitive search), and the GetInterfaces method returns an array of all the interfaces implemented on a particular type. You want a more focused searching mechanism that might involve searching for interfaces that define a method with a specific signature or implemented interfaces that are loaded from the Global Assembly Cache (GAC). You need more flexible and more advanced searching for interfaces that does not involve creating your own interface search engine.

Solution

The FindInterfaces method of a Type object can be used along with a callback to perform complex searches of interfaces on a type. The following method will call a custom interface searching method, SearchInterfacesOfType:

```
using System;
using System.Reflection;

public class SearchType
{
    public void FindSpecificInterfaces()
    {
        Type[] names = new Type[3] {Type.GetType("System.ICloneable"),
                        Type.GetType("System.Collections.ICollection"),
                        Type.GetType("System.IAppDomainSetup")};
        Type[] interfaces = SearchInterfacesOfType(Type.GetType(
                        "System.Collections.ArrayList"), names);

        if (interfaces.Length > 0)
        {
            Console.WriteLine("Matches found:");
            for(int counter =0; counter < interfaces.Length; counter++)
            {
```

```
                Console.WriteLine("\tIFace Name: " +
                            interfaces[counter].ToString());
                Console.WriteLine("\tIFace Base Type: " +
                            interfaces[counter].BaseType);
                foreach (object attr in
                        interfaces[counter].GetCustomAttributes(false))
                {
                    Console.WriteLine("\t\tIFace attr: " + attr.ToString());
                }
            }
        }
        else
        {
            Console.WriteLine("\t\tNo matches found");
        }
    }

    public Type[] SearchInterfacesOfType(Type searchedType,
      Type[] ifaceNames)
    {
        TypeFilter filter = new TypeFilter(IfaceFilterCallback);
        Type[] interfaces =
            searchedType.FindInterfaces(filter, ifaceNames);

        return (interfaces);
    }

    public bool IfaceFilterCallback(Type type, object criteria)
    {
        foreach (Type ifaceName in (Type[])criteria)
        {
            if(type.FullName == ifaceName.FullName)
            {
                return (true);
            }
        }

        return (false);
    }
}
```

The FindSpecificInterfaces method searches for any of the three interface types, contained in the Names array that are implemented by the System.Collections. ArrayList type.

The SearchInterfacesOfType method accepts a type (*searchedType*) on which to search for interfaces and an object (*ifaceNames*) that contains criteria for the search. For this method, the criterion is a Type array of interfaces. This method then calls the FindInterfaces method on the *searchedType* parameter and passes in a delegate and the Type array criteria of interfaces. (The delegate will be called back to for each found interface.) This method then returns an array of interface types that match the criterion.

The TypeFilter delegate, filter, defines the IfaceFilterCallback method to be called for each interface found on the *searchedType* object. The real power of this search mechanism lies in the IfaceFilterCallback callback method.

This callback searches for each of the interface types in the *criteria* array that is implemented by the *searchedType* parameter of the SearchInterfacesOfType method.

Discussion

Most complex member searches can be performed only through the use of the FindInterfaces method of a Type object. This method makes use of the TypeFilter delegate, which is passed to the *filter* parameter. This delegate is supplied by the FCL and allows an extra layer of filtering (of any type that you want) to occur. This delegate returns a Boolean value, where true indicates that the *ifaceType* object passed to this delegate should be included in the Type array that the FindInterfaces method returns; false indicates that this *ifaceType* object should not be included.

 The FindInterfaces method will take into account all interfaces implemented by the type being searched as well as all of its base types when performing a search. In addition, if any of the interfaces implemented by any of these types also implements one or more interfaces, those interfaces are included in the search.

There are many ways to use this TypeFilter delegate to search for interfaces implemented on a type—here are just a few other searches that can be performed:

- A filter to search for all implemented interfaces that are defined within a particular namespace (in this case, the System.Collections namespace):

```
public bool IfaceFilterCallback(Type type, object criteria)
{
    if (type.Namespace.Equals("System.Collections"))
    {
        return (true);
    }
    else
    {
        return (false);
    }
}
```

- A filter to search for all implemented interfaces that contain a method called Add, which returns an Int32 value:

```
public bool IfaceFilterCallback(Type type, object criteria)
{
    if (type.GetMethod("Add") != null &&
        type.GetMethod("Add").ReturnType == Type.GetType("System.Int32"))
    {
        return (true);
    }
```

```
    else
    {
        return (false);
    }
}
```

- A filter to search for all implemented interfaces that are loaded from the Global Assembly Cache (GAC):

```
public bool IfaceFilterCallback(Type type, object criteria)
{
    if (type.Assembly.GlobalAssemblyCache)
    {
        return (true);
    }
    else
    {
        return (false);
    }
}
```

- A filter to search for all implemented interfaces that are defined within an assembly with the version number 1.0.3300.0:

```
public bool IfaceFilterCallback(Type type, object criteria)
{
    if (type.Assembly.FullName.IndexOf("Version=1.0.3300.0") >= 0)
    {
        return (true);
    }
    else
    {
        return (false);
    }
}
```

See Also

See Recipe 7.8; see the "Delegate Class" and "Type.FindInterfaces Method" topics in the MSDN documentation.

7.8 An Advanced Member Search Mechanism

Problem

You are searching for a member within a type using the Type class. However, complex member searches are not available through the GetMember and GetMembers methods of a Type object. The GetMember method searches for a member name only within a type limited by the set of BindingFlags used, and the GetMembers method searches for all members limited by the set of BindingFlags used. BindingFlags is an enumeration of various member types that can be searched. The BindingFlags related to this recipe are defined here:

DeclaredOnly
> Include inherited members in the search.

Default
> No binding flags are used.

FlattenHierarchy
> Include all static members in the inheritance hierarchy in the search (do not include static members of nested types in the search).

IgnoreCase
> Perform a case-insensitive search.

Instance
> Include instance members in the search.

NonPublic
> Include nonpublic members in the search.

Public
> Include public members in the search.

Static
> Include static members in the search.

You need to create more flexible and advanced searches for members that do not involve creating your own member search engine.

Solution

The FindMembers method of a Type object can be used, along with a callback, to create your own complex searches. The following method will call our custom member searching method, SearchMembers:

```
using System;
using System.Reflection;

public class SearchType
{
    public void TestSearchMembers( )
    {
        MemberInfo[] members = SearchMembers(this.GetType( ),
                                     Type.GetType("System.Int32"));

        if (members.Length > 0)
        {
            Console.WriteLine("Matches found:");

            // Display information for each match
            for(int counter = 0; counter < members.Length; counter++)
            {
                Console.WriteLine("\tMember Name: " +
                                members[counter].ToString( ));
                Console.WriteLine("\tMember Type: " +
```

```
                            members[counter].MemberType);
            foreach (object attr in
                    members[counter].GetCustomAttributes(false))
            {
                Console.WriteLine("\t\tMember attr: " +
                    attr.ToString());
            }
        }
    }
    else
    {
        Console.WriteLine("\t\tNo matches found");
    }
}

public MemberInfo[] SearchMembers(Type searchedType, Type returnType)
{
    // Delegate that compares the member's return type
    //     against the returnType parameter
    MemberFilter filterCallback = new MemberFilter(ReturnTypeFilter);

    MemberInfo[] members = searchedType.FindMembers(MemberTypes.All,
                BindingFlags.Instance | BindingFlags.Public |
                BindingFlags.NonPublic | BindingFlags.Static,
                filterCallback,
                returnType);

    return (members);
}

private bool ReturnTypeFilter(MemberInfo member, object criteria)
{
    // Obtain the return type of either a method or property
    string returnType = "";
    if (member is MethodInfo)
    {
        returnType = ((MethodInfo)member).ReturnType.FullName;
    }
    else if (member is PropertyInfo)
    {
        returnType = ((PropertyInfo)member).PropertyType.FullName;
    }
    else
    {
        return (false);
    }

    // Match return type
    if (returnType == ((Type)criteria).FullName)
    {
        return (true);
    }
    else
    {
```

```
        return (false);
      }
    }
  }
```

This method will search for any member in the current type that has a return value of System.Int32.

The SearchMembers method accepts a Type object in which to search and a string representation of the full name of a return type. This method simply calls the FindMembers method of the *searchType* object passed to it. Notice that the *returnType* parameter is passed to the FindMembers method as the last parameter.

The MemberFilter delegate, filterCallback, defines the ReturnTypeFilter method to be called for each member that meets the specified criteria of the FindMembers method (i.e, MemberTypes.All, BindingFlags.Instance, BindingFlags.Public, BindingFlags.NonPublic, and BindingFlags.Static). The real power of this search mechanism lies in the ReturnTypeFilter callback method.

This callback method casts the member parameter to the correct member type (i.e., MethodInfo or PropertyInfo), obtains the return type, and compares that return type to the one passed in to the *returnType* parameter of the SearchMembers method. A return value of true indicates that the return types matched; a false indicates they did not match.

Discussion

Most complex member searches can be performed only through the use of the FindMembers method of a Type object. This method returns an array of MemberInfo objects that contain all members that match the *memberType*, *bindingAttr*, and *filterCriteria* parameters.

This method makes use of the MemberFilter delegate, which is passed in to the *filter* parameter. This delegate is supplied by the FCL and allows an extra layer of member filtering to occur. This filtering can be anything you want. This delegate returns a Boolean value, where true indicates that the *member* object passed in to this delegate should be included in the MemberInfo array that the FindMembers method returns, and false indicates that this *member* object should not be included.

There are many ways to use this MemberFilter delegate to search for members within a type. Here are just a few other items that can be searched for:

- A filter callback to search for only fields marked as const:

```
private bool ReturnTypeFilter(MemberInfo member, object criteria)
{
    if (member is FieldInfo)
    {
        if (((FieldInfo)member).IsLiteral)
        {
            return (true);
```

```
        }
        else
        {
            return (false);
        }
    }

    return (false);
}
```

- A filter callback to search for only fields marked as readonly:

```
private bool ReturnTypeFilter(MemberInfo member, object criteria)
{
    if (member is FieldInfo)
    {
        if (((FieldInfo)member).IsInitOnly)
        {
            return (true);
        }
        else
        {
            return (false);
        }
    }

    return (false);
}
```

- A filter to search for a read-only property (note that in VB.NET, this filter finds methods marked with the readonly modifier, and in C#, this filter finds methods that only have a get accessor):

```
private bool ReturnTypeFilter(MemberInfo member, object criteria)
{
    if (member is PropertyInfo)
    {
        if (((PropertyInfo)member).CanRead && !((PropertyInfo)member).CanWrite)
        {
            return (true);
        }
        else
        {
            return (false);
        }
    }

    return (false);
}
```

- A filter to search for any methods that contain out parameters:

```
private bool ReturnTypeFilter(MemberInfo member, object criteria)
{
    if (member is MethodInfo)
    {
        ParameterInfo[] params = ((MethodInfo)member).GetParameters();
        foreach (ParameterInfo param in params)
```

```
        {
            if (param.IsOut)
            {
                return (true);
                break;
            }
        }

        return (false);
    }

    return (false);
}
```

- A filter to search for any members that are marked with the System. ObsoleteAttribute attribute:

```
private bool ReturnTypeFilter(MemberInfo member, object criteria)
{
    object[] attrs = member.GetCustomAttributes(false);
    foreach (object attr in attrs)
    {
        if (attr.ToString().Equals("System.ObsoleteAttribute"))
        {
            return (true);
        }
    }

    return (false);
}
```

Creating a filter that searches for delegates or some ingredient of a delegate must be done in a roundabout way, as there is no DelegateInfo object, and the MemberTypes enumeration does not contain a value for delegates. A delegate type shows up as a nested type in the reflection API; this nested type's base class can then be checked to see whether it is a System.MulticastDelegate or a System.Delegate type (note that we can test the base class because both the MulticastDelegate and Delegate types are sealed). This is the code to determine whether a nested type is a delegate:

```
private bool ReturnTypeFilter(MemberInfo member, Object criteria)
{
    if (member.MemberType == MemberTypes.NestedType)
    {
        if (((Type)member).BaseType.ToString().Equals(
                "System.MulticastDelegate") ||
            ((Type)member).BaseType.ToString().Equals("System.Delegate"))
        {
            return (true);
        }

        return (false);
    }

    return (false);
}
```

See Also

See Recipe 7.7; see the "Delegate Class" and "Type.FindMembers Method" topics in the MSDN documentation.

7.9 Observing Additions and Modifications to a Hashtable

Problem

You have multiple objects that need to observe modifications to a Hashtable. When an item is added, deleted, or modified in the Hashtable, each of these observer objects should be able to vote to allow or disallow the action. In order for an action to be allowed to complete, all observer objects must vote to allow the action. If even one observer object votes to disallow the action, the action is prevented.

Solution

Use the HashtableObserver class to observe additions and modifications to a HashtableSubject object that is registered with this object. The HashtableSubject class is an extension of the regular Hashtable class and allows itself to be observed by the HashtableObserver class. Its source code is:

```
public class HashtableSubject : Hashtable
{
    public event HashtableEventHandler BeforeAddItem;
    public event HashtableEventHandler AfterAddItem;
    public event HashtableEventHandler BeforeChangeItem;
    public event HashtableEventHandler AfterChangeItem;

    protected virtual bool OnBeforeAdd(HashtableEventArgs e)
    {
        if (BeforeAddItem != null)
        {
            BeforeAddItem(this, e);
            return (e.KeepChanges);
        }

        return (true);
    }

    protected virtual void OnAfterAdd(HashtableEventArgs e)
    {
        if (AfterAddItem != null)
        {
            AfterAddItem(this, e);
        }
    }
```

```csharp
protected virtual bool OnBeforeChange(HashtableEventArgs e)
{
    if (BeforeChangeItem != null)
    {
        BeforeChangeItem(this, e);
        return (e.KeepChanges);
    }

    return (true);
}

protected virtual void OnAfterChange(HashtableEventArgs e)
{
    if (AfterChangeItem != null)
    {
        AfterChangeItem(this, e);
    }
}

public override void Add(object key, object value)
{
    HashtableEventArgs hashArgs = new HashtableEventArgs(key, value);
    OnBeforeAdd(hashArgs);

    if (hashArgs.KeepChanges)
    {
        base.Add(key, value);
    }
    else
    {
        Console.WriteLine("Addition of key/value cannot be performed");
    }

    OnAfterAdd(hashArgs);
}

public override object this[object key]
{
    get
    {
        return (base[key]);
    }
    set
    {
        HashtableEventArgs hashArgs = new HashtableEventArgs(key, value);
        OnBeforeChange(hashArgs);

        if (hashArgs.KeepChanges)
        {
            base[key] = value;
        }
        else
        {
            Console.WriteLine("Change of value cannot be performed");
```

```
        }

            OnAfterChange(hashArgs);
        }
    }
}
```

The `HashtableEventHandler` is defined as follows:

```
[Serializable]
public delegate void HashtableEventHandler(object sender, HashtableEventArgs e);
```

The code for the `HashtableObserver` class is:

```
using System;
using System.Collections;

// The observer object that will observe a registered HashtableSubject object
public class HashtableObserver
{
    public HashtableObserver() {}

    public void Register(HashtableSubject hashtable)
    {
        hashtable.BeforeAddItem += new HashtableEventHandler(BeforeAddListener);
        hashtable.AfterAddItem += new HashtableEventHandler(AfterAddListener);
        hashtable.BeforeChangeItem +=
            new HashtableEventHandler(BeforeChangeListener);
        hashtable.AfterChangeItem +=
            new HashtableEventHandler(AfterChangeListener);
    }

    public void UnRegister(HashtableSubject hashtable)
    {
        hashtable.BeforeAddItem -= new HashtableEventHandler(BeforeAddListener);
        hashtable.AfterAddItem -= new HashtableEventHandler(AfterAddListener);
        hashtable.BeforeChangeItem -=
            new HashtableEventHandler(BeforeChangeListener);
        hashtable.AfterChangeItem -=
            new HashtableEventHandler(AfterChangeListener);
    }

    public void BeforeAddListener(object sender, HashtableEventArgs e)
    {
        if (((string)e.Value).Length > 3)
        {
            e.KeepChanges = false;
        }
        else
        {
            e.KeepChanges = true;
        }

        Console.WriteLine("[NOTIFY] Before Add...");
    }
```

```
    public void AfterAddListener(object sender, HashtableEventArgs e)
    {
        Console.WriteLine("[NOTIFY] ...After Add\r\n");
    }

    public void BeforeChangeListener(object sender, HashtableEventArgs e)
    {
        if (((string)e.Value).Length > 3)
        {
            e.KeepChanges = false;
        }
        else
        {
            e.KeepChanges = true;
        }

        Console.WriteLine("[NOTIFY] Before Change...");
    }

    public void AfterChangeListener(object sender, HashtableEventArgs e)
    {
        Console.WriteLine("[NOTIFY] ...After Change\r\n");
    }
}
```

The HashtableEventArgs class is a specialization of the EventArgs class, which provides the Hashtable key and value being added or modified to the HashtableObserver object, as well as a Boolean flag, KeepChanges, that's passed by reference. This flag indicates whether the addition or modification in the HashtableSubject object will succeed or be rolled back. The source code for the HashtableEventArgs class is:

```
// Event arguments for HashtableSubject
public class HashtableEventArgs : EventArgs
{
    public HashtableEventArgs(object key, object value)
    {
        this.key = key;
        this.value = value;
    }

    private object key = null;
    private object value = null;
    private bool keepChanges = true;

    public bool KeepChanges
    {
        get {return (keepChanges);}
        set {keepChanges = value;}
    }

    public object Key
    {
        get {return (key);}
    }
```

```
        public object Value
        {
            get {return (value);}
        }
    }
```

Discussion

The *observer design pattern* allows one or more observer objects to act as spectators over one or more subject objects. Not only do the observer objects act as spectators, but they can also induce change in the subject objects. According to this pattern, any subject object is allowed to register itself with one or more observer objects. Once this is done, the subject can operate as it normally does. The key feature is that the subject doesn't have to know what it is being observed by—this allows the coupling between subjects and observers to be minimized. The observer object(s) will then be notified of any changes in state to the subject objects. When the subject object's state changes, the observer object(s) can change the state of other objects in the system to bring them into line with changes that were made to the subject object(s). In addition, the observer could even make changes or refuse changes to the subject object(s) themselves.

The observer pattern is best implemented with events in C#. The event object provides a built-in way of implementing the observer design pattern. This recipe implements this pattern on a Hashtable. The Hashtable object must raise events for any listening observer objects to handle. But the Hashtable class found in the FCL does not raise any events. In order to make a Hashtable raise events at specific times, we must derive a new class, HashtableSubject, from the Hashtable class. This HashtableSubject class overrides the Add and indexer members of the base Hashtable. In addition, four events (BeforeAddItem, AfterAddItem, BeforeChangeItem, and AfterChangeItem) are created that will be raised before and after items are added or modified in the HashtableSubject object. To raise these events, the following four methods are created, one to raise each event:

- The OnBeforeAdd method raises the BeforeAddItem event.
- The OnAfterAdd method raises the AfterAddItem event.
- The OnBeforeChange method raises the BeforeChangeItem event.
- The OnAfterChange method raises the AfterChangeItem event.

The Add method calls the OnBeforeAdd method, which then raises the event to any listening observer objects. The OnBeforeAdd method is called before the base.Add method—which adds the key/value pair to the Hashtable—is called. After the key/value pair has been added, the OnAfterAdd method is called. This operation is similar to the indexer set method.

The On*xxx* methods that raise the events in the HashtableSubject class are marked as protected virtual to allow classes to subclass this class and implement their own method of dealing with the events. Note that this statement is not applicable to sealed classes. In those cases, you can simply make the methods public.

The HashtableEventArgs class contains three private fields defined as follows:

key
> The key that is to be added to the Hashtable.

value
> The value that is to be added to the Hashtable.

keepChanges
> A flag indicating whether the key/value pair should be added to the Hashtable. true indicates that this pair should be added to the Hashtable.

The keepChanges field is used by the observer to determine whether an add or change operation should proceed. This flag is discussed further when we look at the HashtableObserver observer object.

The HashtableObserver is the observer object that watches any HashtableSubject objects it is told about. Any HashtableSubject object can call the HashtableObserver.Register method in order to tell the HashtableObserver object that it wants to be observed. This method accepts a pointer to a HashtableSubject object (hashtable) as its only parameter. This method then hooks up the event handlers in the HashtableObserver object to the events that can be raised by the HashtableSubject object passed in through the hashtable parameter. Therefore, the following events and event handlers are bound together:

- The HashtableSubject.BeforeAddItem event is bound to the HashtableObserver.BeforeAddListener event handler.

- The HashtableSubject.AfterAddItem event is bound to the HashtableObserver.AfterAddListener event handler.

- The HashtableSubject.BeforeChangeItem event is bound to the HashtableObserver.BeforeChangeListener event handler.

- The HashtableSubject.AfterChangeItem event is bound to the HashtableObserver.AfterChangeListener event handler.

The BeforeAddListener and BeforeChangeListener methods watch for additions and changes to the key/value pairs of the watched HashtableSubject object(s). Since we have an event firing before and after an addition or modification occurs, we can determine whether the addition or change should occur. This is where the keepChanges field of the HashtableEventArgs object comes into play. The HashtableObserver object will set this flag according to whether it determines that the action should proceed or be prematurely terminated. The HashtableEventArgs object is passed back to the OnBeforeAdd and OnBeforeChange methods. These methods then return the value of the KeepChanges property to either the calling Add method or indexer. The Add method or indexer then uses this flag to determine whether the base Hashtable object should be updated.

The following code shows how to instantiate subjects and observers, and to register, use, and unregister them:

```
// Create three subject objects
ObserverPattern.HashtableSubject H1 =
    new ObserverPattern.HashtableSubject();
ObserverPattern.HashtableSubject H2 =
    new ObserverPattern.HashtableSubject();
ObserverPattern.HashtableSubject H3 =
    new ObserverPattern.HashtableSubject();

// Create an observer for the three subject objects
ObserverPattern.HashtableObserver observer =
    new ObserverPattern.HashtableObserver();

// Register the three subjects with the observer
observer.Register(H1);
observer.Register(H2);
observer.Register(H3);

// Use the subjects
H1.Add(1,"one");
H2.Add(2,"two");
H3.Add(3,"three");

// Unregister the subjects
observer.UnRegister(H3);
observer.UnRegister(H2);
observer.UnRegister(H1);
```

Note that if the subject objects are used without registering them, no events will be raised. Since no events are raised, the observer cannot do its job, and values may be added to the unregistered subjects that are out of bounds for the application.

Many other scenarios exist in which the observer design pattern can be used. For example, if you wanted another Hashtable object to be updated to reflect the additions or modifications of a HashtableSubject object, you could modify the HashtableObserver object as shown in the highlighted text here:

```
public void Register(Hashtable hashtable)
{
    MirrorTable = hashtable;
}

Hashtable MirrorTable = null;

public void BeforeAddListener(object sender, EventArgs e)
{
```

```
        HashtableEventArgs hashE = (HashtableEventArgs)e;

        if (((string)hashE.Value).Length > 3)
        {
            hashE.KeepChanges = false;
        }
        else
        {
            hashE.KeepChanges = true;
            if (MirrorTable != null)
            {
                MirrorTable.Add(hashE.Key, hashE.Value);
            }
        }

        Console.WriteLine("[NOTIFY] Before Add...");
    }

    public void BeforeChangeListener(object sender, EventArgs e)
    {
        HashtableEventArgs hashE = (HashtableEventArgs)e;

        if (((string)hashE.Value).Length > 3)
        {
            hashE.KeepChanges = false;
        }
        else
        {
            hashE.KeepChanges = true;
            if (MirrorTable != null)
            {
                MirrorTable[hashE.Key] = hashE.Value;
            }
        }

        Console.WriteLine("[NOTIFY] Before Change...");
    }
```

A new field, MirrorTable, has been added; it points to a Hashtable mirroring the observed HashtableSubject object. The MirrorTable object is set through the constructor of this class. The MirrorTable object is updated whenever the observed object is successfully modified. With these modifications to the HashtableObserver object, you should observe only one HashtableSubject object at any one time. If you are observing more than one subject object, you run the risk of attempting to add duplicate keys to the MirrorTable object.

When using the observer design pattern, you should keep in mind that fine-grained events, such as the ones in this recipe, should be watched carefully so that they do not drag down performance. If you have many subjects raising many events, your application could fail to meet performance expectations. If this occurs, you need to either minimize the number of actions that cause events to be raised or remove some events.

See Also

See the "Event" keyword, "EventHandler Delegate," "EventArgs Class," and "Handling and Raising Events" topics in the MSDN documentation.

7.10 Using the Windows Keyboard Hook

Problem

You need to watch and respond to specific user keyboard input, and, based on the input, you want to perform one or more actions. For example, pressing the Windows key and the E key at the same time launches Windows Explorer. You would like to add other Windows key combinations for your own applications. In addition, you could prevent the user from using specific keys (such as the Windows key) from within your application.

Solution

The following Windows Forms application uses the WH_KEYBOARD Windows hook:

```
using System;
using System.Windows.Forms;
using System.Runtime.InteropServices;

namespace WindowsApplication2
{
    public class Form1 : System.Windows.Forms.Form
    {
        // Required designer variable.
        private System.ComponentModel.Container components = null;

        private System.Windows.Forms.Button button1;
        private System.Windows.Forms.Button button2;
        private System.Windows.Forms.TextBox textBox1;

        public Form1( )
        {
            // Required for Windows Form Designer support
            InitializeComponent( );
        }

        protected override void Dispose( bool disposing )
        {
            if( disposing )
            {
                if (components != null)
                {
                    components.Dispose( );
                }
            }
```

```csharp
        base.Dispose( disposing );
}

#region Windows Form Designer generated code
/// <summary>
/// Required method for Designer support - do not modify
/// the contents of this method with the code editor.
/// </summary>
private void InitializeComponent()
{
    this.button1 = new System.Windows.Forms.Button( );
    this.button2 = new System.Windows.Forms.Button( );
    this.textBox1 = new System.Windows.Forms.TextBox( );
    this.SuspendLayout( );
    //
    // button1
    //
    this.button1.Name = "button1";
    this.button1.TabIndex = 0;
    this.button1.Text = "Start";
    this.button1.Click +=
      new System.EventHandler(this.button1_Click);
    //
    // button2
    //
    this.button2.Location = new System.Drawing.Point(0, 48);
    this.button2.Name = "button2";
    this.button2.TabIndex = 1;
    this.button2.Text = "End";
    this.button2.Click +=
      new System.EventHandler(this.button2_Click);
    //
    // textBox1
    //
    this.textBox1.Location = new System.Drawing.Point(80, 0);
    this.textBox1.Multiline = true;
    this.textBox1.Name = "textBox1";
    this.textBox1.ScrollBars =
      System.Windows.Forms.ScrollBars.Vertical;
    this.textBox1.Size = new System.Drawing.Size(752, 504);
    this.textBox1.TabIndex = 2;
    this.textBox1.Text = "";
    this.textBox1.WordWrap = false;
    //
    // Form1
    //
    this.AutoScaleBaseSize = new System.Drawing.Size(5, 13);
    this.ClientSize = new System.Drawing.Size(832, 509);
    this.Controls.AddRange(new System.Windows.Forms.Control[] {
                            this.textBox1,
                            this.button2,
                            this.button1});
    this.Name = "Form1";
    this.Text = "Form1";
    this.ResumeLayout(false);
```

```
    }
    #endregion

    [STAThread]
    static void Main( )
    {
        Application.Run(new Form1( ));
    }

    // Declare Windows API calls used to access Windows hooks
    [DllImport("user32.dll")]
    public static extern int SetWindowsHookEx(int hookType,
                                            HookProc callback,
                                            int instance,
                                            int threadID);
    [DllImport("user32.dll")]
    public static extern int CallNextHookEx(int hookHandle, int code,
                                            int wparam, int lparam);
    [DllImport("user32.dll")]
    public static extern bool UnhookWindowsHookEx(int hookHandle);
    [DllImport("user32.dll")]
    public static extern int GetAsyncKeyState(int vKey);

    // Fields, constants, and structures used by the keyboard hook
    int hookHandle = 0;
    HookProc cb = null;

    public const int WH_KEYBOARD = 2;

    public const int HC_ACTION = 0;
    public const int HC_NOREMOVE = 3;

    public const int VK_CONTROL = 0x11;
    public const int VK_LWIN = 0x5B;
    public const int VK_RWIN = 0x5C;
    public const int VK_APPS = 0x5D;
    public const int VK_LSHIFT = 0xA0;
    public const int VK_RSHIFT = 0xA1;
    public const int VK_LCONTROL = 0xA2;
    public const int VK_RCONTROL = 0xA3;
    public const int VK_LMENU = 0xA4;
    public const int VK_RMENU = 0xA5;
    public const int VK_BROWSER_BACK = 0xA6;
    public const int VK_BROWSER_FORWARD = 0xA7;
    public const int VK_BROWSER_REFRESH = 0xA8;
    public const int VK_BROWSER_STOP = 0xA9;
    public const int VK_BROWSER_SEARCH = 0xAA;
    public const int VK_VOLUME_MUTE = 0xAD;
    public const int VK_VOLUME_DOWN = 0xAE;
    public const int VK_VOLUME_UP = 0xAF;
    public const int VK_MEDIA_NEXT_TRACK = 0xB0;
    public const int VK_MEDIA_PREV_TRACK = 0xB1;
    public const int VK_MEDIA_STOP = 0xB2;
    public const int VK_MEDIA_PLAY_PAUSE = 0xB3;
```

```csharp
// Keyboard hook delegate
public delegate int HookProc(int code, int wparam, int lparam);

public int Proc(int code, int wparam, int lparam)
{
    if (code == HC_ACTION)
    {
        switch (wparam)
        {
            case VK_BROWSER_BACK:
                // Handle Back keyboard button here
                textBox1.Text += "Browser Back key caught" +
                                    Environment.NewLine;
                break;
            case VK_BROWSER_FORWARD:
                // Handle Forward keyboard button here
                textBox1.Text += "Browser Forward key caught" +
                                    Environment.NewLine;
                break;
            case VK_BROWSER_REFRESH:
                // Handle Refresh keyboard button here
                textBox1.Text += "Browser Refresh key caught" +
                                    Environment.NewLine;
                break;
            case VK_BROWSER_STOP:
                // Handle Stop keyboard button here
                textBox1.Text += "Browser Stop key caught" +
                                    Environment.NewLine;
                break;
            case VK_BROWSER_SEARCH:
                // Handle Search keyboard button here
                textBox1.Text += "Browser Search key caught" +
                                    Environment.NewLine;
                break;
            case VK_VOLUME_MUTE:
                // Handle Mute keyboard button here
                textBox1.Text += "Volume Mute key caught" +
                                    Environment.NewLine;
                break;
            case VK_VOLUME_DOWN:
                // Handle Volume - keyboard button here
                textBox1.Text += "Volume Down key caught" +
                                    Environment.NewLine;
                break;
            case VK_VOLUME_UP:
                // Handle Volume + keyboard button here
                textBox1.Text += "Volume Up key caught" +
                                    Environment.NewLine;
                break;
            case VK_MEDIA_NEXT_TRACK:
                // Handle Next Track keyboard button here
                textBox1.Text += "Media Next Track key caught" +
                                    Environment.NewLine;
                break;
```

```
                        case VK_MEDIA_PREV_TRACK:
                            // Handle Previous Track keyboard button here
                            textBox1.Text += "Media Previous Track key caught" +
                                               Environment.NewLine;
                            break;
                        case VK_MEDIA_STOP:
                            // Handle Stop keyboard button here
                            textBox1.Text += "Media Stop key caught" +
                                               Environment.NewLine;
                            break;
                        case VK_MEDIA_PLAY_PAUSE:
                            // Handle Play keyboard button here
                            textBox1.Text += "Media Play/Pause key caught" +
                                               Environment.NewLine;
                            break;
                }
            }
            return (CallNextHookEx(hookHandle, code, wparam, lparam));
        }

        // Click event handlers for button1 and button2
        private void button1_Click(object sender, System.EventArgs e)
        {
            // Set the keyboard hook
            if (hookHandle == 0)
            {
                cb = new HookProc(Proc);
                hookHandle = SetWindowsHookEx(WH_KEYBOARD, cb, 0,
                                       AppDomain.GetCurrentThreadId( ));
            }
            else
            {
                textBox1.Text += "Hook already set" + Environment.NewLine;
            }
            textBox1.Text += "Start: " + hookHandle + Environment.NewLine;
        }

        private void button2_Click(object sender, System.EventArgs e)
        {
            // Unhook the keyboard hook
            textBox1.Text += "End: " + UnhookWindowsHookEx(hookHandle) +
                        Environment.NewLine;
            hookHandle = 0;
        }
    }
}
```

Discussion

The hooks provided by the Windows operating system allow for very powerful
code to be written with a minimum of work. The hook used in this recipe is the
WH_KEYBOARD hook, which watches messages that are generated by the keyboard.

The WH_KEYBOARD hook allows keyboard messages to be watched or discarded. To discard a keyboard message, return a 1 from the Proc hook callback method. The HookProc delegate is used as the method to which the keyboard hook calls back whenever a keyboard message is received. This hook does not allow the message to be modified.

To use a hook, as the code in the Solution section shows, you first need to declare the following three Windows API functions:

SetWindowsHookEx

> This API creates the hook specified by the first parameter and attaches it to the callback method specified in the second parameter. The return value of this function is the handle to the newly created hook. This handle needs to be stored so that it can later be used to remove the hook.

CallNextHookEx

> This API calls the next hook in the hook chain if SetWindowsHookEx has been called multiple times for a single type of hook. The return value is dependent on the type of hook that is installed.

UnhookWindowsHookEx

> This API removes the callback to the hook specified by the hook handle passed as its only parameter. The hook handle is returned by the SetWindowsHookEx method. This hook handle is returned by the SetWindowHookEx function.

Once these functions are declared, the next step is to declare the delegate for the hook callback method. This hook callback method is automatically invoked whenever a keyboard message is sent. The return value of both the delegate and callback methods is the return value of the CallNextHookEx API method.

The keyboard hook used in this recipe will intercept only messages that are sent to the message queue of the thread on which the hook is installed. The thread on which to install the hook is passed as the fourth argument of the SetWindowsHookEx API method. For this recipe, the current thread is passed as an argument using the static AppDomain.GetCurrentThreadId method. Therefore, if you have a multithreaded application and you want each thread to intercept messages sent by the keyboard, you will have to call SetWindowsHookEx on each thread to set up the WH_KEYBOARD hook.

The keyboard hook can also be used to capture keys pressed in combination. For example, if the Windows Menu key is pressed along with the V key, a keyboard hook callback procedure can be implemented to capture this action:

```
// Hook callback method
public int Proc(int code, int wparam, int lparam)
{
    if (code == HC_ACTION)
    {
        // Check the state of the Window's keyboard Pop-Up Menu key
        int state = GetAsyncKeyState(VK_APPS);
```

```
        // Is the Menu key already down?
        if ((state & 0x8000) == 0x8000)
        {
            // Is the key up?
            if ((lparam & 0x80000000) == 0x80000000)
            {
                // Is this the v key?
                if (wparam == 0x56)
                {
                    // Handle AppMenu-v key combination here...
                    textBox1.Text += "AppMenu-v action caught" +
                                        Environment.NewLine;
                }
            }
        }
    }
    return (CallNextHookEx(hookHandle, code, wparam, lparam));
}
```

This callback gets the state of the Menu key and determines whether it is depressed ((state & 0x8000) == 0x8000). If it is depressed, the V key is checked to see if it is being released ((lparam & 0x80000000) == 0x80000000). If these conditions are true, a message is displayed. (Of course, you could add your own code here to do something more interesting.)

See Also

See Recipe 7.11; *Subclassing & Hooking with Visual Basic* by Stephen Teilhet (O'Reilly); and see the "Delegate Class" and "Hooks" topics in the MSDN documentation.

7.11   Using Windows Hooks to Manipulate the Mouse

Problem

Many new mice have more than just a left and right button. Nowadays mice come with several additional buttons and a mouse wheel. You need to allow your application to take advantage of these new mice features. Additionally, you might need to know where the current location of the mouse is on a particular window, whether it is on the client area of the window (where your menus, toolbars, and controls are placed in the window), the nonclient area of the window (window border, title bar, close button, etc.), or the *x* and *y* coordinates of the mouse pointer.

Solution

Use the mouse events that are built into the System.Windows.Forms.Form class.

Discussion

There are seven mouse events that exist in the System.Windows.Forms.Form class. These are, in the order in which they occur:

- MouseEnter
- MouseMove
- MouseHover or MouseDown or MouseWheel
- MouseUp (if MouseDown was the previously raised event)
- MouseLeave

Most of these events accept a MouseEventArgs object that contains all the information about the mouse when the event is raised. The MouseEventArgs class contains the following data:

- Which button the user is acting on
- The number of times the mouse button was clicked
- The direction and speed of the mouse wheel
- The x and y coordinate of the mouse pointer

Your code can make use of any one or more of these events on the Form class along with the MouseEventArgs object.

See Also

See Recipe 7.10; *Subclassing & Hooking with Visual Basic* by Stephen Teilhet (O'Reilly); see the "Form Class," "MouseEventArgs Class," "Control.MouseDown Event," "Control.MouseEnter Event," "Control.MouseHover Event," "Control. MouseLeave Event," "Control.MouseMove Event," "Control.MouseWheel Event," "Control.MouseUp Event," and "Control.MouseMove Event" topics in the MSDN documentation.

CHAPTER 8
Regular Expressions

Included in the .NET Framework Class Library is the System.Text.RegularExpressions namespace that is devoted to creating, executing, and obtaining results from regular expressions executed against a string.

Regular expressions take the form of a pattern that can be matched to zero or more characters within a string. The simplest of these patterns, such as .* (match anything and everything) and [A-Za-z] (match any letter) are easy to learn, but more advanced patterns can be difficult to learn and even more difficult to implement correctly. Learning and understanding regular expressions can take considerable time and effort, but the work will pay off.

Regular expression patterns can take a simple form—such as a single word or character—or a much more complex pattern. The more complex patterns can recognize and match such things as the year portion of a date, all of the <SCRIPT> tags in an ASP page, or a phrase in a sentence that varies with each use. The .NET regular expression classes provide a very flexible and powerful way to do such things as recognize text, replace text within a string, and split up text into individual sections based on one or more complex delimiters.

Despite the complexity of regular expression patterns, the regular expression classes in the FCL are easy to use in your applications. Executing a regular expression consists of the following steps:

1. Create an instance of the Regex object that contains the regular expression pattern along with any options for executing that pattern.

2. Retrieve a reference to an instance of the Match object by calling the Match instance method if you want only the first match found, or to an instance of the MatchesCollection object by calling the Matches instance method if you want more than just the first match found.

3. If you've called the Matches method to retrieve a MatchCollection object, iterate over the MatchCollection using a foreach loop. Each iteration will allow access to every Match object that the regular expression produced.

8.1 Enumerating Matches

Problem

You need to find one or more substrings corresponding to a particular pattern within a string. You need to be able to inform the searching code to return either all matching substrings or only the matching substrings that are unique within the set of all matched strings.

Solution

Call the FindSubstrings method, which executes a regular expression and obtains all matching text. This method returns either all matching results or only the unique matches; this behavior is controlled by the findAllUnique parameter. Note that if the findAllUnique parameter is set to true, the unique matches are returned sorted alphabetically. Its source code is as follows:

```
using System;
using System.Collections;
using System.Text.RegularExpressions;

public static Match[] FindSubstrings(string source, string matchPattern,
                                     bool findAllUnique)
{
    SortedList uniqueMatches = new SortedList( );
    Match[] retArray = null;

    Regex RE = new Regex(matchPattern, RegexOptions.Multiline);
    MatchCollection theMatches = RE.Matches(source);

    if (findAllUnique)
    {
        for (int counter = 0; counter < theMatches.Count; counter++)
        {
            if (!uniqueMatches.ContainsKey(theMatches[counter].Value))
            {
                uniqueMatches.Add(theMatches[counter].Value,
                                  theMatches[counter]);
            }
        }

        retArray = new Match[uniqueMatches.Count];
        uniqueMatches.Values.CopyTo(retArray, 0);
    }
    else
    {
        retArray = new Match[theMatches.Count];
        theMatches.CopyTo(retArray, 0);
    }

    return (retArray);
}
```

The following method searches for any tags in an XML string; it does this by searching for a block of text that begins with the < character and ends with the > character.

This method first displays all unique tag matches present in the XML string and then displays all tag matches within the string:

```
public static void TestFindSubstrings()
{
    string matchPattern = "<.*>";

    string source = @"<?xml version='1.0' encoding='UTF-8'?>
            <!-- my comment -->
            <![CDATA[<escaped> <><chars>>>>>]]>
            <Window ID='Main'>
              <Control ID='TextBox'>
                <Property Top='0' Left='0' Text='BLANK'/>
              </Control>
              <Control ID='Label'>
                <Property Top='0' Left='0' Caption='Enter Name Here'/>
              </Control>
              <Control ID='Label'>
                <Property Top='0' Left='0' Caption='Enter Name Here'/>
              </Control>
            </Window>";

    Console.WriteLine("UNIQUE MATCHES");
    Match[] x1 = FindSubstrings(source, matchPattern, true);
    foreach(Match m in x1)
    {
        Console.WriteLine(m.Value);
    }

    Console.WriteLine();
    Console.WriteLine("ALL MATCHES");
    Match[] x2 = FindSubstrings(source, matchPattern, false);
    foreach(Match m in x2)
    {
        Console.WriteLine(m.Value);
    }
}
```

The following text will be displayed:

```
UNIQUE MATCHES
<!-- my comment -->
<![CDATA[<escaped> <><chars>>>>>]]>
</Control>
</Window>
<?xml version="1.0\" encoding=\"UTF-8\"?>
<Control ID="Label">
<Control ID="TextBox">
<Property Top="0" Left="0" Caption="Enter Name Here"/>
<Property Top="0" Left="0" Text="BLANK"/>
<Window ID="Main">
```

```
ALL MATCHES
<?xml version="1.0\" encoding=\"UTF-8\"?>
<!-- my comment -->
<![CDATA[<escaped> <><chars>>>>>]]>
<Window ID="Main">
<Control ID="TextBox">
<Property Top="0" Left="0" Text="BLANK"/>
</Control>
<Control ID="Label">
<Property Top="0" Left="0" Caption="Enter Name Here"/>
</Control>
<Control ID="Label">
<Property Top="0" Left="0" Caption="Enter Name Here"/>
</Control>
</Window>
```

Discussion

As you can see, the regular expression classes in the FCL are quite easy to use. The first step is to create an instance of the Regex object that contains the regular expression pattern along with any options for running this pattern. The second step is to get a reference to an instance of the Match object, if you only need the first found match, or a MatchCollection object, if you need more than just the first found match. To get a reference to this object, the two instance methods Match and Matches can be called from the Regex object that was created in the first step. The Match method returns a single match object (Match) and Matches returns a collection of match objects (MatchCollection).

The FindSubstrings method returns an array of Match objects that can be used by the calling code. You might have noticed that the unique elements are returned sorted, and the nonunique elements are not sorted. A SortedList, which is used by the FindSubstrings method to store unique strings that match the regular expression pattern, automatically sorts its items when they are added.

The regular expression used in the TestFindSubstrings method is very simplistic and will work in most—but not all—conditions. For example, if two tags are on the same line, as shown here:

the regular expression will catch the entire line, not each tag separately. You could change the regular expression from <.*> to <[^>]*> to match only up to the closing > ([^>]* matches everything that is *not* a >). However, this will fail in the CDATA section, matching <![CDATA[<escaped>, <>, and <chars> instead of <![CDATA[<escaped> <> <chars>>>>>]]>. The more complicated @"(<!\[CDATA.*>|<[^>]*>)" will match either <!\[CDATA.*> (a greedy match for everything within the CDATA section) or <[^>]*>, described previously.

See Also

See the ".NET Framework Regular Expressions" and "SortedList Class" topics in the MSDN documentation.

8.2 Extracting Groups from a MatchCollection

Problem

You have a regular expression that contains one or more named groups, such as the following:

```
\\\\(?<TheServer>\w*)\\(?<TheService>\w*)\\
```

where the named group TheServer will match any server name within a UNC string, and TheService will match any service name within a UNC string.

You need to store the groups that are returned by this regular expression in a keyed collection (such as a Hashtable) in which the key is the group name.

Solution

The RegExUtilities class contains a method, ExtractGroupings, that obtains a set of Group objects keyed by their matching group name:

```csharp
using System;
using System.Collections;
using System.Text.RegularExpressions;

public static ArrayList ExtractGroupings(string source,
                                         string matchPattern,
                                         bool wantInitialMatch)
{
    ArrayList keyedMatches = new ArrayList();
    int startingElement = 1;
    if (wantInitialMatch)
    {
        startingElement = 0;
    }

    Regex RE = new Regex(matchPattern, RegexOptions.Multiline);
    MatchCollection theMatches = RE.Matches(source);

    foreach(Match m in theMatches)
    {
        Hashtable groupings = new Hashtable();

        for (int counter = startingElement;
          counter < m.Groups.Count; counter++)
        {
            // If we had just returned the MatchCollection directly, the
            //  GroupNameFromNumber method would not be available to use
```

```
                groupings.Add(RE.GroupNameFromNumber(counter),
                            m.Groups[counter]);
            }

            keyedMatches.Add(groupings);
        }

        return (keyedMatches);
    }
```

The ExtractGroupings method can be used in the following manner to extract named groups and organize them by name:

```
public static void TestExtractGroupings()
{
    string source = @"Path = ""\\MyServer\MyService\MyPath;
                        \\MyServer2\MyService2\MyPath2\""";
    string matchPattern = @"\\\\(?<TheServer>\w*)\\(?<TheService>\w*)\\";

    foreach (Hashtable grouping in
            ExtractGroupings(source, matchPattern, true))
    {
        foreach (DictionaryEntry DE in grouping)
            Console.WriteLine("Key / Value = " + DE.Key + " / " +
                                DE.Value);
        Console.WriteLine("");
    }
}
```

This test method creates a source string and a regular expression pattern in the MatchPattern variable. The two groupings in this regular expression are highlighted here:

```
string matchPattern = @"\\\\(?<TheServer>\w*)\\(?<TheService>\w*)\\";
```

The names for these two groups are: TheServer and TheService. Text that matches either of these groupings can be accessed through these group names.

The source and matchPattern variables are passed in to the ExtractGroupings method, along with a Boolean value, which we will discuss shortly. This method returns an ArrayList containing Hashtable objects. These Hashtable objects contain the matches for each of the named groups in the regular expression, keyed by their group name.

This test method, TestExtractGroupings, returns the following:

```
Key / Value = 0 / \\MyServer\MyService\
Key / Value = TheService / MyService
Key / Value = TheServer / MyServer

Key / Value = 0 / \\MyServer2\MyService2\
Key / Value = TheService / MyService2
Key / Value = TheServer / MyServer2
```

If the last parameter to the `ExtractGroupings` method were to be changed to `false`, the following output would result:

```
Key / Value = TheService / MyService
Key / Value = TheServer / MyServer

Key / Value = TheService / MyService2
Key / Value = TheServer / MyServer2
```

The only difference between these two outputs are that the first grouping is not displayed when the last parameter to `ExtractGroupings` is changed to `false`. The first grouping is always the complete match of the regular expression.

Discussion

Groups within a regular expression can be defined in one of two ways. The first way is to add parentheses around the subpattern that you wish to define as a grouping. This type of grouping is sometimes labeled as *unnamed*. This grouping can later be easily extracted from the final text in each `Match` object returned by running the regular expression. The regular expression for this recipe could be modified, as follows, to use a simple unnamed group:

```
string matchPattern = @"\\\\(\w*)\\(\w*)\\";
```

After running the regular expression, you can access these groups using a numeric integer value starting with 1.

The second way to define a group within a regular expression is to use one or more *named groups*. A named group is defined by adding parentheses around the subpattern that you wish to define as a grouping and, additionally, adding a named value to each grouping, using the following syntax:

```
(?<Name>\w*)
```

The *Name* portion of this syntax is the name you specify for this group. After executing this regular expression, you can access this group by the name *Name*.

To access each group, you must first use a loop to iterate each `Match` object in the `MatchCollection`. For each `Match` object, you access the `GroupCollection`'s indexer, using the following unnamed syntax:

```
string group1 = m.Groups[1].Value;
string group2 = m.Groups[2].Value;
```

or the following named syntax where `m` is the `Match` object:

```
string group1 = m.Groups["Group1_Name"].Value;
string group2 = m.Groups["Group2_Name"].Value;
```

If the `Match` method was used to return a single `Match` object instead of the `MatchCollection`, use the following syntax to access each group:

```
// Un-named syntax
string group1 = theMatch.Groups[1].Value;
string group2 = theMatch.Groups[2].Value;
```

```
// Named syntax
string group1 = theMatch.Groups["Group1_Name"].Value;
string group2 = theMatch.Groups["Group2_Name"].Value;
```

where theMatch is the Match object returned by the Match method.

See Also

See the ".NET Framework Regular Expressions" and "Hashtable Class" topics in the MSDN documentation.

8.3   Verifying the Syntax of a Regular Expression

Problem

You have either constructed a regular expression dynamically from your code or based on user input. You need to test the validity of this regular expression's syntax before you actually use it.

Solution

Use the following method to test the validity of a regular expression's syntax:

```
using System;
using System.Text.RegularExpressions;

public static bool VerifyRegEx(string testPattern)
{
    bool isValid = true;

    if ((testPattern != null) && (testPattern.Trim().Length > 0))
    {
        try
        {
            Regex.Match("", testPattern);
        }
        catch (ArgumentException)
        {
            // BAD PATTERN: Syntax error
            isValid = false;
        }
    }
    else
    {
        //BAD PATTERN: Pattern is null or blank
        isValid = false;
    }

    return (isValid);
}
```

To use this method, pass it the regular expression that you wish to verify:

```
public static void TestUserInputRegEx(string regEx)
{
    if (VerifyRegEx(regEx))
        Console.WriteLine("This is a valid regular expression.");
    else
        Console.WriteLine("This is not a valid regular expression.");
}
```

Discussion

The `VerifyRegEx` method calls the static `Regex.Match` method, which is useful for running quick regular expressions against a string. The static `Regex.Match` method returns a single `Match` object. By using this static method to run a regular expression against a string (in this case a blank string), we can determine whether the regular expression is invalid by watching for a thrown exception. The `Regex.Match` method will throw an `ArgumentException` if the regular expression is not syntactically correct. The `Message` property of this exception contains the reason the regular expression failed to run, and the `ParamName` property contains the regular expression passed to the `Match` method. Both of these properties are read-only.

Before testing the regular expression with the static `Match` method, the regular expression is tested to see if it is `null` or blank. A `null` regular expression string returns an `ArgumentNullException` when passed in to the `Match` method. On the other hand, if a blank regular expression is passed in to the `Match` method, no exception is thrown (as long as a valid string is also passed to the first parameter of the `Match` method).

8.4   Quickly Finding Only the Last Match in a String

Problem

You need to find the last pattern match in a string, but you do not want the overhead of finding all matches in a string and having to move to the last match in the collection of matches.

Solution

Using the `RegexOptions.RightToLeft` option, the match starts at the end of the string and proceeds toward the beginning. The first found match is the last match in the string. You supply the `RegexOptions.RightToLeft` constant as an argument to the `Match` method. The instance `Match` method can be used as follows:

```
Regex RE = new Regex(Pattern, RegexOptions.RightToLeft);
Match theMatch = RE.Match(Source);
```

or use the static `Regex.Match` method:

```
Match theMatch = Regex.Match(Source, Pattern, RegexOptions.RightToLeft);
```

where *Pattern* is the regular expression pattern and *Source* is the string against which to run the pattern.

Discussion

The `RegexOptions.RightToLeft` regular expression option will force the regular expression engine to start searching for a pattern starting with the end of the string and proceeding backward toward the beginning of the string. The first match encountered will be the match closest to the end of the string—in other words, the last match in the string.

See Also

See the ".NET Framework Regular Expressions" topic in the MSDN documentation.

8.5 Replacing Characters or Words in a String

Problem

You are given a string in which a complex pattern of characters needs to be replaced with a new string.

Solution

Using the `Replace` instance method on the `Regex` class allows for easy replacement of text within a string. The following overloaded `Replace` methods accept a *source* string that contains characters or words to be replaced, a *matchPattern* to match the replaceable text in the *source* parameter, and a *replaceStr* string to replace the text matched by *matchPattern*. In addition there are two parameters, *count* and *startPos*, to control the number of replacements allowed and where the replacements start from in the *source* string, respectively:

```
using System;
using System.Text.RegularExpressions;

public static string Replace(string source, char matchPattern,
                                            string replaceStr)
{
    return (Replace(source, matchPattern.ToString( ), replaceStr, -1, 0));
}

public static string Replace(string source, char matchPattern,
                             string replaceStr, int count)
{
    return (Replace(source.ToString( ), matchPattern.ToString( ), replaceStr,
                    count, 0));
}

public static string Replace(string source, char matchPattern,
                             string replaceStr, int count, int startPos)
```

```
    {
        return (Replace(source.ToString( ), matchPattern.ToString( ), replaceStr,
                        count, startPos));
    }

    public static string Replace(string source, string matchPattern,
                                 string replaceStr)
    {
        return (Replace(source, matchPattern, replaceStr, -1, 0));
    }

    public static string Replace(string source, string matchPattern,
                                 string replaceStr, int count)
    {
        return (Replace(source, matchPattern, replaceStr, count, 0));
    }

    public static string Replace(string source, string matchPattern,
                                 string replaceStr, int count, int startPos)
    {
        Regex RE = new Regex(matchPattern);
        string newString = RE.Replace(source, replaceStr, count, startPos);

        return (newString);
    }
```

To use the overloaded Replace methods to replace the word FOO with the word BAR in a sentence, you could write the following:

```
public static void TestReplace( )
{
    string source = "Replace the FOO in this text block of text FOO.";
    string matchPattern = "FOO";
    string replaceStr = "BAR";

    Console.WriteLine(Replace(source, matchPattern, replaceStr));
    Console.WriteLine(Replace(source, matchPattern, replaceStr, -1));
    Console.WriteLine(Replace(source, matchPattern, replaceStr, -1, 0));
    Console.WriteLine(Replace(source, matchPattern, replaceStr, 1));
    Console.WriteLine(Replace(source, matchPattern, replaceStr, 1, 0));
    Console.WriteLine(Replace(source, matchPattern, replaceStr, 1));
    Console.WriteLine(Replace(source, matchPattern, replaceStr, 1, 20));

    Console.WriteLine(Replace(source, matchPattern, replaceStr, -1, 0));
    Console.WriteLine(Replace(source, matchPattern, replaceStr, 1, 0));
    Console.WriteLine(Replace(source, matchPattern, replaceStr, 1, 20));
}
```

which would produce the following output:

```
Replace the BAR in this text block of text BAR.
Replace the BAR in this text block of text BAR.
Replace the BAR in this text block of text BAR.
Replace the BAR in this text block of text FOO.
Replace the BAR in this text block of text FOO.
Replace the BAR in this text block of text FOO.
```

```
Replace the FOO in this text block of text BAR.
Replace the BAR in this text block of text BAR.
Replace the BAR in this text block of text FOO.
Replace the FOO in this text block of text BAR.
```

This code looks for the word "FOO", and each time this pattern is found, the string "BAR" is substituted for the matched string ("FOO").

Discussion

Using the overloaded instance Replace method on the Regex class, we can easily define a replacement string that is substituted for a regular expression pattern each time that pattern is found. Several overloads of this method provide even more flexibility in determining where to replace matches and how many matches will be replaced.

An overloaded static Replace method is also provided on the Regex class. This method is somewhat different than its instance method counterpart. This static Replace method does not allow for the flexibility of a *startPos* or a *count* parameter. In lieu of these parameters, an *options* parameter is used. This parameter allows for modification of the *RegexOptions* options. If you require that the regular expression options (RegexOptions) be controllable, rather than using the less flexible static Regex.Replace method, you can modify the overloaded Replace methods as follows:

```csharp
// Constant to provide a default set of options for the regular expression
const RegexOptions defaultOptions = RegexOptions.IgnorePatternWhitespace |
                                    RegexOptions.Multiline;

public static string Replace(string source, char matchPattern,
                             string replaceStr)
{
    return (Replace(source, matchPattern.ToString( ), replaceStr, -1, 0,
                defaultOptions));
}

public static string Replace(string source, char matchPattern,
                             string replaceStr, int count)
{
    return (Replace(source.ToString( ), matchPattern.ToString( ), replaceStr,
                count, 0, defaultOptions));
}

public static string Replace(string source, char matchPattern,
                             string replaceStr, int count, int startPos)
{
    return (Replace(source.ToString( ), matchPattern.ToString( ), replaceStr,
                count, startPos, defaultOptions));
}

public static string Replace(string source, char matchPattern,
                             string replaceStr, int count, int startPos,
                             RegexOptions options)
{
    return (Replace(source.ToString( ), matchPattern.ToString( ), replaceStr,
```

```
                            count, startPos, options));
    }

    public static string Replace(string source, string matchPattern,
                            string replaceStr)
    {
        return (Replace(source, matchPattern, replaceStr, -1, 0,
                    defaultOptions));
    }

    public static string Replace(string source, string matchPattern,
                            string replaceStr, int count)
    {
        return (Replace(source, matchPattern, replaceStr, count, 0,
                    defaultOptions));
    }

    public static string Replace(string source, string matchPattern,
                                string replaceStr, int count, int startPos)
    {
        return (Replace(source, matchPattern, replaceStr, count, startPos,
                    defaultOptions));
    }

    public static string Replace(string source, string matchPattern,
                                string replaceStr, int count, int startPos,
                                RegexOptions options)
    {
        Regex RE = new Regex(matchPattern, options);
        string newString = RE.Replace(source, replaceStr, count, startPos);

        return (newString);
    }
```

An *options* parameter of type RegexOptions has been added to the end of each
method's parameter list. The last Replace method uses this *options* parameter to
define how the Regex object will use the regular expression. Note also that a constant defaultOptions of type RegexOptions has been defined to provide a uniform way
to represent the default set of options in each overloaded method.

See Also

See the ".NET Framework Regular Expressions" topic in the MSDN documentation.

8.6   Augmenting the Basic String Replacement Function

Problem

You need to replace character patterns within the target string with a new string.
However, in this case, each replacement operation has a unique set of conditions

that must be satisfied in order to allow the replacement to occur. Consider, for example, that you receive a string in the form of XML (or possibly HTML). You wish to modify an attribute of a specific XML tag to a particular number, but only if that number is within a specified range (or possibly outside of a particular range).

Solution

Use the overloaded instance `Replace` method that accepts a `MatchEvaluator` delegate along with its other parameters. The `MatchEvaluator` delegate, which is a callback method that overrides the default behavior of the `Replace` method, is shown here:

```csharp
using System;
using System.Text.RegularExpressions;

public static string MatchHandler(Match theMatch)
{
    // Handle Top property of the Property tag
    if (theMatch.Value.StartsWith("<Property"))
    {
        long topPropertyValue = 0;

        // Obtain the numeric value of the Top property
        Match topPropertyMatch = Regex.Match(theMatch.Value,
                                    "Top=\"([-]*\\d*)");
        if (topPropertyMatch.Success)
        {
            if (topPropertyMatch.Groups[1].Value.Trim().Equals(""))
            {
                // If blank, set to zero
                return (theMatch.Value.Replace("Top=\"\"", "Top=\"0\""));
            }
            else if (topPropertyMatch.Groups[1].Value.Trim().Equals("-"))
            {
                // If only a negative sign (syntax error), set to zero
                return (theMatch.Value.Replace("Top=\"-\"", "Top=\"0\""));
            }
            else
            {
                // We have a valid number
                // Convert the matched string to a numeric value
                topPropertyValue = long.Parse(
                            topPropertyMatch.Groups[1].Value,
                            System.Globalization.NumberStyles.Any);

                // If the Top property is out of the specified
                //     range, set it to zero
                if (topPropertyValue < 0 || topPropertyValue > 5000)
                {
                    return (theMatch.Value.Replace("Top=\"" +
                                            topPropertyValue +
                                            "\"", "Top=\"0\""));
                }
            }
        }
```

```
        }
    }

    return (theMatch.Value);
}
```

The callback method for the Replace method is shown here:

```
public static void ComplexReplace(string matchPattern, string source)
{
    MatchEvaluator replaceCallback = new MatchEvaluator(MatchHandler);
    Regex RE = new Regex(matchPattern, RegexOptions.Multiline);
    string newString = RE.Replace(source, replaceCallback);

    Console.WriteLine("Replaced String = " + newString);
}
```

To use this callback method with the static Replace method, modify the previous ComplexReplace method as follows:

```
public void ComplexReplace(string matchPattern, string source)
{
    MatchEvaluator replaceCallback = new MatchEvaluator(MatchHandler);
    string newString = Regex.Replace(source, matchPattern,
                                     replaceCallback);

    Console.WriteLine("Replaced String = " + newString);
}
```

where *source* is the original string to run the replace operation against, and *matchPattern* is the regular expression pattern to match in the *source* string.

If the ComplexReplace method is called from the following code:

```
public static void TestComplexReplace()
{
    string matchPattern = "<.*>";
    string source = @"<?xml version=""1.0\"" encoding=\""UTF-8\""?>
<Window ID=""Main"">
    <Control ID=""TextBox"">
        <Property Top=""-100"" Left=""0"" Text=""BLANK""/>
    </Control>
    <Control ID=""Label"">
    <Property Top=""99990"" Left=""0"" Caption=""Enter Name Here""/>
    </Control>
</Window>";

    ComplexReplace(matchPattern, source);
}
```

only the Top attributes of the Property tags are changed from their original values to 0.

The result of this replace action will change only the Top property value of a Property tag to zero if it is less than zero or greater than 5000. Any other tag that contains a Top property will remain unchanged. The following two lines of the source string will be changed from:

```
<Property Top="100" Left="0" Text="BLANK"/>
<Property Top="99999" Left="0" Caption="Enter Name Here"/>
```

to:

```
<Property Top="100" Left="0" Text="BLANK"/>
<Property Top="0" Left="0" Caption="Enter Name Here"/>
```

Discussion

The MatchEvaluator delegate, which is automatically invoked when it is supplied as a parameter to the Regexp class's Replace method, allows for custom replacement of each string that conforms to the regular expression pattern.

If the current Match object is operating on a Property tag whose Top property is out of the specified range, the code within the MatchHandler callback method returns a new modified string. Otherwise, the currently matched string is returned unchanged. This ability allows you to override the default Replace functionality by replacing only that part of the source string that meets certain criteria. The code within this callback method gives you some idea of what can be accomplished using this replacement technique.

To make use of this callback method, we need a way to call it from the ComplexReplace method. First, a variable of type System.Text.RegularExpressions. MatchEvaluator is created. This variable (replaceCallback) is the delegate that is used to call the MatchHandler method:

```
MatchEvaluator replaceCallback = new MatchEvaluator(MatchHandler);
```

Finally, the Replace method is called with the reference to the MatchEvaluator delegate passed in as a parameter:

```
string newString = RE.Replace(source, replaceCallback);
```

See Also

See the ".NET Framework Regular Expressions" topic in the MSDN documentation.

8.7   A Better Tokenizer

Problem

A simple method of *tokenizing*—or breaking up a string into its discrete elements—was presented in Recipe 2.6. However, this is not powerful enough to handle all your string-tokenizing needs. You need a tokenizer—also referred to as a *lexer*—that can split up a string based on a well-defined set of characters.

Solution

Using the Split method of the Regex class, we can use a regular expression to indicate the types of tokens and separators that we are interested in gathering. This technique works especially well with equations, since the tokens of an equation are well-defined. For example, the code:

```
using System;
using System.Text.RegularExpressions;

public static string[] Tokenize(string equation)
{
    Regex RE = new Regex(@"([\+\-\*\(\)\^\\])");
    return (RE.Split(equation));
}
```

will divide up a string according to the regular expression specified in the Regex constructor. In other words, the string passed in to the Tokenize method will be divided up based on the delimiters +, -, *, (,), ^, or \. The following method will call the Tokenize method to tokenize the equation: (y - 3)(3111*x^21 + x + 320):

```
public void TestTokenize()
{
    foreach(string token in Tokenize("(y - 3)(3111*x^21 + x + 320)"))
        Console.WriteLine("String token = " + token.Trim());
}
```

which displays the following output:

```
String token =
String token = (
String token = y
String token = -
String token = 3
String token = )
String token =
String token = (
String token = 3111
String token = *
String token = x
String token = ^
String token = 21
String token = +
String token = x
String token = +
String token = 320
String token = )
String token =
```

Notice that each individual operator, parenthesis, and number has been broken out into its own separate token.

Discussion

The tokenizer created in Recipe 2.6 would be useful in specific controlled circumstances. However, in real-world projects, we do not always have the luxury of being able to control the set of inputs to our code. By making use of regular expressions, we can take the original tokenizer and make it flexible enough to allow it to be applied to any type or style of input we desire.

The key method used here is the Split instance method of the Regex class. The return value of this method is a string array whose elements include each individual token of the source string—the equation, in this case.

Notice that the static method allows RegexOptions enumeration values to be used, while the instance method allows for a starting position to be defined and a maximum amount of matches to occur. This may have some bearing on whether you choose the static or instance method.

See Also

See Recipe 2.6; see the ".NET Framework Regular Expressions" topic in the MSDN documentation.

8.8   Compiling Regular Expressions

Problem

You have a handful of regular expressions to execute as quickly as possible over many different strings. Performance is of the utmost importance.

Solution

The best way to do this task is to use compiled regular expressions. However, there are some drawbacks to using this technique, which we will examine.

There are two ways to compile regular expressions. The easiest way is to use the RegexOptions.Compiled enumeration value in the Options parameter of the static Match or Matches methods on the Regex class:

```
Match theMatch = Regex.Match(source, pattern, RegexOptions.Compiled);

MatchCollection theMatches = Regex.Matches(source, pattern, RegexOptions.Compiled);
```

If more than a few expressions will be compiled and/or the expressions need to be shared across applications, consider precompiling all of these expressions into their own assembly. Do this by using the static CompileToAssembly method on the Regex class. The following method accepts an assembly name and compiles two simple regular expressions into this assembly:

```
public static void CreateRegExDLL(string assmName)
{
    RegexCompilationInfo[] RE = new RegexCompilationInfo[2]
        {new RegexCompilationInfo("PATTERN", RegexOptions.Compiled,
                                  "CompiledPATTERN", "Chapter_Code", true),
         new RegexCompilationInfo("NAME", RegexOptions.Compiled,
                                  "CompiledNAME", "Chapter_Code", true)};

    System.Reflection.AssemblyName aName =
        new System.Reflection.AssemblyName();
    aName.Name = assmName;
```

```
        Regex.CompileToAssembly(RE, aName);
}
```

Now that the expressions are compiled to an assembly, the assembly can be added as a reference to your project and used as follows:

```
Chapter_Code.CompiledNAME CN = new Chapter_Code.CompiledNAME();
Match mName = CN.Match("Get the NAME from this text.");
Console.WriteLine("mName.Value = " + mName.Value);
```

This code displays the following text:

```
mName.Value = NAME
```

Discussion

Compiling regular expressions allows the expression to run faster. To understand how, we need to examine the process that an expression goes through as it is run against a string. If an expression is not compiled, the regular expression engine converts the expression to a series of internal codes that are recognized by the regular expression engine; it is not converted to MSIL. As the expression runs against a string, the engine interprets the series of internal codes. This can be a slow process, especially as the source string becomes very large and the expression becomes much more complex.

To fix this performance problem, you can compile the expression so that it gets converted directly to a series of MSIL instructions, which perform the pattern matching for the specific regular expression. Once the Just-In-Time (JIT) compiler is run on this MSIL, the instructions are converted to machine code. This allows for an extremely fast execution of the pattern against a string.

There are two drawbacks to using the `RegexOptions.Compiled` enumerated value to compile regular expressions. The first is that the first time an expression is used with the `Compiled` flag, it performs very slowly, due to the compilation process. Fortunately, this is a one-time expense since every unique expression is compiled only once. The second drawback is that an in-memory assembly gets generated to contain the IL, which can never be unloaded. An assembly can never be unloaded from an AppDomain. The garbage collector cannot remove it from memory. If large numbers of expressions are compiled, the amount of heap resources that will be used up and not released will be larger. So use this technique wisely.

Compiling regular expressions into their own assembly immediately gives you two benefits. First, precompiled expressions do not require any extra time to be compiled while your application is running. Second, they are in their own assembly and therefore can be used by other applications.

 Consider precompiling regular expressions and placing them in their own assembly rather than using the `RegexOptions.Compiled` flag.

To compile one or more expressions into an assembly, the static `CompileToAssembly` method of the Regex class must be used. To use this method, a `RegexCompilationInfo` array must be created and filled with `RegexCompilationInfo` objects. The next step is to create the assembly in which the expression will live. An instance of the `AssemblyName` class is created using the default constructor. Next, this assembly is given a name (do not include the `.dll` file extension in the name, it is added automatically). Finally, the `CompileToAssembly` method can be called with the `RegexCompilationInfo` array and the `AssemblyName` object supplied as arguments.

In our example, this assembly is placed in the same directory that the executable was launched from.

See Also

See the ".NET Framework Regular Expressions" and "AssemblyName Class" topics in the MSDN documentation.

8.9   Counting Lines of Text

Problem

You need to count lines of text within a string or within a file.

Solution

Read in the entire file and count the number of linefeeds, as shown in the following method:

```
using System;
using System.Text.RegularExpressions;
using System.IO;

public static long LineCount(string source, bool isFileName)
{
    if (source != null)
    {
        string text = source;

        if (isFileName)
        {
            FileStream FS = new FileStream(source, FileMode.Open,
                                     FileAccess.Read, FileShare.Read);
            StreamReader SR = new StreamReader(FS);
            text = SR.ReadToEnd( );
            SR.Close( );
            FS.Close( );
        }
```

```
        Regex RE = new Regex("\n", RegexOptions.Multiline);
        MatchCollection theMatches = RE.Matches(text);

        // Needed for files with zero length
        //   Note that a string will always have a line terminator
        //        and thus will always have a length of 1 or more
        if (isFileName)
        {
            return (theMatches.Count);
        }
        else
        {
            return (theMatches.Count) + 1;
        }
    }
    else
    {
        // Handle a null source here
        return (0);
    }
}
```

An alternative version of this method uses the StreamReader.ReadLine method to count lines in a file and a regular expression to count lines in a string:

```
public static long LineCount2(string source, bool isFileName)
{
    if (source != null)
    {
        string text = source;
        long numOfLines = 0;

        if (isFileName)
        {
            FileStream FS = new FileStream(source, FileMode.Open,
                                    FileAccess.Read, FileShare.Read);
            StreamReader SR = new StreamReader(FS);

            while (text != null)
            {
                text = SR.ReadLine();

                if (text != null)
                {
                    ++numOfLines;
                }
            }

            SR.Close();
            FS.Close();
            return (numOfLines);
        }
        else
        {
```

```
                    Regex RE = new Regex("\n", RegexOptions.Multiline);
                    MatchCollection theMatches = RE.Matches(text);

                    return (theMatches.Count + 1);
                }
        }
        else
        {
            // Handle a null source here
            return (0);
        }
    }
```

The following method counts the lines within a specified text file and a specified string:

```
public static void TestLineCount( )
{
    // Count the lines within the file TestFile.txt
    LineCount(@"C:\TestFile.txt", true);

    // Count the lines within a string
    // Notice that a \r\n characters start a new line
    //     as well as just the \n character
    LineCount("Line1\r\nLine2\r\nLine3\nLine4", false);
}
```

Discussion

Every line ends with a special character. For Windows files, the line terminating characters are a carriage return followed by a linefeed. This sequence of characters is described by the regular expression pattern \r\n. Unix files terminate their lines with just the linefeed character (\n). The regular expression "\n" is the lowest common denominator for both sets of line-terminating characters. Consequently, this method runs a regular expression that looks for the pattern "\n" in a string or file.

 Macintosh files usually end with a carriage-return character (\r). To count the number of lines in this type of file, the regular expression should be changed to the following in the constructor of the Regex object:

```
            Regex RE = new Regex("\r", RegexOptions.Multiline);
```

Simply running this regular expression against a string returns the number of lines minus one because the last line does not have a line-terminating character. To account for this, one is added to the final count of linefeeds in the string.

The LineCount method accepts two parameters. The first is a string that either contains the actual text that will have its lines counted or the path and name of a text file whose lines are to be counted. The second parameter, isFileName, determines whether the first parameter (source) is a string or a file path. If this parameter is true, the source parameter is a file path; otherwise, it is simply a string.

See Also

See the ".NET Framework Regular Expressions," "FileStream Class," and "Stream-Reader Class" topics in the MSDN documentation.

8.10   Returning the Entire Line in Which a Match Is Found

Problem

You have a string or file that contains multiple lines. When a specific character pattern is found on a line, you want to return the entire line, not just the matched text.

Solution

Use the `StreamReader.ReadLine` method to obtain each line in a file in which to run a regular expression against:

```
public static ArrayList GetLines(string source, string pattern,
                                 bool isFileName)
{
    string text = source;
    ArrayList matchedLines = new ArrayList( );

    // If this is a file, get the entire file's text
    if (isFileName)
    {
        FileStream FS = new FileStream(source, FileMode.Open,
                                      FileAccess.Read, FileShare.Read);
        StreamReader SR = new StreamReader(FS);

        while (text != null)
        {
            text = SR.ReadLine( );

            if (text != null)
            {
                // Run the regex on each line in the string
                Regex RE = new Regex(pattern, RegexOptions.Multiline);
                MatchCollection theMatches = RE.Matches(text);

                if (theMatches.Count > 0)
                {
                    // Get the line if a match was found
                    matchedLines.Add(text);
                }
            }
        }
    }
```

```
            SR.Close( );
            FS.Close( );
        }
        else
        {
            // Run the regex once on the entire string
            Regex RE = new Regex(pattern, RegexOptions.Multiline);
            MatchCollection theMatches = RE.Matches(text);

            // Get the line for each match
            foreach (Match m in theMatches)
            {
                int lineStartPos = GetBeginningOfLine(text, m.Index);
                int lineEndPos = GetEndOfLine(text, (m.Index + m.Length - 1));
                string line = text.Substring(lineStartPos,
                                             lineEndPos - lineStartPos);
                matchedLines.Add(line);
            }
        }

        return (matchedLines);
    }

    public static int GetBeginningOfLine(string text, int startPointOfMatch)
    {
        if (startPointOfMatch > 0)
        {
            --startPointOfMatch;
        }

        if (startPointOfMatch >= 0 && startPointOfMatch < text.Length)
        {
            // Move to the left until the first '\n' char is found
            for (int index = startPointOfMatch; index >= 0; index--)
            {
                if (text[index] == '\n')
                {
                    return (index + 1);
                }
            }

            return (0);
        }

        return (startPointOfMatch);
    }

    public static int GetEndOfLine(string text, int endPointOfMatch)
    {
        if (endPointOfMatch >= 0 && endPointOfMatch < text.Length)
        {
            // Move to the right until the first '\n' char is found
            for (int index = endPointOfMatch; index < text.Length; index++)
            {
```

```
            if (text[index] == '\n')
            {
                return (index);
            }
        }

        return (text.Length);
    }

    return (endPointOfMatch);
}
```

The following method shows how to call the GetLines method with either a filename or a string:

```
public static void TestGetLine( )
{
    // Get each line within the file TestFile.txt as a separate string
    Console.WriteLine( );
    ArrayList lines = GetLines(@"C:\TestFile.txt", "\n", true);
    foreach (string s in lines)
        Console.WriteLine("MatchedLine: " + s);

    // Get the lines matching the text "Line" within the given string
    Console.WriteLine( );
    lines = GetLines("Line1\r\nLine2\r\nLine3\nLine4", "Line", false);
    foreach (string s in lines)
        Console.WriteLine("MatchedLine: " + s);
}
```

Discussion

The GetLines method accepts three parameters:

source

> The string or filename in which to search for a pattern.

pattern

> The regular expression pattern to apply to the *source* string.

isFileName

> Pass in true if the *source* is a filename or false if *source* is a string.

This method returns an ArrayList of strings that contains each line in which the regular expression match was found.

The GetLines method can obtain the lines on which matches occur, within a string or a file. When running a regular expression against a file whose name is passed in to the *source* parameter (when *isFileName* equals true) in the GetLines method, the file is opened and read line-by-line. The regular expression is run against each line and if a match is found, that line is stored in the matchedLines ArrayList. Using the ReadLine method of the StreamReader object saves us from having to determine where

---

each line starts and ends. Determining where a line starts and ends in a string requires some work, as you shall see.

Running the regular expression against a string passed in to the *source* parameter (when *isFileName* equals false) in the GetLines method produces a MatchCollection. Each Match object in this collection is used to obtain the line on which it is located in the *source* string. The line is obtained by starting at the position of the first character of the match in the *source* string and moving one character to the left until either a '\n' character is found or the beginning of the *source* string is found (this code is found in the GetBeginningOfLine method). This gives you the beginning of the line, which is placed in the variable LineStartPos. Next, the end of the line is found by starting at the last character of the match in the *source* string and moving to the right until either a '\n' character is found or the end of the *source* string is found (this code is found in the GetEndOfLine method). This ending position is placed in the LineEndPos variable. All of the text between the LineStartPos and LineEndPos will be the line in which the match is found. Each of these lines is added to the matchedLines ArrayList and returned to the caller.

Something interesting you can do with the GetLines method is to pass in the string "\n" in the pattern parameter of this method. This trick will effectively return each line of the string or file as a string in the ArrayList.

Note that if more than one match is found on a line, each matching line will be added to the ArrayList.

See Also

See the ".NET Framework Regular Expressions," "FileStream Class," and "Stream-Reader Class" topics in the MSDN documentation.

8.11 Finding a Particular Occurrence of a Match

Problem

You need to find a specific occurrence of a match within a string. For example, you want to find the third occurrence of a word or the second occurrence of a Social Security Number. In addition, you may need to find every third occurrence of a word in a string.

Solution

To find a particular occurrence of a match in a string, simply subscript the array returned from Regex.Matches:

```
public static Match FindOccurrenceOf(string source, string pattern,
                                     int occurrence)
```

```
    {
        if (occurrence < 1)
        {
            throw (new ArgumentException("Cannot be less than 1",
                                        "occurrence"));
        }

        // Make occurrence zero-based
        --occurrence;

        // Run the regex once on the source string
        Regex RE = new Regex(pattern, RegexOptions.Multiline);
        MatchCollection theMatches = RE.Matches(source);

        if (occurrence >= theMatches.Count)
        {
            return (null);
        }
        else
        {
            return (theMatches[occurrence]);
        }
    }
}
```

To find each particular occurrence of a match in a string, build an `ArrayList` on the fly:

```
public static ArrayList FindEachOccurrenceOf(string source, string pattern,
                                             int occurrence)
{
    ArrayList occurrences = new ArrayList();

    // Run the regex once on the source string
    Regex RE = new Regex(pattern, RegexOptions.Multiline);
    MatchCollection theMatches = RE.Matches(source);

    for (int index = (occurrence - 1);
         index < theMatches.Count; index += occurrence)
    {
        occurrences.Add(theMatches[index]);
    }

    return (occurrences);
}
```

The following method shows how to invoke the two previous methods:

```
public static void TestOccurrencesOf()
{
    Match matchResult = FindOccurrenceOf(
                "one two three one two three one two three one"
                + " two three one two three one two three", "two", 2);
    if (matchResult != null)
        Console.WriteLine(matchResult.ToString() + "\t" +
                            matchResult.Index);
```

```
      Console.WriteLine( );
      ArrayList results = FindEachOccurrenceOf(
                  "one one two three one two three one two" +
                  " three one two three", "one", 2);
      foreach (Match m in results)
          Console.WriteLine(m.ToString( ) + "\t" + m.Index);
  }
```

Discussion

This recipe contains two similar but distinct methods. The first method, FindOccurrenceOf, returns a particular occurrence of a regular expression match. The occurrence you want to find is passed in to this method via the occurrence parameter. If the particular occurrence of the match does not exist—for example, you ask to find the second occurrence, but only one occurrence exists—a null is returned from this method. Because of this, you should check that the returned object of this method is not null before using that object. If the particular occurrence exists, the Match object that holds the match information for that occurrence is returned.

The second method in this recipe, FindEachOccurrenceOf, works similar to the FindOccurrenceOf method, except that it continues to find a particular occurrence of a regular expression match until the end of the string is reached. For example, if you ask to find the second occurrence, this method would return an ArrayList of zero or more Match objects. The Match objects would correspond to the second, fourth, sixth, and eighth occurrence of a match and so on until the end of the string is reached.

See Also

See the ".NET Framework Regular Expressions" and "ArrayList Class" topics in the MSDN documentation.

8.12 Using Common Patterns

Problem

You need a quick list from which to choose regular expression patterns that match standard items. These standard items could be a Social Security Number, a zip code, a word containing only characters, an alphanumeric word, an email address, a URL, dates, or one of many other possible items used throughout business applications.

These patterns can be useful in making sure that a user has input the correct data and that it is well-formed. These patterns can also be used as an extra security measure to keep hackers from attempting to break your code by entering strange or malformed input (e.g., SQL injection or cross-site-scripting attacks). Note that these regular expressions are not a silver bullet that will stop all attacks on your system; rather, they are an added layer of defense.

Solution

- Match only alphanumeric characters along with the characters -, +, ., and any whitespace:

    `^([\w\.+-]|\s)*$`

     Be careful using the - character within a character class—a regular expression enclosed within [and]. That character is also used to specify a range of characters, as in a–z for a through z inclusive. If you want to use a literal - character, either escape it with \ or put it at the end of the expression, as shown in the previous and next examples.

- Match only alphanumeric characters along with the characters -, +, ., and any whitespace, with the stipulation that there is at least one of these characters and no more than 10 of these characters:

    `^([\w\.+-]|\s){1,10}$`

- Match a date in the form ##/##/#### where the day and month can be a one- or two-digit value, and year can either be a two- or four-digit value:

    `^\d{1,2}\/\d{1,2}\/\d{2,4}$`

- Match a time to be entered with an optional am or pm extension (note that this regular expression also handles military time):

    `^\d{1,2}:\d{2}\s?([ap]m)?$`

- Match an IP address:

    `^([0-2]?[0-5]?[0-5]\.){3}[0-2]?[0-5]?[0-5]$`

- Verify that an email address is in the form *name@address* where *address* is not an IP address:

    `^[A-Za-z0-9_\-\.]+@(([A-Za-z0-9\-])+\.)+([A-Za-z\-])+$`

- Verify that an email address is in the form *name@address* where *address* is an IP address:

    `^[A-Za-z0-9_\-\.]+@([0-2]?[0-5]?[0-5]\.){3}[0-2]?[0-5]?[0-5]$`

- Match only a dollar amount with the optional $ and + or - preceding characters (note that any number of decimal places may be added):

    `^\$?[+-]?[\d,]*(\.\d*)?$`

    This is similar to the previous regular expression except that only up to two decimal places are allowed:

    `^\$?[+-]?[\d,]*\.?\d{0,2}$`

- Match a credit card number to be entered as four sets of four digits separated with a space, -, or no character at all:

    `^((\d{4}[- ]?){3}\d{4})$`

- Match a zip code to be entered either as five digits with an optional four-digit extension:

    `^\d{5}(-\d{4})?$`

- Match a North American phone number with an optional area code and an optional - character to be used in the phone number and no extension:

    ```
    ^(\(?[0-9]{3}\)?)?\-?[0-9]{3}\-?[0-9]{4}$
    ```

- Match a phone number similar to the previous regular expression, but allow an optional five-digit extension prefixed with either ext or extension:

    ```
    ^(\(?[0-9]{3}\)?)?\-?[0-9]{3}\-?[0-9]{4}(\s*ext(ension)?[0-9]{5})?$
    ```

- Match a full path beginning with the drive letter and optionally match a file-name with a three-character extension (note that no .. characters signifying to move up the directory hierarchy are allowed, nor is a directory name with a . followed by an extension):

    ```
    ^[a-zA-Z]:[\\/]([_a-zA-Z0-9]+[\\/]?)*([_a-zA-Z0-9]+\.[_a-zA-Z0-9]{0,3})?$
    ```

Discussion

Regular expressions are effective at finding specific information, and they have a wide range of uses. Many applications use them to locate specific information within a larger range of text, as well as to filter out bad input. The filtering action is very useful in tightening the security of an application and preventing an attacker from attempting to use carefully formed input to gain access to a machine on the Internet or a local network. By using a regular expression to allow only good input to be passed to the application, you can reduce the likelihood of many types of attacks, such as SQL injection or cross-site-scripting.

The regular expressions presented in this recipe only provide a minute cross-section of what can be accomplished with them. By taking these expressions and manipulating parts of them, you can easily modify them to work with your application. Take, for example, the following expression which allows only between 1 and 10 alphanumeric characters, along with a few symbols to be allowed as input:

```
^([\w\.+-]|\s){1,10}$
```

By changing the {1,10} part of the regular expression to {0,200}, this expression will now match a blank entry or an entry of the specified symbols up to and including 200 characters.

Note the use of the ^ character at the beginning of the expression and the $ character at the end of the expression. These characters start the match at the beginning of the text and match all the way to the end of the text. Adding these characters forces the regular expression to match the entire string or none of it. By removing these characters, you can search for specific text within a larger block of text. For example, the following regular expression matches only a string containing nothing but a U.S. zip code (there can be no leading or trailing spaces):

```
^\d{5}(-\d{4})?$
```

This version matches only a zip code with leading or trailing spaces (notice the addition of the \s* to the start and end of the expression):

```
^\s*\d{5}(-\d{4})?\s*$
```

However, this modified expression matches a zip code found anywhere within a string (including a string containing just a zip code):

```
\d{5}(-\d{4})?
```

Use the regular expressions in this recipe and modify them to suit your needs.

See Also

Two good books that cover regular expressions are *Regular Expression Pocket Reference* by Tony Stubblebine (O'Reilly) and *Mastering Regular Expressions*, Second Edition, by Jeffrey Friedl (O'Reilly).

8.13   Documenting Your Regular Expressions

Problem

You have one or more complex regular expressions that may exist in a file outside of your code. You need a way to place comments within the regular expression itself. These comments will aid others in being able to read and maintain your regular expressions later on.

Solution

Add comments to the regular expression using the # comment character:

```
string matchPattern = @"\\\\           # Find this:  \\
                (?<TheServer>\w*)    # Server name
                \\                   # Find this:  \
                (?<TheService>\w*)\\ # Service name";
```

or add C#-style comments outside of the regular expression string:

```
string matchPattern = @"\\\\" +          // Find this:  \\
                @"(?<TheServer>\w*)" +   // Server name
                @"\\" +                  // Find this:  \
                @"(?<TheService>\w*)\\"; // Service name
```

When using these expressions in a Regex object, the RegexOptions. IgnorePatternWhitespace enumeration value must be added to the options parameter of the Regex object constructor:

```
Regex RE = new Regex(matchPattern,
    RegexOptions.Multiline | RegexOptions.IgnorePatternWhitespace);
MatchCollection theMatches = RE.Matches("The source text goes here...");
```

Discussion

With large and complex regular expressions, it is desirable to break up the expression into manageable pieces and to identify what each piece does. For example, the regular expression in the Solution section will pull the server and service pieces out of a UNC string. By breaking up the regular expression onto separate lines and adding comments to each line, we have allowed other developers (who might not be familiar with regular expressions) to more quickly and easily read and maintain our regular expression.

Typically, you would use the string concatenation and C#-style commenting to comment a regular expression string. However, if you are retrieving the regular expression from an external source, such as a text file, regular expression style commenting (#) is the type to use.

With simpler regular expressions, you can get away with adding a C# comment outside of the regular expression string to indicate what it does. But adding comments to the regular expression itself greatly aids in understanding it.

CHAPTER 9
Collections

Collections are groups of items; in .NET, collections contain objects (including boxed value types). Each object contained in a collection is called an *element*. Some collections contain a straightforward list of elements, while others (dictionaries) contain a list of key and value pairs. The following collection types consist of a straightforward list of elements:

```
ArrayList
BitArray
Queue
Stack
```

The following collection types are dictionaries:

```
Hashtable
SortedList
```

These collection classes are organized under the System.Collections namespace. In addition to this namespace, there is also another namespace called System.Collections.Specialized, which contains a few more useful collection classes. These classes might not be as well known as the previous classes, so here is a short explanation of the list:

ListDictionary

    This class operates very similar to the Hashtable. However, this class beats out the Hashtable on performance when it contains 10 or fewer elements.

HybridDictionary

    This class consists of two internal collections, the ListDictionary and the Hashtable. Only one of these classes is used at any one time. The ListDictionary is used while the collection contains 10 or fewer elements, and then a switch is made to use a Hashtable when the collection grows beyond 10 elements. This switch is made transparently to the developer. Once the Hashtable is used, this collection cannot revert to using the ListDictionary even if the elements number

10 or fewer. Also note that when using strings as the key, this class supports both case-sensitive (with respect to the invariant culture) and case-insensitive string searches through setting a Boolean value in the constructor.

CollectionsUtil

This class contains two static methods: one to create a case-insensitive Hashtable and another to create a case-insensitive SortedList. By directly creating a Hashtable and SortedList object, you will always create a case-sensitive Hashtable or SortedList, unless you use one of the constructors that take an IComparer and pass CaseInsensitiveComparer.Default to it.

NameValueCollection

This collection consists of key and value pairs, which are both of type String. The interesting thing about this collection is that it can store multiple string values with a single key. The multiple string values are comma-delimited. The String.Split method is useful when breaking up multiple strings in a value.

StringCollection

This collection is a simple list containing string elements. This list accepts null elements as well as duplicate strings. This list is case-sensitive.

StringDictionary

This is a Hashtable that stores both the key and value as strings. Keys are converted to all lowercase letters before being added to the Hashtable, allowing for case-insensitive comparisons. Keys cannot be null, but values may be set to null.

The C# compiler also supports a fixed-size array. Arrays of any type may be created using the following syntax:

```
int[] foo = new int[2];
```

where foo is an integer array containing exactly 2 elements.

Arrays come in several styles as well: multidimensional, jagged, and even multidimensional jagged. Multidimensional arrays are defined as shown here:

```
int[,] foo = new int[2,3];      // A 2-dimensional array containing up to 6 elements
int[,,] bar = new int[2,3,4];   // A 3-dimensional array containing up to 24 elements
```

A two-dimensional array is usually described as a table with rows and columns. The foo array would be described as a table of two rows each containing three columns of elements. A three-dimensional array can be described as a cube with layers of tables. The bar array could be described as four layers of two rows each containing three columns of elements.

Jagged arrays are arrays of arrays. Therefore, if you picture a jagged array as a type of two-dimensional array, it could have a different number of elements on each row. A jagged array is defined as follows:

```
int[][] baz = new int[2][] {new int[2], new int[3]};
```

The baz array consists of a one-dimensional array containing two elements. Each of these elements consists of another array, the first array having two elements and the second array having three.

The rest of this chapter contains recipes dealing with arrays and the various collection types.

9.1   Swapping Two Elements in an Array

Problem

You want an efficient method to swap two elements that exist within a single array.

Solution

Use a temporary object to hold one of the items being swapped:

```
public static void SwapElementsInArray(object[] theArray, int index1, int index2)
{
    object tempHolder = theArray[index1];
    theArray[index1] = theArray[index2];
    theArray[index2] = tempHolder;
}
```

You can make this method strongly typed by setting theArray parameter type to a specific type. The following overload of the SwapElementsInArray method has been modified to accept an array of integers. This fix will prevent any costly boxing operations in the code that actually swaps the two elements:

```
public static void SwapElementsInArray(int[] theArray, int index1, int index2)
{
    int tempHolder = theArray[index1];
    theArray[index1] = theArray[index2];
    theArray[index2] = tempHolder;
}
```

Discussion

There is no specific method in the .NET Framework that allows only two specific elements to be swapped within an array. The SwapElementsInArray method presented in this recipe allows for only two specified elements of an array (specified in the index1 and index2 arguments to this method).

The following code uses the SwapElementsInArray method to swap the zeroth and fourth elements in an array of integers:

```
public static void TestSwapArrayElements()
{
    int[] someArray = new int[5] {1,2,3,4,5};

    for (int counter = 0; counter < someArray.Length; counter++)
    {
```

```
        Console.WriteLine("Element " + counter + " = " + someArray[counter]);
    }

    SwapElementsInArray(someArray, 0, 4);

    for (int counter = 0; counter < someArray.Length; counter++)
    {
        Console.WriteLine("Element " + counter + " = " + someArray[counter]);
    }
}
```

This code produces the following output:

```
Element 0 = 1      ← The original array
Element 1 = 2
Element 2 = 3
Element 3 = 4
Element 4 = 5

Element 0 = 5      ← The array with reversed elements
Element 1 = 2
Element 2 = 3
Element 3 = 4
Element 4 = 1
```

9.2   Quickly Reversing an Array

Problem

You want an efficient method to reverse the order of elements within an array.

Solution

You can use the static Reverse method, as in this snippet of code:

```
int[] someArray = new int[5] {1,2,3,4,5};
Array.Reverse(someArray);
```

or you can write your own reversal method:

```
public static void DoReversal(int[] theArray)
{
    int tempHolder = 0;

    if (theArray.Length > 0)
    {
        for (int counter = 0; counter < (theArray.Length / 2); counter++)
        {
            tempHolder = theArray[counter];
            theArray[counter] = theArray[theArray.Length - counter - 1];
            theArray[theArray.Length - counter - 1] = tempHolder;
        }
    }
    else
    {
```

```
        Console.WriteLine("Nothing to reverse");
    }
}
```

While there is more code to write, the benefit of the DoReversal method is that it is about twice as fast as the Array.Reverse method. In addition, you can tailor the DoReversal method to a specific situation. For example, the DoReversal method accepts a value type array (int), whereas the Array.Reverse method accepts only a reference type (System.Array). This means that a boxing operation will occur for the int value types. The DoReversal method removes any boxing operations.

Discussion

The following TestArrayReversal method creates a test array of five integers and displays the elements in their initial order. Next, the DoReversal method is called to reverse the elements in the array. After this method returns, the array is then displayed a second time as a reversed array:

```
public unsafe static void TestArrayReversal()
{
    int[] someArray = new int[5] {1,2,3,4,5};

    for (int counter = 0; counter < someArray.Length; counter++)
    {
        Console.WriteLine("Element " + counter + " = " + someArray[counter]);
    }

    DoReversal(someArray);

    for (int counter = 0; counter < someArray.Length; counter++)
    {
        Console.WriteLine("Element " + counter + " = " + someArray[counter]);
    }
}
```

This code displays the following:

```
Element 0 = 1      ← The original array
Element 1 = 2
Element 2 = 3
Element 3 = 4
Element 4 = 5

Element 0 = 5      ← The reversed array
Element 1 = 4
Element 2 = 3
Element 3 = 2
Element 4 = 1
```

Reversing the elements in an array is a fairly common routine. The algorithm here swaps elements in the array until it is fully reversed. The DoReversal method accepts two parameters. The first (*theArray*) is a pointer to the first element in the array that is to be reversed. The second (*theArray.Length*) is an integer describing the length of this array; in this case it is set to five.

The array is actually reversed inside of the for loop. The for loop counts from zero (the first element in the array) to a value equal to the array's length divided by two:

```
for (int counter = 0; counter < (theArray.Length / 2); counter++)
```

Note that this is *integer division*, so if the array length is an odd number, any digits to the right of the decimal point are truncated. Since our array length is five, the for loop counts from zero to two.

Inside of the loop are three lines of code:

```
tempHolder = theArray[counter];
theArray[counter] = theArray[theArray.Length - counter - 1];
theArray[theArray.Length - counter - 1] = tempHolder;
```

These three lines swap the first half of the array with the second half. As the for loop counts from zero, these three lines swap the first and last elements in the array. The loop increments the counter by one, allowing the second element and the next to last element to be swapped. This continues on until all elements in the array have been swapped.

There is one element in the array that cannot be swapped; this is the middle element of an array with an odd number for the length. For example, in our code, we have five elements in the array. The third element should not be swapped. Put another way, all of the other elements pivot on this third element when they are swapped. This does not occur when the length of the array is an even number.

By dividing the array length by two, we can compensate for even or odd array elements. Since we get back an integer number from this division, we can easily skip over the middle element in an array with an odd length.

See Also

See Recipes 9.3 and 9.4; see the "Array.Reverse Method" topic in the MSDN documentation.

9.3   Reversing a Two-Dimensional Array

Problem

You need to reverse each row in a two-dimensional array. The Array.Reverse method does not support this.

Solution

Use two loops; one to iterate over rows, the other to iterate over columns:

```
public static void Reverse2DimArray(int[,] theArray)
{
    for (int rowIndex = 0;
        rowIndex <= (theArray.GetUpperBound(0)); rowIndex++)
```

```
            {
                for (int colIndex = 0;
                    colIndex <= (theArray.GetUpperBound(1) / 2); colIndex++)
                {
                    int tempHolder = theArray[rowIndex, colIndex];
                    theArray[rowIndex, colIndex] =
                        theArray[rowIndex, theArray.GetUpperBound(1) - colIndex];
                    theArray[rowIndex, theArray.GetUpperBound(1) - colIndex] =
                        tempHolder;
                }
            }
        }
    }
```

Discussion

The following TestReverse2DimArray method shows how the Reverse2DimArray method is used:

```
public static void TestReverse2DimArray()
{
    int[,] someArray =
        new int[5,3] {{1,2,3},{4,5,6},{7,8,9},{10,11,12},{13,14,15}};

    // Display the original array
    foreach (int i in someArray)
    {
        Console.WriteLine(i);
    }
    Console.WriteLine();

    Reverse2DimArray(someArray);

    // Display the reversed array
    foreach (int i in someArray)
    {
        Console.WriteLine(i);
    }
}
```

This method displays the following:

```
1
2
3
4
5
6
7
8
9
10
11
12
13
14
15
```

```
3      ← Note that each row of 3 elements are reversed
2
1
6      ← This is the start of the next row
5
4
9
8
7
12
11
10
15
14
13
```

The `Reverse2DimArray` method uses the same logic presented in the previous recipe to reverse the array; however, a nested for loop is used instead of a single for loop. The outer for loop iterates over each row of the array (there are five rows in the `someArray` array). The inner for loop is used to iterate over each column of the array (there are three columns in the `someArray` array). The reverse logic is then applied to the elements handled by the inner for loop, which allows each row in the array to be reversed.

See Also

Recipes 9.2 and 9.4.

9.4   Reversing a Jagged Array

Problem

The `Array.Reverse` method does not provide a way to reverse each subarray in a jagged array. You need this functionality.

Solution

Use the `ReverseJaggedArray` method:

```
public static void ReverseJaggedArray(int[][] theArray)
{
    for (int rowIndex = 0;
      rowIndex <= (theArray.GetUpperBound(0)); rowIndex++)
    {
        for (int colIndex = 0;
            colIndex <= (theArray[rowIndex].GetUpperBound(0) / 2);
            colIndex++)
        {
            int tempHolder = theArray[rowIndex][colIndex];
            theArray[rowIndex][colIndex] =
              theArray[rowIndex][theArray[rowIndex].GetUpperBound(0) -
```

```
                            colIndex];
            theArray[rowIndex][theArray[rowIndex].GetUpperBound(0) -
                    colIndex] = tempHolder;
        }
    }
}
```

Discussion

The following TestReverseJaggedArray method shows how the ReverseJaggedArray method is used:

```
public static void TestReverseJaggedArray()
{
    int[][] someArray =
      new int[][] {new int[3] {1,2,3}, new int[6]{10,11,12,13,14,15}};

    // Display the original array
    for (int rowIndex = 0; rowIndex < someArray.Length; rowIndex++)
    {
        for (int colIndex = 0;
          colIndex < someArray[rowIndex].Length; colIndex++)
        {
            Console.WriteLine(someArray[rowIndex][colIndex]);
        }
    }
    Console.WriteLine();

    ReverseJaggedArray(someArray);

    // Display the reversed array
    for (int rowIndex = 0; rowIndex < someArray.Length; rowIndex++)
    {
        for (int colIndex = 0;
          colIndex < someArray[rowIndex].Length; colIndex++)
        {
            Console.WriteLine(someArray[rowIndex][colIndex]);
        }
    }
}
```

This method displays the following:

```
1
2
3
10
11
12
13
14
15

3     ← The first reversed subarray
2
```

```
1
15    ← The second reversed subarray
14
13
12    ← The third reversed subarray
11
10
```

The logic used to reverse each subarray of a jagged array is very similar to the reversal logic discussed in the previous recipe. The ReverseJaggedArray method uses the same basic logic presented in Recipe 9.2 to reverse each element in the array; however, a nested for loop is used instead of a single for loop. The outer for loop iterates over each element of the first dimensioned array of the jagged array (there are two elements in this array). The inner for loop is used to iterate over each array contained within the second dimensioned array of the jagged array. The reverse logic is then applied to the elements handled by the inner for loop. This allows each array contained by the first dimensioned array in the jagged array to be reversed.

See Also

Recipes 9.2 and 9.3.

9.5   A More Flexible StackTrace Class

Problem

You have a StackTrace class containing a listing of stack frames. You need to iterate through these stack frames as if you were using an Array type object.

Solution

Use the *adapter design pattern* to adapt the public interface of a StackTrace object to look like a Collection type object. The StackTraceArray class implements this design pattern:

```
using System;
using System.Collections;
using System.Diagnostics;
using System.Reflection;
using System.Text;
using System.Threading;

public class StackTraceArray : StackTrace, IList
{
    public StackTraceArray() : base()
    {
        InitInternalFrameArray();
    }

    public StackTraceArray(bool needFileInfo) : base(needFileInfo)
```

```csharp
{
    InitInternalFrameArray();
}

public StackTraceArray(Exception e) : base(e)
{
    InitInternalFrameArray();
}

public StackTraceArray(int skipFrames) : base(skipFrames)
{
    InitInternalFrameArray();
}

public StackTraceArray(StackFrame frame) : base(frame)
{
    InitInternalFrameArray();
}

public StackTraceArray(Exception e, bool needFileInfo) : base(e, needFileInfo)
{
    InitInternalFrameArray();
}

public StackTraceArray(Exception e, int skipFrames) : base(e, skipFrames)
{
    InitInternalFrameArray();
}

public StackTraceArray(int skipFrames, bool needFileInfo) :
    base(skipFrames, needFileInfo)
{
    InitInternalFrameArray();
}

public StackTraceArray(Thread targetThread, bool needFileInfo) :
    base(targetThread, needFileInfo)
{
    InitInternalFrameArray();
}

public StackTraceArray(Exception e, int skipFrames, bool needFileInfo) :
        base(e, skipFrames, needFileInfo)
{
    InitInternalFrameArray();
}

private StackFrame[] internalFrameArray = null;

private void InitInternalFrameArray()
{
    internalFrameArray = new StackFrame[this.FrameCount];

    for (int counter = 0; counter < base.FrameCount; counter++)
```

```csharp
    {
        internalFrameArray[counter] = base.GetFrame(counter);
    }
}

public string GetFrameAsString(int index)
{
    StringBuilder str = new StringBuilder("\tat ");
    str.Append(GetFrame(index).GetMethod().DeclaringType.FullName);
    str.Append(".");
    str.Append(GetFrame(index).GetMethod().Name);
    str.Append("(");
    foreach (ParameterInfo PI in GetFrame(index).GetMethod().GetParameters())
    {
        str.Append(PI.ParameterType.Name);
        if (PI.Position < (GetFrame(index).GetMethod().GetParameters().Length - 1))
        {
            str.Append(", ");
        }
    }
    str.Append(")");

    return (str.ToString());
}

// IList properties/methods
public bool IsFixedSize
{
    get {return (internalFrameArray.IsFixedSize);}
}

public bool IsReadOnly
{
    get {return (true);}
}

// Note that this indexer must return an object to comply
//      with the IList interface for this indexer
public object this[int index]
{
    get {return (internalFrameArray[index]);}
    set {throw (new NotSupportedException(
        "The set indexer method is not supported on this object."));}
}

public int Add(object value)
{
    return (((IList)internalFrameArray).Add(value));
}

public void Insert(int index, object value)
{
    ((IList)internalFrameArray).Insert(index, value);
}
```

```csharp
        public void Remove(object value)
        {
            ((IList)internalFrameArray).Remove(value);
        }

        public void RemoveAt(int index)
        {
            ((IList)internalFrameArray).RemoveAt(index);
        }

        public void Clear()
        {
            // Throw an exception here to prevent the loss of data
            throw (new NotSupportedException(
                    "The Clear method is not supported on this object."));
        }

        public bool Contains(object value)
        {
            return (((IList)internalFrameArray).Contains(value));
        }

        public int IndexOf(object value)
        {
            return (((IList)internalFrameArray).IndexOf(value));
        }

        // IEnumerable method
        public IEnumerator GetEnumerator()
        {
            return (internalFrameArray.GetEnumerator());
        }

        // ICollection properties/methods
        public int Count
        {
            get {return (internalFrameArray.Length);}
        }

        public bool IsSynchronized
        {
            get {return (internalFrameArray.IsSynchronized);}
        }

        public object SyncRoot
        {
            get {return (internalFrameArray.SyncRoot);}
        }

        public void CopyTo(Array array, int index)
        {
            internalFrameArray.CopyTo(array, index);
        }
    }
}
```

Discussion

The *adapter design pattern* allows an existing object to be tailored to operate like a different object. Basically, a new class is created to act the same as the original class. This new object exposes an interface of the desired type, and the exposed members adapt and forward their calls to the underlying original class.

This can be done using several techniques. One technique involves using containment. A new class is created that contains a reference to the original class. This new class acts as an intermediary class and forwards calls to the contained original class. A second technique, which is used in this recipe, is to use inheritance to create a totally new class, which then exposes a different interface used to forward calls to the base class members.

This recipe adapts the System.Diagnostics.StackTrace class to look and act like a collection of stack frames. The StackTrace class provides a convenient way to obtain a stack trace from the current point in code, an exception object, or a specific thread. Unfortunately, the StackTrace provides only a very simplified way to get at each stack frame. It would be much better if the StackTrace object operated like an array. To make this happen, an intermediate object called StackTraceArray is created that inherits from StackTrace and implements the ICloneable, IList, ICollection, and IEnumerable interfaces—the same interfaces that the Array class implements.

The constructors for the StackTraceArray class mimic the StackTrace constructors. Each StackTraceArray constructor passes its work along to the base class using the base keyword:

```
public StackTraceArray() : base()
```

Each StackTraceArray constructor contains a call to the private method InitInternalFrameArray. This private method copies all of the individual StackFrame objects from the base StackTrace object into a private field of type StackFrame[] called internalFrameArray. The StackTraceArray uses the internalFrameArray field as a convenient storage mechanism for each individual StackFrame object; in addition, we get a free implementation of the IEnumerator interface. It also makes it easier to make the StackTraceArray class look and feel more like an array as opposed to a StackTrace object.

Another useful method added to the StackTraceArray class is the public GetFrameAsString method. This method accepts an index of a specific StackFrame object in the internalFrameArray field. From this StackFrame object, it constructs a string similar to the string output for each StackFrame.

The methods implemented from the IList, ICollection, and IEnumerable interfaces forward their calls on to the internalFrameArray field, which implements the same interfaces—throwing the NotSupportedException for most of these interface methods.

The StackTrace object can now be used as if it were an array, through the intermediate StackTraceArray object. To obtain a StackTraceArray object for the current point in code, use the following code:

```
StackTraceArray arrStackTrace = new StackTraceArray();
```

To display a portion or all of the stack trace, use the following code:

```
// Display the first stack frame
Console.WriteLine(arrStackTrace[0].ToString());

// Display all stack frames
foreach (StackFrame SF in arrStackTrace)
{
    Console.WriteLine("stackframe: " + SF.ToString());
}
```

To obtain a StackTraceArray object from a thrown exception, use the following code:

```
...
catch (Exception e)
{
    StackTraceArray EST = new StackTraceArray(e, true);

    Console.WriteLine("TOSTRING: " + Environment.NewLine + EST.ToString());
    foreach (StackFrame SF in EST)
    {
        Console.WriteLine(SF.ToString());
    }
}
```

To copy the StackFrame objects to a new array, use the following code:

```
StackFrame[] myNewArray = new StackFrame[arrStackTrace.Count];
arrStackTrace.CopyTo(myNewArray, 0);
```

You will notice that the first StackFrame object in the stack trace contains something like the following:

```
at AdapterPattern.StackTraceArray..ctor()
```

This is actually the constructor call to our StackTraceArray object. This information is usually not necessary to display and can be removed quite easily. When creating the StackTraceArray object, pass in an integer one as an argument to the constructor. This will force the first stack frame (the one containing the call to the StackTraceArray constructor) to be discarded:

```
StackTraceArray arrStackTrace = new StackTraceArray(1);
```

You should note that the Add, Insert, Remove, and RemoveAt methods on the IList interface of an Array type throw the NotSupportedException because an array is fixed in length, and these methods will alter the length of the array.

See Also

See the "StackTrace Class" and "IList Interface" topics in the MSDN documentation. Also see the "Adapter Design Pattern" chapter in *Design Patterns* by Erich Gamma et al. (Addison Wesley).

9.6 Determining the Number of Times an Item Appears in an ArrayList

Problem

You need the number of occurrences of one type of object contained in an ArrayList. The ArrayList contains methods, such as Contains and BinarySearch to find a single item. Unfortunately, these methods cannot find all duplicated items at one time—essentially, there is no *count all* functionality. If you want to find multiple items, you need to implement your own routine.

Solution

The following class inherits from the ArrayList class in order to extend its functionality. Two methods are added to return the number of times a particular object appears in a sorted and an unsorted ArrayList:

```
using System;
using System.Collections;

public class ArrayListEx : ArrayList
{
    // Count the number of times an item appears in this
    //   unsorted or sorted ArrayList
    public int CountAll(object searchValue)
    {
        int foundCounter = 0;

        for (int index = 0; index < this.Count; index++)
        {
            if (this[index].Equals(searchValue))
            {
                foundCounter++;
            }
        }

        return (foundCounter);
    }

    // Count the number of times an item appears in this sorted ArrayList
    public int BinarySearchCountAll(object searchValue)
    {
```

```
// Sort ArrayList
this.Sort();

bool done = false;
int count = 0;

// Search for first item
int center = this.BinarySearch(searchValue);
int left = center - 1;
int right = center + 1;
int position = -1;

if (center >= 0)
{
    // Increment counter for found item
    ++count;

    // Search to the left
    do
    {
        if (left < 0)
        {
            done = true;
        }
        else
        {
            if (this[left].Equals(searchValue))
            {
                position = left;
            }
            else
            {
                position = -1;
            }

            if (position < 0)
            {
                done = true;
            }
            else
            {
                // Increment counter for found item
                ++count;
            }
        }

        --left;
    }while (!done);

    // Reset done flag
    done = false;

    // Search to the right
    do
```

```
            {
                if (right >= (this.Count))
                {
                    done = true;
                }
                else
                {
                    if (this[right].Equals(searchValue))
                    {
                        position = right;
                    }
                    else
                    {
                        position = -1;
                    }

                    if (position < 0)
                    {
                        done = true;
                    }
                    else
                    {
                        // Increment counter for found item
                        ++count;
                    }
                }

                ++right;
            }while (!done);
        }

        return (count);
    }
}
```

Discussion

The CountAll method accepts a search value (searchValue) of type object. This method then proceeds to count the number of times the search value appears in the ArrayListEx class. This method may be used when the ArrayListEx is sorted or unsorted. If the ArrayListEx is sorted (an ArrayListEx is sorted by calling the Sort method), the BinarySearchCountAll method can be used to increase the efficiency of the searching. This is done by making use of the BinarySearch method on the ArrayListEx class, which is much faster than iterating through the entire ArrayListEx. This is especially true as the ArrayListEx grows in size.

The following code exercises these two new methods of the ArrayListEx class:

```
class CTest
{
    static void Main()
    {
        ArrayListEx arrayExt = new ArrayListEx();
```

```
        arrayExt.Add(-2);
        arrayExt.Add(-2);
        arrayExt.Add(-1);
        arrayExt.Add(-1);
        arrayExt.Add(1);
        arrayExt.Add(2);
        arrayExt.Add(2);
        arrayExt.Add(2);
        arrayExt.Add(2);
        arrayExt.Add(3);
        arrayExt.Add(100);
        arrayExt.Add(4);
        arrayExt.Add(5);

        Console.WriteLine("--CONTAINS TOTAL--");
        int count = arrayExt.CountAll(2);
        Console.WriteLine("Count2: " + count);

        count = arrayExt.CountAll(3);
        Console.WriteLine("Count3: " + count);

        count = arrayExt.CountAll(1);
        Console.WriteLine("Count1: " + count);

        Console.WriteLine("\r\n--BINARY SEARCH COUNT ALL--");
        count = arrayExt.BinarySearchCountAll(2);
        Console.WriteLine("Count2: " + count);

        count = arrayExt.BinarySearchCountAll(3);
        Console.WriteLine("Count3: " + count);

        count = arrayExt.BinarySearchCountAll(1);
        Console.WriteLine("Count1: " + count);
    }
}
```

This code outputs the following:

```
--CONTAINS TOTAL--
Count2: 4
Count3: 1
Count1: 1

--BINARY SEARCH COUNT ALL--
Count2: 4
Count3: 1
Count1: 1
```

The CountAll method uses a sequential search that is performed in a for loop. A linear search must be used since the ArrayList is not sorted. The if statement determines whether each element in the ArrayList is equal to the search criteria (searchValue). If the element is found to be a match, the counter (foundCounter) is incremented by one. This counter is returned by this method to indicate the number of items matching the search criteria in the ArrayList.

The `BinarySearchCountAll` method is somewhat more complex. This method implements a binary search to locate the first item matching the search criteria (searchValue) in the `ArrayList`. If one is found, the count variable is incremented by one and the algorithm proceeds to search to the left and right of the first found element. This first found item is used as a pivot point to locate all other matching items that exist around it. First, it searches to the left of the initially found item. Once it encounters the start of the `ArrayList` or an item that does not match searchValue, the searching to the left stops and searching to the right of the initially found item starts. Searching to the right continues until the end of the `ArrayList` is reached or an item is found that does not match searchValue. Every time an element is found to the right or left of the initially found item, the count variable is incremented by one; the value of this variable is then returned to the caller.

Recipe 9.7 contains a variation of this recipe that returns the actual items found, rather than a count.

See Also

See Recipe 9.7; see the "ArrayList Class" topic in the MSDN documentation.

9.7 Retrieving All Instances of a Specific Item in an ArrayList

Problem

You need to retrieve every object that matches a search criteria contained in an `ArrayList`. The `ArrayList` contains the `BinarySearch` method to find a single item— essentially, there is no *find all* functionality. If you want to find all items duplicated in an `ArrayList`, you must write your own routine.

Solution

The following class inherits from the `ArrayList` class in order to extend its functionality. Two methods are added to return an array of all the matching objects found in this sorted or unsorted `ArrayList`:

```
using System;
using System.Collections;

public class ArrayListEx : ArrayList
{
    // The method to retrieve all matching objects in a
    //   sorted or unsorted ArrayListEx
    public object[] GetAll(object searchValue)
    {
        ArrayList foundItem = new ArrayList();
```

```csharp
        for (int index = 0; index < this.Count; index++)
        {
            if (this[index].Equals(searchValue))
            {
                foundItem.Add(this[index]);
            }
        }

        return (foundItem.ToArray());
    }

    // The method to retrieve all matching objects in a sorted ArrayListEx
    public object[] BinarySearchAll(object searchValue)
    {
        // Sort ArrayList
        this.Sort();

        bool done = false;
        ArrayList RetObjs = new ArrayList();

        // Search for first item
        int center = this.BinarySearch(searchValue);
        int left = center - 1;
        int right = center + 1;
        int position = -1;

        if (center >= 0)
        {
            // Add first found
            RetObjs.Add(this[center]);

            // Search to the left
            do
            {
                if (left < 0)
                {
                    done = true;
                }
                else
                {
                    if (this[left].Equals(searchValue))
                    {
                        position = left;
                    }
                    else
                    {
                        position = -1;
                    }

                    if (position < 0)
                    {
                        done = true;
                    }
                    else
                    {
```

```
                            // Add next found to left
                            RetObjs.Add(this[left]);
                        }
                }

                --left;
            }while (!done);

            // Reset done flag
            done = false;

            // Search to the right
            do
            {
                if (right >= (this.Count))
                {
                    done = true;
                }
                else
                {
                    if (this[right].Equals(searchValue))
                    {
                        position = right;
                    }
                    else
                    {
                        position = -1;
                    }

                    if (position < 0)
                    {
                        done = true;
                    }
                    else
                    {
                        // Add next found to right
                        RetObjs.Add(this[right]);
                    }
                }

                ++right;
            }while (!done);
        }

        return (RetObjs.ToArray());
    }
}
```

Discussion

These methods are very similar to the methods used in the previous recipe. The main difference is that these methods return the actual items found in an `object` array instead of a count of the number of times an item was found. The main thing to keep in mind when choosing a method to use is whether you are going to be searching an

ArrayList that is sorted. Choose the GetAll method to obtain an array of all found items from an unsorted ArrayList, and choose the BinarySearchAll method to get all items in a sorted ArrayList.

The following code exercises these two new methods of the ArrayListEx class:

```
class CTest
{
    static void Main()
    {
        ArrayListEx arrayExt = new ArrayListEx();
        arrayExt.Add(-1);
        arrayExt.Add(-1);
        arrayExt.Add(1);
        arrayExt.Add(2);
        arrayExt.Add(2);
        arrayExt.Add(2);
        arrayExt.Add(2);
        arrayExt.Add(3);
        arrayExt.Add(100);
        arrayExt.Add(4);
        arrayExt.Add(5);

        Console.WriteLine("--GET All--");
        object[] objects = arrayExt.GetAll(2);
        foreach (object o in objects)
        {
            Console.WriteLine("obj2: " + o);
        }

        Console.WriteLine();
        objects = arrayExt.GetAll(-2);
        foreach (object o in objects)
        {
            Console.WriteLine("obj-2: " + o);
        }

        Console.WriteLine();
        objects = arrayExt.GetAll(5);
        foreach (object o in objects)
        {
            Console.WriteLine("obj5: " + o);
        }

        Console.WriteLine("\r\n--BINARY SEARCH GET ALL--");
        objects = arrayExt.BinarySearchAll(-2);
        foreach (object o in objects)
        {
            Console.WriteLine("obj-2: " + o);
        }

        Console.WriteLine();
        objects = arrayExt.BinarySearchAll(2);
        foreach (object o in objects)
```

```
        {
            Console.WriteLine("obj2: " + o);
        }

        Console.WriteLine( );
        objects = arrayExt.BinarySearchAll(5);
        foreach (object o in objects)
        {
            Console.WriteLine("obj5: " + o);
        }
    }
}
```

This code outputs the following:

```
--GET All--
obj2: 2
obj2: 2
obj2: 2
obj2: 2

obj5: 5

--BINARY SEARCH GET ALL--

obj2: 2
obj2: 2
obj2: 2
obj2: 2

obj5: 5
```

The BinarySearchAll method is faster than the GetAll method, especially if the array has already been sorted. In the BinarySearchAll method, we have added a call to the Sort method for the current ArrayListEx object; this is done to make absolutely sure that the ArrayListEx has been sorted. You can remove this call if you are absolutely sure that the ArrayListEx will be sorted. If a BinarySearch is used on an unsorted ArrayList, it is highly likely that the results returned by the search will be incorrect.

See Also

See Recipe 9.6; see the "ArrayList Class" topic in the MSDN documentation.

9.8   Inserting and Removing Items from an Array

Problem

You need the ability to insert and remove items from a standard array (System. Array). When an item is inserted, it should not overwrite the item where it is being inserted; instead, it should be inserted between the element at that index and the previous index. When an item is removed, the void left by the element should be closed by shifting around the other elements in the array. However, the Array type has no usable method to perform these operations.

Solution

If possible, switch to an ArrayList instead. If this is not possible, use the approach shown in the following class. Two methods insert and remove items from the array. The InsertIntoArray method will insert an item into the array without overwriting any data that already exists in the array. The RemoveFromArray will remove an element from the array:

```
using System;

public class ArrayUtilities
{
    public void InsertIntoArray(Array target,
      object value, int index)
    {
        if (index < target.GetLowerBound(0) ||
            index > target.GetUpperBound(0))
        {
            throw (new ArgumentOutOfRangeException("index", index,
              "Array index out of bounds."));
        }
            else
        {
            Array.Copy(target, index, target, index + 1,
                    target.Length - index - 1);
        }

        target.SetValue(value, index);
    }

    public void RemoveFromArray(Array target, int index)
    {
        if (index < target.GetLowerBound(0) ||
            index > target.GetUpperBound(0))
        {
            throw (new ArgumentOutOfRangeException("index", index,
              "Array index out of bounds."));
        }
        else if (index < target.GetUpperBound(0))
        {
            Array.Copy(target, index + 1, target, index,
                    target.Length - index - 1);
        }

        target.SetValue(null, target.GetUpperBound(0));
    }
}
```

Discussion

The `InsertIntoArray` and `RemoveFromArray` methods make use of the `Array.Copy` static method to perform their operations. Initially, both methods test to see whether an item is being added or removed within the bounds of the array target. If the item passes this test, the `Array.Copy` method is used to shift items around to either make room for an element to be inserted or to overwrite an element being removed from the array.

The `RemoveFromArray` method accepts two parameters. The first parameter, *target*, is the array from which an element is to be removed; the second parameter, *index*, is the zero-based position of the element to be removed in the array. Elements at and above the inserted element are shifted down by one. The last element in the array is set to the default value for the array type.

The `InsertIntoArray` method accepts three parameters. The first parameter, *target*, is the array that is to have an element added, *value* is the element to be added, and *index* is the zero-based position at which *value* is to be added. Elements at and above the inserted element are shifted up by one. The last element in the array is discarded.

The following code illustrates the use of the `InsertIntoArray` and `RemoveFromArray` methods:

```
class CTest
{
    static void Main( )
    {
        ArrayUtilities arrlib = new ArrayUtilities ( );
        string[] numbers = {"one", "two", "four", "five", "six"} ;

        arrlib.InsertIntoArray(numbers, "three", 2);
        foreach (string number in numbers)
        {
            Console.WriteLine(number);
        }

        Console.WriteLine( );
        arrlib.RemoveFromArray(numbers, 2);
        foreach (string number in numbers)
        {
            Console.WriteLine(number);
        }
    }
}
```

This code displays the following:

```
one
two
three
four
five
```

```
one
two
four
five
```

See Also

See the "Array Class" and "ArrayList Class" topics in the MSDN documentation.

9.9   Keeping Your ArrayList Sorted

Problem

You will be using the `BinarySearch` method of the `ArrayList` to periodically search the `ArrayList` for specific elements. The addition, modification, and removal of elements will be interleaved with the searches. The `BinarySearch` method, however, presupposes a sorted array; if the `ArrayList` is not sorted, the `BinarySearch` method will possibly return incorrect results. You do not want to have to remember to always call the `ArrayList.Sort` method before calling the `ArrayList.BinarySearch` method, not to mention incurring all the overhead associated with this call. You need a way of keeping the `ArrayList` sorted without always having to call the `ArrayList.Sort` method.

Solution

The following class enhances the adding and modifying of elements within an `ArrayList`. These methods keep the array sorted when items are added to it and modified. Note that a `DeleteSorted` method is not required since this method would not disturb the sorting:

```
using System;
using System.Collections;

public class SortedArrayList : ArrayList
{
    public void AddSorted(object item)
    {
        int position = this.BinarySearch(item);
        if (position < 0)
        {
            position = ~position;
        }

        this.Insert(position, item);
    }

    public void ModifySorted(object item, int index)
    {
        this.RemoveAt(index);

        int position = this.BinarySearch(item);
```

```
        if (position < 0)
        {
            position = ~position;
        }

        this.Insert(position, item);
    }
}
```

Discussion

Instead of calling ArrayList.Add directly to add elements, use the AddSorted method to add elements while at the same time keeping the ArrayList sorted. The AddSorted method accepts an object (*item*) to add to *source*.

Likewise, instead of using the ArrayList indexer directly to modify elements, use the ModifySorted method to modify elements while at the same time keeping the ArrayList sorted. Call this method, passing in the object to replace the existing object (*item*), and the index of the object to modify (*index*).

The following code exercises the SortedArrayList class:

```
class CTest
{
    static void Main( )
    {
        // Create a SortedArrayList and populate it with
        //     randomly choosen numbers
        SortedArrayList sortedAL = new SortedArrayList( );
        sortedAL.AddSorted(200);
        sortedAL.AddSorted(20);
        sortedAL.AddSorted(2);
        sortedAL.AddSorted(7);
        sortedAL.AddSorted(10);
        sortedAL.AddSorted(0);
        sortedAL.AddSorted(100);
        sortedAL.AddSorted(-20);
        sortedAL.AddSorted(56);
        sortedAL.AddSorted(55);
        sortedAL.AddSorted(57);
        sortedAL.AddSorted(200);
        sortedAL.AddSorted(-2);
        sortedAL.AddSorted(-20);
        sortedAL.AddSorted(55);
        sortedAL.AddSorted(55);

        // Display it
        foreach (int i in sortedAL)
        {
            Console.WriteLine(i);
        }

        // Now modify a value at a particular index
```

```
        sortedAL.ModifySorted(0, 5);
        sortedAL.ModifySorted(1, 10);
        sortedAL.ModifySorted(2, 11);
        sortedAL.ModifySorted(3, 7);
        sortedAL.ModifySorted(4, 2);
        sortedAL.ModifySorted(2, 4);
        sortedAL.ModifySorted(15, 0);
        sortedAL.ModifySorted(0, 15);
        sortedAL.ModifySorted(223, 15);

        // Display it
        Console.WriteLine( );
        foreach (int i in sortedAL)
        {
            Console.WriteLine(i);
        }
    }
}
```

This method automatically places the new item in the `ArrayList` while keeping its sort order; this is done without having to explicitly call `ArrayList.Sort`. The reason this works is because the `AddSorted` method first calls the `BinarySearch` method and passes it to the object to be added to the ArrayList. The `BinarySearch` method will either return the index where it found an identical item or a negative number that we can use to determine where the item that we are looking for should be located. If the `BinarySearch` method returns a positive number, we can use the `ArrayList.Insert` method to insert our new element at that location, keeping the sort order within the `ArrayList`. If the `BinarySearch` method returns a negative number, we can use the bitwise complement operator ~ to determine where the item should have been located, had it existed in the sorted list. Using this number, we can use the `ArrayList.Insert` method to add the item to the correct location in *source* while keeping the correct sort order.

You can remove an element from *source* without disturbing the sort order, but modifying an element's value in the `ArrayList` most likely will cause *source* to become unsorted. The `ModifySorted` method alleviates this problem. This method works similarly to the `AddSorted` method, except that it will initially remove the element from the `ArrayList` and then insert the new element into the correct location.

See Also

See the "ArrayList Class" topic in the MSDN documentation.

9.10   Sorting a Hashtable's Keys and/or Values

Problem

You want to sort the keys and/or values contained in a `Hashtable` in order to display the entire `Hashtable` to the user sorted in either ascending or descending order.

Solution

Use the Keys and Values properties of a Hashtable object to obtain an ICollection of its key and value objects. The methods shown here return an ArrayList of objects containing the keys or values of a Hashtable:

```
using System;
using System.Collections;

// Return an ArrayList of Hashtable keys
public static ArrayList GetKeys(Hashtable table)
{
    return (new ArrayList(table.Keys));
}

// Return an ArrayList of Hashtable values
public static ArrayList GetValues(Hashtable table)
{
    return (new ArrayList(table.Values));
}
```

The following code creates a Hashtable object and displays first keys, and then values, sorted in ascending and descending order:

```
public static void TestSortKeyValues()
{
    // Define a hashtable object
    Hashtable hash = new Hashtable();
    hash.Add(2, "two");
    hash.Add(1, "one");
    hash.Add(5, "five");
    hash.Add(4, "four");
    hash.Add(3, "three");

    // Get all the keys in the hashtable and sort them
    ArrayList keys = GetKeys(hash);
    keys.Sort();

    // Display sorted key list
    foreach (object obj in keys)
        Console.WriteLine("Key: " + obj + "    Value: " + hash[obj]);

    // Reverse the sorted key list
    Console.WriteLine();
    keys.Reverse();

    // Display reversed key list
    foreach (object obj in keys)
        Console.WriteLine("Key: " + obj + "    Value: " + hash[obj]);

    // Get all the values in the hashtable and sort them
    Console.WriteLine();
    Console.WriteLine();
    ArrayList values = GetValues(hash);
```

```
        values.Sort( );
        foreach (object obj in values)
            Console.WriteLine("Value: " + obj);

        // Reverse the sorted value list
        Console.WriteLine( );
        values.Reverse( );
        foreach (object obj in values)
            Console.WriteLine("Value: " + obj);
}
```

The key/value pairs are displayed as shown:

```
Key: 1    Value: one
Key: 2    Value: two
Key: 3    Value: three
Key: 4    Value: four
Key: 5    Value: five

Key: 5    Value: five
Key: 4    Value: four
Key: 3    Value: three
Key: 2    Value: two
Key: 1    Value: one

Value: five      ← Notice that the values are sorted alphabetically
Value: four
Value: one
Value: three
Value: two

Value: two
Value: three
Value: one
Value: four
Value: five
```

Discussion

The Hashtable object exposes two useful properties for obtaining a collection of its keys or values. The Keys property returns an ICollection containing all the keys currently in the Hashtable. The Values property returns the same for all values currently contained in the Hashtable.

The GetKeys method uses the Keys property. Once the ICollection of keys is returned through this property, a new ArrayList is created to hold the keys. This ArrayList is then returned to the caller. The GetValues method works in a similar manner except that it uses the Values property.

The ICollection object returned either from the Keys or Values properties of a Hashtable object are direct references to the key and value collections within the Hashtable. This means that if the keys and/or values change in a Hashtable, the key and value collections will be altered accordingly.

See Also

See the "Hashtable Class" and "ArrayList Class" topics in the MSDN documentation.

9.11 Creating a Hashtable with Max and Min Size Boundaries

Problem

You need to use a Hashtable in your project that allows you to set the maximum and/or minimum number of elements that it can hold.

Solution

Use the MaxMinSizeHashtable class defined here. This class allows a definition of a maximum and a minimum size beyond which this MaxMinSizeHashtable cannot grow or shrink:

```
using System;
using System.Collections;

[Serializable]
public class MaxMinSizeHashtable : Hashtable
{
    public MaxMinSizeHashtable( ) : base(10)
    {
    }

    public MaxMinSizeHashtable(int minSize, int maxSize)
        : base(maxSize)
    {
        if (minSize >= 0 && maxSize > 0)
        {
            this.minSize = minSize;
            this.maxSize = maxSize;
        }
    }

    protected int minSize = 0;
    protected int maxSize = 10; // Initial size for a regular Hashtable
    protected bool readOnly = false;

    public bool ReadOnly
    {
        get {return (readOnly);}
        set {readOnly = value;}
    }

    public override bool IsReadOnly
    {
```

```csharp
        get{return readOnly;}
    }

    public override object this[object key]
    {
        get
        {
            return (base[key]);
        }
        set
        {
            if (!readOnly)
            {
                if (key is long)
                {
                    if (long.Parse(key.ToString()) < maxSize &&
                        long.Parse(key.ToString()) > minSize)
                    {
                        base[key] = value;
                    }
                    else
                    {
                        throw (new ArgumentOutOfRangeException("key", key,
                          "The key is outside the minimum/maximum" +
                          " boundaries."));
                    }
                }
                else
                {
                    base[key] = value;
                }           }
            else
            {
                throw (new ArgumentOutOfRangeException("value", value,
                    "This Hashtable is currently set to read-only."));
            }
        }
    }

    public override void Add(object key, object value)
    {
        if (!readOnly)
        {
            if (this.Count < maxSize)
            {
                base.Add(key, value);
            }
            else
            {
                throw (new ArgumentOutOfRangeException("value", value,
                    "No more values can be added to this Hashtable, " +
                    "until one is removed"));
            }
        }
```

```csharp
        else
        {
            throw (new ArgumentOutOfRangeException("value", value,
                "This Hashtable is currently set to read-only."));
        }
    }

    public override void Remove(object key)
    {
        if (!readOnly)
        {
            if (this.Count > minSize)
            {
                base.Remove(key);
            }
            else
            {
                throw (new InvalidOperationException(
                "No more values can be removed from this Hashtable, " +
                "until one is added"));
            }
        }
        else
        {
            throw (new NotSupportedException(
                "This Hashtable is currently set to read-only."));
        }
    }

    public override void Clear()
    {
        if (!readOnly)
        {
            if (minSize == 0)
            {
                base.Clear();
            }
            else
            {
                throw (new InvalidOperationException(
                "Clearing this Hashtable would go below the minimum " +
                "size of " + minSize));
            }
        }
        else
        {
            throw (new InvalidOperationException(
                "This Hashtable is currently set to read-only."));
        }
    }
}
```

Discussion

The `MaxMinSizeHashtable` class inherits from `Hashtable` and overrides the members that allow `Hashtable` values to be added, removed, and modified. The overloaded constructor for the `MaxMinSizeHashtable` class is defined here:

```
public MaxMinSizeHashtable(int minSize, int maxSize)
```

Its parameters are:

minSize

> The smallest number of elements this class can contain

maxSize

> The largest number of elements this class can contain

A public Boolean property called `ReadOnly` has been added to this class to allow or prevent the use of the `Add`, `Remove`, and `Clear` methods.

The overloaded `Add` method will add the object to the `MaxMinSizeHashtable` only when it is not read-only and the current size is less than the `maxSize` field. If all tests pass, the value is added to the `MaxMinSizeHashtable`.

The overloaded `Remove` method is overloaded to validate that the size of the `MaxMinSizeHashtable` does not fall below the number specific by the `minSize` field. The `Clear` method is also overridden to verify that the `minSize` field is zero before this operation is allowed to proceed, since this operation will leave zero elements in this `MaxMinSizeHashtable`.

As a final point, the overloaded constructor accepts *minSize* and *maxSize* as signed integers. Obviously the `MaxMinSizeHashtable` cannot have a negative size. The reason for this is compliance with other .NET languages that may use this class. The unsigned numeric types are not included in the CLS; therefore, they are not CLS-compliant.

Consider what would happen if a Visual Basic .NET object—which does not handle unsigned numeric types—tried to use this object. If the `MaxMinSizeHashtable` constructor accepted only `uint` types and a Visual Basic .NET class attempted to instantiate an instance of the `MaxMinSizeHashtable`:

```
' Visual Basic .NET code
Dim Table As New MaxMinSizeHashtable(2, 4)
```

the Visual Basic .NET compiler would complain that a value of type `Integer` could not be converted to a `System.UInt32` type. Visual Basic .NET has no ability to convert types to and from unsigned types. To make this object and many others in this book compliant, we choose to use signed rather than unsigned numeric types where possible.

See Also

See the "Hashtable Class" topic in the MSDN documentation.

9.12 Creating a Hashtable with Max and Min Value Boundaries

Problem

You need to use a Hashtable in your project that stores only numeric data between a set maximum and minimum value.

Solution

Create a class whose accessors and methods enforce these boundaries. This class, MaxMinValueHashtable, allows only integer values that fall between a maximum and minimum size to be stored:

```
using System;
using System.Collections;

[Serializable]
public class MaxMinValueHashtable : Hashtable
{
    public MaxMinValueHashtable() : base()
    {
    }

    public MaxMinValueHashtable(int minValue, int maxValue)
        : base()
    {
        this.minValue = minValue;
        this.maxValue = maxValue;
    }

    protected int minValue = int.MinValue;
    protected int maxValue = int.MaxValue;
    protected bool readOnly = false;

    public bool ReadOnly
    {
        get {return (readOnly);}
        set {readOnly = value;}
    }

    public override bool IsReadOnly
    {
        get{return readOnly;}
    }

    public override object this[object key]
    {
        get
        {
            return (base[key]);
        }
```

```
        set
        {
            if (!readOnly)
            {
                if (value is int)
                {
                    if ((int)value >= minValue && (int)value <= maxValue)
                    {
                        base[key] = value;
                    }
                    else
                    {
                        throw (new ArgumentOutOfRangeException("value",
                            value,
                            "Value must be within the range " + minValue +
                            " to " + maxValue));
                    }
                }
                else
                {
                    base[key] = value;
                }
            }
            else
            {
                throw (new ArgumentOutOfRangeException("value", value,
                    "This Hashtable is currently set to read-only."));
            }
        }
    }

// This method has been overridden to allow objects to be
// stored in this Hashtable, as well as integers.
//   If you do not wish objects to be stored in this
//   Hashtable alongside numeric values, simply throw an
//   InvalidOperationException when this method is called.

    public override void Add(object key, object value)
    {
        if (!readOnly)
        {
            base.Add(key, value);
        }
        else
        {
            throw (new ArgumentOutOfRangeException("value", value,
                "This Hashtable is currently set to read-only."));
        }
    }

    public void Add(object key, int value)
    {
        if (!readOnly)
        {
```

```
            if (value >= minValue && value <= maxValue)
            {
                base.Add(key, value);
            }
            else
            {
                throw (new ArgumentOutOfRangeException("value", value,
                    "Value must be within the range " + minValue +
                    " to " + maxValue));
            }
        }
        else
        {
            throw (new ArgumentOutOfRangeException("value", value,
                "This Hashtable is currently set to read-only."));
        }
    }

    public override void Remove(object key)
    {
        if (!readOnly)
        {
            base.Remove(key);
        }
        else
        {
            throw (new ArgumentOutOfRangeException(
                "This Hashtable is currently set to read-only."));
        }
    }

    public override void Clear()
    {
        if (!readOnly)
        {
            base.Clear();
        }
        else
        {
            throw (new ArgumentOutOfRangeException(
                "This Hashtable is currently set to read-only."));
        }
    }
}
```

Discussion

The MaxMinValueHashtable class inherits from Hashtable and overrides the members
that allow Hashtable values to be added, removed, and modified. The overloaded
constructor for the MaxMinValueHashtable class is defined here:

```
public MaxMinValueHashtable(int minValue, int maxValue)
```

This constructor allows the range of values to be set. Its parameters are:

minValue

> The smallest integer value that can be added as a value in a key/value pair.

maxValue

> The largest integer value that can be added as a value in a key/value pair.

A public Boolean property called ReadOnly has been added to this class to allow or prevent the use of the Add, Remove, and Clear methods. The IsReadOnly property of the base Hashtable object cannot be used in this situation, since the IsReadOnly property is a read-only property. For the MaxMinValueHashtable, we needed read/write access to this property. However, the IsReadOnly property is overloaded in the MaxMinValueHashtable to return the value of the ReadOnly property.

The overridden indexer has both get and set. The get returns the value that matches the provided *key*. The set verifies that this object is not read-only; if it is not, the *value* parameter is checked to determine whether it is an integer. If the *value* parameter is an integer, it is checked to determine whether it is within the boundaries of the minValue and maxValue fields before it is set. If the *value* parameter is not an integer, it is set using the *key*.

There are two Add methods: one takes an object and the other takes an integer for its *value* parameter. The Add method that accepts an object will add the object to the MaxMinValueHashtable only when it is not read-only. The other Add method that accepts an integer for its *value* parameter performs the same tests and adds a new test to determine whether the integer value is between, or equal to, the minValue and maxValue fields. If all tests pass, the integer is added to the MaxMinValueHashtable.

See Also

See the "Hashtable Class" topic in the MSDN documentation.

9.13 Displaying an Array's Data as a Delimited String

Problem

You have an array or type that implements ICollection, and that you wish to display or store as a comma-delimited string (note that another delimiter character can be substituted for the comma). This ability will allow you to easily save data stored in an array to a text file as delimited text.

Solution

The `ConvertCollectionToDelStr` method will accept any object that implements the `ICollection` interface. This collection object's contents are converted into a delimited string:

```
public static string ConvertCollectionToDelStr(ICollection theCollection,
    char delimiter)
{
    string delimitedData = "";

    foreach (string strData in theCollection)
    {
        if (strData.IndexOf(delimiter) >= 0)
        {
            throw (new ArgumentException(
            "Cannot have a delimiter character in an element of the array.",
            "theCollection"));
        }

        delimitedData += strData + delimiter;
    }

    // Return the constructed string minus the final
    //    appended delimiter char.
    return (delimitedData.TrimEnd(delimiter));
}
```

Discussion

The following `TestDisplayDataAsDelStr` method shows how to use the overloaded `ConvertCollectoinToDelStr` method to convert an array of strings to a delimited string:

```
public static void TestDisplayDataAsDelStr( )
{
    string[] numbers = {"one", "two", "three", "four", "five", "six"} ;

    string delimitedStr = ConvertCollectionToDelStr(numbers, ',');
    Console.WriteLine(delimitedStr);
}
```

This code creates a delimited string of all the elements in the array and displays it as follows:

```
one,two,three,four,five,six
```

Of course, instead of a comma as the delimiter, we could also have used a semicolon, dash, or any other character. The delimiter type was made a char because it is best to use only a single delimiting character if you are going to use the `String.Split` method to restore the delimited string to an array of substrings, as the `String.Split` method works only with delimiters that consist of one character.

See Also

See the "ICollection Interface" topic in the MSDN documentation.

9.14 Storing Snapshots of Lists in an Array

Problem

You have an ArrayList, Queue, or Stack object and you want to take a snapshot of its current state. (Note that this recipe also works for any other data type that implements the ICollection interface.)

Solution

Use the CopyTo method declared in the ICollection interface. The following method, TakeSnapshotOfList, accepts any type that implements the ICollection interface and takes a snapshot of the entire object's contents. This snapshot is returned as an object array:

```
public static object[] TakeSnapshotOfList(ICollection theList)
{
    object[] snapshot = new object[theList.Count];
    theList.CopyTo(snapshot, 0);
    return (snapshot);
}
```

Discussion

The following method creates a Queue object, enqueues some data, and then takes a snapshot of it:

```
public static void TestListSnapshot( )
{
    Queue someQueue = new Queue( );
    someQueue.Enqueue(1);
    someQueue.Enqueue(2);
    someQueue.Enqueue(3);

    object[] queueSnapshot = TakeSnapshotOfList(someQueue);
}
```

The TakeSnapshotOfList is useful when you want to record the state of an object that implements the ICollection interface. This "snapshot" can be compared to the original list later on to determine what, if anything, has changed in the list. Multiple snapshots can be taken at various points in an applications run to show the state of the list or lists over time.

The TakeSnapshotOfList method could easily be used as a logging/debugging tool for developers. Take, for example, an ArrayList that is being corrupted at some point in the application. You can take snapshots of the ArrayList at various points in the

---

application using the TakeSnapshotOfList method and then compare the snapshots to narrow down the list of possible places where the ArrayList is being corrupted.

See Also

See the "ICollection Interface" and "Array Class" topics in the MSDN documentation.

9.15 Creating a Strongly Typed Collection

Problem

You have some particular data type (and its descendent types) that you wish to store in a collection, and you do not want users of your collection to store any other data types within it.

Solution

Create a strongly typed collection by inheriting from the CollectionBase abstract base class. There are two ways to create a strongly typed collection; the first is to modify the parameters for all the overloaded methods to accept only a particular type. For example, instead of the Add method accepting a generic Object data type, you can change it to accept only one particular data type. A collection base that accepts only objects of a particular type (Media) or its descendents (Magnetic, Optical, or PunchCard) is shown here (note that the Media class and its descendents are defined in Recipe 3.4):

```
public class MediaCollection : CollectionBase
{
    public MediaCollection() : base()
    {
    }

    public Media this[int index]
    {
        get
        {
            return ((Media)List[index]);
        }
        set
        {
            List[index] = value;
        }
    }

    public int Add(Media item)
    {
        return (List.Add(item));
    }

    public int IndexOf(Media item)
```

```
        {
            return(List.IndexOf(item));
        }

        public void Insert(int index, Media item)
        {
            List.Insert(index, item);
        }

        public void Remove(Media item)
        {
            List.Remove(item);
        }

        public bool Contains(Media item)
        {
            return(List.Contains(item));
        }
    }
```

The next method of writing a strongly typed collection involves the OnValidate event.
This event is fired immediately before any action that modifies the data within the
collection. The next strongly typed collection operates the same as the previous
MediaCollection class, except that it uses an event to make sure that only a particular type and/or its descendents are operated on:

```
public class MediaCollectionEv : CollectionBase
{
    public MediaCollectionEv() : base()
    {
    }

    public object this[int index]
    {
        get
        {
            return (List[index]);
        }
        set
        {
            List[index] = value;
        }
    }

    public int Add(object item)
    {
        return (List.Add(item));
    }

    public int IndexOf(object item)
    {
        return(List.IndexOf(item));
    }

    public void Insert(int index, object item)
```

```
    {
        List.Insert(index, item);
    }

    public void Remove(object item)
    {
        List.Remove(item);
    }

    public bool Contains(object item)
    {
        return(List.Contains(item));
    }

    protected override void OnValidate(object item)
    {
        if (!(item is Media))
        {
            throw new ArgumentException("This collection only accepts " +
                "the Media type or types that derive from Media");
        }
    }
}
}
```

Discussion

Most of the collection types built in to the FCL are generic; that is, they accept only the most basic type—the Object type. Sometimes it is good to have a more specialized collection type (usually referred to as *strongly typed collections*) that can contain only objects of one particular type. Of course, this collection would also be able to contain objects of types descending from this one particular type.

There are several benefits to writing a strongly typed collection, such as reducing the number of potential errors that can be coded into your application. If you are only expecting a particular type to be contained within a collection, and a piece of code inadvertently adds objects not of this type, your code might fail when attempting to operate on this unexpected type. If the first of the two strongly typed collections were used, the compiler would catch this mistake earlier in the development phase. Note that the OnValidate event will work only at runtime.

Another useful side effect of using the first of the two strongly typed collections is that you do not have to cast the object being returned from the collection to its correct type before using it. A strongly typed collection automatically returns the type you expect, as opposed to an Object type, which must then be cast to the expected type.

A benefit of either strongly typed collection is that you can add specialized code to your collection to more easily allow you to operate on the objects contained in your collection. For example, if you wrote a strongly typed collection to contain only Invoice type objects, you could add methods to this collection to do the following:

- Retrieve only those invoices that match a specific criteria, such as being overdue.

- Reject attempts to add invoices to this collection that do not meet a criterion, such as a minimum amount.
- Prevent invoice objects from being removed by throwing a `NotImplementedException` when a `Remove` method is called and overloading the `RemoveAt` method to do the same, so that invoices cannot be removed.

Now that you have a reason for building a strongly typed collection, you have three choices for doing so:

1. Inherit from the `CollectionBase` abstract base class and implement the members so that they operate on a specific type, other than `Object`, as in the `MediaCollection` class defined in the Solution section.
2. Inherit from `CollectionBase` and override the `OnValidate` event, as with the `MediaCollectionEv` class defined in the Solution section.
3. Build your own from scratch (this technique is not covered in this recipe since the previous two ways are much easier to implement).

Many developers opt for the first technique, which involves adding methods to the collection, such as `Add`, `Remove`, `IndexOf`, and others that operate on a specific type. This technique best aids the developer for two important reasons. First, the developer can examine the exact type that this collection is expecting by using the Intellisense features of the IDE. Second, the developer is alerted at compile time when the collection is not being used as it should, via compile-time errors.

The second technique is very similar to the first technique, but instead of writing strongly typed methods such as `Add`, `Remove`, and so on, these methods are written to accept and return the `Object` type. Instead of preventing other data types from being contained in this collection, an event handler, called `OnValidate`, is added to validate the object being added to, removed from, and so on, with regard to the collection. If the object is of the correct type, the event handler does nothing, allowing the collection to perform the specified action. If the object is not of the correct type, an exception is thrown, preventing the collection from performing the specified action.

Note that when using weakly typed methods with the `OnValidate` event handler, the compiler will not be able to validate any use of the strongly typed collection. However, this event handler is useful when you want to consolidate all validation routines for your collection. In fact, there is no reason why the first and second techniques cannot be combined (i.e., strongly typed methods along with the `OnValidate` event handler for further validations).

See Also

See Recipe 3.4; see the "CollectionBase Class" and "Creating and Manipulating Collections" topics in the MSDN documentation.

9.16 Persisting a Collection Between Application Sessions

Problem

You have a collection such as an `ArrayList` or a `Hashtable` in which you are storing application information. This information can be used to tailor the application's environment to the last known settings (e.g., window size, window placement, currently displayed toolbars), or the information can be used to allow the user to start using the application at the same point where the application was last shut down. In other words, if the user were editing an invoice and needed to shut down the computer for the night, the application would know exactly which invoice to initially display when the application was started next time.

Solution

Serialize the object(s) to and from a file:

```
public static void SaveObj(object obj)
{
    FileStream FS = File.Create(dataFile);
    BinaryFormatter binSerializer = new BinaryFormatter();
    binSerializer.Serialize(FS, obj);
    FS.Close();
}

public static object RestoreObj()
{
    FileStream FS = File.OpenRead(dataFile);
    BinaryFormatter binSerializer = new BinaryFormatter();
    object obj = binSerializer.Deserialize(FS);
    FS.Close();

    return (obj);
}
```

Discussion

The `DataFile` constant defines a string value to use as a filename. The `SaveObj` method accepts an object and attempts to serialize it to a file. Conversely, the `RestoreObj` method removes the serialized object from the file created in the `SaveObj` method.

The following code shows how to use these methods to serialize a `Hashtable` object (note that this will work for any type that is marked with the `SerializableAttribute`):

```
public static void TestSerialization()
{
    // Create an object to save/restore to/from a file
```

```
Hashtable HT = new Hashtable();
HT.Add(0, "Zero");
HT.Add(1, "One");
HT.Add(2, "Two");

// Display this object's contents and save it to a file
foreach (DictionaryEntry DE in HT)
    Console.WriteLine(DE.Key + " : " + DE.Value);
SaveObj(HT);

// Restore this object from the same file and display its contents
Hashtable HTNew = new Hashtable();
HTNew = (Hashtable)RestoreObj();
foreach (DictionaryEntry DE in HTNew)
    Console.WriteLine(DE.Key + " : " + DE.Value);
}
```

If you serialize your objects to disk at specific points in your application, you can then deserialize them and return to a known state; for instance, in the event of an unintended shutdown.

See Also

See the "ArrayList Class," "Hashtable Class," "File Class," and "BinaryFormatter Class" topics in the MSDN documentation.

CHAPTER 10

Data Structures and Algorithms

In this chapter, we look at certain data structures and algorithms that are not available for you in the Framework Class Library (FCL) through Version 1.1. Examples are provided for algorithms like hash code creation and string balancing. The FCL does not support every data structure you might need, so this chapter provides solutions for priority and double queues, binary and *n*-ary trees, sets, and a multimap, as well as many other things.

10.1 Creating a Hash Code for a Data Type

Problem

You have created a class or structure that will be used as a key in a Hashtable. You need to overload the GetHashCode method in order to return a good distribution of hash values to be used in a Hashtable (the Discussion section defines a good distribution of hash values). You also need to choose the best hash code algorithm to use in the GetHashCode method of your object.

Solution

The following procedures implement hash code algorithms and can be used to override the GetHashCode method. Included in the discussion of each method are the pros and cons of using it, as well as why you would want to use one instead of another.

In addition, it is desirable, for performance reasons, to use the return value of the GetHashCode method to determine whether the data contained within two objects is equal. Calling GetHashCode to return a hash value of two objects and comparing their hash values can be faster than calling Equals, which individually tests the equality of all pertinent data within two objects. In fact, some developers even opt to compare hash code values returned from GetHashCode, within their overloaded Equals method.

The simple hash

This hash accepts a variable number of integer values and XORs each value to obtain a hash code. This simple algorithm has a good chance of producing an adequate distribution and good performance. Remember to profile and measure it to confirm that it works as well for your particular data set. It fails when you need to integrate more than just numeric values equal or smaller in size to an integer. Its code is:

```
public int SimpleHash(params int[] values)
{
    int hashCode = 0;
    if (values != null)
    {
        foreach (int val in values)
        {
            hashCode ^= val;
        }
    }

    return (hashCode);
}
```

The folding hash

This hash allows you to integrate the long data type into a hash algorithm. It takes the upper 32 bits of the long value and folds them over the lower 32 bits of this value. The actual process of folding the two values is implemented by XORing them and using the result. Once again, this is a good performing algorithm with good distribution properties, but, again, it fails when you need to go beyond the long data type. A sample implementation is:

```
public int FoldingHash(params long[] values)
{
    int hashCode = 0;
    if (values != null)
    {
        int tempLowerVal = 0;
        int tempUpperVal = 0;
        foreach (long val in values)
        {
            tempLowerVal = (int)(val & 0x000000007FFFFFFF);
            tempUpperVal = (int)((val >> 32) & 0xFFFFFFFF);
            hashCode^= tempLowerVal ^ tempUpperVal;
        }
    }

    return (hashCode);
}
```

The contained object cache

This hash obtains the hash codes from a variable number of object types. The only types that should be passed in to this method are reference type fields contained within your object. This method XORs all the values returned by the GetHashCode method of each object. Its source code is:

```
public int ContainedObjHash(params object[] values)
{
    int hashCode = 0;
    if (values != null)
    {
        foreach (int val in values)
        {
            hashCode ^= val.GetHashCode( );
        }
    }

    return (hashCode);
}
```

The CryptoHash method

Potentially the best method of obtaining a hash value for an object is to use the hashing classes built in to the FCL. The CryptoHash method returns a hash value for some input using the MACTripleDES class. This method returns a very good distribution for the hash value, although you may pay for it in performance. If you do not require a near perfect hash value and are looking for an excellent distribution, consider using this approach to calculate a hash value:

```
public int CryptoHash(string strValue)
{
    int hashCode = 0;
    if (strValue != null)
    {
        byte[] encodedUnHashedString =
         Encoding.Unicode.GetBytes(strValue);

        // Replace the following Key with your own
        // key value
        byte[] Key = new byte[16] {1,122,3,11,65,7,9,45,42,98,
                        77,34,99,45,167,211};

        MACTripleDES hashingObj = new MACTripleDES(Key);
        byte[] code =
         hashingObj.ComputeHash(encodedUnHashedString);

        // use the BitConverter class to take the
        // first 4 bytes and use them as an int for
        // the hash code
        hashCode = BitConverter.ToInt32(code,0);
    }

    return (hashCode);
}
```

The CryptoHash method using a nonstring

This method shows how other, nonstring data types can be used with the built-in hashing classes to obtain a hash code. This method converts a numeric value to a string and then to a byte array. The array is then used to create the hash value using the SHA256Managed class. Finally, each value in the byte array is added together to obtain a hash code. The code is:

```
public int CryptoHash(long intValue)
{
    int hashCode = 0;
    byte[] encodedUnHashedString =
        Encoder.Unicode.GetBytes(intValue.ToString());

    SHA256Managed hashingObj = new SHA256Managed();
    byte[] code = hashingObj.ComputeHash(encodedUnHashedString);

    // use the BitConverter class to take the
    // first 4 bytes and use them as an int for
    // the hash code
    hashCode = BitConverter.ToInt32(code,0);

    return (hashCode);
}
```

The shift and add hash

This method uses each character in the input string, strValue, to determine a hash value. This algorithm produces a good distribution of hash codes even when this method is fed similar strings. However, this method will break down when long strings that end with the same characters are passed. While this may not happen many times with your applications, it is something to be aware of. If performance is critical, this is an excellent method to use. Its code is:

```
public int ShiftAndAddHash (string strValue)
{
    int hashCode = 0;
    long workHashCode = 0;

    if (strValue != null)
    {
        for (int counter=0; counter<strValue.Length; counter++)
        {
            workHashCode = (workHashCode << (counter % 4)) +
                        (int)strValue[counter];
        }
        workHashCode = workHashCode % (127);
    }
    hashCode = (int)workHashCode;

    return (hashCode);
}
```

The calculated hash

This method is a rather widely accepted method of creating a good hash value that accepts several different data types and uses a different algorithm to compute the hash value for each. It calculates the hash code as follows:

- It assigns an arbitrary odd primary number to the HashCode variable. This variable will eventually contain the final hash code. Good primary numbers to use are 3, 5, 7, 11, 13, 17, 19, 23, 29, 31, 37, 41, 43, 47, 53, 59, 61, or 67. Obviously, others exist beyond this set, but this should give you a good starting point.

- For numeric types equal to or less than the size of an int and char data types, it multiplies the current HashCode by the primary number selected and then adds to this value the value of the numeric type cast to an integer.

- For numeric types greater than the size of an int, it multiplies the current HashCode by the primary number selected and then adds to this the folded version of this numeric value. (For more information on folding, see "The folding hash" method earlier in this recipe.)

- For char, floating point, or decimal data types, it multiplies the current HashCode by the primary number selected, casts the numeric value to an integer, and then uses the folding method to calculate its value.

- For bool data types, it multiplies the current HashCode by the primary number selected and then adds a 1 for true and 0 for false (you can reverse this behavior if you wish).

- For object data types, it multiplies the current HashCode by the primary number selected and then adds the return value of GetHashCode called on this object. If an object is set to null, use the value 0 in your calculations.

- For an array or collection, it determines the contained type(s) and uses each element of the array or collection to calculate the hash value, as follows (in the case of an integer array named MyArray):

```
foreach (int element in myArray)
{
    hashCode = (hashCode * 31) + element;
}
```

This algorithm will produce a good distributed hash code for your object and has the added benefit of the flexibility to employ any type of data type. This is a high performing algorithm for simple, moderately complex, and even many complex objects. However, for extremely complex objects—ones that contain many large arrays, large Hashtables, or other objects that use a slower hash code algorithm—this algorithm will start performing badly. In this extreme case, you may want to consider switching to another hash code algorithm to speed performance or simply paring down the amount of fields used in the calculation. Be careful if you choose this second method to increase performance; you could inadvertently cause the algorithm to produce similar values for differing objects. The code for the calculated hash method is:

```
public int CalcHash(short someShort, int someInt, long someLong,
                    float someFloat, object someObject)
{
    int hashCode = 7;
    hashCode = hashCode * 31 + (int)someShort;
    hashCode = hashCode * 31 + someInt;
    hashCode = hashCode * 31 +
                        (int)(someLong ^ (someLong >> 32));
    long someFloatToLong = (long)someFloat;
    hashCode = hashCode * 31 +
            (int)(someFloatToLong ^ (someFloatToLong >> 32));

    if (someObject != null)
    {
        hashCode = hashCode * 31 +
                            someObject.GetHashCode( );
    }

    return (hashCode);
}
```

The string concatenation hash

This technique converts its input into a string, and then uses that string's GetHashCode method to automatically generate a hash code for an object. It accepts an integer array, but you could substitute any type that can be converted into a string. You could also use several different types of arguments as input to this method. This method iterates through each integer in the array passed as an argument to the method. The ToString method is called on each value to return a string. The ToString method of an int data type returns the value contained in that int. Each string value is appended to the string variable HashString. Finally, the GetHashCode method is called on the HashString variable to return a suitable hash code.

This method is simple and efficient, but it does not work well with objects that have not overridden the ToString method to return something other than their data type. It may be best to simply call the GetHashCode method on each of these objects individually. You should use your own judgment and the rules found in this recipe to make your decision:

```
public int ConcatStringGetHashCode(int[] someIntArray)
{
    int hashCode = 0;
    StringBuilder hashString = new StringBuilder( );

    if (someIntArray != null)
    {
        foreach (int i in someIntArray)
        {
            hashString.Append(i.ToString( ) + "^");
```

```
        }
    }
    hashCode = hashString.GetHashCode();

    return (hashCode);
}
```

The following using directives must be added to any file containing this code:

```
using System;
using System.Text;
using System.Security.Cryptography;
```

Discussion

The GetHashCode method is called when you are using an instance of this class as the key in a Hashtable object. Whenever your object is added to a Hashtable as a key, the GetHashCode method is called on your object to obtain a hash code to be used by the Hashtable. A hash code is also obtained from your object when a search is performed for your object in the Hashtable.

The following class implements the SimpleHash algorithm for the overloaded GetHashCode method:

```
public class SimpleClass
{
    private int x = 0;
    private int y = 0;

    public override int GetHashCode()
    {
        return(SimpleHash(x, y));
    }

    public int SimpleHash(params int[] values)
    {
        int hashCode = 0;
        if (values != null)
        {
            foreach (int val in values)
            {
                hashCode ^= val;
            }
        }

        return (hashCode);
    }
}
```

This class could then be used as a key in a Hashtable through the following code:

```
SimpleClass simpleClass = new SimpleClass();

Hashtable hashTable = new Hashtable();
hashTable.Add(simpleClass, 100);
```

There are several rules for writing a good GetHashCode method and a good hash code algorithm:

- This method should return the same value for two different objects that have value equality. Value equality means that two objects contain the same data.

- The hash algorithm should return a good distribution of values for the best performance in a Hashtable. A good distribution of values means that the hash values returned by the GetHashCode method are usually different for objects of the same type, unless those objects have value equality. Note that objects containing very similar data should also return a unique hash value. This distribution allows the Hashtable to work more efficiently and thus perform better.

- This method should not throw an exception.

- Both the Equals method and GetHashCode method should be overridden together.

- The GetHashCode method should compute the hash code using the exact set of variables that the overridden Equals method uses when calculating equality.

- The hash algorithm should be as fast as possible to speed up the process of adding and searching for keys in a Hashtable.

- When creating structures, it is always best to override the GetHashCode method if you think this hash code will ever be used, since the ValueType.GetHashCode method is slow. (ValueType.GetHashCode makes use of reflection to obtain a hash value from a type's internal fields.)

- Unless the base class is object, use the base class's GetHashCode value when calculating the hash code.

- Use the GetHashCode values of any contained objects when calculating the hash code of the parent object.

- Use the GetHashCode values of all elements of an array when calculating the array's hash code.

The System.Int32, System.UInt32, and System.IntPtr data types in the FCL use an additional hash code algorithm not covered in the Solution section. Basically, these data types return the value that they contain as a hash code. Most likely, your objects will not be so simple as to contain a single numeric value, but if they are, this method works extremely well.

You may also want to combine specific algorithms to suit your purposes. For instance, if your object contains one or more string types and one or more long data types, you could combine the ContainedObjHash method and the FoldingHash method to create a hash value for your object. The return values from each method could either be added or XORed together.

Once an object is in use as a key in a Hashtable, it should never return a different value for the hash code. Originally, it was documented that hash codes must be immutable, as the authors of Hashtable thought that this should be dealt with by whomever writes GetHashCode. It doesn't take much thought to realize that for mutable types, if you require both that the hashcode never changes, *and* that Equals represents the equality of the mutable objects, *and* that if a.Equals(b), then a.GetHashCode( ) == b.GetHashCode( ), then the only possible value implementation of GetHashCode is one that returns the same integer constant for all values.

The GetHashCode method is called when you are using this object as the key in a Hashtable object. Whenever your object is added to a Hashtable as a key, the GetHashCode method is called on your object to obtain a hash code. This hash code must not change while your object is a key in the Hashtable. If it does, the Hashtable will not be able to find your object.

The GetHashCode method is called when you are using this object as the key in a Hashtable object. Whenever your object is added to a Hashtable as a key, the GetHashCode method is called on your object to obtain a hash code. This hash code must not change while your object is a key in the Hashtable. If it does, the Hashtable will not be able to find your object.

From the perspective of memory consumption, this object will not be able to have its memory freed until the Hashtable is collected causing a noteworthy degree of memory retention.

See Also

See the "GetHashCode Method" and "Hashtable Class" topics in the MSDN documentation.

10.2   Creating a Priority Queue

Problem

You need a data structure that operates similarly to a Queue but that returns objects based on a specific order. When objects are added to this queue, they are located in the queue according to their priority. When objects are retrieved from the queue, the queue simply returns the highest or lowest priority element based on which one you ask for.

Solution

Create a priority queue that orders items as they are added to the queue and return items based on their priority. The PriorityQueue class shows how this is accomplished:

```
using System;
using System.Collections;

public class PriorityQueue : IEnumerable, ICloneable
{
    public PriorityQueue( ) {}
    public PriorityQueue(IComparer icomparer)
    {
```

```csharp
            specialComparer = icomparer;
    }

    protected ArrayList internalQueue = new ArrayList();
    protected IComparer specialComparer = null;

    public int Count
    {
        get {return (internalQueue.Count);}
    }

    public void Clear()
    {
        internalQueue.Clear();
    }

    public object Clone()
    {
        // Make a new PQ and give it the same comparer
        PriorityQueue newPQ = new PriorityQueue(specialComparer);
        newPQ.CopyTo(internalQueue.ToArray(),0);
        return newPQ;
    }

    public int IndexOf(string str)
    {
        return (internalQueue.BinarySearch(str));
    }

    public bool Contains(string str)
    {
        if (internalQueue.BinarySearch(str) >= 0)
        {
            return (true);
        }
        else
        {
            return (false);
        }
    }

    public int BinarySearch(string str)
    {
        return (internalQueue.BinarySearch(str, specialComparer));
    }

    public bool Contains(string str, IComparer specialComparer)
    {
        if (internalQueue.BinarySearch(str, specialComparer) >= 0)
        {
            return (true);
        }
        else
        {
            return (false);
```

```csharp
        }
    }

    public void CopyTo(Array array, int index)
    {
        internalQueue.CopyTo(array, index);
    }

    public virtual object[] ToArray()
    {
        return (internalQueue.ToArray());
    }

    public virtual void TrimToSize()
    {
        internalQueue.TrimToSize();
    }

    public void Enqueue(string str)
    {
        internalQueue.Add(str);
        internalQueue.Sort(specialComparer);
    }

    public string DequeueSmallest()
    {
        string s = (string)internalQueue[0];
        internalQueue.RemoveAt(0);

        return (s);
    }

    public string DequeueLargest()
    {
        string s = (string)internalQueue[internalQueue.Count - 1];
        internalQueue.RemoveAt(internalQueue.Count - 1);

        return (s);
    }

    public string PeekSmallest()
    {
        return ((string)internalQueue[0]);
    }

    public string PeekLargest()
    {
        return ((string)internalQueue[internalQueue.Count - 1]);
    }

    public IEnumerator GetEnumerator()
    {
        return (internalQueue.GetEnumerator());
    }
```

For example, perhaps your application or component needs to send packets of data of differing sizes across a network. The algorithm for sending these packets of data states that the smallest (or perhaps the largest) packets will be sent before the larger (or smaller) ones. An analogous programming problem involves queuing up specific jobs to be run. Each job could be run based on its type, order, or size.

This priority queue is designed so that items—in this case, string values—may be added in any order; but when they are removed from the head or tail of the queue, they are dequeued in a specific order. The `IComparer` type object, a `specialComparer` that is passed in through the constructor of this object, determines this order. The queued string objects are stored internally in a field called `internalQueue` of type `ArrayList`. This was the simplest way to construct this type of queue, since an `ArrayList` has most of the functionality built into it that we wanted to implement for this type of queue.

Many of the methods of this class delegate to the `internalQueue` in order to perform their duties. These types of methods include `Count`, `Clear`, `TrimToSize`, and many others. Some of the more important methods to examine are `Enqueue`, `DequeueSmallest`, `DequeueLargest`, `PeekSmallest`, and `PeekLargest`.

The `Enqueue` method accepts a `string` as an argument and adds it to the end of the `internalQueue`. Next, this `ArrayList` is sorted according to the `specialComparer` object. If the `specialComparer` object is `null`, the comparison defaults to the `IComparer` of the string object. By sorting the `ArrayList` after each item is added, we do not have to perform a sort before every search, dequeue, and peek method. A small performance hit will occur when an item is added, but this is a one-time-only penalty. Keep in mind that when items are removed from the head or tail of this queue, the internal `ArrayList` does not have to be resorted.

There are two dequeue methods: `DequeueSmallest` and `DequeueLargest`. These methods remove items from the head (index equals 0) of the `internalQueue` and from the tail (index equals `internalQueue.Length`), respectively. Before returning the string, these methods will remove that string from the queue. The `PeekSmallest` and `PeekLargest` methods work in a similar manner, except that they do not remove the string from the queue.

Two other methods of interest are the `ContainsString` and `Contains` methods. The only real difference between these two methods is that the `Contains` method uses the `IComparer` interface of the `string` object, whereas the `Contains` method uses the `specialComparer` interface to use when searching for a string in the `internalQueue`, if one is provided.

The `PriorityQueue` class members are listed in Table 10-1.

Table 10-1. PriorityQueue class members

Member	Description
Count property	Returns an int indicating the number of items in the queue.
Clear method	Removes all items from the queue.
Clone method	Returns a copy of the PriorityQueue object.
IndexOf method	Returns the zero-based index of the queue item that contains a particular search string. Its syntax is: IndexOf(string *str*) where *str* is the string to be found in the queue.
Contains method	Returns a bool indicating whether a particular search string is found in the queue. Its syntax is: Contains(string *str*) where *str* is the string to be found in the queue.
BinarySearch method	Returns the zero-based index of the queue item that contains a particular search string. Its syntax is: BinarySearch(string *str*) where *str* is the string to be found in the queue. The comparison of *str* with the strings found in the queue is handled by the IComparer implementation, if one was passed as an argument to one of the overloads of the PriorityQueue class constructor.
Contains method	Returns a bool indicating whether a particular search string is found in the queue. Its syntax is: Contains(string *str*) where *str* is the string to be found in the queue. The comparison of *str* with the strings found in the queue is handled by the IComparer implementation, if one was passed as an argument to one of the overloads of the PriorityQueue class constructor.
CopyTo method	Copies the queue items to a one-dimensional array starting at a particular position in the queue. Its syntax is: CopyTo(array *array*, int *arrayIndex*) where *array* is the array to receive the copy of the queue items and *arrayIndex* is the position in the queue from which to begin copying items.
ToArray method	Copies the items in the queue to an object array.
TrimToSize method	Sets the capacity of the queue to the current count of its items. If the TrimToSize method is called when no items are in the queue, its capacity is set to a default value.
Enqueue method	Adds an item to the queue and sorts the queue based on either the default sort behavior of each item or on the IComparer implementation passed as an argument to one of the overloads of the PriorityQueue class constructor. Its syntax is: Enqueue(string *str*) where *str* is the string to be added to the queue.
DequeueLargest method	Returns and removes the item at the tail of the queue (i.e., the last item in the queue).
DequeueSmallest method	Returns and removes the item at the head of the queue (i.e., the first item in the queue).
PeekSmallest method	Returns the item at the head of the queue (i.e., the first item in the queue).
PeekLargest method	Returns the item at the tail of the queue (i.e., the last item in the queue).
GetEnumerator method	Returns an enumerator that allows iteration of the items in the queue.

The PriorityQueue can be created and filled with strings using code like the following:

```
class CTest
{
    static void Main( )
    {
        // Create ArrayList of messages
        ArrayList msgs = new ArrayList( );
        msgs.Add("foo");
        msgs.Add("This is a longer message.");
        msgs.Add("bar");
        msgs.Add(@"Message with odd characters
                    !@#$%^&*( )_+=-0987654321~|}{[]\\;:?/>.<,");
        msgs.Add(@"<
                        >");
        msgs.Add("<text>one</text><text>two</text><text>three</text>" +
                "<text>four</text>");
        msgs.Add("");
        msgs.Add("1234567890");

        // Create a Priority Queue with the appropriate comparer
        CompareStrLen comparer = new CompareStrLen( );
        PriorityQueue pqueue = new PriorityQueue(comparer);

        // Add all messages from the ArrayList to the priority queue
        foreach (string msg in msgs)
        {
            pqueue.Enqueue(msg);
        }

        // Display messages in the queue in order of priority
        foreach (string msg in pqueue)
        {
            Console.WriteLine("Msg: " + msg);
        }

        // Dequeue messages starting with the smallest
        int currCount = pqueue.Count;
        for (int index = 0; index < currCount; index++)
        {
            // In order to dequeue messages starting with the largest uncomment
            //    the following line and comment the following lines that
            //    dequeue starting with the smallest message
            //Console.WriteLine("pqueue.DequeueLargest( ): " +
            //                    pqueue.DequeueLargest( ).ToString( ));

            Console.WriteLine("pqueue.DequeueSmallest( ): " +
                                pqueue.DequeueSmallest( ).ToString( ));
        }
    }
}
```

An ArrayList of string messages is created that will be used to fill the queue. A new CompareStrLen IComparer type object is created and passed in to the constructor of the PriorityQueue. If we did not pass in this IComparer object, the output would be much different; instead of retrieving items from the queue based on length, they would be retrieved based on their alphabetical order. (The IComparer interface is covered in detail in the Discussion section.) Finally, a foreach loop is used to enqueue all messages into the PriorityQueue object.

At this point, the PriorityQueue object can be used in a manner similar to the Queue class contained in the FCL, except for the ability to remove items from both the head and tail of the queue.

Discussion

You can instantiate the PriorityQueue class with or without a special comparer object. In the case of our example, this special comparer object is defined as follows:

```
public class CompareStrLen : IComparer
{
    public int Compare(object obj1, object obj2)
    {
        int result = 0;

        if ((obj1 is string) && (obj2 is string))
        {
            result = Compare((string)obj1, (string)obj2);
        }
        else
        {
            throw (new ArgumentException("Arguments are not both strings"));
        }

        return (result);
    }

    public int Compare(string str1, string str2)
    {
        if (str1.Length == str2.Length)
        {
            return (0);
        }
        else if (str1.Length > str2.Length)
        {
            return (1);
        }
        else
        {
            return (-1);
        }
    }
}
```

This special comparer is required because we want to prioritize the elements in the queue by size. The default string IComparer interface compares strings alphabetically. Implementing the IComparer interface requires that we implement a single method, Compare, with the following signature:

```
int Compare(object x, object y);
```

where x and y are the objects being compared. When implementing custom Compare methods, the method is to return 0 if x equals y, less than 0 if x is less than y, and greater than 0 if x is greater than y. This method is called automatically by the .NET runtime whenever the custom IComparer implementation is used. It attempts to convert its two object arguments to strings and, in turn, calls a second overload of the Compare method that accepts two string type arguments. This second Compare method simply returns a 0 if both strings are of the same length, a 1 if the first string argument is larger than the second, and a -1 if the reverse is true.

If we wanted to compare objects other than strings, the previous IComparer interface could be modified as follows:

```
public class CompareObjs : IComparer
{
    public int Compare(object obj1, object obj2)
    {
        int result = 0;

        IComparable comparableObj1 = obj1 as IComparable;
        IComparable comparableObj2 = obj2 as IComparable;
        if(comparableObj1 != null && comparableObj2 != null)
        {
            result = comparableObj1.CompareTo(comparableObj2);
        }
        else
        {
            throw (new ArgumentException(
                        "Arguments do not both implement IComparable"));
        }

        return (result);
    }

    public int Compare(string str1, string str2)
    {
        if (str1.Length == str2.Length)
        {
            return (0);
        }
        else if (str1.Length > str2.Length)
        {
            return (1);
        }
        else
        {
```

```
        return (-1);
      }
   }
}
```

This `CompareObjs` method requires that both objects implement the `IComparable` interface. If they do not, you will need to modify the type to implement this interface. This interface requires the `CompareTo` method to be implemented in the type. The definition of this method is as follows:

```
int CompareTo(object obj)
```

This method accepts an object to compare with this instance. The return value is calculated as follows:

- A negative number less than zero is returned if the current instance is less than *obj*.

- A zero is returned if the current instance is equal to *obj*.

- A positive number greater than zero is returned if the current instance is greater than *obj*.

It is up to you to decide how the `CompareTo` method is implemented and to define what makes two of these objects equal, greater than, or less than one another.

See Also

See the "ArrayList Class," "IEnumerable Interface," "ICloneable Interface," "IComparer Interface," and "IComparable Interface" topics in the MSDN documentation.

10.3   Creating a More Versatile Queue

Problem

You need a queue object in which you can explicitly control the adding and removing of objects to either the head (top) or tail (bottom).

Solution

A queue that allows explicit removal of items from the head and the tail is called a *double-queue*.

This class is defined as follows:

```
using System;
using System.Collections;

[Serializable]
public class DblQueue : ICollection, IEnumerable, ICloneable
{
    public DblQueue( )
```

```csharp
{
    internalList = new ArrayList();
}

public DblQueue(ICollection coll)
{
    internalList = new ArrayList(coll);
}

protected ArrayList internalList = null;

public virtual int Count
{
    get {return (internalList.Count);}
}

public virtual bool IsSynchronized
{
    get {return (false);}
}

public virtual object SyncRoot
{
    get {return (this);}
}

public static DblQueue Synchronized(DblQueue dqueue)
{
    if (dqueue == null)
    {
        throw (new ArgumentNullException("dqueue"));
    }

    return (new SyncDeQueue(dqueue));
}

public virtual void Clear()
{
    internalList.Clear();
}

public virtual object Clone()
{
    // Make a new DQ
    DblQueue newDQ = new DblQueue(this);
    return newDQ;
}

public virtual bool Contains(object obj)
{
    return (internalList.Contains(obj));
}

public virtual void CopyTo(Array array, int index)
```

```
{
    internalList.CopyTo(array, index);
}

public virtual object DequeueHead()
{
    object retObj = internalList[0];
    internalList.RemoveAt(0);
    return (retObj);
}

public virtual object DequeueTail()
{
    object retObj = internalList[InternalList.Count - 1];
    internalList.RemoveAt(InternalList.Count - 1);
    return (retObj);
}

public virtual void EnqueueHead(object obj)
{
    internalList.Insert(0, obj);
}

public virtual void EnqueueTail(object obj)
{
    internalList.Add(obj);
}

public virtual object PeekHead()
{
    return (internalList[0]);
}

public virtual object PeekTail()
{
    return (internalList[internalList.Count - 1]);
}

public virtual IEnumerator GetEnumerator()
{
    return (internalList.GetEnumerator());
}

public virtual object[] ToArray()
{
    return (internalList.ToArray());
}

public virtual void TrimToSize()
{
    internalList.TrimToSize();
}

// Nested Synchronized class
```

```
[Serializable]
public class SyncDeQueue : DblQueue
{
    public SyncDeQueue(DblQueue q)
    {
        wrappedQ = q;
        root = q.SyncRoot;
    }

    private DblQueue wrappedQ = null;
    private object root = null;

    public override int Count
    {
        get
        {
            lock(this)
            {
                return (wrappedQ.Count);
            }
        }
    }

    public override bool IsSynchronized
    {
        get {return (true);}
    }

    public override object SyncRoot
    {
        get {return (root);}
    }

    public override void Clear()
    {
        lock(this)
        {
            wrappedQ.Clear();
        }
    }

    public override object Clone()
    {
        lock(this)
        {
            return (this.MemberwiseClone());
        }
    }

    public override bool Contains(object obj)
    {
        lock(this)
        {
            return (wrappedQ.Contains(obj));
```

```csharp
        }
    }

    public override void CopyTo(Array array, int index)
    {
        lock(this)
        {
            wrappedQ.CopyTo(array, index);
        }
    }

    public override object DequeueHead( )
    {
        lock(this)
        {
            return (wrappedQ.DequeueHead( ));
        }
    }

    public override void EnqueueHead(object obj)
    {
        lock(this)
        {
            wrappedQ.EnqueueHead(obj);
        }
    }

    public override object PeekHead( )
    {
        lock(this)
        {
            return (wrappedQ.PeekHead( ));
        }
    }

    public override object DequeueTail( )
    {
        lock(this)
        {
            return (wrappedQ.DequeueTail( ));
        }
    }

    public override void EnqueueTail(object obj)
    {
        lock(this)
        {
            wrappedQ.EnqueueTail(obj);
        }
    }

    public override object PeekTail( )
    {
        lock(this)
```

```
            {
                return (wrappedQ.PeekTail());
            }
        }

        public override IEnumerator GetEnumerator()
        {
            lock(this)
            {
                return (wrappedQ.GetEnumerator());
            }
        }

        public override object[] ToArray()
        {
            lock(this)
            {
                return (wrappedQ.ToArray());
            }
        }

        public override void TrimToSize()
        {
            lock(this)
            {
                wrappedQ.TrimToSize();
            }
        }
    }
}
```

The double-queue class created for this recipe was developed in a fashion similar to the PriorityQueue in Recipe 10.2. It exposes most of the ArrayList members through wrapper methods. For instance, the DblQueue.Count and DblQueue.Clear methods, among others, simply delegate their calls to the ArrayList.Count and ArrayList.Clear methods, respectively.

The methods defined in Table 10-2 are of particular interest to constructing a double-queue.

Table 10-2. Members of the DblQueue class

Member	Description
Count property	Returns an int indicating the number of items in the queue.
Clear method	Removes all items from the queue.
Clone method	Returns a copy of the DblQueue object.
Contains method	Returns a bool indicating whether the queue contains a particular search object. Its syntax is: Contains(object *obj*) where *obj* is the object to be found in the queue.

Table 10-2. Members of the DblQueue class (continued)

Member	Description
CopyTo method	Copies a range of items from this queue into an array. Its syntax is: `CopyTo(Array array, int index)` where *array* is the array in which the queue will be copied into, and *index* is the index in the queue to start copying items. The head of the queue is at index 0.
DequeueHead method	Removes and returns the object at the head (i.e., position 0) of the queue. This method makes use of the indexer and RemoveAt methods of the internal ArrayList to return the first (zeroth) element in the ArrayList. Its syntax is: `DequeueHead( )`
DequeueTail method	Removes and returns the object at the tail (i.e., position (ArrayList.Count – 1) of the queue. This method makes use of the indexer and RemoveAt methods of the internal ArrayList to return the last element in the ArrayList. Its syntax is: `DequeueTail( )`
EnqueueHead method	Accepts an object type to add to the head of the queue. This method makes use of the Insert method of the internal ArrayList to add an element to the start (zeroth position) in the ArrayList. Its syntax is: `EnqueueHead(object obj)` where *obj* is the object to add to the head of the queue.
EnqueueTail method	Accepts an object type to add to the tail of the queue. This method makes use of the Add method of the internal ArrayList to add an element to the end of the ArrayList. Its syntax is: `EnqueueTail(object obj)` where *obj* is the object to add to the tail of the queue.
PeekHead method	Returns, but does not remove, the object at the head of the queue. This method makes use of the indexer of the internal ArrayList to obtain the first (zeroth) element in the ArrayList. Its syntax is: `PeekHead( )`
PeekTail method	Returns, but does not remove, the object at the tail of the queue. This method makes use of the indexer of the internal ArrayList to obtain the last element in the ArrayList. Its syntax is: `PeekTail( )`
ToArray method	Returns the entire queue as an object array. Its syntax is: `ToArray( )` The first element in the object array (index 0) is the item at the head object in the queue and the last element in the array is the tail object in the queue.
TrimToSize method	Sets the capacity of the queue to the number of elements currently in the queue. Its syntax is: `TrimToSize( )`

The following code exercises the DblQueue class:

```
class CTest
{
    static void Main( )
    {
        DblQueue dqueue = new DblQueue( );
```

```
// Count should be zero
Console.WriteLine("dqueue.Count: " + dqueue.Count);
try
{
    // Attempt to remove an item from an empty queue
    object o = dqueue.DequeueHead();
}
catch (Exception e)
{
    Console.WriteLine(e.ToString());
}

// Add items to queue
dqueue.EnqueueHead(1);
dqueue.EnqueueTail(2);
dqueue.EnqueueHead(0);
dqueue.EnqueueTail(3);

// Clone queue
DblQueue dqueueClone = (DblQueue) dqueue.Clone();
Console.WriteLine("dqueueClone.Count: " + dqueueClone.Count);

// Find these items in the cloned queue
Console.WriteLine("dqueueClone.Contains(1): " + dqueueClone.Contains(1));
Console.WriteLine("dqueueClone.Contains(0): " + dqueueClone.Contains(0));
Console.WriteLine("dqueueClone.Contains(15): " + dqueueClone.Contains(15));

// Display all items in cloned queue
foreach (object o in dqueueClone.ToArray())
{
    Console.WriteLine("Queued Item (Cloned): " + o);
}
dqueueClone.TrimToSize();

// Display all items in original queue
foreach (int i in dqueue)
{
    Console.WriteLine("Queued Item: " + i.ToString());
}

// Find these items in original queue
Console.WriteLine("dqueue.Contains(1): " + dqueue.Contains(1));
Console.WriteLine("dqueue.Contains(10): " + dqueue.Contains(10));

// Peek at head and tail values without removing them
Console.WriteLine("dqueue.PeekHead(): " + dqueue.PeekHead().ToString());
Console.WriteLine("dqueue.PeekTail(): " + dqueue.PeekTail().ToString());

// Remove one item from the queue's head and two items from the tail
Console.WriteLine("dqueue.DequeueHead(): " + dqueue.DequeueHead());
Console.WriteLine("dqueue.DequeueTail(): " + dqueue.DequeueTail());
Console.WriteLine("dqueue.DequeueTail(): " + dqueue.DequeueTail());
```

```
        // Display the count of items and the items themselves
        Console.WriteLine("dqueue.Count: " + dqueue.Count);
        foreach (int i in dqueue)
        {
            Console.WriteLine("Queued Item: " + i.ToString( ));
        }

        // Clear the cloned queue of all items (items are also removed from the
        //  original queue, since this is a shallow copy
        dqueueClone.Clear( );
    }
}
```

Discussion

The `DblQueue` class implements the same three interfaces as the `Queue` class found in the `System.Collections` namespace of the FCL. These are the `ICollection`, `IEnumerable`, and `ICloneable` interfaces. The `IEnumerable` interface forces the `DblQueue` to implement the `GetEnumerator` method. The implementation of the `DblQueue.GetEnumerator` method returns the `IEnumerator` object for the internal `ArrayList`, used to store the queued items.

The `ICloneable` interface forces the `Clone` method to be implemented in the `DblQueue` class. This method returns a shallow copy of the `DblQueue` object.

The `ICollection` interface forces three properties and a method to be implemented by the `DblQueue` class. The `IsSynchronized` and `SyncRoot` methods obtain a synchronized `DblQueue` object that is thread-safe. In addition to these two properties, a static method called `Synchronized` is added to enable clients of this object to obtain a synchronized version of this class. These synchronization properties and methods will be discussed at length in Recipe 13.4.

The `ICollection` interface also forces the `Count` property and the `CopyTo` method to be implemented by the `DblQueue` class. Both of these delegate to the corresponding `ArrayList` property and method for their implementations.

The `Enqueue` and `Dequeue` methods of the `Queue` class found in the FCL operate only on the head of the queue. The `DblQueue` class allows these operations to be performed on both the head and tail of a queue. The `DblQueue` class has the flexibility of being used as a first-in, first-out (FIFO) queue, which is similar in operation to the `System.Collection.Queue` class; or of being used as a first-in, last-out (FILO) stack, which is similar in operation to the `System.Collection.Stack` class. In fact, with a `DblQueue`, you can start off using it as a FIFO queue and then change in midstream to using it as a FILO stack. This can be done without having to do anything special, such as creating a new class.

See Also

See the "ArrayList Class," "IEnumerable Interface," "ICloneable Interface," and "ICollection Interface" topics in the MSDN documentation.

10.4 Determining Where Characters or Strings Do Not Balance

Problem

It is not uncommon to accidentally create strings that contain unbalanced parentheses. For example, a user might enter the following equation in your calculator application:

(((a) + (b)) + c * d

This equation contains four (characters while only matching them with three) characters. You cannot solve this equation, since the user did not supply the fourth) character. Likewise, if a user enters a regular expression, you might want to do a simple check to see that all the (, {, [, and < characters match up to every other), },], and > character.

In addition to determining whether the characters/strings/tags match, you should also know where the unbalanced character/string/tag exists in the string.

Solution

Use the various Check methods of the Balance class to determine whether and where the character/string is unbalanced:

```
using System;
using System.Collections;

public class Balance
{
    public Balance( ) {}

    private Stack bookMarks = new Stack ( );

    public int Check(string source, char openChar, char closeChar)
    {
        return (Check(source.ToCharArray( ), openChar, closeChar));
    }

    public int Check(char[] source, char openChar, char closeChar)
    {
        bookMarks.Clear( );

        for (int index = 0; index < source.Length; index++)
        {
            if (source[index] == openChar)
            {
                bookMarks.Push(Index);
            }
            else if (source[index] == closeChar)
            {
                if (bookMarks.Count <= 0)
                {
```

```
                    return (index);
                }
                else
                {
                    bookMarks.Pop();
                }
            }
        }

        if (bookMarks.Count > 0)
        {
            return ((int)bookMarks.Pop());
        }
        else
        {
            return (-1);
        }
    }

    public int Check(string source, string openChars, string closeChars)
    {
        return (Check(source.ToCharArray(), openChars.ToCharArray(),
                closeChars.ToCharArray()));
    }

    public int Check(char[] source, char[] openChars, char[] closeChars)
    {
        bookMarks.Clear();

        for (int index = 0; index < source.Length; index++)
        {
            if (source[index] == openChars[0])
            {
                if (CompareArrays(source, openChars, index))
                {
                    bookMarks.Push(index);
                }
            }

            if (source[index] == closeChars[0])
            {
                if (CompareArrays(source, closeChars, index))
                {
                    if (bookMarks.Count <= 0)
                    {
                        return (index);
                    }
                    else
                    {
                        bookMarks.Pop();
                    }
                }
            }
        }
```

```
        if (bookMarks.Count > 0)
        {
            return ((int)bookMarks.Pop( ));
        }
        else
        {
            return (-1);
        }
    }

    public bool CompareArrays(char[] source, char[] targetChars, int startPos)
    {
        bool isEqual = true;

        for (int index = 0; index < targetChars.Length; index++)
        {
            if (targetChars[index] != source[startPos + index])
            {
                isEqual = false;
                break;
            }
        }

        return (isEqual);
    }
}
```

The Check method determines whether there is one closing element for every opening element. There are four overloaded Check methods, and each takes three parameters of varying types. These methods return an integer indicating where the offending
character is located, or a negative number if each *openChar* has a matching *closeChar*.

These methods return an integer indicating where the offending string is located, or a
negative number if each *openChars* has a matching *closeChars*.

The code to exercise the Balance class is shown here:

```
class CTest
{
    static void Main( )
    {
        Balance balanceUtil = new Balance( );

        // A string with an unbalanced } char. This unbalanced char is the final
        //      } char in the string.
        string unbalanced = @"{namespace Unbalanced
                            {
                                public class Tipsy
                                {
                                    public Tipsy( )
                                    {
                            }}}}}
                            ";
```

```
// Use the various overloaded Check methods
//     to check for unbalanced } chars
Console.WriteLine("Balance {}: " +
                 balanceUtil.Check(unbalanced, '{', '}'));
Console.WriteLine("Balance {}: " +
                 balanceUtil.Check(unbalanced.ToCharArray(), '{', '}'));

Console.WriteLine("Balance {}: " +
                 balanceUtil.Check(unbalanced.ToCharArray(),
                          new char[1] {'{'}, new char[1] {'}'}));
Console.WriteLine("Balance {}: " +
                 balanceUtil.Check(unbalanced.ToCharArray(),
                          new char[1] {'{'}, new char[1] {'}'}));
    }
}
```

This code produces the following output:

```
Balance {}: 136
Balance {}: 136
Balance {}: 136
Balance {}: 136
Balance {}: -1
```

where a -1 means that the items are balanced and a number greater than -1 indicates the character position that contains the unbalanced character.

Discussion

Determining whether characters have a matching character is actually quite easy when a Stack object is used. A stack works on a first-in, last-out (FILO) principle. The first item added to a stack is always the last one to be removed; conversely, the last item added to a stack is always the first removed.

To see how the stack is used in matching characters, let's see how we'd use it to handle the following equation:

```
((a + (b)) + c) * d
```

The algorithm works like this: we iterate through all characters in the equation, then any time we come upon a left or right parenthesis, we push or pop an item from the stack. If we see a left parenthesis, we know to push it onto the stack. If we see a right parenthesis, we know to pop a left parenthesis from the stack. In fact, the left parenthesis that was popped off of the stack is the matching left parenthesis to the current right parenthesis. If all parentheses are balanced, the stack will be empty after iterating through all characters in the equation. If the stack is not empty, the top left parenthesis on the stack is the one that does not have a matching right parenthesis. If there are two or more items in the stack, there is more than one unbalanced parenthesis in the equation.

For the previous equation, starting at the lefthand side, we would push one left parenthesis on the stack and then immediately push a second one. We consume the a and + characters and then come upon a third left parenthesis; our stack now contains three left parentheses. We consume the b character and come upon two right parentheses in a row. For each right parenthesis, we will pop one matching left parenthesis off of the stack. Our stack now contains only one left parenthesis. We consume the + and c characters and come upon the last right parenthesis in the equation. We pop the final left parenthesis off of the stack and then check the rest of the equation for any other parenthesis. Since the stack is empty and we are at the end of the equation, we know that each left parenthesis has a matching right parenthesis.

For our Check methods in this recipe, the location in the string where each left parenthesis is located is pushed onto the stack. This allows us to immediately locate the offending parenthesis.

See Also

See the "Stack Class" topic in the MSDN documentation.

10.5   Creating a One-to-Many Map (MultiMap)

Problem

A Hashtable can map only a single key to a single value, but you need to map a key to one or more values. In addition, it may also be possible to map a key to null.

Solution

Use a Hashtable whose values are ArrayLists. This structure allows you to add multiple values (in the ArrayList) for each key of the Hashtable. The MultiMap class, which is used in practically the same manner as a Hashtable class, does this:

```
using System;
using System.Collections;

public class MultiMap
{
    private Hashtable map = new Hashtable();

    public ArrayList this[object key]
    {
        get    {return ((ArrayList)map[key]);}
        set {map[key] = value;}
    }

    public void Add(object key, object item)
    {
        AddSingleMap(key, item);
    }

    public void Clear()
    {
```

```
        map.Clear( );
    }

    public int Count
    {
        get {return (map.Count);}
    }

    public bool ContainsKey (object key)
    {
        return (map.ContainsKey(key));
    }

    public bool ContainsValue(object item)
    {
        if (item == null)
        {
            foreach (DictionaryEntry de in map)
            {
                if (((ArrayList)de.Value).Count == 0)
                {
                    return (true);
                }
            }

            return (false);
        }
        else
        {
            foreach (DictionaryEntry de in map)
            {
                if (((ArrayList)de.Value).Contains(item))
                {
                    return (true);
                }
            }

            return (false);
        }
    }

    public IEnumerator GetEnumerator( )
    {
        return (map.GetEnumerator( ));
    }

    public void Remove(object key)
    {
        RemoveSingleMap(key);
    }

    public object Clone( )
    {
        MultiMap clone = new MultiMap( );
```

```csharp
        foreach (DictionaryEntry de in map)
        {
            clone[de.Key] = (ArrayList)((ArrayList)de.Value).Clone( );
        }

        return (clone);
    }

    protected virtual void AddSingleMap(object key, object item)
    {
        // Search for key in map Hashtable
        if (map.ContainsKey(key))
        {
            if (item  == null)
            {
                throw (new ArgumentNullException("value",
                        "Cannot map a null to this key"));
            }
            else
            {
                // Add value to ArrayList in map
                ArrayList values = (ArrayList)map[key];

                // Add this value to this existing key
                values.Add(item);
            }
        }
        else
        {
            if (item == null)
            {
                // Create new key and mapping to an empty ArrayList
                map.Add(key, new ArrayList( ));
            }
            else
            {
                ArrayList values = new ArrayList( );
                values.Add(item);

                // Create new key and mapping to its value
                map.Add(key, values);
            }
        }
    }

    protected virtual void RemoveSingleMap(object key)
    {
        if (this.ContainsKey(key))
        {
            // Remove the key from KeysTable
            map.Remove(key);
        }
        else
        {
```

```
                throw (new ArgumentOutOfRangeException("key", key.ToString(),
                    "This key does not exists in the map."));
        }
    }
}
```

The methods defined in Table 10-3 are of particular interest to using a MultiMap object.

Table 10-3. Members of the MultiMap class

Member	Description
Indexer	The get accessor obtains an ArrayList of all values that are associated with a key. The set accessor adds an entire ArrayList of values to a key. Its syntax is: `this[object key]` where *key* is the key to be added to the MultiMap through the set accessor, or it is the key in which to retrieve all of its associated values via the get accessor.
Add method	Adds a key to the Hashtable and its associated value. Its syntax is: `Add(object key, object value)` where *key* is the key to be added to the MultiMap, and *value* is the value to add to the internal ArrayList of the private map field.
Clear method	Removes all items from the MultiMap object.
Count method	Returns a count of all keys in the MultiMap object.
Clone method	Returns a deep copy of the MultiMap object.
ContainsKey method	Returns a bool indicating whether the MultiMap contains a particular value as its key. Its syntax is: `ContainsValue(object value)` where *value* is the key to be found in the MultiMap.
ContainsValue method	Returns a bool indicating whether the MultiMap contains a particular value. Its syntax is: `ContainsValue(object value)` where *value* is the object to be found in the MultiMap.
Remove method	Removes a key from the Hashtable and all its referent values in the internal valuesTable Hashtable. Its syntax is: `Remove(object key)` where *key* is the key to be removed.

Items may be added to a MultiMap object in the following manner:

```
public static void TestMultiMap()
{
    string s = "foo";

    // Create and populate a MultiMap object
    MultiMap myMap = new MultiMap();
    myMap.Add("0", "zero");
    myMap.Add("1", "one");
    myMap.Add("2", "two");
    myMap.Add("3", "three");
    myMap.Add("3", "duplicate three");
```

```
myMap.Add("3", "duplicate three");
myMap.Add("4", null);
myMap.Add("5", s);
myMap.Add("6", s);

// Display contents
foreach (DictionaryEntry entry in myMap)
{
    Console.Write("Key: " + entry.Key.ToString() + "\tValue: ");
    foreach (object o in myMap[entry.Key])
    {
        Console.Write(o.ToString() + " : ");
    }
    Console.WriteLine();
}

MultiMap otherMap = (MultiMap)myMap.Clone();

// Obtain values through the indexer
Console.WriteLine();
Console.WriteLine("((ArrayList) myMap[3])[0]: " + myMap["3"][0]);
Console.WriteLine("((ArrayList) myMap[3])[1]: " + myMap["3"][1]);

// Add items to MultiMap using an ArrayList
ArrayList testArray = new ArrayList();
testArray.Add("BAR");
testArray.Add("BAZ");
myMap["10"] = testArray;
myMap["10"] = testArray;

// Remove items from MultiMap
myMap.Remove("0");
myMap.Remove("1");

// Display MultiMap
Console.WriteLine();
Console.WriteLine("myMap.Count: " + myMap.Count);
foreach (DictionaryEntry entry in myMap)
{
    Console.Write("entry.Key: " + entry.Key.ToString() +
                "\tentry.Value(s): ");
    foreach (object o in myMap[entry.Key])
    {
        if (o == null)
        {
            Console.Write("null : ");
        }
        else
        {
            Console.Write(o.ToString() + " : ");
        }
    }
    Console.WriteLine();
}
```

```
        // Determine if the map contains the key("2") or the value("two")
        Console.WriteLine( );
        Console.WriteLine("myMap.ContainsKey(2): " + myMap.ContainsKey("2"));
        Console.WriteLine("myMap.ContainsValue(two): " +
        myMap.ContainsValue("two"));

        // Clear all items from MultiMap
        myMap.Clear( );
    }
```

This code displays the following:

```
Key: 2  Value: two :
Key: 3  Value: three : duplicate three : duplicate three :
Key: 0  Value: zero :
Key: 1  Value: one :
Key: 6  Value: foo :
Key: 4  Value:
Key: 5  Value: foo :

((ArrayList) myMap[3])[0]: three
((ArrayList) myMap[3])[1]: duplicate three

myMap.Count: 6
entry.Key: 2    entry.Value(s): two :
entry.Key: 3    entry.Value(s): three : duplicate three : duplicate three :
entry.Key: 6    entry.Value(s): foo :
entry.Key: 4    entry.Value(s):
entry.Key: 5    entry.Value(s): foo :
entry.Key: 10   entry.Value(s): BAR : BAZ :

myMap.ContainsKey(2): True
myMap.ContainsValue(two): True
```

Discussion

A one-to-many map, or multimap, allows one object, a key, to be associated, or *mapped*, to zero or more objects. The MultiMap class presented here operates similarly to a Hashtable. The MultiMap class contains a Hashtable field called map that contains the actual mapping of keys to values. Several of the MultiMap methods are delegated to the methods on the map Hashtable object.

A Hashtable operates on a one-to-one principle: only one key may be associated with one value at any time. However, if you need to associate multiple values with a single key, you must use the approach used by the MultiMap class. The private map field associates a key with a single ArrayList of values, which allows multiple mappings of values to a single key and mappings of a single value to multiple keys. As an added feature, a key can also be mapped to a null value.

Here's what happens when key/value pairs are added to a MultiMap object:

1. The MultiMap.Add method is called with a *key* and *value* provided as parameters.
2. The Add method checks to see whether *key* exists in the map Hashtable object.

3. If *key* does not exist, it is added as a key in the map Hashtable object. This key is associated with a new ArrayList as the value associated with *key* in this Hashtable.

4. If the *key* does exist, the *key* is looked up in the map Hashtable object and the *value* is added to the *key*'s ArrayList.

To remove a key using the Remove method, the key and ArrayList pair are removed from the map Hashtable. This allows removal of all values associated with a single key. The MultiMap.Remove method calls the RemoveSingleMap method, which encapsulates this behavior. Removal of key "0", and all values mapped to this key, is performed with the following code:

```
myMap.Remove(1);
```

To remove all keys and their associated values, use the MultiMap.Clear method. This method removes all items from the map Hashtable.

The other major member of the MultiMap class to discuss is its indexer. The indexer returns the ArrayList of values for a particular key through its get accessor. The set accessor simply adds the ArrayList provided to a single key. This code creates an array of values and attempts to map them to key "5" in the myMap object:

```
ArrayList testArray = new ArrayList();
testArray.Add("BAR");
testArray.Add("BAZ");
myMap["5"] = testArray;
```

The following code makes use of the get accessor to access each value associated with key "3":

```
Console.WriteLine(myMap["3"][0]);
Console.WriteLine(myMap["3"][1]);
Console.WriteLine(myMap["3"][2]);
```

This looks somewhat similar to using a jagged array. The first indexer is used to pull the ArrayList from the map Hashtable and the second indexer is used to obtain the value in the ArrayList. This code displays the following:

```
three
duplicate three
duplicate three
```

This MultiMap class also allows the use of the foreach loop to enumerate its key/value pairs. The following code displays each key/value pair in the MyMap object:

```
foreach (DictionaryEntry entry in myMap)
{
    Console.Write("Key: " + entry.Key.ToString() + "\tValue: ");
    foreach (object o in myMap[entry.Key])
    {
        Console.Write(o.ToString() + " : ");
    }
    Console.WriteLine();
}
```

The outer foreach loop is used to retrieve all the keys and the inner foreach loop is used to display each value mapped to a particular key. This code displays the following for the initial MyMap object:

```
Key: 2  Value: two :
Key: 3  Value: three : duplicate three : duplicate three :
Key: 0  Value: zero :
Key: 1  Value: one :
Key: 4  Value:
```

There are two methods that allow searching of the MultiMap object: ContainsKey and ContainsValue. The ContainsKey method searches for the specified key in the map Hashtable. The ContainsValue method searches for the specified value in an ArrayList in the map Hashtable. Both methods return true if the key/value was found or false otherwise:

```
Console.WriteLine("Contains Key 2: " + myMap.ContainsKey("2"));
Console.WriteLine("Contains Key 12: " + myMap.ContainsKey("12"));

Console.WriteLine("Contains Value two: " + myMap.ContainsValue("two"));
Console.WriteLine("Contains Value BAR: " + myMap.ContainsValue("BAR"));
```

Note that the ContainsKey and ContainsValue methods are both case-sensitive.

See Also

See the "ArrayList Class," "Hashtable Class," and "IEnumerator Interface" topics in the MSDN documentation.

10.6   Creating a Binary Tree

Problem

You need to store information in a tree structure, where the left node is less than its parent node, and the right node is greater than or equal to (in cases where the tree can contain duplicates) its parent. The stored information must be easily inserted into the tree, removed from the tree, and found within the tree.

Solution

Each node must be an object that inherits from the IComparable interface. This means that every node that wishes to be included in the binary tree must implement the CompareTo method. This method will allow one node to determine whether it is less than, greater than, or equal to another node.

Use the following BinaryTree class, which contains all of the nodes in a binary tree and lets you traverse it:

```
using System;
using System.Collections;
```

```
public class BinaryTree
{
    public BinaryTree( ) {}

    public BinaryTree(IComparable value, int index)
    {
        BinaryTreeNode node = new BinaryTreeNode(value, index);
        root = node;
        counter = 1;
    }

    // Use this .ctor when you need to flatten this tree (see recipe 9.15)
    public BinaryTree(IComparable value)
    {
        BinaryTreeNode node = new BinaryTreeNode(value);
        root = node;
        counter = 1;
    }

    protected int counter = 0;              // Number of nodes in tree
    protected BinaryTreeNode root = null;  // Pointer to root node in this tree

    public  void AddNode(IComparable value, int index)
    {
        BinaryTreeNode node = new BinaryTreeNode(value, index);
        ++counter;

        if (root == null)
        {
            root = node;
        }
        else
        {
            root.AddNode(node);
        }
    }

    // Use this method to add a node
    //    when you need to flatten this tree (see recipe 9.15)
    public int AddNode(IComparable value)
    {
        BinaryTreeNode node = new BinaryTreeNode(value);
        ++counter;

        if (root == null)
        {
            root = node;
        }
        else
        {
            root.AddNode(node);
        }

        return (counter - 1);
    }
```

```
    public BinaryTreeNode SearchDepthFirst(IComparable value)
    {
        return (root.DepthFirstSearch(value));
    }

    public void Print()
    {
        root.PrintDepthFirst();
    }

    public BinaryTreeNode GetRoot()
    {
        return (root);
    }

    public int TreeSize
    {
        get {return (counter);}
    }
}
```

The BinaryTreeNode encapsulates the data and behavior of a single node in the binary tree:

```
public class BinaryTreeNode
{
    public BinaryTreeNode() {}

    public BinaryTreeNode(IComparable value)
    {
        nodeValue = value;
    }

    // These 2 ctors Added to allow tree to be flattened
    public BinaryTreeNode(int index)
    {
        nodeIndex = index;
    }

    public BinaryTreeNode(IComparable value, int index)
    {
        nodeValue = value;
        nodeIndex = index;
    }

    protected int nodeIndex = 0;           // Added to allow tree to be flattened
    protected IComparable nodeValue = null;
    protected BinaryTreeNode leftNode = null;    //  leftNode.Value < Value
    protected BinaryTreeNode rightNode = null;   //  rightNode.Value >= Value

    public int NumOfChildren
    {
        get {return (CountChildren());}
    }
```

```
public int CountChildren()
{
    int currCount = 0;

    if (leftNode != null)
    {
        ++currCount;
        currCount += leftNode.CountChildren();
    }

    if (rightNode != null)
    {
        ++currCount;
        currCount += rightNode.CountChildren();
    }

    return (currCount);
}

public int Index
{
    get {return (nodeIndex);}
}

public BinaryTreeNode Left
{
    get {return (leftNode);}
}

public BinaryTreeNode Right
{
    get {return (rightNode);}
}

public IComparable GetValue
{
    get {return (nodeValue);}
}

public void AddNode(BinaryTreeNode node)
{
    if (node.nodeValue.CompareTo(nodeValue) < 0)
    {
        if (leftNode == null)
        {
            leftNode = node;
        }
        else
        {
            leftNode.AddNode(node);
        }
    }
    else if (node.nodeValue.CompareTo(nodeValue) >= 0)
    {
```

```
        if (rightNode == null)
        {
            rightNode = node;
        }
        else
        {
            rightNode.AddNode(node);
        }
    }
}

public bool AddUniqueNode(BinaryTreeNode node)
{
    bool isUnique = true;

    if (node.nodeValue.CompareTo(nodeValue) < 0)
    {
        if (leftNode == null)
        {
            leftNode = node;
        }
        else
        {
            leftNode.AddNode(node);
        }
    }
    else if (node.nodeValue.CompareTo(nodeValue) > 0)
    {
        if (rightNode == null)
        {
            rightNode = node;
        }
        else
        {
            rightNode.AddNode(node);
        }
    }
    else    //node.nodeValue.CompareTo(nodeValue) = 0
    {
        isUnique = false;
        // Could throw exception here as well...
    }

    return (isUnique);
}

public BinaryTreeNode DepthFirstSearch(IComparable targetObj)
{
    // NOTE: foo.CompareTo(bar) == -1   -->   (foo < bar)
    BinaryTreeNode retObj = null;
    int comparisonResult = targetObj.CompareTo(nodeValue);

    if (comparisonResult  == 0)
    {
```

```
                retObj = this;
        }
        else if (comparisonResult > 0)
        {
            if (rightNode != null)
            {
                retObj = rightNode.DepthFirstSearch(targetObj);
            }
        }
        else if (comparisonResult < 0)
        {
            if (leftNode != null)
            {
                retObj = leftNode.DepthFirstSearch(targetObj);
            }
        }

        return (retObj);
}

public void PrintDepthFirst()
{
    if (leftNode != null)
    {
        leftNode.PrintDepthFirst();
    }

    Console.WriteLine(this.nodeValue.ToString());

    try
    {
        Console.WriteLine("\tContains Left: " +
        leftNode.nodeValue.ToString());
    }
    catch
    {
        Console.WriteLine("\tContains Left:  NULL");
    }
    try
    {
        Console.WriteLine("\tContains Right: " +
        rightNode.nodeValue.ToString());
    }
    catch
    {
        Console.WriteLine("\tContains Right: NULL");
    }

    if (rightNode != null)
    {
        rightNode.PrintDepthFirst();
    }
}
```

```
        public void RemoveLeftNode()
        {
            leftNode = null;
        }

        public void RemoveRightNode()
        {
            rightNode = null;
        }
    }
```

The methods defined in Table 10-4 are of particular interest to using a BinaryTree object.

Table 10-4. Members of the BinaryTree class

Member	Description
Overloaded constructor	This constructor creates a BinaryTree object with a root node and a node index *id*. Its syntax is: `BinaryTree(IComparable value, int index)` where *value* is the root node for the tree, and *index* is used for flattening the tree.
Overloaded constructor	This constructor creates a BinaryTree object with a root node. Its syntax is: `BinaryTree(IComparable value)` where *value* is the root node for the tree. Note that this tree may not be flattened.
AddNode method	Adds a node to the tree. Its syntax is: `AddNode(IComparable value, int id)` where *value* is the object to be added and *id* is the node index. Use this method if the tree will be flattened.
AddNode method	Adds a node to the tree. Its syntax is: `AddNode(IComparable value)` where *value* is the object to be added. Use this method if the tree will not be flattened.
SearchDepthFirst method	Searches for and returns a BinaryTreeNode object in the tree, if one exists. This method searches the depth of the tree first. Its syntax is: `SearchDepthFirst(IComparable value)` where *value* is the object to be found in the tree.
Print method	Displays the tree in depth-first format. Its syntax is: `Print()`
GetRoot method	Returns the BinaryTreeNode object that is the root of the tree. Its syntax is: `GetRoot()`
TreeSize property	A read-only property that gets the number of nodes in the tree. Its syntax is: `int TreeSize {get;}`

The methods defined in Table 10-5 are of particular interest to using a BinaryTreeNode object.

Table 10-5. Members of the BinaryTreeNode class

Member	Description

Overloaded constructor	This constructor creates a `BinaryTreeNode` object. Its syntax is:
	 `BinaryTreeNode(IComparable value)`
	 If a tree is to be flattened, the following constructors should be used instead:
	 `BinaryTreeNode(int nodeIndex)`
	 `BinaryTreeNode(IComparable value, int nodeIndex)`
	 where *value* is the object contained in this node, which will be used to compare to its parent. The *nodeIndex* is used for flattening the tree.

NumOfChildren property	A read-only property to retrieve the number of children below this node. Its syntax is: `int NumOfChildren {get;}`
Index property	A read-only property to retrieve the index number of this node. This index value was set in the *nodeIndex* parameter of its constructor. Its syntax is: `int Index {get;}`
Left property	A read-only property to retrieve the left child node below this node. Its syntax is: `BinaryTreeNode Left {get;}`
Right property	A read-only property to retrieve the right child node below this node. Its syntax is: `BinaryTreeNode Right {get;}`
CountChildren method	Retrieves the number of child nodes below this node. Its syntax is: `CountChildren( )`
GetValue method	Returns the `IComparable` object that this node contains. Its syntax is: `GetValue( )`
AddNode method	Adds a new node recursively to either the left or right side. Its syntax is: `AddNode(BinaryTreeNode node)` where *node* is the node to be added. Duplicate nodes may be added using this method.
AddUniqueNode method	Adds a new node recursively to either the left side or the right side. Its syntax is: `AddUniqueNode(BinaryTreeNode node)` where *node* is the node to be added. Duplicate nodes may not be added using this method. A Boolean value is returned; `true` indicates a successful operation, `false` indicates an attempt to add a duplicate node.
DepthFirstSearch method	Searches for and returns a `BinaryTreeNode` object in the tree, if one exists. This method searches the depth of the tree first. Its syntax is: `DepthFirstSearch(IComparable targetObj)` where *targetObj* is the object to be found in the tree.
PrintDepthFirst method	Displays the tree in depth first format. Its syntax is: `PrintDepthFirst( )`
RemoveLeftNode method	Removes the left node and any child nodes of this node. Its syntax is: `RemoveLeftNode( )`
RemoveRightNode method	Removes the right node and any child nodes of this node. Its syntax is: `RemoveRightNode( )`

The following code illustrates the use of the `BinaryTree` and `BinaryTreeNode` classes when creating and using a binary tree:

```
public static void TestBinaryTree( )
{
    BinaryTree tree = new BinaryTree("d");
    tree.AddNode("a");
    tree.AddNode("b");
    tree.AddNode("f");
    tree.AddNode("e");
    tree.AddNode("c");
    tree.AddNode("g");

    tree.Print( );
    tree.Print( );

    Console.WriteLine("tree.TreeSize: " + tree.TreeSize);
    Console.WriteLine("tree.GetRoot( ).DepthFirstSearch(a).NumOfChildren: " +
            tree.GetRoot( ).DepthFirstSearch("b").NumOfChildren);
    Console.WriteLine("tree.GetRoot( ).DepthFirstSearch(a).NumOfChildren: " +
            tree.GetRoot( ).DepthFirstSearch("a").NumOfChildren);
    Console.WriteLine("tree.GetRoot( ).DepthFirstSearch(g).NumOfChildren: " +
            tree.GetRoot( ).DepthFirstSearch("g").NumOfChildren);

    Console.WriteLine("tree.SearchDepthFirst(a): " +
            tree.SearchDepthFirst("a").GetValue.ToString( ));
    Console.WriteLine("tree.SearchDepthFirst(b): " +
            tree.SearchDepthFirst("b").GetValue.ToString( ));
    Console.WriteLine("tree.SearchDepthFirst(c): " +
            tree.SearchDepthFirst("c").GetValue.ToString( ));
    Console.WriteLine("tree.SearchDepthFirst(d): " +
            tree.SearchDepthFirst("d").GetValue.ToString( ));
    Console.WriteLine("tree.SearchDepthFirst(e): " +
            tree.SearchDepthFirst("e").GetValue.ToString( ));
    Console.WriteLine("tree.SearchDepthFirst(f): " +
            tree.SearchDepthFirst("f").GetValue.ToString( ));

    tree.GetRoot( ).RemoveLeftNode( );
    tree.Print( );

    tree.GetRoot( ).RemoveRightNode( );
    tree.Print( );
}
```

Discussion

Trees are data structures where each node has exactly one parent and possibly many children. The root of the tree is a single node that branches out into one or more child nodes. A node is the part of the tree structure that contains data and contains the branches (or in more concrete terms, *references*) to its children node(s).

A tree can be used for many things, such as to represent a management hierarchy with the president of the company at the root node and the various vice-presidents as child nodes of the president. The vice-presidents may have managers as child nodes, and so on. A tree can be used to make decisions, where each node of the tree contains a question and the answer given depends on which branch is taken to a child node. The tree described in this recipe is called a *binary tree*. A binary tree can have zero, one, or two child nodes for every node in the tree. A binary tree node can never have more than two child nodes; this is where this type of tree gets its name. (There are other types of trees. For instance, the *n*-ary tree can have zero to *n* nodes for each node in the tree. This type of tree is defined in Recipe 10.7.)

A binary tree is very useful for storing objects and then efficiently searching for those objects. The following algorithm is used to store objects in a binary tree:

1. Start at the root node
2. Is this node free?
   a. If yes, add the object to this node, and we are done.
   b. If no, continue.
3. Is the object to be added to the tree less than ("less than" is determined by the IComparable.CompareTo method of the node being added) the current node?
   a. If yes, follow the branch to the node on the left side of the current node, and go to step 2.
   b. If no, follow the branch to the node of the right side of the current node, and go to step 2.

Basically, this algorithm states that the node to the left of the current node contains an object or value less than the current node, and the node to the right of the current node contains an object or value greater than (or equal to, if the binary tree can contain duplicates) the current node.

Searching for an object in a tree is easy. Just start at the root and ask yourself, "Is the object I am searching for less than the current node's object?" If it is, follow the left branch to the next node in the tree. If it is not, check the current node to determine whether it contains the object you are searching for. If this is still not the correct object, continue down the right branch to the next node. When you get to the next node, start the process over again.

The binary tree used in this recipe is made up of two classes. The BinaryTree class is not a part of the actual tree; rather, it acts as a starting point from which we can create a tree, add nodes to it, search the tree for items, and retrieve the root node to perform other actions.

The second class, BinaryTreeNode, is the heart of the binary tree and represents a single node in the tree. This class contains all the members that are required to create and work with a binary tree.

The BinaryTreeNode class contains a protected field, nodeValue, that contains an object implementing the IComparable interface. This structure allows us to perform searches and add nodes in the correct location in the tree. The Compare method of the IComparable interface is used in searching and adding methods to determine whether we need to follow the left or right branch. See the AddNode, AddUniqueNode, and DepthFirstSearch methods to see this in action.

There are two methods to add nodes to the tree, AddNode and AddUniqueNode. The AddNode method allows duplicates to be introduced to the tree, whereas the AddUniqueNode allows only unique nodes to be added.

The DepthFirstSearch method allows the tree to be searched by first checking the current node to see whether it contains the value searched for; if not, recursion is used to check the left and then the right node. If no matching value is found in any node, this method returns null.

It is interesting to note that even though the BinaryTree class is provided to create and manage the tree of BinaryTreeNode objects, we could merely use the BinaryTreeNode class as long as we keep track of the root node ourselves. The following code creates and manages the tree without the use of the BinaryTree class:

```
public static void TestManagedTreeWithNoBinaryTreeClass()
{
    // Create the root node
    BinaryTreeNode topLevel = new BinaryTreeNode("d");

    // Create all nodes that will be added to the tree
    BinaryTreeNode one = new BinaryTreeNode("b");
    BinaryTreeNode two = new BinaryTreeNode("c");
    BinaryTreeNode three = new BinaryTreeNode("a");
    BinaryTreeNode four = new BinaryTreeNode("e");
    BinaryTreeNode five = new BinaryTreeNode("f");
    BinaryTreeNode six = new BinaryTreeNode("g");

    // Add nodes to tree through the root
    topLevel.AddNode(three);
    topLevel.AddNode(one);
    topLevel.AddNode(five);
    topLevel.AddNode(four);
    topLevel.AddNode(two);
    topLevel.AddNode(six);

    // Print the tree starting at the root node
    topLevel.PrintDepthFirst();

    // Print the tree starting at node 'Three'
    three.PrintDepthFirst();

    // Display the number of child nodes of various nodes in the tree
    Console.WriteLine("topLevel.NumOfChildren: " + topLevel.NumOfChildren);
    Console.WriteLine("one.NumOfChildren: " + one.NumOfChildren);
    Console.WriteLine("three.NumOfChildren: " + three.NumOfChildren);
    Console.WriteLine("six.NumOfChildren: " + six.NumOfChildren);

    // Search the tree using the depth-first searching method
    Console.WriteLine("topLevel.DepthFirstSearch(a): " +
            topLevel.DepthFirstSearch("a").GetValue.ToString());
    Console.WriteLine("topLevel.DepthFirstSearch(b): " +
            topLevel.DepthFirstSearch("b").GetValue.ToString());
```

```
Console.WriteLine("topLevel.DepthFirstSearch(c): " +
        topLevel.DepthFirstSearch("c").GetValue.ToString( ));
Console.WriteLine("topLevel.DepthFirstSearch(d): " +
        topLevel.DepthFirstSearch("d").GetValue.ToString( ));
Console.WriteLine("topLevel.DepthFirstSearch(e): " +
        topLevel.DepthFirstSearch("e").GetValue.ToString( ));
Console.WriteLine("topLevel.DepthFirstSearch(f): " +
        topLevel.DepthFirstSearch("f").GetValue.ToString( ));

// Remove the left child node from the root node and display the entire tree
topLevel.RemoveLeftNode( );
topLevel.PrintDepthFirst( );

// Remove all nodes from the tree except for the root and display the tree
topLevel.RemoveRightNode( );
topLevel.PrintDepthFirst( );
}
```

See Also

See the "Queue Class" and "IComparable Interface" topics in the MSDN documentation.

10.7   Creating an n-ary Tree

Problem

You need a tree that can store a number of child nodes in each of its nodes. A binary tree would work if each node needs to have only two children, but, in this case, each node needs to have a fixed number of child nodes greater than two.

Solution

Use the following NTree class to create the root node for the *n*-ary tree:

```
using System;
using System.Collections;

public class NTree
{
    public NTree( )
    {
        maxChildren = int.MaxValue;
    }

    public NTree(int maxNumChildren)
    {
        maxChildren = maxNumChildren;
    }

    // The root node of the tree
    protected NTreeNodeFactory.NTreeNode root = null;
```

```
    // The maximum number of child nodes that a parent node may contain
    protected int maxChildren = 0;

    public void AddRoot(NTreeNodeFactory.NTreeNode node)
    {
        root = node;
    }

    public NTreeNodeFactory.NTreeNode GetRoot()
    {
        return (root);
    }

    public int MaxChildren
    {
        get {return (maxChildren);}
    }
}
```

The methods defined in Table 10-6 are of particular interest to using an NTree object.

Table 10-6. Members of the NTree class

Member	Description
Overloaded constructor	This constructor creates an NTree object. Its syntax is: NTree(int *maxNumChildren*) where *maxNumChildren* is the maximum number of children that one node may have at any time.
MaxChildren property	A read-only property to retrieve the maximum number of children any node may have. Its syntax is: int *MaxChildren* {get;} The value this property returns is set in the constructor.
AddRoot method	Adds a node to the tree. Its syntax is: AddRoot(NTreeNodeFactory.NTreeNode *node*) where *node* is the node to be added as a child to the current node.
GetRoot method	Returns the root node of this tree. Its syntax is: GetRoot()

The NTreeNodeFactory class is used to create nodes for the *n*-ary tree. These nodes are defined in the class NTreeNode, which is nested inside of the NTreeNodeFactory class. You are not able to create an NTreeNode without the use of this factory class. The code is:

```
public class NTreeNodeFactory
{
    public NTreeNodeFactory(NTree root)
    {
        maxChildren = root.MaxChildren;
    }

    private int maxChildren = 0;
```

```csharp
public int MaxChildren
{
    get {return (maxChildren);}
}

public NTreeNode CreateNode(IComparable value)
{
    return (new NTreeNode(value, maxChildren));
}

// Nested Node class
public class NTreeNode
{
    public NTreeNode(IComparable value, int maxChildren)
    {
        if (value != null)
        {
            nodeValue = value;
        }

        childNodes = new NTreeNode[maxChildren];
    }

    protected IComparable nodeValue = null;
    protected NTreeNode[] childNodes = null;

    public int NumOfChildren
    {
        get {return (CountChildren());}
    }

    public int CountChildren()
    {
        int currCount = 0;

        for (int index = 0; index <= childNodes.GetUpperBound(0); index++)
        {
            if (childNodes[index] != null)
            {
                ++currCount;
                currCount += childNodes[index].CountChildren();
            }
        }

        return (currCount);
    }

    public int CountImmediateChildren()
    {
        int currCount = 0;

        for (int index = 0; index <= childNodes.GetUpperBound(0); index++)
        {
            if (childNodes[index] != null)
            {
```

```
                    ++currCount;
            }
        }

        return (currCount);
    }

    public NTreeNode[] Children
    {
        get {return (childNodes);}
    }

    public NTreeNode GetChild(int index)
    {
        return (childNodes[index]);
    }

    public IComparable GetValue()
    {
        return (nodeValue);
    }

    public void AddNode(NTreeNode node)
    {
        int numOfNonNullNodes = CountImmediateChildren();

        if (numOfNonNullNodes < childNodes.Length)
        {
            childNodes[numOfNonNullNodes] = node;
        }
        else
        {
            throw (new Exception("Cannot add more children to this node."));
        }
    }

    public NTreeNode DepthFirstSearch (IComparable targetObj)
    {
        NTreeNode retObj = null;

        if (targetObj.CompareTo(nodeValue) == 0)
        {
            retObj = this;
        }
        else
        {
            for (int index=0; index<=childNodes.GetUpperBound(0); index++)
            {
                if (childNodes[index] != null)
                {
                    retObj = childNodes[index].DepthFirstSearch(targetObj);
                    if (retObj != null)
                    {
                        break;
```

```
                }
            }
        }
    }

    return (retObj);
}

public NTreeNode BreadthFirstSearch (IComparable targetObj)
{
    Queue row = new Queue();
    row.Enqueue(this);

    while (row.Count > 0)
    {
        // Get next node in queue
        NTreeNode currentNode = (NTreeNode)row.Dequeue();

        // Is this the node we are looking for?
        if (targetObj.CompareTo(currentNode.nodeValue) == 0)
        {
            return (currentNode);
        }

        for (int index = 0;
             index < currentNode.CountImmediateChildren();
             index++)
        {
            if (currentNode.Children[index] != null)
            {
                row.Enqueue(currentNode.Children[index]);
            }
        }
    }

    return (null);
}

public void PrintDepthFirst()
{
    Console.WriteLine("this: " + nodeValue.ToString());

    for (int index = 0; index < childNodes.Length; index++)
    {
        if (childNodes[index] != null)
        {
            Console.WriteLine("\tchildNodes[" + index + "]:  " +
            childNodes[index].nodeValue.ToString());
        }
        else
        {
            Console.WriteLine("\tchildNodes[" + index + "]:  NULL");
        }
    }
```

```
            for (int index = 0; index < childNodes.Length; index++)
            {
                if (childNodes[index] != null)
                {
                    childNodes[index].PrintDepthFirst();
                }
            }
        }

        public void RemoveNode(int index)
        {
            // Remove node from array and Compact the array
            if (index < childNodes.GetLowerBound(0) ||
                index > childNodes.GetUpperBound(0))
            {
                throw (new ArgumentOutOfRangeException("index", index,
                        "Array index out of bounds."));
            }
            else if (index < childNodes.GetUpperBound(0))
            {
                Array.Copy(childNodes, index + 1, childNodes, index,
                childNodes.Length - index - 1);
            }

            childNodes.SetValue(null, childNodes.GetUpperBound(0));
        }
    }
}
```

The methods defined in Table 10-7 are of particular interest to using an NTreeNodeFactory object.

Table 10-7. Members of the NTreeNodeFactory class

Member	Description
Constructor	Creates a new NTreeNodeFactory object that will create NTreeNode objects with the same number of MaxChildren that the NTree object passed in supports. Its syntax is: `NTreeNodeFactory(NTree root)` where *root* is an NTree object.
MaxChildren property	Read-only property that returns the maximum number of children that the NTree object supports. Its syntax is: `int MaxChildren {get;}`
CurrentValue property	Read-only property that returns the IComparable object that the node created by the NTreeNodeFactory contains. Its syntax is: `IComparable CurrentValue {get;}`

CreateNode method	Overloaded. Returns a new NTreeNode object. Its syntax is:
	
	`CreateNode()`
	`CreateNode(IComparable value)`
	
	where *value* is the IComparable object this new node object will contain.

The methods defined in Table 10-8 are of particular interest to using the nested NTreeNode object.

Table 10-8. Members of the NTreeNode class

Member	Description
Constructor	Creates a new NTreeNode object from the NTreeNodeFactory object passed in to it. Its syntax is: NTreeNode(NTreeNodeFactory *factory*) where *factory* is an NTreeNodeFactory object.
NumOfChildren property	Read-only property that returns the total number of children below this node. Its syntax is: int NumOfChildren {get;}
Children property	Read-only property that returns all of non-null child node objects in an array that the current node contains. Its syntax is: NTreeNode[] Children {get;}
CountChildren method	Recursively counts the number of non-null child nodes below the current node and returns this value as an integer. Its syntax is: CountChildren( )
CountImmediateChildren method	Counts only the non-null child nodes contained in the current node. Its syntax is: CountImmediateChildren( )
GetChild method	Uses an index to return the NTreeNode contained by the current node. Its syntax is: GetChild(int *index*) where *index* is the array index where the child object is stored.
GetValue method	Returns the IComparable object that the current node contains. Its syntax is: GetValue( )
AddNode method	Adds a new child node to the current node. Its syntax is: AddNode(NTreeNode *node*) where *node* is the child node to be added.
DepthFirstSearch method	Attempts to locate an NTreeNode by the IComparable object that it contains. An NTreeNode is returned if the IComparable object is located or a null if it is not. Its syntax is: DepthFirstSearch(IComparable *targetObj*) where *targetObj* is the IComparable object to locate in the tree. Note that this search starts with the current node, which may or may not be the root of the tree. The tree traversal is done in a depth-first manner.
BreadthFirstSearch method	Attempts to locate an NTreeNode by the IComparable object that it contains. An NTreeNode is returned if the IComparable object is located or a null if it is not. Its syntax is: DepthFirstSearch(IComparable *targetObj*) where *targetObj* is the IComparable object to locate in the tree. Note that this search starts with the current node, which may or may not be the root of the tree. The tree traversal is done in a breadth-first manner.

Table 10-8. Members of the NTreeNode class (continued)

Member	Description
PrintDepthFirst method	Displays the tree structure on the console window starting with the current node. Its syntax is: PrintDepthFirst( ) This method uses recursion to display each node in the tree.
RemoveNode method	Removes the child node at the specified *index* on the current node. Its syntax is: RemoveNode(int *index*) where *index* is the array index where the child object is stored. Note that when a node is removed, all of its children nodes are removed as well.

The following code illustrates the use of the NTree, NtreeNodeFactory, and the NTreeNode classes when creating and using an *n*-ary tree:

```
public static void TestNTree( )
{
    NTree topLevel = new NTree(3);
    NTreeNodeFactory nodeFactory = new NTreeNodeFactory(topLevel);

    NTreeNodeFactory.NTreeNode one = nodeFactory.CreateNode("One");
    NTreeNodeFactory.NTreeNode two = nodeFactory.CreateNode("Two");
    NTreeNodeFactory.NTreeNode three = nodeFactory.CreateNode("Three");
    NTreeNodeFactory.NTreeNode four = nodeFactory.CreateNode("Four");
    NTreeNodeFactory.NTreeNode five = nodeFactory.CreateNode("Five");
    NTreeNodeFactory.NTreeNode six = nodeFactory.CreateNode("Six");
    NTreeNodeFactory.NTreeNode seven = nodeFactory.CreateNode("Seven");
    NTreeNodeFactory.NTreeNode eight = nodeFactory.CreateNode("Eight");
    NTreeNodeFactory.NTreeNode nine = nodeFactory.CreateNode("Nine");

    topLevel.AddRoot(one);
    Console.WriteLine("topLevel.GetRoot( ).CountChildren: " +
            topLevel.GetRoot( ).CountChildren( ));

    topLevel.GetRoot( ).AddNode(two);
    topLevel.GetRoot( ).AddNode(three);
    topLevel.GetRoot( ).AddNode(four);

    topLevel.GetRoot( ).Children[0].AddNode(five);
    topLevel.GetRoot( ).Children[0].AddNode(eight);
    topLevel.GetRoot( ).Children[0].AddNode(nine);
    topLevel.GetRoot( ).Children[1].AddNode(six);
    topLevel.GetRoot( ).Children[1].Children[0].AddNode(seven);

    Console.WriteLine("Display Entire tree:");
    topLevel.GetRoot( ).PrintDepthFirst( );

    Console.WriteLine("Display tree from node [two]:");
    topLevel.GetRoot( ).Children[0].PrintDepthFirst( );
```

```
            Console.WriteLine("Depth First Search:");
            Console.WriteLine("topLevel.DepthFirstSearch(One): " +
                    topLevel.GetRoot().DepthFirstSearch("One").GetValue().ToString());
            Console.WriteLine("topLevel.DepthFirstSearch(Two): " +
                    topLevel.GetRoot().DepthFirstSearch("Two").GetValue().ToString());
            Console.WriteLine("topLevel.DepthFirstSearch(Three): " +
                    topLevel.GetRoot().DepthFirstSearch("Three").GetValue().ToString());
            Console.WriteLine("topLevel.DepthFirstSearch(Four): " +
                    topLevel.GetRoot().DepthFirstSearch("Four").GetValue().ToString());
            Console.WriteLine("topLevel.DepthFirstSearch(Five): " +
                    topLevel.GetRoot().DepthFirstSearch("Five").GetValue().ToString());

            Console.WriteLine("\r\n\r\nBreadth First Search:");
            Console.WriteLine("topLevel.BreadthFirstSearch(One): " +
                    topLevel.GetRoot().BreadthFirstSearch("One").GetValue().ToString());
            Console.WriteLine("topLevel.BreadthFirstSearch(Two): " +
                    topLevel.GetRoot().BreadthFirstSearch("Two").GetValue().ToString());
            Console.WriteLine("topLevel.BreadthFirstSearch(Three): " +
                    topLevel.GetRoot().BreadthFirstSearch("Three").GetValue().ToString());
            Console.WriteLine("topLevel.BreadthFirstSearch(Four): " +
                    topLevel.GetRoot().BreadthFirstSearch("Four").GetValue().ToString());
        }
```

Discussion

An *n*-ary tree is one that has no limitation on the number of children each parent node may contain. This is in contrast to the binary tree in Recipe 10.6, in which each parent node may only contain two children nodes.

NTree is a simple class that contains only a constructor and three public methods. Through this object, you can create an *n*-ary tree, set the root node, and obtain the root node in order to navigate and manipulate the tree. An NTree object that can contain at most three children is created in the following manner:

```
    NTree topLevel = new NTree(3);
```

An NTree object that can contain at most int.MaxValue children, which allows greater flexibility, is created in the following manner:

```
    NTree topLevel = new NTree();
```

The real work is done in the NTreeNodeFactory object and the NTreeNode object, which is nested in the NTreeNodeFactory class. The NTreeNodeFactor class is an object factory that facilitates the construction of all NTreeNode objects. When the factory object is created, the NTree object is passed in to the constructor, as shown here:

```
    NTreeNodeFactory nodeFactory = new NTreeNodeFactory(topLevel);
```

Therefore, when the factory object is created, it knows the maximum number of children that a parent node may have. The factory object provides an overloaded public method, CreateNode, that allows for the creation of an NTreeNode object. If an IComparable type object is passed into this method, the IComparable object will be contained within this new node in the Value field. If no IComparable object is passed in, the new NTreeNode object will contain the IComparable object that was passed in to the CreateNode method of the NTreeNodeFactory object the last time it was called, or null if this is the first time this method has been called. Since the String object implements the IComparable interface, it can be passed in to this parameter with no modifications. Passing in no parameters allows the CreateNode method to be called within a loop to make it easier to create many duplicate nodes at one time. Node creation is performed in the following manner:

```
NTreeNodeFactory.NTreeNode one = nodeFactory.CreateNode("One");
NTreeNodeFactory.NTreeNode two = nodeFactory.CreateNode("Two");
NTreeNodeFactory.NTreeNode three = nodeFactory.CreateNode("Three");
NTreeNodeFactory.NTreeNode four = nodeFactory.CreateNode("Four");
NTreeNodeFactory.NTreeNode five = nodeFactory.CreateNode("Five");
NTreeNodeFactory.NTreeNode six = nodeFactory.CreateNode("Six");
NTreeNodeFactory.NTreeNode seven = nodeFactory.CreateNode("Seven");
NTreeNodeFactory.NTreeNode eight = nodeFactory.CreateNode("Eight");
NTreeNodeFactory.NTreeNode nine = nodeFactory.CreateNode("Nine");
```

The NTreeNode class is nested within the factory class; it is not actually supposed to be used directly to create a node object. Instead, the factory will create a node object and return it to the caller. NTreeNode has one constructor that accepts an NTreeNodeFactory object. This factory object exposes critical information used to initialize this instance of the NTreeNode object; namely, the maximum number of child nodes allowed. This value is stored in the ChildNodes field of the NTreeNode object. This object also contains a second field, Value, that is used to store an object that implements the IComparable interface. It is this Value field that we use when we are searching the tree for a particular item.

Adding a root node to the TopLevel NTree object is performed using the AddRoot method of the NTree object:

```
topLevel.AddRoot(one);
```

Each NTreeNode object contains a field called ChildNodes. This field is an array containing all child nodes attached to this parent node object. The maximum number of children—obtained from the factory class—provides this number, which is used to create the fixed size array. This array is initialized in the constructor of the NTreeNode object.

The following code shows how to add nodes to this tree:

```
// Add nodes to root
topLevel.GetRoot( ).AddNode(two);
topLevel.GetRoot( ).AddNode(three);
topLevel.GetRoot( ).AddNode(four);

// Add node to the first node Two of the root
topLevel.GetRoot( ).Children[0].AddNode(five);

// Add node to the previous node added, node five
topLevel.GetRoot( ).BreadthFirstSearch("Five").AddNode(six);
```

The searching method `BreadthFirstSearch` is constructed similar to the way the same method was constructed for the binary tree in Recipe 9.14. The `DepthFirstSearch` method is constructed a little differently from the same method in the binary tree. This method uses recursion to search the tree, but it uses a `for` loop to iterate over the array of child nodes, searching each one in turn. In addition, the current node is checked first to determine whether it matches the `targetObj` parameter to this method. This is a better-performing design, as opposed to moving this test to the end of the method.

If the `RemoveNode` method is successful, the array containing all child nodes of the current node is compacted to prevent fragmentation, which allows nodes to be added later in a much simpler manner. The `AddNode` method only has to add the child node to the end of this array as opposed to searching the array for an open element. The following code shows how to remove a node:

```
// Remove all nodes below node 'Two'
// Nodes 'Five' and 'Six' are removed
topLevel.GetRoot().BreadthFirstSearch("Two").RemoveNode(0);

// Remove node 'Three' from the root node
topLevel.GetRoot().RemoveNode(1);
```

It is easy to modify the `NTreeNodeFactory` and `NTreeNode` classes to accept an object instead of an `IComparable` type object. To do this:

1. Search for every occurrence of `IComparable` and replace it with `object`.

2. Search for all occurrences of the `CompareTo` method and replace them with the `==` operator.

See Also

See the "Queue Class" and "IComparable Interface" topics in the MSDN documentation.

10.8 Creating a Set Object

Problem

You need an object that contains a group of unordered objects. This object containing a set of data must be able to be compared to other objects containing sets of data, as well as have the following actions performed on them:

- Union of the items contained by the two objects containing sets of data.

- Intersection of the items contained by the two objects containing sets of data.

- Difference of the items contained by the two objects containing sets of data.

Solution

Create a Set object, shown here:

```
using System;
using System.Collections;
using System.Text;

public class Set : IEnumerable
{
    private ArrayList internalSet = new ArrayList();

    public int Count
    {
        get {return (internalSet.Count);}
    }

    public object this[int index]
    {
        get
        {
            return (internalSet[index]);
        }
        set
        {
            if (internalSet.Contains(value))
            {
                throw (new ArgumentException(
                        "Duplicate object cannot be added to this set."));
            }
            else
            {
                internalSet[index] = value;
            }
        }
    }

    public void Add(object obj)
    {
        if (internalSet.Contains(obj))
        {
            throw (new ArgumentException(
                    "Duplicate object cannot be added to this set."));
        }
        else
        {
            internalSet.Add(obj);
        }
    }

    public void Remove(object obj)
    {
        if (internalSet.Contains(obj))
        {
```

```
            throw (new ArgumentException("Object cannot be removed from " +
                    "this set because it does not exist in this set."));
    }
    else
    {
        internalSet.Remove(obj);
    }
}

public void RemoveAt(int index)
{
    internalSet.RemoveAt(index);
}

public bool Contains(object obj)
{
    return (internalSet.Contains(obj));
}

public static Set operator |(Set lhs, Set rhs)
{
    return (lhs.UnionOf(rhs));
}

public Set UnionOf(Set set)
{
    Set unionSet = new Set();
    Set sourceSet = null;
    Set mergeSet = null;

    if (set.Count > this.Count)    // An optimization
    {
        sourceSet = set;
        mergeSet = this;
    }
    else
    {
        sourceSet = this;
        mergeSet = set;
    }

    // Initialize unionSet with the entire SourceSet
    for (int index = 0; index < sourceSet.Count; index++)
    {
        unionSet.Add(sourceSet.internalSet[index]);
    }

    // mergeSet OR sourceSet
    for (int index = 0; index < mergeSet.Count; index++)
    {
        if (!sourceSet.Contains(mergeSet.internalSet[index]))
        {
            unionSet.Add(mergeSet.internalSet[index]);
        }
```

```
    }

    return (unionSet);
}

public static Set operator &(Set lhs, Set rhs)
{
    return (lhs.IntersectionOf(rhs));
}

public Set IntersectionOf(Set set)
{
    Set intersectionSet = new Set( );
    Set sourceSet = null;
    Set mergeSet = null;

    if (set.Count > this.Count)    // An optimization
    {
        sourceSet = set;
        mergeSet = this;
    }
    else
    {
        sourceSet = this;
            mergeSet = set;
    }

    // mergeSet AND sourceSet
    for (int index = 0; index < mergeSet.Count; index++)
    {
        if (sourceSet.Contains(mergeSet.internalSet[index]))
        {
            intersectionSet.Add(mergeSet.internalSet[index]);
        }
    }

    return (intersectionSet);
}

public static Set operator ^(Set lhs, Set rhs)
{
    return (lhs.DifferenceOf(rhs));
}

public Set DifferenceOf(Set set)
{
    Set differenceSet = new Set( );

    // mergeSet XOR sourceSet
    for (int index = 0; index < set.Count; index++)
    {
        if (!this.Contains(set.internalSet[index]))
        {
            differenceSet.Add(set.internalSet[index]);
```

```
        }
    }

    for (int index = 0; index < this.Count; index++)
    {
        if (!set.Contains(internalSet[index]))
        {
            differenceSet.Add(internalSet[index]);
        }
    }

    return (differenceSet);
}

public static bool operator ==(Set lhs, Set rhs)
{
    return (lhs.Equals(rhs));
}

public static bool operator !=(Set lhs, Set rhs)
{
    return (!lhs.Equals(rhs));
}

public override bool Equals(object obj)
{
    bool isEquals = false;

    if (obj != null)
    {
        if (obj is Set)
        {
            if (this.Count == ((Set)obj).Count)
            {
                if (this.IsSubsetOf((Set)obj) &&
                    ((Set)obj).IsSubsetOf(this))
                {
                    isEquals = true;
                }
            }
        }
    }

    return (isEquals);
}

public override int GetHashCode()
{
    return (internalSet.GetHashCode());
}

public bool IsSubsetOf(Set set)
{
    for (int index = 0; index < this.Count; index++)
```

```csharp
        {
            if (!set.Contains(internalSet[index]))
            {
                return (false);
            }
        }

        return (true);
    }

    public bool IsSupersetOf(Set set)
    {
        for (int index = 0; index < set.Count; index++)
        {
            if (!this.Contains(set.internalSet[index]))
            {
                return (false);
            }
        }

        return (true);
    }

    public string DisplaySet()
    {
        if (this.Count == 0)
        {
            return ("{}");
        }
        else
        {
            StringBuilder displayStr = new StringBuilder("{ ");

            for (int index = 0; index < (this.Count - 1); index++)
            {
                displayStr.Append(internalSet[index]);
                displayStr.Append(", ");
            }

            displayStr.Append(internalSet[internalSet.Count - 1]);
            displayStr.Append(" }");

            return (displayStr.ToString());
        }
    }

    public IEnumerator GetEnumerator()
    {
        return(new SetEnumerator(this));
    }

    // Nested enumerator class
    public class SetEnumerator : IEnumerator
    {
```

```
public SetEnumerator(Set theSet)
{
    setObj = theSet;
}

private Set setObj;
private int index = -1;

public bool MoveNext()
{
    index++;
    if (index >= setObj.Count)
    {
        return(false);
    }
    else
    {
        return(true);
    }
}

public void Reset()
{
    index = -1;
}

public object Current
{
    get{return(setObj[index]);}
}
    }
}
```

The methods defined in Table 10-9 are of particular interest to using a Set object.

Table 10-9. Members of the Set class

Member	Description
Count property	Read-only property to return the number of objects within this Set object. Its syntax is: `    int Count {get;}`
Indexer	Allows the Set object to operate in a manner similar to an array. Its syntax is: `    this[int index] {get; set;}`
Add method	Add a new object to the current Set object. Its syntax is: `    Add(object obj)` where *obj* is the object to add to this Set.
Remove method	Removes an existing object from the current Set object. Its syntax is: `    Remove(object obj)` where *obj* is the object to remove from this Set.
RemoveAt method	Removes an existing object from the current Set object using an index. Its syntax is: `    Add(int index)` where *index* is the index where the object to be removed is stored.

Table 10-9. Members of the Set class (continued)

Member	Description
Contains method	Returns a Boolean indicating whether the object passed in exists within this Set object. If a true is returned, the object exists; otherwise, it does not. Its syntax is: Contains(int *obj*) where *obj* is the object to be searched for.
BinarySearch method	Returns the object searched for, if the object passed in exists within this Set object. Its syntax is: BinarySearch(int *obj*) where *obj* is the object to be searched for.
UnionOf method	Performs a union operation on the current Set object and a second Set object. A new Set object is returned containing the union of these two Set objects. Its syntax is: UnionOf(Set *set*) where *set* is the second Set object.
Overloaded | operator	This operator delegates its work to the UnionOf method.
IntersectionOf method	Performs an intersection operation on the current Set object and a second Set object. A new Set object is returned containing the intersection of these two Set objects. Its syntax is: IntersectionOf(Set *set*) where *set* is the second Set object.
Overloaded & operator	This operator delegates its work to the IntersectionOf method.
DifferenceOf method	Performs a difference operation on the current Set object and a second Set object. A new Set object is returned containing the difference of these two Set objects. Its syntax is: DifferenceOf(Set *set*) where *set* is the second Set object.
Overloaded ^ operator	This operator delegates its work to the DifferenceOf method.
Overloaded Equals method	Returns a Boolean indicating whether a second Set object is equal to the current Set object. Its syntax is: Equals(object *obj*) where *obj* is the second Set object.
Overloaded == operator	This operator delegates its work to the Equals method.
Overloaded != operator	This operator delegates its work to the Equals method. However, this operator takes the inverse of the Boolean returned from the Equals method and returns this new value.
Overridden GetHashCode method	Returns the hash code of the internal ArrayList used to hold the objects contained in this Set object. Its syntax is: GetHashCode( )
IsSubsetOf method	Returns a Boolean indicating whether the current Set object is a subset of a second Set object. Its syntax is: IsSubsetOf(Set *set*) where *set* is the second Set object.
IsSupersetOf method	Returns a Boolean indicating whether the current Set object is a superset of a second Set object. Its syntax is: IsSupersetOf(Set *set*) where *set* is the second Set object.

Table 10-9. Members of the Set class (continued)

Member	Description
DisplaySet method	Displays all objects within the current Set object in the following format:
	{Obj1, Obj2, Obj3, ...}
	Its syntax is:
	DisplaySet( )

The following code illustrates the use of the Set class:

```
public static void TestSet( )
{
    Set set1 = new Set( );
    Set set2 = new Set( );
    Set set3 = new Set( );

    set1.Add(1);
    set1.Add(2);
    set1.Add(3);
    set1.Add(4);
    set1.Add(5);
    set1.Add(6);

    set2.Add(-10);
    set2.Add(2);
    set2.Add(40);

    set3.Add(3);
    set3.Add(6);

    foreach (object o in set2)
    {
        Console.WriteLine(o.ToString( ));
    }

    Console.WriteLine("set1.Contains(2): " + set1.Contains(2));
    Console.WriteLine("set1.Contains(0): " + set1.Contains(0));

    Console.WriteLine("\r\nset1.Count: " + set1.Count);
    Console.WriteLine( );
    Console.WriteLine("set1.DisplaySet: " + set1.DisplaySet( ));
    Console.WriteLine("set2.DisplaySet: " + set2.DisplaySet( ));
    Console.WriteLine("set3.DisplaySet: " + set3.DisplaySet( ));
    Console.WriteLine( );
    Console.WriteLine("set1.UnionOf(set2): " +
            set1.UnionOf(set2).DisplaySet( ));
    Console.WriteLine("set1.IntersectionOf(set2): " +
            set1.IntersectionOf(set2).DisplaySet( ));
    Console.WriteLine("set1.DifferenceOf(set2): " +
            set1.DifferenceOf(set2).DisplaySet( ));
    Console.WriteLine("set1 | set2: " + (set1 | set2).DisplaySet( ));
    Console.WriteLine("set1 & set2: " + (set1 & set2).DisplaySet( ));
    Console.WriteLine("set1 ^ set2: " + (set1 ^ set2).DisplaySet( ));
```

```
Console.WriteLine("set1.Equals(set2): " + set1.Equals(set2));
Console.WriteLine("set1 == set2: " + (set1 == set2));
Console.WriteLine("set1 != set2: " + (set1 != set2));
Console.WriteLine("set1.IsSubsetOf(set2): " + set1.IsSubsetOf(set2));
Console.WriteLine("set1.IsSupersetOf(set2): " + set1.IsSupersetOf(set2));
Console.WriteLine();
Console.WriteLine("set2.UnionOf(set1): " +
        set2.UnionOf(set1).DisplaySet());
Console.WriteLine("set2.IntersectionOf(set1): " +
        set2.IntersectionOf(set1).DisplaySet());
Console.WriteLine("set2.DifferenceOf(set1): " +
        set2.DifferenceOf(set1).DisplaySet());
Console.WriteLine("set2.Equals(set1): " + set2.Equals(set1));
Console.WriteLine("set2 == set1): " + (set2 == set1));
Console.WriteLine("set2 != set1): " + (set2 != set1));
Console.WriteLine("set2.IsSubsetOf(set1): " + set2.IsSubsetOf(set1));
Console.WriteLine("set2.IsSupersetOf(set1): " + set2.IsSupersetOf(set1));
Console.WriteLine();
Console.WriteLine("set3.UnionOf(set1): " +
        set3.UnionOf(set1).DisplaySet());
Console.WriteLine("set3.IntersectionOf(set1): " +
        set3.IntersectionOf(set1).DisplaySet());
Console.WriteLine("set3.DifferenceOf(set1): " +
        set3.DifferenceOf(set1).DisplaySet());
Console.WriteLine("set3.Equals(set1): " + set3.Equals(set1));
Console.WriteLine("set3 == set1: " + (set3 == set1));
Console.WriteLine("set3 != set1: " + (set3 != set1));
Console.WriteLine("set3.IsSubsetOf(set1): " + set3.IsSubsetOf(set1));
Console.WriteLine("set3.IsSupersetOf(set1): " + set3.IsSupersetOf(set1));
Console.WriteLine("set1.IsSubsetOf(set3): " + set1.IsSubsetOf(set3));
Console.WriteLine("set1.IsSupersetOf(set3): " + set1.IsSupersetOf(set3));
Console.WriteLine();
Console.WriteLine("set3.UnionOf(set2): " +
        set3.UnionOf(set2).DisplaySet());
Console.WriteLine("set3.IntersectionOf(set2): " +
        set3.IntersectionOf(set2).DisplaySet());
Console.WriteLine("set3.DifferenceOf(set2): " +
        set3.DifferenceOf(set2).DisplaySet());
Console.WriteLine("set3 | set2: " + (set3 | set2).DisplaySet());
Console.WriteLine("set3 & set2: " + (set3 & set2).DisplaySet());
Console.WriteLine("set3 ^ set2: " + (set3 ^ set2).DisplaySet());
Console.WriteLine("set3.Equals(set2): " + set3.Equals(set2));
Console.WriteLine("set3 == set2: " + (set3 == set2));
Console.WriteLine("set3 != set2: " + (set3 != set2));
Console.WriteLine("set3.IsSubsetOf(set2): " + set3.IsSubsetOf(set2));
Console.WriteLine("set3.IsSupersetOf(set2): " + set3.IsSupersetOf(set2));
Console.WriteLine();
Console.WriteLine("set3.Equals(set3): " + set3.Equals(set3));
Console.WriteLine("set3 == set3: " + (set3 == set3));
Console.WriteLine("set3 != set3: " + (set3 != set3));
Console.WriteLine("set3.IsSubsetOf(set3): " + set3.IsSubsetOf(set3));
Console.WriteLine("set3.IsSupersetOf(set3): " + set3.IsSupersetOf(set3));
```

```
        Console.WriteLine("set1[1]: " + set1[1].ToString());
        set1[1] = 100;

        set1.RemoveAt(1);
        set1.RemoveAt(2);
        Console.WriteLine("set1: " + set1.DisplaySet());
    }
```

Discussion

Sets are containers that hold a group of homogeneous object types. Various mathematical operations can be performed on sets, including the following:

Union

(A ∪ B)

Combines all elements of set A and set B into a resulting Set object. If an object exists in both sets, the resulting unioned Set object contains only one of those elements, not both.

Intersection

(A ∩ B)

Combines all elements of set A and set B that are common to both A and B into a resulting Set object. If an object exists in one set and not the other, the element is not added to the intersectioned Set object.

Difference

(A–B)

Combines all elements of set A, except for the elements that are also members of set B, into a resulting Set object. If an object exists in both sets A and B, it is not added to the final differenced Set object. The difference is equivalent to taking the union of both sets and the intersection of both sets and then removing all elements in the unioned set that exist in the intersectioned set.

Subset

(A ⊂ B)

Returns true if all elements of set A are contained in a second set B; otherwise, it returns false. Set B may contain elements not found in A.

Superset

(A ⊃ B)

Returns true if all elements of set A are contained in a second set B; otherwise, it returns false. Set A may contain elements not found in B.

Equivalence

(A == B)

Returns true if both Set objects contain the same number and value of each element; otherwise, it returns false. This is equivalent to stating that (A ⊂ B) and (B ⊂ A). Nonequivalence is defined by the != operator. Note that the .NET Equals method could be used to test for equivalence.

The Set class wraps an ArrayList (InternalSet), which contains all elements of that set. Many of the methods exposed by the Set class are delegated to the internalSet ArrayList. Of these wrapped methods, the Add method requires some discussion. This method prevents a duplicate object from being added to the Set object. This is a property of sets—no set may contain duplicate elements at any time. Calling the Contains method of the internalSet ArrayList, to determine whether the new object is already contained in this Set object, performs this check. This check is also performed in the set accessor of the indexer. The following code creates and populates two Set objects:

```
Set set1 = new Set();
Set set2 = new Set();

set1.Add(1);
set1.Add(2);
set1.Add(3);
set1.Add(4);
set1.Add(5);
set1.Add(6);

set2.Add(-10);
set2.Add(2);
set2.Add(40);
```

The union operation can be performed in one of two ways. The first is to use the UnionOf method and pass in a Set with which to union this Set. The Set class also overrides the | operator to provide this same functionality. Notice that the OR operator is shorthand for the union operation. Essentially, the resulting set contains elements that exist in either of the two Set objects or both Set objects. The following code shows how both of these operations are performed:

```
Set resultingUnionSet = set1.UnionOf(set2);
resultingUnionSet = set1 | set2;
```

The intersection operation is set up similarly to the union operation. There are two ways to perform an intersection between two Set objects: the first is to use the IntersectionOf method; and the second is to use the overloaded & operator. Once again, notice that the logic of the AND operator is the same as the intersection operation. Essentially, an element must be in both Set A and Set B in order for it to be placed in the resulting Set object. The following code demonstrates the intersection operation:

```
Set resultingIntersectSet = set1.IntersectionOf(set2);
resultingIntersectSet = set1 & set2;
```

The difference operation is performed either through the overloaded ^ operator or the DifferenceOf method. Notice that the XOR operation is similar to taking the difference of two sets. Essentially, only elements in either set, but not both, are placed in the resulting set. The following code demonstrates the difference operation:

```
Set resultingDiffSet = set1.DifferenceOf(set2);
resultingDiffSet = set1 ^ set2;
```

The subset operation is only performed through a single method called `IsSubsetOf`. The superset operation is also performed using a single method called `IsSupersetOf`. The following code demonstrates these two operations:

```
bool isSubset = set1.IsSubsetOf(set2);
bool isSuperset = set1.IsSupersetOf(set2);
```

The equivalence operation is performed using either the overloaded `==` operator or the `Equals` method. Since the `==` operator was overloaded, the `!=` operator must also be overloaded. The `!=` operator returns the inverse of the `==` operator or `Equals` method. The following code demonstrates these three operations:

```
bool isEqual = set1.Equals(set2);
isEqual = set1 == set2;
bool isNotEqual = set1 != set2;
```

See Also

See the "ArrayList Class," "Overloadable Operators," and "Operator Overloading Tutorial" topics in the MSDN documentation.

CHAPTER 11

Filesystem I/O

This chapter deals with the filesystem in four distinct ways. The first set of recipes looks at typical file interactions like creation, reading and writing, deletion, attributes, encoding methods for character data, and how to select the correct way (based on usage) to access files via streams. The second set looks at directory- or folder-based programming tasks like file creation as well as renaming, deleting, and determining attributes. The third set deals with the parsing of paths and the use of temporary files and paths, and the fourth set deals with more advanced topics in filesystem I/O, like asynchronous reads and writes, monitoring for certain filesystem actions, version information in files, and using P/Invoke to perform file I/O.

The file interactions section comes first since it sets the stage for many of the recipes in the temporary file and advanced sections. This is foundational knowledge that will help you understand the other file I/O recipes and how to modify them for your purposes. The various file and directory I/O techniques are used throughout the more advanced examples to help show a couple of different ways to approach the problems you will encounter working with filesystem I/O.

Unless otherwise specified, you need the following using statements in any program that uses snippets or methods from this chapter:

```
using System;
using System.IO;
```

11.1 Creating, Copying, Moving, and Deleting a File

Problem

You need to create a new file, copy an existing file, move an existing file, or delete a file.

Solution

The System.IO namespace contains two classes to perform these actions: the File and FileInfo classes. The File class contains only static methods, while the FileInfo class contains only instance methods.

File's static Create method returns an instance of the FileStream class, which you can use to read from or write to the newly created file. For example, the following code uses the static Create method of the File class to create a new file:

```
FileStream fileStream = null;
if (!File.Exists(@"c:\delete\test\test.txt"))
{
    fileStream = File.Create(@"c:\delete\test\test.txt");
}
```

The Create instance method of the FileInfo class takes no parameters. You should supply the path with a filename as the only parameter to the FileInfo class constructor. The method returns an instance of the FileStream class that you can use to read from or write to the newly created file. For example, the following code uses the Create instance method of the FileInfo class to create a new file:

```
FileInfo fileInfo = null;
FileStream fileStream = null;
if (!File.Exists (@"c:\delete\test\test.txt"))
{
    fileInfo = new FileInfo(@"c:\delete\test\test.txt");
    fileStream = fileInfo.Create();
}
```

You can copy a file using the overloaded static File.Copy method that returns void. The third parameter of one of the overrides for this function allows you to pass true or false depending upon whether you want to overwrite an existing destination file, as shown in the following code, which uses the static Copy method of the File class to copy a file:

```
if (File.Exists(@"c:\delete\test\test.txt"))
{
    File.Copy(@"c:\delete\test\test.txt ",
              Directory.GetCurrentDirectory() + @"\test.txt", true);
}
```

The overloaded CopyTo instance method returns a FileInfo object that represents the newly copied file. This method can also take a Boolean in one of the overrides to signify your intent to overwrite an existing file. For example, the following code uses the CopyTo instance method of the FileInfo class to copy a file:

```
FileInfo fileInfo = new FileInfo(@"c:\delete\test\test.txt");
fileInfo.CopyTo(@"c:\test.txt", true);
```

You can move a file using the static Move method of the File class, which returns void. For example, the following code uses the static Move method to move a file after checking for its existence:

```
        if (!File.Exists(Directory.GetCurrentDirectory() + @"\test.txt"))
        {
            File.Move(@"c:\delete\test\test.txt ",
                Directory.GetCurrentDirectory() + @"\test.txt");
        }
```

The MoveTo instance method returns void and is the way to move a file using the FileInfo class. For example, the following code moves a file using the MoveTo instance method of the FileInfo class after checking for the file's existence:

```
        FileInfo fileInfo = new FileInfo(@"c:\delete\test\test.txt");
        if (!File.Exists(@"c:\test.txt "))
        {
            fileInfo.MoveTo(@"c:\test.txt ");
        }
```

You can delete a file using the static Delete method of the File class that returns void. For example, the following code uses the static Delete method to delete a file:

```
        if (File.Exists(Directory.GetCurrentDirectory() + @"\test.txt"))
        {
            File.Delete(Directory.GetCurrentDirectory() + @"\test.txt", true);
        }
```

The Delete instance method on the FileInfo class takes no parameters and returns void. For example, the following code uses the Delete instance method of the FileInfo class to delete a file:

```
        if(File.Exists(@"c:\delete\test\test.txt")
        {
            FileInfo fileInfo = new FileInfo(@"c:\delete\test\test.txt");
            fileInfo.Delete();
        }
```

Discussion

Whether you choose to call the static file operation methods or the instance file operation methods depends on what you are trying to accomplish. If you need a quick way of creating, moving, copying, or deleting a file, consider using the static methods. If you will be performing multiple operations on a file, such as creating, moving, and changing its attributes, you should consider the instance methods of the FileInfo class. Another consideration is that static methods on a class do not require an object to be created on the managed heap and subsequently destroyed by the garbage collector. Instance methods require an object to be created before the methods can be called. If you are trying to minimize the number of objects the garbage collector has to manage, consider using static methods.

A few items to note when using the file functions:

- If the directory doesn't exist, the method won't create it and you'll get an exception. See how to check whether a directory exists in Recipe 11.4.

- If no path is provided, the file will land in the current working directory. If the user does not have permission to write to the current working directory (such as the case of a normal user writing to the *Program Files* directory), this will result in an UnauthorizedAccessException.

- If a relative path is provided (for example, *C:\dir1\dir2\.\.\file.txt*), it will be evaluated properly.
- If an absolute path is provided, the method will succeed as expected.

When creating a new file, you should first determine whether that file already exists. This is a good idea since the default creation behavior of the file classes is to either overwrite the existing file silently or, if the file is read-only, to throw an exception. The File and FileInfo classes both contain a method, Exists, to perform this operation. Once it is determined that the file does not exist, we can create it using either the static or instance Create methods. Note that this does leave a small window open between the time you checked and the time that the creation starts, so it is not a replacement for proper exception and error handling of the Create call.

See Also

See the "File Class" and "FileInfo Class" topics in the MSDN documentation.

11.2   Manipulating File Attributes

Problem

You need to display or manipulate a file's attributes or timestamps.

Solution

To display a file's timestamps, you can use either the static methods of the File class or the instance properties of the FileInfo class. The static methods are GetCreationTime, GetLastAccessTime, and GetLastWriteTime. Each has a single parameter, the path and name of the file whose timestamp information is to be returned, and returns a DateTime value containing the relevant timestamp. For example:

```
public void DisplayFileAttr(string path)
{
    Console.WriteLine(File.GetCreationTime(path).ToString( ));
    Console.WriteLine(File.GetLastAccessTime(path).ToString( ));
    Console.WriteLine(File.GetLastWriteTime(path).ToString( ));
}
```

The instance properties of the FileInfo class are CreationTime, LastAccessTime, and LastWriteTime. Each returns a DateTime value containing the respective timestamp of the file represented by the FileInfo object. The following code illustrates their use:

```
public void DisplayFileAttr(string path)
{
    FileInfo fileInfo = new FileInfo(path);
```

```
        Console.WriteLine(fileInfo.CreationTime.ToString( ));
        Console.WriteLine(fileInfo.LastAccessTime.ToString( ));
        Console.WriteLine(fileInfo.LastWriteTime.ToString( ));
}
```

To modify a file's timestamps, you can use either the static methods of the File class or the instance properties of the FileInfo class. The static methods are SetCreationTime, SetLastAccessTime, and SetLastWriteTime. All of them take the path and name of the file whose timestamp is to be modified as the first parameter and a DateTime value containing the new timestamp as the second, and each returns void. For example:

```
public void ModifyFileAttr(string path)
{
    File.SetCreationTime(path, DateTime.Parse(@"May 10, 2003"));
    File.SetLastAccessTime(path, DateTime.Parse(@"May 10, 2003"));
    File.SetLastWriteTime(path, DateTime.Parse(@"May 10, 2003"));
}
```

The instance properties are the same as the properties used to display timestamp information: CreationTime, LastAccessTime, or LastWriteTime. To set the timestamp, assign a value of type DateTime to the relevant timestamp property. For example:

```
public void ModifyFileAttr(string path)
{
    FileInfo fileInfo  = new FileInfo(path);

    DateTime dt = new DateTime(2001,2,8);
    fileInfo.CreationTime = dt;
    fileInfo.LastAccessTime = dt;
    fileInfo.LastWriteTime = dt;
}
```

To display or modify a file's attributes, use the instance Attributes property. The property's value is a bitmask consisting of one or more members of the FileAttributes enumeration. For example, the following code:

```
public void ViewModifyFileAttr(string path, FileAttributes fileAttribute)
{
    if(File.Exists(path)
    {
        FileInfo fileInfo = new FileInfo(path);

        // Display this file's attributes
        Console.WriteLine(fileInfo.Attributes.ToString( ));

        // Display whether this file is hidden
        Console.WriteLine("Is file hidden? = " +
        ((fileInfo.Attributes & FileAttributes.Hidden) == FileAttributes.Hidden));

        // Modify this file's attributes
        fileInfo.Attributes |= FileAttributes.Hidden;
    }
}
```

Discussion

One of the easier methods of creating a `DateTime` object is to use the static `DateTime.Parse` method. This method accepts a string defining a particular date and is converted to a `DateTime` object.

In addition to timestamp information, a file's attributes may also be obtained and modified. This is accomplished through the use of the public instance `Attributes` property found on a `FileInfo` object. This property returns or modifies a `FileAttributes` enumeration. The `FileAttributes` enumeration is made up of bit flags that can be turned on or off through the use of the bitwise operators &, |, or ^.

Table 11-1 lists each of the flags in the `FileAttributes` enumeration.

Table 11-1. FileAttributes enumeration values

Member name	Description
Archive	Represents the file's archive status that marks the file for backup or removal.
Compressed	Indicates that the file is compressed.
Device	This option is reserved for future use.
Directory	Indicates that this is a directory.
Encrypted	Indicates that a file or directory is encrypted. In the case of a file, its contents are encrypted. In the case of a directory, newly created files will be encrypted by default.
Hidden	Indicates a hidden file.
Normal	Indicates that the file has no other attributes, and, as such, this attribute cannot be used in combination with others.
NotContentIndexed	Indicates that the file is excluded from the content index service.
Offline	Indicates that the state of the file is offline, and its contents will be unavailable.
ReadOnly	Indicates that the file is read-only.
ReparsePoint	Indicates a *reparse point*, a block of data associated with a directory or file.
SparseFile	Indicates a sparse file, which may take up less space on the filesystem than its reported size because zeros in the file are not actually allocated on-disk.
System	Indicates that the file is a system file.
Temporary	Indicates a temporary file. It may reside entirely in memory.

In many cases, more than one of these flags can be set at one time, but see the description for the `Normal` flag, which must be used alone.

See Also

See the "File Class," "FileInfo Class," and "FileAttributes Enumeration" topics in the MSDN documentation.

11.3   Renaming a File

Problem

You need to rename a file.

Solution

With all of the bells and whistles hanging off of the .NET Framework, you would figure that renaming a file is easy. Unfortunately, there is no specific rename method that can be used to rename a file. Instead, you can use the static Move method of the File class or the instance MoveTo method of the FileInfo class. The static File.Move method can be used to rename a file in the following manner:

```
public void RenameFile(string originalName, string newName)
{
    File.Move(originalName, newName);
}
```

This code has the effect of renaming the originalName file to the newName file.

The FileInfo.MoveTo instance method can also be used to rename a file in the following manner:

```
public void RenameFile(FileInfo originalFile, string newName)
{
    originalFile.MoveTo(newName);
}
```

Discussion

The Move and MoveTo methods allow a file to be moved to a different location, but they can also be used to rename files. For example, you could use RenameFile to rename a file from *foo.txt* to *bar.dat*:

```
RenameFile("foo.txt","bar.dat");
```

You could also use fully qualified paths to rename them:

```
RenameFile("c:\mydir\foo.txt","c:\mydir\bar.dat");
```

See Also

See the "File Class" and "FileInfo Class" topics in the MSDN documentation.

11.4   Determining Whether a File Exists

Problem

You need to determine whether a file exists prior to creating or performing an action on that file.

Solution

Use the static `Exists` method of the `File` class to determine whether a file currently exists:

```
if (File.Exists(@"c:\delete\test\test.txt"))
{
    // Operate on that file here
}
```

Discussion

Determining whether a file exists is often critical to your code. If a file exists and you try to create it using one of the file creation methods, one of three things will happen: either the existing file will be overwritten; or, if the file is read-only, an exception will be thrown; or, an exception will be thrown indicating that the state of the filesystem is not what you think it is. There is a small window between the `Exists` call and the actions you take where another process could change the filesystem, so you should be prepared for that with proper exception handling.

See Also

See the "File Class" topic in the MSDN documentation.

11.5   Choosing a Method of Opening a File or Stream for Reading and/or Writing

Problem

When you are first learning the .NET Framework—and even for some time after—the proper way to read to, write from, or otherwise interact with files can be unclear because the framework provides so many different ways of attacking this problem. How should you determine which approach fits your scenario?

Solution

Use file streams to perform various file functions. There are five basic types of built-in file stream manipulation classes that you can use in order to read and/or write to the file stream:

FileStream
> For the most fine-grained control, use `FileStream` for file manipulation since it provides the most low-level access to the file, and, therefore, the most complex actions become available. Some of these actions are reading and writing files in both synchronous and asynchronous fashions, methods to lock and unlock part or all of a file, seek a particular position in a file, or even read the file as a stream of either characters or bytes.

StreamReader

This type is derived from the abstract base class TextReader. The StreamReader class is designed for reading character or string input from a file. This class contains methods to read single characters, blocks of characters, lines of characters, or even the whole file into a single string variable.

StreamWriter

This class derives from the TextWriter class. It is designed for writing character or string output to a file. This class contains methods to write single characters or lines of characters.

BinaryReader

This type is derived from the Object class, as is the BinaryWriter class. It is designed for reading primitive data types—including byte or char data—from a file. This class contains methods to read any of the simple types (int, long, float, etc.), including char arrays and byte arrays.

BinaryWriter

This type derives from the Object class. It is designed for writing primitive data types—including byte or char data—to a file. This class contains methods to write any of the primitive types (int, long, float, etc.), including char arrays and byte arrays.

There are other stream readers and writers (XmlTextReader/Writer, StringReader/Writer) that can also perform file stream functions but at a higher level. This recipe is meant to give you a more fundamental approach to file operations.

Here are a few examples of using the various built-in streams:

```
// create a temp file to work with
string tempFile = Path.GetTempFileName();

// FileStream
FileStream fileStream = null;
try
{
    // open the file
    fileStream = File.Open(tempFile,FileMode.Append);

    string text = "Hello World ";
    byte [] bytes = Encoding.ASCII.GetBytes(text.ToCharArray());

    // write to the file
    fileStream.Write(bytes,0,bytes.Length);
}
finally
{
    //make sure the file is closed if it was opened
    if(fileStream != null)
        fileStream.Close();
}
```

```csharp
// StreamReader
StreamReader streamReader = null;
try
{
    streamReader = new StreamReader(tempFile);
    char[] chars = new char[64];
    // read a block of characters
    streamReader.Read(chars,0,64);
    string charsFound = new string(chars);
    Console.WriteLine("Chars in stream {0}",charsFound);
}
finally
{
    if(streamReader != null)
        streamReader.Close();
}


// StreamWriter
StreamWriter streamWriter = null;
try
{
    // open for append
    streamWriter = new StreamWriter(tempFile,true);
    // append some text
    streamWriter.WriteLine(", It's the StreamWriter!");
}
finally
{
    if(streamWriter != null)
        streamWriter.Close();
}


// BinaryWriter
BinaryWriter binaryWriter = null;
long pos = 0;
int twentyFive = 25;
try
{
    // start up the binary writer with the base stream from the streamwriter
    // since it is open
    binaryWriter = new BinaryWriter(streamWriter.BaseStream);
    // move to end
    pos = binaryWriter.Seek(0, SeekOrigin.End);
    // write out 25
    binaryWriter.Write(twentyFive);
}
finally
{
    // close up
    if(binaryWriter != null)
        binaryWriter.Close();
}


// BinaryReader
StreamReader streamReader2 = null;
```

```
    BinaryReader binaryReader = null;
    try
    {
        // open a new reader
        streamReader2 = new StreamReader(tempFile);
        binaryReader = new BinaryReader(streamReader2.BaseStream);

        // advance the stream to the number we stored
        for(long i=0;i<pos;i++)
            binaryReader.ReadByte();
        // read our number (should be 25)
        int num = binaryReader.ReadInt32();
        // is this the same number...?
        if(num == twentyFive)
            Console.WriteLine("Successfully read 25 back from stream");
        else
            Console.WriteLine("Failed to successfully read 25 back from stream");
    }
    finally
    {
        // close up
        if(binaryReader != null)
            binaryReader.Close();
        // close stream
        if(streamReader2 != null)
            streamReader2.Close();
    }
```

Discussion

There are many different ways to create a stream. First, we will examine the FileStream class, referring to useful recipes that will help create objects of this type. We will then look at the StreamWriter and StreamReader classes, followed by the BinaryWriter and BinaryReader classes.

The most straightforward method of creating an object is to use the new keyword. The FileStream class has several overloaded class constructors that enable creating a new FileStream from scratch. The FileStream's constructor enables a new FileStream object to be created from either a filename or a file handle. See Recipe 11.19.

The FileStream constructor can also accept a FileAccess, FileMode, and/or FileShare enumeration value. These enumeration values are defined in Tables 11-2, 11-3, and 11-4, respectively.

Table 11-2. FileMode enumeration values

Value name	Definition	Specifics
Append	Opens an existing file and prepares it to be written to, starting at the end of the file. If the file does not exist, a new zero-length file is created.	This value can be used only in tandem with the FileAccess.Write enumeration value; otherwise, an ArgumentException is thrown.

Table 11-2. FileMode enumeration values (continued)

Value name	Definition	Specifics
Create	Creates a new file. If the specified file exists, it is truncated.	If you do not wish to lose data, consider employing the CreateNew enumeration value instead. This value can be used only in tandem with the FileAccess.Write or FileAccess.ReadWrite enumeration values; otherwise, an ArgumentException is thrown.
CreateNew	Creates a new file.	An IOException is thrown if the file already exists. This prevents accidental data loss. This value can be used only in tandem with the FileAccess.Write or FileAccess.ReadWrite enumeration values; otherwise, an ArgumentException is thrown.
Open	Opens an existing file.	A FileNotFoundException is thrown if the file does not exist. Use OpenOrCreate if it is possible that the file might not already exist.
OpenOrCreate	Opens a file if it exists or creates a new one if it does not exist.	Consider using Open if you expect the file to always exist before it is opened. An ArgumentException is *not* thrown if this enumeration value is used in tandem with the FileAccess.Read enumeration value.
Truncate	Opens an existing file and deletes all information in that file.	A FileNotFoundException is thrown if the file does not exist. This value can be used in tandem with the FileAccess.Write or FileAccess.ReadWrite enumeration values; otherwise, an ArgumentException is thrown.

Table 11-3. FileAccess enumeration values

Value name	Definition
Read	Allows data only to be read from a file.
ReadWrite	Allows data to be read from and written to a file. Same as FileAccess.Read | FileAccess.Write.
Write	Allows data only to be written to a file.

Table 11-4. FileShare enumeration values

Value name	Definition
Inheritable	Not supported in Win32.
None	The file cannot be accessed (read from or written to) or deleted by this or any other process.
Read	The file cannot be written to or deleted by this or any other process. It can be read from.
Write	The file cannot be read from or deleted by this or any other process. It can be written to.
ReadWrite	The file can be read from or written to by this or any other process. The file still cannot be deleted while it is being shared in this mode. Same as using FileShare.Read | FileShare.Write.

In addition to these enumerations that define how a file is opened, the `FileStream` constructor allows you to define whether this stream will be opened in a synchronous or asynchronous manner. This is the only class—of the ones discussed in this chapter—that allows a file to be opened in an asynchronous manner.

The `FileStream` class also has methods for seeking to a point within a file stream, as well as locking or unlocking a portion or an entire file; *locking* will prevent other processes or threads from modifying the file. The other stream types discussed in this chapter do not have the ability to lock or unlock portions or an entire file. This locking/unlocking functionality cannot even be accessed through the `BaseStream` property of any of these types. Seeking within a file can be done directly using the `BinaryReader` or `BinaryWriter` classes. The `StreamReader` and `StreamWriter` classes cannot directly access the seek functionality. However, by using the `BaseStream` property of either the `StreamReader` or `StreamWriter` classes, the base stream's seek functionality can be used.

`FileStreams` can also be created using the static methods of the `File` class. Table 11-5 shows these methods, along with their equivalent `FileStream` object constructor parameters.

Table 11-5. Static methods of the File class and their equivalent FileStream constructor calls

Static methods in File class	Equivalent FileStream constructor call
`FileStream fileStream = File.Create("File.txt");`	`FileStream fileStream = new FileStream("File.txt", FileMode.Create, FileAccess.ReadWrite, FileShare.None);`
`FileStream fileStream = File.Open("File.txt");`	`FileStream fileStream = new FileStream("File.txt");`
`FileStream fileStream = File.OpenRead("File.txt");`	`FileStream fileStream = new FileStream("File.txt", FileMode.Open, FileAccess.Read, FileShare.Read);`
`FileStream fileStream = File.OpenWrite("File.txt");`	`FileStream fileStream = new FileStream("File.txt", FileMode.OpenOrCreate, FileAccess.Write, FileShare.None);`

The `File.Open` method is overloaded to accept `FileMode`, `FileAccess`, and `FileShare` enumeration values. The `FileStream` constructor is also overloaded to accept these same parameters. Therefore, to make an equivalent `FileStream` constructor for the `File.Open` method, we need to use the same parameters for each of these three enumeration values in both parameter lists.

The `File` class has a complementary class called `FileInfo` that contains similar methods, but these methods are instance, not static, methods. Table 11-6 shows the `FileInfo` methods, which are similar to the `File` static methods, along with their equivalent `FileStream` object constructor parameters.

Table 11-6. Instance methods of the FileInfo class and equivalent FileStream constructor calls

Instance methods in FileInfo class	Equivalent FileStream constructor call

``FileInfo fileInfo =
new FileInfo("File.txt");```
 	
``FileStream fileStream =
fileInfo.Create();```
	``FileStream fileStream = new FileStream("File.txt",
	FileMode.Create, FileAccess.ReadWrite, FileShare.None);```

``FileInfo fileInfo =
new FileInfo("File.txt");```
 	
``FileStream fileStream =
fileInfo.Open(FileMode.open);```
	```FileStream fileStream = new FileStream("File.txt");```

``FileInfo fileInfo =
new FileInfo("File.txt");```
 	
``FileStream fileStream =
fileInfo.OpenRead();```
	``FileStream fileStream = new FileStream("File.txt",
	FileMode.Open, FileAccess.Read, FileShare.Read);```

``FileInfo fileInfo =
new FileInfo("File.txt");```
 	
``FileStream fileStream =
fileInfo.OpenWrite();```
	``FileStream fileStream = new FileStream("File.txt",
	FileMode.OpenOrCreate, FileAccess.Write, FileShare.
	None);```

The `FileInfo.Open` instance method is overloaded to accept `FileMode`, `FileAccess`, and `FileShare` enumeration values. These values should be matched in the `FileStream` constructor parameter list.

The `StreamReader` and `StreamWriter` objects can be created using their overloaded constructors. These overloaded constructors accept as parameters either a file path and name or a `FileStream` object. Therefore, we can use any of the previously mentioned ways of creating a `FileStream` object in the construction of either a `StreamReader` or `StreamWriter` object.

In addition, we can use three of the static methods in the `File` class or three of the instance methods in the `FileInfo` class to create a `StreamReader` or `StreamWriter` object. Table 11-7 describes the static methods of the `File` class used to create `StreamReader` and `StreamWriter` objects and their equivalent `StreamReader` and `StreamWriter` object constructor parameters.

Table 11-7. Static methods of the File class and their equivalent StreamReader/StreamWriter constructor calls

Static methods in File class	Equivalent StreamReader/StreamWriter constructor calls
```StreamReader streamReader = File.OpenText("File.txt");```	```StreamReader streamReader = new StreamReader("File. txt");```
```StreamWriter streamWriter = File.AppendText("File.txt");```	```StreamWriter streamWriter = new StreamWriter("File. txt", true);```
```StreamWriter streamWriter = File.CreateText("File.txt");```	```StreamWriter streamWriter = new StreamWriter("File. txt", false);```

Table 11-8 describes the instance methods of the FileInfo class used to create StreamReader and StreamWriter object and their equivalent StreamReader and StreamWriter object constructor parameters.

Table 11-8. Instance methods of the FileInfo class and their equivalent StreamReader/ StreamWriter constructor calls

Instance methods in FileInfo class	Equivalent StreamReader/StreamWriter constructor calls

`FileInfo fileInfo = new FileInfo("File.txt");`
 	
`StreamReader streamReader = fileInfo.OpenText();`
	`StreamReader streamReader = new StreamReader("File.txt");`

`FileInfo fileInfo = new FileInfo("File.txt");`
 	
`StreamWriter streamWriter = fileInfo.AppendText();`
	`StreamWriter streamWriter = new StreamWriter("File.txt", true);`

`FileInfo fileInfo = new FileInfo("File.txt");`
 	
`StreamWriter streamWriter = fileInfo.AppendText();`
	`StreamWriter streamWriter = new StreamWriter("File.txt", false);`

The methods of the File and FileInfo classes do not return BinaryReader and BinaryWriter classes; therefore, we rely on their constructors to create these types of objects. The overloaded BinaryReader and BinaryWriter class constructors accept only a Stream object; they do not accept a filename.

To create a BinaryReader or BinaryWriter object, we first need to create a Stream type object. Since Stream is an abstract class, we need to create one of its derived classes, such as the FileStream class. Any of the prior ways of creating a FileStream object may be employed as a parameter in the constructor of either a BinaryReader or BinaryWriter. The following code creates both a BinaryReader and a BinaryWriter object from a single FileStream object:

```
fileStream = File.Create("filename.file");
BinaryWriter binaryWriter1 = new BinaryWriter(fileStream);
BinaryReader binaryReader1 = new BinaryReader(fileStream);
```

There are many different ways of combining the techniques discussed in this recipe to create and open files. For example, if you require file locking and/or asynchronous file processing, you will need a FileStream object. If you are dealing with text streams in memory and on disk, perhaps the StreamReader and StreamWriter might be a better choice. Finally, if you are dealing with binary data or mixed binary and text data in different encodings, you should consider BinaryReader and BinaryWriter.

See Also

See Recipe 11.19; see the "FileStream Class," "StreamReader Class," "StreamWriter Class," "BinaryReader," and "BinaryWriter" topics in the MSDN documentation.

11.6 Randomly Accessing Part of a File

Problem

When reading a file, you sometimes need to move from the current position in a file to a position some number of characters before or after the current position, including to the beginning or the end of a file. After moving to this point, you can add, modify, or read the information at this new point in the file.

Solution

To move around in a stream, use the Seek method. The following method writes the string contained in the variables theFirstLine and theSecondLine to a file in this same order. The stream is then flushed to the file on disk:

```
public void CreateFile(string theFirstLine, int theSecondLine)
{
    FileStream fileStream = new FileStream("data.txt",
        FileMode.Create,
        FileAccess.ReadWrite,
        FileShare.None);
    StreamWriter streamWriter = new StreamWriter(fileStream);

    streamWriter.WriteLine(theFirstLine);
    streamWriter.WriteLine(theSecondLine);
    streamWriter.Flush();
    streamWriter.Close();
    fileStream.Close();
}
```

If the following code is used to call this method:

```
CreateFile("This is the first line.", 1020304050);
```

the resulting *data.txt* file will contain the following text:

```
This is the first line.
1020304050
```

The following method, ModifyFile, uses the Seek method to reposition the current file position at the end of the first line. A new line of text is then added between the first and second lines of text in the file. Finally, the Seek method is used to place the current position pointer in the file to the end, and a final line of text is written to this file:

```
public void ModifyFile(int theSecondLine)
{
    // open the file for read/write
    FileStream fileStream =
    File.Open("data.txt",
        FileMode.Open,
        FileAccess.ReadWrite,
        FileShare.None);

    StreamWriter streamWriter = new StreamWriter(fileStream);
```

```
            // backup over the newline
            int offset = streamWriter.NewLine.Length;
            // backup over the second line
            offset += (theSecondLine.ToString( ).Length);
            // make negative
            offset = offset - (2 * offset);
            // move file pointer to just after first line
            streamWriter.BaseStream.Seek(offset, SeekOrigin.End);

            StringBuilder stringBuilder
                = new StringBuilder("This line added by seeking ");
            stringBuilder.AppendFormat("{0} chars from the end of this file.",offset);

            streamWriter.WriteLine(sb.ToString( ));
            streamWriter.Flush( );

            streamWriter.BaseStream.Seek(0, SeekOrigin.End);
            streamWriter.WriteLine("This is the last line" +
                ", added by seeking to the end of the file.");

            streamWriter.Close( );
    }
```

If the following code is used to call this method:

```
    ModifyFile(1020304050);
```

the resulting *data.txt* file will contain the following text:

```
    This is the first line.
    This line added by seeking -12 chars from the end of this file.
    This is the last line, added by seeking to the end of the file.
```

The next method, ReadFile, reads the file that we just created. First, the current position pointer in the file is moved to the end of the first line (this line contains the string in the variable theFirstLine). The ReadToEnd method is invoked reading the rest of the file (the second and third lines in the file) and the results are displayed:

```
    public void ReadFile(string theFirstLine)
    {
        StreamReader streamReader = new StreamReader("data.txt");

        streamReader.BaseStream.Seek(
            theFirstLine.Length + Environment.NewLine.Length, SeekOrigin.Begin);

        Console.WriteLine(streamReader.ReadToEnd( ));
        streamReader.Close( );
    }
```

The following text is displayed:

```
    This line added by seeking -12 chars from the end of this file.
    This is the last line, added by seeking to the end of the file.
```

If you are wondering where the line of text that reads:

```
    1020304050
```

is located, it was overwritten when we did the first Seek while writing data to this file.

Discussion

File seeking is the placement of the pointer to the current location in an opened file anywhere between—and including—the beginning and ending bytes of a file. Seeking is performed through the use of the Seek method.

This method returns the new location of the file pointer in the file.

Seeking is performed in one of three ways: as an offset from the beginning of the file, as an offset from the end of the file, or as an offset from the current location in the file, as shown here:

```
public void MoveInFile(int offsetValue)
{
    FileStream fileStream =
    File.Open("data.txt",
        FileMode.Open,
        FileAccess.ReadWrite,
        FileShare.None);

    StreamWriter streamWriter = new StreamWriter(fileStream);

    // move from the beginning of the file
    streamWriter.BaseStream.Seek(offsetValue, SeekOrigin.Begin);

    // move from the end of the file
    streamWriter.BaseStream.Seek(offsetValue, SeekOrigin.End);

    // move from the current file pointer location in the file
    streamWriter.BaseStream.Seek(offsetValue, SeekOrigin.Current);

    streamWriter.Close( );
}
```

offsetValue may be any positive or negative number as long as it does not attempt to force the file pointer before the beginning of the file or after the end. The SeekOrigin. Begin enumeration value starts the offset at the beginning of the file; likewise, the SeekOrigin.End value starts the offset at the end of the file. The SeekOrigin.Current value starts the offset at the current location of the file pointer. You must take extra care not to force the file pointer to a point before the start of the file when using the seek method with a negative offset, since this action could move the file pointer before the beginning of the file. If you think about it logically, you should be giving positive values when specifying SeekOrigin.Begin, negative values when specifying SeekOrigin.End, and any value makes sense for SeekOrigin.Current, so long as it doesn't cause the pointer to roll over the beginning or the end. To prevent the IOException from being thrown in this circumstance, you can test for this condition in the following manner:

```
long offsetValue = -20;
FileStream fileStream =
    File.Open("data.txt",
```

```
        FileMode.Open,
        FileAccess.ReadWrite,
        FileShare.None);

StreamWriter streamWriter = new StreamWriter(fileStream);

if ((offsetValue + streamWriter.BaseStream.Position) >= 0)
{
    streamWriter.BaseStream.Seek(OffsetValue, SeekOrigin.Current);
}
else
{
    Console.WriteLine("Cannot seek before the beginning of the file.");
}

if ((offsetValue + streamWriter.BaseStream.Length) >= 0)
{
    streamWriter.BaseStream.Seek(offsetValue, SeekOrigin.End);
}
else
{
    Console.WriteLine("Cannot seek before the beginning of the file.");
}

if (offsetValue >= 0)
{
    streamWriter.BaseStream.Seek(offsetValue, SeekOrigin.Begin);
}
else
{
    Console.WriteLine("Cannot seek before the beginning of the file.");
}
```

To seek to the beginning of a file, use the following code:

```
streamWriter.BaseStream.Seek(0, SeekOrigin.Begin);
```

To seek to the end of a file, use the following code:

```
streamWriter.BaseStream.Seek(0, SeekOrigin.End);
```

The SeekOrigin enumeration value sets the file pointer to the beginning or end of a file and then the offset, which is zero, does not force the file pointer to move. With this in mind, realize that using zero as an offset to SeekOrigin.Current is pointless because you just don't move the pointer at all, and you are killing clock cycles to no effect.

See Also

See the "FileStream Class," "StreamReader Class," "StreamWriter Class," "Binary-Reader Class," "BinaryWriter Class," and "SeekOrigin Enumeration" topics in the MSDN documentation.

11.7 Outputting a Platform-Independent EOL Character

Problem

Your application will run on more than one platform. Each platform uses a different end-of-line (EOL) character. You want your code to output the correct EOL character without having to write code to handle the EOL character specially for each platform.

Solution

The .NET Framework provides the `Environment.NewLine` constant, which represents a newline on the given platform. This is the newline string used by all of the framework-provided `WriteLine` methods internally (including `Console`, `Debug`, and `Trace`).

There are a few different scenarios when this could be useful:

1. Formatting a block of text with newlines embedded within it:

```
// 1) Remember to use Environment.NewLine on every block of text
// we format that we want platform correct newlines inside of
string line;
line = String.Format("FirstLine {0} SecondLine {0} ThirdLine {0}",
                Environment.NewLine);

// get a temp file to work with
string file = Path.GetTempFileName( );
FileStream stream = File.Create(file);
byte[] bytes = Encoding.Unicode.GetBytes(line);
stream.Write(bytes,0,bytes.Length);
// close the file
stream.Close( );

// remove the file (good line to set a breakpoint to check out the file
// we created)
File.Delete(file);
```

2. You need to use a different newline character than the default one used by `StreamWriter` (which happens to be `Environment.NewLine`). You can set the newline that a `StreamWriter` will use once so that all `WriteLines` performed by the `StreamWriter` use that newline instead of having to manually do it each time:

```
// 2) Set up a text writer and tell it to use the certain newline
// string
// get a new temp file
file = Path.GetTempFileName( );
line = "Double spaced line";
StreamWriter streamWriter = new StreamWriter(file);
// make this always write out double lines
streamWriter.NewLine = Environment.NewLine + Environment.NewLine;
// WriteLine on this stream will automatically use the newly specified
// newline sequence (double newline in our case)
streamWriter.WriteLine(line);
```

```
    streamWriter.WriteLine(line);
    streamWriter.WriteLine(line);
    // close the file
    streamWriter.Close( );
    // remove the file (good line to set a breakpoint to check out the file
    // we created)
    File.Delete(file);
```

3. Normal WriteLine calls:

```
    // 3) Just use any of the normal WriteLine methods as they use the
    // Environment.NewLine by default
    line = "Default line";
    Console.WriteLine(line);
```

Discussion

Environment.NewLine allows you to have peace of mind whether the platform is using \n or \r\n as the newline or possibly something else. Your code will be doing things the right way for each platform.

One word of caution here: if you are interoperating with a non-Windows operating system via SOAP and Web Services, the Environment.NewLine defined here might not be accurate for a stream you send to or receive from that other operating system. Of course, if you are doing Web Services, newlines aren't your biggest concern.

See Also

See the "Environment Class" topic in the MSDN documentation.

11.8   Create, Write to, and Read from a File

Problem

You need to create a file—possibly for logging information to or storing temporary information—and then write information to it. You also need to be able to read the information that you wrote to this file.

Solution

To create, write to, and read from a log file, we will use the FileStream and its reader and writer classes. For example, we will create methods to allow construction, reading to, and writing from a log file. To create a log file, you can use the following code:

```
    public FileStream CreateLogFile(string logFileName)
    {
        FileStream fileStream = new FileStream(logFileName,
                                    FileMode.Create,
                                    FileAccess.ReadWrite,
                                    FileShare.None);
        return (fileStream);
    }
```

To write text to this file, you can create a `StreamWriter` object wrapper around the previously created `FileStream` object (`fileStream`). You can then use the `WriteLine` method of the `StreamWriter` object. The following code writes three lines to the file: a string, followed by an integer, followed by a second string:

```
public void WriteToLog(FileStream fileStream, string data)
{
    // make sure we can write to this stream
    if(!fileStream.CanWrite)
    {
        // close it and reopen for append
        string fileName = fileStream.Name;
        fileStream.Close();
        fileStream = new FileStream(fileName,FileMode.Append);
    }
    StreamWriter streamWriter = new StreamWriter(fileStream);
    streamWriter.WriteLine(data);
    streamWriter.Close();
}
```

Now that the file has been created and data has been written to it, you can read the data from this file. To read text from a file, create a `StreamReader` object wrapper around the file. If the code had not closed the `FileStream` object (`fileStream`), it could use that object in place of the filename used to create the `StreamReader`. To read the entire file in as a single string, use the `ReadToEnd` method:

```
public string ReadAllLog(FileStream fileStream)
{
    if(!fileStream.CanRead)
    {
        // close it and reopen for read
        string fileName = fileStream.Name;
        fileStream.Close();
        fileStream = new FileStream(fileName,FileMode.Open,FileAccess.Read);
    }
    StreamReader streamReader = new StreamReader(fileStream);
    string contents = streamReader.ReadToEnd();
    streamReader.Close();
    return contents;
}
```

If you need to read the lines in one by one, use the `Peek` method, as shown in `ReadLogPeeking`, or the `ReadLine` method, as shown in `ReadLogByLines`:

```
public static void ReadLogPeeking(FileStream fileStream)
{
    if(!fileStream.CanRead)
    {
        // close it and reopen for read
        string fileName = fileStream.Name;
        fileStream.Close();
        fileStream = new FileStream(fileName,FileMode.Open,FileAccess.Read);
    }
```

```
            Console.WriteLine("Reading file stream peeking at next line:");
            StreamReader streamReader = new StreamReader(fileStream);
            while (streamReader.Peek() != -1)
            {
                Console.WriteLine(streamReader.ReadLine());
            }
            streamReader.Close();
        }
```

or:

```
    public static void ReadLogByLines(FileStream fileStream)
    {
        if(!fileStream.CanRead)
        {
            // close it and reopen for read
            string fileName = fileStream.Name;
            fileStream.Close();
            fileStream = new FileStream(fileName,FileMode.Open,FileAccess.Read);
        }
        Console.WriteLine("Reading file stream as lines:");
        StreamReader streamReader = new StreamReader(fileStream);
        string text = "";
        while ((text = streamReader.ReadLine()) != null)
        {
            Console.WriteLine(text);
        }
        streamReader.Close();
    }
```

If you need to read in each character of the file as a byte value, use the Read method, which returns a byte value:

```
    public static void ReadAllLogAsBytes(FileStream fileStream)
    {
        if(!fileStream.CanRead)
        {
            // close it and reopen for read
            string fileName = fileStream.Name;
            fileStream.Close();
            fileStream = new FileStream(fileName,FileMode.Open,FileAccess.Read);
        }
        Console.WriteLine("Reading file stream as bytes:");
        StreamReader streamReader = new StreamReader(fileStream);
        while (streamReader.Peek() != -1)
        {
            Console.Write(streamReader.Read());
        }
        streamReader.Close();
    }
```

This method displays numeric byte values instead of the characters that they represent. For example, if the log file contained the following text:

```
This is the first line.
100
This is the third line.
```

it would be displayed by the ReadAllLogAsBytes method, as follows:

```
8410410511532105115321161041013210210511411511632108 10
5110101461310494848131084104105115321051153211610410 13
2116104105114100321081051101014613 10
```

If you need to read in the file by chunks, create and fill a buffer of an arbitrary length based on your performance needs. This buffer can then be displayed or manipulated as needed:

```
public static void ReadAllBufferedLog (FileStream fileStream)
{
    if(!fileStream.CanRead)
    {
        // close it and reopen for read
        string fileName = fileStream.Name;
        fileStream.Close();
        fileStream = new FileStream(fileName,FileMode.Open,FileAccess.Read);
    }
    Console.WriteLine("Reading file stream as buffers of bytes:");
    StreamReader streamReader = new StreamReader(fileStream);
    while (streamReader.Peek() != -1)
    {
        char[] buffer = new char[10];
        int bufferFillSize = streamReader.Read(buffer, 0, 10);
        foreach (char c in buffer)
        {
            Console.Write(c);
        }
        Console.WriteLine(bufferFillSize);
    }
    streamReader.Close();
}
```

This method displays the log file's characters in 10-character chunks, followed by the number of characters actually read. For example, if the log file contained the following text:

```
This is the first line.
100
This is the third line.
```

it would be displayed by the ReadAllBufferedLog method as follows:

```
This is th10
e first li10
ne.
100
10
This is th10
e third li10
ne.
        5
```

Notice that at the end of every tenth character (the buffer is a char array of size 10), the number of characters read in is displayed. During the last read performed, only

---

five characters were left to read from the file. In this case, a 5 is displayed at the end of the text, indicating that the buffer was not completely filled.

The previous code could have been modified to use the ReadBlock method as shown in the ReadAllBufferedLogBlock method instead of the Read method. The output is the same in both cases:

```
public static void ReadAllBufferedLogBlock(FileStream fileStream)
{
    if(!fileStream.CanRead)
    {
        // close it and reopen for read
        string fileName = fileStream.Name;
        fileStream.Close();
        fileStream = new FileStream(fileName,FileMode.Open,FileAccess.Read);
    }
    Console.WriteLine("Reading file stream as buffers of bytes using ReadBlock:");
    StreamReader streamReader = new StreamReader(fileStream);
    while (streamReader.Peek() != -1)
    {
        char[] buffer = new char[10];
        int bufferFillSize = streamReader.ReadBlock(buffer, 0, 10);
        foreach (char c in buffer)
        {
            Console.Write(c);
        }
        Console.WriteLine(bufferFillSize);
    }
    streamReader.Close();
}
```

This displays the following text:

```
This is th10
e first li10
ne.
100
10
This is th10
e third li10
ne.
    5
```

Discussion

There are many mechanisms for recording state information about applications, other than creating a file full of the information. One example of this type of mechanism is the Windows Event Log, where informational, security, and error states can be logged during an application's progress. One of the primary reasons for creating a log file is to assist in troubleshooting or to debug your code in the field. If you are shipping code without some sort of debugging mechanism for your support staff (or possibly for you in a small company), we suggest you consider adding some logging support. Any developer who has spent a late night debugging a problem on a QA machine, or worse yet, at a customer site, can tell you the value of a log of the program's actions.

If you are writing character information to a file, the simplest method is to use the Write and WriteLine methods of the StreamWriter class to write data to the file. These two methods are overloaded to handle any of the primitive values (except for the byte data type), as well as character arrays. These methods are also overloaded to handle various formatting techniques discussed in Chapter 1. All of this information is written to the file as character text, not as the underlying primitive type.

If you need to write byte data to a file, consider using the Write and WriteByte methods of the FileStream class. These methods are designed to write byte values to a file. The WriteByte method accepts a single byte value and writes it to the file, after which the pointer to the current position in the file is advanced to the next value after this byte. The Write method accepts an array of bytes that can be written to the file, after which the pointer to the current position in the file is advanced to the next value after this array of bytes. The Write method can also choose a range of bytes in the array in which to write to the file.

The Write method of the BinaryWriter class overloaded similarly to the Write method of the StreamWriter class. The main difference is that the BinaryWriter class's Write method does not allow formatting. This allows the BinaryReader to read the information written by the BinaryWriter as its underlying type, not as a character or a byte. See Recipe 11.18 for an example of the BinaryReader and BinaryWriter classes in action.

Once we have the data written to the file, we can read it back out. The first concern when reading data from a file is not to go past the end of the file. The StreamReader class provides a Peek method that looks—but does not retrieve—the next character in the file. If the end of the file has been reached, a -1 is returned. Likewise, the Read method of this class also returns a -1 if it has reached the end of the file. The Peek and Read methods can be used in the following manner to make sure that you do not go past the end of the file:

```
StreamReader streamReader = new StreamReader("data.txt");
while (streamReader.Peek() != -1)
{
    Console.WriteLine(streamReader.ReadLine());
}
streamReader.Close();
```

or:

```
StreamReader streamReader = new StreamReader("data.txt");
string text = "";
while ((text = streamReader.Read()) != -1)
{
    Console.WriteLine(text);
}
streamReader.Close();
```

The main differences between the Read and Peek methods are that the Read method actually retrieves the next character and increments the pointer to the current position in the file by one character, and the Read method is overloaded to return an array of characters instead of just one. If the Read method is used that returns an array buffer of characters and the buffer is larger than the file, the extra elements in the buffer array are set to an empty string.

The StreamReader also contains a method to read an entire line up to and including the newline character. This method is called ReadLine. This method returns a null if it goes past the end of the file. The ReadLine method can be used in the following manner to make sure that you do not go past the end of the file:

```
StreamReader streamReader = new StreamReader("data.txt");
string text = "";
while ((text = streamReader.ReadLine()) != null)
{
    Console.WriteLine(text);
}
streamReader.Close();
```

If you simply need to read the whole file in at one time, use the ReadToEnd method to read the entire file in to a string. If the current position in the file is moved to a point other than the beginning of the file, the ReadToEnd method returns a string of characters starting at that position in the file and ending at the end of the file.

The FileStream class contains two methods, Read and ReadByte, which read one or more bytes of the file. The Read method reads a byte value from the file and casts that byte to an int before returning the value. If you are explicitly expecting a byte value, consider casting the return type to a byte value:

```
FileStream fileStream = new FileStream("data.txt", FileMode.Open);
byte retVal = (byte) fileStream.ReadByte();
```

However, if retVal is being used to determine whether the end of the file has been reached (i.e., retVal == -1 or retVal == 0xffffffff in hexadecimal), you will run into problems. When the return value of ReadByte is cast to a byte, a –1 is cast to 0xff, which is not equal to –1 but is equal to 255 (the byte data type is not signed). If you are going to cast this return type to a byte value, you cannot use this value to determine whether you are at the end of the file. You must instead rely on the Length Property. The following code block shows the use of the return value of the ReadByte method to determine when we are at the end of the file:

```
FileStream fileStream = new FileStream("data.txt", FileMode.Open);
int retByte = 0;
while ((retByte = fileStream.ReadByte()) != -1)
{
    Console.WriteLine((byte)retByte);
}
fileStream.Close();
```

This code block shows the use of the `Length` property to determine when to stop reading the file:

```
FileStream fileStream = new FileStream("data.txt", FileMode.Open);
long currPosition = 0;
while (currPosition < fileStream.Length)
{
    Console.WriteLine((byte) fileStream.ReadByte());
    currPosition++;
}
fileStream.Close();
```

The `BinaryReader` class contains several methods for reading specific primitive types, including character arrays and byte arrays. These methods can be used to read specific data types from a file. Recipe 11.18 contains more on this topic. All of these methods, except for the `Read` method, indicate that the end of the file has been reached by throwing the `EndOfStreamException`. The `Read` method will return a –1 if it is trying to read past the end of the file. This class contains a `PeekChar` method that is very similar to the `Peek` method in the `StreamReader` class. The `PeekChar` method is used as follows:

```
FileStream fileStream = new FileStream("data.txt", FileMode.Open);
BinaryReader binaryReader = new BinaryReader(fileStream);
while (binaryReader.PeekChar() != -1)
{
    Console.WriteLine(binaryReader.ReadChar());
}
binaryReader.Close();
```

In this code, the `PeekChar` method is used to determine when to stop reading values in the file. This will prevent a costly `EndOfStreamException` from being thrown by the `ReadChar` method if it tries to read past the end of the file.

See Also

See the "FileStream Class," "StreamReader Class," "StreamWriter Class," "Binary-Reader Class," and "BinaryWriter Class" topics in the MSDN documentation.

11.9 Determining Whether a Directory Exists

Problem

You need to determine whether a directory exists prior to creating or performing an action on that directory.

Solution

Use the static `Exists` method on the `Directory` class to determine whether a directory currently exists:

```
if (Directory.Exists(@"c:\delete\test"))
{
    // Operate on that directory here
}
```

Discussion

Determining whether a directory exists can be critical to your code. If you try to delete a directory that no longer exists, a System.IO.DirectoryNotFoundException will be thrown. This can be handled by catching the exception and reporting the failure accordingly for your application.

This method returns a bool indicating if the directory was found (true) or not (false).

See Also

See the "Directory Class" topic in the MSDN documentation.

11.10 Creating, Moving, and Deleting a Directory

Problem

You need to create a new directory, move an existing directory, or delete a directory.

Solution

The System.IO namespace contains two classes to perform these actions: the Directory and DirectoryInfo classes. The Directory class contains only static methods, while the DirectoryInfo class contains only instance methods.

To create a directory, you can use the static CreateDirectory method of the Directory class. The return value for this method is an instance of the DirectoryInfo class. This class can be used to invoke instance methods on the newly created directory. For example:

```
DirectoryInfo dirInfo = null;
if (!Directory.Exists(@"c:\delete\test"))
{
    dirInfo = Directory.CreateDirectory(@"c:\delete\test");
}
```

You can also use the instance Create method of the DirectoryInfo class—a method that takes no parameters and returns void. For example:

```
DirectoryInfo dirInfo = null;
if (!Directory.Exists(@"c:\delete\test"))
{
    dirInfo = new DirectoryInfo(@"c:\delete\test");
    dirInfo.Create();
}
```

To move a directory, you can use the static `Move` method of the `Directory` class, which returns void. For example:

```
if (!Directory.Exists(@"c:\MovedDir"))
{
    Directory.Move(@"c:\delete", @"c:\MovedDir");
}
```

You can also use the instance `MoveTo` method of the `DirectoryInfo` class, which returns void. For example:

```
DirectoryInfo dirInfo = null;
if (!Directory.Exists(@"c:\MovedDir"))
{
    dirInfo = new DirectoryInfo(@"c:\delete\test");
    dirInfo.MoveTo(@"c:\MovedDir");
}
```

To delete a directory, you can use the static `Delete` method of the `Directory` class, which returns void. There are two overloads for this method: one that will attempt to delete just the directory and one that you can pass a Boolean value to tell it to delete recursively. If you elect to delete the directory recursively, all subdirectories and files will be deleted as well. If you do not use the recursive flag, the `Delete` method will throw an exception if you attempt to delete a directory that has either files or subdirectories still in it:

```
if (Directory.Exists(@"c:\MovedDir"))
{
    Directory.Delete(@"c:\MovedDir", true);
}
```

You can also use the instance `Delete` method of the `DirectoryInfo` class, which returns a void. For example:

```
DirectoryInfo dirInfo = null;
if (Directory.Exists(@"c:\MovedDir"))
{
    dirInfo = new DirectoryInfo(@"c:\delete\test");
    dirInfo.Delete(true);
}
```

Discussion

Creating, moving, and deleting are the basic operations that you can perform on directories. It makes sense that there are specific methods to address each of these operations. In fact, there are two methods to perform each of these actions: one static and one instance method.

Which method you choose depends on what you are trying to accomplish. If you need a quick way of creating, moving, or deleting a directory, use the static methods since you don't incur the overhead of instantiating an object before performing the operation. If you will be performing multiple operations on a directory, you should use instance methods. Another consideration is that static methods on a class do not require an object to be created on the managed heap. Instance methods require an object to be created before the methods can be called. If you are trying to minimize the number of objects the garbage collector has to manage, consider using static methods.

Before creating a new directory, you should first determine whether that directory already exists. The Directory class contains a static method, Exists, to perform this operation (note that there are no instance classes to do this).

To move a directory, you must first determine whether the destination directory exists. If it does exist, the move operation will fail and throw an exception.

To delete a directory, you must first determine whether it exists. If it does not exist, the delete operation will fail and throw an exception.

See Also

See the "Directory Class" and "DirectoryInfo Class" topics in the MSDN documentation.

11.11 Manipulating Directory Attributes

Problem

You need to display or manipulate a directory's attributes or timestamps.

Solution

To display a directory's timestamps, you can use either the set of static methods from the Directory object or the set of instance properties from the DirectoryInfo object. The static methods are GetCreationTime, GetLastAccessTime, or GetLastWriteTime. For example:

```
public void DisplayDirAttr(string path)
{
    Console.WriteLine(Directory.GetCreationTime(path).ToString());
    Console.WriteLine(Directory.GetLastAccessTime(path).ToString());
    Console.WriteLine(Directory.GetLastWriteTime(path).ToString());
}
```

In each case, *path* is the path to the directory whose timestamp you wish to retrieve, and the method returns a DateTime value containing the relevant timestamp. The instance properties are CreationTime, LastAccessTime, or LastWriteTime. For example:

```
public void DisplayDirAttr(string path)
{
    DirectoryInfo dirInfo = Directory.CreateDirectory(path);

    Console.WriteLine(dirInfo.CreationTime.ToString());
    Console.WriteLine(dirInfo.LastAccessTime.ToString());
    Console.WriteLine(dirInfo.LastWriteTime.ToString());
}
```

Each property returns a `DateTime` value containing the timestamp from the directory represented by the `DirInfo` object.

To modify a directory's timestamps, you can use either set of static methods of the `Directory` class or a set of instance properties of the `DirectoryInfo` class. The static methods are `SetCreationTime`, `SetLastAccessTime`, or `SetLastWriteTime`. For example:

```
public void ModifyDirAttr(string path)
{
    DateTime dt = new DateTime(2003,5,10);
    Directory.SetCreationTime(path, dt);
    Directory.SetLastAccessTime(path, dt);
    Directory.SetLastWriteTime(path, dt);
}
```

Each method has two parameters: the first is the path to the directory whose timestamp is to be set, and the second is a `DateTime` value containing the new timestamp. Each method returns void. The instance properties, all of which are of type `DateTime`, are `CreationTime`, `LastAccessTime`, and `LastWriteTime`. For example:

```
public void ModifyDirAttr(string path)
{
    DirectoryInfo dirInfo = Directory.CreateDirectory(path);

    DateTime dt = new DateTime(2001,2,8);
    dirInfo.CreationTime = dt;
    dirInfo.LastAccessTime = dt;
    dirInfo.LastWriteTime = dt;
}
```

To display or modify a directory's attributes, use the instance property `Attributes`:

```
public void ViewModifyDirAttr(string path, FileAttributes fileAttributes)
{
    DirectoryInfo dirInfo = new DirectoryInfo(@"C:\Windows\System32");
    // Display this directory's attributes
    Console.WriteLine(dirInfo.Attributes);

    // Display whether this directory is hidden
    Console.WriteLine("Is directory hidden? = " +
        ((dirInfo.Attributes & FileAttributes.Hidden) == FileAttributes.Hidden));

    // Modify this directory's attributes
    dirInfo.Attributes |= fileAttributes;
    // Display whether this directory is hidden
    Console.WriteLine("Is directory hidden? = " +
        ((dirInfo.Attributes & FileAttributes.Hidden) == FileAttributes.Hidden));
}
```

Discussion

There are three distinct timestamps associated with any particular directory. These timestamps are creation time, last access time, and last write time.

In addition to timestamp information, a directory's attributes may also be obtained and modified. This is accomplished through the use of the public instance Attributes property found on a DirectoryInfo object. This property either returns or modifies a FileAttributes enumeration (see Table 11-9). The FileAttributes enumeration is made up of bit flags that can be turned on or off through the use of the bitwise operators &, |, or ^.

Table 11-9. Definitions of each bit flag in the FileAttributes enumeration

Flag name	Definition
Archive	The current directory is archived.
Compress	The current directory uses compression.
Directory	The current item is a directory.
Encrypted	The current directory is encrypted.
Hidden	The current directory is hidden.
Normal	The current directory has no other attributes set. When this attribute is set, no others can be set.
NotContentIndexed	The current directory is not being indexed by the Indexing service.
Offline	The current directory is offline, and its contents are not accessible unless it is online.
ReadOnly	The current directory is read only.
ReparsePoint	The current directory contains a reparse point.
SparseFile	The current directory contains large files consisting mostly of zeros.
System	The current directory is used by the system.
Temporary	The current directory is classified as a temporary directory.

In many cases, more than one of these flags may be set at one time. The Normal flag is the exception; when this flag is set, no other flag may be set.

See Also

See the "Directory Class," "DirectoryInfo Class," and "FileAttributes Enumeration" topics in the MSDN documentation.

11.12 Renaming a Directory

Problem

You need to rename a directory.

Solution

Unfortunately, there is no specific rename method that can be used to rename a directory. However, you can use the instance MoveTo method of the DirectoryInfo class or the static Move method of the Directory class instead. The static Move method can be used to rename a directory in the following manner:

```
public void DemonstrateRenameDir(string originalName, string newName)
{
    try
    {
        Directory.CreateDirectory(originalName);
        // "rename" it
        Directory.Move(originalName, newName);
        // clean up after ourselves
        Directory.Delete(newName);
    }
    catch(IOException ioe)
    {
        // most likely given the directory exists or isn't empty
        Console.WriteLine(ioe.ToString());
    }
    catch(Exception e)
    {
        // catch any other exceptions
        Console.WriteLine(e.ToString());
    }
}
```

This code creates a directory using the *originalName* parameter, renames it to the value supplied in the *newName* parameter and removes it once complete.

The instance MoveTo method of the DirectoryInfo class can also be used to rename a directory in the following manner:

```
public void DemonstrateRenameDir (string originalName, string newName)
{
    try
    {
        DirectoryInfo dirInfo = new DirectoryInfo(originalName);
        // create the dir
        dirInfo.Create();
        // "rename" it
        dirInfo.MoveTo(newName);
        // clean up after ourselves
        dirInfo.Delete(false);
    }
    catch(IOException ioe)
    {
        // most likely given the directory exists or isn't empty
        Console.WriteLine(ioe.ToString());
    }
    catch(Exception e)
    {
        // catch any other exceptions
        Console.WriteLine(e.ToString());
    }
}
```

This code creates a directory using the *originalName* parameter, renames it to the value supplied in the *newName* parameter and removes it once complete.

Discussion

The Move and MoveTo methods allow a directory to be moved to a different location. However, when the path remains unchanged up to the directory that will have its name changed, the Move methods act as a Rename method.

See Also

See the "Directory Class" and "DirectoryInfo Class" topics in the MSDN documentation

11.13 Searching for Directories or Files Using Wildcards

Problem

You are attempting to find one or more specific files or directories that might or might not exist within the current filesystem. The search might need to use wildcard characters in order to widen the search; for example, searching for all user mode dump files in a filesystem. These files have a *.dmp* extension.

Solution

There are several methods of obtaining this information. The first three methods return a string array containing the full path of each item. The next three methods return an object that encapsulates a directory, a file, or both.

The static GetFileSystemEntries method on the Directory class returns a string array containing the names of all files and directories within a single directory. For example, the following method retrieves a string array containing the names of all files and subdirectories in a particular directory, then displays them:

```
public void DisplayFilesDirs(string path)
{
    string[] items = Directory.GetFileSystemEntries(path);
    foreach (string item in items)
    {
        Console.WriteLine(item);
    }
}
```

The static GetDirectories method on the Directory class returns a string array containing the names of all directories within a single directory. For example, the following method retrieves a string array containing the names of all subdirectories in a particular directory, then displays them:

```
public void DisplayDirs(string path)
{
    string[] items = Directory.GetDirectories(path);
    foreach (string item in items)
    {
        Console.WriteLine(item);
    }
}
```

The static `GetFiles` method on the `Directory` class returns a string array containing the names of all files within a single directory. For example, the following method retrieves a string array containing the name of a file in a particular directory, then displays it:

```
public void DisplayFiles(string path)
{
    string[] items = Directory.GetFiles(path);
    foreach (string item in items)
    {
        Console.WriteLine(item);
    }
}
```

These next three methods return an object instead of simply a string. The `GetFileSystemInfos` method of the `DirectoryInfo` object returns a strongly typed array of `FileSystemInfo` objects (that is, of `DirectoryInfo` and `FileInfo` objects) representing the directories and files within a single directory. For example, the following code calls the `GetFileSystemInfos` method to retrieve an array of `FileSystemInfo` objects representing all the items in a particular directory, and then lists the Name property of each item to the console window:

```
public void DisplayFilesDirs(string path)
{
    DirectoryInfo mainDir = new DirectoryInfo(path);
    FileSystemInfo[] items = mainDir.GetFileSystemInfos();
    foreach (FileSystemInfo item in items)
    {
        if (item is DirectoryInfo)
        {
            Console.WriteLine("DIRECTORY: " + ((DirectoryInfo)item).Name);
        }
        else if (item is FileInfo)
        {
            Console.WriteLine("FILE: " + item.Name);
        }
        else
        {
            Console.WriteLine("Unknown");
        }
    }
}
```

The GetDirectories instance method of the DirectoryInfo object returns an array of DirectoryInfo objects representing only subdirectories in a single directory. For example, the following code calls the GetDirectories method to retrieve an array of DirectoryInfo objects, then displays the Name property of each object to the console window:

```
public void DisplayDirs(string path)
{
    DirectoryInfo mainDir = new DirectoryInfo(path);
    DirectoryInfo[] items = mainDir.GetDirectories();
    foreach (DirectoryInfo item in items)
    {
        Console.WriteLine("DIRECTORY: " + ((DirectoryInfo)item).Name);
    }
}
```

The GetFiles instance method of the FileInfo object returns an array of FileInfo objects representing only the files in a single directory. For example, the following code calls the GetFiles method to retrieve an array of FileInfo objects, then it displays the Name property of each object to the console window:

```
public void DisplayFiles(string path)
{
    DirectoryInfo mainDir = new DirectoryInfo(path);
    FileInfo[] items = mainDir.GetFiles();
    foreach (FileInfo item in items)
    {
        Console.WriteLine("FILE: " + item.Name);
    }
}
```

There are several ways to obtain this information. The first three methods return a string representing the full path of the directory and/or file. The next three methods return an object that encapsulates a directory, a file, or both.

The static GetFileSystemEntries method on the Directory class returns all files and directories in a single directory that match pattern:

```
public void DisplayFilesDirs(string path, string pattern)
{
    string[] items = Directory.GetFileSystemEntries(path, pattern);
    foreach (string item in items)
    {
        Console.WriteLine(item);
    }
}
```

The static GetDirectories method on the Directory class returns only those directories in a single directory that match pattern:

```
public void DisplayDirs(string path, string pattern)
{
    string[] items = Directory.GetDirectories(path, pattern);
    foreach (string item in items)
```

```
    {
        Console.WriteLine(item);
    }
}
```

The static `GetFiles` method on the `Directory` class returns only those files in a single directory that match pattern:

```
public void DisplayFiles(string path, string pattern)
{
    string[] items = Directory.GetFiles(path, pattern);
    foreach (string item in items)
    {
        Console.WriteLine(item);
    }
}
```

These next three methods return an object instead of simply a string. The first instance method is `GetFileSystemInfos`, which returns both directories and files in a single directory that match pattern:

```
public void DisplayFilesDirs(string path, string pattern)
{
    DirectoryInfo mainDir = new DirectoryInfo(path);
    FileSystemInfo[] items = mainDir.GetFileSystemInfos(pattern);
    foreach (FileSystemInfo item in items)
    {
        if (item is DirectoryInfo)
        {
            Console.WriteLine("DIRECTORY: " + ((DirectoryInfo)item).Name);
        }
        else if (item is FileInfo)
        {
            Console.WriteLine("FILE: " + item.Name);
        }
        else
        {
            Console.WriteLine("Unknown");
        }
    }
}
```

The `GetDirectories` instance method returns only directories (contained in the `DirectoryInfo` object) in a single directory that match pattern:

```
public void DisplayDirs(string path, string pattern)
{
    DirectoryInfo mainDir = new DirectoryInfo(@"C:\TEMP ");
    DirectoryInfo[] items = mainDir.GetDirectories(pattern);
    foreach (DirectoryInfo item in items)
    {
        Console.WriteLine("DIRECTORY: " + ((DirectoryInfo)item).Name);
    }
}
```

The `GetFiles` instance method returns only file information (contained in the `FileInfo` object) in a single directory that match pattern:

```
public void DisplayFiles(string path, string pattern)
{
    DirectoryInfo mainDir = new DirectoryInfo(@"C:\TEMP ");
    FileInfo[] items = mainDir.GetFiles(pattern);
    foreach (FileInfo item in items)
    {
        Console.WriteLine("FILE: " + item.Name);
    }
}
```

Discussion

If you need just an array of strings containing paths to both directories and files, you can use the static method `Directory.GetFileSystemEntries`. The string array returned does not include any information about whether an individual element is a directory or a file. Each string element contains the entire path to either a directory or file contained within the specified path.

To quickly and easily distinguish between directories and files, use the `Directory.GetDirectories` and `Directory.GetFiles` static methods. These methods return arrays of directory names and filenames. These methods return an array of string objects. Each element contains the full path to the directory or file.

Returning a string is fine if you do not need any other information about the directory or file returned to you or if you are going to need more information for only one of the files returned. It is more efficient to use the static methods to get the list of filenames and just retrieve the `FileInfo` for the ones you need than to have all of the `FileInfo`s constructed for the directory that the instance methods will do. If you are going to have to access attributes, lengths, or times on every one of the files, you should consider using the instance methods described here.

The instance method `GetFileSystemInfos` returns an array of strongly typed `FileSystemInfo` objects. (The `FileSystemInfo` object is the base class to the `DirectoryInfo` and `FileInfo` objects.) Therefore, you can test whether the returned type is a `DirectoryInfo` or `FileInfo` object using the is or as keywords. Once you know what subclass this object really is, you can cast it to that type and begin using it.

To get only `DirectoryInfo` objects, use the overloaded `GetDirectories` instance method. To get only `FileInfo` objects, use the overloaded `GetFiles` instance method. These methods return an array of `DirectoryInfo` and `FileInfo` objects respectively; each element of which encapsulates a directory or file.

See Also

See the "DirectoryInfo Class," "FileInfo Class," and "FileSystemInfo Class" topics in the MSDN documentation.

11.14 Obtaining the Directory Tree

Problem

You need to get a directory tree, potentially including filenames, extending from any point in the directory hierarchy. In addition, each directory or file returned must be in the form of an object encapsulating that item. This will allow you to perform operations on the returned objects, such as deleting the file, renaming the file, or examining/changing its attributes. Finally, you potentially need the ability to search for a specific subset of these items based on a pattern, such as finding only files with the .pdb extension.

Solution

By placing a call to the GetFileSystemInfos instance method in a recursive method, you can iterate down the directory hierarchy from any starting point and get all files and directories:

```
public void GetAllDirFilesRecurse(string Dir)
{
    DirectoryInfo mainDir = new DirectoryInfo(dir);
    FileSystemInfo[] items = mainDir.GetFileSystemInfos();
    foreach (FileSystemInfo item in items)
    {
        if (item is DirectoryInfo)
        {
            Console.WriteLine("DIRECTORY: " + ((DirectoryInfo)item).FullName);
            GetAllDirFilesRecurse(((DirectoryInfo)item).FullName);
        }
        if (item is FileInfo)
        {
            Console.WriteLine("FILE: " + ((FileInfo)item).FullName);
        }
        else
        {
            Console.WriteLine("Unknown");
        }
    }
}
```

It isn't necessarily true that you have to use recursion to retrieve information about *all* files and directories. The following recursive method uses both the GetFiles and GetDirectories instance methods with pattern matching to obtain a listing of all files with the extension of .pdb that exist in directories that begin with a "Chapter 1":

```
public void GetAllFilesInPatternRecurse(string Dir)
{
    DirectoryInfo mainDir = new DirectoryInfo(dir);
    FileSystemInfo[] items = mainDir.GetFileSystemInfos("Chapter 1*");
    foreach (FileSystemInfo item in items)
    {
```

```
            if (item is DirectoryInfo)
            {
                GetAllFilesInPatternRecurse(((DirectoryInfo)item).FullName);
            }
            if (item is FileInfo)
            {
                FileInfo fileInfo = item as FileInfo;
                if(fileInfo.Extension.ToUpper( ).CompareTo(".PDB")==0)
                    Console.WriteLine("FILE: " + (fileInfo.FullName));
            }
        }
    }
```

Discussion

To obtain a tree representation of a directory with its respective files, you can use a simple recursive method. This recursive method first creates a DirectoryInfo object that begins in the directory with which you wish to start creating a hierarchy; in the first code example in the Solution section, this directory is represented by the mainDir object. It must then check the pattern for this directory to see whether it should be reported before moving down the directory trees.

Next, it can call the GetFileSystemInfos method on the mainDir object to obtain both DirectoryInfo and FileInfo objects representing the files and directories in that initial folder. Alternatively, it could call both the GetFiles and GetDirectories methods on the mainDir object; the latter two methods return a string array containing the paths and names of files and directories.

Simply calling the GetFileSystemInfos method is easy enough, but you need to cast the returned FileSystemInfo objects to their correct subtype, which is either a DirectoryInfo or a FileInfo object. Once cast to the correct type, you can perform operations on that object.

The final step is to add a recursive method call every time you find a DirectoryInfo object. This DirectoryInfo object is then passed as an argument to this same function, making it the starting directory for the new function call. This continues on until every directory under the initial directory has been returned along with its contents.

You will note that the check of the FileSystemInfos in the if statements are not an if–else tree. This is done deliberately so that you catch the files in a directory as you traverse back upwards.

See Also

See the "DirectoryInfo Class," "FileInfo Class," and "FileSystemInfo Class" topics in the MSDN documentation.

11.15 Parsing a Path

Problem

You need to separate the constituent parts of a path and place them into separate variables.

Solution

Use the static methods of the Path class:

```
public static void ParsePath(string path)
{
    string root = Path.GetPathRoot(path);
    string dirName = Path.GetDirectoryName(path);
    string fullFileName = Path.GetFileName(path);
    string fileExt = Path.GetExtension(path);
    string fileNameWithoutExt = Path.GetFileNameWithoutExtension(path);
    StringBuilder format = new StringBuilder();
    format.Append("ParsePath of {0} breaks up into the following" +
            "pieces:\r\n\tRoot: {1}\r\n\t");
    format.Append("Directory Name: {2}\r\n\tFull File Name: {3}\r\n\t");
    format.Append("File Extension: {4}\r\n\tFile Name Without Extension: {5}\r\n");
    Console.WriteLine(format.ToString(),path,root,dirName,
            fullFileName,fileExt,fileNameWithoutExt);
}
```

If the string @"c:\test\tempfile.txt" is passed to this method, the output would look like this:

```
ParsePath of C:\test\tempfile.txt breaks up into the following pieces:
        Root: C:\
        Directory Name: C:\test
        Full File Name: tempfile.txt
        File Extension: .txt
        File Name Without Extension: tempfile
```

Discussion

The Path class contains methods that can be used to parse a given path. Using these classes is much easier and less error-prone than writing path- and filename-parsing code. There are five main methods used to parse a path: GetPathRoot, GetDirectoryName, GetFileName, GetExtension, and GetFileNameWithoutExtension. Each has a single parameter, *path*, which represents the path to be parsed:

GetPathRoot
> This method returns the root directory of the path. If no root is provided in the path, such as when a relative path is used, this method returns an empty string, not null.

GetDirectoryName
> This method returns the complete path to a file.

GetFileName

This method returns the filename, including the file extension. If no filename is provided in the path, this method returns an empty string, not null.

GetExtension

This method returns the file's extension. If no extension is provided for the file or no file exists in the path, this method returns an empty string, not null.

GetFileNameWithoutExtension

This method returns the root filename without the file extension. If no extension is provided on the file, this method returns an empty string, not null.

Be aware that these methods do not actually determine whether the drives, directories, or even files exist on the system that runs these methods. These methods are string parsers and if you pass one of them a string in some strange format (such as "\\ZY:\foo"), it will try to do what it can with it anyway:

```
ParsePath of \\ZY:\foo breaks up into the following pieces:
        Root: \\ZY:\foo
        Directory Name:
        Full File Name: foo
        File Extension:
        File Name Without Extension: foo
```

These methods will, however, throw an exception if illegal characters are found in the path. To determine whether files or directories exist, use the static `Directory.Exists` or `File.Exists` methods.

See Also

See the "Path Class" topic in the MSDN documentation.

11.16 Parsing Paths in Environment Variables

Problem

You need to parse multiple paths contained in environment variables, such as PATH or Include.

Solution

You can use the `Path.PathSeparator` field or the `;` character to extract individual paths from an environment variable whose value consists of multiple paths, and place them in an array. Then you can use a `foreach` loop to iterate over each individual path in the PATH environment variable and parse each path. This process is illustrated by the `ParsePathEnvironmentVariable` method:

```
public static void ParsePathEnvironmentVariable()
{
    string originalPathEnv = Environment.GetEnvironmentVariable("PATH");
```

```
        string[] paths = originalPathEnv.Split(new char[1] {Path.PathSeparator});
        foreach (string s in paths)
        {
            string pathEnv = Environment.ExpandEnvironmentVariables(s);
            Console.WriteLine("Path = " + pathEnv);
            if(pathEnv.Length > 0)
            {
                Console.WriteLine("Individual Path = " + pathEnv);
            }
            else
            {
                Console.WriteLine("Skipping blank environment path details " +
                        " as it causes exceptions...");
            }
            Console.WriteLine();
        }
    }
```

If the PATH environment variable contains the following:

```
PATH=Path=C:\WINDOWS\system32;C:\WINDOWS
```

then the output of the ParsePathEnvironmentVariable method is as follows:

```
Path = C:\WINDOWS\system32
GetDirectoryName = C:\WINDOWS
GetExtension =
GetFileName = system32
GetFileNameWithoutExtension = system32
GetFullPath = C:\WINDOWS\system32
GetPathRoot = C:\
HasExtension = False
IsPathRooted = True

Path = C:\WINDOWS
GetDirectoryName = C:\
GetExtension =
GetFileName = WINDOWS
GetFileNameWithoutExtension = WINDOWS
GetFullPath = C:\WINDOWS
GetPathRoot = C:\
HasExtension = False
IsPathRooted = True
```

Discussion

When working with environment variables in particular, there are a number of cases
in which several paths may be concatenated together and you need to parse each one
individually. To distinguish each individual path from the others, Microsoft Windows uses the semicolon character. (Other operating systems might use a different
character; Unix, Linux, and Mac OS X use a colon.) To make sure that we always
use the correct path separation character, the Path class contains a public static field
called PathSeparator. This field contains the character used to separate paths in the
current platform. This field is marked as read-only, so it cannot be modified.

To obtain each individual path contained in a single string, use the Split instance method from the String class. This method accepts a param array of character values that are used to break apart the string instance. These individual strings containing the paths are returned in a string array. We can then simply use the foreach loop construct to iterate over each string in this string array, and we can use the various static methods of the Path class to operate on each individual path string.

See Also

See the "Path Class" and "Environment Class" topics in the MSDN documentation.

11.17 Verifying a Path

Problem

You have a path—possibly entered by the user—and you need to verify that it has no illegal characters and that a filename and extension exist.

Solution

We use several of the static fields and methods in the Path class. We begin by writing a method called CheckUserEnteredPath, which accepts a string containing a path entered by the user and a Boolean value to decide whether we want to find all illegal characters or just the occurrence of any illegal character. Just finding any illegal character is much faster if you don't care which illegal characters are present. This method first calls another method, either FindAnyIllegalChars or FindAllIllegalChars, each of which are described later in the Solution. If there are no illegal characters in this path, it is then checked for the existence of a file and extension:

```
public bool CheckUserEnteredPath(string path, bool any)
{
    try
    {
        Console.WriteLine("Checking path {0}",path);
        bool illegal = false;
        // two ways to do the search, one more expensive than the other...
        if(any == true)
            illegal = FindAnyIllegalChars(path);
        else
            illegal = FindAllIllegalChars(path);

        if (!illegal)
        {
            if (Path.GetFileName(path).Length == 0)
            {
                Console.WriteLine("A filename must be entered");
            }
            else if (!Path.HasExtension(path))
            {
                Console.WriteLine("The filename must have an extension");
```

```
                }
            else
            {
                Console.WriteLine("Path is correct");
                return (true);
            }
        }
    }
    catch(Exception e)
    {
        Console.WriteLine(e.ToString());
    }
    return (false);
}
```

The `FindAllIllegalChars` method, which is called by the `CheckUserEnteredPath` method, accepts a string containing a path. This path is checked for illegal characters by using the `IndexOfAny` method on the string class. The `IndexOfAny` method finds the first occurrence of one of the characters supplied to it in the string being looked at. This method uses the `Path.InvalidPathChars` static field to determine if any illegal characters exist in this path:

```
private bool FindAllIllegalChars(string userEnteredPath)
{
    int  invalidCharPos = -1;
    bool endOfPath = false;
    bool foundIllegalChars = false;

    while (!endOfPath)
    {
        invalidCharPos = userEnteredPath.IndexOfAny(Path.InvalidPathChars,
                                            invalidCharPos + 1);
        if (invalidCharPos == -1)
        {
            endOfPath = true;
        }
        else
        {
            foundIllegalChars = true;
            Console.WriteLine("Invalid char {0} found at position {1}",
userEnteredPath[invalidCharPos],invalidCharPos);
            if (invalidCharPos >= userEnteredPath.Length - 1)
            {
                endOfPath = true;
            }
            else
            {
                invalidCharPos++;
            }
        }
    }
    return (foundIllegalChars);

}
```

The FindAnyIllegalChars method, which is also called by the CheckUserEnteredPath method, accepts a string containing a user entered path. This path is checked for the existence of any illegal characters by using the IndexOfAny method on the string class. If the IndexOfAny method finds anything, we have an illegal path and we return false:

```
private bool FindAnyIllegalChars(string userEnteredPath)
{
    int invalidCharPos = userEnteredPath.IndexOfAny(Path.InvalidPathChars);
    if (invalidCharPos == -1)
    {
        return (false);
    }
    else
    {
        Console.WriteLine("Invalid char {0} found at position {1}",
userEnteredPath[invalidCharPos],invalidCharPos);
        return (true);
    }
}
```

Discussion

This recipe provides a way of verifying a path for invalid characters before it can be used in your application. This recipe does not verify that the directory or path exists; use the Directory.Exists or File.Exists methods to perform this verification.

The CheckUserEnteredPath method starts by calling the FindAnyIllegalChars or FindAllIllegalChars methods and passing the chosen one a path string. Two different mechanisms validate the path against the set of characters supplied by Path.InvalidPathChars. This field contains all of the invalid characters that could be entered into a path string. Both methods return true if there are illegal characters found, but FindAnyIllegalChars prints information to the console only for the first one found, whereas FindAllIllegalChars prints out information for every illegal character found.

See Also

See the "String Class" and "Path Class" topics in the MSDN documentation.

11.18 Using a Temporary File in Your Application

Problem

You need a temporary file in which to store information. This file will exist only as long as the process that created it remains running.

Solution

Use the static `GetTempPath` and `GetTempFileName` methods on the `Path` class. To create the temporary file in the directory set as the temporary directory and get the full path to it, use the following line of code:

```
string tempFilePathWithFileName = Path.GetTempFileName();
```

Before the application terminates, you should delete this temporary file. The following line of code deletes this file:

```
File.Delete(tempFilePathWithFileName);
```

The `GetTempFileName` method creates the temporary file and returns the path, including the name of the file and its extension. To create and obtain just the path without the filename, use the following line of code:

```
string tempFilePathWithoutFileName = Path.GetTempPath();
```

Once all files are closed, before the application terminates, this temporary directory should be deleted as well. The following line of code deletes this directory and any files or subdirectories within it:

```
Directory.Delete(tempFilePathWithoutFileName,true);
```

Discussion

You should use a temporary file whenever you need to store information temporarily for later retrieval. The one thing you must remember is to delete this temporary file before the application that created it is terminated. If it is not deleted, it will remain in the user's temporary directory until the user manually deletes it.

The `Path` class provides two methods for working with temporary files. The first is the static `GetTempPath` method, which returns the path to the temporary directory specified in the `TEMP` environment variable.

The second static method, `GetTempFileName`, will automatically generate a temporary filename, create a zero-length file in the user's temporary directory, and return a string containing this filename and its path.

See Also

See the "Directory Class," "File Class," and "Path Class" topics in the MSDN documentation.

11.19 Opening a File Stream with just a File Handle

Problem

When interoperating with unmanaged code, you encounter a situation where you are provided a file handle and no other information. This file handle must be used to open its corresponding file.

Solution

In order to use an unmanaged file handle to access a file, use the `FileStream` class. The unmanaged file handle could have been generated using P/Invoke to open a file and get the file handle. The code would then pass it to the `WriteToFileHandle` managed method for writing data, then flush and close the unmanaged file handle. This setup is illustrated in the following code:

```
public void UsingAnUnmanagedFileHandle()
{
    IntPtr hFile = IntPtr.Zero;
    // create a file using unmanaged code
    hFile = (IntPtr)FileInteropFunctions.CreateFile("data.txt",
        FileInteropFunctions.GENERIC_WRITE,
        0,
        IntPtr.Zero,
        FileInteropFunctions.CREATE_ALWAYS,
        0,
        0);

    if(hFile.ToInt64() > 0)
    {
        // write to the file using managed code
        WriteToFileHandle(hFile);
        // close the file
        FileInteropFunctions.CloseHandle(hFile);
        // remove the file
        File.Delete("data.txt");
    }
}
```

In order to write to the file handle, we wrap it in a `FileStream`, passing the file handle as the first parameter. Once we have the file stream, we use the capabilities of the `FileStream` to write to the file handle by getting the bytes from a string in ASCII encoding format and calling `Write` on the file stream, as shown here:

```
public static void WriteToFileHandle(IntPtr hFile)
{
    // Open a FileStream object using the passed in file handle
    // pass false so that the stream doesn't own the handle, if this was true,
    // closing the filestream would close the handle
```

```
    FileStream fileStream = new FileStream(hFile, FileAccess.ReadWrite, false);
    // flush before we start to clear any pending unmanaged actions
    fileStream.Flush();
    // Operate on file here...
    string line = "Managed code wrote this line!";
    // write to the file
    byte[] bytes = Encoding.ASCII.GetBytes(line);
    fileStream.Write(bytes,0,bytes.Length);
    // just close the file stream
    fileStream.Close();
}
```

In order to perform the unmanaged functions of creating, flushing, and closing the file handle, we have wrapped the unmanaged Win32 API functions for these functions. The DllImport attribute says that these functions are being used from *kernel32.dll* and the SetLastError attribute is set to true, so that we can see if anything went wrong. A few of the #defines used with file creation have been brought over from unmanaged code for readability:

```
class FileInteropFunctions
{
    public const uint GENERIC_READ = (0x80000000);
    public const uint GENERIC_WRITE = (0x40000000);
    public const uint GENERIC_EXECUTE = (0x20000000);
    public const uint GENERIC_ALL = (0x10000000);

    public const uint CREATE_NEW        = 1;
    public const uint CREATE_ALWAYS     = 2;
    public const uint OPEN_EXISTING     = 3;
    public const uint OPEN_ALWAYS       = 4;
    public const uint TRUNCATE_EXISTING = 5;

    [DllImport("kernel32.dll", SetLastError=true)]
    public static extern bool CloseHandle(IntPtr hObject);

    [DllImport("kernel32.dll", SetLastError=true)]
    public static extern IntPtr CreateFile(
        String lpFileName,              // filename
        uint dwDesiredAccess,             // access mode
        uint dwShareMode,              // share mode
        IntPtr attr,                   // Security Descriptor
        uint dwCreationDisposition,       // how to create
        uint dwFlagsAndAttributes,        // file attributes
        uint hTemplateFile);             // handle to template file

    [DllImport("kernel32.dll", SetLastError=true)]
    public static extern bool FlushFileBuffers(IntPtr hFile);
}
```

Discussion

You can open a file using one of the overloaded constructors of the FileStream class and passing a file handle into it. When opening a file handle, determine whether this object should be able to close this file's handle. If the unmanaged code creating the

---

file intends to hand off ownership to the managed code, the object should set the ownsHandle parameter to true. The ownsHandle parameter is the third parameter on the constructor used with an existing handle. In many cases, this instance should not be allowed to close this file's handle. Instead, let the code that initially opened the file also close the file. If in doubt, set this parameter to false.

Keep your code short when opening a file using a file handle. Call the FileStream. Close method as soon as possible. The reason for this recommendation is that another object might also have this file open, and operating on that file through both FileStream objects can corrupt the data in the file.

See Also

See the "DllImport Attribute," "File Class," and "FileStream Class" topics in the MSDN documentation.

11.20 Write to Multiple Output Files at One Time

Problem

Any output that is written to one file must also be written to at least one other file. Essentially, you want to end up with at least the original file and the duplicate file.

Solution

Create a class called MultiWriter with the ability to write to multiple files from a single WriteLine call.

To create a set of files, just pass the file paths you would like to use to the constructor like this:

```
// Create a list of three file names
string[] names = new string[3];
for (int i=0;i<3;i++)
{
    names[i] = Path.GetTempFileName();
}
MultiWriter multi = new MultiWriter(names);
```

Next, perform the writes and close the instance:

```
multi.WriteLine("First Line");
multi.WriteLine("Second Line");
multi.WriteLine("Third Line");
multi.Close();
```

Here is the implementation of the MultiWriter class:

```
class MultiWriter : IDisposable
{
    FileStream[] _streams;
    string [] _names;
```

```csharp
int _streamCount = 0;
bool _disposed = false;

public MultiStream(string[] fileNames)
{
    try
    {
        // copy the names
        _names = (string[])fileNames.Clone();
        // set the number of streams
        _streamCount = fileNames.Length;
        // make the stream array
        _streams = new FileStream[_streamCount];
        for(int i = 0; i < _streams.Length; i++)
        {
            // create this filestream
            _streams[i] = new FileStream(_names[i],
                FileMode.Create,
                FileAccess.ReadWrite,
                FileShare.None);
        }
    }
    catch(IOException ioe)
    {
        Console.WriteLine(ioe.ToString());
    }
}

public void WriteLine(string text)
{
    // add a newline
    text += Environment.NewLine;
    // get the bytes in unicode format...
    byte[] bytes = Encoding.ASCII.GetBytes(text);
    // roll over the streams
    for(int i = 0; i < _streams.Length; i++)
    {
        // write the text
        _streams[i].Write(bytes,0,bytes.Length);
    }
}

public void Close()
{
    Dispose();
}

public void Dispose()
{
    try
    {
        // only close out once
        if(_disposed == false)
        {
```

```
            // close each stream
            for(int i=0;i<_streams.Length;i++)
            {
                _streams[i].Close();
            }
            // prevent refinalizing
            GC.SuppressFinalize(this);
            // indicate we have done this already
            _disposed = true;
        }
    }
    catch(IOException ioe)
    {
        Console.WriteLine(ioe.ToString());
    }
    }
}
```

Discussion

MultiStream implements the IDisposable interface, which helps the users remember
to close the files this will create. Ultimately, if the user forgets to call Close (a thin
wrapper around Dispose for semantic convenience), the finalizer (~MultiStream) will
call Dispose anyway and close the files when the garbage collector finalizes the
instance. Note that in the Dispose method, we check to see whether the instance has
been disposed before; if not, we close the file streams we created internally and call
the GC.SuppressFinalize method. This is an optimization to keep the garbage collector from having to call our finalizer and subsequently hold on to the object longer.

See Also

See the "FileStream Class," "GC Class," and "IDisposable Interface" topics in the
MSDN documentation.

11.21 Launching and Interacting with Console Utilities

Problem

You have an application that you need to automate and that takes input only from
the standard input stream. You need to drive this application via the commands it
will take over the standard input stream.

Solution

Say we needed to drive the *CMD.EXE* application to display the current time with
the TIME /T command (it is possible to just run this command from the command
line, but this way we can demonstrate an alternative method to drive an application

that responds to standard input). The way to do this is to launch a process that is looking for input on the standard input stream. This is accomplished via the `Process` class `StartInfo` property, which is an instance of a `ProcessStartInfo` class. The `Process.Start` method will launch a new process, but the `StartInfo` property controls many of the details of what sort of environment that process executes in.

First, make sure that the `StartInfo.RedirectStandardInput` property is set to `true`. This setting notifies the process that it should read from standard input. Then set the `StartInfo.UseShellExecute` property to `false` because if you were to let the shell launch the process for you, it would prevent you from redirecting standard input.

Once this is done, launch the process and write to its standard input stream as shown:

```
public void RunProcessToReadStdIn()
{
    Process application = new Process();
    // run the command shell
    application.StartInfo.FileName = @"cmd.exe";

    // turn on standard extensions
    application.StartInfo.Arguments = "/E:ON";

    application.StartInfo.RedirectStandardInput = true;

    application.StartInfo.UseShellExecute = false;

    // start it up
    application.Start();

    // get stdin
    StreamWriter input = application.StandardInput;

    // run the command to display the time
    input.WriteLine("TIME /T");

    // stop the application we launched
    input.WriteLine("exit");
}
```

Discussion

Once the input has been redirected, you can write into the standard input stream of the process by getting the `Process.StandardInput` property that is a `StreamWriter`. Once you have that, you can send things to the process via `WriteLine` calls, as shown earlier.

In order to use `StandardInput`, you have to specify `true` for the `StartInfo` property's `RedirectStandardInput` property. Otherwise, reading the `StandardInput` property throws an exception.

When `UseShellExecute` is false, you can only use `Process` to create executable processes. Normally the Process class can be used to perform operations on the file, like printing a Microsoft Word document. Another difference when using `false` is that the working directory is not used to find the executable, so you should be mindful to pass a full path or have the executable on your `PATH` environment variable.

See Also

See the "Process Class," "ProcessStartInfo Class," "RedirectStandardInput Property," and "UseShellExecute Property" topics in the MSDN documentation.

11.22 Locking Subsections of a File

Problem

You need to read or write data to or from a section of a file, and you want to make sure that no other processes or threads can access, modify, or delete the file until you have finished with it.

Solution

Locking out other processes or threads from accessing your file while you are using it is accomplished through the `Lock` method of the `FileStream` class. The following code creates a file from the *fileName* parameter and writes two lines to it. The entire file is then locked using the `Lock` method. While the file is locked, the code goes off and does some other processing; when this code returns, the file is closed, thereby unlocking it:

```
public void CreateLockedFile(string fileName)
{
    FileStream fileStream = new FileStream(fileName,
        FileMode.Create,
        FileAccess.ReadWrite,
        FileShare.ReadWrite);
    StreamWriter streamWriter = new StreamWriter(fileStream);

    streamWriter.WriteLine("The First Line");
    streamWriter.WriteLine("The Second Line");
    streamWriter.Flush();

    // Lock all of the file
    fileStream.Lock(0, fileStream.Length);

    // Do some lengthy processing here...
    Thread.Sleep(1000);

    // Make sure we unlock the file.
    // If a process terminates with part of a file locked or closes a file
    // that has outstanding locks, the behavior is undefined which is MS
    // speak for bad things....
```

```
        fileStream.Unlock(0, fileStream.Length);

        streamWriter.WriteLine("The Third Line");
        streamWriter.Close();
        fileStream.Close();
    }
```

Discussion

If a file is opened within your application and the FileShare parameter of the FileStream.Open call is set to FileShare.ReadWrite or FileShare.Write, other code in your application can alter the contents of the file while you are using it. To handle file access with more granularity, use the Lock method on the FileStream object to prevent other code from overwriting all or a portion of your file. Once you are done with the locked portion of your file, you can call the Unlock method on the FileStream object to allow other code in your application to write data to the file or that portion of the file.

To lock an entire file, use the following syntax:

```
        fileStream.Lock(0, fileStream.Length);
```

To unlock a portion of a file, use the following syntax:

```
        fileStream.Lock(4, fileStream.Length - 4);
```

This line of code locks the entire file except for the first four characters. Note that you can lock an entire file and still open it multiple times, as well as write to it.

If another thread is accessing this file, it is possible to see an IOException thrown during the call to either the Write, Flush, or Close methods. For example, the following code is prone to such an exception:

```
public void CreateLockedFile(string fileName)
{
    FileStream fileStream = new FileStream(fileName,
                            FileMode.Create,
                            FileAccess.ReadWrite,
                            FileShare.ReadWrite);
    StreamWriter streamWriter = new StreamWriter(fileStream);

    streamWriter.WriteLine("The First Line");
    streamWriter.WriteLine("The Second Line");
    streamWriter.Flush();

    // Lock all of the file
    fileStream.Lock(0, fileStream.Length);

    StreamWriter streamWriter2 = new StreamWriter(new FileStream(fileName,
                                        FileMode.Open,
                                        FileAccess.Write,
                                        FileShare.ReadWrite));
    streamWriter2.Write("foo ");
    try
```

```
    {
        streamWriter2.Close( );  // --> Exception occurs here!
    }
    catch
    {
        Console.WriteLine("The streamWriter2.Close call generated an exception.");
    }
    streamWriter.WriteLine("The Third Line");
    streamWriter.Close( );
    fileStream.Close( );
}
```

Even though `streamWriter2`, the second `StreamWriter` object, writes to a locked file, it is when the `streamWriter2.Close` method is executed that the `IOException` is thrown.

If the code for this recipe were rewritten as follows:

```
public void CreateLockedFile(string fileName)
{
    FileStream fileStream = new FileStream(fileName,
                                FileMode.Create,
                                FileAccess.ReadWrite,
                                FileShare.ReadWrite);
    StreamWriter streamWriter = new StreamWriter(fileStream);

    streamWriter.WriteLine("The First Line");
    streamWriter.WriteLine("The Second Line");
    streamWriter.Flush( );

    // Lock all of the file
    fileStream.Lock(0, fileStream.Length);

    // Try to access the locked file...
    StreamWriter streamWriter2 = new StreamWriter(new FileStream(fileName,
                                        FileMode.Open,
                                        FileAccess.Write,
                                        FileShare.ReadWrite));

    StreamWriter2.Write("foo ");
    streamWriter.Close( );
    streamWriter2.Flush( );
    streamWriter2.Close( );

    streamWriter.Close( );
    fileStream.Close( );
}
```

no exception is thrown. This is due to the fact that the code closed the `FileStream` object that initially locked the entire file. This action also freed all of the locks on the file that this `FileStream` object was holding onto. Since the `streamWriter2.Write("Foo")` method had written Foo to the stream's buffer (but had not flushed it), the string Foo was still waiting to be flushed and written to the actual file. Keep this situation in mind when interleaving the opening, locking, and closing of streams. Mistakes in code sometimes manifest themselves a while after they are written. This leads to some bugs more difficult to track down, so tread carefully when using file locking.

See Also

See the "StreamWriter Class" and "FileStream Class" topics in the MSDN documentation.

11.23 Watching the Filesystem for Specific Changes to One or More Files or Directories

Problem

You want to be notified when a file and/or directory is created, modified, or deleted. In addition, you might also need to be notified of any of these actions for a group of files and/or directories. This can aid in alerting your application as to when a file, such as a log file, grows to a certain size, after which it must be truncated.

Solution

To be notified when an action takes place in the filesystem, you need to employ the FileSystemWatcher class. The following method, TestWatcher, sets up a FileSystemWatcher object to watch the entire *C:* drive for any changes. The changes are limited to any file with the extension *.txt*. At the end of this method, the events are wired up for each one of the changes listed in the NotifyFilter property:

```
public void TestWatcher( )
{
    FileSystemWatcher fsw = new FileSystemWatcher( );
    fsw.Path = @"c:\";
    fsw.Filter = @"*.txt";
    fsw.IncludeSubdirectories = true;

    fsw.NotifyFilter = NotifyFilters.FileName     |
        NotifyFilters.Attributes   |
        NotifyFilters.LastAccess   |
        NotifyFilters.LastWrite    |
        NotifyFilters.Security     |
        NotifyFilters.Size         |
        NotifyFilters.CreationTime |
        NotifyFilters.DirectoryName;

    fsw.Changed += new FileSystemEventHandler(OnChanged);
    fsw.Created += new FileSystemEventHandler(OnCreated);
    fsw.Deleted += new FileSystemEventHandler(OnDeleted);
    fsw.Renamed += new RenamedEventHandler(OnRenamed);
    fsw.Error += new ErrorEventHandler(OnError);

    fsw.EnableRaisingEvents = true;

    string file = @"c:\myfile.txt";
    string newfile = @"c:\mynewfile.txt";
    FileStream stream = File.Create(file);
    stream.Close( );
```

```
        File.Move(file,newfile);
        File.Delete(newfile);

        fsw.Dispose( );
    }
```

The following code implements the event handlers to handle the events that are raised by the FileSystemWatcher object that was created and initialized in the TestWatcher method:

```
    public void OnChanged(object source, FileSystemEventArgs e)
    {
        Console.WriteLine("File " + e.FullPath + " --> " + e.ChangeType.ToString( ));
    }

    public void OnDeleted(object source, FileSystemEventArgs e)
    {
        Console.WriteLine("File " + e.FullPath + " --> " + e.ChangeType.ToString( ));
    }

    public void OnCreated(object source, FileSystemEventArgs e)
    {
        Console.WriteLine("File " + e.FullPath + " --> " + e.ChangeType.ToString( ));
    }

    public void OnRenamed(object source, RenamedEventArgs e)
    {
        Console.WriteLine("File " + e.OldFullPath + " (renamed to)--> " + e.FullPath);
    }

    public void OnError(object source, ErrorEventArgs e)
    {
        Console.WriteLine("Error " + e.ToString( ));
    }
```

Discussion

Watching for changes in the filesystem centers around the FileSystemWatcher class. This class can watch for filesystem changes on the local machine, a networked drive, and even a remote machine. The limitations of watching files on a remote machine are that the watching machine must be running versions of Windows starting from Windows NT 4.0 through 2000, XP, Server 2003, and Longhorn. The one caveat for Windows NT 4.0 is that a Windows NT 4.0 machine cannot watch another remote Windows NT 4.0 machine.

The FileSystemWatcher object cannot watch directories or files on a CD or DVD drive (including rewritables) in the current versions of the framework. This limitation might be revisited in a future version of the framework. This object does watch files regardless of whether their hidden property is set. To start watching a filesystem, we need to create an instance of the FileSystemWatcher class. After creating the FileSystemWatcher object, we can set its properties in order to focus our efforts in watching a filesystem. Table 11-10 examines the various properties that can be set on this object.

Table 11-10. Properties that can be set on the FileSystemWatcher object

Property name	Description

Path	A path to a directory in which to watch. The following are some examples of valid values for this property:
	
	`@"C:\temp"`
	`@"C:\Program Files"`
	`@"C:\Progra~1"`
	`@"..\..\temp"`
	`@"\\MyServer\temp"`
	`@"."`
	`@""`
	
	Note that if a directory is specified, changes to it, such as deleting it or changing its attributes, are not watched. Only changes within the *temp* directory are watched. Assigning an empty string forces the current directory to be watched.

IncludeSubdirectories	Set to `true` to monitor all subdirectories as well, or `false` to watch only the specified directory.

Filter	Specifies a specific subset of files to watch. The following are some examples of valid values for this property:
	
	`@"*.exe"    // Watch only .exe files`
	`@"*"        // Watch all files`
	`@""         // Watch all files`
	`@"a*"       // Watch all files beginning with the letter 'a'`
	`@"test.d??" // Watch all files with the name "test" and`
	`               having a three letter extension starting`
	`               with the letter 'd'`

NotifyFilter	One or more `NotifyFilters` enumeration values. This enumeration is marked with the `FlagsAttribute`, so each enumeration value can be ORed together using the | operator. By default, this property is set to FileName, DirectoryName, and LastWrite. The members of the NotifyFilters enumeration are shown in Table 11-11.
EnableRaisingEvents	When this property is set to `true`, the `FileSystemWatcher` object starts watching the filesystem. To stop this object from watching the filesystem, set this property to `false`.
InternalBufferSize	The internal buffer size in bytes for this object. It is used to store information about the raised filesystem events. This buffer defaults in size to 8192 bytes. See additional information about this property next.

Table 11-11. NotifyFilters enumeration value definitions

Enumeration name	Description
Attributes	Watches for changes to a file or directory's attributes.
CreationTime	Watches for changes to a file or directory's creation time.
DirectoryName	Watches for changes to a directory's name.
FileName	Watches for changes to a file's name.
LastAccess	Watches for changes to a file or directory's last-accessed property.
LastWrite	Watches for changes to a file or directory's last-written-to property.
Security	Watches for changes to a file or directory's security settings.
Size	Watches for changes to a file or directory's size.

The NotifyFilters enumeration values in Table 11-11 determine which events the FileSystemWatcher object watches. For example, the OnChanged event can be raised when any of the following NotifyFilters enumeration values are passed to the NotifyFilter property:

```
NotifyFilters.Attributes
NotifyFilters.Size
NotifyFilters.LastAccess
NotifyFilters.LastWrite
NotifyFilters.Security
NotifyFilters.CreationTime
```

The OnRenamed event can be raised when any of the following NotifyFilters enumeration values are passed to the NotifyFilter property:

```
NotifyFilters.DirectoryName
NotifyFilters.FileName
```

The OnCreated and OnDeleted events can be raised when any of the following NotifyFilters enumeration values are passed to the NotifyFilter property:

```
NotifyFilters.DirectoryName
NotifyFilters.FileName
```

There are times when the FileSystemWatcher object cannot handle the number of raised events coming from the filesystem. In this case, the Error event is raised, informing you that the buffer has overflowed and specific events may have been lost. To reduce the likelihood of this problem, we can limit the number of raised events by minimizing the number of events watched for in the NotifyFilter property. To decrease the number of raised events further, you can set the IncludeSubdirectories property to false. You should note that adding a narrower filter to the Filter property to filter out more files does not affect the number of raised events this object receives. The Filter property is applied to the information already stored in the buffer, so this will not help if you are losing notifications due to the buffer overflows.

If the NotifyFilter and IncludeSubdirectories properties cannot be modified, consider increasing the InternalBufferSize property. To estimate what size to increase this buffer to, Microsoft provides the following tips:

- A 4k byte buffer can keep track of changes for about 80 files in a directory.
- Every event consumes 16 bytes of buffer space.
- In addition to these 16 bytes, the filename is stored as Unicode characters.
- If you are using Windows 2000, consider increasing/decreasing the buffer size by a multiple of 4k bytes. This is the same size as a default memory page.
- If you do not know your operating system's page size, use the following code to increase the FileSystemWatcher's buffer size:

```
FileSystemWatcher fsw = new FileSystemWatcher( );
fsw.InternalBufferSize *= Multiplier;
```

  where *Multiplier* is an integer used to increase the size of the buffer. This makes the most efficient use of the buffer space.

If possible, increase the InternalBufferSize as a last resort since this is an expensive operation due to the buffer space being created in nonpaged memory. Nonpaged memory is memory available to the process that will always be in physical memory. It is a limited resource and is shared across all processes on the machine, so it is possible to affect the operation of other processes using this pool if too much is requested.

In many cases, a single action performed by the user produces many filesystem events. Creating a text file on the desktop yields the following changes:

```
File c:\documents and settings\administrator\ntuser.dat.log --> Changed
File c:\documents and settings\administrator\ntuser.dat.log --> Changed
File c:\documents and settings\administrator\ntuser.dat.log --> Changed
File c:\documents and settings\administrator\ntuser.dat.log --> Changed
File c:\documents and settings\administrator\ntuser.dat.log --> Changed
File c:\documents and settings\administrator\ntuser.dat.log --> Changed
File c:\documents and settings\administrator\ntuser.dat.log --> Changed
File c:\documents and settings\administrator\ntuser.dat.log --> Changed
File c:\documents and settings\administrator\ntuser.dat --> Changed
File c:\documents and settings\administrator\ntuser.dat --> Changed
File c:\documents and settings\administrator\ntuser.dat --> Changed
File c:\documents and settings\administrator\ntuser.dat --> Changed
File c:\documents and settings\administrator\ntuser.dat.log --> Changed
File c:\winnt\system32\config\software.log --> Changed
File c:\winnt\system32\config\software.log --> Changed
File c:\winnt\system32\config\software.log --> Changed
File c:\winnt\system32\config\software --> Changed
File c:\winnt\system32\config\software --> Changed
File c:\winnt\system32\config\software --> Changed
File c:\winnt\system32\config\software --> Changed
File c:\winnt\system32\config\software.log --> Changed
File c:\documents and settings\administrator\desktop\newdoc.txt Created
```

Much of this work is simply registry access, but you notice at the end of this listing that the text file is finally created.

Another example of multiple filesystem events firing for a single action is when this newly created text file is opened by double-clicking on it. The following events are raised by this action:

```
File c:\winnt\system32\notepad.exe --> Changed
File c:\winnt\system32\notepad.exe --> Changed
File c:\documents and settings\administrator\recent\newdoc.txt.lnk --> Deleted
File c:\documents and settings\administrator\recent\newdoc.txt.lnk --> Created
File c:\documents and settings\administrator\recent\newdoc.txt.lnk --> Changed
File c:\winnt\system32\config\software.log --> Changed
File c:\winnt\system32\shell32.dll --> Changed
File c:\winnt\system32\shell32.dll --> Changed
```

Of course, your results may vary, especially if another application accesses the registry or another file while the text file is being opened. Even more events may be raised if a background process or service, such as a virus checker, is accessing the filesystem.

See Also

See the "FileSystemWatcher Class" and "NotifyFilters Enumeration" topics in the MSDN documentation.

11.24 Waiting for an Action to Occur in the Filesystem

Problem

You need to be notified when a particular event occurs in the filesystem, such as the renaming of a particular file or directory, the increasing or decreasing of the size of a file, the user deleting a file or directory, the creation of a file or directory, or even the changing of a file or directory's attribute(s). However, this notification must occur synchronously. In other words, the application cannot continue unless a specific action occurs to a file or directory.

Solution

The WaitForChanged method of the FileSystemWatcher class can be called to wait synchronously for an event notification. This is illustrated in the following method, which waits for an action—more specifically, the action of creating the *Backup.zip* file somewhere on the *C:* drive—to be performed before proceeding on to the next line of code, which is the WriteLine statement. Finally, we ask the ThreadPool to use a thread to go create the file in question using the PauseAndCreateFile method, so that the FileSystemWatcher can detect the file creation:

```
public void WaitForZipCreation(string path, string fileName)
{
    FileSystemWatcher fsw = null;
    try
    {
        fsw = new FileSystemWatcher();
        string [] data = new string[] {path,fileName};
        fsw.Path = path;
        fsw.Filter = fileName;
        fsw.NotifyFilter = NotifyFilters.LastAccess | NotifyFilters.LastWrite
            | NotifyFilters.FileName | NotifyFilters.DirectoryName;

        // Run the code to generate the file we are looking for
        // Normally you wouldn't do this as another source is creating
        // this file
        if(ThreadPool.QueueUserWorkItem(new WaitCallback(PauseAndCreateFile),
                                                        data))
        {
            // block waiting for change
            WaitForChangedResult result =
                        fsw.WaitForChanged(WatcherChangeTypes.Created);
            Console.WriteLine("{0} created at {1}.",result.Name,path);
        }
    }
```

```
        }
        catch(Exception e)
        {
            Console.WriteLine(e.ToString());
        }
        // clean it up
        File.Delete(fileName);

        if(fsw != null)
            fsw.Dispose();
    }
```

The code for `PauseAndCreateFile` is listed here. It is in the form of a `WaitCallback` to be used as an argument to `QueueUserWorkItem` on the `Thread` class. `QueueUserWorkItem` will run `PauseAndCreateFile` on a thread from the .NET thread pool:

```
    void PauseAndCreateFile(Object stateInfo)
    {
        try
        {
            string[] data = (string[])stateInfo;
            // wait a sec...
            Thread.Sleep(1000);
            // create a file in the temp directory
            string path = data[0];
            string file = path + data[1];
            Console.WriteLine("Creating {0} in PauseAndCreateFile...",file);
            FileStream fileStream = File.Create(file);
            fileStream.Close();
        }
        catch(Exception e)
        {
            Console.WriteLine(e.ToString());
        }
    }
```

Discussion

The `WaitForChanged` method returns a `WaitForChangedResult` structure that contains the properties listed in Table 11-12.

Table 11-12. WaitForChangedResult properties

Property	Description
ChangeType	Lists the type of change that occurred. This change is returned as a `WatcherChangeTypes` enumeration. The values of this enumeration can possibly be ORed together.
Name	Holds the name of the file or directory that was changed. If the file or directory was renamed, this property returns the changed name. Its value is set to `null` if the operation method call times out.
OldName	The original name of the modified file or directory. If this file or directory was not renamed, this property will return the same value as the Name property. Its value is set to `null` if the operation method call times out.
TimedOut	Holds a Boolean indicating whether the `WaitForChanged` method timed out (`true`) or not (`false`).

Now, you can certainly add a timeout to the WaitForChanged call to prevent you from hanging forever on the WaitForChanged call, but that is more of a recovery option than actually performing the action you want, which is to see a file change. This mechanism could be set up in a loop to check periodically whether you should continue to monitor for this file change (user could hit "cancel" on your application in another UI thread, for example).

See Also

See the "FileSystemWatcher Class," "NotifyFilters Enumeration," and "Wait-ForChangedResult Structure" topics in the MSDN documentation.

11.25 Comparing Version Information of Two Executable Modules

Problem

You need to programmatically compare the version information of two executable modules. An executable module is a file that contains executable code such as an EXE or DLL file. The ability to compare the version information of two executable modules can be very useful to an application if it is trying to determine if it has all of the "right" pieces present to execute or when deciding on an assembly to dynamically load through reflection. This trick is also useful when an application is looking for the newest version of a file or DLL from many files or DLLs spread out in the local filesystem or on a network.

Solution

Use the CompareFileVersions method to compare executable module version information. This method accepts two filenames, including their paths, as parameters. The version information of each module is retrieved and compared. This file returns a FileComparison enumeration, defined as follows:

```
public enum FileComparison
{
    Error = 0,
    File1IsNewer = 1,
    File2IsNewer = 2,
    FilesAreSame = 3
}
```

The code for the CompareFileVersions method is:

```
public FileComparison CompareFileVersions(string file1, string file2)
{
    FileComparison retValue = FileComparison.Error;
    // do both files exist?
    if (!File.Exists(file1))
```

```csharp
{
    Console.WriteLine(file1 + " does not exist");
}
else if (!File.Exists(file2))
{
    Console.WriteLine(file2 + " does not exist");
}
else
{
    // get the version information
    FileVersionInfo file1Version = FileVersionInfo.GetVersionInfo(file1);
    FileVersionInfo file2Version = FileVersionInfo.GetVersionInfo(file2);

    // check major
    if (file1Version.FileMajorPart > file2Version.FileMajorPart)
    {
        Console.WriteLine(file1 + " is a newer version");
        retValue = FileComparison.File1IsNewer;
    }
    else if (file1Version.FileMajorPart < file2Version.FileMajorPart)
    {
        Console.WriteLine(file2 + " is a newer version");
        retValue = FileComparison.File2IsNewer;
    }
    else // major version is equal, check next...
    {
        // check minor
        if (file1Version.FileMinorPart > file2Version.FileMinorPart)
        {
            Console.WriteLine(file1 + " is a newer version");
            retValue = FileComparison.File1IsNewer;
        }
        else if (file1Version.FileMinorPart < file2Version.FileMinorPart)
        {
            Console.WriteLine(file2 + " is a newer version");
            retValue = FileComparison.File2IsNewer;
        }
        else // minor version is equal, check next...
        {
            // check build
            if (file1Version.FileBuildPart > file2Version.FileBuildPart)
            {
                Console.WriteLine(file1 + " is a newer version");
                retValue = FileComparison.File1IsNewer;
            }
            else if (file1Version.FileBuildPart < file2Version.FileBuildPart)
            {
                Console.WriteLine(file2 + " is a newer version");
                retValue = FileComparison.File2IsNewer;
            }
            else // build version is equal, check next...
            {
                // check private
                if (file1Version.FilePrivatePart > file2Version.FilePrivatePart)
```

```
                {
                    Console.WriteLine(file1 + " is a newer version");
                    retValue = FileComparison.File1IsNewer;
                }
                else if (file1Version.FilePrivatePart <
                        file2Version.FilePrivatePart)
                {
                    Console.WriteLine(file2 + " is a newer version");
                    retValue = FileComparison.File2IsNewer;
                }
                else
                {
                    // identical versions.
                    Console.WriteLine("The files have the same version");
                    retValue = FileComparison.FilesAreSame;
                }
            }
        }
    }
}
        return retValue;
}
```

Discussion

Not all executable modules have version information. If you load a module with no version information using the FileVersionInfo class, you will not throw an exception, nor will you get null back for the object reference. Instead, you will get a valid FileVersionInfo object with all data members in their initial state (which is null for .NET objects).

Assemblies actually have two sets of version information: the version information available in the assembly manifest and the PE (Portable Executable) file version information. FileVersionInfo reads the assembly manifest version information.

The first action this method takes is to determine whether the two files passed in to the *file1* and *file2* parameters actually exist. If so, the static GetVersionInfo method is called on the FileVersionInfo class with each file passed in as a parameter.

The CompareFileVersions method attempts to compare each portion of the file's version number using the following properties of the FileVersionInfo object returned by GetVersionInfo:

FileMajorPart
    The first 2 bytes of the version number.

FileMinorPart
    The second 2 bytes of the version number.

FileBuildPart
    The third 2 bytes of the version number.

FilePrivatePart
    The final 2 bytes of the version number.

The full version number is comprised of these four parts, making up an 8-byte number representing the file's version number.

The CompareFileVersions method first compares the FileMajorPart version information of the two files. If these are equal, the FileMinorPart version information of the two files is compared. This continues through the FileBuildPart and finally the FilePrivatePart version information values. If all four parts are equal, the files are considered to have the same version number. If a file is found to have a higher number than the other file, that first file is considered to be of an earlier version than the one with the higher number.

See Also

See the "FileVersionInfo Class" topic in the MSDN documentation.

Reflection

Reflection is the mechanism provided by the .NET Framework to allow you to inspect how a program is constructed. Using reflection, you can obtain information such as the name of an assembly and what other assemblies a given assembly imports. You can even dynamically call methods on a type in a given assembly. Reflection also allows you to create code dynamically and compile it to an in-memory assembly or to build a symbol table of type entries in an assembly. Reflection is a very powerful feature of the framework, and, as such, is guarded by the runtime, requiring the ReflectionPermission be granted to assemblies doing this type of work. "Code Access Security" has only two permission sets that give all reflection access by default: FullTrust and Everything. The LocalIntranet permission set allows for the ReflectionEmit privilege that allows for emitting metadata and creating assemblies, but not the TypeInformation privilege for inspecting other assemblies or the MemberAccess privilege for performing dynamic invocation of methods on types in assemblies. In this chapter, you will see how you can use reflection to dynamically invoke members on types, figure out all of the assemblies a given assembly is dependent on, and inspect assemblies for different types of information. Reflection is a great way to understand how things are put together in .NET; this chapter provides a starting point.

12.1 Listing Imported Assemblies

Problem

You need to determine each assembly imported by a particular assembly. This information can show you if this assembly is using one or more of your assemblies or if your assembly is using another specific assembly.

Solution

Use the `Assembly.GetReferencedAssemblies` method to obtain the imported assemblies of an assembly:

```
using System;
using System.Reflection;
using System.Collections.Specialized;

public static void BuildDependentAssemblyList(string path,
                                              StringCollection assemblies)
{
    // maintain a list of assemblies the original one needs
    if(assemblies == null)
            assemblies = new StringCollection( );

    // have we already seen this one?
    if(assemblies.Contains(path)==true)
        return;

    Assembly asm = null;
    // look for common path delimiters in the string
    // to see if it is a name or a path
    if((path.IndexOf(@"\",0,path.Length)!=-1)||
        (path.IndexOf("/",0,path.Length)!=-1))
    {
        // load the assembly from a path
        asm = Assembly.LoadFrom(path);
    }
    else
    {
        // try as assembly name
        asm = Assembly.Load(path);
    }
    // add the assembly to the list
    if(asm != null)
    {
        assemblies.Add(path);
    }

    // get the referenced assemblies
    AssemblyName[] imports = asm.GetReferencedAssemblies( );
    // iterate
    foreach (AssemblyName asmName in imports)
    {
        // now recursively call this assembly to get the new modules
        // it references
        BuildDependentAssemblyList(asmName.FullName,assemblies);
    }
}
```

This code fills a `StringCollection` containing the original assembly, all imported assemblies, and the dependent assemblies of the imported assemblies.

If you ran this method against the assembly *C:\CSharpRecipes\bin\Debug\CSharpRecipes.exe*, you'd get the following dependency tree:

```
C:\CSharpRecipes\bin\Debug\CSharpRecipes.exe

mscorlib, Version=1.0.5000.0, Culture=neutral,
   PublicKeyToken=b77a5c561934e089

System, Version=1.0.5000.0, Culture=neutral, PublicKeyToken=b77a5c561934e089

System.Xml, Version=1.0.5000.0, Culture=neutral,
   PublicKeyToken=b77a5c561934e089

System.Runtime.Serialization.Formatters.Soap, Version=1.0.5000.0,
   Culture=neutral, PublicKeyToken=b03f5f7f11d50a3a

REGEX_Test, Version=0.0.0.0, Culture=neutral, PublicKeyToken=null

FileIODenied, Version=1.0.0.0, Culture=neutral, PublicKeyToken=null

FileIOPermitted, Version=1.0.0.0, Culture=neutral, PublicKeyToken=null
```

Discussion

Obtaining the imported types in an assembly is useful in determining what assemblies another assembly is using. This knowledge can greatly aid in learning to use a new assembly. This method can also help determine dependencies between assemblies for shipping purposes.

The GetReferencedAssemblies method of the System.Reflection.Assembly class obtains a list of all the imported assemblies. This method accepts no parameters and returns an array of AssemblyName objects instead of an array of Types. The AssemblyName type is made up of members that allow access to the information about an assembly, such as the name, version, culture information, public/private key pairs, and other data.

Note that this method does not account for assemblies loaded using the Assembly.Load* methods, as it is only inspecting for compile-time references.

See Also

See the "Assembly Class" topic in the MSDN documentation.

12.2   Listing Exported Types

Problem

You need to obtain all the exported types of an assembly. This information allows you to see what types are usable from outside of this assembly.

Solution

Use `Assembly.GetExportedTypes` to obtain the exported types of an assembly:

```
using System;
using System.Reflection;

public static void ListExportedTypes(string path)
{
    // load the assembly
    Assembly asm = Assembly.LoadFrom(path);
    Console.WriteLine("Assembly: {0} imports:",path);
    // get the exported types
    Type[] types = asm.GetExportedTypes();
    foreach (Type t in types)
    {
        Console.WriteLine ("\tExported Type: {0}",t.FullName);
    }
}
```

The previous example will display all exported, or public, types:

```
Assembly: C:\C#Cookbook\CSharpRecipes.exe imports:
        Exported Type: CSharpRecipes.ClassAndStructs
        Exported Type: CSharpRecipes.Line
        Exported Type: CSharpRecipes.Square
        Exported Type: CSharpRecipes.CompareHeight
        Exported Type: CSharpRecipes.Foo
        Exported Type: CSharpRecipes.ObjState
```

Discussion

Obtaining the exported types in an assembly is useful when determining the public interface to that assembly. This ability can greatly aid in learning to use a new assembly or can aid the developer of that assembly in determining all access points to their assembly and seeing whether they are adequately secure from malicious code. To get these exported types, we use the `GetExportedTypes` method on the `System.Reflection.Assembly` type. The exported types consist of all of the types that are publicly accessible from outside of the assembly. A type may have public accessibility but not be accessible from outside of the assembly. Take, for example, the following code:

```
public class Outer
{
    public class Inner {}
    private class SecretInner {}
}
```

The exported types are `Outer` and `Outer.Inner`; the type `SecretInner` is not exposed to the world outside of this assembly. If we change the `Outer` accessibility from public to private, we now have no types accessible to the outside world—the `Inner` class access level is downgraded because of the private on the `Outer` class.

See Also

See the "Assembly Class" topic in the MSDN documentation

12.3   Finding Overridden Methods

Problem

You have an inheritance hierarchy that is several levels deep and has many virtual and overridden methods. You need to determine which method in a derived class overrides what method in one of many possible base classes.

Solution

Use the `MethodInfo.GetBaseDefinition` method to determine which method is overridden in what base class. The following overloaded method, `FindMethodOverrides`, examines all of the static and public instance methods in a class and displays which methods override their respective base class methods. This method also determines which base class the overridden method is in. This overloaded method accepts an assembly path and name along with a type name in which to find overriding methods. Note that the *typeName* parameter must be the fully qualified type name (i.e., the complete namespace hierarchy, followed by any containing classes, followed by the type name you are querying):

```
public void FindMethodOverrides(string asmPath, string typeName)
{
    Assembly asm = Assembly.LoadFrom(asmPath);
    Type asmType = asm.GetType(typeName);

    Console.WriteLine("---[" + asmType.FullName + "]---");

    // get the methods that match this type
    MethodInfo[] methods = asmType.GetMethods(BindingFlags.Instance |
        BindingFlags.NonPublic | BindingFlags.Public |
        BindingFlags.Static | BindingFlags.DeclaredOnly);
    foreach (MethodInfo method in methods)
    {
        Console.WriteLine("Current Method:  " + method.ToString());

        // get the base method
        MethodInfo baseDef = method.GetBaseDefinition();
        if (baseDef != method)
        {
            Console.WriteLine("Base Type FullName:  " +
                baseDef.DeclaringType.FullName);
            Console.WriteLine("Base Method:  " + baseDef.ToString());

            // list the types of this method
            Type[] paramTypes = new Type[method.GetParameters().Length];
            int counter = 0;
            foreach (ParameterInfo param in method.GetParameters())
```

```
        {
            paramTypes[counter] = param.ParameterType;
            Console.WriteLine("\tParam {0}: {1}",
                param.Name,param.ParameterType.ToString());
            counter++;
        }
    }
    Console.WriteLine();
    }
}
```

The second overloaded method allows you to determine whether a particular method overrides a method in its base class. It accepts the same two arguments as the first overloaded method, along with the full method name and an array of Type objects representing its parameter types:

```
public void FindMethodOverrides(string asmPath, string typeName,
    string methodName, Type[] paramTypes)
{
    Console.WriteLine("For [Type] Method:  [" + typeName + "] " + methodName);

    Assembly asm = Assembly.LoadFrom(asmPath);
    Type asmType = null;
    asmType = asm.GetType(typeName,true,true);
    MethodInfo method = asmType.GetMethod(methodName, paramTypes);

    if (method != null)
    {
        MethodInfo baseDef = method.GetBaseDefinition();
        if (baseDef != method)
        {
            Console.WriteLine("Base Type FullName:  " +
                baseDef.DeclaringType.FullName);
            Console.WriteLine("Base Method:  " + baseDef.ToString());
            // get the parameters for the base method
            Type[] baseParamTypes =
                new Type[baseDef.GetParameters().Length];
            bool foundMatch = true;

            // same number of params as we are looking for?
            if(paramTypes.Length == baseParamTypes.Length)
            {
                int counter = 0;
                foreach (ParameterInfo param in baseDef.GetParameters())
                {
                    if(paramTypes[counter].UnderlyingSystemType !=
                        param.ParameterType.UnderlyingSystemType)
                    {
                        // found an unmatching parameter, mark false
                        foundMatch = false;
                    }
                    // list the params so we can see which one we got
                    Console.WriteLine("\tParam {0}: {1}",
                        param.Name,param.ParameterType.ToString());
                    counter++;
```

```
                }
            }
            else
                foundMatch = false;
            // we found the one we were looking for
            if(foundMatch == true)
            {
                Console.WriteLine("Found Match!");
            }
        }
    }
    Console.WriteLine();
}
```

The following code shows how to use each of these overloaded methods:

```
public static void FindOverriddenMethods()
{
    MethodOverrides mo = new MethodOverrides();
    Process current = Process.GetCurrentProcess();
    // get the path of the current module
    string path = current.MainModule.FileName;

    // try the easier one
    mo.FindMethodOverrides(path,"CSharpRecipes.Reflection+DerivedOverrides");

    // try the signature findmethodoverrides
    mo.FindMethodOverrides(path,
        "CSharpRecipes.Reflection+DerivedOverrides",
        "Foo",
        new Type[3] {typeof(long), typeof(double), typeof(byte[])});
}
```

In the usage code, we are getting the path to the test code assembly (*CSharpRecipes.exe*) via the Process class and then using that to find a class that has been defined in the Reflection class, called DerivedOverrides. DerivedOverrides derives from BaseOverrides and they are both shown here:

```
public abstract class BaseOverrides
{
    public abstract void Foo(string str, int i);

    public abstract void Foo(long l, double d, byte[] bytes);
}

public class DerivedOverrides : BaseOverrides
{
    public override void Foo(string str, int i)
    {
    }

    public override void Foo(long l, double d, byte[] bytes)
    {
    }
}
```

The first method only passes in the assembly path and the fully qualified type name. This method returns every overridden method for each method that it finds in the `Reflection.DerivedOverrides` type. If you wanted to display all overriding methods and their corresponding overridden method, you can remove the `BindingFlags.DeclaredOnly` binding enumeration from the `GetMethods` method call:

```
MethodInfo[] methods = asmType.GetMethods(BindingFlags.Instance |
                       BindingFlags.NonPublic | BindingFlags.Public |
                       BindingFlags.Static);
```

The second method passes in the assembly path, the fully qualified type name, a method name, and the parameters for this method to find the override that specifically matches the signature based on the parameters. In this case, the parameter types of method `Foo` are a `long`, `double`, and `byte[]`. This method displays the method that `CSharpRecipes.Reflection+DerivedOverrides.Foo` overrides. The + in the type name represents a nested class.

Discussion

Determining which methods override their base class methods would be a tedious chore if it were not for the `GetBaseDefinition` method of the `System.Reflection.MethodInfo` type. This method takes no parameters and returns a `MethodInfo` object that corresponds to the overridden method in the base class. If this method is used on a `MethodInfo` object representing a method that is not being overridden—as is the case with a virtual or abstract method—`GetBaseDefinition` returns the original `MethodInfo` object.

The code for the `FindMethodOverrides` methods first loads the assembly using the *asmPath* parameter and then gets the type that is specified by the *typeName* parameter.

Once the type is located, its `Type` object's `GetMethod` or `GetMethods` method is called. `GetMethod` is used when both the method name and its parameter array are passed in to `FindMethodOverrides`; otherwise, `GetMethods` is used. If the method is correctly located and its `MethodInfo` object obtained, the `GetBaseDefinition` method is called on that `MethodInfo` object to get the first overridden method in the nearest base class in the inheritance hierarchy. This `MethodInfo` type is compared to the `MethodInfo` type that the `GetBaseDefinition` method was called on. If these two objects are the same, it means that there were no overridden methods in any base classes; therefore, nothing is displayed. This code will display only the overridden method; if no methods are overridden, then nothing is displayed.

See Also

See Recipe 12.11; see the "Process Class," "Assembly Class," "MethodInfo Class," and "ParameterInfo Class" topics in the MSDN documentation.

12.4   Finding Members in an Assembly

Problem

You need to find one or more members in an assembly with a specific name or containing part of a name. This partial name could be, for example, any member starting with the letter 'A' or the string "Test".

Solution

Use the `Type.GetMember` method, which returns all members that match a specified criteria:

```
public static void FindMemberInAssembly(string asmPath, string memberName)
{
    Assembly asm = Assembly.LoadFrom(asmPath);
    foreach(Type asmType in asm.GetTypes())
    {
        // check for static ones first
        MemberInfo[] members = asmType.GetMember(memberName, MemberTypes.All,
            BindingFlags.Public | BindingFlags.NonPublic |
            BindingFlags.Static);

        if(members.Length == 0)
        {
            // check for instance members as well
            members = asmType.GetMember(memberName, MemberTypes.All,
                BindingFlags.Public | BindingFlags.NonPublic |
                BindingFlags.Instance);
        }

        foreach (MemberInfo member in members)
        {
            Console.WriteLine("Found " + member.MemberType + ":  " +
                member.ToString() + " IN " +
                member.DeclaringType.FullName);
        }
    }
}
```

The *memberName* argument can contain the wildcard character * to indicate any character or characters. So to find all methods starting with the string "Test", pass the string "Test*" to the *memberName* parameter. Note that the *memberName* argument is case-sensitive, but the *asmPath* argument is not. If you'd like to do a case-insensitive search for members, add the `BindingFlags.IgnoreCase` flag to the other `BindingFlags` in the call to `Type.GetMember`.

Discussion

The `GetMember` method of the `System.Type` class is useful for finding one or more methods within a type. This method returns an array of `MemberInfo` objects that describe any members that match the given parameters.

The * character may be used as a wildcard character only at the end of the *name* parameter string. In addition, it may be the only character in the *name* parameter; if this is so, all members are returned. No other wildcard characters, such as ?, are supported.

Once we obtain an array of MemberInfo objects, we need to determine what kind of members they are. To do this, the MemberInfo class contains a MemberType property that returns a System.Reflection.MemberTypes enumeration value. This could be any of the values defined in Table 12-1.

Table 12-1. MemberTypes enumeration values

Enumeration value	Definition
All	All member types
Constructor	A constructor member
Custom	A custom member type
Event	An event member
Field	A field member
Method	A method member
NestedType	A nested type
Property	A property member
TypeInfo	A type member that represents a TypeInfo member

See Also

See Recipe 12.11; see the "Assembly Class," "BindingFlags Enumeration," and "MemberInfo Class" topics in the MSDN documentation.

12.5   Finding Members Within an Interface

Problem

You need to find one or more members, with a specific name or a part of a name that belongs to an interface.

Solution

Use the same technique outlined in Recipe 12.4, but filter out all types except interfaces. The first overloaded version of the FindIFaceMemberInAssembly method finds a member specified by the *memberName* parameter in all interfaces contained in an assembly. Its source code is:

```
public static void FindIFaceMemberInAssembly(string asmPath, string memberName)
{
    // delegate to the interface based one passing blank
```

```
        FindIFaceMemberInAssembly(asmPath, memberName, "*");
    }
```

The second overloaded version of the `FindIFaceMemberInAssembly` method finds a member in the interface specified by the *interfaceName* parameter. Its source code is:

```
public static void FindIFaceMemberInAssembly(string asmPath, string memberName,
    string interfaceName)
{
    Assembly asm = Assembly.LoadFrom(asmPath);
    foreach(Type asmType in asm.GetTypes())
    {
        if (asmType.IsInterface &&
            (asmType.FullName.Equals(interfaceName) ||
                            interfaceName.Equals("*")))
        {
            if (asmType.GetMember(memberName, MemberTypes.All,
                BindingFlags.Instance | BindingFlags.NonPublic |
                BindingFlags.Public | BindingFlags.Static |
                BindingFlags.IgnoreCase).Length > 0)
            {
                foreach(MemberInfo iface in asmType.GetMember(memberName,
                    MemberTypes.All,
                    BindingFlags.Instance | BindingFlags.NonPublic |
                    BindingFlags.Public | BindingFlags.Static |
                    BindingFlags.IgnoreCase))
                {
                    Console.WriteLine("Found member {0}.{1}",
                        asmType.ToString(),iface.ToString());
                }
            }
        }
    }
}
```

Discussion

The `FindIFaceMemberInAssembly` method operates very similarly to the `FindMemberInAssembly` method of Recipe 17.3. The main difference between this recipe and the one in Recipe 12.4 is that this method uses the `IsInterface` property of the `System.Type` class to determine whether this type is an interface. If this property returns true, the type is an interface; otherwise, it is a noninterface type.

This recipe also makes use of the `GetMember` method of the `System.Type` class. This name may contain a * wildcard character at the end of the string only. If the * wildcard character is the only character in the name parameter, all members are returned.

If you'd like to do a case-sensitive search, you can omit the `BindingFlags.IgnoreCase` flag from the call to `Type.GetMember`.

See Also

See Recipe 12.11; see the "Assembly Class," "BindingFlags Enumeration," and "MemberInfo Class" topics in the MSDN documentation.

12.6 Obtaining Types Nested Within a Type

Problem

You need to determine which types have nested types contained within them in your assembly. Determining the nested types allows you to programmatically examine various aspects of some design patterns. Various design patterns may specify that a type will contain another type; for example, the *Decorator* and *State* design patterns make use of object containment.

Solution

Use the `DisplayNestedTypes` method to iterate through all types in your assembly and list all of their nested types. Its code is:

```
public static void DisplayNestedTypes(string asmPath)
{
    bool output = false;
    string line;
    Assembly asm = Assembly.LoadFrom(asmPath);
    foreach(Type asmType in asm.GetTypes())
    {
        if (!asmType.IsEnum && !asmType.IsInterface)
        {
            line = asmType.FullName + " Contains:\n" ;
            output = false;

            // Get all nested types
            Type[] nestedTypes = asmType.GetNestedTypes(BindingFlags.Instance |
                BindingFlags.Static |
                BindingFlags.Public |
                BindingFlags.NonPublic);

            // roll over the nested types
            foreach (Type t in nestedTypes)
            {
                line += "    " + t.FullName + "\n";
                output = true;
            }
            if (output)
                Console.WriteLine(line);
        }
    }
}
```

Discussion

The `DisplayNestedTypes` method uses a `foreach` loop to iterate over all nested types in the assembly specified by the `asmPath` parameter. Within this `foreach` loop, any enumeration and interface types are discarded by testing the `IsEnum` and `IsInterface` properties of the System.Type class. Enumeration types will not contain any types, and no further processing on this type needs to be done. Interfaces are also discarded since they cannot contain nested types.

Usually the dot operator is used to delimit namespaces and types; however, nested types are somewhat special. Nested types are set apart from other types by the + operator in their fully qualified name when dealing with them in the Reflection API. By passing this fully qualified name in to the static GetType methods, the actual type that it represents can be acquired.

These methods return a Type object that represents the type identified by the *typeName* parameter.

 Calling Type.GetType on a type in a dynamic assembly (one that is created using the types defined in the System.Reflection.Emit namespace) returns a null if that assembly has not already been persisted to disk.

See Also

See Recipe 12.11; see the "Assembly Class" and "BindingFlags Enumeration" topics in the MSDN documentation.

12.7 Displaying the Inheritance Hierarchy for a Type

Problem

You need to determine all of the base types that make up a specific type. Essentially, you need to determine the inheritance hierarchy of a type starting with the base (least derived) type and ending with the specified (most derived) type.

Solution

Use the DisplayTypeHierarchy method to display the entire inheritance hierarchy for all types existing in an assembly specified by the asmPath parameter. Its source code is:

```
public static void DisplayTypeHierarchy (string asmPath)
{
    Assembly asm = Assembly.LoadFrom(asmPath);
    foreach(Type asmType in asm.GetTypes())
    {
        // Recurse over all base types
        Console.WriteLine ("Derived Type: " + asmType.FullName);
        Console.WriteLine ("Base Type List: " + GetBaseTypeList(asmType));
        Console.WriteLine ();
    }
}
```

DisplayTypeHierarchy in turn calls GetBaseTypeList, a private method that uses recursion to get all base types. Its source code is:

```
private static string GetBaseTypeList(Type type)
{
    if (type != null)
    {
        string baseTypeName = GetBaseType(type.BaseType);
        if (baseTypeName.Length <= 0)
        {
            return (type.Name);
        }
        else
        {
            return (baseTypeName + "::" + type.Name);
        }
    }
    else
    {
        return ("");
    }
}
```

If you want to obtain only the inheritance hierarchy of a specific type as a string, use the following DisplayTypeHierarchy overload:

```
public static void DisplayTypeHierarchy(string asmPath,string baseType)
{
    Assembly asm = Assembly.LoadFrom(asmPath);
    string typeHierarchy = GetBaseTypeList(asm.GetType(baseType));
    Console.WriteLine(typeHierarchy);
}
```

To display the inheritance hierarchy of all types within an assembly, use the first instance of the DisplayTypeHierarchy method call. To obtain the inheritance hierarchy of a single type as a string, use the second instance of the DisplayTypeHierarchy method call. In this instance, we are looking for the type hierarchy of the CSharpRecipes.Reflection+DerivedOverrides nested class:

```
public static void DisplayInheritanceHierarchyType()
{
    Process current = Process.GetCurrentProcess();
    // get the path of the current module
    string asmPath = current.MainModule.FileName;
    // a specific type
    TypeHierarchy.DisplayTypeHierarchy(asmPath,
        "CSharpRecipes.Reflection+DerivedOverrides");
    // all types in the assembly
    TypeHierarchy.DisplayTypeHierarchy(asmPath);
}
```

These methods result in output like the following:

```
Derived Type: CSharpRecipes.Reflection
Base Type List: Object::Reflection
```

```
Derived Type: CSharpRecipes.Reflection+BaseOverrides
Base Type List: Object::BaseOverrides

Derived Type: CSharpRecipes.Reflection+DerivedOverrides
Base Type List: Object::BaseOverrides::DerivedOverrides
```

This output shows that when looking at the Reflection class in the `CSharpRecipes` namespace, its base type list (or inheritance hierarchy) starts with `Object` (like all types in .NET). The nested class `BaseOverrides` also shows a base type list starting with `Object`. The nested class `DerivedOverrides` shows a more interesting base type list, where `DerivedOverrides` derives from `BaseOverrides`, which derives from `Object`.

Discussion

Unfortunately, no property of the `Type` class exists to obtain the inheritance hierarchy of a type. The `DisplayTypeHierarchy` methods in this recipe allow you to obtain the inheritance hierarchy of a type. All that is required is the path to an assembly and the name of the type whose inheritance hierarchy is to be obtained. The `DisplayTypeHierarchy` method requires only an assembly path since it displays only the inheritance hierarchy for all types within that assembly.

The core code of this recipe exists in the `GetBaseTypeList` method. This is a recursive method that walks each inherited type until it finds the ultimate base class—which is always the `object` class. Once it arrives at this ultimate base class, it returns to its caller. Each time the method returns to its caller, the next base class in the inheritance hierarchy is added to the string until the final `GetBaseTypeList` method returns the completed string.

See Also

See the "Process Class," "Assembly Class," and "Type.BaseType Method" topics in the MSDN documentation.

12.8   Finding the Subclasses of a Type

Problem

You have a type and you need to find out whether it is subclassed anywhere in an assembly.

Solution

Use the `Type.IsSubclassOf` method to test all types within a given assembly, which determines whether each type is a subclass of the type specified in the argument to `IsSubClassOf`:

```
public static ArrayList GetSubClasses(string asmPath, Type baseClassType)
{
    Assembly asm = Assembly.LoadFrom(asmPath);
```

```
        ArrayList subClasses = new ArrayList();
        if (baseClassType != null)
        {
            foreach(Type type in asm.GetTypes())
            {
                if (type.IsSubclassOf(baseClassType))
                {
                    subClasses.Add(type);
                }
            }
        }
        else
        {
            throw (new Exception(baseClassType.FullName +
                        " does not exist in assembly " + asmPath));
        }

        return (subClasses);
```

The GetSubClasses method accepts an assembly path string and a second string containing a fully qualified base class name. This method returns an ArrayList of Types representing the subclasses of the type passed to the *baseClass* parameter.

Discussion

The IsSubclassOf method on the Type class allows us to determine whether the current type is a subclass of the type passed in to this method.

To use this method, you could use the following code:

```
public static void FindSubclassOfType()
{
    Process current = Process.GetCurrentProcess();
    // get the path of the current module
    string asmPath = current.MainModule.FileName;
    Type type = Type.GetType("CSharpRecipes.Reflection+BaseOverrides");
    ArrayList subClasses = GetSubClasses(asmPath,type);

    // write out the subclasses for this type
    if(subClasses.Count > 0)
    {
        Console.WriteLine("{0} is subclassed by:",type.FullName);
        foreach(Type t in subClasses)
        {
            Console.WriteLine("\t{0}",t.FullName);
        }
    }
}
```

First we get the assembly path from the current process, and then we set up use of CSharpRecipes.Reflection+BaseOverrides as the type to test for subclasses. We call GetSubClasses, and it returns an ArrayList that we use to produce the following output:

```
CSharpRecipes.Reflection+BaseOverrides is subclassed by:
        CSharpRecipes.Reflection+DerivedOverrides
```

See Also

See the "Assembly Class" and "Type Class" topics in the MSDN documentation.

12.9   Finding All Serializable Types Within an Assembly

Problem

You need to find all the serializable types within an assembly.

Solution

Instead of testing the implemented interfaces and attributes on every type, you can query the `Type.Attributes` property to determine whether it contains the `TypeAttributes.Serializable` flag, as the following method does:

```
public static ArrayList GetSerializableTypeNames(string asmPath)
{
    ArrayList serializableTypes = new ArrayList( );
    Assembly asm = Assembly.LoadFrom(asmPath);

    // look at all types in the assembly
    foreach(Type type in asm.GetTypes( ))
    {
        if ((type.Attributes & TypeAttributes.Serializable) ==
            TypeAttributes.Serializable)
        {
            // add the name of the serializable type
            serializableTypes.Add(type.FullName);
        }
    }

    return (serializableTypes);
}
```

The `GetSerializableTypeNames` method accepts the path of an assembly through its *asmPath* parameter. This assembly is searched for any serializable types, and their full names (including namespaces) are returned in an `ArrayList`. Note that you can just as easily return an `ArrayList` containing the `Type` object for each serializable type by changing the line of code:

```
serializableTypes.Add(asmType.FullName);
```

to:

```
serializableTypes.Add(asmType);
```

In order to use this method to display the serializable types in an assembly, use the following:

```
public static void FindSerializable()
{
    Process current = Process.GetCurrentProcess();
    // get the path of the current module
    string asmPath = current.MainModule.FileName;
    ArrayList serializable = GetSerializableTypeNames(asmPath);
    // write out the serializable types in the assembly
    if(serializable.Count > 0)
    {
        Console.WriteLine("{0} has serializable types:",asmPath);
        for(int i=0;i<serializable.Count;i++)
        {
            Console.WriteLine("\t{0}",serializable[i]);
        }
    }
}
```

Discussion

A type may be marked as serializable in one of two different ways:

- The SerializableAttribute attribute can be added to the type.
- The type can be marked with the SerializableAttribute and/or implement the ISerializable interface.

Testing for either the SerializableAttribute attribute or the ISerializable interface on a type can turn into a fair amount of work. Fortunately, we do not have to do all of this work; it has been done for us. The Attributes enumeration on the Type class contains several flags that describe the current type, one of which is the Serializable flag. This flag is set when either the SerializableAttribute or the ISerializable interface, or both, are added to a type.

To test for this flag, use the following logic:

```
(asmType.Attributes & TypeAttributes.Serializable) == TypeAttributes.Serializable
```

If the Serializable flag is set, this expression will evaluate to true.

See Also

See the "Assembly Class" and "TypeAttributes Enumeration" in the MSDN documentation.

12.10 Controlling Additions to an ArrayList Through Attributes

Problem

You need to allow only certain types of items to be stored within an ArrayList or an ArrayList-derived container, and it is likely that more types will be added to this list of allowed types in the future. You need the added flexibility to mark the types that are allowed to be stored in the ArrayList as such, rather than changing the container.

Solution

First, create a new attribute to mark the types that are allowed to be stored in the ArrayList. The following code defines the AllowedInListAttribute attribute:

```
using System;

[AttributeUsage(AttributeTargets.Interface | AttributeTargets.Struct |
        AttributeTargets.Class, Inherited = false, AllowMultiple = false)]
public class AllowedInListAttribute : Attribute
{
    public AllowedInListAttribute( ) {}

    public AllowedInListAttribute(bool allow)
    {
        allowed = allow;
    }

    // by defaulting to false, we default the usage to preventing the
    // use of the type.
    private bool allowed = false;

    public bool IsAllowed
    {
        get {return (allowed);}
        set {allowed = value;}
    }
}
```

Next, mark all classes that can be stored in the ArrayList with this attribute:

```
[AllowedInListAttribute(true)]
public class ItemAllowed {}

[AllowedInListAttribute(true)]
public class Item {}
```

In addition, this attribute allows types to be disallowed from being stored in the ArrayList by passing false to its constructor or by not passing an argument to the attribute constructor or not applying the attribute:

```
[AllowedInListAttribute(false)]
public class ItemDisallowed {}

public class ItemUnmarked {}
```

Types not marked with this attribute enabled will not be added to the FilteredArrayList shown next.

Finally, create a new class that inherits from ArrayList and overrides both the indexer and Add members. The overridden methods will check the object being added to determine whether it is marked with the AllowedInListAttribute attribute. If it is, and if the IsAllowed property returns true, this object is added to the sub-classed ArrayList:

```
public class FilteredArrayList : ArrayList
{
    private string attributeTypeName =
            "CSharpRecipes.Reflection+AllowedInListAttribute";
    public override object this[int index]
    {
        get
        {
            return (base[index]);
        }

        set
        {
            object[] allowedAttrs = value.GetType( ).GetCustomAttributes(
                Type.GetType(attributeTypeName), false);
            if (allowedAttrs.Length > 0)
            {
                if (((AllowedInListAttribute)allowedAttrs[0]).IsAllowed
                  == true)
                {
                    base[index] = value;
                    return;
                }
            }

            throw (new ArgumentException("Type cannot be added to this list",
                    "obj"));
        }
    }

    public override int Add (object obj)
    {
        object[] allowedAttrs = obj.GetType( ).GetCustomAttributes(
            Type.GetType(attributeTypeName), false);
        if (allowedAttrs.Length > 0)
        {
```

```
            if (((AllowedInListAttribute)allowedAttrs[0]).IsAllowed == true)
            {
                return (base.Add(obj));
            }
        }

        throw (new ArgumentException("Type cannot be added to this list",
                    "obj"));
    }
}
```

You can then instantiate an ArrayList object and add only allowed elements to it, as the following code illustrates:

```
using System;
using System.Collections;
using System.Reflection;

public static void GuardArrayList()
{
    FilteredArrayList list = new FilteredArrayList();
    AddToArray(list, new ItemAllowed() );
    AddToArray(list, new ItemDisallowed() );
    AddToArray(list, new ItemUnmarked() );
    AddToArray(list, new Item() );

    Console.WriteLine("ArrayList contains " + list.Count + " items.");
}

private static void AddToArray(FilteredArrayList fa, object obj)
{
    try
    {
        fa.Add(obj);
    }
    catch (ArgumentException e)
    {
        Console.WriteLine("Unable to add " + obj.ToString()
            + "\n    " + e.Message);
    }
    catch (Exception e)
    {
        Console.WriteLine(e.Message);
    }
}
```

This code produces the following output:

```
Unable to add CSharpRecipes.Reflection+ItemDisallowed
    Type cannot be added to this list
Parameter name: obj
Unable to add CSharpRecipes.Reflection+ItemUnmarked
    Type cannot be added to this list
Parameter name: obj
ArrayList contains 2 items.
```

Discussion

There are times, especially during the initial phases of coding, where the code is constantly changing along with the design specs. This can make it especially difficult to keep your code stable and bug-free. We can alleviate some of these problems by using attributes to mark types in a special way. It is usually easier and much cleaner to add or remove attributes than to add or remove code from within the type.

This recipe uses a custom attribute, `AllowedInListAttribute`, to mark certain types as allowed to be stored in an `ArrayList`. This attribute may be placed on types such as interfaces, structures, or classes. (The targets of an attribute are defined by which members of the `AttributeTargets` enumeration are passed as arguments to the `AttributeUsage` attribute's constructor.) It has one private field, `Allowed`, which is used to determine if the type it marks is able to be stored in an `ArrayList` (true) or not (false).

To use this attribute, subclass `ArrayList` and override both the indexer and `Add` method of the `ArrayList` class. The get accessor of the indexer can simply pass the call through to the base class get accessor, since we're interested in filtering items only as they go into the list. However, the set accessor needs to test for the existence of the `AllowedinListAttribute` on the type of the object being added to the `FilteredArrayList`. If it does not exist, the object may not be added. If this attribute exists, but the `IsAllowed` property returns false, it is still not allowed to be added to this slot. Only when this attribute exists and the `IsAllowed` property returns true can this object be added to this `ArrayList`.

The set accessor of the indexer and the `Add` method both throw an exception if an object cannot be added to the `ArrayList`.

See Also

See the "Attribute Class" topic in the MSDN documentation.

12.11 Filtering Output when Obtaining Members

Problem

You want to get information about one or more members, but you want to retrieve only a subset of members. For example, you need to use `Type.GetConstructor` to obtain only the static constructor of a type, or you need to use `Type.GetField` to obtain only the noninherited nonpublic fields of a type.

Solution

Use the `BindingFlags` enumeration together with the appropriate `Type.Getxxx` methods to find out about the type, as in the following example:

```
public static void FilteringOutputObtainingMembers()
{
    Type reflection = typeof(Reflection);
    ConstructorInfo[] constructors =
        reflection.GetConstructors(BindingFlags.Public |
                                   BindingFlags.NonPublic |
                                   BindingFlags.Instance |
                                   BindingFlags.Static);

    Console.WriteLine("Looking for All Constructors");
    foreach(ConstructorInfo c in constructors)
    {
        Console.WriteLine("\tFound Constructor {0}",c.Name);
    }

    constructors =
        reflection.GetConstructors(BindingFlags.Public |
                                   BindingFlags.Instance);
    Console.WriteLine("Looking for Public Instance Constructors");
    foreach(ConstructorInfo c in constructors)
    {
        Console.WriteLine("\tFound Constructor {0}",c.Name);
    }

    constructors =
        reflection.GetConstructors(BindingFlags.NonPublic |
                                   BindingFlags.Instance |
                                   BindingFlags.Static);
    Console.WriteLine("Looking for NonPublic Constructors");
    foreach(ConstructorInfo c in constructors)
    {
        Console.WriteLine("\tFound Constructor {0}",c.Name);
    }

    FieldInfo[] fields =
        reflection.GetFields(BindingFlags.Static |
                             BindingFlags.Public);
    Console.WriteLine("Looking for Public, Static Fields");
    foreach(FieldInfo f in fields)
    {
        Console.WriteLine("\tFound Field {0}",f.Name);
    }

    fields =
        reflection.GetFields(BindingFlags.Public |
                             BindingFlags.Static |
                             BindingFlags.Instance);
    Console.WriteLine("Looking for Public Fields");
    foreach(FieldInfo f in fields)
    {
        Console.WriteLine("\tFound Field {0}",f.Name);
    }
```

```
        fields =
            reflection.GetFields(BindingFlags.NonPublic |
                                BindingFlags.Static );
        Console.WriteLine("Looking for NonPublic, Static Fields");
        foreach(FieldInfo f in fields)
        {
            Console.WriteLine("\tFound Field {0}",f.Name);
        }

    }
```

In this example, we examine the CSharpRecipes.Reflection type for constructors and fields. The constructors and fields are listed here:

```
#region Fields
    int i = 0;
    public int pi = 0;
    static int si = 0;
    public static int psi = 0;
    object o = null;
    public object po = null;
    static object so = null;
    public static object pso = null;
#endregion

#region Constructors
    static Reflection()
    {
        si++;
        psi = 0;
        so = new Object();
        pso = new Object();
    }

    Reflection()
    {
        i = 0;
        pi = 0;
        o = new Object();
        po = new Object();
    }

    public Reflection(int index)
    {
        i = index;
        pi = index;
        o = new Object();
        po = new Object();
    }
#endregion
```

The output this generates is listed here:

```
Looking for All Constructors
        Found Constructor .cctor
        Found Constructor .ctor
        Found Constructor .ctor
Looking for Public Instance Constructors
        Found Constructor .ctor
Looking for NonPublic Constructors
        Found Constructor .cctor
        Found Constructor .ctor
Looking for Public, Static Fields
        Found Field psi
        Found Field pso
Looking for Public Fields
        Found Field pi
        Found Field po
        Found Field psi
        Found Field pso
Looking for NonPublic, Static Fields
        Found Field si
        Found Field so
```

Discussion

The following methods of the Type object accept a BindingFlags enumerator to filter output:

```
Type.GetConstructor
Type.GetConstructors
Type.GetMethod
Type.GetMethods
Type.GetField
Type.GetFields
Type.GetProperty
Type.GetProperties
Type.Event
Type.Events
Type.GetMember
Type.GetMembers
Type.FindMembers
```

The following are also methods that accept a BindingFlags enumerator to filter members and types to invoke or instantiate:

```
Type.InvokeMember
Type.CreateInstance
```

BindingFlags allows the list of members on which these methods operate to be expanded or limited. For example, if the BindingFlags.Public flag were passed to the Type.GetFields method, only public fields would be returned. If both the BindingFlags.Public and BindingFlags.NonPublic flags were passed to the Type. GetFields method, the list of fields would be expanded to include the protected, internal, protected internal, and private fields of a type. Table 12-2 lists and describes each flag in the BindingFlags enumeration.

Table 12-2. Binding flag definitions

Flag name	Definition
CreateInstance	An instance of a specified type is created while passing in the given arguments to its constructor.
DeclaredOnly	Inherited members are not included when obtaining members of a type.
Default	No binding flags are used.
ExactBinding	The specified parameters must exactly match the parameters on the invoked member.
FlattenHierarchy	Static members up the inheritance hierarchy are returned; nested types won't be returned.
GetField	The specified field's value is to be returned.
GetProperty	The specified property's value is to be returned.
IgnoreCase	Case-sensitivity is turned off.
IgnoreReturn	Ignore the returned value when invoking methods on COM objects.
Instance	Include all instance members when obtaining members of a type.
InvokeMethod	The specified method is to be invoked.
NonPublic	Include all nonpublic members when obtaining members of a type.
OptionalParamBinding	Used with the Type.InvokeMember method to invoke methods that contain parameters with default values and methods with variable numbers of parameters (params).
Public	Include all public members when obtaining members of a type.
PutDispProperty	Invoke the PROPPUT member of a COM object.
PutRefDispProperty	Invoke the PROPPUTREF member of a COM object.
SetField	The specified field's value is to be set.
SetProperty	The specified property's value is to be set.
Static	Include all static members when obtaining members of a type.
SuppressChangeType	Not implemented.

Be aware that to examine or invoke nonpublic members, your assembly must have the correct reflection permissions. The reflection permission flags, and what PermissionSets they are included in by default, are listed in Table 12-3.

Table 12-3. ReflectionPermissionFlags

PermissionFlag	Description	Permission sets including these rights
AllFlags	TypeInformation, MemberAccess, and ReflectionEmit are set.	FullTrust, Everything
MemberAccess	Invocation of operations on all type members is allowed. If this flag is not set, only invocation of operations on visible type members is allowed.	FullTrust, Everything
NoFlags	No reflection is allowed on types that are not visible.	All permission sets
ReflectionEmit	Use of System.Reflection.Emit is allowed.	FullTrust, Everything, LocalIntranet
TypeInformation	Reflection is allowed on members of a type that are not visible.	FullTrust, Everything

One other item to note is that when supplying a `BindingFlags` set of flags for one of the `Get*` methods, you must always pass either `BindingFlags.Instance` or `BindingFlags.Static` in order to get any results back. If you just pass `BindingFlags.Public`, for example, you will not find any results. You need to pass `BindingFlags.Public | BindingFlags.Instance` to get public instance results.

See Also

See the "BindingFlags Enumeration," "Type Class," "ConstructorInfo Class," and "FieldInfo Class" topics in the MSDN documentation.

12.12 Dynamically Invoking Members

Problem

You have a list of method names that you wish to invoke dynamically within your application. As your code executes, it will pull names off of this list and attempt to invoke these methods. This technique would be useful to create a test harness for components that read in the methods to execute from an XML file and execute them with the given parameters.

Solution

The `TestDynamicInvocation` method opens the XML configuration file, reads out the test information, and executes each test method dynamically:

```
public static void TestDynamicInvocation( )
{
    // read in the methods to run from the xml file
    XmlDocument doc = new XmlDocument( );
    doc.Load(@"C:\C#Cookbook\SampleClassLibraryTests.xml");

    // get the tests to run
    XmlNodeList nodes = doc.SelectNodes(@"Tests/Test");

    // run each test method
    foreach(XmlNode node in nodes)
    {
        object obj = DynamicInvoke(node,
                                @"C:\C#Cookbook\SampleClassLibrary.dll");

        // print out the return
        Console.WriteLine("\tReturned object: " + obj);
        Console.WriteLine("\tReturned object: " + obj.GetType( ).FullName);
    }
}
```

The XML document in which the test method information is contained looks like this:

```xml
<?xml version="1.0" encoding="utf-8" ?>
<Tests>
    <Test className='SampleClassLibrary.SampleClass' methodName='TestMethod1'>
        <Parameter>Running TestMethod1</Parameter>
    </Test>
    <Test className='SampleClassLibrary.SampleClass' methodName='TestMethod2'>
        <Parameter>Running TestMethod2</Parameter>
        <Parameter>27</Parameter>
    </Test>
</Tests>
```

The DynamicInvoke method dynamically invokes the method that is passed to it using the information contained in the XmlNode. The parameters types are determined by examining the ParameterInfo items on the MethodInfo, and then the values provided are converted to the actual type from a string via the Convert.ChangeType method. Finally, the return value of the invoked method is returned by this method. Its source code is:

```csharp
public static object DynamicInvoke(XmlNode testNode, string asmPath)
{
    // Load the assembly
    Assembly asm = Assembly.LoadFrom(asmPath);

    // get the name of the type from the className attribute on Test
    string typeName = testNode.Attributes.GetNamedItem("className").Value;

    // get the name of the method from the methodName attribute on Test
    string methodName = testNode.Attributes.GetNamedItem("methodName").Value;

    // create the actual type
    Type dynClassType = asm.GetType(typeName, true, false);

    // Create an instance of this type and verify that it exists
    object dynObj = Activator.CreateInstance(dynClassType);
    if (dynObj != null)
    {
        // Verify that the method exists and get its MethodInfo obj
        MethodInfo invokedMethod = dynClassType.GetMethod(methodName);
        if (invokedMethod != null)
        {
            // Create the parameter list for the dynamically invoked methods
            object[] parameters = new object[testNode.ChildNodes.Count];
            int index = 0;

            // for each parameter, add it to the list
            foreach(XmlNode node in testNode.ChildNodes)
            {
                // get the type of the parameter
                Type paramType =
                        invokedMethod.GetParameters()[index].ParameterType;
```

```
            // change the value to that type and assign it
            parameters[index] =
                Convert.ChangeType(node.InnerText,paramType);
            index++;
        }

        // Invoke the method with the parameters
        object retObj = invokedMethod.Invoke(dynObj, parameters);
        // return the returned object
        return (retObj);
    }
}

return (null);
}
```

These are the dynamically invoked methods located on the `SampleClass` type in the `SampleClassLibrary` assembly:

```
public bool TestMethod1(string text)
{
    Console.WriteLine(text);
    return (true);
}

public bool TestMethod2(string text, int n)
{
    Console.WriteLine(text + " invoked with {0}",n);
    return (true);
}
```

The output from these methods looks like this:

```
Running TestMethod1
        Returned object: True
        Returned object: System.Boolean
Running TestMethod2 invoked with 27
        Returned object: True
        Returned object: System.Boolean
```

Discussion

Reflection possesses the ability to dynamically invoke both static and instance methods existing within a type in either the same assembly or a different one. This can be a very powerful tool to allow your code to determine at runtime which method to call. This determination can be based on an assembly name, a type name, or a method name, though the assembly name is not required if the method exists in the same assembly as the invoking code, or if you already have the `Assembly` object, or if you have a `Type` object for the class the method is on.

This technique may seem similar to delegates since both can dynamically determine at runtime which method is to be called. Delegates, on the whole, require you to know signatures of methods you might call at runtime, whereas with reflection, you can invoke methods where you have no idea of the signature, providing a much looser binding. More dynamic invocation can be achieved with `Delegate.DynamicInvoke`, but this is more of a reflection-based method than the traditional delegate invocation.

The `DynamicInvoke` method shown in the Solution section contains all the code required to dynamically invoke a method. This code first loads the type using its assembly name (passed in through the *asmName* parameter). Next, it gets the `Type` object for the class containing the method to invoke (the class name is gotten from the `Test` element's `className` attribute). The method name is then retrieved (from the `Test` element's `methodName` attribute). Once we have all of the information from the `Test` element, an instance of the `Type` object is created, and we then invoke the specified method on this created instance:

- First, the static `Activator.CreateInstance` method is called to actually create an instance of the `Type` object contained in the local variable `dynClassType`. The method returns an object reference to the instance of *type* that was created, or an exception is thrown if the object cannot be created.

- Once we have successfully obtained the instance of this class, the `MethodInfo` object of the method to be invoked is acquired through a call to `GetMethod` on the object instance just returned by the `CreateInstance` method.

The instance of the object created with the `CreateInstance` method is then passed as the first parameter to the `MethodInfo.Invoke` method. This method returns an object containing the return value of the invoked method, or `null` if the return value is `void`. This object is then returned by the `DynamicInvoke` method. The second parameter to `MethodInfo.Invoke` is an object array containing any parameters to be passed to this method. This array is constructed based on the number of `Parameter` elements under each `Test` element in the XML, we then look at the `ParameterInfo` of each parameter (gotten from `MethodInfo.GetParameters()`) and use the `Convert.ChangeType` method to coerce the string value from the XML to the proper type.

The `TestDynamicInvoke` method finally displays each returned object value and its type. Note that there is no extra logic required to return different return values from the invoked methods since they are all returned as an object, unlike passing differing arguments to the invoked methods.

See Also

See the "Activator Class," "MethodInfo Class," "Convert.ChangeType Method," and "ParameterInfo Class" topics in the MSDN documentation.

Networking

.NET provides many classes to help make network programming easier and more accessible than many environments that preceded it. There is a great deal of functionality to assist you in building "web-aware" applications; performing simple tasks like downloading files, sending and receiving HTTP requests, and writing TCP/IP clients and servers. In areas where Microsoft had not provided a direct managed way to access networking functionality (like named pipes), there is always P/Invoke to allow you to perform networking actions via the Win32 API, which we'll show you in this chapter. With all of the functionality at your disposal in the System.Networking namespace, you'll be writing web utilities in no time.

13.1   Converting an IP Address to a Hostname

Problem

You have an IP address that you need to resolve into a hostname.

Solution

Use the Dns.Resolve method to get the hostname for an IP address. In the following code, an IP address is passed resolved, and the hostname is printed to the console:

```
using System;
using System.Net;

//...

// use the Dnss class to resolve the address
IPHostEntry iphost = Dns.Resolve("127.0.0.1");

// HostName property holds the hostname
string hostName = iphost.HostName;
```

Discussion

The `System.Net.Dns` class is provided for simple DNS resolution functionality. The `Resolve` method returns an `IPHostEntry` that can be used to access the hostname via the `HostName` property.

See Also

See the "DNS Class" and "IPHostEntry Class" topics in the MSDN documentation.

13.2 Converting a Hostname to an IP Address

Problem

You have a string representation of a host (such as *www.oreilly.com*), and you need to obtain the IP address from this hostname.

Solution

Use the `Dns.Resolve` method to get the IP addresses. In the following code, a hostname is provided to the `Resolve` method that returns an `IPHostEntry` from which a string of addresses can be constructed and returned:

```
using System;
using System.Net;
using System.Text;

// ...

public static string HostName2IP(string hostname)
{
    // resolve the hostname into an iphost entry using the dns class
    IPHostEntry iphost = System.Net.Dns.Resolve(hostname);
    // get all of the possible IP addresses for this hostname
    IPAddress[] addresses = iphost.AddressList;
    // make a text representation of the list
    StringBuilder addressList = new StringBuilder();
    // get each ip address
    foreach(IPAddress address in addresses)
    {
        // append it to the list
        addressList.Append("IP Address: ");
        addressList.Append(address.ToString());
        addressList.Append(";");
    }
    return addressList.ToString();
}

// ...

// writes "IP Address: 208.201.239.37;IP Address: 208.201.239.36;"
Console.WriteLine(HostName2IP("www.oreilly.com"));
```

Discussion

An `IPHostEntry` can associate multiple IP addresses with a single hostname via the `AddressList` property. `AddressList` is an array of `IPAddress` objects, each of which holds a single IP address. Once the `IPHostEntry` is resolved, the `AddressList` can be looped over using foreach to create a string that shows all of the IP addresses for the given hostname.

See Also

See the "DNS Class," "IPHostEntry Class," and "IPAddress" topics in the MSDN documentation.

13.3 Parsing a URI

Problem

You need to split a URI (Uniform Resource Identifier) into its constituent parts.

Solution

Construct a `System.Net.Uri` object and pass the URI to the constructor. This class constructor parses out the constituent parts of the URI and allows access to them via the `Uri` properties. We can then display the URI pieces individually:

```
public static void ParseUri(string uriString)
{
    try
    {
        // just use one of the constructors for the System.Net.Uri class
        // this will parse it for us.
         Uri uri = new Uri(uriString);
        // Look at the information we can get at now...
        string uriParts;
        uriParts = "AbsoluteURI: " + uri.AbsoluteUri + Environment.NewLine;
        uriParts += "Scheme: " + uri.Scheme + Environment.NewLine;
        uriParts += "UserInfo: " + uri.UserInfo + Environment.NewLine;
        uriParts += "Host: " + uri.Host + Environment.NewLine;
        uriParts += "Port: " + uri.Port + Environment.NewLine;
        uriParts += "Path: " + uri.LocalPath + Environment.NewLine;
        uriParts += "QueryString: " + uri.Query + Environment.NewLine;
        uriParts += "Fragment: " + uri.Fragment;
        // write out our summary
        Console.WriteLine(uriParts);
    }
    catch(ArgumentNullException e)
    {
        // uriString is a null reference (Nothing in Visual Basic).
        Console.WriteLine("URI string object is a null reference: {0}",e);
    }
```

```
        catch(UriFormatException e)
        {
            Console.WriteLine("URI formatting error: {0}",e);
        }
    }
}
```

Discussion

The Solution code uses the Uri class to do the heavy lifting. The constructor for the Uri class can throw two types of exceptions: an ArgumentNullException and an UriFormatException. The ArgumentNullException is thrown when the uri argument passed is null. The UriFormatException is thrown when the uri argument passed is of an incorrect or indeterminate format. Here are the error conditions that can throw a UriFormatException:

- An empty URI was passed in.
- The scheme specified in the passed in URI is invalid.
- The URI passed in contains too many slashes.
- The password specified in the passed in URI is invalid.
- The hostname specified in the passed in URI is invalid.
- The filename specified in the passed in URI is invalid.

System.Net.Uri provides methods to compare URIs, parse URIs, and combine URIs. It is all you should ever need for URI manipulation and is used by other classes in the framework when a URI is called for. The syntax for the pieces of a URI is this:

```
[scheme]://[user]:[password]@[host/authority]:[port]/[path];[params]?[query
string]#[fragment]
```

If we passed the following URI to ParseURI:

http://user:password@localhost:8080/www.abc.com/home.htm?item=1233#stuff

it would display the following items:

```
AbsoluteURI:
http://user:password@localhost:8080/www.abc.com/home.htm?item=1233#stuff
Scheme: http
UserInfo: user:password
Host: localhost
Port: 8080
Path: /www.abc.com/home.htm
QueryString: ?item=1233
Fragment: #stuff
```

See Also

See the "Uri Class," "ArgumentNullException Class," and "UriFormatException Class" topics in the MSDN documentation.

13.4   Forming an Absolute URI

Problem

You have a base URI of the form *http://www.oreilly.com* and a relative URI of the form *hello_world.htm*; you want to form an absolute URI from them.

Solution

Use the Uri class to combine a base URI and a relative URI via a constructor overload that takes the base and relative paths:

```
public static Uri CreateAbsoluteUri(string uriBase, string uriRelative)
{
    try
    {
        // make the base uri
        Uri baseUri = new Uri(uriBase);
        // create the full uri by combining the base and relative
        return new Uri(baseUri, uriRelative);
    }
    catch(ArgumentNullException e)
    {
        // uriString is a null reference (Nothing in Visual Basic).
        Console.WriteLine("URI string object is a null reference: {0}",e);
    }
    catch(UriFormatException e)
    {
        Console.WriteLine("URI formatting error: {0}",e);

    }
    return null;
}

// ...

Uri myUri = CreateAbsoluteUri("http://www.oreilly.com",
                    "hello_world.htm");

// displays http://www.oreilly.com/hello_world.htm
Console.WriteLine(myUri.AbsoluteUri);
```

Discussion

The System.Net.Uri class has a constructor overload that allows you to create a URI from a base path and a relative path while controlling the escaping of the URI. This creates the absolute URI and places it in the Uri.AbsoluteUri property. Escaping/Unescaping can also be controlled through two other overloads of the Uri constructor that take a bool as the last parameter (dontEscape), but care needs to be taken here: if you unescape the Uri, it will put the URI into a form more readable by a human but no longer usable as a URI (this is because any spaces that were escaped as %20 will now be considered whitespace).

Here are the error conditions that can cause a `UriFormatException` to be thrown when using the `Uri` constructor that takes `baseUri` and `relativeUri`:

- Empty URI formed from combining `baseUri` and `relativeUri`.
- The scheme specified in the combined URI is invalid.
- The combined URI contains too many slashes.
- The password specified in the combined URI is invalid.
- The hostname specified in the combined URI is invalid.
- The filename specified in the combined URI is invalid.

See Also

See the "Uri Class" topic in the MSDN documentation.

13.5   Handling Web Server Errors

Problem

You have obtained a response from a web server and you want to make sure that there were no errors in processing the initial request, such as failing to connect, being redirected, timing out, or failing to validate a certificate. You don't want to have to catch all of the different response codes available.

Solution

Check the `StatusCode` property of the `HttpWebResponse` class to determine what category of status this `StatusCode` falls into, and return an enumeration value (`ResponseCategories`) representing the category. This technique will allow you to use a broader approach to dealing with response codes.

```
public static ResponseCategories VerifyResponse(HttpWebResponse httpResponse)
{
    // Just in case there are more success codes defined in the future
    // by HttpStatusCode, we will check here for the "success" ranges
    // instead of using the HttpStatusCode enum as it overloads some
    // values
    int statusCode = (int)httpResponse.StatusCode;
    if((statusCode >= 100)&& (statusCode <= 199))
    {
        return ResponseCategories.Informational;
    }
    else if((statusCode >= 200)&& (statusCode <= 299))
    {
        return ResponseCategories.Success;
    }
    else if((statusCode >= 300)&& (statusCode <= 399))
    {
        return ResponseCategories.Redirected;
    }
```

```
        else if((statusCode >= 400)&& (statusCode <= 499))
        {
            return ResponseCategories.ClientError;
        }
        else if((statusCode >= 500)&& (statusCode <= 599))
        {
            return ResponseCategories.ServerError;
        }
        return ResponseCategories.Unknown;
    }
```

The ResponseCategories enumeration is defined like this:

```
public enum ResponseCategories
{
    Unknown = 0,        // unknown code  ( < 100 or > 599)
    Informational = 1,  // informational codes (100 <= 199)
    Success = 2,        // success codes (200 <= 299)
    Redirected = 3,     // redirection code (300 <= 399)
    ClientError = 4,    // client error code (400 <= 499)
    ServerError = 5     // server error code (500 <= 599)
}
```

Discussion

There are five different categories of status codes on a response in HTTP:

Category	Available range	HttpStatusCode defined range
Informational	100–199	100–101
Successful	200–299	200–206
Redirection	300–399	300–307
Client Error	400–499	400–417
Server Error	500–599	500–505

Each of the status codes defined by Microsoft in the .NET Framework is assigned an enumeration value in the HttpStatusCode enumeration. These status codes reflect what can happen when a request is submitted. The web server is free to return a status code in the available range even if it is not currently defined for most commercial web servers. The defined status codes are listed in RFC 2616—Section 10 for HTTP/1.1.

We are trying to figure out the broad category of the status of the request. This is achieved where the code inspects the HttpResponse.StatusCode property, compares it to the defined status code ranges for HTTP, and returns the appropriate ResponseCategories value.

When dealing with HttpStatusCode, you will notice that there are certain HttpStatusCode flags that map to the same status code value. An example of this is HttpStatusCode. Ambiguous and HttpStatusCode.MultipleChoices, which both map to HTTP status code 300. If you try to use both of these in a switch statement on the HttpStatusCode, you will get the following error because the C# compiler cannot tell the difference:

```
error CS0152: The label 'case 300:' already occurs in this switch statement.
```

See Also

See *HTTP: The Definitive Guide* by David Gourley and Brian Totty (O'Reilly); see the "HttpStatusCode Enumeration" topic in the MSDN documentation. Also see HTTP/1.1 RFC 2616—Section 10 Status Codes: *http://www.w3.org/Protocols/rfc2616/rfc2616-sec10.html*

13.6   Communicating with a Web Server

Problem

You want to send a request to a web server in the form of a GET or POST request. After you send the request to a web server, you want to get the results of that request (the response) from the web server.

Solution

Use the HttpWebRequest class in conjunction with the WebRequest class to create and send a request to a server.

Take the URI of the resource, the method to use in the request (GET or POST), and the data to send (only for POST requests), and use this information to create an HttpWebRequest:

```
using System.Net;
using System.IO;
using System.Text;

// ...

public static HttpWebRequest GenerateGetOrPostRequest(string uriString,
    string method,
    string postData)
{
    if((method.ToUpper( ) != "GET") &&
       (method.ToUpper( ) != "POST"))
            throw new ArgumentException(method +
                " is not a valid method.  Use GET or POST.","method");

    HttpWebRequest httpRequest = null;
    // get a URI object
    Uri uri = new Uri(uriString);
    // create the initial request
    httpRequest = (HttpWebRequest)WebRequest.Create(uri);

    // check if asked to do a POST request, if so then modify
    // the original request as it defaults to a GET method
    if(method.ToUpper( )=="POST")
    {
```

```
    // Get the bytes for the request, should be pre-escaped
    byte[] bytes = Encoding.UTF8.GetBytes(postData);

    // Set the content type of the data being posted.
    httpRequest.ContentType=
        "application/x-www-form-urlencoded";

    // Set the content length of the string being posted.
    httpRequest.ContentLength=postData.Length;

    // Get the request stream and write the post data in
    Stream requestStream = httpRequest.GetRequestStream( );
    requestStream.Write(bytes,0,bytes.Length);
    // Done updating for POST so close the stream
    requestStream.Close( );
}

// return the request
return httpRequest;
}
```

Once we have an HttpWebRequest, we send the request and get the response using the GetResponse method that takes our newly created HttpWebRequest as input and returns an HttpWebResponse. In this example, we perform a GET for the *index.aspx* page from the *http://localhost/mysite* web site:

```
HttpWebRequest request =
  GenerateGetOrPostRequest("http://localhost/mysite/index.aspx",
                           "GET",
                           null);

HttpWebResponse response = (HttpWebResponse) request.GetResponse( );
// This next line uses VerifyResponse from Recipe 13.5
if(VerifyResponse(response)==ResponseCategories.Success)
{
    Console.WriteLine("Request succeeded");
}
```

We generate the HttpWebRequest, send it and get the HttpWebResponse, and then check the success using the VerifyResponse method from Recipe 13.5.

Discussion

The WebRequest and WebResponse classes encapsulate all of the functionality to perform basic web transactions. HttpWebRequest and HttpWebResponse are derived classes from these, respectively, and provide the HTTP specific web transaction support.

At the most fundamental level, to perform an HTTP-based web transaction, you use the Create method on the WebRequest class to get a WebRequest that can be cast to an HttpWebRequest (so long as the the scheme is http:// or https://). This HttpWebRequest is then submitted to the web server in question when the GetResponse method is called, and it returns an HttpWebResponse that can then be inspected for the response data.

See Also

See the "WebRequest Class," "WebResponse Class," "HttpWebRequest Class," and "HttpWebResponse Class" topics in the MSDN documentation.

13.7   Going Through a Proxy

Problem

Many companies have a web proxy that allows employees to access the Internet, while at the same time preventing outsiders from accessing the company's internal network. The problem is that to create an application that accesses the Internet from within your company, you must first connect to your proxy and then send information through it, rather than directly out to an Internet web server.

Solution

In order to get a HttpWebRequest successfully through a specific proxy server, we need to set up a WebProxy object with the settings to validate our specific request to a given proxy. Since this function is generic for any request, we create the AddProxyInfoToRequest method:

```
public static HttpWebRequest AddProxyInfoToRequest(HttpWebRequest httpRequest,
                        string proxyUri,
                        string proxyID,
                        string proxyPwd,
                        string proxyDomain)
{
    if(httpRequest != null)
    {
        // create the proxy object
        WebProxy proxyInfo = new WebProxy( );
        // add the address of the proxy server to use
        proxyInfo.Address = new Uri(proxyUri);
        // tell it to bypass the proxy server for local addresses
        proxyInfo.BypassProxyOnLocal = true;
        // add any credential information to present to the proxy server
        proxyInfo.Credentials = new NetworkCredential(proxyID,
                                              proxyPwd,
                                              proxyDomain);
        // assign the proxy information to the request
        httpRequest.Proxy = proxyInfo;
    }
    // return the request
    return httpRequest;
}
```

If all requests are going to go through the same proxy, you can use the static Select method on the GlobalProxySelection class to set up the proxy settings for all WebRequests, like so:

```
Uri proxyURI = new Uri("http://webproxy:80");
GlobalProxySelection.Select = new WebProxy(proxyURI);
```

Discussion

AddProxyInfoToRequest takes the URI of the proxy and creates a Uri object, which is used to construct the WebProxy object. The WebProxy object is set to bypass the proxy for local addresses and then the credential information is used to create a NetworkCredential object. The NetworkCredential object represents the authentication information necessary for the request to succeed at this proxy and is assigned to the WebProxy.Credentials property. Once the WebProxy object is completed, it is assigned to the Proxy property of the HttpWebRequest and the request is ready to be submitted.

See Also

See the "WebProxy Class," "NetworkCredential Class," and "HttpWebRequest Class" topics in the MSDN documentation.

13.8   Obtaining the HTML from a URL

Problem

You need to get the HTML returned from a web server in order to examine it for items of interest. For example, you could examine the returned HTML for links to other pages or for headlines from a news site.

Solution

We can use the methods for web communication we have set up in Recipes 13.5 and 13.6 to make the HTTP request and verify the response; then, we can get at the HTML via the ResponseStream property of the HttpWebResponse object:

```
public static string GetHTMLFromURL(string url)
{
    if(url.Length == 0)
        throw new ArgumentException("Invalid URL","url");

    string html = "";
    HttpWebRequest request = GenerateGetOrPostRequest(url,"GET",null);
    HttpWebResponse response = (HttpWebResponse)request.GetResponse();
    try
    {
        if(VerifyResponse(response)== ResponseCategories.Success)
        {
            // get the response stream.
            Stream responseStream = response.GetResponseStream();
            // use a stream reader that understands UTF8
            StreamReader reader = new StreamReader(responseStream,Encoding.UTF8);
```

```
        try
        {
            html = reader.ReadToEnd();
        }
        finally
        {
            // close the reader
            reader.Close();
        }
    }
}
finally
{
    response.Close();
}
return html;
}
```

Discussion

The `GetHTMLFromURL` method is set up to get a web page using the `GenerateGetOrPostRequest` and `GetResponse` methods, verify the response using the `VerifyResponse` method, and then, once we have a valid response, we start looking for the HTML that was returned.

The `GetResponseStream` method on the `HttpWebResponse` provides access to the body of the message that was returned in a `System.IO.Stream` object. In order to read the data, we instantiate a `StreamReader` with the response stream and the UTF8 property of the Encoding class to allow for the UTF8-encoded text data to be read correctly from the stream. We then call `ReadToEnd` on the `StreamReader`, which puts all of the content in the string variable called `html` and return it.

See Also

See the "HttpWebResponse.GetResponseStream Method," "Stream Class," and "StringBuilder Class" topics in the MSDN documentation.

13.9   Writing a TCP Server

Problem

You need to create a server that listens on a port for incoming requests from a TCP client. These client requests can then be processed at the server, and any responses can be sent back to the client. Recipe 13.10 shows how to write a TCP client to interact with this server.

Solution

Use the TcpListener class to create a TCP-based endpoint to listen for requests from TCP based clients. RunServer initiates a one-request TCP-based server running on a given IP address and port:

```
public static void RunServer(string address,int port)
{
    // set up address
    IPAddress addr = IPAddress.Parse(address);
    // set up listener on that address/port
    TcpListener tcpListener = new TcpListener(addr,port);
    if(tcpListener != null)
    {
        // start it up
        tcpListener.Start();
        // wait for a tcp client to connect
        TcpClient tcpClient = tcpListener.AcceptTcpClient();

        byte [] bytes = new byte[1024];
        // get the client stream
        NetworkStream clientStream = tcpClient.GetStream();
        StreamReader reader = new StreamReader(clientStream,Encoding.UTF8);
        try
        {
            string request = reader.ReadToEnd();

            // just send an acknowledgement
            bytes = Encoding.UTF8.GetBytes("Thanks for the message!");
            clientStream.Write(bytes,0,bytes.Length);
        }
        finally
        {
            // close the reader
            reader.Close();
        }

        // stop listening
        tcpListener.Stop();

    }
}
```

Discussion

RunServer takes the IP address and port passed in, creates an IPAddress from the string address, and creates a TcpListener on that IPAddress and port. Once created, the TcpListener.Start method is called to start up the server. The blocking AcceptTcpClient method is called to listen for requests from TCP-based clients. Once the client connects, the request data from the client is read and a brief acknowledgment is given, and then the client stream is closed and the TcpListener is stopped using the TcpListener.Stop method.

See Also

See the "IPAddress Class," "TcpListener Class," and "TcpClient Class" topics in the MSDN documentation.

13.10 Writing a TCP Client

Problem

You want to interact with a TCP-based server.

Solution

Use the TcpClient class to connect to and converse with a TCP-based server by passing the address and port of the server to talk to. This example will talk to the server from Recipe 13.9:

```
public string RunClient(string address,int port)
{
    string response = "";
    // Set up a listener on that address/port
    TcpClient tcpClient = new TcpClient(address,port);
    if(tcpClient != null)
    {
        string message = "Hello there";
        // Translate the passed message into UTF8ASCII and store it as a Byte array.
        byte[] bytes = Encoding.ASCII.GetBytes(message);

        NetworkStream stream = tcpClient.GetStream();

        // Send the message to the connected TcpServer.
        // The write flushes the stream automatically here
        stream.Write(bytes, 0, bytes.Length);

        // Get the response from the server

        StreamReader reader = new StreamReader(stream,Encoding.UTF8);
        try
        {
            response = reader.ReadToEnd();
        }
        finally
        {
            // Close the reader
            reader.Close();
        }

        // Close the client
        tcpClient.Close();
    }
    // Return the response text
    return response;
}
```

Discussion

RunClient is designed to send one message containing "Hello World" to the server, get the response and return it as a string, then terminate. To accomplish this, it creates the TcpClient on the address and port passed in, and then it gets the bytes for the string using the Encoding.UTF8.GetBytes method. Once it has the bytes to send, it gets the NetworkStream from the TcpClient by calling the GetStream method and sends the message using the Write method.

In order to receive the response from the server, the blocking ReadToEnd method is then called. Once ReadToEnd returns, the string contains the response.

See Also

See the "TcpClient Class," "NetworkStream Class," and "Encoding.ASCII Property" topics in the MSDN documentation.

13.11 Simulating Form Execution

Problem

You need to send a collection of name/value pairs to simulate a form being executed on a browser to a location identified by a URI.

Solution

Use the WebClient class to send a set of name/value pairs to the web server using the UploadValues method. This class enables you to act as the browser executing a form by setting up the name/value pairs with the input data. The input field ID is the name, and the value to use in the field is the value:

```
using System;
using System.Net;
using System.Text;
using System.Collections.Specialized;

Uri uri = new Uri("http://localhost/FormSim/WebForm1.aspx");
WebClient client = new WebClient();

// Create a series of name/value pairs to send
NameValueCollection collection = new NameValueCollection();

// Add necessary parameter/value pairs to the name/value container.
collection.Add("Identity","foo@bar.com");
collection.Add("Item","Books");
collection.Add("Quantity","5");
Console.WriteLine("Uploading name/value pairs to URI {0} ...",
                   uri.AbsoluteUri);

// Upload the NameValueCollection.
byte[] responseArray =
```

```
            client.UploadValues(uri.AbsoluteUri,"POST",collection);
        // Decode and display the response.
        Console.WriteLine("\nResponse received was {0}",
            Encoding.ASCII.GetString(responseArray));
```

The webform1.aspx page to receive and process this data looks like this:

```
<%@ Page language="c#" Codebehind="WebForm1.aspx.cs" AutoEventWireup="false"
Inherits="FormSim.WebForm1" %>
<!DOCTYPE HTML PUBLIC "-//W3C//DTD HTML 4.0 Transitional//EN" >
<HTML>
    <HEAD>
        <title>WebForm1</title>
        <meta name="GENERATOR" Content="Microsoft Visual Studio .NET 7.1">
        <meta name="CODE_LANGUAGE" Content="C#">
        <meta name="vs_defaultClientScript" content="JavaScript">
        <meta name="vs_targetSchema"
            content="http://schemas.microsoft.com/intellisense/ie5">
    </HEAD>
    <body MS_POSITIONING="GridLayout">
        <form id="Form1" method="post" runat="server">
            <asp:TextBox id="Identity" style="Z-INDEX: 101; LEFT: 194px;
                    POSITION: absolute; TOP: 52px" runat="server"></asp:TextBox>
            <asp:TextBox id="Item" style="Z-INDEX: 102; LEFT: 193px;
                    POSITION: absolute; TOP: 93px" runat="server"></asp:TextBox>
            <asp:TextBox id="Quantity" style="Z-INDEX: 103; LEFT: 193px;
                    POSITION: absolute; TOP: 132px"
                runat="server"></asp:TextBox>
            <asp:Button id="Button1" style="Z-INDEX: 104; LEFT: 203px;
                    POSITION: absolute; TOP: 183px" runat="server"
                Text="Submit"></asp:Button>
            <asp:Label id="Label1" style="Z-INDEX: 105; LEFT: 58px;
                    POSITION: absolute; TOP: 54px" runat="server"
                Width="122px" Height="24px">Identity:</asp:Label>
            <asp:Label id="Label2" style="Z-INDEX: 106; LEFT: 57px;
                    POSITION: absolute; TOP: 94px" runat="server"
                Width="128px" Height="25px">Item:</asp:Label>
            <asp:Label id="Label3" style="Z-INDEX: 107; LEFT: 57px;
                    POSITION: absolute; TOP: 135px" runat="server"
                Width="124px" Height="20px">Quantity:</asp:Label>
        </form>
    </body>
</HTML>
```

The webform1.aspx code-behind looks like this:

```
using System;
using System.Collections;
using System.ComponentModel;
using System.Data;
using System.Drawing;
using System.Web;
using System.Web.SessionState;
using System.Web.UI;
using System.Web.UI.WebControls;
using System.Web.UI.HtmlControls;
```

```csharp
namespace FormSim
{
    /// <summary>
    /// Summary description for WebForm1.
    /// </summary>
    public class WebForm1 : System.Web.UI.Page
    {
        protected System.Web.UI.WebControls.Button Button1;
        protected System.Web.UI.WebControls.TextBox Item;
        protected System.Web.UI.WebControls.Label Label1;
        protected System.Web.UI.WebControls.Label Label2;
        protected System.Web.UI.WebControls.Label Label3;
        protected System.Web.UI.WebControls.TextBox Identity;
        protected System.Web.UI.WebControls.TextBox Quantity;

        private void Page_Load(object sender, System.EventArgs e)
        {
            // Put user code to initialize the page here
        }

        #region Web Form Designer generated code
        override protected void OnInit(EventArgs e)
        {
            //
            // CODEGEN: This call is required by the ASP.NET Web Form Designer.
            //
            InitializeComponent();
            base.OnInit(e);
        }

        /// <summary>
        /// Required method for Designer support - do not modify
        /// the contents of this method with the code editor.
        /// </summary>
        private void InitializeComponent()
        {
            this.Button1.Click +=
                new System.EventHandler(this.Button1_Click);
            this.Load += new System.EventHandler(this.Page_Load);

        }
        #endregion

        private void Button1_Click(object sender, System.EventArgs e)
        {
            string response = "Thanks for the order!<br/>";
            response += "Identity: " + Request.Form["Identity"] + "<br/>";
            response += "Item: " + Request.Form["Item"] + "<br/>";
            response += "Quantity: " + Request.Form["Quantity"] + "<br/>";
            Response.Write(response);
        }
    }
}
```

Discussion

The WebClient class makes it easy to upload form data to a web server in the common format of a set of name/value pairs. You can see this technique in the call to UploadValues that takes an absolute URI (*http://localhost/FormSim/WebForm1.aspx*), the HTTP method to use (POST), and the NameValueCollection we created (collection). The NameValueCollection is populated with the data for each of the fields on the form by giving the id of the input field as the name, and then the value to put in the field as the value during each call to Add. In this example, we fill in the Identity field with *foo@bar.com*, the Item field with Book, and the Quantity field with 5. We then print out the resulting response from the POST to the console window.

See Also

See the "WebClient Class" topic in the MSDN documentation.

13.12 Downloading Data from a Server

Problem

You need to download data from a location specified by a URI; this data can be either an array of bytes or a file.

Solution

Use the WebClient DownloadData and DownloadFile methods to download the bytes of a file from a URI:

```
string uri = "http://localhost/mysite/upload.aspx";

// make a client
WebClient client = new WebClient( );

// get the contents of the file
Console.WriteLine("Downloading {0} " + uri);
// download the page and store the bytes
byte[] bytes = client.DownloadData (uri);
// Write the HTML out
string page = Encoding.ASCII.GetString(bytes);
Console.WriteLine(page);
```

You could also have downloaded the file itself:

```
// go get the file
Console.WriteLine("Retrieving file from {1}...\r\n", uri);
// get file and put it in a temp file
string tempFile = Path.GetTempFileName( );
client.DownloadFile(uri,tempFile);
Console.WriteLine("Downloaded {0} to {1}",uri,tempFile);
```

Discussion

WebClient simplifies downloading of files and bytes in files, as these are common tasks when dealing with the Web. The more traditional stream-based method for downloading can also be accessed via the OpenRead method on the WebClient.

See Also

See the "WebClient Class" topic in the MSDN documentation.

13.13 Using Named Pipes to Communicate

Problem

You need a way to use named pipes to communicate with another application across the network.

Solution

Create a P/Invoke wrapper class for the named pipe APIs in *Kernel32.dll* to allow for managed access, and then create a managed client and managed server class to work with named pipes.

Here are the named pipe interop wrappers in a class called NamedPipeInterop:

```
namespace NamedPipes
{
/// <summary>
/// Imported namedpipe entry points for p/invoke into native code.
/// </summary>
[SuppressUnmanagedCodeSecurity]
public class NamedPipeInterop
{
    // #defines related to named pipe processing
    public const uint PIPE_ACCESS_OUTBOUND = 0x00000002;
    public const uint PIPE_ACCESS_DUPLEX = 0x00000003;
    public const uint PIPE_ACCESS_INBOUND = 0x00000001;

    public const uint PIPE_WAIT = 0x00000000;
    public const uint PIPE_NOWAIT = 0x00000001;
    public const uint PIPE_READMODE_BYTE = 0x00000000;
    public const uint PIPE_READMODE_MESSAGE = 0x00000002;
    public const uint PIPE_TYPE_BYTE = 0x00000000;
    public const uint PIPE_TYPE_MESSAGE = 0x00000004;

    public const uint PIPE_CLIENT_END = 0x00000000;
    public const uint PIPE_SERVER_END = 0x00000001;

    public const uint PIPE_UNLIMITED_INSTANCES = 255;
```

```csharp
public const uint NMPWAIT_WAIT_FOREVER = 0xffffffff;
public const uint NMPWAIT_NOWAIT = 0x00000001;
public const uint NMPWAIT_USE_DEFAULT_WAIT = 0x00000000;

public const uint GENERIC_READ = (0x80000000);
public const uint GENERIC_WRITE = (0x40000000);
public const uint GENERIC_EXECUTE = (0x20000000);
public const uint GENERIC_ALL = (0x10000000);

public const uint CREATE_NEW        = 1;
public const uint CREATE_ALWAYS     = 2;
public const uint OPEN_EXISTING     = 3;
public const uint OPEN_ALWAYS       = 4;
public const uint TRUNCATE_EXISTING = 5;

public const int INVALID_HANDLE_VALUE = -1;
public const uint ERROR_PIPE_BUSY = 231;
public const uint ERROR_NO_DATA = 232;
public const uint ERROR_PIPE_NOT_CONNECTED = 233;
public const uint ERROR_MORE_DATA = 234;
public const uint ERROR_PIPE_CONNECTED = 535;
public const uint ERROR_PIPE_LISTENING = 536;

public static int GetLastError()
{
    return Marshal.GetLastWin32Error();
}

[DllImport("kernel32.dll", SetLastError=true)]
public static extern bool CallNamedPipe(
    string lpNamedPipeName,
    byte[] lpInBuffer,
    uint nInBufferSize,
    byte[] lpOutBuffer,
    uint nOutBufferSize,
    byte[] lpBytesRead,
    uint nTimeOut);

[DllImport("kernel32.dll", SetLastError=true)]
public static extern bool CloseHandle(int hObject);

[DllImport("kernel32.dll", SetLastError=true)]
public static extern bool ConnectNamedPipe(
    int hNamedPipe,          // handle to named pipe
    IntPtr lpOverlapped      // overlapped structure
    );

[DllImport("kernel32.dll", SetLastError=true)]
public static extern int CreateNamedPipe(
    String lpName,          // pipe name
    uint dwOpenMode,       // pipe open mode
    uint dwPipeMode,       // pipe-specific modes
    uint nMaxInstances,     // maximum number of instances
    uint nOutBufferSize,     // output buffer size
    uint nInBufferSize,      // input buffer size
```

```
    uint nDefaultTimeOut,       // time-out interval
    //SecurityAttributes attr
    IntPtr pipeSecurityDescriptor // security descriptor
    );

[DllImport("kernel32.dll", SetLastError=true)]
public static extern int CreatePipe(
    int hReadPipe,
    int hWritePipe,
    IntPtr lpPipeAttributes,
    uint nSize);

[DllImport("kernel32.dll", SetLastError=true)]
public static extern int CreateFile(
    String lpFileName,          // filename
    uint dwDesiredAccess,         // access mode
    uint dwShareMode,          // share mode
    IntPtr attr,    // security descriptor
    uint dwCreationDisposition,      // how to create
    uint dwFlagsAndAttributes,     // file attributes
    uint hTemplateFile);          // handle to template file

[DllImport("kernel32.dll", SetLastError=true)]
public static extern bool DisconnectNamedPipe(int hNamedPipe);

[DllImport("kernel32.dll", SetLastError=true)]
public static extern bool FlushFileBuffers(int hFile);

[DllImport("kernel32.dll", SetLastError=true)]
public static extern bool GetNamedPipeHandleState(
    int hNamedPipe,
    IntPtr lpState,
    IntPtr lpCurInstances,
    IntPtr lpMaxCollectionCount,
    IntPtr lpCollectDataTimeout,
    string lpUserName,
    uint nMaxUserNameSize);

[DllImport("KERNEL32.DLL", SetLastError=true)]
public static extern bool GetNamedPipeInfo(
    int hNamedPipe,
    out uint lpFlags,
    out uint lpOutBufferSize,
    out uint lpInBufferSize,
    out uint lpMaxInstances);

[DllImport("KERNEL32.DLL", SetLastError=true)]
public static extern bool PeekNamedPipe(
    int hNamedPipe,
    byte[] lpBuffer,
    uint nBufferSize,
    byte[] lpBytesRead,
    out uint lpTotalBytesAvail,
    out uint lpBytesLeftThisMessage);
```

```
[DllImport("KERNEL32.DLL", SetLastError=true)]
public static extern bool SetNamedPipeHandleState(
    int hNamedPipe,
    ref int lpMode,
    IntPtr lpMaxCollectionCount,
    IntPtr lpCollectDataTimeout);

[DllImport("KERNEL32.DLL", SetLastError=true)]
public static extern bool TransactNamedPipe(
    int hNamedPipe,
    byte [] lpInBuffer,
    uint nInBufferSize,
    [Out] byte [] lpOutBuffer,
    uint nOutBufferSize,
    IntPtr lpBytesRead,
    IntPtr lpOverlapped);

[DllImport("kernel32.dll", SetLastError=true)]
public static extern bool WaitNamedPipe(
    string name,
    uint timeout);

[DllImport("kernel32.dll", SetLastError=true)]
public static extern bool ReadFile(
    int hFile,                // handle to file
    byte[] lpBuffer,          // data buffer
    uint nNumberOfBytesToRead,    // number of bytes to read
    byte[] lpNumberOfBytesRead,   // number of bytes read
    uint lpOverlapped          // overlapped buffer
    );

[DllImport("kernel32.dll", SetLastError=true)]
public static extern bool WriteFile(
    int hFile,                  // handle to file
    byte[] lpBuffer,            // data buffer
    uint nNumberOfBytesToWrite,      // number of bytes to write
    byte[] lpNumberOfBytesWritten,  // number of bytes written
    uint lpOverlapped           // overlapped buffer
    );
}

} // end namespace NamedPipes
```

Now, using the interop wrappers, we can create a named pipe client class named
NamedPipeClient:

```
namespace NamedPipes
{
    /// <summary>
    /// NamedPipeClient - An implementation of a synchronous,
    /// message-based, named pipe client
    ///
    ///</summary>
```

```csharp
public class NamedPipeClient : IDisposable
{
    /// <summary>
    ///     the full name of the pipe being connected to
    /// </summary>
    string _pipeName = "";

    /// <summary>
    /// the pipe handle once connected
    /// </summary>
    int _handle = NamedPipeInterop.INVALID_HANDLE_VALUE;

    /// <summary>
    /// default response buffer size (1K)
    /// </summary>
    uint _responseBufferSize = 1024;

    /// <summary>
    /// indicates if this has been closed once which calls
    /// for us to re-register for finalization on subsequent
    /// connect calls
    /// </summary>
    bool disposedOnce = false;

    /// <summary>
    /// WriteMessageResponseDelegate - callback for when a response
    /// to when a WriteMessage returns from the server
    ///
    /// </summary>
    public delegate void WriteMessageResponseDelegate(MemoryStream responseStream);

    /// <summary>
    /// CTOR
    /// </summary>
    /// <param name="pipeName">name of the pipe</param>
    public NamedPipeClient(string pipeName)
    {
        _pipeName = pipeName;
    }

    /// <summary>
    /// Finalizer
    /// </summary>
    ~NamedPipeClient()
    {
        Dispose();
    }

    /// <summary>
    /// Dispose
    /// </summary>
    public void Dispose()
```

```
{
    if(_handle != NamedPipeInterop.INVALID_HANDLE_VALUE)
    {
        NamedPipeInterop.CloseHandle(_handle);
        _handle = NamedPipeInterop.INVALID_HANDLE_VALUE;
    }
    // Suppress Finalization since we have now cleaned up our
    // handle
    System.GC.SuppressFinalize(this);
    // indicate we have disposed at least once
    if(disposedOnce == false)
        disposedOnce = true;
}

/// <summary>
/// Close - because it is more intuitive than Dispose... :)
/// </summary>
public void Close()
{
    Dispose();
}

/// <summary>
/// ResponseBufferSize Property - the size used to create response buffers
/// for messages written using WriteMessage
/// </summary>
public uint ResponseBufferSize
{
    get
    {
        return _responseBufferSize;
    }
    set
    {
        _responseBufferSize = value;
    }
}

/// <summary>
/// Connect - connect to an existing pipe
/// </summary>
/// <returns>true if connected</returns>
public bool Connect()
{
    if(disposedOnce == true)
        System.GC.ReRegisterForFinalize(this);

    if(_handle != NamedPipeInterop.INVALID_HANDLE_VALUE)
        throw new InvalidOperationException("Pipe is already connected!");

    // keep trying to connect
    while (true)
    {
```

```csharp
    // connect to existing pipe
    _handle = NamedPipeInterop.CreateFile(_pipeName,
        NamedPipeInterop.GENERIC_READ |
        NamedPipeInterop.GENERIC_WRITE,
        0,
        IntPtr.Zero,
        NamedPipeInterop.OPEN_EXISTING,
        0,
        0);

    // check to see if we connected
    if(_handle != NamedPipeInterop.INVALID_HANDLE_VALUE)
        break;

    // the pipe could not be opened as all instances are busy
    // any other error we bail for
    if(NamedPipeInterop.GetLastError() !=
        NamedPipeInterop.ERROR_PIPE_BUSY)
    {
        Debug.WriteLine("Could not open pipe: " + _pipeName);
        return false;
    }

    // if it was busy, see if we can wait it out for 20 seconds
    if(!NamedPipeInterop.WaitNamedPipe(_pipeName, 20000))
    {
        Debug.WriteLine("Specified pipe was over-burdened: " +
            _pipeName);
        return false;
    }
}
// indicate connection in debug
Debug.WriteLine("Connected to pipe: " + _pipeName);

// The pipe connected; change to message-read mode.
bool success = false;
int mode = (int) NamedPipeInterop.PIPE_READMODE_MESSAGE;

// set to message mode
success = NamedPipeInterop.SetNamedPipeHandleState(
    _handle,    // pipe handle
    ref mode,   // new pipe mode
    IntPtr.Zero,    // don't set maximum bytes
    IntPtr.Zero);   // don't set maximum time

// currently implemented for just synchronous, message-based pipes,
// so bail if we couldn't set the client up properly
if(false == success)
{
    Debug.WriteLine("Could not change pipe mode to message," +
        " shutting client down.");
                                    Dispose();
    return false;
}
```

```
        return true;
    }

    /// <summary>
    /// WriteMessage - write an array of bytes and return the response from the
    /// server
    /// </summary>
    /// <param name="buffer">bytes to write</param>
    /// <param name="bytesToWrite">number of bytes to write</param>
    /// <param name="ResponseDelegate">callback with the message response</param>
    /// <returns>true if written successfully</returns>
    public bool WriteMessage(byte [] buffer,  // the write buffer
        uint bytesToWrite,  // number of bytes in the write buffer
        WriteMessageResponseDelegate ResponseDelegate) // callback for
        // message responses
    {
        // buffer to get the number of bytes read/written back
        byte[] _numReadWritten = new byte[4];

        bool success = false;
        // Write the byte buffer to the pipe
        success = NamedPipeInterop.WriteFile(_handle,
            buffer,
            bytesToWrite,
            _numReadWritten,
            0);

        if(true == success)
        {
            byte[] responseBuffer = new byte[_responseBufferSize];
            int size = Convert.ToInt32(_responseBufferSize);
            MemoryStream fullBuffer = new MemoryStream(size);
            do
            {
                // Read the response from the pipe.
                success = NamedPipeInterop.ReadFile(
                    _handle,     // pipe handle
                    responseBuffer,    // buffer to receive reply
                    _responseBufferSize,      // size of buffer
                    _numReadWritten,  // number of bytes read
                    0);     // not overlapped

                // failed, not just more data to come
                if (! success && NamedPipeInterop.GetLastError() !=
                  NamedPipeInterop.ERROR_MORE_DATA)
                    break;

                // concat response to stream
                fullBuffer.Write(responseBuffer,
                    0,
                    responseBuffer.Length);

            } while (! success);  // repeat loop if ERROR_MORE_DATA
```

```
                // Callback the caller with this response buffer
                if(ResponseDelegate != null)
                    ResponseDelegate(fullBuffer);
            }
            return success;
        }
    }
} // end namespace NamedPipes
```

Then we need to create a server class for testing, which we will call NamedPipeServer:

```
namespace NamedPipes
{
/// <summary>
/// NamedPipeServer - An implementation of a synchronous, message-based,
/// named pipe server
///
/// </summary>
public class NamedPipeServer : IDisposable
{
    /// <summary>
    /// the pipe handle
    /// </summary>
    int _handle = NamedPipeInterop.INVALID_HANDLE_VALUE;

    /// <summary>
    /// the name of the pipe
    /// </summary>
    string _pipeName = "";

    /// <summary>
    /// the name of the machine the server pipe is on
    /// </summary>
    string _machineName = "";

    /// <summary>
    /// default size of message buffer to read
    /// </summary>
    uint _receiveBufferSize = 1024;

    /// <summary>
    /// indicates if this has been closed once, which calls
    /// for us to re-register for finalization on subsequent
    /// connect calls
    /// </summary>
    bool disposedOnce = false;

    /// <summary>
    /// the internal delegate holder for the callback on message receipt
    /// from clients
    /// </summary>
    MessageReceivedDelegate _messageReceivedDelegate;
```

```csharp
/// <summary>
/// PIPE_SERVER_BUFFER_SIZE set to 8192 by default
/// </summary>
const int PIPE_SERVER_BUFFER_SIZE = 8192;

/// <summary>
/// MessageReceivedDelegate - callback for message received from
/// client
///
/// </summary>
public delegate void MessageReceivedDelegate(MemoryStream message,
    out MemoryStream response);

/// <summary>
/// CTOR
/// </summary>
/// <param name="machineName">name of the machine the pipe is on,
/// use null for local machine</param>
/// <param name="pipeBaseName">the base name of the pipe</param>
/// <param name="msgReceivedDelegate">delegate to be notified when
/// a message is received</param>
public NamedPipeServer(string machineName,
    string pipeBaseName,
    MessageReceivedDelegate msgReceivedDelegate)
{
    // hook up the delegate
    _messageReceivedDelegate =  msgReceivedDelegate;

    if(machineName == null)
        _machineName = ".";
    else
        _machineName = machineName;

    // assemble the pipe name
    _pipeName = "\\\\" + _machineName + "\\PIPE\\" + pipeBaseName;
}

/// <summary>
/// Finalizer
/// </summary>
~NamedPipeServer()
{
    Dispose();
}

/// <summary>
/// Dispose - clean up handle
/// </summary>
public void Dispose()
{
    // if we have a pipe handle, disconnect and clean up
    if(_handle > 0)
    {
```

```
            NamedPipeInterop.DisconnectNamedPipe(_handle);
            NamedPipeInterop.CloseHandle(_handle);
            _handle = 0;
        }
        // Suppress Finalization since we have now cleaned up our
        // handle
        System.GC.SuppressFinalize(this);
        // indicate we have disposed at least once
        if(disposedOnce == false)
            disposedOnce = true;
    }

    /// <summary>
    /// Close - because it is more intuitive than Dispose...
    /// </summary>
    public void Close()
    {
        Dispose();
    }

    /// <summary>
    /// PipeName
    /// </summary>
    /// <returns>the composed pipe name</returns>
    public string PipeName
    {
        get
        {
            return _pipeName;
        }
    }

    /// <summary>
    /// CreatePipe - create the named pipe
    /// </summary>
    /// <returns>true is pipe created</returns>
    public bool CreatePipe()
    {
        if(disposedOnce == true)
            System.GC.ReRegisterForFinalize(this);

        // make a named pipe in message mode
        _handle = NamedPipeInterop.CreateNamedPipe(_pipeName,
            NamedPipeInterop.PIPE_ACCESS_DUPLEX,
            NamedPipeInterop.PIPE_TYPE_MESSAGE |
                NamedPipeInterop.PIPE_READMODE_MESSAGE |
            NamedPipeInterop.PIPE_WAIT,
            NamedPipeInterop.PIPE_UNLIMITED_INSTANCES,
            PIPE_SERVER_BUFFER_SIZE,
            PIPE_SERVER_BUFFER_SIZE,
            NamedPipeInterop.NMPWAIT_WAIT_FOREVER,
            IntPtr.Zero);
```

```csharp
    // make sure we got a good one
    if (_handle == NamedPipeInterop.INVALID_HANDLE_VALUE)
    {
        Debug.WriteLine("Could not create the pipe (" +
            _pipeName + ") - os returned " +
            NamedPipeInterop.GetLastError());

        return false;
    }
    return true;
}

/// <summary>
/// WaitForClientConnect - wait for a client to connect to this pipe
/// </summary>
/// <returns>true if connected, false if timed out</returns>
public bool WaitForClientConnect()
{
    bool success = false;
    // wait for someone to talk to us
    success = NamedPipeInterop.ConnectNamedPipe(_handle,IntPtr.Zero);
    if(true == success)
    {
        // process the first message
        while ( WaitForMessage() );
    }
    return success;
}

/// <summary>
/// WaitForMessage - have the server wait for a message
/// </summary>
/// <returns>true if got a message, false if timed out</returns>
public bool WaitForMessage()
{
    bool success = false;
    // they want to talk to us, read their messages and write
    // replies
    int size = Convert.ToInt32(_receiveBufferSize);
    MemoryStream fullMessageStream = new MemoryStream(size);
    byte [] buffer = new byte[_receiveBufferSize];
    byte [] _numReadWritten = new byte[4];

    // need to read the whole message and put it in one message
    // byte buffer
    do
    {
        // Read the response from the pipe.
        success = NamedPipeInterop.ReadFile(
            _handle,     // pipe handle
            buffer,      // buffer to receive reply
            _receiveBufferSize,     // size of buffer
            _numReadWritten, // number of bytes read
            0);     // not overlapped
```

```
                        // failed, not just more data to come
                        if (! success &&
                            (NamedPipeInterop.GetLastError( ) !=
                            NamedPipeInterop.ERROR_MORE_DATA))
                            break;

                        // concat the message bytes to the stream
                        fullMessageStream.Write(buffer,0,buffer.Length);

                    } while (! success);   // repeat loop if ERROR_MORE_DATA

                    // we read a message from a client
                    if(true == success)
                    {
                        // call delegate if connected for message processing
                        MemoryStream responseStream;
                        if(_messageReceivedDelegate != null)
                        {
                            // call delegate
                            _messageReceivedDelegate(fullMessageStream,
                                out responseStream);

                            if(responseStream != null)
                            {
                                // get raw byte array from stream
                                byte [] responseBytes =
                                    responseStream.ToArray( );
                                uint len =
                                    Convert.ToUInt32(responseBytes.Length);
                                // write the response message provided
                                // by the delegate
                                NamedPipeInterop.WriteFile(_handle,
                                    responseBytes,
                                    len,
                                    _numReadWritten,
                                    0);
                            }
                        }
                    }
                    return success;
                }
            }
        } // end namespace NamedPipes
```

In order to use the NamedPipeClient class, we need some code like the following:

```
using System;
using System.Diagnostics;
using System.Text;
using System.IO;

namespace NamedPipes
{
    class NamedPipesClientTest
```

```
    {
        static void Main(string[] args)
        {
            // create our pipe client
            NamedPipeClient _pc =
                    new NamedPipeClient("\\\\.\\PIPE\\mypipe");

            if(_pc != null)
            {
                // connect to the server
                if(true == _pc.Connect())
                {
                    // set up a dummy message
                    string testString = "This is my message!";
                    UnicodeEncoding UEncoder = new UnicodeEncoding();

                    // turn it into a byte array
                    byte[] writebuffer = UEncoder.GetBytes(testString);
                    uint len = Convert.ToUInt32(writebuffer.Length);

                    // write the message ten times
                    for(int i=0;i<10;i++)
                    {
                        if(false == _pc.WriteMessage(writebuffer,
                                                len,
            new NamedPipeClient.WriteMessageResponseDelegate(WriteMessageResponse)))
                        {
                            Debug.Assert(false,
                                            "Failed to write message!");
                        }
                    }
                    // close up shop
                    _pc.Close();
                }
            }
            Console.WriteLine("Press Enter to exit...");
            Console.ReadLine();
        }

        static void WriteMessageResponse(MemoryStream responseStream)
        {
            UnicodeEncoding UEncoder = new UnicodeEncoding();
            string response = UEncoder.GetString(responseStream.ToArray());
            Console.WriteLine("Received response: {0}",response);
        }
    }
}
```

Then, to set up a server for the client to talk to, we would use the NamedPipeServer class, like this:

```
namespace NamedPipes
{
    class NamedPipesServerTest
    {
```

```csharp
//
// MessageReceived - This is the method used in the delegate for the server
// that gets called after every message is received and before it is replied to
//
static void MessageReceived(MemoryStream message,out MemoryStream response)
{
    // get the bytes of the message from the stream
    byte [] msgBytes = message.ToArray();
    string messageText;

    // I know in the client I used Unicode encoding for the string to
    // turn it into a series of bytes for transmission so just reverse that
    UnicodeEncoding UEncoder = new UnicodeEncoding();
    messageText = UEncoder.GetString(msgBytes);

    // write out our string message from the client
    Console.WriteLine(messageText);

    // now set up response with a polite response using the same
        // Unicode string protocol
    string reply = "Thanks for the message!";
    msgBytes = UEncoder.GetBytes(reply);
    response = new MemoryStream(msgBytes,0,msgBytes.Length);
}


//
// Main - nuff said
//
static void Main(string[] args)
{
    // create pipe server
    NamedPipeServer _ps =
        new NamedPipeServer(null,
                    "mypipe",
            new NamedPipeServer.MessageReceivedDelegate(MessageReceived)
                    );

    // create pipe
    if(true == _ps.CreatePipe())
    {
        // I get the name of the pipe here just to show you can.
        // Normally we would then have to get this name to the client
        // so it knows the name of the pipe to open but hey, I wrote
        // the client too so for now I'm just hard-coding it in the
        // client so we can ignore it :)
        string pipeName = _ps.PipeName();

        // wait for clients to connect and process the first message
        if(true == _ps.WaitForClientConnect())
        {
            // process messages until the read fails
                // (client goes away...)
            bool success = true;
            while(success)
```

```
            {
                success = _ps.WaitForMessage();
            }
        }
        // done; bail and clean up the server
        _ps.Close();
    }
    // make our server hang around so you can see the messages sent
    Console.WriteLine("Press Enter to exit...");
    Console.ReadLine();
      }
    }
}
```

Discussion

Named pipes are a mechanism to allow interprocess or intermachine communications in Windows. As of v1.1, the .NET Framework has not provided managed access to named pipes, so the first thing we need to do is to wrap the functions in *Kernel32.dll* for direct access from managed code in our NamedPipesInterop class.

Once we have this foundation, we can then build a client for using named pipes to talk to a server, exposing a pipe that we did in the NamedPipeClient class. The methods on the NamedPipeClient are listed here with a description:

Method	Description
NamedPipeClient	Constructor for the named pipe client.
~NamedPipeClient	Finalizer for the named pipe client. This ensures the used pipe handle is freed.
Dispose	Dispose method for the named pipe client so that the pipe handle is not held any longer than necessary.
Close	Close method which calls down to the Dispose method.
Connect	Used to connect to a named pipe server.
WriteMessage	Writes a message to the connected server.
WriteMessageResponseDelegate	A delegate to let clients see the server's response if they wish to.

We then create the NamedPipeServer class to be able to have something for the NamedPipeClient to connect to. The methods on the NamedPipeServer are listed here with a description as well:

Method	Description
NamedPipeServer	Constructor for the named pipe server.
~NamedPipeServer	Finalizer for the named pipe server. This ensures the used pipe handles are freed.
Dispose	Dispose method for the named pipe server so that pipe handles are not held on to any longer than necessary.
Close	Close method that calls down to the Dispose method. Many developers use Close, so it is provided for completeness.

Method	Description
PipeName	Returns the composed pipe name.
CreatePipe	Creates a listener pipe on the server.
WaitForClientConnect	Wait on the pipe handle for a client to talk to.
WaitForMessage	Have the server wait for a message from the client.
MessageReceivedDelegate	A delegate to notify users of the server that a message has been received.

Finally we created some code to use NamedPipeClient and NamedPipeServer. The interaction between these two goes like this:

- The server process is started; it fires up a NamedPipeServer, calls CreatePipe to make a pipe, then calls WaitForClientConnect to wait for the NamedPipeClient to connect.

- The client process is then created; it fires up a NamedPipeClient, calls Connect, and connects to the server process.

- The server process sees the connection from the client, and then calls WaitForMessage in a loop. WaitForMessage starts reading the pipe, which blocks until a messages is written to the pipe by the client.

- The client process then writes a message to the server process using WriteMessage.

- The server process sees the message, processes it, and notifies anyone who signed up for notification via the MessageReceivedDelegate, then writes a response to the client, and then starts to wait again.

- When the client process receives the response from the server, it notifies anyone who signed up for the WriteMessageResponseDelegate, closes the NamedPipeClient that closes the pipe connection on the client side, and waits to go away when the user presses Enter.

- The server process notes the closing of the pipe connection by the client via the failed NamedPipesInterop.ReadFile call in WaitForMessage and calls Close on the server to clean up and wait for the user to press Enter to terminate the server process.

See Also

See the "Named Pipes," "DllImport Attribute," "IDisposable Interface," and "GC. SuppressFinalize Method" topics in the MSDN documentation.

CHAPTER 14

Security

There are many ways to secure different parts of your application. The security of running code in .NET revolves around the concept of Code Access Security (CAS). CAS determines the trustworthiness of an assembly based upon its origin. For example, code installed locally on the machine is more trusted than code downloaded from the Internet. The runtime will also validate an assembly's metadata and type safety before that code is allowed to run.

There are many ways to write secure code and protect data using the .NET Framework. In this chapter, we explore such things as controlling access to types, encryption and decryption, random numbers, securely storing data, and using programmatic and declarative security.

14.1 Controlling Access to Types in a Local Assembly

Problem

You have an existing class that contains sensitive data and you do not want clients to have direct access to any objects of this class directly. Instead, you would rather have an intermediary object talk to the clients and allow access to sensitive data based on the client's credentials. What's more, you would also like to have specific queries and modifications to the sensitive data tracked, so that if an attacker manages to access the object, you will have a log of what the attacker was attempting to do.

Solution

Use the *proxy design pattern* to allow clients to talk directly to a proxy object. This proxy object will act as gatekeeper to the class that contains the sensitive data. To keep malicious users from accessing the class itself, make it private, which will at least keep code without the `ReflectionPermissionFlag.TypeInformation` access (which is currently given only in fully trusted code scenarios like executing code interactively on a local machine) from getting at it.

The namespaces we will be using are:

```
using System;
using System.IO;
using System.Security;
using System.Security.Permissions;
using System.Security.Principal;
```

We start this design by creating an interface that will be common to both the proxy objects and the object that contains sensitive data:

```
internal interface ICompanyData
{
    string AdminUserName
    {
        get;
        set;
    }

    string AdminPwd
    {
        get;
        set;
    }

    string CEOPhoneNumExt
    {
        get;
        set;
    }

    void RefreshData();
    void SaveNewData();
}
```

The CompanyData class is the underlying object that is "expensive" to create:

```
internal class CompanyData : ICompanyData
{
    public CompanyData()
    {
        Console.WriteLine("[CONCRETE] CompanyData Created");
        // Perform expensive initialization here
    }

    private string adminUserName = "admin";
    private string adminPwd = "password";
    private string ceoPhoneNumExt = "0000";

    public string AdminUserName
    {
        get {return (adminUserName);}
        set {adminUserName = value;}
    }
```

```
    public string AdminPwd
    {
        get {return (adminPwd);}
        set {adminPwd = value;}
    }

    public string CEOPhoneNumExt
    {
        get {return (ceoPhoneNumExt);}
        set {ceoPhoneNumExt = value;}
    }

    public void RefreshData()
    {
        Console.WriteLine("[CONCRETE] Data Refreshed");
    }

    public void SaveNewData()
    {
        Console.WriteLine("[CONCRETE] Data Saved");
    }
}
```

The following is the code for the security proxy class, which checks the caller's permissions to determine whether the CompanyData object should be created and its methods or properties called:

```
public class CompanyDataSecProxy : ICompanyData
{
    public CompanyDataSecProxy()
    {
        Console.WriteLine("[SECPROXY] Created");

        // Must set principal policy first
        AppDomain.CurrentDomain.SetPrincipalPolicy(PrincipalPolicy.
            WindowsPrincipal);
    }

    private ICompanyData coData = null;
    private PrincipalPermission admPerm =
        new PrincipalPermission(null, @"BUILTIN\Administrators", true);
    private PrincipalPermission guestPerm =
        new PrincipalPermission(null, @"BUILTIN\Guest", true);
    private PrincipalPermission powerPerm =
        new PrincipalPermission(null, @"BUILTIN\PowerUser", true);
    private PrincipalPermission userPerm =
        new PrincipalPermission(null, @"BUILTIN\User", true);

    public string AdminUserName
    {
        get
        {
            string userName = "";
            try
```

```
    {
        admPerm.Demand( );
        Startup( );
        userName = coData.AdminUserName;
    }
    catch(SecurityException e)
    {
    Console.WriteLine("AdminUserName_get failed! {0}",e.ToString());
    }
    return (userName);
}
set
{
    try
    {
        admPerm.Demand( );
        Startup( );
        coData.AdminUserName = value;
    }
    catch(SecurityException e)
    {
    Console.WriteLine("AdminUserName_set failed! {0}",e.ToString( ));
    }
}
}

public string AdminPwd
{
    get
    {
        string pwd = "";
        try
        {
            admPerm.Demand( );
            Startup( );
            pwd = coData.AdminPwd;
        }
        catch(SecurityException e)
        {
        Console.WriteLine("AdminPwd_get Failed! {0}",e.ToString( ));
        }

        return (pwd);
    }
    set
    {
        try
        {
            admPerm.Demand( );
            Startup( );
            coData.AdminPwd = value;
        }
        catch(SecurityException e)
        {
```

```
                Console.WriteLine("AdminPwd_set Failed! {0}",e.ToString());
            }
        }
    }

    public string CEOPhoneNumExt
    {
        get
        {
            string ceoPhoneNum = "";
            try
            {
                admPerm.Union(powerPerm).Demand();
                Startup();
                ceoPhoneNum = coData.CEOPhoneNumExt;
            }
            catch(SecurityException e)
            {
                Console.WriteLine("CEOPhoneNum_set Failed! {0}",e.ToString());
            }
            return (ceoPhoneNum);
        }
        set
        {
            try
            {
                admPerm.Demand();
                Startup();
                coData.CEOPhoneNumExt = value;
            }
            catch(SecurityException e)
            {
            Console.WriteLine("CEOPhoneNum_set Failed! {0}",e.ToString());
            }
        }
    }

    public void RefreshData()
    {
        try
        {
            admPerm.Union(powerPerm.Union(userPerm)).Demand();
            Startup();
            Console.WriteLine("[SECPROXY] Data Refreshed");
            coData.RefreshData();
        }
        catch(SecurityException e)
        {
        Console.WriteLine("RefreshData Failed! {0}",e.ToString());
        }
    }

    public void SaveNewData()
    {
```

```
        try
        {
            admPerm.Union(powerPerm).Demand( );
            Startup( );
            Console.WriteLine("[SECPROXY] Data Saved");
            coData.SaveNewData( );
        }
        catch(SecurityException e)
        {
        Console.WriteLine("SaveNewData Failed! {0}",e.ToString( ));
        }
    }

    // DO NOT forget to use [#define DOTRACE] to control the tracing proxy
    private void Startup( )
    {
        if (coData == null)
        {
#if (DOTRACE)
            coData = new CompanyDataTraceProxy( );
#else
            coData = new CompanyData( );
#endif
            Console.WriteLine("[SECPROXY] Refresh Data");
            coData.RefreshData( );
        }
    }
}
```

When creating the PrincipalPermissions as part of the object construction, we are using string representations of the built in objects ("BUILTIN\Administrators") to set up the principal role. However, the names of these objects may be different depending on the locale the code runs under. It would be appropriate to use the WindowsAccountType.Administrator enumeration value to ease localization since this value is defined to represent the administrator role as well. We used text here to clarify what was being done and also to access the PowerUsers role, which is not available through the WindowsAccountType enumeration.

If the call to the CompanyData object passes through the CompanyDataSecProxy, then the user has permissions to access the underlying data. Any access to this data may be logged to allow the administrator to check for any attempted hacking of the CompanyData object. The following code is the tracing proxy used to log access to the various method and property access points in the CompanyData object (note that the CompanyDataSecProxy contains the code to turn on or off this proxy object):

```
public class CompanyDataTraceProxy : ICompanyData
{
    public CompanyDataTraceProxy( )
    {
        Console.WriteLine("[TRACEPROXY] Created");
        string path = Path.GetTempPath( ) + @"\CompanyAccessTraceFile.txt";
        fileStream = new FileStream(path, FileMode.Append,
```

```
        FileAccess.Write, FileShare.None);
    traceWriter = new StreamWriter(fileStream);
    coData = new CompanyData( );
}

private ICompanyData coData = null;
private FileStream fileStream = null;
private StreamWriter traceWriter = null;

public string AdminPwd
{
    get
    {
        traceWriter.WriteLine("AdminPwd read by user.");
        traceWriter.Flush( );
        return (coData.AdminPwd);
    }
    set
    {
        traceWriter.WriteLine("AdminPwd written by user.");
        traceWriter.Flush( );
        coData.AdminPwd = value;
    }
}

public string AdminUserName
{
    get
    {
        traceWriter.WriteLine("AdminUserName read by user.");
        traceWriter.Flush( );
        return (coData.AdminUserName);
    }
    set
    {
        traceWriter.WriteLine("AdminUserName written by user.");
        traceWriter.Flush( );
        coData.AdminUserName = value;
    }
}

public string CEOPhoneNumExt
{
    get
    {
        traceWriter.WriteLine("CEOPhoneNumExt read by user.");
        traceWriter.Flush( );
        return (coData.CEOPhoneNumExt);
    }
    set
    {
        traceWriter.WriteLine("CEOPhoneNumExt written by user.");
        traceWriter.Flush( );
        coData.CEOPhoneNumExt = value;
```

```
        }
    }

    public void RefreshData()
    {
        Console.WriteLine("[TRACEPROXY] Refresh Data");
        coData.RefreshData();
    }

    public void SaveNewData()
    {
        Console.WriteLine("[TRACEPROXY] Save Data");
        coData.SaveNewData();
    }
}
```

The proxy is used in the following manner:

```
// Create the security proxy here
CompanyDataSecProxy companyDataSecProxy = new CompanyDataSecProxy();

// Read some data
Console.WriteLine("CEOPhoneNumExt: " + companyDataSecProxy.CEOPhoneNumExt);

// Write some data
companyDataSecProxy.AdminPwd = "asdf";
companyDataSecProxy.AdminUserName = "asdf";

// Save and refresh this data
companyDataSecProxy.SaveNewData();
companyDataSecProxy.RefreshData();
```

Note that as long as the CompanyData object were accessible, we could have also written this to access the object directly:

```
// Instantiate the CompanyData object directly without a proxy
CompanyData companyData = new CompanyData();

// Read some data
Console.WriteLine("CEOPhoneNumExt: " + companyData.CEOPhoneNumExt);

// Write some data
companyData.AdminPwd = "asdf";
companyData.AdminUserName = "asdf";

// Save and refresh this data
companyData.SaveNewData();
companyData.RefreshData();
```

If these two blocks of code are run, the same fundamental actions occur: data is read, data is written, and data is updated/refreshed. This shows us that our proxy objects are set up correctly and function as they should.

Discussion

The *proxy design pattern* is useful for several tasks. The most notable, in COM and
.NET Remoting, is for marshaling data across boundaries such as AppDomains or
even across a network. To the client, a proxy looks and acts exactly the same as its
underlying object; fundamentally, the proxy object is a wrapper around the underlying object.

A proxy can test the security and/or identity permissions of the caller before the
underlying object is created or accessed. Proxy objects can also be chained together
to form several layers around an underlying object. Each proxy could be added or
removed depending on the circumstances.

For the proxy object to look and act the same as its underlying object, both should
implement the same interface. The implementation in this recipe uses an
ICompanyData interface on both the proxies (CompanyDataSecProxy and
CompanyDataTraceProxy) and the underlying object (CompanyData). If more proxies are
created, they too need to implement this interface.

The CompanyData class represents an expensive object to create. In addition, this class
contains a mixture of sensitive and nonsensitive data that require permission checks
to be made before the data is accessed. For this recipe, the CompanyData class simply
contains a group of properties to access company data and two methods for updating and refreshing this data. You can replace this class with one of your own and create a corresponding interface that both the class and its proxies implement.

The CompanyDataSecProxy object is the object that a client must interact with. This
object is responsible for determining whether the client has the correct privileges to
access the method or property that it is calling. The get accessor of the AdminUserName
property shows the structure of the code throughout most of this class:

```
public string AdminUserName
{
    get
    {
        string userName = "";
        try
        {
            admPerm.Demand( );
            Startup( );
            userName = coData.AdminUserName;
        }
        catch(SecurityException e)
        {
        Console.WriteLine("AdminUserName_get Failed!: {0}",e.ToString( ));
        }
        return (userName);
    }
    set
    {
```

```
            try
            {
                admPerm.Demand( );
                Startup( );
                coData.AdminUserName = value;
            }
            catch(SecurityException e)
            {
            Console.WriteLine("AdminUserName_set Failed! {0}",e.ToString( ));
            }
        }
    }
```

Initially, a single permission (AdmPerm) is demanded. If this demand fails, a SecurityException, which is handed by the catch clause, is thrown. (Other exceptions will be handed back to the caller.) If the Demand succeeds, the Startup method is called. It is in charge of instantiating either the next proxy object in the chain (CompanyDataTraceProxy) or the underlying CompanyData object. The choice depends on whether the DOTRACE preprocessor symbol has been defined. You may use a different technique, such as a registry key to turn tracing on or off, if you wish. Notice that if a security demand fails, the expensive object CompanyData is not created, saving our application time and resources.

This proxy class uses the private field CoData to hold a reference to an ICompanyData type, which could either be a CompanyDataTraceProxy or the CompanyData object. This reference allows us to chain several proxies together.

The CompanyDataTraceProxy simply logs any access to the CompanyData object's information to a text file. Since this proxy will not attempt to prevent a client from accessing the CompanyData object, the CompanyData object is created and explicitly called in each property and method of this object.

See Also

See *Design Patterns* by Erich Gamma et al. (Addison Wesley).

14.2 Encrypting/Decrypting a String

Problem

You have a string you want to be able to encrypt and decrypt—perhaps a password or software key—which will be stored in some form accessible by users, such as in a file, the registry, or even a field, that may be open to attack from malicious code.

Solution

Encrypting the string will prevent users from being able to read and decipher the information. The following class, CryptoString, contains two static methods to encrypt and decrypt a string and two static properties to retrieve the generated key and inititialization vector (IV—a random number used as a starting point to encrypt data) after encryption has occurred:

```
using System;
using System.Security.Cryptography;

public sealed class CryptoString
{
    private CryptoString() {}

    private static byte[] savedKey = null;
    private static byte[] savedIV = null;

    public static byte[] Key
    {
        get { return savedKey; }
        set { savedKey = value; }
    }

    public static byte[] IV
    {
        get { return savedIV; }
        set { savedIV = value; }
    }

    private static void RdGenerateSecretKey(RijndaelManaged rdProvider)
    {
        if (savedKey == null)
        {
            rdProvider.KeySize = 256;
            rdProvider.GenerateKey();
            savedKey = rdProvider.Key;
        }
    }

    private static void RdGenerateSecretInitVector(RijndaelManaged rdProvider)
    {
        if (savedIV == null)
        {
            rdProvider.GenerateIV();
            savedIV = rdProvider.IV;
        }
    }

    public static string Encrypt(string originalStr)
    {
        // Encode data string to be stored in memory
        byte[] originalStrAsBytes = Encoding.ASCII.GetBytes(originalStr);
        byte[] originalBytes = {};

        // Create MemoryStream to contain output
        MemoryStream memStream = new MemoryStream(originalStrAsBytes.Length);

        RijndaelManaged rijndael = new RijndaelManaged();
```

```
        // Generate and save secret key and init vector
        RdGenerateSecretKey(rijndael);
        RdGenerateSecretInitVector(rijndael);

        if (savedKey == null || savedIV == null)
        {
            throw (new NullReferenceException(
                    "savedKey and savedIV must be non-null."));
        }

        // Create encryptor, and stream objects
        ICryptoTransform rdTransform = rijndael.CreateEncryptor((byte[])savedKey.
                        Clone(),(byte[])savedIV.Clone());
        CryptoStream cryptoStream = new CryptoStream(memStream, rdTransform,
                        CryptoStreamMode.Write);

        // Write encrypted data to the MemoryStream
        cryptoStream.Write(originalStrAsBytes, 0, originalStrAsBytes.Length);
        cryptoStream.FlushFinalBlock();
        originalBytes = memStream.ToArray();

        // Release all resources
        memStream.Close();
        cryptoStream.Close();
        rdTransform.Dispose();
        rijndael.Clear();

        // Convert encrypted string
        string encryptedStr = Convert.ToBase64String(originalBytes);
        return (encryptedStr);
    }

    public static string Decrypt(string encryptedStr)
    {
        // Unconvert encrypted string
        byte[] encryptedStrAsBytes = Convert.FromBase64String(encryptedStr);
        byte[] initialText = new Byte[encryptedStrAsBytes.Length];

        RijndaelManaged rijndael = new RijndaelManaged();
        MemoryStream memStream = new MemoryStream(encryptedStrAsBytes);

        if (savedKey == null || savedIV == null)
        {
            throw (new NullReferenceException(
                    "savedKey and savedIV must be non-null."));
        }

        // Create decryptor, and stream objects
        ICryptoTransform rdTransform = rijndael.CreateDecryptor((byte[])savedKey.
                        Clone(),(byte[])savedIV.Clone());
        CryptoStream cryptoStream = new CryptoStream(memStream, rdTransform,
                        CryptoStreamMode.Read);
```

```
        // Read in decrypted string as a byte[]
        cryptoStream.Read(initialText, 0, initialText.Length);

        // Release all resources
        memStream.Close();
        cryptoStream.Close();
        rdTransform.Dispose();
        rijndael.Clear();

        // Convert byte[] to string
        string decryptedStr = Encoding.ASCII.GetString(initialText);
        return (decryptedStr);
    }
}
```

Discussion

The CryptoString class follows a singleton design pattern. This class contains only static members, except for the private instance constructor, which prevents anyone from directly creating an object from this class.

This class uses the *Rijndael algorithm* to encrypt and decrypt a string. This algorithm is found in the System.Security.Cryptography.RijndaelManaged class. This algorithm requires a secret key and an initialization vector; both are byte arrays. A random secret key can be generated for you by calling the GenerateKey method on the RijndaelManaged class. This method accepts no parameters and returns void. The generated key is placed in the Key property of the RijndaelManaged class. The GenerateIV method generates a random initialization vector and places this vector in the IV property of the RijndaelManaged class.

The byte array values in the Key and IV properties must be stored for later use and not modified. This is due to the nature of private-key encryption classes, such as RijndaelManaged. The Key and IV values must be used by both the encryption and decryption routines to successfully encrypt and decrypt data.

The SavedKey and SavedIV private static fields contain the secret key and initialization vector, respectively. The secret key is used by the encryption and decryption methods to encrypt and decrypt data. This key must be used by both the encryption and decryption methods in order to successfully encrypt and then decrypt the data. This is why there are public properties for these values, so they can be stored somewhere secure for later use. This means that any strings encrypted by this object must be decrypted by this object. The initialization vector is used to prevent anyone from attempting to decipher the secret key.

There are two methods in the CryptoString class, RdGenerateSecretKey and RdGenerateSecretInitVector, that are used to generate a secret key and initialization vector, when none exist. The RdGenerateSecretKey method generates the secret key, which is placed in the SavedKey field. Likewise, the RdGenerateSecretInitVector generates the initialization vector, which is placed in the SavedIV field. There is only one key and one IV generated for this class. This enables the encryption and decryption routines to have access to the same key and IV information at all times.

The `Encrypt` and `Decrypt` methods of the `CryptoString` class do the actual work of encrypting and decrypting a string, respectively. The `Encrypt` method accepts a string that you want to encrypt and returns an encrypted string. The following code calls this method and passes in a string to be encrypted:

```
string encryptedString = CryptoString.Encrypt("MyPassword");
Console.WriteLine("encryptedString: " + encryptedString);
// get the key and IV used so you can decrypt it later
byte [] key = CryptoString.Key;
byte [] IV = CryptoString.IV;
```

Once the string is encrypted, the key and IV are stored for later decryption. This method displays:

```
encryptedString: Ah4vkmVKpwMYRT97Q8cVgQ==
```

The following code sets the key and IV used to encrypt the string, then calls the `Decrypt` method to decrypt the previously encrypted string:

```
CryptoString.Key = key;
CryptoString.IV = IV;
string decryptedString = CryptoString.Decrypt(encryptedString);
Console.WriteLine("decryptedString: " + decryptedString);
```

This method displays:

```
decryptedString: MyPassword
```

There does not seem to be any problems with using escape sequences such as \r, \n, \r\n, or \t in the string to be encrypted. In addition, using a quoted string literal, with or without escaped characters, works without a problem:

```
@"MyPassword"
```

See Also

See Recipe 3.32; see the "System.Cryptography Namespace," "MemoryStream Class," "ICryptoTransform Interface," and "RijndaelManaged Class" topics in the MSDN documentation.

14.3 Encrypting and Decrypting a File

Problem

You have sensitive information that must be encrypted before it is written to a file that might be in a nonsecure area. This information must also be decrypted before it is read back in to the application.

Solution

Use multiple cryptography providers and write the data to a file in encrypted format. This is accomplished in the following class, whose constructor expects an instance of the System.Security.Cryptography.SymmetricAlgorithm class and a path for the file. The SymmetricAlgorithm class is an abstract base class for all cryptographic providers in .NET, so we can be reasonably assured that this class could be extended to cover all of them. This example implements support for TripleDES and Rijndael. It could easily be extended for DES and RC2, which are also provided by the framework.

The following namespaces are needed for this solution:

```
using System;
using System.Text;
using System.IO;
using System.Security.Cryptography;
```

The class SecretFile can be used for TripleDES as shown:

```
// Use TripleDES
TripleDESCryptoServiceProvider tdes = new TripleDESCryptoServiceProvider( );
SecretFile secretTDESFile = new SecretFile(tdes,"tdestext.secret");

string encrypt = "My TDES Secret Data!";

Console.WriteLine("Writing secret data: {0}",encrypt);
secretTDESFile.SaveSensitiveData(encrypt);
// save for storage to read file
byte [] key = secretTDESFile.Key;
byte [] IV = secretTDESFile.IV;

string decrypt = secretTDESFile.ReadSensitiveData( );
Console.WriteLine("Read secret data: {0}",decrypt);

// release resources
tdes.Clear( );
```

To use SecretFile with Rijndael, just substitute the provider in the constructor like this:

```
// Use Rijndael
RijndaelManaged rdProvider = new RijndaelManaged( );
SecretFile secretRDFile = new SecretFile(rdProvider,"rdtext.secret");

string encrypt = "My Rijndael Secret Data!";

Console.WriteLine("Writing secret data: {0}",encrypt);
secretRDFile.SaveSensitiveData(encrypt);
// save for storage to read file
byte [] key = secretRDFile.Key;
byte [] IV = secretRDFile.IV;
```

```
        string decrypt = secretRDFile.ReadSensitiveData();
        Console.WriteLine("Read secret data: {0}",decrypt);

        // release resources
        rdProvider.Clear();
```

Here is the implementation of SecretFile:

```
public class SecretFile
{
    private byte[] savedKey = null;
    private byte[] savedIV = null;
    private SymmetricAlgorithm symmetricAlgorithm;
    string path;

     public byte[] Key
    {
        get { return savedKey; }
        set { savedKey = value; }
    }

     public byte[] IV
    {
        get { return savedIV; }
        set { savedIV = value; }
    }

    public SecretFile(SymmetricAlgorithm algorithm, string fileName)
    {
        symmetricAlgorithm = algorithm;
        path = fileName;
    }

    public void SaveSensitiveData(string sensitiveData)
    {
        // Encode data string to be stored in encrypted file
        byte[] encodedData = Encoding.Unicode.GetBytes(sensitiveData);

        // Create FileStream and crypto service provider objects
        FileStream fileStream = new FileStream(path,
                                                FileMode.Create,
                                                FileAccess.Write);

        // Generate and save secret key and init vector
        GenerateSecretKey();
        GenerateSecretInitVector();

        // Create crypto transform and stream objects
        ICryptoTransform transform = symmetricAlgorithm.CreateEncryptor(savedKey,
                                    savedIV);
        CryptoStream cryptoStream =
            new CryptoStream(fileStream, transform, CryptoStreamMode.Write);
```

```csharp
        // Write encrypted data to the file
        cryptoStream.Write(encodedData, 0, encodedData.Length);

        // Release all resources
        cryptoStream.Close();
        transform.Dispose();
        fileStream.Close();
    }

    public string ReadSensitiveData()
    {
        // Create file stream to read encrypted file back
        FileStream fileStream = new FileStream(path,
                                               FileMode.Open,
                                               FileAccess.Read);

        //print out the contents of the encrypted file
        BinaryReader binReader = new BinaryReader(fileStream);
        Console.WriteLine("---------- Encrypted Data ---------");
        int count = (Convert.ToInt32(binReader.BaseStream.Length));
        byte [] bytes = binReader.ReadBytes(count);
        char [] array = Encoding.Unicode.GetChars(bytes);
        string encdata = new string(array);
        Console.WriteLine(encdata);
        Console.WriteLine("---------- Encrypted Data ---------\r\n");

        // reset the file stream
        fileStream.Seek(0,SeekOrigin.Begin);

        // Create Decryptor
        ICryptoTransform transform = symmetricAlgorithm.CreateDecryptor(savedKey,
                                                                        savedIV);
        CryptoStream cryptoStream = new CryptoStream(fileStream,
                                                     transform,
                                                     CryptoStreamMode.Read);

        //print out the contents of the decrypted file
        StreamReader srDecrypted = new StreamReader(cryptoStream,
                                                    new UnicodeEncoding());
        Console.WriteLine("---------- Decrypted Data ---------");
        string decrypted = srDecrypted.ReadToEnd();
        Console.WriteLine(decrypted);
        Console.WriteLine("---------- Decrypted Data ---------");

        // Release all resources
        binReader.Close();
        srDecrypted.Close();
        cryptoStream.Close();
        transform.Dispose();
        fileStream.Close();
        return decrypted;
    }
```

```
        private void GenerateSecretKey( )
        {
            if(null != (symmetricAlgorithm as TripleDESCryptoServiceProvider))
            {
                TripleDESCryptoServiceProvider tdes;
                tdes = symmetricAlgorithm as TripleDESCryptoServiceProvider;
                tdes.KeySize = 192; //  Maximum key size
                tdes.GenerateKey( );
                savedKey = tdes.Key;
            }
            else if(null != (symmetricAlgorithm as RijndaelManaged))
            {
                RijndaelManaged rdProvider;
                rdProvider = symmetricAlgorithm as RijndaelManaged;
                rdProvider.KeySize = 256; // Maximum key size
                rdProvider.GenerateKey( );
                savedKey = rdProvider.Key;
            }
        }

        private void GenerateSecretInitVector( )
        {
            if(null != (symmetricAlgorithm as TripleDESCryptoServiceProvider))
            {
                TripleDESCryptoServiceProvider tdes;
                tdes = symmetricAlgorithm as TripleDESCryptoServiceProvider;
                tdes.GenerateIV( );
                savedIV = tdes.IV;
            }
            else if(null != (symmetricAlgorithm as RijndaelManaged))
            {
                RijndaelManaged rdProvider;
                rdProvider = symmetricAlgorithm as RijndaelManaged;
                rdProvider.GenerateIV( );
                savedIV = rdProvider.IV;
            }
        }
    }
```

If the SaveSensitiveData method is used to save the following text to a file:

```
This is a test
This is sensitive data!
```

the ReadSensitiveData method will display the following information from this same file:

```
---------- Encrypted Data ---------
?????????????????????????????????????????????
---------- Encrypted Data ---------

---------- Decrypted Data ---------
This is a test
This is sensitive data!
---------- Decrypted Data ---------
```

Discussion

Encrypting data is essential to many applications, especially ones that store information in easily accessible locations. Once data is encrypted, a decryption scheme is required to restore the data back to an unencrypted form without losing any information. The same underlying algorithms can be used to authenticate the source of a file or message.

The encryption schemes used in this recipe are TripleDES and Rijndael. The reason for using Triple DES are:

- TripleDES employs symmetric encryption, meaning that a single private key is used to encrypt and decrypt data. This process allows much faster encryption and decryption, especially as the streams of data become larger.
- TripleDES encryption is much harder to crack than the older DES encryption.
- If you wish to use another type of encryption, this recipe can be easily converted using any provider derived from the SymmetricAlgorithm class.

The main drawback to TripleDES is that both the sender and receiver must use the same key and Initialization Vector (IV) in order to encrypt and decrypt the data successfully. If you wish to have an even more secure encryption scheme, use the Rijndael scheme. This type of encryption scheme is highly regarded as a solid encryption scheme, since it is fast and can use larger key sizes than TripleDES. However, it is still a symmetric cryptosystem, which means that it relies on shared secrets. Use an asymmetric cryptosystem, such as RSA or DSA, for a cryptosystem that uses shared public keys with private keys that are never shared between parties.

See Also

See the "SymmetricAlgorithm Class," "TripleDESCryptoServiceProvider Class," and "RijndaelManaged Class" topics in the MSDN documentation.

14.4 Cleaning Up Cryptography Information

Problem

You will be using the cryptography classes in the FCL to encrypt and/or decrypt data. In doing so, you want to make sure that no data (e.g., seed values or keys) is left in memory for longer than you are using the cryptography classes. Hackers can sometimes find this information in memory and use it to break your encryption; or worse, to break your encryption, modify the data, and then re-encrypt the data and pass it on to your application.

Solution

In order to clear out the key and initialization vector (or seed), we need to call the Clear method on whichever SymmetricAlgorithm derived or AsymmetricAlgorithm derived class we are using. Clear reinitializes the Key and IV properties preventing them from being found in memory. This is done after saving the key and IV so that we can decrypt later. The following example shows a series of actions that encodes a string and uses this approach to clean up immediately after the encryption is performed to provide the smallest window possible for potential attackers:

```
using System;
using System.Text;
using System.IO;
using System.Security.Cryptography;

string originalStr = "SuperSecret information";
// Encode data string to be stored in memory
byte[] originalStrAsBytes = Encoding.ASCII.GetBytes(originalStr);
byte[] originalBytes = {};

// create MemoryStream to contain output
MemoryStream memStream = new MemoryStream(originalStrAsBytes.Length);

RijndaelManaged rijndael = new RijndaelManaged();

// generate secret key and init vector
rijndael.KeySize = 256;
rijndael.GenerateKey();
rijndael.GenerateIV();

// save the key and IV for later decryption
byte [] key = rijndael.Key;
byte [] IV = rijndael.IV;

// create encryptor, and stream objects
ICryptoTransform transform = rijndael.CreateEncryptor(rijndael.Key,
    rijndael.IV);
CryptoStream cryptoStream = new CryptoStream(memStream, transform,
    CryptoStreamMode.Write);

// write encrypted data to the MemoryStream
cryptoStream.Write(originalStrAsBytes, 0, originalStrAsBytes.Length);
cryptoStream.FlushFinalBlock();

// release all resources as soon as we are done with them
// to prevent retaining any information in memory
memStream.Close();
memStream = null;
cryptoStream.Close();
cryptoStream = null;
transform.Dispose();
transform = null;
// this clear statement regens both the key and the init vector so that
// what is left in memory is no longer the values you used to encrypt with
rijndael.Clear();
// make this eligible for GC as soon as possible
rijndael = null;
```

Discussion

To be on the safe side, we also close the MemoryStream and CryptoStream objects as soon as possible, as well as calling Dispose on the ICryptoTransform implementation to clear out any resources used in this encryption. Finally, we set the references for all of the objects involved to null to allow the garbage collector to collect them as soon as possible.

See Also

See the "SymmetricAlgorithm.Clear Method" and "AsymmetricAlgorithm.Clear Method" topics in the MSDN documentation.

14.5 Verifying that a String Is Uncorrupted During Transmission

Problem

You have some text that will be sent across a network to another machine for processing. It is critical that you are able to verify that this text remains intact and unmodified when it arrives at its destination.

Solution

Calculate a hash value from this string and append it to the string before it is sent to its destination. Once the destination receives the string, it can remove the hash value and determine whether the string is the same one that was initially sent. The CreateStringHash method takes a string as input, adds a hash value to the end of it, and returns the new string:

```
public class HashOps
{
  public static string CreateStringHash(string unHashedString)
  {
      byte[] encodedUnHashedString = Encoding.Unicode.GetBytes(unHashedString);

      SHA256Managed hashingObj = new SHA256Managed( );
      byte[] hashCode = hashingObj.ComputeHash(encodedUnHashedString);

      string hashBase64 = Convert.ToBase64String(hashCode);
      string stringWithHash = unHashedString + hashBase64;

      hashingObj.Clear( );

      return (stringWithHash);
  }

  public static bool TestReceivedStringHash(string stringWithHash,
                                            out string originalStr)
```

```
        {
            // Code to quickly test the handling of a tampered string
            //stringWithHash = stringWithHash.Replace('a', 'b');

            if (stringWithHash.Length < 45)
            {
                originalStr = null;
                return (true);
            }

            string hashCodeString =
                stringWithHash.Substring(stringWithHash.Length - 44);
            string unHashedString =
                stringWithHash.Substring(0, stringWithHash.Length - 44);

            byte[] hashCode = Convert.FromBase64String(hashCodeString);

            byte[] encodedUnHashedString = Encoding.Unicode.GetBytes(unHashedString);

            SHA256Managed hashingObj = new SHA256Managed();
            byte[] receivedHashCode = hashingObj.ComputeHash(encodedUnHashedString);

            bool hasBeenTamperedWith = false;
            for (int counter = 0; counter < receivedHashCode.Length; counter++)
            {
                if (receivedHashCode[counter] != hashCode[counter])
                {
                    hasBeenTamperedWith = true;
                    break;
                }
            }

            if (!hasBeenTamperedWith)
            {
                originalStr = unHashedString;
            }
            else
            {
                originalStr = null;
            }

            hashingObj.Clear();

            return (hasBeenTamperedWith);
        }
    }
```

The `TestReceivedStringHash` method is called by the code that receives a string with a hash value appended. This method removes the hash value, calculates a new hash value for the string, and checks to see whether both hash values match. If they match, both strings are exactly the same, and the method returns `false`. If they don't match, the string has been tampered with, and the method returns `true`.

Since the `CreateStringHash` and `TestReceivedStringHash` methods are static members of a class named `HashOps`, we can call these methods with code like the following:

```
public static void VerifyNonStringCorruption( )
{
    string testString = "This is the string that we'll be testing.";
    string unhashedString;
    string hashedString = HashOps.CreateStringHash(testString);

    bool result = HashOps.TestReceivedStringHash(hashedString, out unhashedString);
    Console.WriteLine(result);
    if (!result)
        Console.WriteLine("The string sent is: " + unhashedString);
    else
        Console.WriteLine("The string " + unhashedString +
            " has become corrupted.");
}
```

Discussion

You can use a hash, checksum, or *cyclic redundancy check* (CRC) to calculate a value based on a message. This value is then used at the destination to determine whether the message has been modified during transmission between the source and destination.

This recipe uses a hash value as a reliable method of determining whether a string has been modified. The hash value for this recipe is calculated using the SHA256Managed class. This hash value is 256 bits in size and produces greatly differing results when calculated from strings that are very similar, but not exactly the same. In fact, if a single letter is removed or even capitalized, the resulting hash value will change.

By appending this value to the string, both the string and hash value can be sent to its destination. The destination then removes the hash value and calculates a hash value of its own based on the received string. These two hash values are then compared. If they are equal, the strings are exactly the same. If they are not equal, you can be sure that somewhere between the source and destination, the string was corrupted. This technique is great for verifying that transmission succeeded without errors, but it does not guarantee against malicious tampering. To protect against malicious tampering, use an asymmetric algorithm: sign the string with a private key and verify the signature with a public key.

The `CreateStringHash` method first converts the unhashed string into a byte array using the GetBytes method of the UnicodeEncoding class. This byte array is then passed into the ComputeHash method of the SHA256Managed class.

Once the hash value is calculated, the byte array containing the hash code is converted to a string containing base64 digits, using the `Convert.ToBase64String` method. This method accepts a byte array, converts it to a string of base64 digits, and returns that string. The reason for doing this is to convert all unsigned integers in the byte array to values that can be represented in a string data type. The last thing that this method does is to append the hash value to the end of the string and return the newly hashed string.

The TestReceivedStringHash method accepts a hashed string and an out parameter that will return the unhashed string. This method returns a Boolean; as previously mentioned, true indicates that the string has been modified, false indicates that the string is unmodified.

This method first removes the hash value from the end of the StringWithHash variable. Next, a new hash is calculated using the string portion of the StringWithHash variable. These two hash values are compared. If they are the same, the string has been received, unmodified. Note that if you change the hashing algorithm used, you must change it both in this method and the CreateStringHash method. You must also change the numeric literal 44 in the TestReceivedStringHash method to an appropriate size for the new hashing algorithm. This number is the exact length of the base64 representation of the hash value, which was appended to the string.

See Also

See the "SHA256Managed Class," "Convert.ToBase64String Method," and "Convert.FromBase64String Method" topics in the MSDN documentation.

14.6 Wrapping a String Hash for Ease of Use

Problem

You need to create a class to protect other developers on your team from having to deal with the details of how to add a hash to a string, as well as how to use the hash to verify if the string has been modified or corrupted.

Solution

The following classes decorate the StringWriter and StringReader classes to handle a hash added to its contained string. The WriterDecorator and StringWriterHash classes allow the StringWriter class to be decorated with extra functionality to add a hash value to the StringWriter's internal string. Note that the method calls to create the hash value in the CreateStringHash method was defined in Recipe 14.5:

The code for the WriterDecorator abstract base class is:

```
using System;
using System.Text;
using System.IO;

[Serializable]
public abstract class WriterDecorator : TextWriter
```

```
{
    public WriterDecorator() {}

    public WriterDecorator(StringWriter stringWriter)
    {
        internalStringWriter = stringWriter;
    }

    protected bool isHashed = false;
    protected StringWriter internalStringWriter = null;

    public void SetWriter(StringWriter stringWriter)
    {
        internalStringWriter = stringWriter;
    }
}
```

This is the concrete implementation of the WriterDecorator class:

```
[Serializable]
public class StringWriterHash : WriterDecorator
{
    public StringWriterHash( ) : base( ) {}

    public StringWriterHash(StringWriter stringWriter) : base(stringWriter)
    {
    }

    public override Encoding Encoding
    {
        get {return (internalStringWriter.Encoding);}
    }

    public override void Close( )
    {
        internalStringWriter.Close( );
        base.Dispose(true);                    // Completes the cleanup
    }

    public override void Flush( )
    {
        internalStringWriter.Flush( );
        base.Flush( );
    }

    public virtual StringBuilder GetStringBuilder( )
    {
        return (internalStringWriter.GetStringBuilder( ));
    }

    public override string ToString( )
    {
        return (internalStringWriter.ToString( ));
    }
```

```
        public void WriteHash( )
        {
            int originalStrLen = internalStringWriter.GetStringBuilder( ).Length;

            // Call hash generator here for whole string.
            string hashedString = HashOps.CreateStringHash(this.ToString( ));
            internalStringWriter.Write(hashedString.Substring(originalStrLen));

            isHashed = true;
        }

        public override void Write(char value)
        {
            if (isHashed)
            {
                throw (new Exception("A hash has already been added to this string"+
                                    ", it cannot be modified."));
            }
            else
            {
                internalStringWriter.Write(value);
            }
        }

        public override void Write(string value)
        {
            if (isHashed)
            {
                throw (new Exception("A hash has already been added to this string"+
                                    ", it cannot be modified."));
            }
            else
            {
                internalStringWriter.Write(value);
            }
        }

        public override void Write(char[] buffer, int index, int count)
        {
            if (isHashed)
            {
                throw (new Exception("A hash has already been added to this string"+
                                    ", it cannot be modified."));
            }
            else
            {
                internalStringWriter.Write(buffer, index, count);
            }
        }
    }
}
```

These are the ReaderDecorator and StringReaderHash classes, which allow the StringReader class to be decorated with extra functionality to handle the verification

of a string's hash value. Note that the method calls to verify the hash value in the
TestRecievedStringHash method were defined in Recipe 14.5:

```
[Serializable]
public abstract class ReaderDecorator : TextReader
{
    public ReaderDecorator() {}

    public ReaderDecorator(StringReader stringReader)
    {
        internalStringReader = stringReader;
    }

    protected StringReader internalStringReader = null;

    public void SetReader(StringReader stringReader)
    {
        internalStringReader = stringReader;
    }
}
```

This is the concrete implementation of the ReaderDecorator class:

```
[Serializable]
public class StringReaderHash : ReaderDecorator
{
    public StringReaderHash() : base() {}

    public StringReaderHash(StringReader stringReader) : base(stringReader)
    {
    }

    public override void Close()
    {
        internalStringReader.Close();
        base.Dispose(true);// Completes the cleanup
    }

    public string ReadToEndHash()
    {
        string hashStr = internalStringReader.ReadToEnd();

        string originalStr = "";
        // Call hash reader here.
        bool isInvalid = HashOps.TestReceivedStringHash(hashStr,
                                                        out originalStr);

        if (isInvalid)
        {
            throw (new Exception("This string has failed its hash check."));
        }

        return (originalStr);
    }
```

```
    public override int Read( )
    {
        return (internalStringReader.Read( ));
    }

    public override int Read(char[] buffer, int index, int count)
    {
        return (internalStringReader.Read(buffer, index, count));
    }

    public override string ReadLine( )
    {
        return (internalStringReader.ReadLine( ));
    }

    public override string ReadToEnd( )
    {
        return (internalStringReader.ReadToEnd( ));
    }
}
```

The following code creates a StringWriter object (stringWriter) and decorates it with a StringWriterHash object:

```
StringWriter stringWriter = new StringWriter(new StringBuilder("Initial Text"));
StringWriterHash stringWriterHash = new StringWriterHash( );
stringWriterHash.SetWriter(stringWriter);
stringWriterHash.Write("-Extra Text-");
stringWriterHash.WriteHash( );
Console.WriteLine("stringWriterHash.ToString( ): " + stringWriterHash.ToString( ));
```

The string "Initial Text" is added to the StringWriter on initialization, and later the string "-Extra Text-" is added. Next, the WriteHash method is called to handle adding a hash value to the end of the complete string. Notice that if the code attempts to write more text to the StringWriterHash object after the WriteHash method has been called, an exception will be thrown. The string cannot be modified once the hash has been calculated and added.

The following code takes a StringReader object (stringReader) that was initialized with the string and hash produced by the previous code and decorates it with a StringReaderHash object:

```
StringReader stringReader = new StringReader(stringWriterHash.ToString( ));
StringReaderHash stringReaderHash = new StringReaderHash( );
stringReaderHash.SetReader(stringReader);
Console.WriteLine("stringReaderHash.ReadToEndHash( ): " +
                    stringReaderHash.ReadToEndHash( ));
```

If the original string is modified after the hash is added, the ReadToEndHash method throws an exception.

Discussion

The *decorator design pattern* provides the ability to modify individual objects without having to modify or subclass the object's class. This allows for the creation of both decorated and undecorated objects. The implementation of a decorator pattern is sometimes hard to understand at first. An abstract decorator class is created that inherits from the same base class as the class we will decorate. In the case of this recipe, we will decorate the StringReader/StringWriter classes to allow a hash to be calculated and used. The StringReader class inherits from TextReader, and the StringWriter class inherits from TextWriter. Knowing this, we will create two abstract decorator classes: ReaderDecorator, which inherits from TextReader; and WriterDecorator, which inherits from TextWriter.

The abstract decorator classes contain two constructors: a private field named internalStreamReader\internalStreamWriter and a method named SetReader\SetWriter. Basically, the field stores a reference to the contained StringReader or StringWriter object that is being decorated. This field can be set through either a constructor or the SetReader\SetWriter method. The interesting thing about this pattern is that each of the decorator objects must also contain an instance of the class that they decorate. The StringReaderHash class contains a StringReader object in its internalStreamReader field, and the StringWriterHash class contains a StringWriter object in its internalStreamWriter field.

A concrete decorator class is created that inherits from the abstract decorator classes. The StringReaderHash class inherits from ReaderDecorator, while the StringWriterHash inherits from WriterDecorator. This pattern allows us the flexibility to add concrete decorator classes without having to touch the existing code.

Most of the methods in the StringReaderHash and StringWriterHash classes simply act as wrappers to the internalStreamReader or internalStreamWriter objects, respectively. The method that actually decorates the StringReader object with a hash is the StringReaderCRC.ReadToEndHash method, and the method that actually decorates the StringWriter object is StringWriterCRC.WriteHash. These two methods allow the hash to be attached to a string and later used to determine whether the string contents have changed.

The attractiveness of the decorator pattern is that we can add any number of concrete decorator classes that derives from either ReaderDecorator or WriterDecorator. If we need to use a different hashing algorithm, or even a quick and dirty hash algorithm, we can subclass the ReaderDecorator or WriterDecorator classes and add functionality to use these new algorithms. Now we have more choices of how to decorate these classes.

See Also

See the "StringWriter Class" and "StringReader Class" topics in the MSDN documentation.

14.7   A Better Random Number Generator

Problem

You need a random number with which to generate items such as a sequence of session keys. The random number must be as unpredictable as possible so that the likelihood of predicting the sequence of keys is as low as possible.

Solution

Use the classes System.Security.Cryptography.RNGCryptoServiceProvider and System.Random.

The RNGCryptoServiceProvider is used to populate a random byte array using the GetBytes method that is then printed out as a string in the following example:

```
public static void BetterRandomString()
{
    // create a stronger hash code using RNGCryptoServiceProvider
    byte[] random = new byte[64];
    RNGCryptoServiceProvider rng = new RNGCryptoServiceProvider();
    // populate with random bytes
    rng.GetBytes(random);

    // convert random bytes to string
    string randomBase64 = Convert.ToBase64String(random);
    // display
    Console.WriteLine("Random string: {0}\r\n ",randomBase64);
}
```

Discussion

Random provides methods like Next, NextBytes, and NextDouble to generate random information for integers, arrays of bytes, and doubles, respectively. These methods can produce a moderate level of unpredictability, but to truly generate a more unpredictable random series, you would want to use the RNGCryptoServiceProvider.

RNGCryptoServiceProvider can be customized to use any of the underlying Win32 Crypto API providers by passing a CspParameters structure in the constructor to determine exactly which provider is responsible for generating the random bytes sequence. CspParameters allows you to customize items such as the key container name, the provider type code, the provider name, and the key number used. The GetBytes method populates the entire length of the byte array with random bytes.

See Also

See the "RNGCryptoServiceProvider Class," "CspParameters Class," and "Cryptographic Provider Types" topics in the MSDN documentation.

14.8   Securely Storing Data

Problem

You need to store settings data about individual users for use by your application that is isolated from other instances of your application run by different users.

Solution

You can use isolated storage to establish per user data stores for your application data, and then use hashed values for critical data in your data store.

To illustrate how to do this for settings data, we create the following `UserSettings` class. `UserSettings` holds only two pieces of information, the user identity (current `WindowsIdentity`) and the password for our application. The user identity is accessed via the `User` property, and the password is accessed via the `Password` property. Note that the password field is being created the first time and is stored as a salted hashed value to keep it secure. The combination of the isolated storage and the hashing of the password value helps to strengthen the security of the password by using the "defense in depth" principle. The settings data is held in XML that is stored in the isolated storage scope and accessed via an `XmlDocument` instance.

This solution uses the following namespaces:

```
using System;
using System.IO;
using System.IO.IsolatedStorage;
using System.Xml;
using System.Text;
using System.Diagnostics;
using System.Security.Principal;
using System.Security.Cryptography;
```

Here is the `UserSettings` class:

```
// class to hold user settings
public class UserSettings
{
    IsolatedStorageFile isoStorageFile = null;
    IsolatedStorageFileStream isoFileStream = null;
    XmlDocument settingsDoc = null;
    XmlTextWriter writer = null;
    const string storageName = "SettingsStorage.xml";

    // constructor
    public UserSettings(string password)
    {
        // get the isolated storage
        isoStorageFile = IsolatedStorageFile.GetUserStoreForDomain( );
        // create an internal DOM for settings
        settingsDoc = new XmlDocument( );
```

```
                // if no settings, create default
                if(isoStorageFile.GetFileNames(storageName).Length == 0)
                {
                    isoFileStream =
                        new IsolatedStorageFileStream(storageName,
                                                      FileMode.Create,
                                                      isoStorageFile);

                    writer = new XmlTextWriter(isoFileStream,Encoding.UTF8);
                    writer.WriteStartDocument();
                    writer.WriteStartElement("Settings");
                    writer.WriteStartElement("User");
                    // get current user as that is the user
                    WindowsIdentity user = WindowsIdentity.GetCurrent();
                    writer.WriteString(user.Name);
                    writer.WriteEndElement();
                    writer.WriteStartElement("Password");
                    // pass null as the salt to establish one
                    string hashedPassword = CreateHashedPassword(password,null);
                    writer.WriteString(hashedPassword);
                    writer.WriteEndElement();
                    writer.WriteEndElement();
                    writer.WriteEndDocument();
                    writer.Flush();
                    writer.Close();
                    Console.WriteLine("Creating settings for " + user.Name);
                }

                // set up access to settings store
                isoFileStream =
                    new IsolatedStorageFileStream(storageName,
                                                  FileMode.Open,
                                                  isoStorageFile);

                // load settings from isolated filestream
                settingsDoc.Load(isoFileStream);
                Console.WriteLine("Loaded settings for " + User);
            }
```

The User property provides access to the WindowsIdentity of the user that this set of settings belongs to:

```
// User Property
public string User
{
    get
    {
        XmlNode userNode = settingsDoc.SelectSingleNode("Settings/User");
        if(userNode != null)
        {
            return userNode.InnerText;
        }
        return "";
    }
}
```

The `Password` property gets the salted and hashed password value from the XML store, and, when updating the password, takes the plain text of the password and creates the salted and hashed version, which is then stored:

```
// Password Property
public string Password
{
    get
    {
        XmlNode pwdNode =
                    settingsDoc.SelectSingleNode("Settings/Password");
        if(pwdNode != null)
        {
            return pwdNode.InnerText;
        }
        return "";
    }
    set
    {
        XmlNode pwdNode =
                    settingsDoc.SelectSingleNode("Settings/Password");

        string hashedPassword = CreateHashedPassword(value,null);
        if(pwdNode != null)
        {
            pwdNode.InnerText = hashedPassword;
        }
        else
        {
            XmlNode settingsNode =
                        settingsDoc.SelectSingleNode("Settings");
            XmlElement pwdElem =
                        settingsDoc.CreateElement("Password");
            pwdElem.InnerText=hashedPassword;
            settingsNode.AppendChild(pwdElem);
        }
    }
}
```

The `CreateHashedPassword` method performs the creation of the salted and hashed password. The `password` parameter is the plain text of the password and the `existingSalt` parameter is the salt to use when creating the salted and hashed version. If no salt exists, like the first time a password is stored, `existingSalt` should be passed null and a random salt will be generated.

Once we have the salt, it is combined with the plain text password and hashed using the `SHA512Managed` class. The salt value is then appended to the end of the hashed value and returned. The salt is appended so that when we attempt to validate the password, we know what salt was used to create the hashed value. The entire value is then base64-encoded and returned:

```
// Make a hashed password
private string CreateHashedPassword(string password,
                                    byte[] existingSalt)
{
    byte [] salt = null;
    if(existingSalt == null)
    {
        // Make a salt of random size
        Random  random = new Random( );
        int size = random.Next(16, 64);

        // create salt array
        salt = new byte[size];

        // Use the better random number generator to get
        // bytes for the salt
        RNGCryptoServiceProvider rng =
                new RNGCryptoServiceProvider( );
        rng.GetNonZeroBytes(salt);
    }
    else
        salt = existingSalt;

    // Turn string into bytes
    byte[] pwd = Encoding.UTF8.GetBytes(password);

    // make storage for both password and salt
    byte[] saltedPwd = new byte[pwd.Length + salt.Length];

    // add pwd bytes first
    pwd.CopyTo(saltedPwd,0);
    // now add salt
    salt.CopyTo(saltedPwd,pwd.Length);

    // Use SHA512 as the hashing algorithm
    SHA512Managed sha512 = new SHA512Managed( );

    // Get hash of salted password
    byte[] hash = sha512.ComputeHash(saltedPwd);

    // append salt to hash so we have it
    byte[] hashWithSalt = new byte[hash.Length + salt.Length];

    // copy in bytes
    hash.CopyTo(hashWithSalt,0);
    salt.CopyTo(hashWithSalt,hash.Length);

    // return base64 encoded hash with salt
    return Convert.ToBase64String(hashWithSalt);
}
```

To check a given password against the stored salted and hashed value, we call
CheckPassword and pass in the plain text password to check. First, the stored value is
retrieved using the Password property and converted from base64. Then we know we

used SHA512, so there are 512 bits in the hash, but we need the byte size so we do the math and get that size in bytes. This allows us to figure out where to get the salt from in the value, so we copy it out of the value and call CreateHashedPassword using that salt and the plain text password parameter. This gives us the hashed value for the password that was passed in to verify, and once we have that, we just compare it to the Password property to see whether we have a match and return true or false appropriately:

```
// Check the password against our storage
public bool CheckPassword(string password)
{
    // Get bytes for password
    // this is the hash of the salted password and the salt
    byte[] hashWithSalt = Convert.FromBase64String(Password);

    // We used 512 bits as the hash size (SHA512)
    int hashSizeInBytes = 512 / 8;

    // make holder for original salt
    int saltSize = hashWithSalt.Length - hashSizeInBytes;
    byte[] salt = new byte[saltSize];

    // copy out the salt
    Array.Copy(hashWithSalt,hashSizeInBytes,salt,0,saltSize);

    // Figure out hash for this password
    string passwordHash = CreateHashedPassword(password,salt);

    // If the computed hash matches the specified hash,
    // the plain text value must be correct.
    // see if Password (stored) matched password passed in
    return (Password == passwordHash);
}
```

The code to use the UserSettings class is shown here:

```
class IsoApplication
{
    static void Main(string[] args)
    {
        if(args.Length > 0)
        {
            UserSettings settings = new UserSettings(args[0]);
            if(settings.CheckPassword(args[0]))
            {
                Console.WriteLine("Welcome");
                return;
            }
        }
        Console.WriteLine("The system could not validate your credentials");
    }
}
```

The way to use this application is to pass the password on the command line as the first argument. This password is then checked against the UserSettings, which is stored in the isolated storage for this particular user. If the password is correct, the user is welcomed; if not, the user is shown the door.

Discussion

Isolated storage allows applications to store data that is unique to the application and the user running the application. This storage allows the application to write out state information that is not visible to other applications or even other users of the same application. Isolated storage is based on the code identity as determined by the CLR, and it stores the information either directly on the client machine or in isolated stores that can be opened and roam with the user. The storage space available to the application is directly controllable by the administrator of the machine on which the application operates.

The Solution uses isolation by User, AppDomain, and Assembly by calling IsolatedStorageFile.GetUserStoreForDomain. This creates an isolated store that is accessible by only this user in the current assembly in the current AppDomain:

```
// get the isolated storage
isoStorageFile = IsolatedStorageFile.GetUserStoreForDomain();
```

The Storeadm.exe utility will allow you to see which isolated storage stores have been set up on the machine by running the utility with the /LIST command-line switch. Storeadm.exe is part of the .NET Framework SDK and can be located in your Visual Studio installation directory under the *\SDK\v1.1\Bin* subdirectory.

The output after using the UserSettings class would look like this:

```
C:\>storeadm /LIST
Microsoft (R) .NET Framework Store Admin 1.1.4322.573
Copyright (C) Microsoft Corporation 1998-2002. All rights reserved.

Record #1
[Domain]
<System.Security.Policy.Url version="1">
    <Url>file://D:/PRJ32/Book/IsolatedStorage/bin/Debug/IsolatedStorage.exe</Url>

</System.Security.Policy.Url>

[Assembly]
<System.Security.Policy.Url version="1">
    <Url>file://D:/PRJ32/Book/IsolatedStorage/bin/Debug/IsolatedStorage.exe</Url>

</System.Security.Policy.Url>

        Size : 1024
```

Passwords should never be stored in plain text, period. It is a bad habit to get into, so in the UserSettings class, we have added the salting and hashing of the password value via the CreateHashedPassword method and verification through the

CheckPassword method. Adding a salt to the hash helps to strengthen the protection on the value being hashed so that the isolated storage, the hash, and the salt now protect the password we are storing.

See Also

See the "IsolatedStorageFile Class," "IsolatedStorageStream Class," "About Isolated Storage," and "ComputeHash Method" topics in the MSDN documentation.

14.9   Making a Security Assert Safe

Problem

You want to assert that at a particular point in the call stack, a given permission is understood to be available for all subsequent calls. However, doing this can easily open a security hole to allow other malicious code to spoof your code or to create a back door into your component. You want to assert a given security permission, but you want to do so in a secure and efficient manner.

Solution

In order to make this approach secure, we need to call Demand on the permissions that the subsequent calls need and on which we are using Assert in order to make sure that code that doesn't have these permissions can't slip by due to the Assert. This is demonstrated by the function CallSecureFunctionSafelyAndEfficiently, which performs a Demand, then an Assert before calling into SecureFunction, which performs a Demand for a ReflectionPermission.

The code listing for CallSecureFunctionSafelyAndEfficiently is:

```
public static void CallSecureFunctionSafelyAndEfficiently()
{

    // set up a permission to be able to access nonpublic members
    // via reflection
    ReflectionPermission perm =
        new ReflectionPermission(ReflectionPermissionFlag.MemberAccess);

    // Demand the permission set we have compiled before using Assert
    // to make sure we have the right before we Assert it.  We do
    // the Demand to insure that we have checked for this permission
    // before using Assert to short-circuit stackwalking for it, which
    // helps us stay secure, while performing better.
    perm.Demand();

    // Assert this right before calling into the function that
    // would also perform the Demand to short-circuit the stack walk
    // each call would generate.  The Assert helps us to optimize
    // out use of SecureFunction
    perm.Assert();
```

```
        // We call the secure function 100 times but only generate
        // the stackwalk from the function to this calling function
        // instead of walking the whole stack 100 times.
        for(int i=0;i<100;i++)
        {
            SecureFunction();
        }
    }
```

The code listing for SecureFunction is shown here:

```
public static void SecureFunction()
{
    // set up a permission to be able to access nonpublic members
    // via reflection
    ReflectionPermission perm =
        new ReflectionPermission(ReflectionPermissionFlag.MemberAccess);

    // Demand the right to do this and cause a stackwalk
    perm.Demand();

    // Perform the action here...
}
```

Discussion

In our demonstration function CallSecureFunctionSafelyAndEfficiently, the function we are calling (SecureFunction) performs a Demand on a ReflectionPermission to ensure that the code can access nonpublic members of classes via reflection. Normally, this would result in a stackwalk for every call to SecureFunction. The Demand in CallSecureFunctionSafelyAndEfficiently is only there to protect against the usage of the Assert in the first place. To make this more efficient, we can use Assert to state that all functions called from this one issuing Demands do not have to stack walk any further as the Assert says stop checking for this permission in the call stack. In order to do this, you need the permission to call Assert.

The problem comes in with this Assert as it opens up a potential luring attack where SecureFunction is called via CallSecureFunctionSafelyAndEfficiently, which calls Assert to stop the Demand stack walks from SecureFunction. If unauthorized code without this ReflectionPermission were able to call CallSecureFunctionSafelyAndEfficiently, the Assert would prevent the SecureFunction Demand call from determining that there is some code in the call stack without the proper rights. This is the beauty of the call stack—checking in the CLR when a Demand occurs.

In order to protect against this, we issue a Demand for the ReflectionPermission needed by SecureFunction in CallSecureFunctionSafelyAndEfficiently to close this hole before issuing the Assert. The combination of this Demand and the Assert causes us to do one stack walk instead of the original 100 that would have been caused by the Demand in SecureFunction but to still maintain secure access to this functionality.

Security optimization techniques, such as using Assert, in this case (even though it isn't the primary reason to use Assert), can help class library and controls developers that are trusted to perform Asserts in order to speed the interaction of their code with the runtime; but if used improperly, these techniques can also open up holes in the security picture as well. This example shows that you can have both performance and security where secure access is concerned.

If you are using Assert, be mindful that stackwalk overrides should never be made in a class constructor. Constructors are not guaranteed to have any particular security context, nor are they guaranteed to execute at a specific point in time. This lack leads to the call stack not being well-defined, and Assert used here can produce unexpected results.

One other thing to remember with Assert is that you can only have one active Assert in a function at a given time. If you Assert the same permission twice, a SecurityException is thrown by the CLR. You must revert the original Assert first using RevertAssert and then you can declare the second Assert.

You might have the idea that declarative demands would be faster due to the CLR's knowledge of the call stack; shouldn't it be able to perform the optimization we have done manually here? In the 1.0 and 1.1 versions of the CLR, it turns out that declarative demands are actually slower, since this optimization does not occur.

See Also

See the "CodeAccessSecurity.Assert Method," "CodeAccessSecurity.Demand Method," "CodeAccessSecurity.RevertAssert Method," and "Overriding Security Checks" topics in the MSDN documentation.

14.10 Preventing Malicious Modifications to an Assembly

Problem

You are distributing an assembly, but you want to ensure that nobody can tamper with the internals of that assembly. This tampering could result in its use to gather sensitive information from a user or to act as a back-door mechanism to attack a network. Additionally, you do not want other malicious assemblies to be created that look like yours but operate in malevolent ways (e.g., stealing passwords, reformatting a disk drive). In effect, this malevolent assembly is created to spoof your benevolent assembly.

Solution

This can be averted to a certain degree by using a strong name for your assembly. A strong named assembly has a digital signature that is generated from a public/private key pair. The public key is the part of the pair that provides something well known that your assembly can use to identify as being from you. The private key is the part of the pair that you keep secret and that ensures that people can trust that the assembly came from you and hasn't been tampered with.

In order to generate a key pair, you can use the *SN.EXE* from the Framework SDK:

```
SN -k MyKeys.snk
```

This line creates your key pair in a file called *MyKeys.snk*. Since this file contains both your public and private keys, you need to guard this file carefully; generate it only on a machine that's locked down enough to be consider highly trusted. Never make copies of this key, and store it only on a highly trusted machine or on media that is easy to secure.

Now that you have a key pair, you can get the public key from the pair in order to be able to delay sign your assemblies. Delay signing allows day-to-day development to continue on the assemblies while a trusted system holds the public/private key pair file (*MyKeys.snk*) for final signing of the assemblies.

In order to extract the public key from our key pair, we use the -p switch on *SN.EXE* to produce the *MyPublicKey.snk* file that holds our public key:

```
SN -p MyKeys.snk MyPublicKey.snk
```

Now we can delay-sign the assembly using the public key by placing the public key in two assembly level attributes, like so:

```
[assembly: System.Reflection.AssemblyKeyFile("MyPublicKey.snk")]
[assembly: System.Reflection.AssemblyDelaySign(true)]
```

The `AssemblyKeyFile` attribute tells the compiler where to find the public key to sign with and the `AssemblyDelaySign` attribute tells the compiler to use the delay signing method.

In order to finish the signing process, once you are ready to deploy your assembly, use *SN.EXE* again to add the final signing piece, using the -R option like this:

```
SN -R SignedAssembly.dll MyKeys.snk
```

This line would result in `SignedAssembly` being fully signed using the private key in *MyKeys.snk*. This step would normally be performed on a secure system that has access to the private key.

Discussion

Note that in Visual Studio .NET 2002, the private key file location needs to be relative to the EXE or DLL, not the project, or you will get an error when you try to sign the resulting assembly.

If you don't want to delay-sign your assembly, you could use `MyKeys.snk` as the `AssemblyKeyFile` instead like this:

```
[assembly: System.Reflection.AssemblyKeyFile("MyKeys.snk")]
```

When you do this, you do not need the `AssemblyDelaySign` attribute anymore.

In order to use delay signing, you need to prepare the development environments for assemblies that are only partially signed. To do this, instruct the CLR to skip verification of assemblies using a given public key. Once again, we use *SN.EXE* to accomplish this:

```
SN -Vr *,d15f821006850b34
```

One other approach would be to have a separate key for development and final release versions, which would allow for fully signed development versions without compromising the shipping signed assemblies.

Note that this solution will protect your assembly only as long as the machine it is running on is secure. If the malicious user can access the code that uses the assembly and the assembly itself, he can simply replace them with his own copies. Strong naming ensures that the trusted version of the assembly is deployed, but once it has been installed, it can be modified (as can practically anything else on the system).

See Also

See the "AssemblyKeyFile Attribute" and "AssemblyDelaySign Attribute" topics in the MSDN documentation.

14.11 Verifying that an Assembly Has Been Granted Specific Permissions

Problem

When your assembly requests optional permissions (such as asking for disk access to enable users to export data to disk as a product feature) using the `SecurityAction.RequestOptional` flag, it might or might not get those permissions. Regardless, your assembly will still load and execute. You need a way to verify whether your assembly actually obtained those permissions. This can help prevent many security exceptions from being thrown. For example, if you optionally requested read/write permissions on the registry, but did not receive them, you could disable the user interface controls that are used to read and store application settings in the registry.

Solution

Check to see if your assembly received the optional permissions using the `SecurityManager.IsGranted` method like this:

```
using System;
using System.Text.RegularExpressions;
using System.Web;
using System.Net;
using System.Security;
```

```
Regex regex = new Regex(@"http://www\.oreilly\.com/.*");
WebPermission webConnectPerm = new WebPermission(NetworkAccess.Connect,regex);
if(SecurityManager.IsGranted(webConnectPerm))
{
    // connect to the oreilly site
}
```

This code would set up a Regex for the O'Reilly web site and then use it to create a WebPermission for connecting to that site and all sites containing the *www.oreilly.com* string. We would then check the WebPermission against the SecurityManager to see whether we have the permission to do this.

Discussion

The IsGranted method is a lightweight way of determining whether permission is granted for an assembly without incurring the full stackwalk that a Demand would give you. This method can be helpful not only in determining the permissions available at runtime, but for helping performance by not incurring the stackwalk from a Demand as well. The downside to this approach is that the code would still be subject to a luring attack if Assert were misused, so you need to consider where the call to IsGranted is being made in the overall scheme of your security.

Some of the reasons you might design an assembly to have optional permissions is for deployment in different customer scenarios. In some scenarios (like desktop applications), it might be acceptable to have an assembly that can perform more robust actions (talk to a database, create network traffic via HTTP, etc.). In other scenarios, you would defer these actions if the customer did not wish to grant enough permissions for these extra services to function.

See Also

See the "WebPermission Class," "SecurityManager Class," and "IsGranted Method" topics in the MSDN documentation.

14.12 Minimizing the Attack Surface of an Assembly

Problem

Someone attacking your assembly will first attempt to find out as many things as possible about your assembly and then use this information in constructing the attack(s). The more surface area you give to an attacker, the more they have to work with. You need to minimize what your assembly is allowed to do so that if an attacker is successful in taking over your assembly—possibly through luring it into doing something like executing a small program that attempts to email a password file back to the attacker—the attacker will not have the necessary privileges to do any damage to the system.

Solution

Use the `SecurityAction.RequestRefuse` enumeration member to indicate, at an assembly level, the permissions that you do not wish this assembly to have. This will force the CLR to refuse these permissions to your code and will ensure that even if another part of the system is compromised, your code cannot be used to perform functions that it does not need the rights to do.

The following example allows the assembly to perform file I/O as part of its minimal permission set but explicitly refuses to allow this assembly to have permissions to skip verification:

```
[assembly: FileIOPermission(SecurityAction.RequestMinimal,Unrestricted=true)]
[assembly: SecurityPermission(SecurityAction.RequestRefuse,
            SkipVerification=false)]
```

Discussion

Once you have determined what permissions your assembly needs as part of your normal security testing, you can use `RequestRefuse` to lock down your code. If this seems extreme, think of scenarios where your code could be accessing a data store with sensitive information contained, such as Social Security numbers or salary information. This proactive step can help you show your customers that you take security seriously and can help defend your interests in case of a break-in on a system your code is part of.

One serious consideration with this approach is that the use of `RequestRefuse` marks your assembly as partially trusted and will in turn prevent it from calling any strong-named assembly that hasn't been marked with the `AllowPartiallyTrustedCallers` attribute.

See Also

See the "SecurityAction Enumeration" and "Global Attributes" topics in the MSDN documentation. See Chapter 8, "Code Access Security in Practice," of Microsoft Patterns & Practices Group: *http://msdn.microsoft.com/library/default.asp?url=/library/en-us/dnnetsec/html/THCMCh08.asp*.

Threading

A thread represents a single flow of execution logic in a program. Some programs never need more than a single thread to execute efficiently, but many do. Threading in .NET allows you to build responsive and efficient applications. Many applications need to perform multiple actions at the same time (like supporting simultaneous user interface interaction and data processing)—threading allows the developer to provide this capability. Once you have multiple threads of execution in your application, you need to start thinking about what data in your application needs to be protected from multiple access, what data could cause threads to develop an interdependency that could lead to deadlocking (where Thread A has a resource that Thread B is waiting for and Thread B has a resource that Thread A is waiting for), and how to store data relative to the individual threads. We will explore some of these issues to help you take advantage of this wonderful capability of the .NET Framework, while explaining the areas to beware and items to keep in mind while designing and creating your multithreaded application.

15.1 Creating Per-Thread Static Fields

Problem

Static fields, by default, are shared between threads within an application domain. You need to allow each thread to have its own nonshared copy of a static field, so that this static field can be updated on a per-thread basis.

Solution

Use `ThreadStaticAttribute` to mark any `static` fields as not being shareable between threads:

```
using System;
using System.Threading;

public class Foo
```

```
    {
        [ThreadStaticAttribute( )]
        public static string bar = "Initialized string";
    }
```

Discussion

By default, static fields are shared between the threads that access these fields in an application domain as a whole. To see this, we'll create a class with a static field called bar and a static method used to access and display the value contained in this static field:

```
using System;
using System.Threading;

public class ThreadStaticField
{
    public static string bar = "Initialized string";

    public static void DisplayStaticFieldValue( )
    {
        Console.WriteLine(Thread.CurrentThread.GetHashCode( ) +
                " contains static field value of: " +
                ThreadStaticField.bar);
    }
}
```

Next, create a test method that accesses this static field both on the current thread and on a newly spawned thread:

```
public void TestStaticField( )
{
    ThreadStaticField.DisplayStaticFieldValue( );

    Thread newStaticFieldThread =
        new Thread(new ThreadStart(
            ThreadStaticField.DisplayStaticFieldValue));

    newStaticFieldThread.Start( );

    ThreadStaticField.DisplayStaticFieldValue( );
}
```

This code displays output that resembles the following:

```
21 contains static field value of: Initialized string
21 contains static field value of: Initialized string
23 contains static field value of: Initialized string
```

The current thread's hash value is 21 and the new thread's hash value is 23. Notice that both threads are accessing the same static bar field. Next, add the ThreadStaticAttribute to the static field:

```
public class ThreadStaticField
{
```

```
    [ThreadStaticAttribute( )]
    public static string bar = "Initialized string";

    public static void DisplayStaticFieldValue( )
    {
        //bar = Thread.CurrentThread.ThreadState.ToString( );
        Console.WriteLine(Thread.CurrentThread.GetHashCode( ) +
                " contains static field value of: " + ThreadStaticField.bar);
    }
}
```

Now, output resembling the following is displayed:

```
21 contains static field value of: Initialized string
21 contains static field value of: Initialized string
23 contains static field value of:
```

Notice that the new thread returns a null for the value of the static bar field. This is the expected behavior. The bar field is only initialized in the first thread that accesses it. On all other threads, this field is initialized to null. Therefore, it is imperative that you initialize the bar field on all threads before it is used.

> Remember to initialize any static field that is marked with ThreadStaticAttribute before it is used on any thread. That is, this field should be initialized in the method passed in to the ThreadStart delegate. You should make sure to not initialize the static field using a field initializer as is shown in the prior code since only one thread gets to see that initial value.

The bar field is initialized to the "Initialized string" string literal before it is used on the first thread that accesses this field. In the previous test code, the bar field was accessed first, and, therefore, it was initialized, on the current thread. Suppose we were to remove the first line of the TestStaticField method, as shown here:

```
public void TestStaticField( )
{
//  ThreadStaticField.DisplayStaticFieldValue( );
    Thread newStaticFieldThread =
        new Thread(new ThreadStart(ThreadStaticField.DisplayStaticFieldValue));

    newStaticFieldThread.Start( );

    ThreadStaticField.DisplayStaticFieldValue( );
}
```

This code now displays similar output to the following:

```
21 contains static field value of:
23 contains static field value of: Initialized string
```

The current thread does not access the bar field first and therefore does not initialize it. However, when the new thread accesses it first, it does initialize it.

Note that adding a static constructor to initialize the static field marked with this attribute will still follow the same behavior. Static constructors are executed only one time per application domain.

See Also

See the "ThreadStaticAttribute Attribute" and "static Modifier (C#)" topics in the MSDN documentation.

15.2 Providing Thread Safe Access to Class Members

Problem

You need to provide thread-safe access through accessor functions to an internal member variable.

The following NoSafeMemberAccess class shows three methods: ReadNumericField, IncrementNumericField and ModifyNumericField. While all of these methods access the internal numericField member, the access is currently not safe for multithreaded access:

```
public sealed class NoSafeMemberAccess
{
    private NoSafeMemberAccess () {}

    private static int numericField = 1;

    public static void IncrementNumericField()
    {
        ++numericField;
    }

    public static void ModifyNumericField(int newValue)
    {
        numericField = newValue;
    }

    public static int ReadNumericField()
    {
        return (numericField);
    }
}
```

Solution

NoSafeMemberAccess could be used in a multithreaded application, and, therefore, it must be made thread-safe. Consider what would occur if multiple threads were calling the IncrementNumericField method at the same time. It is possible that two calls could occur to IncrementNumericField while the numericField is updated only once.

In order to protect against this, we will modify this class by creating an object that we can lock against in critical sections:

```
public sealed class SaferMemberAccess
{
    private SaferMemberAccess () {}

    private static int numericField = 1;
    private static object syncObj = new object();

    public static void IncrementNumericField()
    {
        lock(syncObj)
        {
            ++numericField;
        }
    }

    public static void ModifyNumericField(int newValue)
    {
        numericField = newValue;
    }

    public static int ReadNumericField()
    {
        int readValue = 0;
        readValue = numericField;
        return (readValue);
    }
}
```

Using the lock statement on the syncObj object lets us synchronize access to the numericField member. This now makes this method safe for multithreaded access.

Discussion

Marking a block of code as a critical section is done using the lock keyword. This keyword accepts a parameter of either the type object for the class (such as typeof(MyClass)) or a class instance object (new MyClass()). It uses this type or object to control what you are locking.

There is a problem with synchronization using an object like syncObj in the SaferMemberAccess example. If you lock an object or type that can be accessed by other objects within the application, other objects may also attempt to lock this same object. This will manifest itself in poorly written code that locks itself, such as the following code:

```
public class DeadLock
{
    public void Method1()
    {
        lock(this)
        {
```

```
        // Do something
      }
    }
  }
```

When `Method1` is called, it locks the current `DeadLock` object. Unfortunately, any object that has access to the `DeadLock` class may also lock it. This is shown here:

```
using System;
using System.Threading;

public class AnotherCls
{
    public void DoSomething()
    {
        DeadLock deadLock = new DeadLock();
        lock(deadLock)
        {
            Thread thread = new Thread(new ThreadStart(deadLock.Method1));
            thread.Start();

            // Do some time consuming task here
        }
    }
}
```

The `DoSomething` method obtains a lock on the `deadLock` object and then attempts to call the `Method1` method of the `deadLock` object on another thread, after which a very long task is executed. While the long task is executing, the lock on the `deadLock` object prevents `Method1` from being called on the other thread. Only when this long task ends, and execution exits the critical section of the `DoSomething` method, will the `Method1` method be able to acquire a lock on the `this` object. As you can see, this can become a major headache to track down in a much larger application.

Jeffrey Richter has come up with a relatively simple method to remedy this situation, which he details quite clearly in the article "Safe Thread Synchronization" in the January 2003 issue of *MSDN Magazine*. His solution is to create a private field within the class to synchronize on. The object itself can only acquire this private field; no outside object or type may acquire it. The `DeadLock` class can be rewritten, as follows, to fix this problem:

```
public class DeadLock
{
    private object syncObj = new object();

    public void Method1()
    {
        lock(syncObj)
        {
            // Do something
        }
    }
}
```

To clean up your code, you should stop locking any objects or types except for the synchronization objects that are private to your type or object, such as the syncObj in the fixed DeadLock class. This recipe makes use of this pattern by creating a static syncObj object within the SaferMemberAccess class. The IncrementNumericField, ModifyNumericField, and ReadNumericField methods use this syncObj to synchronize access to the numericField field. Note that if you do not need a lock while the numericField is being read in the ReadNumericField method, you can remove this lock block and simply return the value contained in the numericField field.

 Minimizing the number of critical sections within your code can significantly improve performance. Use what you need to secure resource access, but no more.

If you require more control over locking and unlocking of critical sections, you might want to try using the overloaded static Monitor.TryEnter methods. These methods allow more flexibility by introducing a timeout value. The lock keyword will attempt to acquire a lock on a critical section indefinitely. However, with the TryEnter method, you can enter a timeout value in milliseconds (as an integer) or as a TimeSpan structure. The TryEnter methods return true if a lock was acquired and false if it was not. Note that the overload of the TryEnter method that accepts only a single parameter does not block for any amount of time. This method returns immediately, regardless of whether the lock was acquired.

The updated class using the Monitor methods is shown here:

```
using System;
using System.Threading;

public sealed class MonitorMethodAccess
{
    private MonitorMethodAccess () {}

    private static int numericField = 1;
    private static object syncObj = new object();

    public static void IncrementNumericField()
    {
        if (Monitor.TryEnter(syncObj, 250))
        {
            try
            {
                ++numericField;
            }
            finally
            {
                Monitor.Exit(syncObj);
            }
        }
    }
}
```

```
public static void ModifyNumericField(int newValue)
{
    if (Monitor.TryEnter(syncObj, 250))
    {
        try
        {
            numericField = newValue;
        }
        finally
        {
            Monitor.Exit(syncObj);
        }
    }
}

public static int ReadNumericField()
{
    if (Monitor.TryEnter(syncObj, 250))
    {
        int readValue = 0;

        try
        {
            readValue = numericField;
        }
        finally
        {
            Monitor.Exit(syncObj);
        }

        return (readValue);
    }

    return (-1);
}
```

Note that with the TryEnter methods, you should always check to see whether the lock was in fact acquired. If it is not, your code should wait and try again, or return to the caller.

You might think at this point that all of the methods are thread-safe. Individually, they are, but what if you are trying to call them and you expect synchronized access between two of the methods? If ModifyNumericField and ReadNumericField are used one after the other by Class 1 on Thread 1 at the same time Class 2 is using these methods on Thread 2, locking or Monitor calls will not prevent Class 2 from modifying the value before Thread 1 reads it. Here is a series of actions that demonstrates this:

Class 1 Thread 1
    Calls ModifyNumericField with 10.

Class 2 Thread 2
   Calls `ModifyNumericField` with 15.

Class 1 Thread 1
   Calls `ReadNumericField` and gets 15, not 10.

Class 2 Thread 2
   Calls `ReadNumericField` and gets 15, which it expected.

In order to solve this problem of synchronizing reads and writes, the calling class needs to manage the interaction. The external class could accomplish this by using the `Monitor` class to establish a lock on the type object, as shown here:

```
int num = 0;
if(Monitor.TryEnter(typeof(MonitorMethodAccess),250))
{
    MonitorMethodAccess.ModifyNumericField(10);
    num = MonitorMethodAccess.ReadNumericField();
    Monitor.Exit(typeof(MonitorMethodAccess));
}
Console.WriteLine(num);
```

See Also

See the "lock Statement," "Thread Class," and "Monitor Class" topics in the MSDN documentation. Also see the "Safe Thread Synchronization" article in the January 2003 issue of *MSDN Magazine*.

15.3 Preventing Silent Thread Termination

Problem

An exception thrown in a spawned worker thread will cause this thread to be silently terminated if the exception is unhandled. You need to make sure all exceptions are handled in all threads. If an exception happens in this new thread, you want to handle it and be notified of its occurrence.

Solution

You must add exception handling to the method that you pass to the `ThreadStart` delegate with a try/catch, try/finally, or try/catch/finally block. The code to do this is shown here in bold:

```
using System;
using System.Threading;

public class MainThread
{
    public void CreateNewThread()
    {
```

```
            // Spawn new thread to do concurrent work
            Thread newWorkerThread = new Thread(new ThreadStart(Worker.DoWork));
            newWorkerThread.Start( );
        }
    }

    public class Worker
    {
        // Method called by ThreadStart delegate to do concurrent work
        public static void DoWork ( )
        {
            try
            {
                // Do thread work here
            }
            catch
            {
                // Handle thread exception here
                // Do not re-throw exception
            }
            finally
            {
                // Do thread cleanup here
            }
        }
    }
```

Discussion

If an unhandled exception occurs in the main thread of an application, the main thread terminates, along with your entire application. An unhandled exception in a spawned worker thread, however, will terminate only that thread. This will happen without any visible warnings, and your application will continue to run as if nothing happened.

Simply wrapping an exception handler around the Start method of the Thread class will not catch the exception on the newly created thread. The Start method is called within the context of the current thread, not the newly created thread. It also returns immediately once the thread is launched, so it isn't going to wait around for the thread to finish. Therefore, the exception thrown on the new thread will not be caught since it is not visible to any other threads.

If the exception is rethrown from the catch block, the finally block of this structured exception handler will still execute. However, after the finally block is finished, the rethrown exception is, at that point, rethrown. The rethrown exception cannot be handled and the thread terminates. If there is any code after the finally block, it will not be executed, since an unhandled exception occurred.

Never rethrow an exception at the highest point in the exception handling hierarchy within a thread. Since no exception handlers can catch this rethrown exception, it will be considered unhandled and the thread will terminate after all `finally` blocks have been executed.

What if you were using the `ThreadPool` and `QueueUserWorkItem`? This method would still help you because you added the handling code that will execute inside the thread. Just make sure you have the `finally` block set up so that you can notify yourself of exceptions in other threads as shown earlier.

In order to provide a last chance exception handler for your WinForms application, you would need to hook up for two separate events. The first event is the `System.AppDomain.CurrentDomain.UnhandledException` event, which will catch all unhandled exceptions in the current AppDomain on worker threads; it will not catch exceptions that occur on the main UI thread of a WinForms application. In order to catch those, you also need to hook up to the `System.Windows.Forms.Application.ThreadException`, which will catch unhandled exceptions in the main UI thread.

See Also

See the "Thread Class" and "Exception Class" topics in the MSDN documentation.

15.4 Polling an Asynchronous Delegate

Problem

While an asynchronous delegate is executing, you need to continuously poll it to see whether it has completed. This ability is useful when you need to monitor the length of time it takes the asynchronous delegate to execute or if you need to monitor other objects in the system in parallel with this asynchronous delegate, possibly to determine which object finishes first, second, third, and so on. It can also be useful when performing a continuous task, such as displaying an indicator to the user that the asynchronous operation is still running.

Solution

Use the `IsCompleted` property of the `IAsyncResult` interface to determine when the asynchronous call has completed. The following example shows how this is accomplished:

```
using System;
using System.Threading;

public class AsyncAction
{
```

```
public void PollAsyncDelegate()
{
    // Set up the delegate
    AsyncInvoke method1 = new AsyncInvoke(TestAsyncInvoke.Method1);
    // Define the AsyncCallback delegate.
    AsyncCallback callBack = new AsyncCallback(TestAsyncInvoke.CallBack);
    IAsyncResult asyncResult = method1.BeginInvoke(callBack,method1);

    while (!asyncResult.IsCompleted)
    {
        // give up the CPU for 1 second
        Thread.Sleep(1000);
        Console.Write('.');
    }
    Console.WriteLine("Finished Polling");

    try
    {
        int retVal = method1.EndInvoke(asyncResult);
        Console.WriteLine("retVal: " + retVal);
    }
    catch (Exception e)
    {
        Console.WriteLine(e.ToString());
    }
}
```

The following code defines the AsyncInvoke delegate and the asynchronously invoked static method TestAsyncInvoke.Method1:

```
public delegate int AsyncInvoke();

public class TestAsyncInvoke
{
    public static int Method1()
    {
        Console.WriteLine("Invoked Method1");
        return (1);
    }

    public static void CallBack(IAsyncResult ar)
    {
        // Retrieve the delegate.
        AsyncInvoke ai = (AsyncInvoke) ar.AsyncState;

        // Call EndInvoke to retrieve the results.
        int retVal = ai.EndInvoke(ar);
        Console.WriteLine("retVal: " + retVal);
    }
}
```

Discussion

The delegate, `AsyncInvoke`, is invoked asynchronously using its `BeginInvoke` method. The `BeginInvoke` method returns an `IAsyncResult` object, which allows access to the result information from an asynchronous operation.

If the delegate were to accept a `string` and an `int`, in this order, the `BeginInvoke` method would be defined as this:

```
public IAsyncResult BeginInvoke(string s, int i, AsyncCallback callback,
                                object state)
```

For this recipe the *callback* and *state* parameters are set to `null`. The *callback* parameter could call back at completion into the code that invoked it, but for this example, it is a no-op.

To poll for the completion of the `method1` delegate, we get the `IsCompleted` property of the `IAsyncResult` object that is returned by the `BeginInvoke` method. The `IsCompleted` property returns `true` if the `method1` delegate has completed its operation or `false` if it has not. This property can be called continuously within a loop to check whether the delegate has finished.

Once the `method1` delegate has finished its asynchronous processing, the results of the operation can be retrieved through a call to the `EndInvoke` method. The compiler also creates this method dynamically, so that the return value of the delegate can be accessed through the `EndInvoke` method—as well as any `out` or `ref` parameters that the delegate accepts as parameters.

The `EndInvoke` method returns an object of the same type as the return value of the asynchronous delegate. An `EndInvoke` method called on a delegate of the following signature:

```
public delegate long Foo(ref int i, out string s, bool b);
```

will be defined as follows:

```
public long EndInvoke(ref int i, out string s, IAsyncResult result)
```

Notice that the return type is a `long` and only the `ref` and `out` parameters of the original delegate are in the signature for this method. The `EndInvoke` method contains only the output parameters of the delegate or those marked as `ref` or `out`.

 If the asynchronous delegate throws an exception, the only way to obtain that exception object is through the `EndInvoke` method. The `EndInvoke` method should be wrapped in an exception handler.

Once the `while` loop of the `PollAsyncDelegate` method in this recipe is exited—meaning that the asynchronous delegate has completed—the `EndInvoke` method can be safely called to retrieve the return value of the delegate as well as any `ref` or `out`

parameter values. If you want to obtain these values, you must call the EndInvoke method; however, if you do not need any of these values, you may leave out the call to the EndInvoke method.

See Also

See the "IAsyncResult Interface," "AsyncResult Class," "BeginInvoke Method," and "EndInvoke Method" topics in the MSDN documentation.

15.5   Timing Out an Asynchronous Delegate

Problem

You want an asynchronous delegate to operate only within an allowed time span. If it is not finished processing within this time frame, the operation will time out. If the asynchronous delegate times out, it must perform any cleanup before the thread it is running on is terminated.

Solution

The WaitHandle.WaitOne method can indicate when an asynchronous operation times out. The code on the invoking thread needs to periodically wake up to do some work along with timing-out after a specific period of time. Use the approach shown in the following code, which will wake up every 20 milliseconds to do some processing. This method also times out after a specific number of wait/process cycles (note that this code will actually time out after more than two seconds of operation since work is being done between the wait cycles):

```
public class AsyncAction
{
    public void TimeOutWakeAsyncDelegate()
    {
        AsyncInvoke method1 = new AsyncInvoke(TestAsyncInvoke.Method1);
        // Define the AsyncCallback delegate to catch EndInvoke if we timeout.
        AsyncCallback callBack = new AsyncCallback(TestAsyncInvoke.CallBack);
        // Set up the BeginInvoke method with the callback and delegate
        IAsyncResult asyncResult = method1.BeginInvoke(callBack,method1);

        int counter = 0;
        while (counter <= 25 &&
                !asyncResult.AsyncWaitHandle.WaitOne(20, true))
        {
            counter++;
            Console.WriteLine("Processing...");
        }

        if (asyncResult.IsCompleted)
        {
```

```
        int retVal = method1.EndInvoke(asyncResult);
        Console.WriteLine("retVal (TimeOut): " + retVal);
    }
    else
    {
        Console.WriteLine("TimedOut");
    }

    // Clean up
    asyncResult.AsyncWaitHandle.Close();
    }
}
```

The following code defines the AsyncInvoke delegate and the asynchronously invoked static method TestAsyncInvoke.Method1:

```
public delegate int AsyncInvoke();

public class TestAsyncInvoke
{
    public static int Method1()
    {
        Console.WriteLine("Invoked Method1");
        return (1);
    }

    public static void CallBack(IAsyncResult ar)
    {
        // Retrieve the delegate.
        AsyncInvoke ai = (AsyncInvoke) ar.AsyncState;

        // Call EndInvoke to retrieve the results.
        int retVal = ai.EndInvoke(ar);
        Console.WriteLine("retVal: " + retVal);
    }
}
```

Discussion

The asynchronous delegates in this recipe are created and invoked in the same fashion as the asynchronous delegate in Recipe 15.4. However, instead of using the IsCompleted property to determine whether the asynchronous delegate is finished processing, WaitHandle.WaitOne is used. This method blocks the thread that it is called on either indefinitely or for a specified length of time. This method will stop blocking the thread when it is signaled by the ThreadPool that the thread has completed or timed out, and returns a true indicating that the asynchronous processing is finished and the calling thread has been signaled. If the processing is not finished before the allotted time-out value expires, WaitOne returns false. Note that the WaitOne method that accepts no parameters will block the calling thread indefinitely.

It is usually a better idea to include a time-out value when using the WaitOne method, as this will prevent the calling thread from being blocked forever if a deadlock situation occurs (in which case the thread on which the WaitOne method waits is never signaled) or if the thread running the asynchronous delegate never returns, such as when entering into an infinite loop.

The TimeOutAsyncDelegate method in this recipe uses the WaitOne method to block the calling thread for two seconds. If the asynchronous delegate has not finished processing within this two-second period, the WaitOne method will return a false. If the asynchronous delegate finishes processing before the time-out value elapses, the calling thread is signaled by the running thread that the asynchronous delegate is finished and the WaitOne method stops blocking the calling thread and returns a value of true. If the WaitOne method returns true, the EndInvoke method should be called to retrieve any return values, ref parameter values, or out parameter values.

The TimeOutWakeAsyncDelegate method in this recipe approaches the time-out technique a little differently than the first method. The TimeOutWakeAsyncDelegate method will periodically wake up (after 20 milliseconds) and perform some task on the calling thread; unlike the TimeOutAsyncDelegate method, which will continue blocking for the allotted time frame and not wake up. After 25 wait cycles, if the asynchronous delegate has not finished processing, the while loop will be exited, essentially timing out the delegate. If the delegate finishes processing before the 25 wait cycles have completed, the while loop is exited.

The IsCompleted property is checked next to determine whether the asynchronous delegate has finished its processing at this time. If it has finished, the EndInvoke method is called to obtain any return value, ref parameter values, or out parameter values. Otherwise, the delegate has not completed within the allotted time span and the application should be informed that this thread has timed out.

The call to the Close method of the WaitHandle object in effect performs the same function as a Dispose method. Any resources held by this instance of the WaitHandle object are released.

See Also

See the "WaitOne Method" and "AsyncResult Class" topics in the MSDN documentation.

15.6 Being Notified of the Completion of an Asynchronous Delegate

Problem

You need a way of receiving notification from an asynchronously invoked delegate that it has finished. However, it must be more flexible than the notification schemes in the previous two recipes (Recipes 15.4 and 15.5). This scheme must allow your code to continue processing without having to constantly call IsCompleted in a loop or to rely on the WaitOne method. Since the asynchronous delegate will return a value, you must be able to pass this return value back to the invoking thread.

Solution

Use the BeginInvoke method to start the asynchronous delegate, but use the first parameter to pass a callback delegate to the asynchronous delegate:

```
using System;
using System.Threading;

public class AsyncAction
{
    public void CallbackAsyncDelegate()
    {
        AsyncCallback callBack = new AsyncCallback(DelegateCallback);

        AsyncInvoke method1 = new AsyncInvoke(TestAsyncInvoke.Method1);
        IAsyncResult asyncResult = method1.BeginInvoke(callBack, method1);

        // No need to poll or use the WaitOne method here, so return to the calling
        // method.
        return;
    }

    private static void DelegateCallback(IAsyncResult iresult)
    {
        AsyncResult asyncResult = (AsyncResult)iresult;
        AsyncInvoke method1 = (AsyncInvoke)asyncResult.AsyncDelegate;

        int retVal = method1.EndInvoke(asyncResult);
        Console.WriteLine("retVal (Callback): " + retVal);
    }
}
```

This callback delegate will call the DelegateCallback method on the thread the method was ultimately invoked on when the asynchronous delegate is finished processing.

The following code defines the AsyncInvoke delegate and the asynchronously invoked static method TestAsyncInvoke.Method1:

```
public delegate int AsyncInvoke();

public class TestAsyncInvoke
{
    public static int Method1()
    {
        Console.WriteLine("Invoked Method1");
        return (1);
    }
}
```

Discussion

The asynchronous delegates in this recipe are created and invoked in the same fashion as the asynchronous delegate in Recipe 15.4. Instead of using the IsCompleted property to determine when the asynchronous delegate is finished processing (or the WaitOne method to block for a specified time while the asynchronous delegate continues processing), this recipe uses a callback to indicate to the calling thread that the asynchronous delegate has finished processing and that its return value, ref parameter values, and out parameter values are available.

Invoking a delegate in this manner is much more flexible and efficient than simply polling the IsCompleted property to determine when a delegate finishes processing. When polling this property in a loop, the polling method cannot return and allow the application to continue processing. A callback is also better than using a WaitOne method, since the WaitOne method will block the calling thread and allow no processing to occur. You can break up the WaitOne method into a limited number of wait cycles as in Recipe 15.5, but this is simply a merging of the polling technique with the WaitOne operation.

The CallbackAsyncDelegate method in this recipe makes use of the first parameter to the BeginInvoke method of the asynchronous delegate to pass in another delegate that contains a callback method to be called when the asynchronous delegate finishes processing. After calling BeginInvoke, this method can now return and the application can continue processing; it does not have to wait in a polling loop or be blocked while the asynchronous delegate is running.

The AsyncInvoke delegate that is passed into the first parameter of the BeginInvoke method is defined as follows:

```
public delegate void AsyncCallback(IAsyncResult ar)
```

When this delegate is created, as shown here, the callback method passed in, DelegateCallback, will be called as soon as the asynchronous delegate completes:

```
AsyncCallback callBack = new AsyncCallback(DelegateCallback);
```

DelegateCallback will not run on the same thread BeginInvoke ran on. This callback method accepts a parameter of type IAsyncResult. You can cast this parameter to an AsyncResult object within the delegate and use it to obtain information about the completed asynchronous delegate, such as its return value, any ref parameter values, and any out parameter values. If the delegate instance that was used to call BeginInvoke is still in scope, you can just pass the IAsyncResult to the EndInvoke method. In addition, this object can obtain any state information passed into the second parameter of the BeginInvoke method. This state information can be any object type.

The DelegateCallback method casts the IAsyncResult parameter to an AsyncResult object and obtains the asynchronous delegate that was originally called. The EndInvoke method of this asynchronous delegate is called to process any return value, ref parameters, or out parameters. If any state object was passed in to the BeginInvoke method's second parameter, it can be obtained here through the following line of code:

```
object state = asyncResult.AsyncState;
```

See Also

See the "AsyncCallback Delegate" topic in the MSDN documentation.

15.7 Waiting for Worker Thread Completion

Problem

You have two threads currently running in your application. You need the main thread to wait until the worker thread has completed its processing. This ability comes in handy when your application is monitoring activities amongst multiple threads and you don't want your main application thread to terminate until all of the workers are done processing.

Solution

Use the Thread.Join method to detect when a thread terminates:

```
class Worker
{
    static void Main()
    {
        Run();
    }

    static void Run()
    {
        Thread worker = new Thread(new ThreadStart(WorkerThreadProc));
        worker.Start();
        if(worker.Join(4000))
```

```
        {
            // worker thread ended ok
            Console.WriteLine("Worker Thread finished");
        }
        else
        {
            // timed out
            Console.WriteLine("Worker Thread timed out");
        }
    }

    static void WorkerThreadProc()
    {
        Thread.Sleep(2000);
    }
}
```

Discussion

In the Worker class shown previously, the Run method starts off running in the context of the main thread. It then launches a worker thread; it then calls Join on it with a timeout set to four seconds. Since we know that the worker thread should not run for more than two seconds (see WorkerThreadProc), this should be sufficient time to see the worker thread terminate and for the main thread to finish and terminate in an orderly fashion.

It is very important to call Join only after the worker thread has been started, or you will get a ThreadStateException.

See Also

See the "Thread.Join Method" topic in the MSDN documentation.

15.8 Synchronizing the Reading and Writing of a Resource Efficiently

Problem

You have a resource that is shared by multiple threads. You need to provide exclusive access to this resource when a thread is writing to it. However, you do not want the overhead of providing exclusive access to this resource when multiple threads are only reading from it. You want to allow one thread to access a shared resource only if it is writing to it, but you also want to allow multiple threads to read from this resource. While multiple threads can read from a resource, a write operation cannot occur while any thread is reading from this resource.

Solution

Use the ReaderWriterLock class from the FCL. The ReaderWriterLock is optimized for scenarios where you have data that changes infrequently but needs protection for those times when it is updated in a multithreading scenario. To illustrate, the GradeBoard class represents a board where an instructor will post the grades students received from a class. Many students can read the grade board, but only the instructor can post a grade (write) to the grade board. Students will not, however, be able to read from the board while the instructor is updating it:

```
class GradeBoard
{
    // make a static ReaderWriterLock to allow all student threads to check
    // grades and the instructor thread to post grades
    static ReaderWriterLock readerWriter = new ReaderWriterLock();

    // the grade to be posted
    static char studentsGrade = ' ';

    static void Main()
    {
        // create students
        Thread[] students = new Thread[5];
        for(int i=0;i<students.Length;i++)
        {
            students[i] = new Thread(new ThreadStart(StudentThreadProc));
            students[i].Name = "Student " + i.ToString();
            // start the student looking for a grade
            students[i].Start();
        }

        // make those students "wait" for their grades by pausing the instructor
        Thread.Sleep(5000);

        // create instructor to post grade
        Thread instructor = new Thread(new ThreadStart(InstructorThreadProc));
        instructor.Name = "Instructor";
        // start instructor
        instructor.Start();

        // wait for instructor to finish
        instructor.Join();

        // wait for students to get grades
        for(int i=0;i<students.Length;i++)
        {
            students[i].Join();
        }
    }

    static char ReadGrade()
    {
```

```
                // wait ten seconds for the read lock
                readerWriter.AcquireReaderLock(10000);
                try
                {
                    // now we can read safely
                    return studentsGrade;
                }
                finally
                {
                    // Ensure that the lock is released.
                    readerWriter.ReleaseReaderLock();
                }
            }

            static void PostGrade(char grade)
            {
                // wait ten seconds for the write lock
                readerWriter.AcquireWriterLock(10000);
                try
                {
                    // now we can post the grade safely
                    studentsGrade = grade;
                    Console.WriteLine("Posting Grade...");
                }
                finally
                {
                    // Ensure that the lock is released.
                    readerWriter.ReleaseWriterLock();
                }
            }

            static void StudentThreadProc()
            {
                bool isGradeFound = false;
                char grade = ' ';
                while(!isGradeFound)
                {
                    grade = ReadGrade();
                    if(grade != ' ')
                    {
                        isGradeFound = true;
                        Console.WriteLine("Student Found Grade...");
                    }
                    else // check back later
                        Thread.Sleep(1000);
                }
            }

            static void InstructorThreadProc()
            {
                // everyone likes an easy grader :)
                PostGrade('A');
            }
        }
```

Discussion

In the example, the ReaderWriterLock protects access to the grade resource of the GradeBoard class. Lots of students can be continually reading their grades using the ReadGrade method, but once the instructor attempts to post the grades using the PostGrade method, the grade resource is locked so that no one but the instructor can access it. The instructor updates the grades and releases the lock, and the pending student read requests are allowed to resume. All students continue to read the grade board, check to see if the grades have been posted, and then wait before making another request. Once the grades are posted, each student finds it, and the thread for that student terminates.

The Main method calls Join on the instructor and student threads to wait until those threads finish before continuing and ending. If it did not do this, the program could potentially end before the threads finish. It protects against a ThreadInterruptedException, as the Join calls could potentially throw this if the thread aborts. The threads are named using the Name property to ease debugging.

See Also

See the "ReaderWriterLock Class" and "Thread Class" topics in the MSDN documentation.

15.9 Determining Whether a Request for a Pooled Thread Will Be Queued

Problem

Your application will be creating many threads from the thread pool. When creating a thread from this pool, you want to be informed as to whether a thread in the pool is available or if none are available, and the request for a new thread will have to be queued. Basically, you want to know whether a thread is available for immediate use from the thread pool.

Solution

Use the ThreadPool.GetAvailableThreads method to get the number of worker threads currently available in the ThreadPool to determine whether you should queue another request to launch another thread via ThreadPool.QueueUserWorkItem or take an alternate action. The Main method calls a method (SpawnManyThreads) to spawn lots of threads to do work in the ThreadPool, then waits for a bit to simulate processing:

```
public class TestThreads
{
    public static void Main()
    {
```

```
        SpawnManyThreads();
        // have to wait here or the background threads in the thread
        // pool would not run before the main thread exits.
        Console.WriteLine("Main Thread waiting to complete...");
        Thread.Sleep(2000);
        Console.WriteLine("Main Thread completing...");
    }
```

The SpawnManyThreads method launches threads and pauses between each launch to allow the ThreadPool to register the request and act upon it. The isThreadAvailable method is called with the parameter set to true to determine whether there is a worker thread available for use in the ThreadPool:

```
    public static bool SpawnManyThreads()
    {
        try
        {
            for(int i=0;i<500;i++)
            {
                // have to wait or threadpool never gives out threads to
                // requests
                Thread.Sleep(100);
                // check to see if worker threads are available in the pool
                if(true == isThreadAvailable(true))
                {
                    // launch thread if queue isn't full
                    Console.WriteLine("Worker Thread was available...");
                    ThreadPool.QueueUserWorkItem(new WaitCallback(ThreadProc),i);
                }
                else
                    Console.WriteLine("Worker Thread was NOT available...");
            }
        }
        catch(Exception e)
        {
            Console.WriteLine(e.ToString());
            return false;
        }
        return true;
    }
```

The isThreadAvailable method calls ThreadPool.GetAvailableThreads to determine whether the ThreadPool has any available worker threads left. If you pass false as the checkWorkerThreads parameter, it also sees whether there are any completion port threads available. The GetAvailableThreads method compares the current number of threads allocated from the pool against the maximum ThreadPool threads. The worker thread maximum is 25 per CPU, and the completion port thread maximum is 1,000 total, regardless of CPUs on v1.1 of the CLR:

```csharp
public static bool isThreadAvailable(bool checkWorkerThreads)
{
    int workerThreads = 0;
    int completionPortThreads = 0;
    // get available threads
    ThreadPool.GetAvailableThreads(out workerThreads,out completionPortThreads);

    // indicate how many work threads are available
    Console.WriteLine("{0} worker threads available in thread pool.",
                        workerThreads);

    if(checkWorkerThreads)
    {
        if(workerThreads > 0)
            return true;
    }
    else // check completion port threads
    {
        if(completionPortThreads > 0)
            return true;
    }
    return false;
}
```

This is a simple method to call in a threaded fashion:

```csharp
static void ThreadProc(Object stateInfo)
{
    // show we did something with this thread
    Console.WriteLine("Thread {0} running...",stateInfo);
    Thread.Sleep(1000);
}
}
```

Discussion

The ThreadPool is a great way to perform background tasks without having to manage all aspects of the thread yourself. It can be handy to know when the ThreadPool itself is going to become a bottleneck to your application, and the GetAvailableThreads method can help you. However, you might want to check your application design if you are consistently using this many threads as you might be losing performance due to contention or context switching. Queuing up work when the ThreadPool is full simply queues it up for execution once one of the threads comes free; the request isn't lost, just postponed.

See Also

See the "ThreadPool Class" topic in the MSDN documentation. Also see *Applied Microsoft .NET Framework Programming* by Jeffrey Richter (Wintellect).

15.10 Waiting for All Threads in the Thread Pool to Finish

Problem

For threads that are manually created via the Thread class, you can call the Join method to wait for a thread to finish. This works well when you need to wait for all threads to finish processing before an application terminates. Unfortunately, the thread pool threads do not have a Join method. You need to make sure that all threads in the thread pool have finished processing before another thread terminates or your application's main thread terminates.

Solution

Use a combination of the ThreadPool methods—GetMaxThreads and GetAvailableThreads—to determine when the ThreadPool is finished processing the requests:

```
public static void Main()
{
    for(int i=0;i<25;i++)
    {
        // have to wait or threadpool never gives out threads to requests
        Thread.Sleep(50);
        // queue thread request
        ThreadPool.QueueUserWorkItem(new WaitCallback(ThreadProc),i);
    }
    // have to wait here or the background threads in the thread
    // pool would not run before the main thread exits.
    Console.WriteLine("Main Thread waiting to complete...");
    bool working = true;
    int workerThreads = 0;
    int completionPortThreads = 0;
    int maxWorkerThreads = 0;
    int maxCompletionPortThreads = 0;
    // get max threads in the pool
    ThreadPool.GetMaxThreads(out maxWorkerThreads,out maxCompletionPortThreads);
    while(working)
    {
        // get available threads
        ThreadPool.GetAvailableThreads(out workerThreads,out completionPortThreads);
        if(workerThreads == maxWorkerThreads)
        {
            // allow to quit
            working = false;
        }
        else
        {
            // sleep before checking again
```

```
                    Thread.Sleep(500);
            }
        }
        Console.WriteLine("Main Thread completing...");
    }
    Static void ThreadProc(Object stateInfo)
    {
        //show we did something with this thread...
        Console.WriteLine("Thread {0} running...", stateInfo);
        Thread.Sleep(1000);
    }
```

Discussion

This approach is a bit coarse; since the CLR does not allow access to the thread objects being created, the best we can do is to see when the ThreadPool no longer has requests queued. If this approach is not sufficient for your needs, you could implement your own thread pool, but be careful of the many pitfalls that await you because thread pools are not easy to get right in all cases. Some of the issues are having too many or too few threads to service requests, determining initial levels of threads in the pool, and deadlocking threads.

See Also

See the "ThreadPool Class" topic in the MSDN documentation. Also see *Applied Microsoft .NET Framework Programming* by Jeffrey Richter (Wintellect).

15.11 Configuring a Timer

Problem

You have one of the following timer configuration needs:

- You want to use a timer to call a timer callback method at a fixed time after the timer object has been created. Once this callback method has been called the first time, you want to call this same callback method at a specified interval (this interval might be different from the time interval between the creation of the timer and the first time the timer callback method is called).

- You want to use a timer to call a timer callback method immediately upon creation of the System.Threading.Timer object, after which the callback method is called at a specified interval.

- You want to use a timer to call a timer callback method one time only.

- You have been using a System.Threading.Timer object and need to change the intervals at which its timer callback method is called.

Solution

To fire a System.Threading.Timer after an initial delay, and then at a specified period after that, use the System.Threading.Timer constructor to set up different times for the initial and following callbacks:

```
using System;
using System.Threading;

public class TestTimers
{
    public static int count = 0;
    public static Timer timerRef = null;

    public static void Main()
    {
        TimerCallback callback = new TimerCallback(TimerMethod);

        // Create a timer that waits one half second, then invokes
        // the callback every second thereafter.
        Timer timer = new Timer(callback, null,500, 1000);

        // store a reference to this timer so the callback can use it
        timerRef = timer;

        // The main thread does nothing until the timer is disposed.
        while(timerRef != null)
            Thread.Sleep(0);
        Console.WriteLine("Timer example done.");
    }

    static void TimerMethod(Object state)
    {
        count++;
        if(count == 5)
        {
            timerRef.Dispose();
            timerRef = null;
        }
    }
}
```

The previous method showed how to fire the callback after 500 milliseconds. To fire the initial callback immediately, change the value to zero:

```
// Create a timer that doesn't wait, then invokes
// the callback every second thereafter.
Timer timer = new Timer(callback, null,0, 1000);
```

To have the timer call the callback only once, change the constructor to pass Timeout.Infinite for the callback interval. You also have to change the current scheme that waits for five callbacks before disposing of the timer to do it the first time. If you didn't do this, the program would hang since the `Main` function is still waiting for the timer to have `Dispose` called, but the fifth callback will never trigger the `Dispose` call:

```
// Create a timer that waits for half a second, then is disposed
Timer timer = new Timer(callback, null,500, Timeout.Infinite);

// Also change this...to
    static void TimerMethod(Object state)
    {
            timerRef.Dispose( );
            timerRef = null;
    }
```

To change the interval of a running `System.Threading.Timer`, call the `Change` method specifying the delay before the next callback and the new callback interval, like this:

```
static void TimerMethod(Object state)
{
    count++;
    if(count == 5)
    {
        timerRef.Change(1000,2000);
    }
    if(count == 10)
    {
        timerRef.Dispose( );
        timerRef = null;
    }
}
```

This code now checks for the fifth callback and changes the interval from one second to two seconds. The sixth callback will happen one second after, and then callbacks through ten will happen two seconds apart.

Discussion

One item to be aware of when using `System.Threading.Timers` and `TimerCallbacks` is that they are serviced from the `ThreadPool`. This means that if you have other work being farmed out to the `ThreadPool` in your application, it could be contending with the `Timer` callbacks for an available worker thread. The basic timer is enough to serve the earlier scenarios, but if you are doing UI work and want to use timers, you should investigate the `System.Windows.Forms.Timer` class. If you are doing server work, you might also want to look at `System.Timers.Timer` as well. Both of these classes add events for when the timers are disposed and when the timer "ticks"; they also add properties that expose the settings.

See Also

See the "System.Threading.Timer Class," "TimerCallback Delegate," "System.Windows. Forms.Timer Class," and "System.Timers.Timer" topics in the MSDN documentation.

15.12 Storing Thread-Specific Data Privately

Problem

You want to store thread-specific data discovered at runtime on a thread that will be accessible only to code running within that thread.

Solution

Use the `AllocateDataSlot` or `AllocateNamedDataSlot` method on the `Thread` class to reserve a *thread local storage* (TLS) slot. Using TLS, a large structure can be stored in a data slot on a thread and used in many different methods. This can be done without having to pass the structure as a parameter.

For this example, a structure called `Data` here represents a structure that can grow to be very large in size:

```
public struct Data
{
    // Application data is stored here
}
```

Before using this structure, a data slot has to be created in TLS to store the structure. The following code creates an instance of the `Data` structure and stores it in the data slot named `AppDataSlot`:

```
Data appData = new Data();
Thread.SetData(Thread.GetNamedDataSlot("appDataSlot"), appData);
```

Whenever this structure is needed, it can be retrieved with a call to `Thread.GetData`. The following line of code gets the `appData` structure from the data slot named `appDataSlot`:

```
Data storedAppData = (Data)Thread.GetData(Thread.GetNamedDataSlot("appDataSlot"));
```

At this point, the `storedAppData` structure can be read or modified. After the action has been performed on the `storedAppData` structure, `storedAppData` must be placed back into the data slot named `appDataSlot`:

```
Thread.SetData(Thread.GetNamedDataSlot("appDataSlot"), appData);
```

Once the application is finished using this structure, the data slot can be released from memory using the following method call:

```
Thread.FreeNamedDataSlot("appDataSlot");
```

The following simple class shows how TLS can be used to store a structure:

```
using System;
using System.Threading;

public class HandleStructure
{
    public static void Main()
    {
```

```
        // Create structure instance and store it in the named data slot
        Data appData = new Data( );
        Thread.SetData(Thread.GetNamedDataSlot("appDataSlot"), appData);

        // Call another method that will use this structure
        HandleStructure.MethodB( );

        // When done, free this data slot
        Thread.FreeNamedDataSlot("appDataSlot");
    }

    public static void MethodB( )
    {
        // Get the structure instance from the named data slot
        Data storedAppData = (Data)Thread.GetData(
          Thread.GetNamedDataSlot("appDataSlot"));

        // Modify the StoredAppData structure

        // When finished modifying this structure, store the changes back
        // into the named data slot
        Thread.SetData(Thread.GetNamedDataSlot("appDataSlot"),
                       storedAppData);

        // Call another method that will use this structure
        HandleStructure.MethodC( );
    }

    public static void MethodC( )
    {
        // Get the structure instance from the named data slot
        Data storedAppData =
            (Data)Thread.GetData(Thread.GetNamedDataSlot("appDataSlot"));

        // Modify the storedAppData structure

        // When finished modifying this structure, store the changes back into
        //    the named data slot
        Thread.SetData(Thread.GetNamedDataSlot("appDataSlot"), storedAppData);
    }
}
```

Discussion

Thread local storage is a convenient way to store data that is usable across method calls without having to pass the structure to the method or even without knowledge about where the structure was actually created.

Data stored in a named TLS data slot is available only to that thread; no other thread can access a named data slot of another thread. The data stored in this data slot is accessible from anywhere within the thread. This setup essentially makes this data global to the thread.

To create a named data slot, use the static `Thread.GetNamedDataSlot` method. This method accepts a single parameter, *name*, that defines the name of the data slot. This name should be unique; if a data slot with the same name exists, then the contents of that data slot will be returned and a new data slot will not be created. This action occurs silently; there is no exception thrown or error code available to inform you that you are using a data slot someone else created. To be sure that you are using a unique data slot, use the `Thread.AllocateNamedDataSlot` method. This method throws a `System.ArgumentException` if a data slot already exists with the same name. Otherwise, it operates similarly to the `GetNamedDataSlot` method.

It is interesting to note that this named data slot is created on every thread in the process, not just the thread that called this method. This fact should not be much more than an inconvenience to you, though, since the data in each data slot can be accessed only by the thread that contains it. In addition, if a data slot with the same name was created on a separate thread and you call `GetNamedDataSlot` on the current thread with this name, none of the data in any data slot on any thread will be destroyed.

`GetNamedDataSlot` returns a `LocalDataStoreSlot` object that is used to access the data slot. Note that this class is not creatable through the use of the `new` keyword. It must be created through one of the `AllocateDataSlot` or `AllocateNamedDataSlot` methods on the `Thread` class.

To store data in this data slot, use the static `Thread.SetData` method. This method takes the object passed in to the *data* parameter and stores it in the data slot defined by the *dataSlot* parameter.

The static `Thread.GetData` method retrieves the object stored in a data slot. This method accepts a `LocalDataStoreSlot` object that is created through the `Thread.GetNamedDataSlot` method. The `GetData` method then returns the object that was stored in that particular data slot. Note that the object returned might have to be cast to its original type before it can be used.

The static method `Thread.FreeNamedDataSlot` will free the memory associated with a named data slot. This method accepts the name of the data slot as a `string` and, in turn, frees the memory associated with that data slot. Remember that when a data slot is created with `GetNamedDataSlot`, a named data slot is also created on all of the other threads running in that process. This is not really a problem when creating data slots with the `GetNamedDataSlot` method because if a data slot exists with this name, a `LocalDataStoreSlot` object that refers to that data slot is returned, a new data slot is not created, and the original data in that data slot is not destroyed.

This situation becomes more of a problem when using the `FreeNamedDataSlot` method. This method will free the memory associated with the data slot name passed in to it for all threads, not just the thread that it was called on. Freeing a data slot before all threads have finished using the data within that data slot can be disastrous to your application.

A way to work around this problem is to not call the `FreeNamedDataSlot` method at all. When a thread terminates, all of its data slots in TLS are freed automatically. The side effect of not calling `FreeNamedDataSlot` is that the slot is taken up until the garbage collector determines that the thread the slot was created on finished and the slot can be freed.

If you know the number of TLS slots you need for your code at compile time, consider using the `ThreadStaticAttribute` on a static field of your class to set up TLS-like storage.

See Also

See the "Thread Local Storage and Thread Relative Static Fields," "ThreadStatic-Attribute Attribute," and "Thread Class" topics in the MSDN documentation.

CHAPTER 16

Unsafe Code

Visual C# .NET (C#) allows you to step outside of the safe environment of managed code and write code that is considered "unsafe" by the Common Language Runtime (CLR). Running code that is considered unsafe by the CLR presents a certain set of restrictions in exchange for opening up possibilities like accessing memory-mapped data or implementing time-critical algorithms that use pointers directly. These restrictions are mainly based in the Code Access Security (CAS) system of the CLR and are in place to draw a distinct line between code the CLR knows to be playing by the rules (or "safe"), and code that needs to do a bit outside of the traditional sandbox of the CLR (and is thus "unsafe" code). In order to run code that is marked as unsafe by the CLR, you need the CAS SkipVerification privilege granted to the assembly that the unsafe code is implemented in. This tells the CLR to not bother verifying the code and to allow it to run, whereas normally unverified code would not run. This is a highly privileged operation and is not to be done lightly, as you increase the permissions your application will require in order to operate correctly on a user's system. If you use unsafe types in a method signature, you also make the code non-CLS-compliant. This means that interoperability with other .NET based languages, like VB.NET or Managed C++, for this assembly is compromised.

Even though unsafe code allows you to easily write potentially unstable code, it does have several safeguards. Only value types or pointers to value types inside of reference types can be used with unsafe code; reference types cannot. This allows pointer types to be created solely on the stack, so you do not have to use the new and delete operations to allocate and release memory to which the variable points. You only have to wait for the method that declared the pointer type to return, forcing the pointer to go out of scope and clearing any stack space devoted to this method. You can get into a bit of trouble if you are doing exotic things with unsafe code (such as pointing to a value type inside of a reference type) since this behavior allows access to heap-based memory and opens up the possibility for pointer pitfalls such as those seen in C++.

16.1 Controlling Changes to Pointers Passed to Methods

Problem

You must pass a pointer variable in to a method; however, you do not want to allow the called method to change the address that the pointer passed in is pointing to. For example, a developer wants to assume that after passing in a pointer parameter to a method that that parameter is still pointing to the same address when this method returns. If the called method were to change what the pointer pointed to, bugs could be introduced into the code.

In other cases, the converse may be true: the developer *wants* to allow the address to be changed in the method she passes the pointer to. Consider a developer who might create a method that accepts two pointers and switches those pointers by switching the memory locations to which each pointer points to, rather than swapping the values each pointer points to.

Solution

You must decide whether to pass this pointer by value, by reference, or as an out parameter. There are several methods of passing arrays to methods. These methods include using or not using the ref or out keywords to define how the parameters are to be handled.

To make sure that a method does not modify the pointer itself, you would pass the pointer by value, as shown here:

```
unsafe
{
    int num = 1;
    int* numPtr = &num;
    ModifyValue(numPtr);
    // Continue using numPtr...
}
```

The method ModifyValue can still change the value in the memory location to which the NumPtr pointer is pointing to, but it cannot force NumPtr to point to a different memory location after the method ModifyValue returns.

To allow the method to modify the pointer, pass it in by reference:

```
public unsafe void TestSwitchXY()
{
    int x = 100;
    int y = 20;
    int* ptrx = &x;
    int* ptry = &y;
```

```
        Console.WriteLine(*ptrx + "\t" + (int)ptrx);
        Console.WriteLine(*ptry + "\t" + (int)ptry);

        SwitchXY(ref ptrx, ref ptry);

        Console.WriteLine(*ptrx + "\t" + (int)ptrx);
        Console.WriteLine(*ptry + "\t" + (int)ptry);
    }

    public unsafe void SwitchXY(ref int* x, ref int* y)
    {
        int* temp = x;
        x = y;
        y = temp;
    }
```

The SwitchXY method switches the values of the x and y pointers so that they point to the memory location originally pointed to by the other parameter. In this case, you must pass the pointers in to the SwitchXY method by reference (ref). This action allows the SwitchXY method to actually modify where a pointer points to and to return this modified pointer.

Discussion

In safe code, passing a value type to a method *by value* means that the value is passed in, not the reference to that value. Therefore, the called method cannot modify the value that the calling method's reference points to; it can modify only the copy that it received.

It works the same way with unsafe code. When an unsafe pointer is passed in to a method by value, the value of the pointer (which is a memory location) cannot be modified; however, the value that this pointer points to can be modified.

To examine the difference between passing a pointer by reference and by value, we first need to set up a pointer to an integer:

```
int x = 5;
int* ptrx = &x;
```

Next, we write the method that attempts to modify the pointer parameter:

```
private unsafe void CallByValue(int* x)
{
    int newNum = 7;
    x = &newNum;
}
```

Finally, we call the method and pass in ptrx to this method:

```
CallByValue(ptrx);
```

If we examine the pointer variable ptrx before the call to CallByValue, we see that it points to the value 5. The called method CallByValue changes the passed in parameter to point to a different memory location. However, when the CallByValue returns, the ptrx pointer still points to the original memory location that contains the value 5. The reason for this is that the CallByValue method accepts the pointer ptrx by value. This means that whatever value that ptrx holds, a memory location in this case, it cannot be modified, which is similar to when a reference type is passed.

There are other times when we need to allow a called method to modify the memory location that a pointer points to. Passing a pointer *by reference* into a method does this. This means that the called method may, in fact, modify the memory location to which a pointer parameter points. To see this, we again set up a pointer:

```
int x = 5;
int* ptrx = &;
```

Next, we write the method that attempts to modify the parameter:

```
private unsafe void CallByRef(ref int* x)
{
    int newNum = 7;
    x = &newNum;
}
```

Finally, we call the method and pass the pointer by reference:

```
CallByRef(ref ptrx);
```

Now if we examine the value that the pointer ptrx points to, before and after the call is made to CallByRef, we see that it has indeed changed from 5 to 7. Not only this, but the ptrx pointer is actually pointing to a different memory location. Essentially, the ref keyword allows the method CallByRef to modify the value contained in the ptrx variable.

Let's consider the use of the out or ref keywords with pointers. A method that accepts a pointer as an out or ref parameter is called like this:

```
public unsafe void TestOut()
{
    int* ptrx;
    CallUsingOut(out ptrx);

    Console.WriteLine(*ptrx + "\t" + (int)ptrx);
}
```

The CallUsingOut method is written as follows:

```
public unsafe void CallUsingOut(out int* ptrx)
{
    int x = 7;
    ptrx = &x;
}
```

The ptrx variable is initially a null pointer. After the call is made to the CallUsingOut method, the ptrx variable points to the value 7.

The code in this section of this recipe is meant to be as simple as possible in order to explain the difference between passing a pointer by value, by reference, and as an out parameter. However, there is a serious flaw in the design of this example code (the code in the Solution section does not contain this flaw). Take the following code, for example:

```
public unsafe void TestOut()
{
    int* ptrx;
    CallUsingOut(out ptrx);

    Console.WriteLine(*ptrx);
    SomeOtherMethod("Some Text");
    Console.WriteLine(*ptrx);
}
```

The called method is written as follows:

```
public unsafe void CallUsingOut(out int* ptrx)
{
    int temp = 7;
    ptrx = &temp;
}
```

The problem is that the temp variable, pointed to by the out parameter ptrx in the CallUsingOut method, is in the stack frame of the CallUsingOut method. The first call to WriteLine displays the correct value (7) for the pointer variable ptrx since the CallUsingOut method's stack frame is still intact. However, the stack frame to the CallUsingOut method is promptly overwritten when the call to SomeOtherMethod is made, thereby causing the second call to WriteLine to display garbage.

This mistake is easy to make, especially as the code gets more and more complex. This error can also occur when returning a pointer from a method as a return value. To solve this, you need to not assign local variables in the scope of the method that are created on the stack to the pointer since the value being pointed to can "go away" once the scope is exited, creating a dangling pointer.

 Be very careful that you do not create dangling pointers (a pointer that doesn't point at anything valid, such as by assigning a pointer to memory that is collected before leaving the function) when passing pointer parameters as ref or out. This warning also applies to pointers used as return values.

See Also

See the "Method Parameters," "out Parameter," and "ref Parameter" topics in the MSDN documentation.

16.2 Comparing Pointers

Problem

You need to know whether two pointers point to the same memory location. If they don't, you need to know which of the two pointers points to a higher or lower element in the same block of memory.

Solution

Using the == and != operators, we can determine if two pointers point to the same memory location. For example, the code:

```
unsafe
{
    int[] arr = new int[5] {1,2,3,4,5};
    fixed(int* ptrArr = &arr[0])
    {
        int* p1 = (ptrArr + 1);
        int* p2 = (ptrArr + 3);

        Console.WriteLine("p2 > p1");
        Console.WriteLine("(p2 == p1) = " + (p2 == p1));
        Console.WriteLine("(p2 != p1) = " + (p2 != p1));

        p2 = p1;
        Console.WriteLine("p2 == p1");
        Console.WriteLine("(p2 == p1) = " + (p2 == p1));
        Console.WriteLine("(p2 != p1) = " + (p2 != p1));
    }
}
```

displays the following:

```
p2 > p1
(p2 == p1) = False
(p2 != p1) = True

p2 == p1
(p2 == p1) = True
(p2 != p1) = False
```

Using the >, <, >=, or <= comparison operators, we can determine whether two pointers are pointing to a higher, lower, or the same element in an array. For example, the code:

```
unsafe
{
    int[] arr = new int[5] {1,2,3,4,5};
    fixed(int* ptrArr = &arr[0])
    {
        int* p1 = (ptrArr + 1);
        int* p2 = (ptrArr + 3);
```

```
        Console.WriteLine("p2 > p1");
        Console.WriteLine("(p2 > p1) = " + (p2 > p1));
        Console.WriteLine("(p2 < p1) = " + (p2 < p1));
        Console.WriteLine("(p2 >= p1) = " + (p2 >= p1));
        Console.WriteLine("(p2 <= p1) = " + (p2 <= p1));

        p2 = p1;
        Console.WriteLine("p2 == p1");
        Console.WriteLine("(p2 > p1) = " + (p2 > p1));
        Console.WriteLine("(p2 < p1) = " + (p2 < p1));
        Console.WriteLine("(p2 >= p1) = " + (p2 >= p1));
        Console.WriteLine("(p2 <= p1) = " + (p2 <= p1));
    }
}
```

displays the following:

```
p2 > p1
(p2 > p1) = True
(p2 < p1) = False
(p2 >= p1) = True
(p2 <= p1) = False

p2 == p1
(p2 > p1) = False
(p2 < p1) = False
(p2 >= p1) = True
(p2 <= p1) = True
```

Discussion

When manipulating the addresses that pointers point to, it is sometimes necessary to compare their addresses. The ==, !=, >, <, >=, and <= operators have been overloaded to operate on pointer type variables. These comparison operators do not compare the value pointed to by the pointers; instead, they compare the addresses pointed to by the pointers.

To compare the values pointed to by two pointers, dereference the pointers and then use a comparison operator on them. For example:

```
*intPtr == *intPtr2
```

or:

```
structPtr1->value1 != structPtr2->value1
```

will compare the values pointed to by these pointers, rather than their addresses.

See Also

See the "C# Operators," "= = Operator," and "! = Operator" topics in the MSDN documentation.

16.3   Navigating Arrays

Problem

You need to iterate through the elements of a single-dimensional, multidimensional, or jagged array using a pointer to that array.

Solution

To enable iteration, we create an unsafe pointer that points to an array. The manipulation of the array can then be performed through this pointer.

To create a pointer to a single-dimension array, declare and initialize the array:

```
int[] intArray = new int[5] {1, 2, 3, 4, 5};
```

and then set a pointer, arrayPtr, to the address of the first element in this array (we must use the fixed keyword to pin the array in the managed heap so that the garbage collector does not move it):

```
fixed(int* arrayPtr = &intArray[0])
```

Note that this line could also be written as:

```
fixed(int* arrayPtr = intArray)
```

without any address of (&) operator or indexer. This is because the array variable always points to the first element, similar to how C++ array pointers operate.

The following code creates and initializes a pointer to a single-dimension array and then displays the last item in that array:

```
unsafe
{
    int[] intArray = new int[5] {1, 2, 3, 4, 5};
    fixed(int* arrayPtr = &intArray[0])
    {
        Console.WriteLine(*(arrayPtr + 4)); //Display the last value '5'
    }
}
```

Creating a pointer to an array of enumeration values is very similar:

```
unsafe
{
    Colors[] intArray = new Colors[2] {Colors.Red, Colors.Blue};
    fixed(Colors* arrayPtr = &intArray[0])
    {
        // Use arrayPtr here
    }
}
```

where Colors is declared as follows:

```
public enum Colors{Red, Green, Blue}
```

The last element of the array can then be displayed with the following code:

```
Console.WriteLine(*(arrayPtr + intArray.GetLength(0) - 1));
```

Creating a pointer to a multidimensional array is performed by declaring and initializing a multidimensional array:

```
int[,] intMultiArray = new int[2,5] {{1,2,3,4,5},{6,7,8,9,10}};
```

and then setting a pointer to the address of the first element in this array:

```
fixed(int* arrayPtr = &intMultiArray[0,0])
```

For example, the following code creates and initializes a pointer to a multidimensional array and then displays the last item in that array:

```
unsafe
{
    int[,] intMultiArray = new int[2,5] {{1,2,3,4,5},{6,7,8,9,10}};
    fixed(int* arrayPtr = &intMultiArray[0,0])
    {
        Console.WriteLine(*(arrayPtr + 9)); //Display the last value '10'
    }
}
```

A jagged array can be pointed to as well, but it is much harder to navigate this type of array using a pointer. This code creates and initializes a pointer to a jagged array and then displays each item in that array:

```
unsafe
{
    int[][] intJaggedArray = new int[3][];
    intJaggedArray[0] = new int[2] {100,200};
    intJaggedArray[1] = new int[3] {300,400,500};
    intJaggedArray[2] = new int[4] {600,700,800,900};
    fixed(int* arrayPtr = &intJaggedArray[0][0])
    {
        for(int counter = -3; counter <= 15; counter++)
        {
            Console.WriteLine(*(arrayPtr + counter));
        }
    }
}
```

This code creates and initializes a pointer to a jagged array whose second array is defined as a multidimensional array, and then displays each item in that array:

```
unsafe
{
    int[][,] intJaggedArray2 = new int[3][,];
    intJaggedArray2[0] = new int[2,1] {{100},{200}};
    intJaggedArray2[1] = new int[3,1] {{300},{400},{500}};
    intJaggedArray2[2] = new int[4,1] {{600},{700},{800},{900}};
    fixed(int* arrayPtr = &intJaggedArray2[0][0,0])
    {
```

```
        for(int counter = -5; counter <= 23; counter++)
        {
            Console.WriteLine(*(arrayPtr + counter));
        }
    }
}
```

See Also

See the "Multidimensional Arrays" and "Jagged Arrays" topics and the "Unsafe at the Limit" article in the MSDN documentation.

16.4   Manipulating a Pointer to a Fixed Array

Problem

One limitation of a pointer to a fixed array is that you may not reassign this pointer to any other element of that array using pointer arithmetic. The following code will not compile since we are attempting to modify where the fixed pointer, arrayPtr, is pointing. The line of code in error is highlighted and results in a compile-time error:

```
unsafe
{
    int[] intArray = new int[5] {1,2,3,4,5};
    fixed(int* arrayPtr = &intArray[0])
    {
        arrayPtr++;
    }
}
```

We need a way to increment the address stored in the arrayPtr to access other elements in the array.

Solution

To allow this operation, create a new temporary pointer to the fixed array, shown here:

```
unsafe
{
    int[] intArray = new int[5] {1,2,3,4,5};
    fixed(int* arrayPtr = &intArray[0])
    {
        int* tempPtr = arrayPtr;
        tempPtr++;
    }
}
```

By assigning a pointer that points to the fixed pointer (arrayPtr), we now have a variable (tempPtr) that we can manipulate as we wish.

Discussion

Any variables declared in a fixed statement cannot be modified or passed as ref or out parameters to other methods. This limitation can pose a problem when attempting to move a pointer of this type through the elements of an array. Fixing this problem involves creating a temporary variable, tempPtr, that points to the same memory locations as the pointer declared in the fixed statement. Pointer arithmetic can then be applied to this temporary variable to cause the pointer to point to any of the elements in the array.

The compiler does not allow passing the pointer declared in the fixed statement, arrayPtr, as a ref or out parameter. However, the tempPtr variable can be passed to a method as a ref or out parameter. Passing pointers by reference or as out parameters can easily introduce errors into your code.

See Also

See the "unsafe" and "fixed" keywords in the MSDN documentation.

16.5 Returning a Pointer to a Particular Element in an Array

Problem

You need to create a method that accepts a pointer to an array, searches that array for a particular element, and returns a pointer to the found element.

Solution

The FindInArray method, shown here, returns a pointer to an element found in an array:

```
public unsafe int* FindInArray(int* theArray, int arrayLength, int valueToFind)
{
    for (int counter = 0; counter < arrayLength; counter++)
    {
        if (theArray[counter] == valueToFind)
        {
            return (&theArray[counter]);
        }
    }

    return (null);
}
```

This method is strongly typed for arrays that contain integers. To modify this method to use another type, change the int* types to the pointer type of your choice. Note that if no elements are found in the array, a null pointer is returned.

The method that creates an array of integers and passes a pointer to this array into the FindInArray method is shown here:

```
public void TestFind( )
{
    unsafe
    {
        int[] numericArr = new int[3] {2,4,6};
        fixed(int* ptrArr = &numericArr[0])
        {
            int* foundItem = FindInArray(ptrArr, numericArr.Length, 4);
            if (foundItem != null)
            {
                Console.WriteLine(*foundItem);
            }
            else
            {
                Console.WriteLine("Not Found");
            }
        }
    }
}
```

Discussion

The FindInArray method accepts three parameters. The first parameter, theArray, is a pointer to the first element in the array that will be searched. The second parameter, arrayLength, is the length of the array, and the final parameter, valueToFind, is the value we wish to find in the array theArray.

The second parameter, arrayLength, informs the for loop when the last element is reached. We cannot determine the length of an array from just a pointer to that array, so this parameter is needed. Many unmanaged APIs that accept a pointer to an array also require that the length of the array be passed.

 We could pass a pointer to any element in the array through the theArray parameter, but in doing so, we calculate the remaining length by subtracting the element location from the length of the array and passing the result to the arrayLength parameter.

The loop iterates over each element in the array and looks for the element that has a value equal to the parameter valueToFind. Once this element is found, a pointer to it is returned to the caller. We could have returned the actual value or the index value (Counter), but by returning a pointer to the element, more flexibility is offered to the calling method. A pointer can be dereferenced to get the value pointed to or it can be manipulated to point to the next or previous elements in the array using simple pointer arithmetic.

The FindInArray method could also be written as follows:

```
public unsafe int* FindInArray(int* theArray, int arrayLength, int valueToFind)
{
    for (int counter = 0; counter < arrayLength; counter++, theArray++)
    {
        if (*theArray == valueToFind)
        {
            return (theArray);
        }
    }

    return (null);
}
```

This version of this method uses pointer arithmetic to obtain the correct element in the array to be returned by this method.

Note that it is possible to return null from this method even though the return value is a pointer to a primitive type. If it were simply a primitive type and not a pointer to one, we could not return null from this method.

 Make sure you check for null pointers on return when calling a method that may return a null pointer. Proper exception handling can also mitigate this.

See Also

See the "unsafe" keyword in the MSDN documentation.

16.6   Creating and Using an Array of Pointers

Problem

You need to create, initialize, and use an array containing pointers.

Solution

The following code creates three pointers (TheNewBrush1, TheNewBrush2, and TheNewBrush3) that are inserted as elements in an array. The array of pointers to the NewBrush structure is created and set to a size of 3 so that it can hold each NewBrush structure. This newly defined array now contains undefined pointers. These undefined pointers should be initialized either to point to a value or to point to null. Here, all of the pointers in the array are initialized as null pointers. Finally, each NewBrush structure is then added to this array. Now we have a fully initialized array of pointers. From here we can use this array as we wish:

```
unsafe
{
    NewBrush theNewBrush1 = new NewBrush();
    NewBrush theNewBrush2 = new NewBrush();
    NewBrush theNewBrush3 = new NewBrush();

    NewBrush*[] arrayOfNewBrushPtrs = new NewBrush*[3];
    for (int counter = 0; counter < 3; counter++)
    {
        arrayOfNewBrushPtrs[counter] = null;
    }

    arrayOfNewBrushPtrs[0] = &theNewBrush1;
    arrayOfNewBrushPtrs[1] = &theNewBrush2;
    arrayOfNewBrushPtrs[2] = &theNewBrush3;
}
```

Notice that the for loop initializes each pointer in the array to null before the array is used. This is usually a good practice so that you do not inadvertently use an uninitialized pointer. Using a pointer that points to null results in a NullReferenceException being thrown on current versions of the CLR. This device makes it easier to track down pointer problems.

Using this newly created array of pointers to NewBrush objects allows you to use a pointer to a pointer. The following code shows how to dereference each pointer within the array arrayOfNewBrushPtrs:

```
unsafe
{
    fixed(NewBrush** ptrArrayOfNewBrushPtrs = arrayOfNewBrushPtrs)
    {
        for (int counter = 0; counter < 3; counter++)
        {
            ptrArrayOfNewBrushPtrs[counter]->BrushType = counter;
            Console.WriteLine(ptrArrayOfNewBrushPtrs[counter]->BrushType);
            Console.WriteLine((int)ptrArrayOfNewBrushPtrs[counter]);
        }
    }
}
```

The for loop initializes the BrushType field of each of the pointers to NewBrush objects in the array. This field is initialized to the current value of the loop counter (counter). The next two lines display this newly initialized field and the address of where the structure is located in memory. This code displays the following output:

```
0
1243292
1
1243284
2
1243276
```

Discussion

When using an array of pointers, the fixed statement pins the array in memory. Even though this array consists of pointers to value types, the array itself is created on the managed heap. Notice that ptrArrayOfNewBrushPtrs is defined as a pointer to a pointer. This stems from our creation of a pointer (ptrArrayOfNewBrushPtrs) that will initially point to the first element in an array of pointers. Therefore, to be able to dereference this pointer to get to the value that the pointer in the array is pointing to, we must dereference it once to get to the pointer in the array and then a second time to get the value that the array pointer is pointing to. The NewBrush structure used here is defined like this:

```
public struct NewBrush
{
public int BrushType;
}
```

See Also

See the "Unsafe Code Tutorial" in the MSDN documentation.

16.7 Creating and Using an Array of Pointers to Unknown Types

Problem

You need to create and operate on elements of an array that holds objects of unknown types.

Solution

The solution is to create an array of void pointers so that we do not need to know at design time what type(s) we will be pointing to:

```
unsafe
{
    long x = 10;
    long y = 20;
    long z = 1;

    void*[] arrayOfPtrs = new void*[3];
    arrayOfPtrs[0] = &X;
    arrayOfPtrs[1] = &Y;
    arrayOfPtrs[2] = &Z;

    Console.WriteLine(*((long*)arrayOfPtrs[0]));
    Console.WriteLine(*((long*)arrayOfPtrs[1]));
    Console.WriteLine(*((long*)arrayOfPtrs[2]));
}
```

This code creates an array, arrayOfPtrs, that will contain three void pointers. The pointers that are saved to this array are pointers to the three variables x, y, and z of type long. It is a simple matter to change the long data type to something different such as a byte or char. However, when the pointers in this array are used, they must be cast back to their original type. This cast is shown in the last three lines, where each pointer in the array is being dereferenced and displayed. If you do the wrong cast, you get undefined results, but the next example helps address this.

The following code creates an array of two void pointers and points the first pointer at a NewBrush structure and the second at an integer type variable:

```
unsafe
{
    NewBrush theNewBrush1 = new NewBrush();
    int* theInt = stackalloc int[1];

    void*[] arrayOfPtrs = new void*[2];

    arrayOfPtrs[0] = &theNewBrush1;
    arrayOfPtrs[1] = theInt;

    Console.WriteLine("arrayOfPtrs[0] = " + (
                      (NewBrush*)arrayOfPtrs[0])->BrushType);
    Console.WriteLine("arrayOfPtrs[1] = " +
                      ((int*)arrayOfPtrs[1])->ToString());
}
```

This code starts by creating a new NewBrush structure and a new pointer to an integer and the integer itself on the stack using the stackalloc statement. Next, the array of void pointers is created. At this point, we could opt to set all of the void pointers to null, but here we will immediately initialize each void pointer in the array to point to one of the previously declared types. However, this solution presents a problem with casting the pointers in the array back to their original types. This solution requires you to keep track of the data type that is stored in each element of the array so that you can correctly cast it back to its original type.

Discussion

Notice that each of the pointers in the array must be cast to their proper pointer type before the value they point to can be used, as shown in the following code:

```
((NewBrush*)arrayOfPtrs[0])->BrushType = 5;
*((int*)arrayOfPtrs[1]) = 111;
```

We cannot simply write *arrayOfPtrs[0] to dereference the pointer at the first element of the array. The compiler cannot accurately determine what type to dereference it as. Therefore the array element must be cast to some type before it is dereferenced.

When you cast a void pointer to an incorrect type, an exception will never be thrown. Using this incorrectly cast pointer can result in corruption of the original data that the pointer pointed to. This is one of the things that makes unsafe code so unsafe to use.

See Also

See the "Void Sample" article and the "stackalloc" keyword in the MSDN documentation.

16.8   Switching Unknown Pointer Types

Problem

You need a generic method that accepts two pointers and switches the addresses that each pointer points to. In other words, if X points to an integer variable Foo and Y points to an integer variable Bar, you want to switch X so that it points to Bar and switch Y so that it points to Foo.

Solution

Create a method that accepts two void pointers. The following method accepts two pointers to void by reference. The *by reference* is required since we are actually switching the values contained in the pointer variables, not the value that the pointer is pointing to:

```
public unsafe void Switch(ref void* x, ref void* y)
{
    void* temp = x;
    x = y;
    y = temp;
}
```

The following test code calls the Switch method with two integer variables that point to different memory locations:

```
public unsafe void TestSwitch( )
{
    int x = 100;
    int y = 20;
    int* ptrx = &x;
    int* ptry = &y;

    Console.WriteLine(*ptrx + "\t" + (int)ptrx);
    Console.WriteLine(*ptry + "\t" + (int)ptry);

    // Convert int* to void*
    void* voidx = (void*)ptrx;
    void* voidy = (void*)ptry;

    // Switch pointer values
    Switch(ref voidx, ref voidy);

    // Convert returned void* to a usable int*
    ptrx = (int*)voidx;
    ptry = (int*)voidy;
```

```
        Console.WriteLine(*ptrx + "\t" + (int)ptrx);
        Console.WriteLine(*ptry + "\t" + (int)ptry);
    }
```

The following is displayed:

```
100     1243108
 20     1243104
 20     1243104
100     1243108
```

The TestSwitch method could just have easily been written with another data type, such as a byte, shown here:

```
public unsafe void TestSwitch()
{
    byte x = 100;
    byte y = 20;
    byte* ptrx = &x;
    byte* ptry = &y;

    Console.WriteLine(*ptrx + "\t" + (int)ptrx);
    Console.WriteLine(*ptry + "\t" + (int)ptry);

    // Convert byte* to void*
    void* voidx = (void*)ptrx;
    void* voidy = (void*)ptry;

    // Switch pointer values
    Switch(ref voidx, ref voidy);

    // Convert returned void* to a usable byte*
    ptrx = (byte*)voidx;
    ptry = (byte*)voidy;

    Console.WriteLine(*ptrx + "\t" + (int)ptrx);
    Console.WriteLine(*ptry + "\t" + (int)ptry);
}
```

All that had to be done is to change the int* types to byte* types.

Discussion

A void pointer has no type and therefore cannot be dereferenced, nor can pointer arithmetic be applied to this type of pointer. A void pointer does have one very useful function, though; it can be cast to a pointer of any other type. A void pointer is also able to be cast to the following other value types as well:

sbyte	int
byte	uint
short	long
ushort	ulong

In the Switch method, used in the Solution for this recipe, we notice that it takes two parameters by reference of type void*. We are declaring that any pointer type may be passed to these two parameters on this method. Once inside the Switch method, we can manipulate the value contained in the void pointers. However, since we do not know the original type that the void* was cast from, we cannot dereference the void*.

The one drawback to this technique is that before the Switch method is called in the TestSwitch method, the int* or byte* pointers must be cast to a void*. When the Switch method returns, the void* pointers must be cast back to their original types before they may be used. The reason for this casting is that we are passing the void* pointers by reference instead of by value.

We could pass the void* pointers by value instead, and simply switch the values pointed to, rather than the memory locations pointed to, in the Switch method. This new SwitchValues method would look something like this:

```
public unsafe void SwitchValues(void* x, void* y)
{
    void* temp = x;
    *x = *y;
    *y = *temp;
}
```

Unfortunately, this code will not compile, since you cannot dereference a void*. The void* must be cast to its original type before it can be dereferenced. To do this, we must also pass along the type information to the SwitchValues method. This can become very cumbersome, and it will reduce the genericity of this method as well.

See Also

See section A.4 Pointer conversions in the C# specification.

16.9 Breaking Up Larger Numbers into Their Equivalent Byte Array Representation

Problem

You have a larger number, such as an integer or a floating-point value, that you want to break up into its equivalent byte array representation. For example, you have the integer value 0x1120FFED and you want to obtain the following byte array: 0x11, 0x20, 0xFF, and 0xED.

Solution

Convert the larger number to a byte*, and operate on the byte* as if it were a pointer to an array of bytes. The following example creates a byte* to an int value and displays each byte value starting with the leftmost byte and working to the right:

```
unsafe
{
    int myInt = 1;
    byte* myIntPointer = (byte*)&myInt;    // Convert to a byte*

    // Display all bytes of this integer value
    for (int counter = sizeof(int) - 1; counter >= 0; counter--)
    {
        Console.WriteLine(myIntPointer[counter]);
    }
}
```

The following code shows how this can also be done with a decimal value:

```
unsafe
{
    decimal myDec = 1M;
    byte* myBytePointer = (byte*)&myDec;    // Convert to a byte*

    // Display all bytes of this decimal value
    for (int counter = sizeof(decimal) - 1; counter >= 0; counter--)
    {
        Console.WriteLine(myBytePointer[counter]);
    }
}
```

You'll notice that the byte representation for a decimal value (and floating-point values) is quite different from non-floating-point values.

Discussion

When using this technique to extract bytes from a larger number, keep in mind the *endianness* of the machine you are working on. For example, my Intel machine uses *little-endian* format, while others may use *big-endian* format.

With little-endian format, the least-significant byte is stored as the first byte of a 32-bit value, and the most-significant byte is stored as the last byte. It's as if you were reading the bytes backward in memory. Big-endian stores the least-significant byte on the right and the most-significant byte on the left.

On Intel machines, if you want to walk the array starting with the most-significant byte, you must use the following for loop:

```
for (int counter = sizeof(int) - 1; counter >= 0; counter--)
```

Notice that the loop starts with the last element of the array and moves toward the first element.

If you want to walk the array starting with the least-significant byte, you would use the following modified for loop:

```
for (int counter = 0; counter < sizeof(decimal); counter++)
```

Notice now that the loop starts at the first element in the array and works its way to the last element.

Always determine the endianness of the machine you are working on (consult `System.BitConverter.IsLittleEndian`) if you are using the code in this recipe. Otherwise, you could make the mistake of looking at the most-significant byte when, in fact, it is the least-significant byte.

See Also

See the "unsafe" keyword in the MSDN documentation.

16.10 Converting Pointers to a Byte[], SByte[], or Char[] to a String

Problem

You have obtained a pointer to a byte array, an sbyte array, or a char array. You want to convert this array into its string equivalent.

Solution

Use one of the string object's constructors that build a string from either a byte*, sbyte*, or char* passed in as a parameter. The following overloaded ConvertToString methods accept a byte[], an sbyte[], or a char[] and return the equivalent string object created from these arrays:

```
public string ConvertToString(byte[] arr)
{
    unsafe
    {
        string returnStr;
        fixed(byte* fixedPtr = arr)
        {
            returnStr = new string((sbyte*)fixedPtr);
        }
    }

    return (returnStr);
}

public string ConvertToString(sbyte[] arr)
{
    unsafe
    {
        string returnStr;
        fixed(sbyte* fixedPtr = arr)
        {
            returnStr = new string(fixedPtr);
        }
    }
}
```

```
        return (returnStr);
    }

    public string ConvertToString(char[] arr)
    {
        unsafe
        {
            string returnStr;
            fixed(char* fixedPtr = arr)
            {
                returnStr = new string(fixedPtr);
            }
        }

        return (returnStr);
    }
```

The following code calls these methods, passing in one of the required array types:

```
Console.WriteLine(ConvertToString(new byte[3] {0x61,0x62,0x63}));
Console.WriteLine(ConvertToString(new char[3] {'a','b','c'}));
Console.WriteLine(ConvertToString(new sbyte[3] {0x61,0x62,0x63}));
```

Discussion

The System.String constructor that takes an sbyte* in the Solution code is expecting
a null-terminated string in the buffer. There are also constructors on System.String
that take an sbyte* and default to Unicode, or allow you to pass an Encoding object.
One method to create a string from these arrays is to use a foreach loop to iterate
over each element in the array and append the character value of each array element
to the end of a StringBuilder object. However, this would operate slower than using
the technique in this recipe. In fact, assuming a null-terminated string is in the byte
array, the following unsafe code to convert a byte array to a string executes in 46% of
the time of its equivalent safe code:

```
public string ConvertToString(byte[] arr)
{
    unsafe
    {
        string returnStr;
        fixed(byte* fixedPtr = arr)
        {
            returnStr = new string((sbyte*)fixedPtr);
        }
    }

    return (returnStr);
}
```

The safe code is shown here:

```
public string ConvertToStringSlow(byte[] arr)
{
    System.Text.StringBuilder returnStr = new System.Text.StringBuilder();
```

```
    foreach (sbyte C in arr)
    {
        returnStr.Append(C);
    }

    return (returnStr.ToString());
}
```

In addition, the unsafe code is twice as fast as the following code, which uses the Encoding.ASCII class to convert a byte array to a string:

```
public string ConvertToASCIIStringSlow(byte[] arr)
{
    String retStr = Encoding.ASCII.GetString(arr);

    return (retStr);
}
```

This recipe uses two overloaded string constructors that accept either a pointer to a byte array or a pointer to a char array. The constructor then uses this array to construct a string from the array. The newly created string object is then initialized to this string created from the array. The constructors used in this recipe are defined as follows:

```
unsafe public String(char* value)
unsafe public String(sbyte* value)
```

The parameter for this constructor is defined as follows:

value

A pointer to either a char array or an sbyte array.

Note that if a pointer to a byte array is passed in, it must be cast to an sbyte:

```
returnStr = new string((sbyte*)fixedPtr);
```

Notice that the array's length is not passed in to the string constructor. Instead, the constructor will keep appending array values to the string until a null character is reached. If you know how many characters are in the array, then you should use the string overload that allows you to pass in the length.

See Also

See the "Unsafe Code Tutorial" and the "Encoding Class" topics in the MSDN documentation.

XML

XML (Extensible Markup Language) is a simple, portable, and flexible way to represent data in a structured format. XML is used in a myriad of ways, from acting as the foundation of web-based messaging protocols like SOAP, to being one of the more popular ways to store configuration data (such as the *web.config*, *machine.config*, or *security.config* files in the .NET Framework). Microsoft recognized the usefulness of XML to developers and has done a nice job of giving the developer choices around the tradeoffs one encounters when using XML. Sometimes you want to simply run though an XML document looking for a value in a read-only cursor-like fashion, and other times you need to be able to randomly access various pieces of the document. Microsoft provides classes like `XmlTextReader` and `XmlTextWriter` for lighter access and `XmlDocument` for full DOM (Document Object Model) processing support. It is likely that if you use .NET you will be dealing with XML to one degree or another, and in this chapter we explore some of the uses for XML and XML-based technologies like XPath and XSLT, as well as explore topics like validation of XML and transformation of XML to HTML.

17.1 Reading and Accessing XML Data in Document Order

Problem

You need to read in all the elements of an XML document and obtain information about each element, such as its name and attributes.

Solution

Create an `XMLTextReader` and use its `Read` method to process the document:

```
using System;
using System.Xml;
```

```
// ...

public static void Indent(int level)
{
    for (int i = 0; i < level; i++)
      Console.Write(" ");
}

public static void AccessXML()
{
    string xmlFragment = "<?xml version='1.0'?>" +
    "<!-- My sample XML -->" +
    "<?pi myProcessingInstruction?>" +
    "<Root>" +
    "<Node1 nodeId='1'>First Node</Node1>" +
    "<Node2 nodeId='2'>Second Node</Node2>" +
    "<Node3 nodeId='3'>Third Node</Node3>" +
    "</Root>";

    XmlTextReader reader = new XmlTextReader(xmlFragment,
        XmlNodeType.Element, null);
    int level = 0;

    while (reader.Read())
    {
        switch (reader.NodeType)
        {
            case XmlNodeType.CDATA:
                Indent(level);
                Console.WriteLine("CDATA: {0}", reader.Value);
                break;
            case XmlNodeType.Comment :
                Indent(level);
                Console.WriteLine("COMMENT: {0}", reader.Value);
                break;
            case XmlNodeType.DocumentType :
                Indent(level);
                Console.WriteLine("DOCTYPE: {0}={1}",
                  reader.Name, reader.Value);
                break;
            case XmlNodeType.Element :
                Indent(level);
                Console.WriteLine("ELEMENT: {0}", reader.Name);
                level++;
                while(reader.MoveToNextAttribute())
                {
                    Indent(level);
                    Console.WriteLine("ATTRIBUTE: {0}='{1}'",
                        reader.Name, reader.Value);
                }
                break;
            case XmlNodeType.EndElement :
                level--;
                break;
```

```
            case XmlNodeType.EntityReference :
                Indent(level);
                Console.WriteLine("ENTITY: {0}", reader.Name);
                break;
            case XmlNodeType.ProcessingInstruction :
                Indent(level);
                Console.WriteLine("INSTRUCTION: {0}={1}",
                    reader.Name, reader.Value);
                break;
            case XmlNodeType.Text :
                Indent(level);
                Console.WriteLine("TEXT: {0}", reader.Value);
                break;
            case XmlNodeType.XmlDeclaration :
                Indent(level);
                Console.WriteLine("DECLARATION: {0}={1}",
                    reader.Name, reader.Value);
                break;
        }
    }
    reader.Close( );
}
```

This code dumps the XML document in a hierarchical format:

```
DECLARATION: xml=version='1.0'
COMMENT:  My sample XML
INSTRUCTION: pi=myProcessingInstruction
ELEMENT: Root
 ELEMENT: Node1
  ATTRIBUTE: nodeId='1'
  TEXT: First Node
 ELEMENT: Node2
  ATTRIBUTE: nodeId='2'
  TEXT: Second Node
 ELEMENT: Node3
  ATTRIBUTE: nodeId='3'
  TEXT: Third Node
```

Discussion

Reading existing XML and identifying different node types is one of the fundamental actions that you will need to perform when dealing with XML. The code in the Solution shows how to create an XmlTextReader from either a string or from a stream, and then iterate over the nodes while recreating the formatted XML for output to the console window.

See Also

See the "XmlTextReader Class," "XmlNodeType Enumeration," and "StringReader Class" topics in the MSDN documentation.

17.2   Reading XML on the Web

Problem

Given a URL that points to an XML document, you need to grab the XML.

Solution

Use the XmlTextReader constructor that takes a URL as a parameter:

```
string url = "http://localhost/xml/sample.xml";

// use the XmlTextReader to get the xml at the url
XmlTextReader reader = new XmlTextReader (url);

    while (reader.Read())
    {
        switch (reader.NodeType)
        {
            case XmlNodeType.Element :
                Console.Write("<{0}>", reader.Name);
                break;
        }
    }
    reader
```

Discussion

The *sample.xml* file being referenced in this code is set up in a virtual directory named *xml* on the local system. The code retrieves the *sample.xml* file from the web server and displays all of the elements in the XML.

Sample.xml contains the following XML data:

```
<?xml version='1.0'?>
<!-- My sample XML -->
<?pi myProcessingInstruction?>
<Root>
    <Node1 nodeId='1'>First Node</Node1>
    <Node2 nodeId='2'>Second Node</Node2>
    <Node3 nodeId='3'>Third Node</Node3>
    <Node4><![CDATA[<>\&']]></Node4>
</Root>
```

See Also

See the "XmlTextReader Class" topic in the MSDN documentation.

17.3 Querying the Contents of an XML Document

Problem

You have a large and complex XML document and you need to find various pieces of information, such as all the information contained within a specific element and having a particular attribute setting. You want to query the XML structure without having to iterate through all the nodes in the XML document and searching for a particular item by hand.

Solution

In order to query a database, you normally would use SQL. In order to query an XML document, you would use XPath. In .NET, this means using the System.Xml. XPath namespace and classes like XPathDocument, XPathNavigator, and XPathNodeIterator.

In the following example, we use these classes to select nodes from an XML document we construct holding members from the board game "Clue" (or "Cluedo", as it is known abroad) and their various roles. We want to be able to select the married female participants who were witnesses to the crime. In order to do this, we pass an XPath expression to query the XML data set as follows:

```
public static void QueryXML( )
{
    string xmlFragment = "<?xml version='1.0'?>" +
        "<Clue>" +
        "<Participant type='Perpetrator'>Professor Plum</Participant>" +
        "<Participant type='Witness'>Colonel Mustard</Participant>" +
        "<Participant type='Witness'>Mrs. White</Participant>" +
        "<Participant type='Witness'>Mrs. Peacock</Participant>" +
        "<Participant type='Witness'>Mr. Green</Participant>" +
        "</Clue>";

    XmlTextReader reader = new XmlTextReader(xmlFragment,
                        XmlNodeType.Element,null);

    // Instantiate an XPathDocument using the XmlTextReader.
    XPathDocument xpathDoc = new XPathDocument(reader, XmlSpace.Preserve);

    // get the navigator
    XPathNavigator xpathNav = xpathDoc.CreateNavigator( );

    // set up the query looking for the married female participants
    // who were witnesses
    string xpathQuery =
      "/Clue/Participant[attribute::type='Witness'][contains(text( ),'Mrs.')]";
```

```
    // get the nodeset from the query
    XPathNodeIterator xpathIter = xpathNav.Select(xpathQuery);

    // write out the nodes found (Mrs. White and Mrs.Peacock in this instance)
    while(xpathIter.MoveNext())
    {
        Console.WriteLine(xpathIter.Current.Value);
    }

    // close the reader.
    reader.Close();
}
```

This outputs the following:

```
Mrs. White
Mrs. Peacock
```

Discussion

XPath is a very versatile language for performing queries on XML-based data. In order to accomplish our goal, we first created an XML fragment that looks like this:

```
<?xml version='1.0'?>
<Clue>
    <Participant type='Perpetrator'>Professor Plum</Participant>
    <Participant type='Witness'>Colonel Mustard</Participant>
    <Participant type='Witness'>Mrs. White</Participant>
    <Participant type='Witness'>Mrs. Peacock</Participant>
    <Participant type='Witness'>Mr. Green</Participant>
</Clue>;
```

We then load this fragment into an XmlTextReader, as shown in Recipe 17.1, then construct an XPathDocument to allow us to create an XPathNavigator, which lets us use XPath syntax to query the XML document shown in the preceding listing. The XmlTextReader reads over the document, checking for well-formedness; the XPathDocument instance wraps the XmlTextReader so we can use XPath to locate nodes (as well as perform XSLT transforms directly), and the XPathNavigator gets the set of nodes selected by the XPath expression.

```
XmlTextReader reader = new XmlTextReader(xmlFragment,
                    XmlNodeType.Element,null);

// Instantiate an XPathDocument using the XmlTextReader.
XPathDocument xpathDoc = new XPathDocument(reader, XmlSpace.Preserve);

// get the navigator
XPathNavigator xpathNav = xpathDoc.CreateNavigator();
```

Now we have to determine the XPath-based query to get all of the married female participants who were witnesses. This is set up in the xpathQuery string like this:

```
// set up the query looking for the married female participants
// who were witnesses
string xpathQuery =
  "/Clue/Participant[attribute::type='Witness'][contains(text(),'Mrs.')]";
```

In order to get a bit of comprehension of what is going on here, let me explain the syntax a bit:

- /Clue/Participant says "Get all of the Participants under the root level node Clue."
- Participant[attribute::type='Witness'] says "Select only Participants with an attribute called type with a value of Witness."
- Participant[contains(text( ),'Mrs.')] says "Select only Participants with a value that contains 'Mrs.'"

Put them all together and we get all of the married female participants who were witnesses.

Once we have an XPathNavigator, we call the Select method on it, passing the XPath-based query to select the nodes we are looking for that are returned via the XPathNodeIterator. We use the XPathNodeIterator to write out the names of the Participants we found and close the XmlTextReader.

See Also

See the "XPathDocument Class," "XPathNavigator Enumeration," and "XPath-NodeIterator Class" topics in the MSDN documentation.

17.4 Validating XML

Problem

You are accepting an XML document created by another source and you want to verify that it conforms to a specific schema. This schema may be in the form of an XSD or XDR schema; alternatively, you want the flexibility to use a DTD to validate the XML.

Solution

Use the XmlValidatingReader to validate XML documents against any descriptor document, such as an XSD (XML Schema), a DTD (Document Type Definition), or an XDR (Xml-Data Reduced):

```
public static void ValidateXML( )
{
    // create XSD schema collection with book.xsd
    XmlSchemaCollection schemaCollection = new XmlSchemaCollection( );
    // wire up handler to get any validation errors
    schemaCollection.ValidationEventHandler +=
        new ValidationEventHandler(ValidationCallBack);
    // add book.xsd
    schemaCollection.Add(null, @"..\..\Book.xsd");
    // make sure we added
    if(schemaCollection.Count > 0)
```

```
        {
            // open the book.xml file
            XmlTextReader reader = new XmlTextReader(@"..\..\Book.xml");
            // set up the validating reader
            XmlValidatingReader validReader =
                new XmlValidatingReader(reader);

            // set the validation type and add the schema collection
            validReader.ValidationType = ValidationType.Schema;
            validReader.Schemas.Add(schemaCollection);

            // wire up for any validation errors from the validating
            // reader
            validReader.ValidationEventHandler +=
                new ValidationEventHandler(ValidationCallBack);
            // read all nodes and print out
            while (validReader.Read())
            {
                if(validReader.NodeType == XmlNodeType.Element)
                {
                    Console.Write("<{0}", validReader.Name);
                    while(validReader.MoveToNextAttribute())
                    {
                        Console.Write(" {0}='{1}'",validReader.Name,
                            validReader.Value);
                    }
                    Console.Write(">");
                }
                else if(validReader.NodeType == XmlNodeType.Text)
                {
                    Console.Write(validReader.Value);
                }
                else if(validReader.NodeType == XmlNodeType.EndElement)
                {
                    Console.WriteLine("</{0}>",validReader.Name);
                }
            }
        }
    }

    private static void ValidationCallBack(object sender, ValidationEventArgs e)
    {
        Console.WriteLine("Validation Error: {0}", e.Message);
    }
```

Discussion

The Solution illustrates how to use the XmlValidatingReader to validate the *book.xml*
document against a *book.xsd* XML Schema definition file. DTDs were the original way
to specify the structure of an XML document, but it has become more common to use
XML Schema since it reached W3C Recommendation status in May 2001. XDR was
an early form of the final XML Schema syntax provided by Microsoft, and, while it
might be encountered in existing systems, it should not be used for new development.

The first thing to do is create an XmlSchemaCollection to hold our XSD (*book.xsd*):

```
// create XSD schema collection with book.xsd
XmlSchemaCollection schemaCollection = new XmlSchemaCollection( );
// wire up handler to get any validation errors
schemaCollection.ValidationEventHandler +=
    new ValidationEventHandler(ValidationCallBack);
// add book.xsd
schemaCollection.Add(null, @"..\..\Book.xsd");
```

This code also hooks up the schema collection event handler for validation errors to the ValidationCallback function that writes out the validation error message:

```
private static void ValidationCallBack(object sender, ValidationEventArgs e)
{
    Console.WriteLine("Validation Error: {0}", e.Message);
}
```

Once we have the schema collection, we create an XmlTextReader to load the *book.xml* file and then use the XmlTextReader to create our XmlValidatingReader:

```
// open the book.xml file
XmlTextReader reader = new XmlTextReader(@"..\..\Book.xml");
// set up the validating reader
XmlValidatingReader validReader =
    new XmlValidatingReader(reader);
```

The XmlValidatingReader error handler is also wired up to the ValidationCallback function; we then proceed to roll over the XML document and write out the elements and attributes. Setting the XmlValidationReader.ValidationType to ValidationType.Schema tells the XmlValidatingReader to perform XML Schema validation. To perform DTD validation, use a DTD and ValidationType.DTD, and to perform XDR validation, use an XDR schema and ValidationType.XDR:

```
// set the validation type and add the schema collection
validReader.ValidationType = ValidationType.Schema;
validReader.Schemas.Add(schemaCollection);

// wire up for any validation errors from the validating
// reader
validReader.ValidationEventHandler +=
    new ValidationEventHandler(ValidationCallBack);

// read all nodes and print out
while (validReader.Read( ))
{
    if(validReader.NodeType == XmlNodeType.Element)
    {
        Console.Write("<{0}", validReader.Name);
        while(validReader.MoveToNextAttribute( ))
        {
        Console.Write(" {0}='{1}'",validReader.Name,
            validReader.Value);
        }
```

```
                    Console.Write(">");
                }
                else if(validReader.NodeType == XmlNodeType.Text)
                {
                    Console.Write(validReader.Value);
                }
                else if(validReader.NodeType == XmlNodeType.EndElement)
                {
                    Console.WriteLine("</{0}>",validReader.Name);
                }
            }
        }
```

The *book.xml* file contains the following:

```
<?xml version="1.0" encoding="utf-8"?>
<Book xmlns="http://tempuri.org/Book.xsd" name="C# Cookbook">
    <Chapter>File System IO</Chapter>
    <Chapter>Security</Chapter>
    <Chapter>Data Structures and Algorithms</Chapter>
    <Chapter>Reflection</Chapter>
    <Chapter>Threading</Chapter>
    <Chapter>Numbers</Chapter>
    <Chapter>Strings</Chapter>
    <Chapter>Classes And Structures</Chapter>
    <Chapter>Collections</Chapter>
    <Chapter>XML</Chapter>
    <Chapter>Delegates And Events</Chapter>
    <Chapter>Diagnostics</Chapter>
    <Chapter>Enums</Chapter>
    <Chapter>Unsafe Code</Chapter>
    <Chapter>Regular Expressions</Chapter>
</Book>
```

The *book.xsd* file contains the following:

```
<?xml version="1.0" ?>
<xs:schema id="NewDataSet" targetNamespace="http://tempuri.org/Book.xsd" xmlns:
mstns="http://tempuri.org/Book.xsd"
    xmlns="http://tempuri.org/Book.xsd"
    xmlns:xs="http://www.w3.org/2001/XMLSchema"
    xmlns:msdata="urn:schemas-microsoft-com:xml-msdata"
    attributeFormDefault="qualified" elementFormDefault="qualified">
    <xs:element name="Book">
        <xs:complexType>
            <xs:sequence>
                <xs:element name="Chapter" nillable="true"
                            minOccurs="0" maxOccurs="unbounded">
                    <xs:complexType>
                        <xs:simpleContent
msdata:ColumnName="Chapter_Text" msdata:Ordinal="0">
                            <xs:extension base="xs:string">
                            </xs:extension>
                        </xs:simpleContent>
                    </xs:complexType>
                </xs:element>
            </xs:sequence>
```

```
        <xs:attribute name="name" form="unqualified" type="xs:string"/>
      </xs:complexType>
    </xs:element>
  </xs:schema>
```

See Also

See the "XmlValidatingReader Class," "XmlSchemaCollection Class," "Validation-EventHandler Class," "ValidationType Enumeration," and "Introduction to XML Schemas" topics in the MSDN documentation.

17.5 Creating an XML Document Programmatically

Problem

You have data that you want to put into a more structured form, such as an XML document.

Solution

Suppose you have the following information for an address book that you want to turn into XML:

Name	Phone
Tim	999-888-0000
Newman	666-666-6666
Harold	777-555-3333

Use the XmlTextWriter to create XML for this table:

```
XmlTextWriter writer = new XmlTextWriter(Console.Out);
writer.Formatting = Formatting.Indented;
writer.WriteStartElement("AddressBook");
writer.WriteStartElement("Contact");
writer.WriteAttributeString("name", "Tim");
writer.WriteAttributeString("phone", "999-888-0000");
writer.WriteEndElement( );
writer.WriteStartElement("Contact");
writer.WriteAttributeString("name", "Newman");
writer.WriteAttributeString("phone", "666-666-6666");
writer.WriteEndElement( );
writer.WriteStartElement("Contact");
writer.WriteAttributeString("name", "Harold");
writer.WriteAttributeString("phone", "777-555-3333");
writer.WriteEndElement( );
writer.WriteEndElement( );
writer.Close( );
```

Or you can use the XmlDocument class to programmatically construct XML from other data:

```
public static void CreateXML()
{
    // Start by making an XmlDocument
    XmlDocument xmlDoc = new XmlDocument();
    // create a root node for the document
    XmlElement addrBook = xmlDoc.CreateElement("AddressBook");
    xmlDoc.AppendChild(addrBook);
    // create the Tim contact
    XmlElement contact = xmlDoc.CreateElement("Contact");
    contact.SetAttribute("name","Tim");
    contact.SetAttribute("phone","999-888-0000");
    addrBook.AppendChild(contact);
    // create the Newman contact
    contact = xmlDoc.CreateElement("Contact");
    contact.SetAttribute("name","Newman");
    contact.SetAttribute("phone","666-666-6666");
    addrBook.AppendChild(contact);
    // create the Harold contact
    contact = xmlDoc.CreateElement("Contact");
    contact.SetAttribute("name","Harold");
    contact.SetAttribute("phone","777-555-3333");
    addrBook.AppendChild(contact);

    // Display XML
    Console.WriteLine("Generated XML:\r\n{0}",addrBook.OuterXml);
    Console.WriteLine();
}
```

Both of these methods generate XML that looks like this:

```
<AddressBook>
    <Contact name="Tim" phone="999-888-0000" />
    <Contact name="Newman" phone="666-666-6666" />
    <Contact name="Harold" phone="777-555-3333" />
</AddressBook>
```

Discussion

Now that you have seen two ways to do this, the question arises: "Which one to use?" The XMLDocument uses the traditional DOM method of interacting with XML, while the XmlTextReader/XmlTextWriter combination deals with XML in a streaming format. If you are dealing with larger documents, you are probably better off using the XmlTextReader/XmlTextWriter combination than the XmlDocument. The XmlTextReader/XmlTextWriter combination is the better-performing of the two when you do not need the whole document in memory. If you need the power of being able to traverse back over what you have written already, use XmlDocument.

XmlDocument is the class that implements the DOM model for XML processing in the .NET Framework. The DOM holds all of the nodes in the XML in memory at the same time, which enables tree traversal both forward and backward. DOM also allows for a writable interface to the whole XML document, which other XML classes do not provide in .NET. XmlDocument allows you to manipulate any aspect of the XML tree, is eligible to be used for XSLT transformations via the XslTransform class through its support of the IXPathNavigable interface, and allows you to run XPath queries against the document without having to create an XPathDocument first.

See Also

See the "XmlDocument Class," "XML Document Object Model (DOM)," "Xsl-Transform Class," and "IXPathNavigable Interface" topics in the MSDN documentation.

17.6   Detecting Changes to an XML Document

Problem

You need to inform one or more classes or components that a node in an XML document has been inserted, removed, or had its value changed.

Solution

In order to track changes to an active XML document, subscribe to the events published by the XmlDocument class. XmlDocument publishes events for node creation, insertion, and removal for both the pre- and post-conditions of these actions. In the following example, we have a number of event handlers defined in the same scope as the DetectXMLChanges method, but they could just as easily be callbacks to functions on other classes that are interested in the manipulation of the live XML document.

DetectXMLChanges loads an XML fragment we define in the method, wires up the event handlers for the node events, adds, changes, and removes some nodes to trigger the events, then writes out the resulting XML:

```
public static void DetectXMLChanges()
{
    string xmlFragment = "<?xml version='1.0'?>" +
        "<!-- My sample XML -->" +
        "<?pi myProcessingInstruction?>" +
        "<Root>" +
        "<Node1 nodeId='1'>First Node</Node1>" +
        "<Node2 nodeId='2'>Second Node</Node2>" +
        "<Node3 nodeId='3'>Third Node</Node3>" +
        @"<Node4><![CDATA[<>\&']]></Node4>" +
        "</Root>";

    XmlDocument doc = new XmlDocument();
    doc.LoadXml(xmlFragment);
```

```
        //Create the event handlers.
        doc.NodeChanging += new XmlNodeChangedEventHandler(NodeChangingEvent);
        doc.NodeChanged += new XmlNodeChangedEventHandler(NodeChangedEvent);
        doc.NodeInserting += new XmlNodeChangedEventHandler(NodeInsertingEvent);
        doc.NodeInserted += new XmlNodeChangedEventHandler(NodeInsertedEvent);
        doc.NodeRemoving += new XmlNodeChangedEventHandler(NodeRemovingEvent);
        doc.NodeRemoved += new XmlNodeChangedEventHandler(NodeRemovedEvent);

        // Add a new element node.
        XmlElement elem = doc.CreateElement("Node5");
        XmlText text = doc.CreateTextNode("Fifth Element");
        doc.DocumentElement.AppendChild(elem);
        doc.DocumentElement.LastChild.AppendChild(text);

        // Change the first node
        doc.DocumentElement.FirstChild.InnerText = "1st Node";

        // remove the fourth node
        XmlNodeList nodes = doc.DocumentElement.ChildNodes;
        foreach(XmlNode node in nodes)
        {
            if(node.Name == "Node4")
            {
                doc.DocumentElement.RemoveChild(node);
                break;
            }
        }

        // write out the new xml
        Console.WriteLine(doc.OuterXml);
    }
```

These are the event handlers from the XmlDocument along with one formatting method, WriteNodeInfo, that takes an action string and gets the name and value of the node being manipulated. All of the event handlers invoke this formatting method, passing the corresponding action string:

```
    private static void WriteNodeInfo(string action, XmlNode node)
    {
        if (node.Value != null)
        {
            Console.WriteLine("Element: <{0}> {1} with value {2}",
                node.Name,action,node.Value);
        }
        else
            Console.WriteLine("Element: <{0}> {1} with null value",
                node.Name,action);
    }

    public static void NodeChangingEvent(object source, XmlNodeChangedEventArgs e)
    {
        WriteNodeInfo("changing",e.Node);
    }
```

```
public static void NodeChangedEvent(object source, XmlNodeChangedEventArgs e)
{
    WriteNodeInfo("changed",e.Node);
}

public static void NodeInsertingEvent(object source, XmlNodeChangedEventArgs e)
{
    WriteNodeInfo("inserting",e.Node);
}

public static void NodeInsertedEvent(object source, XmlNodeChangedEventArgs e)
{
    WriteNodeInfo("inserted",e.Node);
}

public static void NodeRemovingEvent(object source, XmlNodeChangedEventArgs e)
{
    WriteNodeInfo("removing",e.Node);
}

public static void NodeRemovedEvent(object source, XmlNodeChangedEventArgs e)
{
    WriteNodeInfo("removed",e.Node);
}
```

The DetectXmlChanges method results in the following output:

```
Element: <Node5> inserting with null value
Element: <Node5> inserted with null value
Element: <#text> inserting with value Fifth Element
Element: <#text> inserted with value Fifth Element
Element: <#text> changing with value First Node
Element: <#text> changed with value 1st Node
Element: <Node4> removing with null value
Element: <Node4> removed with null value
<?xml version="1.0"?><!-- My sample XML --><?pi myProcessingInstruction?><Root><
Node1 nodeId="1">1st Node</Node1><Node2 nodeId="2">Second Node</Node2><Node3 nod
eId="3">Third Node</Node3><Node5>Fifth Element</Node5></Root>
```

Discussion

With an XmlDocument, you can traverse both forward and backward on the XML stream, as well as use XPath navigation to find nodes. If you are just reading XML and not modifying it, and you have no need for traversing backward through the nodes, you should avoid using XmlDocument, since XmlTextReader is faster for reading and XmlTextWriter is faster for writing (both have less overhead than XmlDocument). The .NET Framework team did a nice job of giving XML processing flexibility, but if you use a class with more functionality than you need, you will pay the resulting performance penalty.

See Also

See the "XmlDocument Class" and "XmlNodeChangedEventHandler Class" topics in the MSDN documentation.

17.7 Handling Invalid Characters in an XML String

Problem

You are creating an XML string. Before adding a tag containing a text element, you want to check it to determine whether the string contains any of the following invalid characters:

```
<
>
\"
\'
&
```

If any of these characters are encountered, you want them to be replaced with their escaped form:

```
&lt;
&gt;
&quot;
&apos;
&amp;
```

Solution

There are different methods to accomplish this, depending on which XML creation approach you are using. If you are using XmlTextWriter, the WriteCData and WriteElementString methods take care of this for you. If you are using XmlDocument and XmlElements, the XmlElement.InnerXML and XmlElement.InnerText methods will handle these characters.

The two ways to handle this using an XmlTextWriter work like this. The WriteCData method will wrap the invalid character text in a CDATA section, as shown in the creation of the InvalidChars1 element in the example that follows. The other method, using XmlTextWriter, is to use the WriteElementString method that will automatically escape the text for you, as shown while creating the InvalidChars2 element:

```
// set up a string with our invalid chars
string invalidChars = @"<>\&'";
XmlTextWriter writer = new XmlTextWriter(Console.Out);
writer.WriteStartElement("Root");
writer.WriteStartElement("InvalidChars1");
writer.WriteCData(invalidChars);
writer.WriteEndElement();
writer.WriteElementString("InvalidChars2",invalidChars);
writer.WriteEndElement();
writer.Close();
```

The output from this is:

```
<Root>
    <InvalidChars1><![CDATA[<>\&']]></InvalidChars1>
    <InvalidChars2>&lt;&gt;\&amp;'</InvalidChars2>
</Root>
```

The two ways you can handle this problem with XmlDocument and XmlElement are as follows: the first way is to surround the text you are adding to the XML element with a CDATA section, and add it to the InnerXML property of the XmlElement like this:

```
// set up a string with our invalid chars
string invalidChars = @"<>\&'";
XmlElement invalidElement1 = xmlDoc.CreateElement("InvalidChars1");
invalidElement1.InnerXml = "<![CDATA[" + invalidChars + "]]>";
```

The second way is to let the XmlElement class escape the data for you by assigning the text directly to the InnerText property like this:

```
// set up a string with our invalid chars
string invalidChars = @"<>\&'";
XmlElement invalidElement2 = xmlDoc.CreateElement("InvalidChars2");
invalidElement2.InnerText = invalidChars;
```

The whole XmlDocument is created with these XmlElements in this code:

```
public static void HandlingInvalidChars()
{
    // set up a string with our invalid chars
    string invalidChars = @"<>\&'";

    XmlDocument xmlDoc = new XmlDocument();
    // create a root node for the document
    XmlElement root = xmlDoc.CreateElement("Root");
    xmlDoc.AppendChild(root);

    // create the first invalid character node
    XmlElement invalidElement1 = xmlDoc.CreateElement("InvalidChars1");
    // wrap the invalid chars in a CDATA section and use the
    // InnerXML property to assign the value as it doesn't
    // escape the values, just passes in the text provided
    invalidElement1.InnerXml = "<![CDATA[" + invalidChars + "]]>";
    // append the element to the root node
    root.AppendChild(invalidElement1);

    // create the second invalid character node
    XmlElement invalidElement2 = xmlDoc.CreateElement("InvalidChars2");
    // Add the invalid chars directly using the InnerText
    // property to assign the value as it will automatically
    // escape the values
    invalidElement2.InnerText = invalidChars;
    // append the element to the root node
    root.AppendChild(invalidElement2);
```

```
        Console.WriteLine("Generated XML with Invalid Chars:\r\n{0}",xmlDoc.OuterXml);
        Console.WriteLine();
    }
```

The XML created by this procedure (and output to the console) looks like this:

```
<Root>
    <InvalidChars1><![CDATA[<>\&']]></InvalidChars1>
    <InvalidChars2>&lt;&gt;\&amp;'</InvalidChars2>
</Root>
```

Discussion

One of the more interesting types of nodes is the CDATA type of node. A CDATA node allows you to represent the items in the text section as character data, not as escaped XML, for ease of entry. Normally these characters would need to be in their escaped format (< for < and so on) but the CDATA section allows us to enter them as regular text.

When the CDATA tag is used in conjunction with the InnerXML property of the XmlElement class, you can submit characters that would normally need to be escaped first. The XmlElement class also has an InnerText property that will automatically escape any markup found in the string assigned. This allows you to add these characters without having to worry about them.

See Also

See the "XmlDocument Class," "XmlElement Class," and "CDATA Sections" topics in the MSDN documentation.

17.8   Transforming XML to HTML

Problem

You have a raw XML document that you need to convert into a more readable format. For example, you have personnel data that is stored as an XML document and you need to display it on a web page or in a text file. Unfortunately, not everyone wants to sort through reams of XML all day; they would rather read the data as a formatted list or within a grid with defined columns and rows. You need a method of transposing the XML data into a more readable form.

Solution

The solution for this is to use an XSLT stylesheet to transform the XML into another format using the XslTransform class. In the example code, we are transforming some personnel data from a fictitious business stored in *Personnel.xml*. First, we load the stylesheet for generating HTML output, then we perform the transformation to HTML via XSLT using the *PersonnelHTML.xsl* stylesheet. After that, we transform the data to comma-delimited format using the *PersonnelCSV.xsl* stylesheet:

```
public static void TransformXML( )
{
    // Create a resolver with default credentials.
    XmlUrlResolver resolver = new XmlUrlResolver( );
    resolver.Credentials = System.Net.CredentialCache.DefaultCredentials;

    // transform the personnel.xml file to html

    XslTransform transform = new XslTransform( );
    // load up the stylesheet
    transform.Load(@"..\..\PersonnelHTML.xsl",resolver);
    // perform the transformation
    transform.Transform(@"..\..\Personnel.xml",@"..\..\Personnel.html",resolver);

    // transform the personnel.xml file to comma delimited format

    // load up the stylesheet
    transform.Load(@"..\..\PersonnelCSV.xsl",resolver);
    // perform the transformation
    transform.Transform(@"..\..\Personnel.xml",
      @"..\..\Personnel.csv",resolver);

}
```

The *Personnel.xml* file contains the following items:

```
<?xml version="1.0" encoding="utf-8"?>
<Personnel>
    <Employee name="Bob" title="Customer Service" companyYears="1"/>
    <Employee name="Alice" title="Manager" companyYears="12"/>
    <Employee name="Chas" title="Salesman" companyYears="3"/>
    <Employee name="Rutherford" title="CEO" companyYears="27"/>
</Personnel>
```

The *PersonnelHTML.xsl* stylesheet looks like this:

```
<?xml version="1.0" encoding="UTF-8"?>
<xsl:stylesheet version="1.0"
    xmlns:xsl="http://www.w3.org/1999/XSL/Transform"
    xmlns:xs="http://www.w3.org/2001/XMLSchema">
    <xsl:template match="/">
      <html>
        <head />
          <body title="Personnel">
            <xsl:for-each select="Personnel">
              <p>
                <xsl:for-each select="Employee">
                    <xsl:if test="position( )=1">
                        <table border="1">
                            <thead>
                                <tr>
                                    <td>Employee Name</td>
                                    <td>Employee Title</td>
                                    <td>Years with Company</td>
```

```
                            </tr>
                          </thead>
                          <tbody>
                            <xsl:for-each select="../Employee">
                              <tr>
                                <td>
                                  <xsl:for-each select="@name">
                                      <xsl:value-of select="." />
                                  </xsl:for-each>
                                </td>
                                <td>
                                  <xsl:for-each select="@title">
                                      <xsl:value-of select="." />
                                  </xsl:for-each>
                                </td>
                                <td>
                                  <xsl:for-each select="@companyYears">
                                      <xsl:value-of select="." />
                                  </xsl:for-each>
                                </td>
                              </tr>
                            </xsl:for-each>
                          </tbody>
                        </table>
                      </xsl:if>
                    </xsl:for-each>
                  </p>
                </xsl:for-each>
              </body>
            </html>
          </xsl:template>
        </xsl:stylesheet>
```

The output from the *PersonnelHTML.xsl* stylesheet and the *Personnel.xml* generates the HTML shown in Figure 17-1.

Employee name	Employee title	Year with company
Bob	Customer service	1
Alice	Manager	12
Chas	Salesman	3
Rutherford	CEO	27

Figure 17-1. Personnel HTML table generated from Personnel.xml

Here is the HTML source:

```
<html xmlns:xs="http://www.w3.org/2001/XMLSchema">
  <head>
    <META http-equiv="Content-Type" content="text/html; charset=utf-8">
```

```
      </head>
    <body title="Personnel">
      <p>
        <table border="1">
          <thead>
            <tr>
              <td>Employee Name</td>
              <td>Employee Title</td>
              <td>Years with Company</td>
            </tr>
          </thead>
          <tbody>
            <tr>
              <td>Bob</td>
              <td>Customer Service</td>
              <td>1</td>
            </tr>
            <tr>
              <td>Alice</td>
              <td>Manager</td>
              <td>12</td>
            </tr>
            <tr>
              <td>Chas</td>
              <td>Salesman</td>
              <td>3</td>
            </tr>
            <tr>
              <td>Rutherford</td>
              <td>CEO</td>
              <td>27</td>
            </tr>
          </tbody>
        </table>
      </p>
    </body>
  </html>
```

The comma-delimited output is generated using *PersonnelCSV.xsl* and *Personnel.xml*; the stylesheet is shown here:

```
<?xml version="1.0" encoding="UTF-8"?>
<xsl:stylesheet version="1.0" xmlns:xsl="http://www.w3.org/1999/XSL/Transform" xmlns:
xs="http://www.w3.org/2001/XMLSchema">
<xsl:output method="text" encoding="UTF-8"/>
    <xsl:template match="/">
                <xsl:for-each select="Personnel">
                    <xsl:for-each select="Employee">
                        <xsl:for-each select="@name">
                            <xsl:value-of select="." />
                        </xsl:for-each>,<xsl:for-each select="@title">
                            <xsl:value-of select="." />
                        </xsl:for-each>,<xsl:for-each select="@companyYears">
                            <xsl:value-of select="." />
                        </xsl:for-each>
```

```
            <xsl:text> &#xd;&#xa;</xsl:text>
          </xsl:for-each>
        </xsl:for-each>
    </xsl:template>
  </xsl:stylesheet>
```

The output from the *PersonnelCSV.xsl* stylesheet is shown here:

```
Bob,Customer Service,1
Alice,Manager,12
Chas,Salesman,3
Rutherford,CEO,27
```

Discussion

There are many overrides for the XslTransform.Transform method. As of .NET 1.1, the majority of these are now marked as obsolete because they do not take an XmlResolver as one of the parameters. If you attempt to use one of these overloads without an XmlResolver, the compiler will issue a warning:

```
xml.cs(354,13): warning CS0618: 'System.Xml.Xsl.XslTransform.Transform(string,
string)' is obsolete: 'You should pass XmlResolver to Transform( ) method'
```

Since XmlResolver is an abstract class, you need to either use the XmlUrlResolver, the XmlSecureResolver, or pass null as the XmlResolver typed argument. The XmlUrlResolver will resolve URLs to external resources, such as schema files, using the *file*, *http*, and *https* protocols. The XmlSecureResolver restricts the resources that you can access by requiring you to pass in evidence, which helps prevent cross-domain redirection in XML. If you are accepting XML from the Internet, it could easily have a redirection in it to a site where malicious XML would be waiting to be downloaded and executed if you were not using the XmlSecureResolver. If you pass null for the XmlResolver, you are saying you do not want to resolve any external resources. Microsoft has declared the null option to be obsolete, and it shouldn't be used anyway since you should always use some type of XmlResolver.

XSLT is a very powerful technology that allows you to transform XML into just about any format you can think of, but it can be frustrating at times. The simple need of a carriage return/linefeed combination in the XSLT output was such a trial that we were able to find over 20 different message board requests for help on how to do this! After looking at the W3C spec for XSLT, we found you could do this using the xsl:text element like this:

```
<xsl:text> &#xd;&#xa;</xsl:text>
```

The & xd; stands for a hexadecimal 13, or a carriage return, and the & xa; stands for a hexadecimal 10, or a linefeed. This is output at the end of each employee's data from the XML.

See Also

See the "XslTransform Class," "XmlResolver Class," "XmlUrlResolver Class," "XmlSecureResolver Class," and "xsl:text" topics in the MSDN documentation.

17.9 Tearing Apart an XML Document

Problem

You have an XML document that needs to be broken apart into its constituent parts. Each part can then be sent to a different destination (possibly a web service) to be processed individually. This solution is useful when you have a large document, such as an invoice, in XML form. For example, with an invoice, you would want to tear off the billing information and send this to accounting while sending the shipping information to shipping, and then send the invoice items to fulfillment to be processed.

Solution

In order to separate the invoice items, we will load an XmlDocument with the invoice XML from the *Invoice.xml* file:

```
<?xml version="1.0" encoding="UTF-8"?>
<Invoice invoiceDate='2003-10-05' invoiceNumber='INV-01'>
    <shipInfo>
        <name>Beerly Standing</name>
        <attn>Receiving</attn>
        <street>47 South Street</street>
        <city>Intox</city>
        <state>NH</state>
    </shipInfo>
    <billInfo>
        <name>Beerly Standing</name>
        <attn>Accounting</attn>
        <street>98 North Street</street>
        <city>Intox</city>
        <state>NH</state>
    </billInfo>
    <Items>
        <item partNum="98745">
            <productName>Brown Eyed Stout</productName>
            <quantity>12</quantity>
            <price>23.99</price>
            <shipDate>2003-12-20</shipDate>
        </item>
        <item partNum="34987">
            <productName>Diamond Pearl Lager</productName>
            <quantity>22</quantity>
            <price>35.98</price>
            <shipDate>2003-12-20</shipDate>
        </item>
        <item partNum="AK254">
            <productName>Job Site Ale</productName>
            <quantity>50</quantity>
            <price>12.56</price>
            <shipDate>2003-11-12</shipDate>
        </item>
    </Items>
</Invoice>
```

The code to tear this invoice apart, and send the various information pieces to their respective departments, is shown here:

```csharp
public static void ProcessInvoice()
{
    XmlDocument xmlDoc = new XmlDocument();
    // pick up invoice from deposited directory
    xmlDoc.Load(@"..\..\Invoice.xml");
    // get the Invoice element node
    XmlNode Invoice = xmlDoc.SelectSingleNode("/Invoice");

    // get the invoice date attribute
    XmlAttribute invDate =
        (XmlAttribute)Invoice.Attributes.GetNamedItem("invoiceDate");
    // get the invoice number attribute
    XmlAttribute invNum =
        (XmlAttribute)Invoice.Attributes.GetNamedItem("invoiceNumber");

    // Process the billing information to Accounting
    XmlElement billingEnvelope = xmlDoc.CreateElement("BillingEnvelope");

    // correlate this information back to the original invoice number and date
    billingEnvelope.Attributes.Append((XmlAttribute)invDate.Clone());
    billingEnvelope.Attributes.Append((XmlAttribute)invNum.Clone());

    XmlNodeList billList = xmlDoc.SelectNodes("/Invoice/billInfo");
    // add the billing information to the envelope
    foreach(XmlNode billInfo in billList)
    {
        billingEnvelope.AppendChild(billInfo.Clone());
    }
    Console.WriteLine("BillingEnvelope:\r\n{0}",billingEnvelope.OuterXml);

    // Save a copy of the envelope
    FileStream fileStream = File.Create(@"..\..\BillingEnvelope.xml");
    byte [] bytes = Encoding.ASCII.GetBytes(billingEnvelope.OuterXml);
    fileStream.Write(bytes,0,bytes.Length);
    fileStream.Close();

    // Process the shipping information to Shipping
    XmlElement shippingEnvelope = xmlDoc.CreateElement("ShippingEnvelope");
    // correlate this information back to the original invoice number and date
    shippingEnvelope.Attributes.Append((XmlAttribute)invDate.Clone());
    shippingEnvelope.Attributes.Append((XmlAttribute)invNum.Clone());

    XmlNodeList shipList = xmlDoc.SelectNodes("/Invoice/shipInfo");
    // add the shipping information to the envelope
    foreach(XmlNode shipInfo in shipList)
    {
        shippingEnvelope.AppendChild(shipInfo.Clone());
    }
    Console.WriteLine("ShippingEnvelope:\r\n{0}",shippingEnvelope.OuterXml);
```

```
    // Save a copy of the envelope
    fileStream = File.Create(@"..\..\ShippingEnvelope.xml");
    bytes = Encoding.ASCII.GetBytes(shippingEnvelope.OuterXml);
    fileStream.Write(bytes,0,bytes.Length);
    fileStream.Close();

    // Process the item information to Fulfillment
    XmlElement fulfillmentEnvelope = xmlDoc.CreateElement("FulfillmentEnvelope");
    // correlate this information back to the original invoice number and date
    fulfillmentEnvelope.Attributes.Append((XmlAttribute)invDate.Clone());
    fulfillmentEnvelope.Attributes.Append((XmlAttribute)invNum.Clone());

    XmlNodeList itemList = xmlDoc.SelectNodes("/Invoice/Items/item");
    // add the item information to the envelope
    foreach(XmlNode item in itemList)
    {
        fulfillmentEnvelope.AppendChild(item.Clone());
    }
    Console.WriteLine("FulfillmentEnvelope:\r\n{0}",fulfillmentEnvelope.OuterXml);

    // Save a copy of the envelope
    fileStream = File.Create(@"..\..\FulfillmentEnvelope.xml");
    bytes = Encoding.ASCII.GetBytes(fulfillmentEnvelope.OuterXml);
    fileStream.Write(bytes,0,bytes.Length);
    fileStream.Close();

    // Now send the data to the web services ...
}
```

The "envelopes" containing the various pieces of XML data for the web services are listed in the following sections:

BillingEnvelope XML

```
<BillingEnvelope invoiceDate="2003-10-05" invoiceNumber="INV-01">
    <billInfo>
        <name>Beerly Standing</name>
        <attn>Accounting</attn>
        <street>98 North Street</street>
        <city>Intox</city>
        <state>NH</state>
    </billInfo>
</BillingEnvelope>
```

ShippingEnvelope XML

```
<ShippingEnvelope invoiceDate="2003-10-05" invoiceNumber="INV-01">
    <shipInfo>
        <name>Beerly Standing</name>
        <attn>Receiving</attn>
        <street>47 South Street</street>
        <city>Intox</city>
        <state>NH</state>
    </shipInfo>
</ShippingEnvelope>
```

FulfillmentEnvelope XML

```
<FulfillmentEnvelope invoiceDate="2003-10-05" invoiceNumber="INV-01">
    <item partNum="98745">
        <productName>Brown Eyed Stout</productName>
        <quantity>12</quantity>
        <price>23.99</price>
        <shipDate>2003-12-20</shipDate>
    </item>
    <item partNum="34987">
        <productName>Diamond Pearl Lager</productName>
        <quantity>22</quantity>
        <price>35.98</price>
        <shipDate>2003-12-20</shipDate>
    </item>
    <item partNum="AK254">
        <productName>Job Site Ale</productName>
        <quantity>50</quantity>
        <price>12.56</price>
        <shipDate>2003-11-12</shipDate>
    </item>
</FulfillmentEnvelope>
```

Discussion

In order to tear apart the invoice, we needed to establish what pieces would go to which departments. The breakdown of this is that each of the envelopes would get the invoice date and invoice number from the main invoice to give context to the information in the envelope. The `billInfo` element and children would go to the `BillingEnvelope`, the `shipInfo` element and children would go to the `ShippingEnvelope`, and the `item` elements would go to the `FulfillmentEnvelope`. Once these envelopes were constructed, they would be sent to the web services for each department that accepts the data to perform their function for this invoice.

In the example program from the solution, we first loaded the *Invoice.xml* file and got the attributes we were going to give to each of the envelopes:

```
XmlDocument xmlDoc = new XmlDocument();
// pick up invoice from deposited directory
xmlDoc.Load(@"..\..\Invoice.xml");
// get the Invoice element node
XmlNode Invoice = xmlDoc.SelectSingleNode("/Invoice");

// get the invoice date attribute
XmlAttribute invDate =
    (XmlAttribute)Invoice.Attributes.GetNamedItem("invoiceDate");
// get the invoice number attribute
XmlAttribute invNum =
    (XmlAttribute)Invoice.Attributes.GetNamedItem("invoiceNumber");
```

Then we established each envelope with the sections of the invoice that matter to the respective functions (the `BillingEnvelope` is handled by Accounting, the `ShippingEnveloper` is handled by Shipping, and the `FulfillmentEnvelope` is handled by Fulfillment, starting with the `BillingEnvelope`:

```
// Process the billing information to Accounting
XmlElement billingEnvelope = xmlDoc.CreateElement("BillingEnvelope");

// correlate this information back to the original invoice number and date
billingEnvelope.Attributes.Append((XmlAttribute)invDate.Clone());
billingEnvelope.Attributes.Append((XmlAttribute)invNum.Clone());

XmlNodeList billList = xmlDoc.SelectNodes("/Invoice/billInfo");
// add the billing information to the envelope
foreach(XmlNode billInfo in billList)
{
    billingEnvelope.AppendChild(billInfo.Clone());
}
Console.WriteLine("BillingEnvelope:\r\n{0}",billingEnvelope.OuterXml);

// Save a copy of the envelope
FileStream fileStream = File.Create(@"..\..\BillingEnvelope.xml");
byte [] bytes = Encoding.ASCII.GetBytes(billingEnvelope.OuterXml);
fileStream.Write(bytes,0,bytes.Length);
fileStream.Close();
```

Then the ShippingEnvelope was created:

```
// Process the shipping information to Shipping
XmlElement shippingEnvelope = xmlDoc.CreateElement("ShippingEnvelope");
// correlate this information back to the original invoice number and date
shippingEnvelope.Attributes.Append((XmlAttribute)invDate.Clone());
shippingEnvelope.Attributes.Append((XmlAttribute)invNum.Clone());

XmlNodeList shipList = xmlDoc.SelectNodes("/Invoice/shipInfo");
// add the shipping information to the envelope
foreach(XmlNode shipInfo in shipList)
{
    shippingEnvelope.AppendChild(shipInfo.Clone());
}
Console.WriteLine("ShippingEnvelope:\r\n{0}",shippingEnvelope.OuterXml);

    // Save a copy of the envelope
    fileStream = File.Create(@"..\..\ShippingEnvelope.xml");
    bytes = Encoding.ASCII.GetBytes(shippingEnvelope.OuterXml);
    fileStream.Write(bytes,0,bytes.Length);
    fileStream.Close();
```

Finally, the FulfillmentEnvelope was created:

```
// Process the item information to Fulfillment
XmlElement fulfillmentEnvelope = xmlDoc.CreateElement("FulfillmentEnvelope");
// correlate this information back to the original invoice number and date
fulfillmentEnvelope.Attributes.Append((XmlAttribute)invDate.Clone());
fulfillmentEnvelope.Attributes.Append((XmlAttribute)invNum.Clone());

XmlNodeList itemList = xmlDoc.SelectNodes("/Invoice/Items/item");
// add the item information to the envelope
foreach(XmlNode item in itemList)
{
    fulfillmentEnvelope.AppendChild(item.Clone());
}
```

```
Console.WriteLine("FulfillmentEnvelope:\r\n{0}",fulfillmentEnvelope.OuterXml);

// Save a copy of the envelope
fileStream = File.Create(@"..\..\FulfillmentEnvelope.xml");
bytes = Encoding.ASCII.GetBytes(fulfillmentEnvelope.OuterXml);
fileStream.Write(bytes,0,bytes.Length);
fileStream.Close( );
```

At this point, each of the envelopes could be posted to the respective web service interfaces.

Note that when we appended the attributes from the Invoice to the envelopes, we called the XmlNode.Clone method on the XmlAttributes. This is done so that each of the elements had their own separate copy. If you do not do this, then the attribute will appear only on the last element it was assigned to.

See Also

See the "XmlDocument Class," "XmlElement Class," and "XmlAttribute Class" topics in the MSDN documentation.

17.10 Putting Together an XML Document

Problem

You have various pieces of a document in XML form that need to be put together to form a single XML document—this is the opposite of what was done in Recipe 17.9. In this case, you have received various pieces of an invoice in XML form. For example, one department sent the shipping information as an XML document, one sent the billing information in XML, and another sent invoice line items, also as an XML document. You need a way to put these XML pieces together to form a single XML invoice document.

Solution

In order to reconstitute the original invoice, we need to reverse the process used to create the pieces of the invoice using multiple XmlDocuments. There are three parts being sent back to us to help in reforming the original invoice XML: *BillingEnvelope.xml*, *ShippingEnvelope.xml*, and *Fulfillment.xml*. These are shown listed in the following sections:

BillingEnvelope XML

```
<BillingEnvelope invoiceDate="2003-10-05" invoiceNumber="INV-01">
    <billInfo>
        <name>Beerly Standing</name>
        <attn>Accounting</attn>
        <street>98 North Street</street>
```

```
            <city>Intox</city>
            <state>NH</state>
        </billInfo>
    </BillingEnvelope>
```

ShippingEnvelope XML

```
<ShippingEnvelope invoiceDate="2003-10-05" invoiceNumber="INV-01">
    <shipInfo>
        <name>Beerly Standing</name>
        <attn>Receiving</attn>
        <street>47 South Street</street>
        <city>Intox</city>
        <state>NH</state>
    </shipInfo>
</ShippingEnvelope>
```

FulfillmentEnvelope XML

```
<FulfillmentEnvelope invoiceDate="2003-10-05" invoiceNumber="INV-01">
    <item partNum="98745">
        <productName>Brown Eyed Stout</productName>
        <quantity>12</quantity>
        <price>23.99</price>
        <shipDate>2003-12-20</shipDate>
    </item>
    <item partNum="34987">
        <productName>Diamond Pearl Lager</productName>
        <quantity>22</quantity>
        <price>35.98</price>
        <shipDate>2003-12-20</shipDate>
    </item>
    <item partNum="AK254">
        <productName>Job Site Ale</productName>
        <quantity>50</quantity>
        <price>12.56</price>
        <shipDate>2003-11-12</shipDate>
    </item>
</FulfillmentEnvelope>
```

To put these back together as a single invoice, we reverse the process we went through to break it apart, while inferring the invoice date and invoice number from the BillingEnvelope to help reestablish the invoice:

```
public static void ReceiveInvoice()
{
    XmlDocument invoice = new XmlDocument();
    XmlDocument billing = new XmlDocument();
    XmlDocument shipping = new XmlDocument();
    XmlDocument fulfillment = new XmlDocument();

    // set up root invoice node
    XmlElement invoiceElement = invoice.CreateElement("Invoice");
    invoice.AppendChild(invoiceElement);
```

```
// load the billing
billing.Load(@"..\..\BillingEnvelope.xml");
// get the invoice date attribute
XmlAttribute invDate =           (XmlAttribute)
  billing.DocumentElement.Attributes.GetNamedItem("invoiceDate");
// get the invoice number attribute
XmlAttribute invNum = (XmlAttribute)
  billing.DocumentElement.Attributes.GetNamedItem("invoiceNumber");
// set up the invoice with this info
invoice.DocumentElement.Attributes.SetNamedItem(invDate.Clone( ));
invoice.DocumentElement.Attributes.SetNamedItem(invNum.Clone( ));
// add the billInfo back in
XmlNodeList billList = billing.SelectNodes("/BillingEnvelope/billInfo");
foreach(XmlNode billInfo in billList)
{
    invoice.DocumentElement.AppendChild(invoice.ImportNode(billInfo,true));
}

// load the shipping
shipping.Load(@"..\..\ShippingEnvelope.xml");
// add the shipInfo back in
XmlNodeList shipList = shipping.SelectNodes("/ShippingEnvelope/shipInfo");
foreach(XmlNode shipInfo in shipList)
{
    invoice.DocumentElement.AppendChild(invoice.ImportNode(shipInfo,true));
}

// load the items
fulfillment.Load(@"..\..\FulfillmentEnvelope.xml");

// Create an Items element in the Invoice to add these under
XmlElement items = invoice.CreateElement("Items");

// add the items back in under Items
XmlNodeList itemList = fulfillment.SelectNodes("/FulfillmentEnvelope/item");
foreach(XmlNode item in itemList)
{
    items.AppendChild(invoice.ImportNode(item,true));
}

// add it in
invoice.DocumentElement.AppendChild(items.Clone( ));

// display Invoice XML
Console.WriteLine("Invoice:\r\n{0}",invoice.OuterXml);

// save our reconstitued invoice
FileStream fileStream = File.Create(@"..\..\ReceivedInvoice.xml");
byte [] bytes = Encoding.ASCII.GetBytes(invoice.OuterXml);
fileStream.Write(bytes,0,bytes.Length);
fileStream.Close( );
}
```

The code reconstitutes the invoice and saves it as *ReceivedInvoice.xml*, the contents of which are shown here:

```xml
<Invoice invoiceDate="2003-10-05" invoiceNumber="INV-01">
    <billInfo>
        <name>Beerly Standing</name>
        <attn>Accounting</attn>
        <street>98 North Street</street>
        <city>Intox</city>
        <state>NH</state>
    </billInfo>
    <shipInfo>
        <name>Beerly Standing</name>
        <attn>Receiving</attn>
        <street>47 South Street</street>
        <city>Intox</city>
        <state>NH</state>
    </shipInfo>
    <Items>
        <item partNum="98745">
            <productName>Brown Eyed Stout</productName>
            <quantity>12</quantity>
            <price>23.99</price>
            <shipDate>2003-12-20</shipDate>
        </item>
        <item partNum="34987">
            <productName>Diamond Pearl Lager</productName>
            <quantity>22</quantity>
            <price>35.98</price>
            <shipDate>2003-12-20</shipDate>
        </item>
        <item partNum="AK254">
            <productName>Job Site Ale</productName>
            <quantity>50</quantity>
            <price>12.56</price>
            <shipDate>2003-11-12</shipDate>
        </item>
    </Items>
</Invoice>
```

Discussion

In the Solution code, the first thing we did was to create a set of XmlDocuments for the Invoice, BillingEnvelope, ShippingEnvelope, and FulfillmentEnvelope. Then we created the new root Invoice element in the invoice XmlDocument:

```csharp
XmlDocument invoice = new XmlDocument();
XmlDocument billing = new XmlDocument();
XmlDocument shipping = new XmlDocument();
XmlDocument fulfillment = new XmlDocument();

// set up root invoice node
XmlElement invoiceElement = invoice.CreateElement("Invoice");
invoice.AppendChild(invoiceElement);
```

Next, we processed the `BillingEnvelope` first, taking the invoice date and number from it and adding it to the Invoice. Then we added the billing information back in to the invoice:

```
// load the billing
billing.Load(@"..\..\BillingEnvelope.xml");
// get the invoice date attribute
XmlAttribute invDate = (XmlAttribute)
 billing.DocumentElement.Attributes.GetNamedItem("invoiceDate");
// get the invoice number attribute
XmlAttribute invNum = (XmlAttribute)
 billing.DocumentElement.Attributes.GetNamedItem("invoiceNumber");
// set up the invoice with this info
invoice.DocumentElement.Attributes.SetNamedItem(invDate.Clone( ));
invoice.DocumentElement.Attributes.SetNamedItem(invNum.Clone( ));
// add the billInfo back in
XmlNodeList billList = billing.SelectNodes("/BillingEnvelope/billInfo");
foreach(XmlNode billInfo in billList)
{
    invoice.DocumentElement.AppendChild(invoice.ImportNode(billInfo,true));
}
```

The `ShippingEnvelope` came next:

```
// load the shipping
shipping.Load(@"..\..\ShippingEnvelope.xml");
// add the shipInfo back in
XmlNodeList shipList = shipping.SelectNodes("/ShippingEnvelope/shipInfo");
foreach(XmlNode shipInfo in shipList)
{
    invoice.DocumentElement.AppendChild(invoice.ImportNode(shipInfo,true));
}
```

And finally, the items from the `FulfillmentEnvelope` were placed back under an Items element under the main Invoice element:

```
// load the items
fulfillment.Load(@"..\..\FulfillmentEnvelope.xml");

// Create an Items element in the Invoice to add these under
XmlElement items = invoice.CreateElement("Items");

// add the items back in under Items
XmlNodeList itemList = fulfillment.SelectNodes("/FulfillmentEnvelope/item");
foreach(XmlNode item in itemList)
{
    items.AppendChild(invoice.ImportNode(item,true));
}

// add it in
invoice.DocumentElement.AppendChild(items.Clone( ));
```

One item to be aware of when dealing with multiple `XmlDocuments` is that when you take a node from one `XmlDocument`, you cannot just append it as a child to a node in a different `XmlDocument` because the node has the context of the original `XmlDocument`. If you try to do this, you will get the following exception message:

```
The node to be inserted is from a different document context.
```

To fix this, use the `XmlDocument.ImportNode` method, which will make a copy (deep or shallow) of the node you are bringing over to the new `XmlDocument`, as shown, when we add the shipping information like so:

```
invoice.DocumentElement.AppendChild(invoice.ImportNode(shipInfo,true));
```

This line takes the `shipInfo` node, clones it deeply, then it appends it to the main invoice node.

See Also

See the "XmlDocument Class," "XmlElement Class," and "XmlAttribute Class" topics in the MSDN documentation.

Index

Symbols

<> (angle brackets), balanced, 492
*= (assignment operator), 99–102
+= (assignment operator), 99–102
-= (assignment operator), 99–102
/= (assignment operator), 99–102
\ (backslash)
    in regular expression patterns, 416
    on command line, 153
& (bitwise AND operator), 110, 236–237, 531, 535
~ (bitwise complement operator), 5
| (bitwise OR operator), 110, 236–237, 531, 535
^ (bitwise XOR operator), 110, 531, 535
{} (braces), balanced, 492
^ (caret), on command line, 153
() (cast operator), 124
(comment character), 418
// (comment characters), 418
?: (conditional operator), 102–105
"" (double quotes), on command line, 153
== (equality operator)
    comparing pointers with, 751
    comparing strings with, 66
    overriding, 108, 278
    Set class, 531, 536
> (greater than operator), 751
>= (greater than or equal operator), 751
- (hyphen)
    in regular expression patterns, 416
    on command line, 153
!= (inequality operator)
    comparing pointers with, 751

    overriding, 108, 278
    Set class, 531, 536
< (less than operator), 751
<= (less than or equal operator), 751
?? (logical AND operator), 102–105
|| (logical OR operator), 102–105
//... (omitted C# code in examples), xx
<!--...--> (omitted XML code in
        examples), xx
() (parentheses)
    balanced, 492
    in equations, 111
; (semicolon), on command line, 153
' (single quotes), on command line, 153
/ (slash), on command line, 153
[] (square brackets), balanced, 492
?: (ternary operator), 112
* (wildcard character), 614

A

abstract base classes, implementing
        polymorphism with, 85–89
AccessException exception, 259
Acos method, Math class, 27
adapter design pattern, 429, 433, 435
Add method
    MultiMap class, 499, 501
    Set class, 530
    SortedList class, 91–95
AddNode method
    BinaryTree class, 509
    BinaryTreeNode class, 510, 513
    NTreeNode class, 520, 524
AddProxyInfoToRequest method, 644

We'd like to hear your suggestions for improving our indexes. Send email to *index@oreilly.com*.

AddRoot method, NTree class, 515, 523
AddUniqueNode method, BinaryTreeNode
    class, 510, 513
AllFlags privilege, 630
AllocateDataSlot method, Thread class, 742,
    744
AllocateNamedDataSlot method, Thread
    class, 742, 744
Allocation Profiler, 223
AmbiguousMatchException exception, 259
angle brackets (<>), balanced, 492
angles
    calculating one angle of triangle, 27
    converting degrees to radians, 3
    converting radians to degrees, 4
AppDomainUnloadedException
    exception, 259
Append method, StringBuilder class, 64
AppendText method
    File class, 550
    FileInfo class, 551
AppendText method, FileInfo class, 551
AppEvents class, 314
application
    command-line parameters for, 150–158
    conditionally compiling blocks
        of, 310–312
    data for, storing securely, 700–706
    event logs for (see event logs)
    performance counters for, 330–333,
        333–336
    persisting collections between
        sessions, 465–466
    processes not responding for,
        determining, 312–313
    production, trace output from, 290–293
    selective debugging and tracing
        for, 294–297
    versioning with multiple entry
        points, 144–145
    versions of modules, comparing, 601–604
application configuration file
    selecting components to trace in, 294,
        296
    selecting level of tracing in, 295, 297
    turning on tracing with, 291–293
ApplicationException exception, 247, 259
Applied Microsoft .NET Framework
    Programming (Richter), 737
AppSpecificSwitch class, 298
AppSpecificSwitchLevel enumeration, 298
arccosine function, 27

arcsine function, 27
arctangent function, 27
ArgumentException exception, 85, 122, 243,
    244, 245, 259, 396
ArgumentNullException exception, 57, 85,
    243, 245, 247, 259, 396, 638
ArgumentOutOfRangeException
    exception, 63, 243, 244, 247, 259
ArithmeticException exception, 259
Array class
    BinarySearch method, 95–99
    Copy method, 445
    Reverse method, 423
    Sort method, 90–95
ArrayList class
    as values in Hashtable, 496–503
    BinarySearch method, 95–99, 435, 439,
        443
    Contains method, 435
    controlling additions to, through
        attributes, 623–626
    counting occurrences of an object type
        in, 435–439
    Hashtable keys or values stored in, 449
    maintaining sort when adding or
        modifying elements, 446–448
    persisting between application
        sessions, 465–466
    retrieving all instances of an object
        type, 439–443
    snapshot of, 460
    Sort method, 90–95
    (see also collections)
ArrayListEx class, 435, 439, 442
arrays, 421
    byte arrays, breaking large numbers
        into, 764
    displaying values as a delimited
        string, 458
    exceptions for, 247, 248
    fixed-size, 421, 755
    inserting elements into, 443–446
    jagged, 421
        navigating with pointer, 754
        reversing, 427
    multidimensional, 421, 754
    navigating with pointers, 753–755
    of objects, nested, 167–174
    of pointers, 758–760
    of pointers to unknown types, 760–762
    pointers to, manipulating, 755
    removing elements from, 443–446

returning pointers to an element
      in, 756–758
reversing order of elements in, 423–425
searching class or structure objects
      in, 95–99
snapshots of, 460
sorting class or structure objects
      in, 90–95
StackTrace class acting as, 429–435
swapping two elements in, 422
two-dimensional, reversing, 425
types of, 421
ArrayTypeMismatchException
      exception, 247, 259
ArrayUtilities class, 444
as operator
      casting with, 125–127
      when to use, 124
ASCII values, byte array of, converting to a
      string, 52
ASCIIEncoding class
      GetBytes method, 53
      GetString method, 52
Asin method, Match class, 27
ASP.NET cache, 181
ASPNET user account, performance counters
      prevented by, 331, 334
ASP.NET, Windows NT 4.0 not
      supporting, xvi
assemblies
      access to types in, controlling, 670–679
      assemblies imported by, listing, 605–607
      attack surface of, minimizing, 711
      CLSCompliantAttribute for, 165
      digital signature for, 708
      exported types of, listing, 607
      inheritance hierarchies of types
            in, 617–619
      loading, exceptions generated by, 257
      malicious modifications to,
            preventing, 708–710
      members in
            finding, 613–614
            retrieving filtered list of, 626–631
      nested types in, finding, 616–617
      permissions for, verifying, 710–711
      reflection and, 605
      regular expressions compiled
            into, 405–407
      serializable types in, finding, 621–622
      strong name for, 708
      subclasses of types in, 619–621

Assembly class
      GetExportedTypes method, 608
      GetReferencedAssemblies method, 606,
            607
      LoadFrom method, 257
assembly registration tool, 158
Assert method
      CodeAccessSecurity class, 706, 707
      Debug class, 245
assignment operators, overloading, 99–102
Associative Law, 114
asterisk (*) as wildcard character, 614
AsymmetricAlgorithm class, Clear
            method, 688
AsyncAction class, 288, 723, 726, 729
asynchronous delegates
      exceptions thrown by, 288
      notification of completion, 729–731
      polling, 723–726
      synchronous delegates converted
            to, 348–351
      timing out, 726–728
Atan method, Math class, 27
attributes
      custom, exceptions for, 247
      of files, 541, 542, 568
Attributes property, DirectoryInfo class, 568
Attributes property, FileInfo class, 541, 542
AverageCount64 counter, 335
AverageTimer32 counter, 336

B

backslash (\)
      in regular expression patterns, 416
      on command line, 153
BadImageFormatException exception, 257,
            259
Balance class, 492
base 10, converting to, from another base, 9
base classes, overridden methods in, listing
            for derived class, 609–612
Base64 data
      decoding into byte array, 50
      encoding byte array as, 49
Base64DecodeString method, 50
Base64EncodeBytes method, 49
BeginInvoke method, 725, 729
BetterRandomString method, 699
big-endian format, 765
binary data
      decoding Base64 data into, 50
      encoding as a string, 49

binary trees, 503–514
BinaryReader class, 545, 551
    PeekChar method, 564
    Read method, 564
BinarySearch method
    Array class, 95–99
    ArrayList class, 95–99, 435, 439, 443
    PriorityQueue class, 479
    Set class, 531
BinarySearchAll method, 439
BinarySearchCountAll method, 435
BinaryTree class, 503, 509, 512
BinaryTreeNode class, 505, 509, 512
BinaryWriter class, 545, 551, 562
BindingFlags enumeration, 366, 626, 629
bit flags
    in enumerations, testing, 235–237
    turning on or off, 108–111
BitArray class, 420
    (see also collections)
bitmaps (see binary data; byte array)
bitmask, 109, 232–237
bitwise AND operator (&), 110, 236–237,
    531, 535
bitwise complement operator (~), 5
bitwise OR operator (|), 110, 236–237, 531,
    535
bitwise XOR operator (^), 110, 531, 535
blittable objects, 71
books
    about adapter design pattern, 435
    about C#, xix
    about design patterns, 679
    about HTTP, 642
    about .NET Framework
        programming, 737
    about regular expressions, 418
    about security, 712
    about Visual Studio .NET, xix
bool data type, 1
Boolean equations
    ensuring correctness of, 111–113
    simplifying, 114–116
boolean values, conversions to, 55–58, 119,
    120
BooleanSwitch class, controlling tracing
        with, 294, 296
boxing, 74
    finding where it occurs, 221–223
    preventing, 222
braces ({}), balanced, 492

brackets (see angle brackets; braces; square
        brackets)
BreadthFirstSearch method, NTreeNode
        class, 520, 524
BuildDependentAssemblyList method, 606
byte array
    breaking large numbers into, 764
    converting to a string, 51
    decoding Base64 data into, 50
    encoding as a string, 49
    passing strings to methods as, 53–54
byte data type, 1, 766–768

C

C# in a Nutshell (O'Reilly), xix
C# language, xv
    books about, xix
    specification for, 6
    web sites with sample code for, xv, xvi
C language, compared to C#, xv
C++ language, compared to C#, xv
C# Language Pocket Reference
        (O'Reilly), xix
cache
    ASP.NET, 181
    for objects, 181–191
caching, 189
CalcHash method, 472
calculated hash algorithm, 471
calculations, ensuring correctness
        of, 111–113
CallbackAsyncDelegate method, 729, 730
callbacks
    delegates implementing, 139, 729–731
    interfaces used for, 136–144
CallBackThroughIFace method, 137, 143
CallCOMMethod method, 240
CallNextHookEx function, 385
CallSecureFunctionSafelyAndEfficiently
        method, 706, 707
CannotUnloadAppDomainException
        exception, 259
Capacity property, StringBuilder class, 69,
        70
caret (^), on command line, 153
CAS (Code Access Security), 670, 746
case sensitivity
    comparing characters using, 33
    comparing strings using, 43
    searching for strings at head or tail of
        string using, 44

searching for strings within strings
    using, 37–41
cast operator (()), 124
casting
    as operator used for, 124, 125–127
    cast operator (()) used for, 124
    exceptions thrown as result of, 120
    is operator used for, 124
    predetermining success of, with is
        operator, 127–130
    to narrower data type, 15–25
catch blocks, 239–241
    multiple, handling exceptions
        individually, 249–251
    preventing unhandled exceptions
        with, 263–265
    within finally blocks, 251–254
    (see also exception handling)
CDATA nodes, 786
Celsius
    converting Fahrenheit to, 14
    converting to Fahrenheit, 14
char data type, 1, 766–768
characters
    byte array of, converting to a string, 51
    case-sensitive or case-insensitive, 33
    comparison operators and, 32
    conversions to, 55–58, 119, 120
    ensuring maximum number in string, 63
    inserting into strings, 45–46
    iterating over characters in string, 64
    removing from head or tail of string, 72
    removing or replacing within a
        string, 46–49
    searching strings for, 35–36, 39
    type of, determining, 28–32
    within a range, determining, 32
CharKind enumeration, 29
Check for Arithmetic Overflow/Underflow
    project property, 24
Check method, Balance class, 492
/checked compiler switch, 24
checked context, 24, 118
checked keyword, 15, 24
CheckPassword method, 704, 705
CheckUserEnteredPath method, 581
Children property, NTreeNode class, 520
classes
    abstract base classes, 85–89
    base classes, 609–612
    cloneable, 174–177
    COM objects using, 158–162

concrete classes, 89
    Equals method for, overloading, 105
    operating as union types, 76
    overridden methods in, listing, 609–612
    performance of, 73
    polymorphism for, 85–89, 130–133
    represented as a string, 77–83
    sealed, adding events to, 351–357
    single instance of, 191–195
    static fields, initializing, 284–288
    when to use, 74
    (see also objects)
Clear method
    AsymmetricAlgorithm class, 688
    classes using, 218
    DblQueue class, 488
    MultiMap class, 499, 502
    PriorityQueue class, 479
    SymmetricAlgorithm class, 688
ClientABC class, 144
Clone method
    DblQueue class, 488
    MultiMap class, 499
    PriorityQueue class, 479
    XmlNode class, 796
cloneable classes, 174–177
cloning, 176
Close method, 218
CLS compliance
    ensuring compatibility with managed
        languages, 165
    simple types not conforming to, 2
CLSCompliantAttribute for assembly, 165
coarse-grained exception handling, 239
Code Access Security (CAS), 670, 746
Code Access Security in Practice (Microsoft
    Patterns & Practices Group), 712
code samples, xx
    in this book, system requirements for, xvi
    permission requirements, xx
    web sites for, xv, xvi
CollectionBase abstract base class, 461–464
collections, 420
    displaying values as a delimited
        string, 458
    persisting between application
        sessions, 465–466
    StackTrace class acting as, 429–435
    strongly typed (restricted to specific data
        type), 461–464
    types of, 420

CollectionsUtil class, 421
COM components
    exceptions for, 247, 258–262
    releasing, 180
    user-defined exceptions for, 262
    using C# classes, 158–162
COMException exception, 247, 259, 262
command-line parameters, parsing, 150–158
comment characters, 418
comments regarding this book, xxi
Commutative Law, 114
CompanyData class, 671, 678
CompanyDataSecProxy class, 672, 678
CompanyDataTraceProxy class, 675, 679
Compare method, string class, 43, 44
CompareFileVersions method, 601
CompareHeight class, 91
CompareTo method, 503
comparison operators
    characters used with, 32
    pointers and, 751
    Set objects used with, 531, 536
    strings used with, 66
    (see also Equals method)
CompileToAssembly method, Regex
        class, 405–407
compiling
    conditionally, 310–312
    /main switch, 145
    regular expressions, 405–407
ComplexReplace method, 402
component, as source for event log,
        determining, 327–330
ConcatStringGetHashCode method, 472
concrete classes, implementing
        polymorphism with, 89
conditional operator (?:),
        overloading, 102–105
ConditionalAttribute attribute, 311
configuration, exceptions for, 247
configuration files (see application
        configuration file; machine
        configuration file)
ConfigurationException exception, 247
console utilities, reading from and
        responding to, 589
const field, 163–165
constants, initializing at runtime, 163–165
constructors
    default, removing, 146
    overloaded, initializing objects
        with, 146–148

contact information for this book, xxi
contained object cache algorithm, 468
ContainedObjHash method, 469
Container class, 201
Contains method
    ArrayList class, 435
    DblQueue class, 488
    PriorityQueue class, 478, 479
    Set class, 531
    SortedList class, 95–99
Contains method, PriorityQueue class, 479
ContainsKey method
    MultiMap class, 499, 503
    SortedList class, 95–99
ContainsString method, PriorityQueue
        class, 478
ContainsValue method
    MultiMap class, 499, 503
    SortedList class, 95–99
ContextMarshalException exception, 259
control character, determining if character
        is, 28–32
conventions used in this book, xix
Convert class
    FromBase64CharArray method, 50
    ToBase64CharArray method, 49
    ToBoolean method, 119
    ToByte method, 119
    ToChar method, 119
    ToDateTime method, 119
    ToDecimal method, 119
    ToDouble method, 119
    ToInt16 method, 119
    ToInt32 method, 9, 119
    ToInt64 method, 119
    ToSByte method, 119
    ToSingle method, 119
    ToString method, 119
    ToUInt16 method, 119
    ToUInt32 method, 119
    ToUInt64 method, 119
ConvertCollectionToDelStr method, 459
ConvertDegreesToRadians method, 4
ConvertObj method, 125
ConvertRadiansToDegrees method, 4
ConvertToASCIIStringSlow method, 768
ConvertToString method, 766, 767
ConvertToStringSlow method, 767
Copy method
    Array class, 445
    File class, 538

CopyTo method
    DblQueue class, 489
    FileInfo class, 538
    ICollection interface, 460
    PriorityQueue class, 479
Cos method, Math class, 25
cosine function, 26
Count method, MultiMap class, 499
Count property
    DblQueue class, 488
    PriorityQueue class, 479
    Set class, 530
CountAll method, 435
CountChildren method
    BinaryTreeNode class, 510
    NTreeNode class, 520
CounterDelta32 counter, 332
CounterDelta64 counter, 332
CounterMultiTimer counter, 336
CounterMultiTimer100Ns counter, 336
CounterMultiTimer100NsInverse
    counter, 336
CounterMultiTimerInverse counter, 336
counters (see performance counters)
CounterTimer counter, 332
CounterTimerInverse counter, 332
CountImmediateChildren method,
    NTreeNode class, 520
CountPerTimeInterval32 counter, 332
CountPerTimeInterval64 counter, 332
CRC (cyclic redundancy check), 692
Create method
    DirectoryInfo class, 565
    File class, 538, 549
    FileInfo class, 538, 550
CreateAbsoluteUri method, 639
CreateAndHandlePoint method, 128
CreateComplexCounter method, 333
CreateDirectory method, Directory
    class, 565
CreateFile method, 552
CreateHashedPassword method, 702, 705
CreateInternedStr method, 66
CreateLockedFile method, 592
CreateLogFile method, 557
CreateNestedObjects method, 173
CreateNode method, NTreeNodeFactory
    class, 519, 523
CreatePoint method, 127
CreateRegExDLL method, 405
CreateSimpleCounter method, 330
CreateStringHash method, 690, 692

CreateText method, File class, 550
CreationTime property
    DirectoryInfo class, 567, 568
    FileInfo class, 540, 541
credit card number, regular expression
    patterns for, 416
critical sections, locking objects against, 717
CryptographicException exception, 259
CryptographicUnexpectedOperationException
    exception, 259
cryptography (see encryption; security)
CryptoHash method, 469, 470
CryptoHash method algorithm, 469, 470
CryptoStream class, 690
CryptoString class, 680, 682
    Decrypt method, 683
    Encrypt method, 683
    RdGenerateSecretInitVector method, 682
    RdGenerateSecretKey method, 682
CtoF method, 14
currency, formatting strings as, 59
CurrentValue property, NTreeNodeFactory
    class, 519
CustomAttributeFormatException
    exception, 247, 259
cyclic redundancy check (CRC), 692

D

dangling pointers, 750
dash (-)
    in regular expression patterns, 416
    on command line, 153
data
    controlling and tracking access
        to, 670–679
    encrypting (see encryption)
    isolated storage of, 705
    securely storing, 700–706
    synchronizing reading and writing by
        multiple threads, 732–735
    thread-specific, storing privately, 742–745
    (see also files)
data types
    casting (see casting)
    collections restricted to specific data
        type, 461–464
    conversions between, 117–123
        (see also specific data types)
    hash codes for, 467–475
    of variables, determining with is
        operator, 127–130
    simple, 1, 117–123

dates, regular expression patterns for, 416
DateTime object, creating, 542
date/time values, conversions to, 119, 121
DblQueue class, 483, 488
DeadLock class, 718
deadlocks, preventing, 717
Debug class, 290
    Assert method, 245
    interchanging with Trace class, 290
    (see also Trace class)
debugging, 290
    configuring to break on
        exceptions, 282–284
    enabling for specific
        components, 294–297
    (see also tracing)
decimal data type, 1
decorator design pattern, 698
Decrypt method, CryptoString class, 683
deep copying, 174, 176
DeepClone class, 174
#define preprocessor directive, 310, 311
degrees
    converting Celsius to Fahrenheit, 14
    converting Fahrenheit to Celsius, 14
    converting radians to, 4
    converting to radians, 3
DelegateCallback method, 729, 731
delegates, 340
    asynchronous
        exceptions thrown by, 288
        notification of completion, 729–731
        polling, 723–726
        timing out, 726–728
    callbacks implemented by, 139, 729–731
    compared to dynamic invocation using
        reflection, 633
    for keyboard hook callback, 385
    MatchEvaluator, 401–403
    MemberFilter delegate, 369
    multicast
        controlling delegates executed
          in, 340–344
        handling exceptions for each delegate
          in, 346–348
        invocation list for, 343
        return values from each delegate
          in, 344–346
    synchronous, converting to
        asynchronous, 348–351
    TypeFilter delegate, 365
DelegateUtilities class, 346, 349, 350

Delete method
    Directory class, 566
    DirectoryInfo class, 566
    File class, 539
    FileInfo class, 539
Demand method, 706, 707
DemonstrateRenameDir method, 570
DeMorgan's Theorem, 114
DepthFirstSearch method
    BinaryTreeNode class, 510, 513
    NTreeNode class, 520, 524
DequeueHead method, DblQueue class, 489
DequeueLargest method, PriorityQueue
        class, 478, 479
DequeueSmallest method, PriorityQueue
        class, 478, 479
DequeueTail method, DblQueue class, 489
derived classes, overriding methods in,
        listing, 609–612
design patterns
    adapter design pattern, 429, 433
    books about, 435, 679
    decorator design pattern, 698
    dispose design pattern, 214–221
    façade design pattern, 195–200
    iterator design pattern, 204
    memento design pattern, 208–213
    observer design pattern, 376–379
    proxy design pattern, 670, 678
    simple factory design pattern, 337–339
    singleton design pattern, 191–195, 682
Design Patterns: Elements of Reusable Object
        Oriented Software (Gamma, Helm,
        Johnson, Vlissides), 435, 679
DetectXMLChanges method, 781
DevPartner Profiler Community Edition, 223
DevPartner Studio Professional Edition, 223
diagnostics, 290
dictionary collections, 420
difference of set objects, 524, 531, 534, 535
DifferenceOf method, Set class, 531, 535
digit, determining if character is, 28–32
digital signatures, for assemblies, 708
directories
    creating, 565, 567
    deleting, 566, 567
    determining if it exists, 564, 567
    monitoring for changes to, 594–599
    moving, 566, 567
    not existing when creating file, 539
    not found, exceptions for, 247
    renaming, 569–571

searching for, using wildcards, 571–575
timestamps of, manipulating, 567
waiting for changes to, 599–601
(see also files)
Directory class, 565
   CreateDirectory method, 565
   Delete method, 566
   Exists method, 564
   GetCreationTime method, 567
   GetDirectories method, 571, 573, 575
   GetFiles method, 572, 574
   GetFileSystemEntries method, 571, 573, 575
   GetLastAccessTime method, 567
   GetLastWriteTime method, 567
   Move method, 566, 570
   SetCreationTime method, 568
   SetLastAccessTime method, 568
   SetLastWriteTime method, 568
directory trees, retrieving and manipulating, 576
DirectoryInfo class, 565
   Attributes property, 568
   Create method, 565
   creating instance of, 565
   CreationTime property, 567, 568
   Delete method, 566
   GetDirectories method, 573, 574, 575, 576
   GetFiles method, 576
   GetFileSystemInfos method, 572, 574, 575, 576
   LastAccessTime property, 567, 568
   LastWriteTime property, 567, 568
   MoveTo method, 566, 570
DirectoryInfoNotify class, 351, 358
DirectoryInfoObserver class, 353, 360
DirectoryNotFoundException exception, 247, 259, 565
disassembler tool, 221
DisplayDirAttr method, 567
DisplayDirs method, 572, 573, 574
DisplayException method, 265
DisplayFileAttr method, 540
DisplayFiles method, 573, 574
DisplayFilesDirs method, 571, 572, 573, 574
DisplayInheritanceHierarchyType method, 618
DisplayNestedTypes method, 616
DisplaySet method, Set class, 532
DisplayTypeHierarchy method, 617, 618
dispose design pattern, 214–221

Dispose method, 177–180, 217–221
Distributive Law, 114
DivideByZeroException exception, 259
DllNotFoundException exception, 259
.dmp file extension, 571
Dns class, Resolve method, 635, 636
dollar amounts, regular expression patterns for, 416
DOM model, 780
DoReversal method, 423
double data type, 1, 2
double quotes (""), on command line, 153
double-queue, 483–491
DownloadData method, WebClient class, 652
DownloadFile method, WebClient class, 652
DTD, validating XML conformance to, 775–779
dump files, searching for, 571
DuplicateWaitObjectException exception, 259
DynamicInvoke method, 632

E

ElapsedTime counter, 332
elements, in a collection, 420
#elif preprocessor directive, 310, 312
ellipses (...), omitted code in examples, xx
email address
   for this book, xxi
   regular expression patterns for, 416
Encrypt method, CryptoString class, 683
encryption, 688
   clearing key and initialization vector afterwards, 688
   cryptography providers, 684
   digital signatures for assemblies, 708
   of files, 683–688
   random number generator for, 699
   of strings, 679–683
endianness, 765
EndInvoke method, 288, 725
end-of-line character (see EOL character; linefeed character)
EndOfStreamException exception, 259, 564
EndsWith method, string class, 44
EnhancedLog class, 147
Enqueue method, PriorityQueue class, 478, 479
EnqueueHead method, DblQueue class, 489
EnqueueTail method, DblQueue class, 489

EnsureCapacity method, StringBuilder
        class, 71
entry points, multiple, 144–145
EntryPointNotFoundException
        exception, 259
EntryWrittenEventHandler delegate, 327
Enum class
    IsDefined method, 228–229
    Parse method, 227
enumerations, 224
    All member of, 231
    conditional testing of bit flags
            for, 235–237
    converting strings to, 55–58
    converting text of to enumeration
            value, 227
    displaying as strings, 225–227
    exceptions for, 248
    Flags attribute, 232–234
    testing for valid value of, 228–230,
            230–231
    used as bitmask, 232–237
    used as flags, 226, 230–231
enumerators, custom, 201–207
Environment class
    StackTrace method, 280
    StackTrace property, 279
environment variables, parsing paths
        in, 579–581
Environment.NewLine constant, 556
EOL (end-of-line) character, 556
    (see also linefeed character)
equality operator (==)
    comparing pointers with, 751
    comparing strings with, 66
    overriding, 108, 278
    Set class, 531, 536
Equals method, 105, 474
    GetHashCode method as alternative
            to, 467
    improving performance of, 105–108
    overriding for user-defined
            exceptions, 278
    Set class, 531, 536
    string class, 33, 66
equations
    balanced, determining, 492–496
    complex, ensuring correctness
            of, 111–113
    complex, simplifying, 114–116
    (see also calculations)

error handling
    web server errors, 640–642
    (see also exception handling)
ErrorCode property, COMException
        exception, 263
even values, determining if number is, 6
event logs
    custom, maximum size of, 321–322
    monitoring for specific entries, 326–327
    multiple, 314–321
    searching, 322–326
    sources for, determining, 327–330
events
    adding to sealed class, 351–357
    listener for, canceling action that raised an
            event, 357–363
    mouse events, 387
    observing object modifications, 372–380
    specialized parameters for, 357–363
EventSearchLog class, 323
Everything permissions set, 605, 630
examples (see code samples)
Exception class, 247
    creating, 269–278
    GetBaseException method, 268
    mapped to HRESULT, 259
exception event handlers, 263–265
exception handling, 238–244
    for asynchronous delegates, 288, 351
    coarse-grained, 239
    for delegates in multicast
            delegate, 346–348
    fine-grained, 238
    incorrect parameters, 244–246
    performance of, 239, 242, 246
    with threads, 721–723, 725
    when to throw specific
            exceptions, 247–249
exceptions
    asynchronous delegate throwing, 288
    breaking application before
            handling, 281–284
    casting, 120
    determining object originating, 246
    displaying information from, 265–268
    generated by method using
            reflection, 254–257
    handling individually, 249–251
    HRESULTs mapped to, 258–262
    innermost, finding, 268
    list of, 247–249

not losing with finally blocks, 251–254
rethrowing, 246
throwing, 243
unhandled, preventing, 263–265
user-defined, creating, 269–278
when to throw, 247–249
(see also specific exceptions)
executable modules, comparing versions
        of, 601–604
ExecutionEngineException exception, 244, 259
Exists method
    Directory class, 564
    File class, 540, 544
    FileInfo class, 540
exported types of an assembly, listing, 607
expressions
    balanced, determining, 492–496
    complex, ensuring correctness
        of, 111–113
    (see also equations)
Extensible Markup Language (see XML)
ExternalException class, 241
ExternalException exception, 259
ExtractGroupings method, RegExUtilities
        class, 392

F

façade design pattern, 195–200
factory design pattern, simple, 337–339
Fahrenheit
    converting Celsius to, 14
    converting to Celsius, 14
FieldAccessException exception, 259
File class, 538
    AppendText method, 550
    Copy method, 538
    Create method, 538, 549
    CreateText method, 550
    Delete method, 539
    Exists method, 540, 544
    GetCreationTime method, 540
    GetLastAccessTime method, 540
    GetLastWriteTime method, 540
    Move method, 538, 543
    Open method, 549
    OpenRead method, 549
    OpenText method, 550
    OpenWrite method, 549
    SetCreationTime method, 541
    SetLastAccessTime method, 541
    SetLastWriteTime method, 541

file handle, opening file from, 585–587
file streams, types of, 544
    (see also BinaryReader class; BinaryWriter
        class; FileStream class;
        StreamReader class; StreamWriter
        class)
FileAccess enumeration, 548
FileAttributes enumeration, 542, 569
FileInfo class, 538
    AppendText method, 551
    Attributes property, 541, 542
    CopyTo method, 538
    Create method, 538, 550
    CreationTime property, 540, 541
    Delete method, 539
    Exists method, 540
    GetFiles method, 573, 575
    LastAccessTime property, 540, 541
    LastWriteTime property, 540, 541
    MoveTo method, 539, 543
    Open method, 550
    OpenRead method, 550
    OpenText method, 551
    OpenWrite method, 550
FileLoadException exception, 257
FileMode enumeration, 547
FileNotFoundException exception, 257,
        259, 548
files
    attributes for, 541, 542, 568
    copying, 538
    counting lines of text in, 407–410
    creating, 538, 540, 557
    deleting, 539
    determining whether it exists, 543
    encrypting and decrypting, 683–688
    EOL character in,
        platform-independent, 556
    linefeed character in (see linefeed
        character)
    loading, exceptions generated by, 257
    locking portions of, 591–594
    monitoring for changes to, 594–599
    moving, 538
    not found, exception for, 247
    opening for reading and/or
        writing, 544–551
    opening from file handle, 585–587
    persisting collections to, between
        application sessions, 465
    reading, 558–561, 562–564

files (*continued*)
  regular expression pattern for path
      name, 417
  renaming, 543
  returning all lines in an ArrayList, 413
  searching, 410–413
  searching for, using wildcards, 571–575
  seeking (randomly accessing), 552–555
  temporary, 583
  timestamp of, manipulating, 540, 542
  waiting for changes to, 599–601
  writing to, 558, 562
  writing to multiple files at one
      time, 587–589
  (see also directories)
FileShare enumeration, 548
FileStream class, 544, 547–550
  creating instance of, 538, 557
  creating instance of, from file handle, 586
  Lock method, 591
  Read method, 563
  ReadByte method, 563
  Seek method, 552
  Unlock method, 592
  Write method, 562
  WriteByte method, 562
FileSystemWatcher class, 594, 595–598
  as alternative to DirectoryInfoNotify
      class, 351
  properties of, 596
  WaitForChanged method, 599, 600
FileVersionInfo class, 603
FilteredArrayList class, 624
FilteringOutputObtainingMembers
      method, 626
finalizers, 217
finally blocks, 241–243
  catch blocks within, 251–254
  for each delegate in multicast
      delegate, 348
  not losing exceptions with, 251–254
  preventing unhandled exceptions
      with, 263–265
  (see also exception handling)
FindAll method, 37
FindAllIllegalChars method, 582
FindAllOccurrences method, 35
FindAnEntryInEventLog method, 325
FindAny method, 39
FindAnyIllegalChars method, 583
FindIFaceMemberInAssembly method, 614
FindInArray method, 756–758

FindInterfaces method, Type class, 363, 365
FindMemberInAssembly method, 613
FindMembers method, Type class, 367
FindMethodOverrides method, 609
FindOccurrenceOf method, 413
FindOverriddenMethods method, 611
FindSerializable method, 622
FindSourceNamesFromAllLogs method, 328
FindSourceNamesFromLog method, 327
FindSpecificInterfaces method, 364
FindSubclassOfType method, 620
FindSubstrings method, 389, 391
fine-grained exception handling, 238
FinishedProcessingGroup method,
      INotificationCallbacks
      interface, 136–138
FinishedProcessingSubGroup method,
      INotificationCallbacks
      interface, 136–138
fixed statement, 756, 760
fixed-size arrays, 421, 755
Flags attribute, enumerations, 232–234
flags, enumerations used as, 226, 230–231
  (see also bit flags)
FlipBit method, 108
float data type, 1, 2
floating-point values
  equality with fractions, 2
  rounding, 12–14
Floor method, Math class, 13
folding hash algorithm, 468
FoldingHash method, 468
fonts used in this book, xix
for loop, iterating over characters in
      string, 65
foreach loop
  iterating over characters in string
      using, 64
  iterating over interfaces with, 134
  nested, iterating across nested arrays of
      objects, 167–174
  optimizing, 65
  polymorphic use of, 201–207
Format method, string class, 58–61
FormatException exception, 11, 57, 122,
      244, 247, 259
formatting strings, 58–62
forms, simulating execution of, 649–652
fractions, equality with floating-point
      values, 2
FreeNamedDataSlot method, Thread
      class, 744

FromASCIIByteArray method, 52
FromBase64CharArray method, Convert
    class, 50
FromUnicodeByteArray method, 52
FtoC method, 14
FullTrust permission set, 605, 630
FusionLog property, 257

G

GenerateGetOrPostRequest method, 642,
    646
GenerateIV method, RijndaelManaged
    class, 682
GenerateKey method, RijndaelManaged
    class, 682
generics, xv
Get methods, Type class, 626
GET request, sending to web
    server, 642–644
GetAll method, 439
GetAllDirFilesRecurse method, 576
GetAllFilesInPatternRecurse method, 576
GetAvailableThreads method, ThreadPool
    class, 735, 737, 738
GetBaseDefinition method, MethodInfo
    class, 609, 612
GetBaseException method, Exception
    class, 268
GetBaseTypeList method, 618, 619
GetBytes method
    ASCIIEncoding class, 53
    UnicodeEncoding class, 53
GetCharKind method, 29
GetCharKindInString method, 30
GetChild method, NTreeNode class, 520
GetCreationTime method
    Directory class, 567
    File class, 540
GetData method, Thread class, 744
GetDirectories method
    Directory class, 571, 573, 575
    DirectoryInfo class, 573, 574, 575, 576
GetDirectoryName method, Path class, 578
GetEnumerator method, PriorityQueue
    class, 479
GetExportedTypes method, Assembly
    class, 608
GetExtension method, Path class, 579
GetFileName method, Path class, 579
GetFileNameWithoutExtension method,
    Path class, 579

GetFiles method
    Directory class, 572, 574, 575
    DirectoryInfo class, 576
    FileInfo class, 573, 575
GetFileSystemEntries method, Directory
    class, 571, 573, 575
GetFileSystemInfos method, DirectoryInfo
    class, 572, 574, 575, 576
GetHashCode method, 467–475
    overriding, 105, 107, 278
    Set class, 531
GetHTMLFromURL method, 645
GetInterface method, Type class, 363
GetInterfaces method, Type class, 363
GetInvocationList method, MulticastDelegate
    class, 341, 343, 344, 346
GetKeys method, 449
GetLastAccessTime method
    Directory class, 567
    File class, 540
GetLastWriteTime method
    Directory class, 567
    File class, 540
GetLines method, 410
GetLSB method, 8
GetMaxThreads method, ThreadPool
    class, 738
GetMember method, Type class, 366, 613,
    615
GetMembers method, Type class, 366
GetMethod method, 612
GetMethods method, 612
GetMSB method, 7
GetNamedDataSlot method, Thread
    class, 744
GetPathRoot method, Path class, 578
GetReferencedAssemblies method, Assembly
    class, 606, 607
GetResponse method, HttpWebResponse
    class, 643, 646
GetResponseStream method,
    HttpWebResponse class, 646
GetRoot method
    BinaryTree class, 509
    NTree class, 515
GetSerializableTypeNames method, 621
GetStackTraceDepth method, 280
GetStream method, TcpClient class, 649
GetString method
    ASCIIEncoding class, 52
    UnicodeEncoding class, 52
GetSubClasses method, 619

GetTempFileName method, Path class, 584
GetTempPath method, Path class, 584
GetType method, Type class, 617
GetValues method, 449
GetVersionInfo method, FileVersionInfo
    class, 603
GradeBoard class, 733, 735
greater than operator (>), 751
greater than or equal operator (>=), 751
groups in regular expressions, 392–395
GUIDs, created by assembly registration
    tool, 158

H

HandleEnum method, 228, 229
HandleFlagsEnum method, 231
HandlingInvalidChars method, 785
hash code algorithms
    calculated hash, 471
    contained object cache, 468
    CryptoHash method, 469, 470
    folding hash, 468
    guidelines for, 474
    shift and add hash, 470
    simple hash, 468
    string concatenation hash, 472
hash values
    appending to strings for
      verification, 690–693, 693–698
    creating for a data type, 467–475
hashed passwords, 702, 705
HashOps class, 690
Hashtable class, 189
    displaying sorted by keys and/or
      values, 448–451
    maximum size for, setting, 451–454
    maximum values stored in,
      setting, 455–458
    minimum size for, setting, 451–454
    minimum values stored in,
      setting, 455–458
    one-to-many map (multimap)
      using, 496–503
    persisting between application
      sessions, 465–466
    (see also collections)
Hashtable object
    observing additions and modifications
      to, 372–380
    storing grouped search results in, 392,
      393

HashtableEventArgs class, 375, 377
HashtableObserver class, 372, 374, 377
HashtableSubject class, 372, 376
hexadecimal values, formatting strings as, 60
hooks, Windows keyboard, 380–386
host name
    converting to IP address, 636
    resolving IP address to, 635
HostName2IP method, 636
HRESULT
    for user-defined exceptions, 276
    mapping to exceptions, 258–262
    throwing exceptions as alternative to, 243
    unknown, exception for, 247
    user-defined, handling, 262
HTML
    converting XML to, 786–790
    obtaining from URL, 645
    tags, checking if balanced, 492–496
HTTP status codes, 641
HTTP: The Definitive Guide (Gourley,
    Totty), 642
HttpStatusCode enumeration, 641
HttpWebRequest class, 642
HttpWebResponse class
    GetResponse method, 643
    GetResponseStream method, 646
    StatusCode property, 640
HybridDictionary class, 420
hyphen (-)
    in regular expression patterns, 416
    on command line, 153
hypotenuse of a triangle, 27

I

IAsynchResult interface, IsCompleted
    property, 723, 725
ICloneable interface, 491
ICollection class, 449
ICollection interface, 460, 491
ICompanyData interface, 671
IComparable interface, 90–95, 95–99, 503
IComparer interface, 95–99, 482
icons used in this book, xx
IDisposable interface, 217
IEnumerable interface, 167, 171, 205, 491
IEnumerator interface, 171, 205
#if preprocessor directive, 310, 312
IFormattable interface, ToString method
    and, 82
Ildasm disassembler tool, 221

Index property, BinaryTreeNode class, 510
indexers
    MultiMap class, 499, 502
    parameters for, verifying correctness
        of, 244–246
    Set class, 530
IndexOf method
    PriorityQueue class, 479
    string class, 35, 37, 39
IndexOfAny method, string class, 37, 39,
        582, 583
IndexOutOfRangeException exception, 244,
        248, 259
inequality operator (!=)
    comparing pointers with, 751
    overriding, 108, 278
    Set class, 531, 536
inheritance hierarchies, of types in
        assemblies, 617–619
InnerException property,
        TargetInvocationException
        exception, 255
InnerXML property, XmlElement class, 786
INotificationCallbacks interface, 136–138
input/output (see files)
Insert method
    string class, 45
    StringBuilder class, 46
InsertIntoArray method, 444
InstallException exception, 248
instance methods, when to use, 539, 566
int data type, 1
interfaces
    callbacks provided with, 136–144
    implementing polymorphism with, 89
    members in, finding, 614
    polymorphism implemented
        with, 130–133, 133–135
    searching, advanced mechanisms
        for, 363–366
Intern method, string class, 66–68
intern pool, 66–68
InternedStrCls class, 66
Internet
    accessing through proxy, 644–645
    reading XML data from, 772
intersection of set objects, 524, 531, 534,
        535
IntersectionOf method, Set class, 531, 535
InvalidCastException exception, 120, 124,
        125, 135, 259

InvalidComObjectException exception, 259
InvalidEnumArgumentException
        exception, 244, 245, 248
InvalidFilterCriteriaException
        exception, 259
InvalidOleVariantTypeException
        exception, 259
InvalidOperationException exception, 241,
        243, 248, 259
InvalidPathChars field, Path class, 582, 583
InvalidProgramException exception, 260
InvokeEveryOther method, 341
InvokeInReverse method, 341
I/O (see files)
IOException exception, 248, 260, 548, 554,
        592, 593
IP address
    converting host name to, 636
    regular expression patterns for, 416
    resolving to host name, 635
IPHostEntry class, 637
is operator
    determining variable's type
        with, 127–130
    when to use, 124
IsApproximatelyEqualTo method, 2
IsCharEqual method, 33
IsCompleted property, 723, 725, 728
IsDefined method, Enum class, 228–229
IsEven method, 6
IsGranted method, SecurityManager
        class, 710
IsInRange method, 32
IsIntegerRegEx method, 12
IsInterned method, string class, 66–68
IsMatch method, Regex class, 11
IsNumeric method, 10
IsNumericFromTryParse method, 10
IsNumericRegEx method, 11
IsOdd method, 6
IsolatedStorageException exception, 260
IsProcessResponding method, 312
IsSafeToConvert method, 16
IsSubclassOf method, Type class, 619
IsSubsetOf method, Set class, 531, 536
IsSupersetOf method, Set class, 531, 536
isThreadAvailable method, 736
IsUnsignedIntegerRegEx method, 12
italic text used in this book, xix
iterator design pattern, 204

J

jagged arrays, 421
    navigating with pointer, 754
    reversing subarrays in, 427
Java language, compared to C#, xv
Join method
    string class, 61
    Thread class, 731, 735

K

keyboard input, monitoring and responding
    to, 380–386
Keys property, Hashtable class, 449, 450

L

Language enumeration, 228, 230, 232, 234
languages
    CLS-compliant, ensuring compatibility
        with, 165
    converting between simple types
        consistently across, 117–123
LastAccessTime property
    DirectoryInfo class, 567, 568
    FileInfo class, 540, 541
LastChanceHandler method, 264
LastWriteTime property
    DirectoryInfo class, 567, 568
    FileInfo class, 540
LastWriteTime property, FileInfo class, 541
Learning C# (O'Reilly), xix
least-significant bits (LSB) of an integer,
    determining, 7
Left property, BinaryTreeNode class, 510
Length property, StringBuilder class, 71
less than operator (<), 751
less than or equal operator (<=), 751
letter, determining if character is, 28–32
    (see also characters)
lexers (see tokenizers)
Line structure, 78, 83
LineCount method, 407
LineCount2 method, 408
linefeed character
    counting in string or file, 407–410
    Macintosh (\r), 409
    Unix (\n), 409
    XSLT, 790
    (see also EOL (end-of-line) character)
ListDictionary class, 189, 420

listeners element, application configuration
    file, 292
ListExportedTypes method, 608
little-endian format, 765
LoadFrom method, Assembly class, 257
LoadMissingDLL method, 257
LocalDataStoreSlot class, 744
LocalIntranet permission set, 605, 630
lock keyword, 717
Lock method, FileStream class, 591
locking
    file streams, 549
    files, 591–594
    objects, 717
Log class, 146
log file, creating and maintaining, 557–564
Log4Net software, 302
logging
    Log4Net software for, 302
    (see also event logs)
logical AND operator (&&),
        overloading, 102–105
logical OR operator (||),
        overloading, 102–105
long data type, 1
LSB (least-significant bits) of an integer,
        determining, 7

M

machine configuration file, 293
Magnetic class, 86
/main compiler switch, 145
managed code
    accessing files created by unmanaged
        code, 587
    blittable and nonblittable types and, 71
    called by COM objects, 243
    dispose design pattern and, 217
    exceptions for, mapping to
        HRESULTs, 258
    P/Invoke and, 74, 653
    releasing COM object through, 180
    (see also unsafe code)
managed execution environment, xv
managed languages, 165
Marshal class, ReleaseComObject
        method, 180
MarshalDirectiveException exception, 260
Mastering Regular Expressions
        (O'Reilly), 418
Mastering Visual Studio .NET (O'Reilly), xix

Match method, Regex class, 388
  compiling regular expressions with, 405, 406
  RightToLeft option for, 396
  verifying syntax of regular expression using, 396
Match object, 388, 391
MatchCollection object, 391, 392–395
Matches method, Regex class, 388
  compiling regular expressions with, 405, 406
  subscripting array returned by, 413
MatchesCollection object, 388
MatchEvaluator delegate, 401–403
MatchHandler method, 401
Math class
  Acos method, 27
  Asin method, 27
  Atan method, 27
  converting degrees to radians for, 3
  converting radians to degrees for, 4
  Cos method, 25
  Floor method, 13
  Pow method, 25
  Round method, 12
  Sin method, 25
  Sqrt method, 25
  Tan method, 25
mathematical equations, ensuring correctness of, 111–113
MaxChildren property
  NTree class, 515
  NTreeNodeFactory class, 519
MaxMinSizeHashtable class, 451
MaxMinValueHashtable class, 455
Media class, 85
MediaCollection class, 461
MemberAccess privilege, 605, 630
MemberAccessException exception, 248
MemberFilter delegate, 369
members
  dynamically invoking using reflection, 631–634
  searching, advanced mechanisms for, 366–372
  thread-safe access to, 716–721
MemberTypes enumeration, 614
Memento class, 211
memento design pattern, 208–213
MementoCareTaker class, 209, 211
MemoryStream class, 690
MethodAccessException exception, 248, 260

MethodInfo class, GetBaseDefinition method, 609, 612
methods
  calling on multiple object types, 133–135
  dynamically invoking using reflection, 631–634
  exceptions for, 248
  format parameters, exceptions for, 247
  instance, when to use, 539, 566
  invoked using reflection, exceptions generated by, 254–257
  overridden, listing for a derived class, 609–612
  parameters for, verifying correctness of, 244–246
  pointers passed to, controlling changes to, 747–750
  preventing compilation of, 311
  raising notifications from non-virtual methods, 354
  returning multiple items from, 148–150
  static, when to use, 539, 566
  thread-safe access to, 716–721
  (see also parameters)
MissingFieldException exception, 260
MissingManifestResourceException exception, 260
MissingMemberException exception, 260
MissingMethodException exception, 260
ModifyDirAttr method, 568
ModifyFile method, 552
ModifyFileAttr method, 541
ModifyNumericField method, 717
monetary values, regular expression patterns for, 416
Monitor class, TryEnter method, 719
MonitorMethodAccess class, 719
most-significant bits (MSB) of an integer, determining, 7
mouse events, 387
mouse, manipulating, 386
Move method
  Directory class, 566, 570
  File class, 538, 543
MoveInFile method, 554
MoveTo method
  DirectoryInfo class, 566, 570
  FileInfo class, 539, 543
MSB (most-significant bits) of an integer, determining, 7
MSDN Library, xix
MultiCallBackThroughIFace method, 140, 143

multicast delegates
    controlling delegates executed
        in, 340–344
    handling exceptions for each delegate
        in, 346–348
    invocation list for, 343
    return values from each delegate
        in, 344–346
MulticastDelegate class, GetInvocationList
        method, 341, 343, 344, 346
MulticastNotSupportedException
        exception, 260
MultiClone class, 175
multidimensional arrays, 421, 754
MultiMap class, 496, 499, 501
MultiMementoCareTaker class, 209, 211
MultiTask class, 139, 141
multithreading (see threading)
MultiWriter class, 587
MyKeys.snk file, 709

N

\n (linefeed character), 409
named groups in regular expressions, 392,
        394
named pipes, 653–669
NamedPipeClient class, 656, 668
NamedPipeInterop class, 653
NamedPipeServer class, 661, 666, 668
NamedPipesInterop class, 668
NameValueCollection class, 421
narrowing conversions, 23, 117
n-ary trees, 514–524
.NET web services, Windows NT 4.0 not
        supporting, xvi
NetworkCredential class, 645
networking, 635
    accessing Internet through web
        proxy, 644–645
    converting host name to IP address, 636
    downloading data from server, 652
    form execution, simulating, 649–652
    forming absolute URI, 639
    named pipes communicating across
        network, 653–669
    parsing a URI, 637–638
    resolving IP address to host name, 635
    sending GET or POST to web
        server, 642–644
    TCP client, creating, 648
    TCP server, creating, 646–648

    URL, obtaining HTML from, 645
    web server errors, handling, 640–642
newline character (see EOL character;
        linefeed character)
NodeChangedEvent method, 782
NodeChangingEvent method, 782
NodeInsertedEvent method, 782
NodeInsertingEvent method, 782
NodeRemovedEvent method, 782
NodeRemovingevent method, 782
NoFlags privilege, 630
nonblittable objects, 71
NotFiniteNumberException exception, 248,
        260
notification callbacks (see callbacks)
notifications, raising from non-virtual
        methods, 354
NotifyClient class, 136
NotifyFilters enumeration, 596
NotImplementedException exception, 248,
        260, 464
NotSupportedException exception, 248,
        260, 433, 434
NTree class, 514, 515, 522
NTreeNode class, 520, 523
NTreeNodeFactory class, 515, 519, 522
NullReferenceException exception, 126,
        138, 181, 242, 244, 248, 260, 759
NumberOfItems32 counter, 332
NumberOfItems64 counter, 332
NumberOfItemsHEX32 counter, 332
NumberOfItemsHEX64 counter, 332
NumberStyles enumeration, 56
numeric data types
    bitwise complement operator used
        with, 5
    casting to narrower data type, 15–25
    equality between fractions and
        floating-point values, 2
    pointers to, converting to
        strings, 766–768
    simple, 1
numeric promotion, 6
numeric values
    big flags in, turning on or off, 108–111
    breaking large numbers into byte
        arrays, 764
    casting to narrower data type, 15–25
    contained in string, determining, 10–12
    conversions to, 119, 120–122
    converting strings to, 55–58

converting to base 10 from another
base, 9
determining if character is, 28–32
determining if even or odd, 6
exceptions for, 248
formatting strings as, 59–60
obtaining most- or least-significant bits
of, 7
regular expression patterns for, 416
rounding floating-point values, 12–14
NumOfChildren property
BinaryTreeNode class, 510
NTreeNode class, 520

O

ObjCache class, 181
ObjectDisposedException exception, 180,
220, 244, 248
objects
cache for, 181–191
determining objects originating
exceptions, 246
disposal of, ensuring, 177–180
disposed, exception for, 248
generating tracing code when
creating, 336–339
initializing with overloaded
constructors, 146–148
locking against critical sections, 717
methods used on multiple object
types, 133–135
nested arrays of, iterating
across, 167–174
observing modifications to a
Hashtable, 372–380
rolling back changes to, 207–213
serializing, 195–200
set objects, creating, 524–536
single instance of, 191–195
stored in arrays
searching, 95–99
sorting, 90–95
strings converted to, 83–85
(see also classes)
ObjState class, 103
observer design pattern, 376–379
odd values, determining if number is, 6
OnEntryWritten method, 326
one-to-many map, 496–503
OnlyOne class, 192
OnlyStaticOne class, 192

Open method
File class, 549
FileInfo class, 550
OpenRead method
File class, 549
FileInfo class, 550
OpenText method
File class, 550
FileInfo class, 551
OpenWrite method
File class, 549
FileInfo class, 550
operators, precedence of, overriding, 111
(see also specific operators)
O'Reilly & Associates, contact information
for, xxi
out parameter
acting as return parameter, 148
passing pointers as, 749
OutOfMemoryException exception, 244,
260
OverFlowException exception, 57, 121
OverflowException exception, 15, 24, 118,
260

P

parameters
command line, parsing, 150–158
exceptions for, 247, 248
out keyword for, 148
verifying correctness of, 244–246
parentheses (())
balanced, 492
in equations, 111
Parse method, 55–58
Enum class, 227
Line structure, 83
numeric types, 10
ParseCmdLine class, 150
ParsePath method, 578
ParsePathEnvironmentVariable method, 579
ParseUri method, 637
passwords, for user settings data, 702, 705
Path class
GetDirectoryName method, 578
GetExtension method, 579
GetFileName method, 579
GetFileNameWithoutExtension
method, 579
GetPathRoot method, 578
GetTempFileName method, 584

Path class (*continued*)
GetTempPath method, 584
InvalidPathChars field, 582, 583
PathSeparator field, 579, 580
path name, regular expression pattern
for, 417
paths
parsing, 578
parsing in environment
variables, 579–581
separator character for, 579, 580
using in file functions, 539
verifying syntax and existence
of, 581–583
PathSeparator field, Path class, 579, 580
PathTooLongException exception, 260
patterns (see design patterns; regular
expressions)
PauseAndCreateFile method, 600
Peek method, StreamReader class, 558, 562
PeekChar method, BinaryReader class, 564
PeekHead method, DblQueue class, 489
PeekLargest method, PriorityQueue
class, 479
PeekSmallest method, PriorityQueue
class, 479
PeekTail method, DblQueue class, 489
percents, formatting strings as, 59
performance
critical sections and, 719
exception handling and, 239, 242, 246
GetHashCode method used to test
equality, 467
observer design pattern and, 379
regular expressions and, 405–407
reversing arrays and, 423–425
performance counters
averages calculated by, 333–336
in .NET Framework, 332
simple counters, 330–333
PerformanceCounter class, 331, 334
permissions
asserting safely, 706–708
for assemblies, 710–711
for reflections, 605, 630
phone number, regular expression patterns
for, 417
P/Invoke method, 74
P/Invoke wrapper class, 653–656
pipes, named, 653–669
Platform Invoke method (see P/Invoke
method)

PlatformNotSupportedException
exception, 260
pluggable protocols, exceptions for, 248
pointers
arrays of, 758–762
comparing, 751
controlling changes to when passed to
methods, 747–750
dangling, 750
navigating arrays with, 753–755
null, checking for, 758
passing as out or ref parameter, 749
passing by reference, 747, 749, 762
passing by value, 747, 748
switching unknown pointer
types, 762–764
to an array element, returning, 756–758
to an array of bytes, 764
to fixed arrays, manipulating, 755
to numeric data types, converting to
strings, 766–768
to unknown types, arrays of, 760–762
unsafe code and, 746
void, 760, 762, 763
PolicyException exception, 260
polymorphism
foreach method and, 201–207
implementing with abstract base
class, 85–89
implementing with concrete class, 89
implementing with interfaces, 89,
130–133
interfaces implementing, 133–135
POST request, sending to web
server, 642–644
Pow method, Math class, 25
preprocessor directives, allowing or
preventing compilation using, 310
PreventLossOfException method, 251, 252
Print method, BinaryTree class, 509
PrintDepthFirst method
BinaryTreeNode class, 510
NTreeNode class, 521
priority queue, 475–483
PriorityQueue class, 475, 479
Process class
Responding property, 313
StartInfo property, 590
processes
launching console utilities with, 589
not responding, determining, 312–313
ProcessInvoice method, 792

ProcessStartInfo class, 590
profiling tools, 221, 223
properties, parameters for, verifying
      correctness of, 244–246
protocol, pluggable, exceptions for, 248
proxy
    accessing Internet through, 644–645
    used for security, 670–679
proxy design pattern, 670, 678
punctuation, determining if character
      is, 28–32
Pythagorean theorem, 25

Q

QueryXML method, 773
Queue class, snapshot of, 460
    (see also collections)
queues
    double-queue, 483–491
    priority, 475–483
quotes, on command line, 153

R

\r (linefeed character, Macintosh), 409
radians
    converting degrees to, 3
    converting to degrees, 4
Random class, 699
random number generator, 699
range, determining if character is in, 32
RankException exception, 260
RateOfCountsPerSecond32 counter, 332
RateOfCountsPerSecond64 counter, 332
RawFraction counter, 336
RdGenerateSecretInitVector method,
      CryptoString class, 682
RdGenerateSecretKey method, CryptoString
      class, 682
Read method
    BinaryReader class, 564
    FileStream class, 563
    StreamReader class, 559, 562
    XMLTextReader class, 769
    XmlTextReader class, 772
ReadAllBufferedLog method, 560
ReadAllBufferedLogBlock method, 561
ReadAllLog method, 558
ReadAllLogAsBytes method, 559
ReadBlock method, StreamReader class, 561
ReadByte method, FileStream class, 563
ReaderDecorator class, 696, 698

ReaderWriterLock class, 733, 735
ReadFile method, 553
ReadLine method, StreamReader class, 408,
      410, 558, 563
ReadLogByLines method, 559
ReadLogPeeking method, 558
ReadNestedObjects method, 173
readonly field, 163–165
ReadSensitiveData method, SecretFile
      class, 687
ReadToEnd method, StreamReader
      class, 558, 563
ReceiveInvoice method, 797
ref parameter, passing pointers as, 749
reference types, unsafe code and, 746
Reflect class, 255
reflection, 605
    dynamically invoking members
      using, 631–634
    handling exceptions generated by
      methods using, 254–257
    permissions for, 605, 630, 706, 707
ReflectionEmit privilege, 605, 630
ReflectionException method, 255
ReflectionTypeLoadException
      exception, 260
Regasm.exe command-line tool, 158
Regex class
    CompileToAssembly method, 405–407
    IsMatch method, 11
    Match method, 405, 406
    Matches method, 405, 406, 413
    Replace method, 397–400, 401–403
    Split method, 403
Regex object, 388, 391
RegExUtilities class, ExtractGroupings
      method, 392
Register for COM interop field, in project
      properties, 158
RegistryKey class
    changing maximum event log size
      using, 322
    determining sources for event logs
      using, 329
Regular Expression Pocket Reference
      (O'Reilly), 418
regular expressions, 388, 417
    balanced, determining, 492–496
    books about, 418
    compiling, 405–407
    conditionally replacing matching text with
      a new string, 400–403

regular expressions (*continued*)
  counting lines of text using, 407–410
  documenting, 418
  finding last match in a string, 396
  finding specific occurrences of a
    match, 413–415
  finding substrings in strings
    using, 389–392
  groups in, 392–395
  list of common patterns for, 415–418
  performance of, 405–407
  replacing matching text with a new
    string, 397–400
  returning line in which match is
    found, 410–413
  testing for numeric value in a string
    using, 10
  tokenizers using, 403–405
  verifying syntax of, 395
ReleaseComObject method, Marshal
    class, 180
RemoteComponentException class, 269, 276
RemotingException exception, 260
RemotingTimeoutException exception, 260
Remove method
  MultiMap class, 499, 502
  Set class, 530
  string class, 47, 48
  StringBuilder class, 48
RemoveAt method, Set class, 530
RemoveFromArray method, 444
RemoveLeftNode method, BinaryTreeNode
    class, 510
RemoveNode method, NTreeNode
    class, 521, 524
RemoveRightNode method, BinaryTreeNode
    class, 510
RenameFile method, 543
Replace method
  Regex class, 397–400
    MatchEvaluator delegate for, 401–403
  string class, 48
  StringBuilder class, 48
Resolve method, Dns class, 635, 636
resources, unmanaged, disposing
    of, 214–221
Responding property, Process class, 313
ResponseCategories enumeration, 641
RestoreObj method, 465
ReThrowException method, 252
ReturnDimensions method, 148
ReturnTypeFilter method, 369

Reverse method, Array class, 423
Reverse2DimArray method, 425
ReverseJaggedArray method, 427
RevertAssert method, 708
Richter, Jeffrey ("Safe Thread
    Synchronization"), 718
Right property, BinaryTreeNode class, 510
RightToLeft constant, 396
Rijndael algorithm, 682, 684
RijndaelManaged class
  GenerateIV method, 682
  GenerateKey method, 682
RNGCryptoServiceProvider class, 699
Round method, Math class, 12
RoundDown method, 13
rounding floating-point values, 12–14
RoundUp method, 13
RunClient method, 648
RunProcessToReadStdIn method, 590
RunServer method, 647

S

Safe Thread Synchronization (MSDN
    Magazine), 721
"Safe Thread Synchronization"
    (Richter), 718
SafeArrayRankMismatchException
    exception, 260
SafeArrayTypeMismatchException
    exception, 260
SaferMemberAccess class, 717
SampleCounter counter, 336
SampleFraction counter, 336
SaveObj method, 465
SaveSensitiveData method, SecretFile
    class, 687
sbyte data type, 1, 766–768
scientific notation, formatting strings as, 59
sealed classes, adding events to, 351–357
SearchDepthFirst method, BinaryTree
    class, 509
searches
  array elements, 95–99, 435, 439, 443
  binary trees, 510, 513
  characters in strings, 35–36, 39
  event logs, 322–326
  files or directories, 571–575
  groups returned by, 392–395
  interfaces, 363–366
  members, 366–372
  n-ary trees, 520, 524
  queue items, 479

set objects, 531
strings in files, 410–413
substrings in strings, 37–41, 44, 389–392, 396, 413–415
tokens in strings, 41–43, 403–405
SearchInterfacesOfType method, 364
SearchMembers method, 367
SearchType class, 363, 367
SecretFile class, 684, 685
   ReadSensitiveData method, 687
   SaveSensitiveData method, 687
SecureFunction method, 707
security, 670
   access to types in an assembly, controlling, 670–679
   assemblies
      minimizing attack surface of, 711
      preventing malicious modifications to, 708–710
      verifying permissions for, 710–711
   asserting a permission safely, 706–708
   clearing cryptography information after using, 688
   encryption and decryption
      of files, 683–688
      of strings, 679–683
   event logs and, 314, 320
   random number generator, 699
   regular expression patterns and, 415
   storing data securely, 700–706
   thread-specific data, storing privately, 742–745
   verifying strings are uncorrupted during transmission, 690–693, 693–698
   (see also permissions)
SecurityAction enumeration, 712
SecurityException exception, 260, 348, 679, 708
SecurityManager class, IsGranted method, 710
Seek method, FileStream class, 552
SeekOrigin enumeration, 554
SEHException exception, 260
semicolon (;), on command line, 153
separator, determining if character is, 28–32
serializable types, finding in an assembly, 621–622
SerializationException exception, 260
serializer, choosing, 195–200
server (see web server)
ServerException exception, 260
Set class, 525, 530

set objects, 534
   creating, 524–536
   difference of, 524, 531, 534, 535
   equivalence and nonequivalence of, 531, 534, 536
   intersection of, 524, 531, 534, 535
   subset of, 531, 534, 536
   superset of, 531, 534, 536
   union of, 524, 531, 534, 535
SetCreationTime method
   Directory class, 568
   File class, 541
SetCustomLogMaxSize method, 321
SetData method, Thread class, 744
SetLastAccessTime method
   Directory class, 568
   File class, 541
SetLastWriteTime method
   Directory class, 568
   File class, 541
SetWindowsHookEx function, 385
shallow copying, 174, 176
ShallowClone class, 174
shift and add hash algorithm, 470
ShiftAndAddHash method, 470
short data type, 1
SignedNumber structure, 75
SignedNumberWithText structure, 76
significant bits of an integer, determining, 7
silent thread termination, 721–723
simple factory design pattern, 337–339
simple hash algorithm, 468
simple types, 1, 117–123
SimpleClass class, 473
SimpleHash method, 468
Sin method, Math class, 25
sine function, 26
single quotes ('), on command line, 153
singleton design pattern, 191–195, 682
SkipVerification privilege, 746
slash (/), on command line, 153
SN.EXE program, 709
SomeDataOriginator class, 208
Sort method, Array class and ArrayList class, 90–95
SortedArrayList class, 446
SortedList class
   Add method, 91–95
   Contains method, 95–99
   ContainsKey method, 95–99
   ContainsValue method, 95–99
   (see also collections)

SourceForge web site, 302
space, determining if character is, 28–32
SpawnManyThreads method, 736
Split method
    Regex class, 403
    string class, 41, 42, 62, 581
Sqrt method, Math class, 25
square brackets ([]), balanced, 492
Square class, 90
Stack class
    finding unbalanced strings using, 495
    snapshot of, 460
    (see also collections)
stack trace, obtaining without exception
        object, 279–281
StackOverflowException exception, 244,
    260
StackTrace class, iterating through like an
        array, 429–435
StackTrace method, Environment class, 280
StackTrace property, Environment class, 279
StackTraceArray class, 429
standard input, reading from and responding
        to, 589
StartInfo property, Process class, 590
StartsWith method, string class, 44
static fields
    initializing with static constructors, 285,
        287
    per-thread, 713–716
static methods, when to use, 539, 566
StatusCode property, HttpWebResponse
        class, 640
StreamReader class, 545, 550
    Peek method, 558, 562
    Read method, 559, 562
    ReadBlock method, 561
    ReadLine method, 408, 410, 558, 563
    ReadToEnd method, 558, 563
streams (see file streams)
StreamWriter class, 545, 550
    Write method, 562
    WriteLine method, 558, 562
string class
    Compare method, 43, 44
    EndsWith method, 44
    Equals method, 33, 66
    Format method, 58–61
    IndexOf method, 35, 37, 39
    IndexOfAny method, 37, 39, 582, 583
    Insert method, 45
    Intern method, 66–68

IsInterned method, 66–68
    Join method, 61
    Remove method, 47, 48
    Replace method, 48
    Split method, 41, 42, 62, 581
    StartsWith method, 44
    ToUpper method, 34
    Trim method, 72
    TrimEnd method, 72
    TrimStart method, 72
string concatenation hash algorithm, 472
string data type, 28
StringBuilder class, 28
    Append method, 64
    Capacity property, 69, 70
    constructor for, 63
    EnsureCapacity method, 71
    improving performance of, 69–71
    Insert method, 46
    Length property, 71
    Remove method, 48
    Replace method, 48
StringCollection class, 421
StringDictionary class, 421
StringReader class, decorating, 693, 698
StringReaderHash class, 696
strings
    array of, formatting as delimited text, 61
    balanced, determining, 492–496
    classes represented as, 77–83
    comparing, 43, 66–68
    conditionally replacing text
        within, 400–403
    conversions to, 51, 119, 123
    converting from pointers to numeric data
        types, 766–768
    converting to value type, 55–58
    counting lines of text in, 407–410
    decoding from Base64 to byte array, 50
    delimited, extracting items from, 62
    displaying enumerations as, 225–227
    encoding byte array as, 49
    encrypting and decrypting, 679–683
    ensuring maximum number of characters
        in, 63
    formatting data in, 58–61
    hash values appended to, 690–693,
        693–698
    inserting character or string into, 45–46
    interning, 66–68
    iterating over characters of, 64
    numeric value in, determining, 10–12

objects represented by, converting to
objects, 83–85
passing to method as byte array, 53–54
performance of, with StringBuilder
class, 69–71
removing characters at head or tail of, 72
removing or replacing characters
in, 46–49
replacing text within, 397–400
returning all lines in an ArrayList, 413
searching, 389–392, 410–413
finding last matching substring in, 396
finding specific occurrences of a
match, 413–415
groups resulting from, 392–395
searching for characters in, 35–36, 39
searching for string at head or tail of, 44
searching for strings in, 37–41
searching for tokens in, 41–43, 403–405
structures represented as, 77–83
type of characters in, determining, 28–32
verifying they are uncorrupted during
transmission, 690–693, 693–698
XML, handling invalid characters
in, 784–786
StringWriter class, decorating, 693, 698
strongly typed collections, 463
structures, 73–75
Equals method for, improving
performance of, 105–108
GetHashCode method for,
overriding, 107
operating as union types, 75–77
performance of, 73
polymorphism for, 130–133
represented as a string, 77–83
static fields, initializing, 284–288
stored in arrays
searching, 95–99
sorting, 90–95
strings converted to, 83–85
when to use, 74
subset of set objects, 531, 534, 536
SUDSGeneratorException exception, 260
SUDSParserException exception, 260
superset of set objects, 531, 534, 536
surrogate character, determining if character
is, 28–32
SwapElementsInArray method, 422
Switch class, custom, 297–301
(see also BooleanSwitch class;
TraceSwitch class)

Switch method, 762
switches element, application configuration
file, 292
symbol, determining if character is, 28–32
SymmetricAlgorithm class, 684
Clear method, 688
SynchronizationLockException
exception, 260
synchronous delegates, converting to
asynchronous delegates, 348–351
SyncInvoke delegate, 348, 349
system requirements for examples in this
book, xvi
System.Collections namespace, 420
System.Diagnostics namespace, 290
SystemException exception, 244, 260
System.Text.RegularExpressions
namespace, 28

T

tags, determining if balanced, 492–496
(see also HTML; XML)
TakeSnapshotOfList method, 460
Tan method, Math class, 25
tangent function, 26
TargetException exception, 260
TargetInvocationException
exception, 255–257, 260
TargetParameterCountException
exception, 261
Task class, 136, 139–143
TCP client, creating, 648
TCP server, creating, 646–648
TcpClient class, 648, 649
TcpListener class, 647
temperatures
converting Celsius to Fahrenheit, 14
converting Fahrenheit to Celsius, 14
ternary operator (?:), 112
TestDynamicInvocation method, 631
TestInit class, 284
TestMediaABC method, 87
TestReceivedStringHash method, 691, 693
TestSort method, 92, 96
TestWatcher method, 594
text (see characters; strings)
theorems for Boolean equations, 114
Thread class
AllocateDataSlot method, 742, 744
AllocateNamedDataSlot method, 742,
744
FreeNamedDataSlot method, 744

Thread class (*continued*)
  GetData method, 744
  GetNamedDataSlot method, 744
  Join method, 731
  SetData method, 744
thread local storage (TLS), 742–745
ThreadAbortException exception, 261
threading, 713
  article about, 721
  asynchronous delegates
    notification of completion, 729–731
    polling, 723–726
    timing out, 726–728
  exception event handlers for, 264
  per-thread static fields, 713–716
  silent thread termination, 721–723
  synchronizing reading and writing of
    resources, 732–735
  thread pool requests, notification of
    availability, 735–737
  thread-safe access to internal
    members, 716–721
  thread-specific data, storing
    privately, 742–745
  timer, configuring, 739–741
  waiting for all threads in pool to
    finish, 738
  worker thread completion, waiting
    for, 731
Threading.Timer class, 740–741
ThreadInterruptedException exception, 261,
  735
ThreadPool class
  GetAvailableThreads method, 735, 737,
    738
  GetMaxThreads method, 738
  timers and, 741
ThreadStart delegate, 721
ThreadStateException exception, 261, 732
ThreadStaticAttribute attribute, 713, 714
ThreadStaticField class, 714
ThreadStopException exception, 261
throw keyword, 246
  (see also exception handling; exceptions)
tilde (~) (see bitwise complement operator)
time, regular expression patterns for, 416
TimeOutAsyncDelegate method, 728
TimeoutException exception, 248
TimeOutWakeAsyncDelegate method, 726,
  728
Timer class, 740–741
timer, configuring, 739–741

Timer100Ns counter, 333
Timer100nsInverse counter, 333
TimerCallback delegate, 741
timestamps
  of directories, 567
  of files, 540, 542
TLS (thread local storage), 742–745
ToArray method
  DblQueue class, 489
  PriorityQueue class, 479
ToASCIIByteArray method, 53
ToBase64CharArray method, Convert
  class, 49
ToBoolean method, Convert class, 119
ToByte method, Convert class, 119
ToChar method, Convert class, 119
ToDateTime method, Convert class, 119
ToDecimal method, Convert class, 119
ToDouble method, Convert class, 119
ToInt16 method, Convert class, 119
ToInt32 method, Convert class, 9, 119
ToInt64 method, Convert class, 119
Tokenize method, 404
tokenizers, 41–43, 403–405
tokens, breaking strings into, 41–43,
  403–405
ToSByte method, Convert class, 119
ToSingle method, Convert class, 119
ToString method, 77–83, 119, 232
  formatting with, 60
  using with enumerations, 225–226
  using with exceptions, 257, 265, 266
ToUInt16 method, Convert class, 119
ToUInt32 method, Convert class, 119
ToUInt64 method, Convert class, 119
ToUnicodeByteArray method, 53
ToUpper method, string class, 34
Trace class, 290
  interchanging with Debug class, 290
  (see also Debug class)
TRACE directive, 309
trace element, application configuration
  file, 292
Traceable class, 293, 294
TraceFactory class, 337
TraceListener class, 302–308
TraceSwitch class, 295, 297
tracing, 290
  configuration file to turn on, 291–293
  customizing levels for, 297–301
  enabling for specific
    components, 294–297

generating code for during object
    creation, 336–339
output from production
    application, 290–293
selecting levels of, 295, 297
stack trace, 279–281
XML output for, 301–310
(see also debugging)
Transform method, XslTransform class, 790
TransformXML method, 786
trees, 511
    (see also binary trees; n-ary trees)
TreeSize property, BinaryTree class, 509
triangles
    calculating length of a side for, 25
    calculating one angle of, 27
trigonometric functions
    calculating an angle of right triangle
        using, 27
    calculating length of a side of right
        triangle using, 26
    converting degrees to radians for, 3
    converting radians to degrees for, 4
Trim method, string class, 72
TrimEnd method, string class, 72
TrimStart method, string class, 72
TrimToSize method
    DblQueue class, 489
    PriorityQueue class, 479
TripleDES algorithm, 684, 688
try-catch blocks (see catch blocks)
try-catch-finally blocks (see catch blocks;
    finally blocks)
TryEnter method, Monitor class, 719
try-finally blocks (see finally blocks)
TryParse method, 10
TurnBitOff method, 108
TurnBitOn method, 108
two-dimensional arrays, reversing, 425
Type class
    FindInterfaces method, 363
    FindMembers method, 367
    Get methods, 626
    GetInterface method, 363
    GetInterfaces method, 363
    GetMember method, 366, 613, 615
    GetMembers method, 366
    GetType method, 617
    IsSubclassOf method, 619
    searching for interfaces with, 363–366
    searching for members with, 366–372
TypeFilter delegate, 365

TypeInformation privilege, 605, 630
TypeInitializationException exception, 261,
    284–288
TypeLoadException exception, 261
types
    inheritance hierarchies of, in
        assemblies, 617–619
    nested, finding in assembly, 616–617
    serializable, finding in an
        assembly, 621–622
    simple, 117–123
    subclasses of, in an assembly, 619–621
TypeUnloadedException exception, 261

U

uint data type, 1
ulong data type, 1
UnauthorizedAccessException
    exception, 261, 540
unchecked context, 24, 118
unchecked keyword, 24
#undef preprocessor directive, 310, 311
UnhookWindowsHookEx function, 385
UnicodeEncoding class
    GetBytes method, 53
    GetString method, 52
Uniform Resource Identifier (see URI)
union of set objects, 524, 531, 534, 535
union types, structures similar to, 75–77
UnionOf method, Set class, 531, 535
Unlock method, FileStream class, 592
unmanaged resources, disposing of, 214–221
unnamed groups in regular expressions, 394
unsafe code, 746
    arrays of pointers, 758–760
    arrays of pointers to unknown
        types, 760–762
    breaking large numbers into byte
        arrays, 764
    converting pointers to numeric data types
        to strings, 766–768
    navigating arrays with pointers, 753–755
    pointers, comparing, 751
    pointers passed to methods, controlling
        changes to, 747–750
    pointers to fixed arrays,
        manipulating, 755
    returning pointers to an element in an
        array, 756–758
    unknown pointer types,
        switching, 762–764
    (see also managed code)

UploadValues method, WebClient
    class, 649, 652
Uri class, 637, 638, 639
URI (Uniform Resource Identifier)
    absolute, forming from base and relative
        URI, 639
    parsing, 637–638
UriFormatException exception, 638, 640
URL
    obtaining HTML from, 645
    reading XML data from, 772
UseChecked method, 15
UseMedia method, 87
UserSettings class, 700
ushort data type, 1
using statement, 178
UsingAnUnmanagedFileHandle
    method, 585

V

ValidateXML method, 775
ValidShape enumeration, 225
Value method, BinaryTreeNode class, 510
Value method, NTreeNode class, 520
value types
    converting strings to, 55–58
    unsafe code and, 746
Values property, Hashtable class, 449, 450
variable, type of, determining, 127–130
vector array, 65
VerificationException exception, 261
VerifyRegEx method, 395
VerifyResponse method, 640, 646
versioning, implementing with multiple entry
    points, 144–145
versions, comparing for executable
    modules, 601–604
ViewModifyDirAttr method, 568
ViewModifyFileAttr method, 541
Visual Basic .NET, compared to C#, xv
Visual Studio .NET
    books about, xix
    requirements for code samples in this
        book, xvii
    versions used for this book, xxi
void pointers, 760, 762, 763

W

WaitForChanged method,
    FileSystemWatcher class, 599, 600
WaitForChangedResult structure, 600
WaitForZipCreation method, 599
WaitOne method, WaitHandle class, 726,
    727
WarningException exception, 248
WatchForAppEvent method, 326
WeakReferenceException exception, 261
web proxy, accessing Internet
    through, 644–645
web server
    downloading data from, 652
    errors from, handling, 640–642
    sending GET or POST request
        to, 642–644
web sites
    C# sample code, xv
    C# sample code for this book, xvi
    for this book, xxi
    MSDN Library, xix
    O'Reilly & Associates, xxi
    profiling tools, 223
    reading XML data from, 772
    SourceForge, Log4Net software, 302
    Visual Studio .NET version
        differences, xxi
WebClient class
    DownloadData method, 652
    DownloadFile method, 652
    UploadValues method, 649, 652
WebException exception, 248
WebProxy class, 644
WebRequest class, 642, 643
WebResponse class, 643
whitespace, determining if character
    is, 28–32
WH_KEYBOARD hook, 380–386
wildcard character (*), 614
wildcards
    searching for files or directories
        using, 571–575
    searching for members in assembly
        using, 613–614
Windows keyboard hook, 380–386
Windows NT 4.0, ASP.NET and .NET web
    services not supported for, xvi

Windows operating system, requirements for code samples in this book, xvi
words, breaking up strings into, 41–43, 403–405
Worker class, 731
Write method
  BinaryWriter class, 562
  FileStream class, 562
  StreamWriter class, 562
WriteByte method, FileStream class, 562
WriteCData method, XmlTextWriter class, 784
WriteElementString method, XmlTextWriter class, 784
WriteLine method
  formatting data using, 58
  newline characters and, 556
  StreamWriter class, 558, 562
  writing to multiple files using, 587
WriteNodeInfo method, 782
WriterDecorator class, 693, 694, 698
WriteToFileHandle method, 585
WriteToLog method, 558

X

XDR schema, validating XML conformance to, 775–779
XML configuration file (see application configuration file)
XML (Extensible Markup Language), 769
  breaking into constituent parts, 791–796
  constructing from separate constituent pieces, 796–801
  converting to HTML, 786–790
  creating programmatically, 779–781
  DOM model for, 780
  exceptions for, 248
  finding tags in an XML string, 390
  invalid characters in, handling, 784–786
  Log4Net logging software for, 302
  querying contents of, 773–775
  reading XML data from the web, 772

  reading XML data in document order, 769–771
  tags, checking if balanced, 492–496
  trace output using, 301–310
  tracking changes to, 781–783
  validating conformance to a schema, 775–779
XmlAttributes class, 796
XmlDocument class, 781
  assembling an XML document using, 796, 799
  breaking apart an XML document using, 791
  constructing XML data using, 780
  handling invalid characters with, 785
  when to use, 769, 780, 783
XmlElement class, 785, 786
XmlException exception, 248
XmlNode class, Clone method, 796
XmlResolver class, 790
XmlSchemaCollection class, 777
XmlSecureResolver class, 790
XmlTextReader class, 769, 772, 774, 780
XmlTextWriter class, 769, 779, 780
  WriteCData method, 784
  WriteElementString method, 784
XMLTraceListener class, 302
XmlUrlResolver class, 790
XmlValidatingReader class, 775, 776
XPath, querying XML data using, 773
XPathDocument class, 773
XPathNavigator class, 773
XPathNodeIterator class, 773
XSD schema, validating XML conformance to, 775–779
XSLT stylesheet, transforming XML using, 786–790
XslTransform class, 786, 790

Z

zip code, regular expression patterns for, 416

About the Authors

Stephen Teilhet earned a degree in electrical engineering but soon afterwards began writing software for the Windows platform. For the last eight years he has worked for several consulting firms on a wide range of projects, specializing in Visual Basic, Visual C++, MTS, COM, MSMQ, and SQL Server. Stephen currently works for Compuware NuMega Lab in Nashua, New Hampshire, where he is immersed in the Microsoft .NET technologies.

Jay Hilyard has been developing applications for the Windows platform for over 10 years, and he is currently a .NET enthusiast. Jay has published an article in *MSDN Magazine* on Profiling and Garbage Collection, and he currently works on the BoundsChecker team at Compuware NuMega Lab in Nashua, New Hampshire. When not immersed in .NET, Jay spends his time with his family and rooting for the New England Patriots.

Colophon

Our look is the result of reader comments, our own experimentation, and feedback from distribution channels. Distinctive covers complement our distinctive approach to technical topics, breathing personality and life into potentially dry subjects.

The animal on the cover of *C# Cookbook* is a garter snake (*Thamnophis sirtalis*). Named because their longitudinal stripes resemble those on garters once used to hold up men's socks, garter snakes are easily identified by their distinctive stripes: a narrow stripe down the middle of the back with a broad stripe on each side of it. Color and pattern variations enable them to blend into their native environments, helping them evade predators. They are the most common snake in North America and the only species of snake found in Alaska.

Garter snakes have keeled scales—one or more ridges down the central axis of the scales—giving them a rough texture and lackluster appearance. Adult garter snakes generally range in length between 46 and 130 centimeters (one and a half feet to over four feet). Females are usually larger than males, with shorter tails and a bulge where the body and tail meet.

Female garters are ovoviviparous, meaning they deliver "live" young that have gestated in soft eggs. Upon delivery, most of the eggs and mucous membranes have broken, which makes their births appear live. Occasionally, a baby will be born still inside its soft shell. A female will usually deliver 10 to 40 babies: the largest recorded number of live babies birthed by a garter snake is 98. Once emerging from their mothers, baby garters are completely independent and must begin fending for themselves. During this time they are most susceptible to predation, and over half of all baby garters die before they are one year old.

Garter snakes are one of the few animals able to eat toads, newts, and other amphibians with strong chemical defenses. Although diets vary depending on their environments, garter snakes mostly eat earthworms and amphibians; however, they occasionally dine on baby birds, fish, and small rodents. Garter snakes have toxic saliva (harmless to humans), which they use to stun or kill their prey before swallowing them whole.

Marlowe Shaeffer was the production editor and proofreader for *C# Cookbook*. Nancy Kotary was the copyeditor. Reg Aubry and Darren Kelly provided quality control. Jamie Peppard and Mary Agner provided production assistance. Angela Howard wrote the index.

Emma Colby designed the cover of this book, based on a series design by Edie Freedman. The cover image is a 19th-century engraving from the Dover Pictorial Archive. Emma Colby produced the cover layout with QuarkXPress 4.1 using Adobe's ITC Garamond font.

David Futato designed the interior layout. This book was converted by Julie Hawks to FrameMaker 5.5.6 with a format conversion tool created by Erik Ray, Jason McIntosh, Neil Walls, and Mike Sierra that uses Perl and XML technologies. The text font is Linotype Birka; the heading font is Adobe Myriad Condensed; and the code font is LucasFont's TheSans Mono Condensed. The illustrations that appear in the book were produced by Robert Romano and Jessamyn Read using Macromedia FreeHand 9 and Adobe Photoshop 6. The tip and warning icons were drawn by Christopher Bing. This colophon was written by Marlowe Shaeffer.

Related Titles Available from O'Reilly

.NET

.NET and XML

.NET Framework Essentials, *3rd Edition*

.NET Windows Forms in a Nutshell

ADO.NET in a Nutshell

ADO.NET Cookbook

ASP.NET in a Nutshell, *2nd Edition*

ASP.NET Cookbook

C# Essentials, *2nd Edition*

C# in a Nutshell, *2nd Edition*

C# Language Pocket Guide

Learning C#

Learning Visual Basic.NET

Mastering Visual Studio.NET

Object Oriented Programming with Visual Basic .NET

Programming .NET Components

Programming .NET Security

Programming .NET Web Services

Programming .NET Windows Applications

Programming ASP.NET, *2nd Edition*

Programming C#, *3rd Edition*

Programming Visual Basic .NET, *2nd Edition*

VB.NET Core Classes in a Nutshell

VB.NET Language in a Nutshell, *2nd Edition*

VB.NET Language Pocket Reference

Keep in touch with O'Reilly

1. Download examples from our books

To find example files for a book, go to:

www.oreilly.com/catalog

select the book, and follow the "Examples" link.

2. Register your O'Reilly books

Register your book at *register.oreilly.com*

Why register your books?
Once you've registered your O'Reilly books you can:

- Win O'Reilly books, T-shirts or discount coupons in our monthly drawing.
- Get special offers available only to registered O'Reilly customers.
- Get catalogs announcing new books (US and UK only).
- Get email notification of new editions of the O'Reilly books you own.

3. Join our email lists

Sign up to get topic-specific email announcements of new books and conferences, special offers, and O'Reilly Network technology newsletters at:

elists.oreilly.com

It's easy to customize your free elists subscription so you'll get exactly the O'Reilly news you want.

4. Get the latest news, tips, and tools

www.oreilly.com

- "Top 100 Sites on the Web"—PC Magazine
- CIO Magazine's Web Business 50 Awards

Our web site contains a library of comprehensive product information (including book excerpts and tables of contents), downloadable software, background articles, interviews with technology leaders, links to relevant sites, book cover art, and more.

5. Work for O'Reilly

Check out our web site for current employment opportunities:

jobs.oreilly.com

6. Contact us

O'Reilly & Associates, Inc.
1005 Gravenstein Hwy North
Sebastopol, CA 95472 USA

TEL: 707-827-7000 or 800-998-9938
(6am to 5pm PST)

FAX: 707-829-0104

order@oreilly.com
For answers to problems regarding your order or our products. To place a book order online, visit:

www.oreilly.com/order_new

catalog@oreilly.com
To request a copy of our latest catalog.

booktech@oreilly.com
For book content technical questions or corrections.

corporate@oreilly.com
For educational, library, government, and corporate sales.

proposals@oreilly.com
To submit new book proposals to our editors and product managers.

international@oreilly.com
For information about our international distributors or translation queries. For a list of our distributors outside of North America check out:

international.oreilly.com/distributors.html

adoption@oreilly.com
For information about academic use of O'Reilly books, visit:

academic.oreilly.com

O'REILLY®

Our books are available at most retail and online bookstores.
To order direct: 1-800-998-9938 • *order@oreilly.com* • *www.oreilly.com*
Online editions of most O'Reilly titles are available by subscription at *safari.oreilly.com*